Southwestern Archaeology

Southwestern Archaeology

Second Edition

by John C. McGregor

UNIVERSITY OF ILLINOIS PRESS   *Urbana, Chicago, London*

Illini Books edition, 1982

© 1965 by the Board of Trustees of the University of Illinois
First edition copyright 1941 by John C. McGregor

Manufactured in the United States of America
P   5   4   3   2   1

Library of Congress Catalog Card No. 65-10079
ISBN 0-252-00989-4

Preface

This book, like the first work of the same title, has been written as a result of the often expressed need, by teachers, laymen, and students, for an organized framework upon which the individual interested in Southwestern archaeology may build. The subject is still advancing so rapidly, and so much detailed information is now at hand, that in general only the broader outlines may be presented. The center of Southwestern culture is considered in greatest detail, outlying cultures much less so, and those which are truly peripheral are omitted. It is hoped that such a review of the information and literature at present available not only will be of immediate value but also will serve as a stimulant for more complete organizations of the subject at some future time.

Certain features of this work will be found of the greatest value to the reader. The maps which show the centers and maximum spread of cultures have been very carefully prepared and have been checked by experts at work in each of these areas and on each of these cultures. They will be found to be of real use in visualizing the areas occupied at the times indicated. The list of pottery types has been meticulously checked as well. It will be found that repeated reference may profitably be made to it, and anyone dealing with actual problems in the Southwest should find it most useful.

At the end of each chapter there is a selected bibliography, some of the items of which have been starred. They will be found to contain much more complete statements of the problems briefly discussed herein. At the end of the book is a much fuller bibliography which should also be useful to the more serious student who wishes to expand further his knowledge of this most fascinating area.

The list of sites which have been dated by tree rings has been dropped from this book for several reasons. The total number of sites, and dates from these sites, has now become so large that it would require too much space to present them. Many of these dates are from sites which are designated by numbers or other symbols which are not intelligible to the average reader. A large number of other sites, or culture stages, have been dated by carbon 14, and these dates again are often so presented that they are not meaningful to the average individual. Finally, even the most exact dates secured by tree-ring dating require expert interpretation, for the date of the construction of a building is not necessarily the date of the associated artifacts. For those individuals who wish to check tree-ring dates, reference may be made to the *Tree Ring Bulletin* of the Tree Ring Society.

Only the most important features of each period or culture have been stressed, so that a more detailed picture may be had by additional reading in the short bibliographies. Since this book is designed as an introduction, and not as a final and complete compendium on the subject, much choice of material has been exercised, and a great deal of available material omitted.

The first part presents a theoretical and general background, the principles of which may be successfully applied to archaeological work in any field. This forms a necessary base upon which later data may be arranged, for the aims and methods of archaeology must be understood before results may be evaluated. The second part is a historical reconstruction of the prehistoric Southwest. Summaries are made of each of the sections of each of the chapters, so for a rapid review of the material in this section these summaries might be read first. In fact the average reader, wishing only the broadest understanding of Southwestern archaeology, might read the introductory chapter, look at the illustrations in the chapters on culture with their dates, and then read the last general summary chapter.

Southwestern archaeologists have never forgotten that their aim is the reconstruction of history, and as a result have directed their research along these lines. Tree-ring dating has done much to make this aim possible, for it has supplied absolute dates in terms of our own calendar to a great many ruins. It has also been possible to extend these dates over larger areas by what is termed herein the "seriation process." Carbon 14 dating has given less accurate dates but has made it possible to secure earlier dates and dates from sites where tree-ring dating is not possible. Most archaeologists have felt that art evaluation of objects, and similar studies, is a phase of the work to be done later, from the material which they have collected and preserved in institutions.

Theoretical interpretations of data have been kept at a minimum, for in any event they are subject to much criticism. Broad and basic interpretations which bear directly on an understanding of historical processes and interrelationships have been pointed out, as it is only in this way that cultural influences and development may be comprehended.

All chapters of this book have been more or less completely revised, and much of it reorganized and rewritten. Many new illustrations have been added to the previous book, and the bibliography has been greatly expanded and brought up to date. So much new material has been added to Southwestern archaeology in the more than two decades since the first book was written that these revisions have been necessary. However, all of the views and interpretations are solely those of the writer and any errors or inconsistencies are his own.

A great deal of interest has been expressed in this revision of an older work, and the assistance of many people freely given is most gratefully acknowledged. The following individuals have been of the greatest aid: Emil W. Haury, Jesse D. Jennings, David Breternetz, Charley Steen, Albert H. Schroeder, Charles Di Peso, W. S. Fulton, Bryant Bannister, Watson Smith, Lyndon L. Hargrave, Lewis Kaywood, E. B. Danson, H. S. Colton, A. J. Lindsey, James Hester, Fred Wendorf, A. E. Dittert, Paul Martin, and John Rinaldo. Personal interviews were had with each of these people, but responsibility for ideas and all statements in this book are those of the writer. A. E. Dittert, E. B. Danson, and Emil W. Haury have each read parts of the manuscript and examined it, and their criticisms and suggestions are gratefully acknowledged.

Part of the funds which have made possible the rewriting of this book were received from the Penrose fund of the American Philosophical Society, and other grants come from the Graduate Research Board of the University of Illinois and the Department of Anthropology of the University of Illinois.

Contents

PART ONE

BACKGROUND

I

Introduction

Archaeology is not the romantic subject of modern fiction, but it does hold much satisfaction for those who have made it a subject of special inquiry. There is always a trace of mystery shrouding the lives of past individuals, and to delve into these ancient histories generally results in new concepts and appreciations of past events. To those of sufficient vision it is possible to perceive, among the clouds of stirred-up dust, something of the character and achievements of the people who composed the prehistoric tribes, and at the same time to attain a better understanding of the processes of history when it is thus extended further back in time.

The Southwest has from the first proved a fertile field for the development of common misconceptions, and perhaps some of these should be corrected immediately. The prehistoric Southwesterners were neither exceptionally small nor exceptionally large, nor were they physically superior to the average Indian of the Southwest today. They were not accomplished engineers, but rule-of-thumb workers, even in the creation of such pretentious structures as massive cliff dwellings, huge ball courts or vast ceremonial chambers, and extensive irrigation ditches. On the whole they were neither more nor less than average human beings attempting to secure their survival in the struggle for existence.

When the Southwest is pictured the archaeology is most commonly thought of as great structures. Picturesque cliff dwellings, unique to this section, are probably best remembered of all, particularly the square or round towers and fine masonry of the Mesa Verde in Colorado, or such sites as sprawling Betatakin and Kiet Siel in their breathtaking Arizona settings. Next to these in impressiveness are the huge open sites in Chaco

Canyon and Aztec Ruin in New Mexico, Casa Grande in southern Arizona, or a thousand more similar villages. Even the cavate dwellings, such as those in Frijoles Canyon, or Old Caves, vividly impress the tourist.

These sites, however, represent only a very small portion of Southwestern prehistory, for by far the greater part of the archaeology still lies most inconspicuously buried. The average individual has much difficulty in locating these ancient homes, but generally the presence of small broken fragments of pottery scattered about on the surface of the ground is of help. If a site choice made now is investigated, ancient house remains will often be found, for the same factors which determined choice then control it today.

A GENERAL STATEMENT OF SOUTHWESTERN ARCHAEOLOGY

The aim of the archaeologist is to make the past understandable and informative in the light of the present. To do this it is necessary to convert prehistory to history—to bring to light unrecorded past events and make of them an alive and dynamic historical account of what happened in the past, and why it happened. The historian is interested in the same ends, and is concerned with the same elements of the same story, as the archaeologist, but the historian has written records from which he may arrive at his conclusions; the archaeologist has not.

Both deal with three elements: events, place, and time. The historian arranges his events, or occurrences, in the proper place group and the proper time sequence, and then he has a history of that place and time. But he must do something more if he is to have a history from which lessons may be drawn and future acts more intelligently directed. He must interpret these events.

The archaeologist, confronted with these problems, must also understand how events came about, and explain them. It is in the interpretation of facts that the most difficult problems of archaeology arise. They must be interpreted correctly, for speculation, or wishful thinking, can play no part in this reconstruction if a true understanding of the past is ever to be achieved. Both the historian and the archaeologist should recognize that history in the making is a dynamic, complex, ever-shifting pageant, and should so present their findings.

When archaeology is mentioned many people immediately think of the Old World, or Central America, where finds have perhaps been more publicized or make a greater appeal to the imagination of the average individual. These fields, however, are not the only fruitful ones, for the Southwest is in many respects even more informative.

More than three quarters of a century of capably collected information concerning the archaeology of the Southwest has accrued to the present. Most well-directed and carefully thought out research has been done within the last few years, but all has been of a relatively high order. Not only has research been well done; this field offers unusual opportunities of re-creating history in two additional particulars. First, an unusually complete, more or less chronological, sequence, from exceedingly simple to very complex remains, is found here. This means that it is possible to examine with some reliability what might be called "cultural evolution." The second important point is that actual dates, in terms of our own calendar, are available for all well-known periods. Tree-ring dating has made this possible, particularly in northern Arizona and New Mexico. One chapter of this book is devoted to a discussion of the history, application, achievements, and limitations of this method.

Early in archaeological work here, and still to some extent in other fields, expeditions have been directed to the collection of remarkable museum specimens, even though a maximum of information might not be secured. The more recent tendency is to dig smaller sites than were investigated in the past. These small sites are most often sufficiently simple that the story they hold may be quite easily read, whereas the larger sites are so complex that their story may be obscure. Small sites were also generally occupied for a shorter time, thus making any dates derived from them more accurate, since houses were not so commonly rebuilt and beams reused.

The nonlogical "logic" of human activities complicates the task of the archaeologist, so that like the detective of popular conception he must have some knowledge of a great many fields, to secure every possible intelligent aid in the solving of past histories. Such fields as biology, chemistry, physics, geology, geography, history, psychology, and such less basic subjects as physiology, anthropometry, ethnology, physiography, ceramics, tree-ring studies, and many others are of the greatest direct aid.

At present Southwestern archaeology is changing rapidly. As information is gradually accumulated toward one end additional data are uncovered, modifying research and altering conclusions before they are fully reached. Even so, it is possible at any one time to summarize and present what at that time constitutes the most acceptable evaluation of known facts, even though these conclusions will probably be altered with the accumulation of more information. Before a brief summary of prehistoric history is presented, certain concepts should be clarified.

Culture, in the sense in which it will be used here, does not mean refinement. It does mean more nearly the average, conventional activities of the group considered. Any group which may be isolated either geographically or in time may be considered distinctive culturally when the total culture of that group is markedly different from the total culture, or means of doing things, of any other. The greater these differences, the more basic to the lives of the people, the more basic the group. The largest and most basic of these cultural groups in the Southwest are referred to as roots.

Smaller cultural divisions form branches, being the various developmental series which have sprung from roots. Branches are composed of a series of sites which may be grouped together to form a time or evolutionary sequence. They are also confined to certain sections, usually occupying much smaller areas than roots. Here branches will not be discussed in detail although one or two must be mentioned.

The smallest division which is commonly made, above the individual site, is the focus, or phase. This unit is composed of several sites which all have essentially the same culture, and hence are of the same time, and must be in at least approximately the same geographical area.

The archaeological unit which might be considered the Southwest should include, at the most, Arizona, New Mexico, the southwestern half of Colorado, most of Utah, the southern tip of Nevada, perhaps the extreme southeastern edge of California, and an undetermined amount of northern Mexico. Throughout all this section the culture is more like that of the center than like that of any other known area. It may therefore be considered a unit. The actual center of Southwestern culture, as now understood, is probably best represented along a line between Arizona and New Mexico from the four corners (Arizona, New Mexico, Colorado, and Utah) south to the Mexican border. This is fortunately also the best-known portion of the Southwest, and it happens to be nearly the center of the section suggested as including the maximum spread of this culture.

In following chapters the center will be considered first and later the outlying portions will be compared to it. It must be remembered that all details upon which proof of the theses suggested in this summary rest will also be found in the following chapters. In this eastern Arizona and western New Mexico section all known major stages in the development of the prehistoric Southwesterner are represented. Other developments are, as now seen, variants of these basic patterns. Though movements are recognizable at various times in the past the most consistently outstanding culture area seems to have been in this center until almost historic times, when the greater numbers of Pueblo people moved east toward, and into, the Rio Grande valley.

Primitive people undoubtedly did not recognize boundaries to their domain other than those imposed by nature, with the result that there was constant interchange and spreading out of influence. Contacts between groups of diverse backgrounds seem to have been much more abundant in the Southwest than has been formerly suspected, and isolation of any group almost nonexistent. Natural environment, however, did affect this development somewhat.

A glance at the accompanying figure will show that the Southwest may easily be divided into two major sections·by an intermediate physiographic zone. The two major sections are the plateau and the desert, while separating them, like a long, carelessly dropped chain, is the mountain section. This also separates the plateau and the desert from the high plains to the east, and seems to have formed an indefinite culture hindrance, if not a barrier, in this direction.

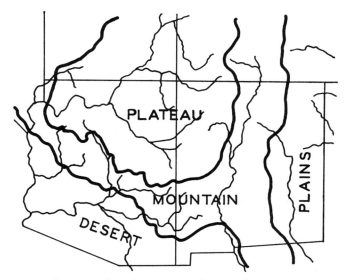

Fig. 1. The major physiographic divisions of the Southwest. Most important are the plateau, mountain, and desert. The plains section is outside the area of typical Southwestern culture. The center of the area is a wide zone along the Arizona–New Mexico border, between the four corners and Mexico.

Not only are these several physical provinces obviously marked, but also each is most characteristic of one broad class of prehistoric remains. To some extent this differentiation is a result of the restrictions imposed on the people by environment. This is particularly apparent in such features as the building of homes of adobe where rocks suitable for building are lacking, or the development of irrigation ditches where natural precipitation is too scanty to make farming possible otherwise. Of all these

provinces it has become increasingly apparent that the most important
in human development is the mountain section.

In almost every respect the mountain section is intermediate between
the plateau and desert. It is also the home of what now appears to have

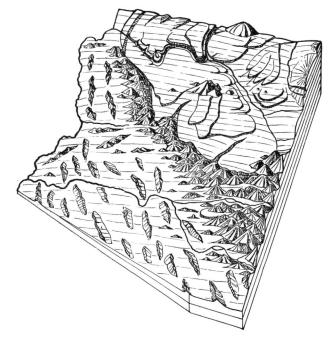

Fig. 2. Block diagram roughly illustrating the topography of the state of Arizona. The
three major divisions of the Southwest, the plateau, mountain, and desert sections, are
even more obvious in this state than in New Mexico, into which all three extend.

been the earliest, or at least one of the earliest highly developed, cultures of the Southwest. These first people, though relying upon hunting,
were also collectors of plant foods and were lesser agriculturists. From
them came style and fad influences, to shape and direct other people and
their histories. Later their own vitality became exhausted, and they were
in turn influenced by the very groups they had helped form.

This important group is now referred to as people of Mogollon culture.
They were originally confined to the mountain section and seem to have
most flourished in the mountains between Arizona and New Mexico. Because of the importance of this culture it is known as the Mogollon Root.
A similarly basic culture is the Basket Maker Root. Possibly as early, or
nearly as early, it began its history in the plateau section of the Southwest, apparently somewhere near the four corners.

Present evidence suggests that both these groups were well established
in their respective quarters by about the beginning of the Christian era, or

Dogoszhibiko Canyon in north central Arizona. This canyon is characteristic of the topography of the northeastern part of the state. It is in the tall sandstone cliffs that natural caves were formed which were commonly occupied by prehistoric Indians.

shortly thereafter, but with an earlier Mogollon development in south-western New Mexico and southeastern Arizona. At about this date a third basic group developed, probably as a modified offshoot of the Mogollon. These people made their homes in the desert section, and had a culture sufficiently distinctive to place them in a separate category, the Hohokam Root.

More recent research along the Colorado River in western Arizona has brought to light an additional distinctive group, the Patayan Root. Much remains to be learned about these people, most recently admitted and least studied, but what is known shows them so different from other roots as to suggest a separate group.

Common usage has grouped Pueblo culture with Basket Maker under the broader heading of Anasazi, and this is a useful and usable concept when dealing with the general cultural history of the plateau area. Pueblo culture now seems to have developed from a Basket Maker base as a result of influences from Mogollon, and hence appears to be a slightly different sort of development than those just mentioned, though not radi-cally so. For these reasons the Basket Maker Root is still considered the base from which these developments have sprung. There is a tendency to make still further root distinctions, but most of these are found upon serious examination to be more nearly variants of the roots here men-tioned than antecedent forms of later developments.

Once these divisions are established it is possible to consider them in the light of their individual historical developments. Groups of prehistoric people, or tribes, are apparent, and various types of cultural groups are also identifiable. In the briefest possible manner the history of each of these broad groups might be summarized as follows.

Early Man

The first known people to occupy the Southwest were living in the area now known as New Mexico and Colorado, and on into the plains at the east, some 12,000 or 13,000 years ago. They were part of what has been regarded as a hunting group, known mostly from kill sites of large, often now extinct, types of animals, which they hunted with spears tipped with leaf-shaped blades. Since they were apparently predominantly hunt-ers they roved about the lakes and stream valleys of this portion of the Southwest and at no place left much in the way of remains. Some of the spear points had flakes running up from the base, and most of them were rather expertly flaked.

We really do not know anything about these earliest people themselves, and little about their culture, except that they had stone projectile points

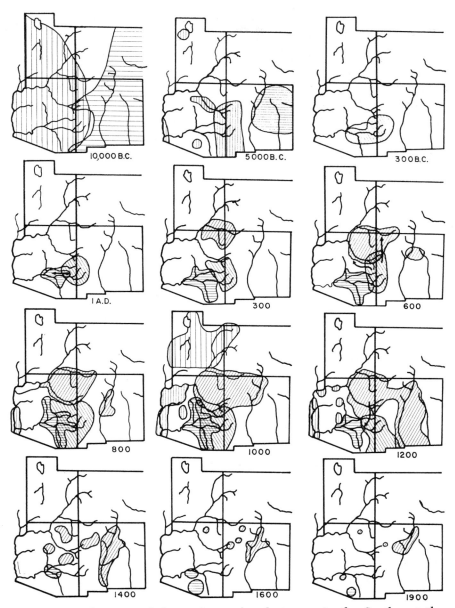

Fig. 3. The development of the various cultural streams in the Southwest through time. The wide-spaced vertical lines are of the Desert culture at 10,000 B.C., the horizontal lines are of the Hunter culture. The diagonal lines from upper left to lower right are Mogollon culture, those from upper right to lower left Anasazi culture, horizontal lines are Hohokam, while vertical fine lines are Patayan. The overlapping of cultures is shown by overlapping lines, and heavy lines with arrows show directions of influence. The growth of these various cultural streams and their movements within the Southwest may be seen in this series of maps.

and shaped bone into tools. Mammoths were among the animals they successfully hunted. In some places they crossed over into what is now Arizona, so that this section of the Southwest is about the western boundary of the area they ranged.

At about the same time, or perhaps a few years later, another group was occupying the basin and range country to the west of this primarily hunter group. These latter people were more gatherers and collectors than they were hunters, though they seem to have hunted some as well. It has been suggested that all of these various gathering groups be referred to as belonging to the Desert culture, mostly in distinction to the hunters to the east.

At 5000 B.C. the Desert culture was probably best represented in the Southwest by the Cochise culture. This culture has been divided into at least three sequential stages which can be distinguished. Grinding stones were more important than spear or projectile points, and the most common chipped stone tool was a rather crudely shaped chopper, or rough scraper. Since Cochise culture apparently lasted, in some areas, until almost the time of Christ, and began 10,000 or 11,000 years ago, it had a life span of some 8,000 or 9,000 years. During all this time the general way of life shows comparatively little change.

Seven thousand years ago the general hunting way of life seems to have still been in vogue in eastern New Mexico, and on east into the plains area. At least such is suggested by the types of projectile points which are found here, and by some of the carbon 14 dates which have been secured.

Certain cave sites, in Utah, Arizona, Nevada, and New Mexico, have been found which were occupied well back into this early time. Perishable materials are preserved in them, and add to the list of artifacts made and used by these people. Toward the end of this period, at perhaps 2000 B.C., corn appears in New Mexico caves but, although it is represented by quantities of cobs, probably did not form the main basis of their subsistence.

At 200 or 300 B.C. some rather important additions were made to the cultural inventory of the Desert culture, notably the use of pottery and the construction of houses. Deliberate burials were also extensively made, and storage pits became much more common. Projectile points were broad, diagonally notched types, and in several other ways this cultural change suggests influences from the plains area, or Midwest.

Mogollon Culture

With the addition of the traits mentioned above to the Desert culture it developed into what has been called the Mogollon culture. The first pottery which was made by the Mogollon people was brown, or reddish, and not decorated in any way. This general kind of pottery enjoyed a widespread distribution in the Southwest during the next several years. It has been assumed that pottery making, or at least the general principle of pottery making, was introduced into this southern desert and mountain portion of the Southwest from Mexico. People at this time, and with this general kind of culture, lived both in the mountain area and in the Gila and Salt River valleys, for pottery of this type is found throughout this entire area. Those individuals who occupied the desert proper soon underwent sufficient change that they may be identified as the Hohokam.

The earliest Mogollon culture shows definite relationships back to the Cochise culture. Stone artifacts are predominantly Cochise in nature, and it is only in other traits that the two may be distinguished.

By about the time of Christ Mogollon culture was well established, and was a vigorous cultural group. Although these people had corn they practiced gathering, and collecting, and hunting as well. From the beginning one of the most striking features of this group is the presence of large structures in each settlement which should probably best be regarded as special ceremonial structures. Other houses were pits dug into the ground, entered by a relatively long passageway sloping down to the floor, and roofed with wood covered with earth.

Present evidence indicates that physically the Mogollon people had more or less rounded heads which tended to be high and were occasionally flattened somewhat in the back, perhaps by the use of a hard cradle board or some other more deliberate means. Interest in the manufacture of pottery led to the creation of more varied forms, and perhaps simple ornamentation. The atlatl was the main hunting implement, but the bow and arrow was introduced either about now or shortly after. At this time the Hohokam had become considerably differentiated.

Some 300 years later, or about A.D. 300, Mogollon culture was still developing and was beginning to exert more influence on other areas surrounding it, although a few years later still it exerted even more influence, especially to the north and the northwest. Mogollon culture does not show any rapid or unusual developments, but rather a gradual and apparently quite successful fitting into the environment. The people were still living in pithouses and they still had the large ceremonial structures. Disposal of the dead was by inhumation in which the body was loosely flexed. Stone carving and working continued much as it had been in the past, and probably their best early achievement was in their pottery, which along with that being developed by the Hohokam was the only pottery being made in the Southwest at this time. It consisted of rather thin red and buff types, with some red painting on the brown backgrounds, and the development of some texturing in surface finish.

By A.D. 600 Mogollon culture was apparently exerting considerable influence on cultures which had been developing to the north. Basket Maker culture had already been established here, and Mogollon was exerting a considerable influence on it. Ceramics were introduced to the Basket Maker people at about this time, as well as houses and other features, and these ideas well may have come through the Mogollon. The house was still a pithouse, had a side entrance, and the economy still included a certain amount of hunting and gathering. Some very simple red-on-brown pottery types were being made. Stone work on the whole seems to have been better, but was never so elaborate as that of the Hohokam culture to the west. Disposal of the dead was by flexed inhumation.

By about A.D. 800 Mogollon culture was expanding somewhat to the west, to overlap in part that of the Hohokam. Probably Mogollon culture, as a distinct entity, was not far from its peak of development. The people were living in relatively deep pithouses, and they were still constructing large ceremonial structures. Even from the beginning Mogollon villages were of some size, consisting of several pithouses more or less grouped on points or ridges.

Some 200 years later, or at about A.D. 1000, Mogollon, or a Mogollon-like culture, had spread northwestward to include the Flagstaff area, and north into the White Mountains. It had also spread into the desert, where it overlapped with Hohokam. Particularly to the south there was a gradual intergrading between Mogollon and Hohokam. In most ways, however, Mogollon had definitely passed its peak of both cultural development and influence and was beginning to wane as a separate entity. The general economy had shifted to a more sedentary type, with greater stress on agriculture. It is interesting that although Mogollon people were the first in the Southwest known to have had corn they did not rely on agriculture at any time during their existence as much as some of the other groups, notably the Hohokam and the Anasazi.

The pottery was changing from the previous red-on-brown types to a red-on-cream, or a black-on-white series which was developing in the south. Most marked alteration in Mogollon culture was the Pueblo influence, which was affecting it from the north.

By A.D. 1200 Mogollon culture was experiencing considerable pressures and undergoing many changes, as a result of the Anasazi influences from the north. Surface masonry structures were being lived in, and pottery was more Anasazi than it was native Mogollon. From about this time on, or shortly thereafter, any vestiges of Mogollon culture which are to be found are in the very southern part of the Southwest, or in northern Mexico.

Hohokam Culture

The development of Hohokam culture in its early part is clearly linked with that of Mogollon. In the beginning they are much alike, and it is probable that they came from the same main stream of cultural influences, the earlier Cochise of the Desert culture. Hohokam, the group which developed in the desert, as opposed to the mountain-dwelling Mogollon, soon took on a very different and distinctive flavor. The Pioneer Hohokam, like the early Mogollon, had pottery, but after the first types of the Hohokam their pottery was predominantly buff in color, was made by the paddle and anvil process, and was fired in an oxidizing atmosphere.

The Hohokam may be further differentiated from their contemporaries by the fact that they cremated their dead. They lived in very shallow pithouses, or at least houses constructed of brush which were built in shallow pits. By about the time of Christ the two groups were clearly differentiated, in the ways just enumerated, and by A.D. 300 they were living quite different ways of life.

By this time Hohokam culture was based almost solely on agriculture, which in turn was dependent on irrigation. Pottery types were a fine red and a plain buff, and in lesser amounts there was a red-on-buff decorated pottery. Interesting human figurines, made of clay, were somewhat suggestive of those of Mexico. Chipped and ground stone work was excellent, particularly an outstandingly well-made long-bitted axe which had a raised ridge about each side of the three-quarter groove. Ornaments of both shell and bone were exceptionally well made, and abundant. Since cremation was universal at this time nothing is known of the physical type.

By A.D. 600 Hohokam culture was very highly developed, possibly also reaching near its peak, or soon to achieve this level. Characteristic features are the presence of huge ball courts, extensive irrigation systems, and excellent shell and ground stone work. Houses were still long pithouses, with more or less rounded ends and short lateral entrances. Pottery was plain buff, and red-on-buff, but considerably specialized from the preceding types. Carved stone vessels, palettes, and mirrors, the last suggesting similar objects known from Mexico, were all outstanding carved stone work.

Some 200 years later, at A.D. 800, Hohokam culture was somewhat overlapping on the east with Mogollon. It had far outstripped Mogollon, however, in regard to exotic traits, many of which suggest they were derived, at least in the form of ideas, from Mexico. The same general type of pithouses prevailed at this time, and the stone work was similar, though perhaps somewhat more ornate. Many of the arrow points were remarkably long, slender, and well made, often with deep serrations along the edges. Both shell and bone were carved in cutout and full round styles,

White House Pueblo in Canyon de Chelly is a good example of a small cliff pueblo in this eastern part of the San Juan drainage.

and were about as well done as any ever produced here. Cremation was still the only method of disposal of the dead.

At about A.D. 1000 the edges of Hohokam and Mogollon cultures were further overlapping, and in the south, along the streams draining into the Gila River, there was a certain amount of intergrading of the cultures. The Hohokam houses were still long oval pithouses. Great irrigation projects were characteristic, but the more abundant ball courts were much smaller than those of the preceding type. Pottery showed an increase in what has been referred to as fabric styles of design in the red-on-buff types. Figurines of clay now consisted of only heads which had hollowed-out backs, and were probably put on sticks or other supports. Ground and chipped stone objects were still on the whole remarkably well made, particularly exotic forms of arrow points. A most interesting feature of Hohokam culture of this age was the inclusion of cast copper bells, made locally by the lost wax method.

Hohokam culture at A.D. 1200 was in no way strikingly outstanding. Beginning at about this time the first of a group of Pueblo-derived people seems to have moved into the drainage of the Gila and Salt rivers, and to have lived peacefully with the declining Hohokam groups. In some cases the two peoples appear to have actually occupied the same villages. The Hohokam clung tenaciously to most of the basic features of their own culture, living in pithouses even though the Puebloans were then occupying compounds, and cremating their dead when the Pueblo people practiced inhumation. They also clung to their typical ceramic industry, producing red, buff, and red-on-buff pottery types, when the Pueblo people were making their much more colorful polychrome pottery.

What became of the Hohokam people is still uncertain. It has been suggested that they survive in some of the desert dwellers of today. If so, the general nature of their culture has considerably altered from that of the peak of Hohokam.

Anasazi Culture

In the plateau country to the north what may eventually prove to be one of the earliest evidences of man is found on the terraces along the Little Colorado River. The date of these artifacts—for the remains consist of very simple and crudely made stone tools—has never been determined, but they may prove to be of some real antiquity.

From about 5000 B.C. on to the time of Christ there is found, widely scattered throughout this northern country, evidence of a very simple gathering-collecting culture. In most respects these stone artifacts are typical of the Cochise culture, which has already been identified. There is

no doubt that they may be related to the early Desert culture, just as
Cochise is, and they are regarded by many archaeologists as being assignable to the postulated Basket Maker I stage of culture. Present evidence suggests that people of this way of life, and this culture stage, were
living here when in the Mogollon and Hohokam cultures such traits as
pottery were already in vogue.

Sometime after the time of Christ what has been defined as Basket
Maker II, or pure Basket Maker, became widespread throughout the plateau area. These people had some agriculture, but apparently extensively
supplemented it with gathering and hunting. They used the atlatl but
lacked the bow and arrow, though by this time there is good evidence
that the Mogollon people had arrows. They did not make any real pottery
of their own, and although they built storage pits, sometimes lined with
rock slabs set on edge, their homes were very impermanent structures at
most, except in the east, where they had simple circular houses. Some of
these people occupied caves, though many others seem to have spent
most of their time in the open. From the caves a good inventory of perishable objects have been recovered, so that considerable of the material
culture of these people is known. They wore sandals, made use of feathers
as ornaments, wove excellent baskets, and made fur or feather blankets.
Rather loosely flexed inhumation of the dead was characteristic. This general way of life survived in the plateau area to probably A.D. 500.

By about A.D. 600 the Basket Maker people were receiving, either directly or indirectly, many innovations presumably from, or by way of, the
Mogollon culture to the south. This included pottery making, and at least
some more permanent and varied houses. The main implement was still
the atlatl, and the people were apparently living much the same general
type of life their ancestors had lived. Arts and crafts, other than pottery
making, consisted largely of better-made examples of the things they had
been making before. Sandals were very expertly made, and many of the
baskets were excellent. Pottery, unlike that of the south, from which they
probably got the general idea of ceramics, was mostly fired in a reducing
atmosphere, which resulted in gray types.

By A.D. 800 many new ideas had reached this northern country, with
the result that this general way of life was changing from what might be
called Basket Maker to Pueblo. Unfortunately this period is not well known
over much of the plateau, but what is known suggests life in small, loosely
knit villages. Pottery was now black-on-white, with generally fine-line
decorations in geometric patterns, and neck corrugations. In some areas
of the plateau at this time this type of pottery seems to have been absent,
or of very brief duration. It is quite probable that the true ceremonial

chambers, or kivas, were in general use at this time by the Anasazi, although what seem to be large, perhaps ceremonial structures were built during the preceding period. Physically the people were changing from a long head to a more rounded one.

A general view of the north end of Kiet Siel Pueblo, a large Pueblo III cliff dwelling in Kiet Siel Canyon, a branch of the Tsegi Canyon system in north central Arizona. A circular kiva is in the foreground. Rectangular rooms with roof-support poles extending beyond the walls are typical. Doorways with recesses for the reception of flat stone covers show in the upper left.

Two hundred years later, or at A.D. 1000, Pueblo culture was well established and exceedingly widespread. This was a period of vigorous development, with many small villages or settlements, some sizable pueblos, and probably about as large a Pueblo population as at any time. The economy had standardized as essentially agricultural. Black-on-white pottery was more varied in shape and even decoration, although the most widespread was a broad-line decoration in geometric patterns. Corrugated pottery was made with the corrugations covering the entire outside of the vessel. In certain parts of the Southwest people were still living in individual pithouses, while in others they had developed unit-type pueblos, or larger pueblo structures. The kiva was well established in many portions of the plateau now. Agriculture had become the main basis of subsistence, and hunting and gathering were relegated to minor roles. In many ways this must have been one of the most pleasant and healthful periods in Anasazi history.

By A.D. 1200 Pueblo culture had spread over a wide area of northeastern Arizona and New Mexico. At this time it was beginning to exert some influence on the Mogollon culture to the south, and this Pueblo stimulus reached as far as the Upper Gila and Salt rivers, and had spread throughout the Rio Grande valley in New Mexico as well. Characteristic features are the presence of larger pueblos, elaborated and regionally varied types of black-on-white pottery, and the shift in ceramics to a greater interest in oxidized types, such as oranges and reds. The bow and arrow had long since replaced the atlatl as the main hunting implement, and the people were everywhere highly oriented to agriculture. This was a sort of peak of geographic expansion and cultural diversification.

By A.D. 1400 Pueblo culture had begun definitely to break up into geographically isolated segments. Most of the San Juan drainage was abandoned by shortly after 1300, and there was a shift of population to the east and south. It did not move in these directions without alteration, however, for it was changed or modified by every local group with which it came in contact. Notable centers were the Hopi country, where the ancestors of the present-day Hopi Indians were living, the Zuñi-Acoma area in northwestern New Mexico, the Rio Grande valley of New Mexico, which was rather widely occupied, the upper Little Colorado area where many large pueblos were flourishing, and even as far west as the Verde valley, where late Sinagua sites with many Pueblo characteristics were occupied. In each of these areas distinctive pottery types and even distinguishable variations of architecture were to be found. It is possible that the nomadic, warlike Athabascan Indians were now putting pressure on these Pueblo people, so that in at least some instances the huge pueblos were probably built for defense.

Although some black-on-white pottery was being made, yellow pottery and other oxidized types were also very common. Many individual ceramic types included decorations in glaze paints, a fad which persisted for some time, particularly in the upper Rio Grande area. This was apparently not a period of marked cultural decline, as has been suggested by some, but rather a time when many innovations of decorative styles and modifications of ceremonial customs took place. The concentration of the population in ever-larger and fewer sites was typical of the period, and carried over into the next.

From roughly A.D. 1600 on the area occupied by Pueblo culture was still further reduced, as a result of this continued concentration of the population in fewer sites. The Hopi Indians became more isolated in northern Arizona, but from Zuñi east, and into the Rio Grande, there were a number of sites which have persisted to today. This was the time when Spaniards were beginning to move into the Southwest in sufficient numbers to have some effect on Pueblo culture, particularly in New Mexico. New agricultural products, and domesticated animals, were being introduced to these people, so that the material culture part of their way of life was beginning gradually to change. There was still a considerable Pueblo population, and it had a well-integrated and vigorous culture.

From 1900 on Pueblo culture has undergone a gradual but accelerating change, particularly since the last war, so that within the last few years certain old and established customs are beginning to be abandoned. The availability of many material objects has rather markedly changed the way of life, particularly of the younger people. Most recently automobiles and trucks have become generally available, and this has tended to break down the isolation and conservatism of these pueblos. On the other hand the tenacity with which many individual pueblo groups have held to their older customs is amazing. There can be little doubt that within the next few years many of the older arts and crafts will be abandoned, except perhaps those produced for sale.

Rio Grande Cultures

In the Rio Grande valley the earliest major cultural development, after the very early hunting groups and the somewhat later gatherers, was about the equivalent of Basket Maker III. At this time, or possibly earlier, there was a rather widespread occurrence of a brown pottery which many feel was related to, or derived from, Mogollon. By A.D. 600 Basket Maker culture, or something related to it, had been established in the upper Rio Grande valley and the headwaters of the Pecos. By 800 a more nearly Pueblo type of culture was flourishing in the middle and upper Rio Grande valley. By 1000, if not before, Pueblo culture in the upper Rio Grande valley had taken on a distinctive New Mexican cast.

In general the material cultures of the two areas, New Mexico and Arizona, were pretty much parallel, with the exception of ceramics, and to a lesser extent architectural features. By A.D. 1200 the Rio Grande valley was quite different ceramically from the western pueblo area, with distinctive types of black-on-white pottery for the various geographic subdivisions of the valley, and the related pueblos to the west. The glaze types were developing, and the first of the so-called "biscuit wares" were being produced.

By A.D. 1400 New Mexico was quite different in details of ceramics from the Hopi development in Arizona. The Zuñi-Acoma culture area was well established, somewhat consolidated, and quite distinctive. Pueblos were found throughout the Rio Grande valley and in the headwaters of the Pecos River. On the east influences from the plains area are distinguish-

A portion of Kiet Siel Pueblo showing characteristic arrangement of house blocks and in the center a circular kiva.

able, and contact through trade was carried on to the west. By 1600 the New Mexico pueblo area had greatly reduced in total size occupied. In the Rio Grande valley the Spaniards were settling, and making the effects of their culture felt for the first time. The Navaho Indians were also a threat to the peaceful pueblos, and as a result Pueblo culture in general began to retrench, both physically, in defendable large villages, and culturally. By 1900 the New Mexico pueblos had reached a sort of balance with American culture which surrounded them and more or less threatened to overwhelm them. Subsequently these pueblos have changed gradually in about the same way as have the Hopi Indians of the West.

Patayan Culture

Along the Colorado River in Arizona, and east from there to the Verde River, another generally different culture existed, which has most commonly been termed the Patayan. The earliest evidence of occupation is probably that of the lower Colorado River, and of the desert areas of California. Here, some 5,000 years ago, people of a general Desert culture type lived. They are represented mostly by distinctive projectile points and a few crudely shaped stone artifacts.

By A.D. 800 there were people again, or perhaps still, living along the lower Colorado River valley. Schroeder has assigned this lower river material to what he has called the Laguish culture. It includes some influences from the east and may have its roots back into much earlier bases. From the Grand Canyon west to the big bend of the Colorado River the Patayan culture is best known from the Cohonina branch. Here pottery was of a type very suggestive of the Pueblo I black-on-whites of the Anasazi, and must somehow be related to it. House types consisted of the considerable use of shades, a supported roof without walls, large brush and clay–walled rooms with associated storage rooms, and what have been called patio houses.

By A.D. 1000 the Patayan culture had reached a sort of peak, with a distinctive kind of black-on-gray pottery found in the Cohonina branch south of the Grand Canyon. One other distinctive ceramic product was the creation of very large storage jars which were covered on the outside with a heavy red paint, and which were rather widely traded to the people to the east. Houses were of the patio house type, and some of the larger structures seem to have developed into what have been called forts. As one moves west through this area the pottery becomes less and less well-fired gray, and more and more brownish.

Two hundred years later, by A.D. 1200, Cohonina culture was much restricted in area, and less vigorous. To the west of it was the Cerbat branch, where more brown pottery was found, and on down the Colorado River there were people who probably were to become the present-day Colorado River tribes. After 1200 what became of these northern Patayan people has been much discussed. It is believed by some that they became the Havasupai Indians, who now inhabit Supai Canyon and the immediate areas about Supai Canyon on the south rim of the Grand Canyon.

Fremont Culture

In Utah by A.D. 1000, or a little later, there was a culture which was much like Pueblo culture but which may be distinguished from it. It may be divided into an eastern and a western phase, the eastern being called Fremont, and the western Sevier Fremont. Of the two, Sevier Fremont seems to show the most Puebloid traits. On the south it grades into, or meets, the Anasazi culture. This represents what may be considered about the northernmost Southwestern cultural development, and in many ways it is more closely related to the older Desert culture than to the more contemporary higher cultural developments to the south.

Modern Peoples

From A.D. 1600 on, with the beginning of written records, the general present pattern of occupation, and all the modern tribes, were established in the Southwest, with the possible exception of the Papago and Yaqui Indians in the extreme south. Although the Papago may be descendants of the desert branch of the Hohokam, this supposition still remains to be demonstrated. Of considerable interest is the postulated time of arrival of the nomadic Indians, the Navaho and Apache. Probably they were originally the same tribe, for the early Spaniards noted them and applied the same name to both of them. They were certainly present in the Southwest by A.D. 1600, and perhaps somewhat earlier, and enjoyed a very rapid rise in numbers, particularly the Navaho.

From about A.D. 1700 on the Navahos and Apaches were a serious menace to the Pueblo Indians, and before that date they had been the cause of some pueblos moving to places of better protection, such as the tops of mesas where the Hopis have mostly remained since. The Navaho Indians occupy most of the eastern portion of the plateau, while the Apaches are scattered throughout the mountain section.

The occupants of the Gila and Salt River drainages of the desert are the Pima, Papago, and Yaqui Indians, with a sprinkling of Maricopa recently moved eastward from the Colorado River. As has been suggested, it is possible that some of these people may be the modern descendants of the Hohokam. Along the Colorado River proper the tribes which belong to the Yuman-speaking group of Indians are found. Northern and eastern representatives are the Walapai and Havasupai, possibly descendants of the ancient Patayan people. Far to the north, in Utah, are the Utes and Paiutes, quite possibly direct descendants of the very ancient Basket Maker Indians of the plateau, for even today their culture is somewhat suggestive of these old people.

Summary

Such in the most general possible terms is the reconstructed history of the prehistoric tribes of the Southwest. In this series the most complete details are known about the later groups, the most incomplete about the earlier. The earliest occupants are the hunter and collector peoples, of which Cochise developed into Mogollon culture, one of the strongest early groups. Some of these in turn were found living in the desert section, and they took on some traits from as far away as Mexico to become the Hohokam. At about the same time, or a little later, another group was either introduced into the Colorado River area, or the Hohokam moved into this section and took on still another type of culture, the Patayan. Little is even yet known in detail about this assumed root, except that it is different from the other known groups. What became of all these people in late prehistoric times still remains an open question.

In the plateau section, at about the time of Christ, the Basket Maker culture became established, an outgrowth of the generalized Desert culture, and developed into a clearly different type of culture despite the fact that it shared many general simple traits with early Mogollon. Later it was strongly influenced from without, probably by the Mogollon people, who were then expanding northward. With many modifications to the original culture, and with many additions, even to a new physical type, it became Pueblo. Late in the prehistory of the Pueblo people they moved southward, only a few stopping in northern Arizona, many going to the mountain section south and east, and a few southwest to the Gila and Salt rivers. This abandonment of the San Juan in the north caused some reshuffling of people to the south so that influences from the north spread out like a stack of toppling cards. To the east, some groups moved into the northern Rio Grande section and intermediate regions, and the most northern group, the Taos Indians, and the most eastern, the Pecos Indians, were in contact with the plains. These Pueblo Indians are obviously the direct descendants of the Anasazi, tracing their ancestry back without any appreciable break to at least the Basket Makers in the plateau section of the Southwest.

GEOLOGY, PHYSIOGRAPHY, CLIMATE, FLORA, FAUNA

As has been pointed out, it is possible to divide the Southwest into four physiographic divisions. These are the plateau, the desert, the mountain, and the plains sections. The last is of little major importance to any discussion of archaeology, but the other three are of extreme importance in understanding the environment which affected Southwestern cultures.

The plateau, extension of the great Colorado Plateau, is an area of relatively flat-lying sedimentary rocks (sandstones, limestones, shales, and occasional conglomerates). Although they are nearly flat they tend to

Photo by Jerry McLain, Phoenix, Arizona

This is a typical view of the desert area showing the desert flora and a mountain rising steeply from the wide-open alluvium-filled valley.

dip gently down as they extend northward, so that, though elevation may be lost in going through some portions in this direction, more recent rocks are progressively traversed. The most commonly exposed rocks are of either Permian or more recent age.

Scattered about over the plateau, particularly in the southern half, are areas which are covered by widespread lava flows, and cinder and lava cones. The great San Francisco volcanic field, which centers at Flagstaff, is an example. The northern half is made up predominantly of sandstones and shales, of which the bright red cliff-forming Navaho and Wingate sandstones are the most prominent.

The desert section is composed of high block-faulted mountains, with huge basins formed between these ranges, which are filled, sometimes to great depths, with such eroded materials as sands, gravels, and clays. The mountain ranges tend to have a northwest-southeast trend, with the steep faces in any direction. The rocks of which they are composed range from very early, often metamorphosed, hard rocks (quartzites, gneisses, and schists) through unaltered sedimentary rocks to relatively recent lava flows, and great series of volcanic tuffs.

The mountain section, both between the plateau and the desert, and between these and the plains, is intermediate in most characteristics, being largely of either volcanic or erosional origin. The high plains are huge, gently sloping accumulations of erosional material swept out from the Rocky Mountains.

Physiographically the plateau is deeply cut by the Colorado River (which forms the Grand Canyon in Arizona) and is widely drained by the Little Colorado River. This latter stream has formed a great basin-like valley which rises from it in every direction. Deep cutting of these rivers and their tributaries has resulted in the sculpturing of the sandstones into the mesas and box canyons so widely recognized as typically Southwestern.

Southern Arizona is cut by only one stream, the Gila, which with its tributary the Salt furnished the major erosional agent of the entire desert section. Typical features are the lava-topped mesas and large Piedmont slopes, but the box canyons characteristic of the plateau are entirely absent.

The mountain region combines some of the features of both the plateau and desert but is largely made up of erosional mountains. Valleys are typically of the mountain type, rather narrow and commonly with abundant streams. This is an area of rugged topography, often with considerable altitudinal variations between valleys.

In New Mexico the Rio Grande, like the Gila and Salt in Arizona, is a major permanent stream which drains a wide area. It flows south through the central part of the state, in a valley which in many places is broad and silt-filled. It proved as attractive to human occupation in New Mexico as did the Gila in Arizona, even from the earliest times. The later Pueblo occupation is clustered along the upper stretches of this river in rather concentrated settlements, and it was here that the Spaniards first seriously settled.

The average annual temperature variations of the Southwest are controlled more by altitude than by location, that of Flagstaff at 7,000 feet being 45.4°, and Yuma with an altitude of 141 feet being 71.9°. Though the entire Southwest may be considered somewhat desertic, Yuma, the lowest point and with the least annual rainfall, has 3.25 inches, while most places of 6,000 feet or more have 20 inches or more. Aside from the mountains most of the desert country has 10 inches or less of rainfall, a condition similar to the desert sections of the Little Colorado valley.

Fig. 4. Diagrammatic section of Arizona from the southwest to the northeast corner, showing block-faulted mountains and alluvial-filled valleys of the desert, eroded mountains of the mountain section, and dipping sedimentaries of the plateau. This represents roughly the path of the moisture-carrying winds as they cross the state, and is a typical section of western New Mexico as well.

The prevailing storm-carrying winds over Arizona and the western portion of New Mexico are southwesterlies, which transport moisture from the Gulf of California or the Pacific coast. In eastern New Mexico many of the storm-bearing winds come from the east or southeast. As a result of the wind direction most of the rain in the plateau section falls upon the porous rocks of the mesas and higher mountains, there either to run off, forming small intermittent streams, or to filter through the sandstones to issue as seep springs. As human occupation of any given locality in this country was largely determined by the presence of an adequate domestic water supply, the population was often clustered about such springs.

In the desert section the chief source of water was the permanent streams, such as the Gila and Salt rivers, or in the small canyons cutting the higher mountains, where streams were fed by summer rains or melting winter snows.

The intermediate mountain region, as a result of the more abundant rain and snowfall, had a greater number of permanent streams, which, winding through rich alluvial valleys, formed ideal locations for agriculture. This more certain growing of crops made a simpler existence possible but was limited to small isolated tracts, none of which could be at too great an altitude (not more than about 7,000 feet) to permit a sufficiently long growing season.

Like rainfall and temperature, the flora of the Southwest is, to a great extent, controlled by altitude. In a very general way the following altitude divisions conform to the suggested types of plant life.

ALTITUDE, FEET	PLANT LIFE
10,000–8,500	Spruce and Douglas fir
8,500–7,000	Yellow pine
7,000–6,000	Piñon and juniper
6,000–3,500	Open country composed of:
6,000–5,000	Sagebrush, rabbitbush, etc.
5,000–4,000	Grassland
4,000–3,500	Sage, salt bush, etc.
3,500 down	Typical desert, cacti, mesquite, etc.

In specific instances this classification does not hold true, for, in sheltered spots in deep canyons, types of trees such as Douglas fir may be found at much lower altitudes than normally. In the plateau the pine, piñon, juniper, sagebrush series prevails, but to the south the transition from pine to oak to grassland is probably more typical.

Because of their ease of mobility and adaptability the larger mammals of the Southwest do not conform closely to regional distinctions. In the heavier forest areas the big mule deer and the elk were most at home, while mountain sheep ranged through this zone from the highest altitudes to the open cactus-filled valleys of the desert. In the most open country of both the north and south whitetail deer were found, and in the southern deserts the big gray variation of the mule deer. Antelope ranged throughout most of the truly open regions of deserts and plains, and in all these zones the predators, mountain lions, wolves, coyotes, and foxes, followed the other game.

Rodents seem to have been more confined by the effects of altitude. Rabbits of several species, including both jacks and cottontails, ranged widely throughout the Southwest. Beaver originally frequented most of the streams, even extending their range well into the deserts of both the plateau and the desert sections. Tree squirrels were plentiful in all timbered sections, while various species and subspecies of pack rats, ground squirrels, gophers, and mice were characteristic of almost every zone, and the kangaroo or jumping rats and mice were found in the desert stretches.

Though one is likely to expect little of bird life in the Southwest, an amazing variety and some abundance are found. The larger birds, like the larger mammals, are generally the most wide-ranging. The wild turkey, king of American game birds, was widely distributed wherever sufficiently brushy cover could be found.

In prehistoric times the bird and animal life must have been very

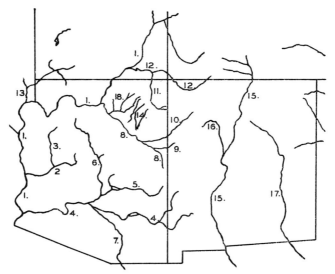

Fig. 5. Major rivers of the archaeological Southwest. 1. Colorado River. 2. Bill Williams River. 3. Big Sandy River. 4. Gila River. 5. Salt River. 6. Verde River. 7. Santa Cruz River. 8. Little Colorado River. 9. Zuñi River. 10. Rio Puerco of the West. 11. Chinlee Wash. 12. San Juan River. 13. Virgin River. 14. Hopi Washes. 15. Rio Grande. 16. Rio Puerco of the East. 17. Pecos River. 18. Moenkopi Wash.

abundant indeed. Records of early trappers, hunters, and military expeditions into the Southwest reported an almost unbelievable abundance of game birds and animals from various sections. The nature of the country probably tended to center animal populations in certain localities, as it does today, and left others relatively sparse. Since wild animals prefer rather dense cover, and agriculture cannot, as a rule, be best practiced there, it is quite likely that with the rise of agriculture the human and animal populations were increasingly separated.

Rainfall in no part of the Southwest is sufficiently abundant to establish many permanently running streams, and as a result those which do exist are advanced to a position of magnified importance. This situation is true of every country where rainfall is at a minimum, and strikingly enough many of the earliest primitive civilizations have had their rise in areas not greatly different, climatically, from that of the Southwest.

Because the waters of a dry country are concentrated in the river valleys and systems, the population of the area, dependent primarily upon water, is also found more or less centered here. Dr. Kidder, in his *Introduction to Southwestern Archaeology* in 1924, clearly recognizing this fact, roughly bounded and appropriately named these areas. In this man-

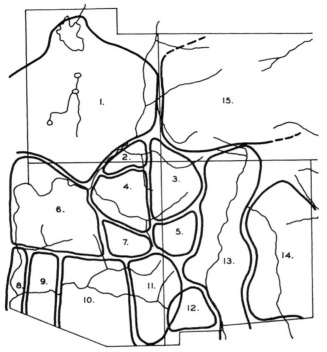

Fig. 6. Rough outline of geographic areas of the Southwest. 1. Northern peripheral area. 2. Western San Juan. 3. Eastern San Juan. 4. Hopi or Little Colorado area. 5. Zuñi area. 6. Kingman area. 7. Mountain area. 8. Colorado River area. 9. Lower Gila. 10. Middle Gila. 11. Upper Gila. 12. Mimbres. 13. Rio Grande. 14. Eastern peripheral area. 15. Western Colorado area.

ner the various culture divisions may still be bounded by drainage provinces. Subsequent investigation, however, has indicated that these divisions, based only on drainages, are not strictly correct, and that they must often be broken up or subdivided into smaller sections on the basis of minute and vital physoiographic or ecological variations.

The accompanying map is an attempt to present the larger of these physiographic divisions for the purpose of fixing in mind the geographical areas. In referring to a general locality and not a specific section it is still most useful to speak of the western San Juan or the Upper Gila.

However, it must be borne in mind that primitive people did not al-

ways hold strictly to any rule, either man-made or of nature; in many instances in various places they spilled over their natural boundaries and
intermingled. The more detailed a study is made of any problem the more
complex it is quite likely to become, as the following chapters will demonstrate is true in Southwestern archaeology.

Sources and Additional References

Colton, Harold S. The Geography of Certain Ruins Near the San Francisco
Mountains, Arizona, *Bulletin of the Geographical Society of Philadelphia*, Vol.
16, No. 2, 1918.

———. * Sunset Crater, the Effect of a Volcanic Eruption on an Ancient Pueblo
People, *Geographical Review*, Vol. 22, No. 4, 1932, American Geographical
Society, New York City. (Environmental change resulting from a cinder fall.)

———. * The Rise and Fall of the Prehistoric Population of Northern Arizona,
Science, Vol. 84, No. 2181, 1936, New York City. (Human ecology of prehistoric and modern Indians of northern Arizona.)

Gregory, H. E. * The Navaho Country, *Bulletin 380*, 1918, United States Geological Survey, Washington, D.C. (Best basic paper on the Navaho country
of northeastern Arizona.)

Hack, John T. The Changing Physical Environment of the Hopi Indians of
Arizona, *Papers of the Peabody Museum of American Archaeology and Eth-
nology*, Vol. 35, No. 1, 1942, Harvard University, Cambridge, Massachusetts.
(As indicated by title.)

Hoover, J. W. The Indian Country of Southern Arizona, *Geographical Review*,
Vol. 19, No. 1, 1929, American Geographical Society, New York City. (The
Papago, Pima country.)

———. Modern Canyon Dwellers of Arizona, *Journal of Geography*, Vol. 27,
No. 7, 1929, Chicago. (Havasupai Indians.)

———. Tusayan, the Hopi Indian Country of Arizona, *Geographical Review*,
Vol. 20, No. 3, 1930, American Geographical Society, New York City. (Hopi
geography.)

———. House and Village Types of the Southwest as Conditioned by Aridity,
Scientific Monthly, Vol. 40, 1935, New York City. (Effect of natural conditions on house types.)

———. * Physiographic Provinces of Arizona, *Pan-American Geologist*, Vol. 65,
1936, Geological Publishing Co., Des Moines, Iowa. (Source from which the
three major and other sections have been taken.)

Kidder, Alfred Vincent. * An Introduction to the Study of Southwestern Archaeology, Phillips Academy, Andover, Massachusetts, 1924. (Basic reference book
for all our work.)

Smith, H. V. The Climate of Arizona, *University of Arizona Bulletin 130*, 1930,
Tucson. (Tables of data on Arizona climate.)

NOTE. An attempt has been made to list only the most pertinent bibliography in
this volume, with an emphasis on those papers which are widely available. The references deemed most important are marked with an asterisk.

II

History of Southwestern Archaeology

Before the problems of Southwestern archaeology can be thoroughly grasped, it is necessary to review history so that past conditions and methods may be more intelligently compared with present ones. For years the remains of prehistoric Southwestern civilizations have been recognized, and from the very beginning of recorded history much interested conjecture has been raised concerning the people who left them. To facilitate discussion, the history has been divided into nine more or less natural sections, each of which may be defined by certain easily recognizable characteristics.

The history of the Southwest is divisible, in its early part, into two major geographically separate groups: the exploration and colonization which went up the Rio Grande valley, and that which centered in northern Sonora and southern Arizona. This latter followed the Santa Cruz River, and eventually worked its way into the Gila drainage. In like manner two great temporal divisions can be established, the first of which may be termed Spanish invasion, and the second American.

SPANISH EXPLORATION AND COLONIZATION—1540 to 1692

The history of Arizona actually begins in 1539 when Fray Marcos de Niza and a negro, Estavanico, "Black Stephen," entered Arizona from Mexico in search of the famed Cibola. Though the negro was killed, Fray Marcos returned with such glowing tales of wealth to be gained in this new country that Coronado sent Diaz and Zaldivar back, in the same year, to verify the story. This expedition probably never got farther than the Gila River but returned to report the finding of the seven cities and to substantiate the claims made for them.

In 1540 Coronado had succeeded in actually organizing his expedition and entered the Southwest with 300 Spaniards and about 800 Indians. During his travels in search of the mythical Cibola, city of gold, he and his men noted and often discussed the ruins which they encountered on the way, particularly those in the vicinity of Zuñi, where they stopped for some time.

It was while at Zuñi that Coronado learned of the province of Tusayan, some 25 leagues to the northwest, where another group of Indians (the Hopis) were living. Coronado dispatched Don Pedro de Tovar to investigate this report. Arriving at the Hopi towns, the small band saw little of interest, certainly nothing comparable to the seven cities. Don Lopez de Cardinas, hearing rumors of a great canyon to the west, pushed on and was undoubtedly the first white man to see the Grand Canyon. This was probably about the extent of the travels of the expedition in northern Arizona, although they went much farther northeast, almost certainly crossing the Canadian River. Coronado arrived at Zuñi about June 6-10, 1540, and returned to Mexico and disbanded by June, 1542.

Because of the difficulties attendant upon any expedition into the Southwest, few explorations were made in the next several years. In 1581 Friar Fay Augustin Rodriguez and two others, with eight or nine soldiers, went up the Rio Grande to the pueblo of Puaray, where they were left with the Indians and the soldiers returned to Mexico. Late in 1582 Don Antonio de Espejo and 14 soldiers left San Bartolome, and visited Puaray in 1583 but, finding all the friars dead, pushed on with a series of explorations. With one friar and 14 soldiers this intrepid Spaniard accomplished as much exploration in Arizona and New Mexico as Coronado with his great band. He went on into northwestern Arizona and there located several valuable mines before he returned to Mexico in the fall of 1583.

One of the most important expeditions of this period was undertaken by Don Juan de Oñate, who, with 400 men (130 of whom had families), 83 wagons, and several thousand cattle reached the Rio Grande in April, 1598, and, following it north, attempted to settle near what is now Santa Fe. One of the outstanding occurrences of the expedition was a battle fought with the pueblo of Acoma, which on January 21, 1599, was destroyed by the Spanish. Explorations were also undertaken by Oñate reaching as far as the mouth of the Colorado River.

In 1610 a history of New Mexico, partly in prose and partly in verse, was published by Captain Gaspar de Villagra, the material of which was gathered on the Oñate expedition. Although this undoubtedly represents the first archaeological treatise on the Southwest, it is actually largely a poetic narrative of the various conquests and battles of the Spaniards, in which the battle at Acoma is recorded in great detail. Probably more than anything else this account crystallized, or summarized, the ideas of the Spaniards regarding the origin of the Mexican cultures, for the many ruins in the Southwest were regarded as early Mexican.

From about 1600 on colonization and missionizing progressed rapidly, being broken only temporarily by the Pueblo Revolt in 1680. By 1642 there was a mild pueblo revolt in which the governor of the territory was killed, but it remained for a San Juan Indian, named Popé, to organize the Indians effectively for the later general uprising. Finally, on August 21, the entire Spanish population abandoned Santa Fe and moved south to El Paso.

With this evacuation of the northern portion of the Rio Grande the first period of occupation of the Southwest was brought to a close. Fray Marcos, having indicated the way, was soon followed by a long series of explorers, missionaries, and treasure seekers, all of whom observed but made very little attempt at investigation of the many prehistoric sites. Toward the end of the period actual settlement took place in northern New Mexico, but it was not truly effective there and could have exerted little or no influence on the Indians of Arizona.

SPANISH SETTLEMENT—1692 to 1821

The Rio Grande in New Mexico

The period from 1692 to 1821 is marked by no great contributions to either archaeology or ethnology. With the exception of the work of such men as Father Garces, Escalante, and Anza, the period may be characterized as one of constant strife between the church and military or governing authorities. This unhappy condition was largely a result of the great distance from the seat of government, as several months were required for reports to reach Spain and authorizations to return.

On August 12, 1692, Don Diego de Vargas left El Paso with 60 soldiers, 100 Indians, and 3 friars to reconquer the Indians of the entire area of the territory of New Mexico. This he accomplished in short order by one of the most astounding military feats of history, for not a shot was fired in the campaign. By enlisting one pueblo against another, he continued to make each in turn capitulate.

Although the Hopi Indians in Arizona were not much affected by the Spaniards during this period, they were occasionally subjected to European diseases. In 1775 there were believed to be 7,494 of these Indians, but by 1780 they were estimated as only 798. This great reduction resulted from three years of drought, between 1777 and 1780, accompanied by disease.

From about 1800 on, the Spanish were very much afraid of both rumored and actual advances which were being made by the Americans and French. At about this same time the Navahos appear to have moved west to the vicinity of the Hopi towns and to have begun serious depredations on this sedentary and peaceful people. As a result the Hopis appealed to the Spaniards for aid, but the Spanish were too occupied by threats of the Americans and French, and too easily hoodwinked by a few insincere and unauthorized Hopi emissaries, to be of much assistance to them.

In 1815 Auguste P. Choteau and Julius de Mun, with 24 trappers and hunters, actually entered New Mexico, camping north of Santa Fe. These first aliens were arrested and their goods confiscated, although by 1821 or 1822 legitimate trade had been established between the Americans and the Spaniards, now under Mexican rule, in Santa Fe.

Southern Arizona

With the exception of the very early explorations of Niza and Coronado little is known regarding southern Arizona until relatively late. No settlement was made in this entire area, with the exception of the Santa Cruz valley, until about 1845, when an American military exploration was undertaken. Even this early American exploration was rather sketchy, but with the gold rush of 1849 the area was definitely opened and settled.

The first reference to southern Arizona is found in 1630 when the Gila was named as an area in the territory comprising New Mexico, from which source the Gila River eventually derived its name. The first definite explorers in Arizona were the Jesuits, the most notable of whom was Father Euseibo Francisco Kino (1680-1710), who alone, and with Indian guides, traveled over much of this state. His purpose was to establish a chain of missions connecting Mexico and California. He kept records of his activities and has given us some excellent ethnographical observations.

In 1694 Kino penetrated alone to the Gila and said mass in Casa Grande, which was then standing with high walls. Again, in 1697, he made a trip to the Casa Grande region in search of ruins which had been described to him by the Indians. These ruins he pictured and in turn described in his copious diaries. After 1711, for more than 20 years, no Spaniard is known to have crossed from Mexico into Arizona. The mission of San Xavier del Bac, established on the Santa Cruz River near the present city of Tucson, probably in 1732, represents the first substantial settlement by Spaniards in this section.

As a result of serious rivalry between the Jesuits and Franciscans the former were removed from the Southwest in 1767, and the entire territory, with all the church properties, was given over to the care of the Franciscans. In 1768 the Franciscan padre, Francisco Garces, took over the mission of San Xavier, in subsequent years traveling widely over the state, much after the manner of Kino. It is an interesting fact that on July 4, 1776, when the Declaration of Independence was being signed, he was in the Hopi towns, where he was very poorly received, being given no food or shelter.

By 1775 the Apaches had begun to cause trouble in southern Arizona, and from then on they were never congenial to the Spanish or to the more peaceful Indians of the desert country. Notwithstanding their raids, the period from 1790 to 1820 was one of prosperity for this region, ending only with the cessation of Spanish rule. Records for this period are in marked contrast to those for the same time from the Rio Grande, where the Indians seem to have constantly suffered at the hands of the Spanish. This may possibly be accounted for by the fact that military forces were largely lacking in southern Arizona.

MEXICAN PERIOD—1821 to 1845

With the change of rule from Spanish to Mexican, the Southwest was thrown into a state where no work in archaeology or ethnology could be accomplished, and a period of exploration was again begun, this time by Americans. One of the earliest American groups to enter the southern portion of the Southwest was James O. Pattie and his party, who trapped on the Upper Gila in the autumn of 1825 and again from 1826 to 1836. Finally trouble developed with the Apaches, and the trappers left this section until it came under American rule. The final serious settlement of southern Arizona occurred in the eighties, when silver and copper had been discovered and were being mined.

During this entire period only a few hunters, traders, and trappers entered the Southwest, and these were mostly confined to the northern portion of New Mexico, where Indian difficulties were not so serious. However, once they gained root, they gradually spread south and west to establish their posts or trapping quarters.

MILITARY RECONNAISSANCE—1845 to 1880

The first exploration of any consequence consisted of a military reconnaissance headed by W. H. Emory, which traveled from Fort Low, Missouri, to San Diego, California. The expedition was reported in detail in Washington in 1848: the routes traveled, the Indians met on the way, their attitude to the party, and some landmarks which consisted of ruins being noted. This expedition seems to have aroused considerable interest in the Southwest. In 1849 J. H. Simpson reported on and sketched the ruins in Canyon de Chelly, thus further adding to the interest in the prehistory of this region.

This marked the beginning of several important military expeditions. In 1851 Lieutenant Sitgreaves followed down the Zuñi River to the Little Colorado and down this river to about Grand Falls, noting ruins in that vicinity and eventually crossing to California. The next expedition was one by J. R. Bartlett, which is reported in the form of a personal narrative, dealing mostly with Texas but touching slightly on New Mexico and southern Arizona. In 1853 Whipple, making a railroad survey for the government, passed through New Mexico and Arizona, visiting Turkey Tanks near Flagstaff. He was followed in 1854 by Aubrey, who crossed approximately the same region, and in 1857 by E. F. Beale, who made a wagon road from the Arkansas River to California. In 1858 Ives traveled overland from Needles to Fort Defiance, and in 1858 and 1859 Beale again went from Albuquerque to the Colorado River and back. Thus military expeditions were crisscrossing the Southwest in every direction for several years.

By 1863 trouble with the Navahos had become so acute that Kit Carson was commissioned to subjugate them. This he did most effectively in that year by rounding them up in Canyon de Chelly and removing them to Bosque Redondo in New Mexico, where they were held by the government as prisoners for several years.

In 1869 and in 1871 Powell made trips through the Grand Canyon from the Green River in Wyoming; he not only reported the geology, topography, and country through which he traveled but also showed a great interest in archaeology and ethnology. This expedition, which became widely known, was of general appeal to the public. It was the interest which Powell developed at this time that carried him into the fields of archaeology and ethnology in the years immediately following.

From all these expeditions into a newly acquired area the general public, for the first time, became truly interested in the Southwest. A country which was so much like portions of native Spain as to impress the Mexicans not at all was so radically different from American ideas of what topography and climate should be that the keen interest in the newly acquired area was not surprising. Not only the type of country, but the large standing ruins as well, so impressed the Americans that it was perfectly natural that the first investigations were concerned with types of houses and with the effect of the country, or nature, upon man. By 1875 cattlemen, sheepmen, and big-game hunters had drifted into much of the Southwest. These individuals settled and thus made scientific work more feasible, or returned to other sections to spread tales which further fired popular interest. As a result, by about 1880 sincere archaeological and ethnological work was undertaken for the first time.

ARCHAEOLOGICAL SURVEY—1880 to 1910

The period from about 1880 to 1910 was the most important in Southwestern archaeological history, for it was then that the science was getting a foothold and principles were being developed which would guide it through later stages. This was the period when general surveys of large areas were being undertaken. Two questions were being seriously considered: first, the effect of the peculiar environment on human beings; and second, a natural outgrowth of the first, the origin and development of the Pueblo groups.

In 1876 and 1877 E. A. Barber, becoming interested in the Southwest, wrote two semipopular articles in which he pictured and described pottery and other artifacts from the Colorado, Utah, Arizona, and New Mexico section. These apparently marked the beginning of an extensive series of such reports, which immediately followed.

A long list of important names characterizes this period, Powell, Holmes, Cushing, Washington Matthews, Stevenson, Victor Mindeleff, Bancroft, Bandelier, the Wetherills, Nordenskiold, Fewkes, and Cosmos Mindeleff being perhaps the most outstanding. Powell was director of the Bureau of Ethnology at this time, and in 1879 and 1880 the first annual report appeared. In it he reported on the beginning of his linguistic studies, to be followed in 1885 and 1886 by his important *Linguistic Families of America North of Mexico*. At the same time William H. Holmes, a member of the United States Geological Survey, and from 1882 to 1893 curator of pottery at the United States National Museum, began publishing reports on his ceramic and textile studies.

In 1879 Cushing took up his life at Zuñi and, in connection with his work in mythology there, later made a survey of the ruins to check the accuracy of these tales. Such an investigation naturally led him to a discussion of Pueblo pottery and Zuñi culture growth. In 1879 and 1880 Stevenson visited several of the pueblos of Arizona and New Mexico and, in making collections of artifacts, particularly from Walpi and Zuñi, evolved a simple pottery classification.

In 1881 Victor Mindeleff, who was later assisted by Cosmos Mindeleff, began his studies of modern and ruined pueblos, with an emphasis primarily on geography and secondarily on clans. This interest in house types and traditions was passed on to Cosmos Mindeleff. His conclusions, published in 1886-87, may be summed up in four points, the third of which, in the light of our present knowledge, is probably the most interesting.

1. He pointed out the contrasts between Tusayan (Hopi) and Cibola (Zuñi).

National Park Service photo

Square Tower House in Mesa Verde Park. This is a typical example of the architecture of these sites. Note the small circular kiva and the square tower.

2. He indicated the importance of the physical conditions of the country in determining the nature of the sites, and also that the press of unfriendly neighbors resulted in a change of architectural type.

3. He indicated an architectural evolution which was largely a result of the materials at hand and was traceable from circular conical structures to pueblos.

4. He pointed out that the defensive motive reached a peak and declined in recent years.

The publications of both Bancroft in 1889 and Bandelier in 1890 continued this theme. Bancroft, in his history, made several observations which are of considerable interest and value even today. For the first time he definitely labeled the Montezuma myth as of Spanish origin, and he maintained that contacts with Mexico or Central America antedated traditional annals. He pointed out the necessity of studying archaeology and ethnology together and indicated the value of such work in the Southwest, where the people were probably the least changed from their aboriginal state of any in the United States at that time.

Bandelier made several points of sufficient present interest that they might be briefly listed somewhat as follows. He was the first to point out that the small house developed into the pueblo. He saw a similarity in structures on mounds in the Gila valley and those of Mexico and Central America and compared them. Areal variations were recognized, but he did not stress time variations. From traditions he postulated a population shift from north to south, but he also suggested other local conflicting movements. These are essentially the same problems with which most Southwestern archaeologists were concerned at the time.

So far as is known at present, Richard Wetherill, a Southwestern cattleman, was the first to make use of natural stratigraphy as applied to archaeological problems in the Southwest. From his work in the western San Juan he established the Basket Maker culture stage as distinct from, and earlier than, that of the later Pueblo people. He published a report of this observation in 1894, and the same facts were written up by Prudden in 1897 and again by Pepper in 1902.

J. Walter Fewkes began his work in northern Arizona about 1893, taking as his main problem the Hopi Indians, and tracing their traditions back through archaeological material. In subsequent years he traveled over much of northeastern and central Arizona in a covered wagon, visiting and describing almost all the standing ruins. Architecture and pottery particularly interested him, and he expended a good deal of effort in trying to decipher symbolic pictographs and pottery decorations. There is little doubt that Fewkes wielded a dominant influence in Southwestern archaeology at least as late as 1910.

Two reports of Mindeleff which were published during this period must be mentioned. Their architectural approach represents the general attitude toward archaeological problems of the time, and they are such complete and excellent studies that they are still of value.

Many of these first workers or investigators branched from other sciences to archaeology, or were essentially untrained in scientific work, and as a result not a few of the earlier expeditions were little more than collecting trips. However, some of the most entertaining writings come from popular works; one of them explains the kivas in the Mesa Verde region as reservoirs, and proposes an ingenious method of piping and viaducts to run water into them around and over the overhanging tops of the caves in which they lie.

The only work of moment in the Gila section of southern Arizona and

New Mexico was that of the Hyde expedition, which was reported on by Hough in 1907. It is regrettable that the true importance of this work was not recognized at this early date. As has been suggested, it was from about 1880 to 1910 that the basic principles of archaeology were being established, so that masonry and house-type classifications, and interpretations of ceramic designs, have naturally played an important part in later studies. Starting with no knowledge, even the better investigators overlooked much, but with the years information piled up, until at last certain periods were recognized. As has been seen, before 1900 two temporal horizons were admitted, the Basket Maker and the Pueblo.

Throughout all this period large collections of material objects were accumulated, some of which were sold abroad, stored in museums where many of them still remain, or scattered among individuals. With the depth of present perspective it would certainly be of value to re-examine these old collections.

GENERAL ARCHAEOLOGY—1910 to 1920

The next period, from 1910 to 1920, saw the introduction of many men into the field. At the beginning of this period the problems of archaeology were considered to be one, and chronology had progressed to the point where only two sequential divisions were recognized in northern Arizona. Regional differentiation in small areas had not been recognized, and the northern and southern roots had not been separated.

Two names, those of Cummings in Arizona and Hewett in New Mexico, stand out most conspicuously. In 1906 Cummings began his archaeological work in Utah, and two years later he made his first trip into Arizona. In 1915 he left the University of Utah and joined the staff of the University of Arizona. Although he did comparatively little writing he undoubtedly was the leading archaeological worker in Arizona at this time, having trained many of the men who were to carry on much of the Southwestern research for the next two or three decades. In New Mexico Hewett fulfilled the same role in much the same way.

At this point it is unnecessary to treat the important names in the history of Southwestern archaeology in detail, for they will be referred to often in the following pages of this book. However, some mention of the most important influences, and the men responsible for them, will be made.

In 1912 N. C. Nelson, working in New Mexico, for the first time made a strict use of statistical methods developed in Europe, and reported on this method in 1916. At about the same time, or a little later, Kidder and

Guernsey were making statistical studies in the San Juan, and Morris was applying the same general attack at Aztec. Once statistical methods of sherd counts and stratigraphic work were introduced, they became not only practically a necessity to any archaeologist working in this field, but actually almost a fad. Probably this method of attack reached its culmination in the work of Kroeber in the Zuñi region, in the establishment of a chronology with little or no excavation.

During this time Kidder, Guernsey, and others began their serious work, laying the foundations of their later classifications based on areal and cultural divisions. The period was characterized by the accumulation of data. Although northern Arizona, and particularly the San Juan, was most intensively studied, this time can hardly be called one of areal specialization, for individuals and institutions excavated or surveyed widely. The less cautious methods of the preceding period, and the attitude that the supply of ruins was inexhaustible, were replaced with conservative principles. Much loot was removed from the earth and carried away, through the activities both of the "pot hunter," who worked for individual gain, and of large institutions which required their field workers to bring back display materials.

AREAL SPECIALIZATION—1920 to 1930

The period of areal specialization, from about 1920 to 1930, marked some of the most radical changes in the work in this area. It was during this time that Kidder's *Introduction to Southwestern Archaeology* appeared, the Pecos classification was fostered, and Dr. Douglass contributed his first series of actual prehistoric dates.

The work of Cummings, Kidder, Guernsey, Morris, Judd, and Hewett was continued, but an attitude of specialization by areas became paramount to most of these workers. Out of the intensive stratigraphical studies of the preceding period, the building of chronology assumed the most importance. Although the idea of areal specialization was not new to Southwestern workers, Kidder's book tended further to accentuate its importance, and the conception of the value of widespread surveys, accompanied by detailed concentrated investigations of restricted areas, naturally ensued.

By 1927 the rapid accumulation of data, which was indicating a definite chronology, led to a general conference at Pecos Pueblo, where Kidder was then at work. The discussions which followed, led mostly by Kidder, Roberts, and Morris, developed the Pecos classification. This was designed as a division of cultures into stages of cultural development, and was felt at that time to be rather generally applicable, though developed from data derived primarily from northern Arizona. Pottery, which had long been recognized as an excellent measure of culture change, rapidly assumed a position of increasing importance as applied to the Pecos classification.

At this time several new purely Southwestern institutions came into being, to give support to the work long under way by the Universities of Arizona and New Mexico and the two state museums, each of which took over the examination of smaller, more or less prescribed, areas. From this work chronology and cultural divisions received a considerable boost, and the way was paved for the attitudes of the next period.

INTENSIVE ANALYSIS—1930 to 1945

The work from about 1930 to 1945 may best be characterized as a period of intensive analysis. Detailed, in most cases almost microscopic, examinations were tending to replace the coarser methods of the preceding periods. Ceramics came into its own, to be subjected to almost every conceivable treatment, with the result that types were established and subdivided until the intricacies of classification approached those of the animal kingdom.

Tree-ring dating progressed at an equal if not faster rate, so that at present a ring chronology has been carried back to 59 B.C., thus covering all the major later stages in the northern part of the Southwest. With much exactness and considerable labor, pottery types and other prehistoric material were dated by correlation with tree-ring dates, and, from these, attempts were made to correlate the various culture stages of the Pecos classification with our own calendar. Dating was a field of peculiarly exciting interest, as it still is.

Neither the field of broad surveys nor areal specialization were neglected in the interest of ceramic studies. In an effort to make all this additional information intelligible, more complex systems of classification were introduced. With the clearer understanding of what constitutes basic cultures and divisions, it was possible to point out culture centers and influence.

Another trend was that of synthesizing. At about the end of this period several general articles, and more pretentious works, began to appear. These represented attempts to summarize specific areas or cultures which had been intensively studied, and to bring together all the data from various fields of specialization into a unified whole. With the war all archaeological work ceased, but at its end began again with renewed vigor and stimulus.

SYNTHESIS AND SALVAGE—1945 on

With the completion of the war interest in Southwestern archaeology was accelerated, and research began again with considerable stimulus from such extensive programs as highway, river basin, and pipeline salvage. All of these activities put a great demand on trained field men, and required the development of new techniques and methods in field work. The most notable new technique was the widespread employment of heavy mechanical tools in excavation on salvage projects, and the working out of techniques for their use. These techniques were then adapted to and utilized for other less hurried excavation. The greatest limitation has been in the supply of workers, and this has led to more and more individuals taking academic training in this field.

During this same period the carbon 14 method of dating was developed and a series of archaeological dates secured. Carbon 14 is not as accurate as tree-ring dating, but it is applicable to far longer periods of time, so that it has been the main instrument of dating Paleo-Indian and Archaic sites. Thus the two methods have proven to be complementary and not competitive. Carbon 14 has been used for the approximate dating of later sites as well, where datable tree-ring material is not available. As a result there has been a great deal of interest in dating, which was carried over from the preceding period.

There has also been much interest in more theoretical problems, with the proposal by Taylor of the use of the conjunctive approach in archaeology, and the introduction and testing of the concept of the "Co-Tradition." Other schemes of organization of the material, and their evaluation, have been proposed, among which are such terms as "Ootam" to cover the desert culture of southeastern Arizona, and "Hakataya" as an inclusive term to group several cultures in western Arizona. In the same general way Jennings has proposed the use of the Desert culture concept to cover all of the small-animal-hunting and gathering cultures found in the Southwest, as distinct from the equally early, or perhaps earlier, more strictly big-game hunter groups.

Many cultures have been much more specifically defined than they were in the past. This has been true of the early big-game hunters, the Patayan and the Sinagua. The validity of the Hohokam as a distinct cultural group has been generally accepted, and the Mogollon culture has been much more clearly defined, as a result of both more extensive and intensive work on this problem.

In general, and perhaps slightly to the detriment of research in this field, detailed work in ceramics has been somewhat less intensive than it was in the period just preceding. Pottery types are still being defined in numbers, but there is a most recent trend to recombine types rather than to split them. This probably is valid, in most cases, but it is very difficult to split types once they have been lumped, whereas it is easy to lump types once they have been split, if it is found they are not shedding light on the particular problem under investigation.

The pressure which has been brought to Southwestern archaeology by the necessity of salvage work has meant that in many cases purely problem-oriented archaeology has had to be shelved. Salvage archaeology has shed much light on problems, but it has generally come as an incidental side of rush salvage work. One good result of intensive salvage has been that regional areas have been both intensively and extensively explored. From this has come an understanding of not only the larger sites in an area but of the more obscure ones as well.

In reviewing the entire history of Southwestern archaeology it is apparent that the science is maturing. There is greater reliance on and cooperation with the specialists in other but related fields. This has had somewhat the effect of fragmenting archaeology, but the often repeated general summaries and syntheses have tended to bring it back together again as a unified whole. In general the men and women who are at work here are being better and better trained, and they are going at problems with an enthusiasm and dedication which promise much in the way of results in the near future. So much is now being done that as usual publication is lagging, but regional meetings, where reports of work and general discussions are held, is doing much to keep everyone more or less abreast of what is developing. Cooperation has for years characterized archaeology in the Southwest.

Sources and Additional References

Bancroft, H. H. * History of Arizona and New Mexico, in The Works of Hubert Howe Bancroft, 1882 to 1890, Vol. 17, A. L. Bancroft & Co., San Francisco, California, 1889. (Review of the early expeditions to the Southwest.)

Bandelier, A. F. Investigations Among the Indians of the Southwestern United States, Carried on Mainly in the Years from 1880 to 1885, *Papers of the Archaeological Institute of America,* American Series III, Part I, 1890, Peabody Museum of American Archaeology and Ethnology, Harvard University, Cambridge, Massachusetts. (Excellent discussion of early conditions in the Southwest.)

Barber, E. A. The Ancient Pottery of Colorado, Utah, Arizona, and New Mexico, *American Naturalist,* Vol. 10, 1876, Cambridge, Massachusetts.

Bickford, F. T. Prehistoric Cave Dwellings, *Century Magazine,* October, 1890,

New York City. (Early review of material and sites from the four corners area.)

Bolton, H. E. Spanish Exploration in the Southwest, 1542 to 1706, Charles Scribner's Sons, New York City, 1916. (Review of early Spanish exploration.)

Brandes, Ray. Archaeological Awareness of the Southwest as Illustrated in Literature to 1890, *Arizona and the West*, Vol. 2, No. 1, 1960, Tucson, Arizona. (As indicated by title.)

Chapin, Frederick H. The Land of the Cliff Dwellers, W. D. Clark and Co., Boston, 1892. (Data on the Wetherills and other early work in northern Arizona.)

Colton, Harold S. * A Brief Survey of the Early Expeditions into Northern Arizona, *Museum Notes*, Vol. 2, No. 9, 1930, Museum of Northern Arizona, Flagstaff. (As implied by title.)

Cummings, Byron. Data supplied by personal letter to the writer.

Daifuku, Hiroshi. A New Conceptual Scheme for Prehistoric Cultures in the Southwestern United States, *American Anthropologist*, Vol. 54, No. 2, 1952, Menasha, Wisconsin. (As indicated by title.)

Hewett, Edgar L. Ancient Life in the American Southwest, Bobbs-Merrill Co., Indianapolis, Indiana, 1930.

Jennings, Jesse D. The American Southwest: A Problem in Cultural Isolation, in Seminars in Archaeology: 1955, *American Antiquity*, Vol. 32, No. 2, Part 2, 1955, Society for American Archaeology, Salt Lake City, Utah. (The Desert culture and its relationships.)

Judd, Neal M. Progress in the Southwest, in Essays in Historical Anthropology of North America, *Smithsonian Miscellaneous Collections*, Vol. 100, 1940, Washington, D.C. (General summary.)

Mindeleff, Victor. A Study of Pueblo Architecture in Tusayan and Cibola, *Eighth Annual Report*, 1891, Bureau of American Ethnology, Washington, D.C.

Pepper, George H. Ancient Basket Makers of Southern Utah, *American Museum Journal*, Vol. 2, No. 4, Supplement, 1902, New York City. (Early report on Basket Maker culture.)

Reed, Erik K. * Trends in Southwestern Archaeology, in New Interpretations of Aboriginal American Culture History, Seventy-fifth Anniversary Volume of the Anthropological Society of Washington, Washington, D.C., 1955. (General summary statement.)

Taylor, Walter W. A Study of Archeology, *American Anthropologist*, Vol. 50, No. 3, Part 2, 1948, Menasha, Wisconsin. (Proposal of the conjunctive approach.)

———. * Southwestern Archeology, Its History and Theory, *American Anthropologist*, Vol. 65, No. 4, Part 1, 1954, Menasha, Wisconsin. (Review of the history of archaeology in the Southwest with emphasis on the more recent trends.)

Wheat, Joe Ben. Mogollon Culture Prior to A.D. 1000, *American Antiquity*, Vol. 20, No. 4, Part 2, 1955, Society for American Archaeology, Salt Lake City, Utah. (Summary of Mogollon culture.)

Winship, George P. * The Coronado Expedition, *Fourteenth Annual Report*, Part I, 1896, Bureau of American Ethnology, Washington, D.C. (Basic account of the Coronado expedition into the Southwest.)

III

Definitions, Aims, and Methods

DEFINITIONS

Unfortunately, in beginning any science, it is necessary to understand thoroughly the various terms which are employed before actual work may be undertaken. For many of these terms usage has established meanings often quite different from the specific uses to which the scientist puts them. It is necessary to define here only the few terms that are so common that further progress without them is impossible, the rest being explained as they occur.

One of the most commonly used, and also misused, terms in any discussion of archaeology is "culture," but before this term can be conveniently defined we must define "culture trait." Dr. Wissler has defined a culture trait as the unit in tribal culture. This is a usable definition, but is hardly specific enough to explain definitely what a trait is. More simply, a culture trait might be explained as the individual things used by man, but this would not quite cover all the traits of a group. Actually there are two types of traits: material and nonmaterial. Obviously the material traits are those things, or objects, used by man, and in our own culture would include all the articles pictured in a mail-order catalogue. The nonmaterial traits, on the other hand, are mental attitudes, or customs, which have no material existence. Such customs of any group are the beliefs, games, religious ideas, and all similar concepts. These are called folkways, morals, and laws. Both of these kinds of traits are stored in the collective mind of the people who had and used them as two kinds of ideas: the idea of how things may be done, which is a sort of storehouse of technology; and the idea of how things should be done, which is the customs just referred to and which may act as a restrictive screen on the application of the former.

Any given *culture* may now be described as being made up of all the material and nonmaterial traits of the people, or the ideas in the collective mind of the people. Obviously any group, to be considered of a distinct culture, must show a total aggregate of traits sufficiently distinct from that of any other people to set them definitely apart. Thus in the Southwest, and on the basis of traits, two contemporaneous but quite different cultures, among others, may be recognized almost immediately, that of the plateau, which has generally been called the Anasazi culture, and that of the desert area, which is known as the Hohokam culture.

Diffusion is a term which is much more difficult to explain but may be briefly characterized as the spreading out, from one center, of a culture trait, traits, or perhaps even an entire culture. It is quite logical to assume that most of our inventions have taken place but once, that is to say, that one man at one place and at one time invented and built the first of each of our modern articles. It is also equally logical to assume that once an invention has been made those people coming in contact with it will, provided that it is of value to them, attempt to copy it and perhaps even improve upon it. This leads to a gradual spreading out from person to person, district to district, country to country, and even continent to continent, of many culture traits, until they become widespread. This process of adoption and spreading is what is known as *diffusion*.

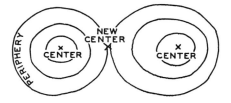 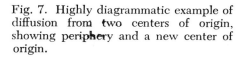

Fig. 7. Highly diagrammatic example of diffusion from two centers of origin, showing periphery and a new center of origin.

Two types of diffusion are known to have taken place: the spread of actual material things, usually, but not always, by trade; and the spread of ideas, frequently as a result of people visiting a new area. In either case, but especially in the latter, the results by copying may be somewhat different from the originals, perhaps because of a lack of detailed technology, or because of limitation of custom on the part of the new group. Traits may also apparently jump over considerable intervening areas before they find a congenial one for development again.

Not always is a given trait quickly and easily transferred from one group to another, for if it is of such a nature as not to be of advantage to the group to which it is offered they will certainly reject it. Rejection of a trait will also take place where its acceptance would cause a considerable disruption of the cultural *balance* of the group. Such is generally true with religious teachings, a fact which is quite often overlooked by missionaries in their zeal to secure converts. On the other hand, some traits seem to have been readily accepted very widely. An example is the use of iron, which replaces stone implements almost universally to advantage, or more strangely tobacco, which has been quickly accepted by many groups throughout the world. This process of acceptance of some traits and rejection of others has led to a very uneven distribution by diffusion, when large areas are considered.

The principle of the flying machine was established in Ohio by the Wright brothers, but as soon as it was seen to have value other individuals adopted it, so that it has now spread throughout the world. The same has been true of primitive traits in the Southwest. The art of pottery making, once established, spread rapidly from person to person, and even group to group, until it covered almost every part of this area.

The central point of distribution of an area of diffusion would tend, all other factors being equal, to be the point at which the discovery was first made, and because this place would be where it had been known for the longest time, new additions in technique or variations in production would be most likely to originate there. This in turn would diffuse, or spread out, and so wave after wave would be sent out from the center of development. The first discovery would be likely to travel the farthest, so that on the edge of the area over which diffusion had taken place would be found the first or most primitive type. The edge of this area of diffusion is called the *periphery*, and any trait found there is said to be *peripheral* to the area of that trait. Thus, if a ring of very primitive pottery types is found surrounding a region, as progress is made toward the center of that area we may rightly expect to find an increasingly involved technique of pottery making.

If diffusion were always ideally regular and uniform the problems of the archaeologist would be greatly simplified. Unfortunately, however, this is generally not true. It has been suggested above that traits, by acceptance and rejection, often travel irregularly over an area, and to this may now be added two further observations. If modifications may be made at the point of origin of a trait, they may also equally well be added as it travels outward by diffusion. As a result the trait may be considerably altered in appearance from its original form by the time it reaches its periphery. Also two somewhat comparable traits, spreading from two centers of origin, may give rise to quite a new form when their two peripheries meet. When complete cultures, instead of simple traits, are concerned, much more complex problems arise, of course, and the life of an archaeologist is anything but an easy one, for a new culture may thus suddenly be created by the combination of the two.

Stratigraphy has been the very backbone upon which archaeology everywhere has been built. Simply stated it is merely the study of the contents of strata. A layer cake is an excellent example of stratigraphy. Here each layer represents a stratum, and to the most uninitiated it is obvious that the lowest layer must have been laid down first to support those resting upon it. Thus the lowest layer is oldest, the next above younger, and so on to the top, where the most recently laid-down layer, or stratum, is found. A study of the contents of these layers will then give some idea of the relative ages of the strata, and this study is stratigraphy.

Almost all people of every age have preserved definite dump grounds where the material that was discarded from their homes was deposited. These accumulations are known under the various names of "trash piles," "dump heaps," "kitchen middens," and "refuse piles." It is to this place that the archaeologist usually turns for his most definite example of stratigraphy. A kitchen midden is located, and a vertical shaft or trench is sunk in it. Each layer or stratum is kept isolated, and all the culture trait material, such as sandals, baskets, and pottery, is collected from its respective layers and studied. The most recent or latest material will come from the top layers; the earliest or most ancient, from the bottom. The archaeologist then need only arrange these objects in the order in which they were uncovered from the bottom up and he has a sequential evolution of the culture of the people who made them. Although the objects

Fig. 8. Diagrammatic section of a double trash mound. The sequence in time of deposition is from A to G. If a second trash mound, with several layers, is found, the lowest of which contain material like that of E, F, and G, these layers are comparable in time, and any additional strata above them will lengthen the chronology.

contained in a trash mound are hardly those of a mail-order catalogue, most trash mounds are the archaeologist's best substitute for such a document.

The correlation of strata containing identical objects from two middens will give a more or less definite time correlation between two sites, for cultural evolution or change is continuous, and any considerable time span would show differences in culture. Additional material in the form of more strata will then extend the chronology, and in this manner archaeological sequence may be built up. However, without recourse to actual dates, any chronology of events such as that produced by stratigraphy will result in only relative and not absolute time.

ARCHAEOLOGICAL AIMS AND METHODS

With this brief identification of a few of the most commonly used archaeological terms it would probably be well now to examine the aims of the archaeologist, and the manner in which he goes about achieving these aims, before turning to more detailed discussions of other methods and problems. It is continually necessary in any work to stop and remind oneself of the ultimate aims of the undertaking; otherwise the temptation to digress or the confusion of pressing problems will often obscure the ultimate aims. It is an example of the trees obscuring the forest, and in an effort to focus the forest more clearly these aims should now be definitely delineated.

As a direct means of opening this problem, and without any specific attempt at definition of either history or prehistory, it may probably most safely be assumed that archaeologists are attempting to make history of prehistory. If this is so, history, and the aims and methods of history, should be of considerable value in further defining the problem.

Any attempt at history must be concerned with three types of phenomena: events, places, and time. History, however, is not simply the notation of these three kinds of things, but is actually the study of their relationships, both to themselves and to each other, plus an explanation or interpretation of these relationships.

The difficulties which confront the archaeologist in determining and interpreting these three kinds of data and their relationships are, of course, much greater than those of the historian. Events, which might be defined as any occurrences or happenings, are indicated only secondarily to the archaeologist, generally by the presence of material traits which have been preserved in the ground. For instance, the presence of one piece of pottery indicates that the trait of pottery making was known, and that this particular object was made by one person at one time and place. Thus traits, as represented by artifacts, once they are in hand, are indisputable. It is in the interpretation of how these traits came to be that real difficulty is encountered. Places, or the areal element, are generally quite easily determined, for any object must have a location in space. Indefiniteness in this matter usually arises from incomplete data in studies concerning trait distribution. Of the three, time is obviously the most difficult to determine with some degree of accuracy. Fortunately, in the Southwest, tree-ring dating has been of the greatest value in this respect, though few persons truly appreciate the difficulties often encountered in the correlation of tree-ring dates and culture. Elsewhere relative chronology is largely the source of dating prehistory.

The determination of both the temporal and areal elements rely upon specialized techniques, which will be briefly discussed later. Once these two factors, and events, are determined, the real task of the archaeologist becomes apparent. This is the interpretation of their relationships.

Though there is a very close parallel between the aims of the archaeologist and those of the historian, a much closer similarity in methods is to be found with those of the detective. Both the detective and the archaeologist are concerned with the reconstruction of past events, and both deal with far from complete data. Each must collect clues, in the form of material objects, and from these deduce the nonmaterial traits which went to produce the situation under consideration. The modern archaeologist, like the modern detective, cannot rely upon guesses, unless they are freely admitted and so labeled. He must work with all the skill and every aid that is at hand, and he must have available or be personally acquainted with whatever help any other science is able to contribute to the solution of his problems. Quite often it is the most fragile clue which will contribute most to the solution of the situation.

Thus the archaeologist, historian, and detective are all confronted with the important problem of the interpretation of the relationship of events in their proper time and space context. Turning again to history, the historian is found to be interested in the developmental sequence of events, one of which arises from another, giving a cultural continuity, or what might be termed a "genetic" relationship of events. Such a relationship may be demonstrated through the building of chronologies, which are simply the notation of a series of events in their proper time sequence from one area. Thus the business of chronology building is actually the basis of both history and archaeology, as it has been defined.

The historian is further interested in three sorts of relationships: a local series of genetically, or developmentally, related events; the influence which this series had on other regions; and the influence outside areas had on its development. These are the same problems which confront the archaeologist.

We may now define *pure archaeology*, as used here, as the interpretation of the interrelationships of three kinds of phenomena: events, time, and space. A somewhat similar sort of study, which has enjoyed considerable popularity at various times and places, might be termed "archae-ography," and may be characterized as the study of only two elements, events and area. The third type of study, for lack of a better term, has been called "chronology," and it too concerns itself with only two characters, events and time. Even a fourth type of work has occasionally laid claim to the title of "archaeology," principally from the fact that it deals with data removed from the ground. This sort of study is simply an interpretation or comment upon artifacts or events, often with little or no regard to the other factors mentioned above. It generally takes the form of artistic evaluation, and so has only a minor part to play in such a study as the one presented in this book.

As has been suggested, the problem which causes the archaeologist the most difficulty is the relationships of the three phenomena, time, space, and events. These relationships may be broadly divided into two types: the first, as suggested just above, is a developmental or "genetic" series; the second, a nongenetic series, or what might be termed a replacement or competition series.

These two basic series may be characterized by four possible situations which, most unfortunately, often tend to overlap somewhat. These are: First, lineal development, or chronological sequences, obviously a pure gentic series. Second, fusional series, wherein varying degrees of fusion or acculturation occur. Two subtypes of this situation may easily be recognized. Third, divergence, or splitting of a cultural sequence, which is usually a result of regional differentiation. And fourth, replacement of one series by another, obviously a nongenetic series.

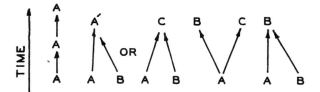

Fig. 9. Illustration of possible chronological variations. Reading from left to right they are: lineal, or genetic development; two variants of fusional series; replacement series.

The question of what indicates a genetic series naturally arises. It has generally been accepted that whenever a close similarity of the total culture elements of two groups is noted these two groups are genetically related. This statement is based on the assumption that a fortuitous identity of one trait, or even of two or three traits, might be imagined, but that mathematically the identity of an entire series of traits, or a total complex, becomes so highly improbable that it may be disregarded.

Following this same principle several similar "laws" may be suggested, most of which have been successfully applied and tested in the Southwest. First, that identical, or almost identical, cultures indicate identical, or almost identical, time (remember that this is based on a detailed similarity, or near identity, of total trait complexes, not individual traits). Second, close cultural similarities indicate close time similarities. Third, nearly identical cultures tend to group into geographical areas (this is the basis of the phase in the Gladwin classification). All this might be summarized in the statement that very close cultural similarities indicate very close genetic, time, and areal relations, while less close similarities indicate less close or in extreme cases no relations. This principle is the basis upon which roots, stems, branches, phases, and components are built.

The determination of the degree of identity or relationship of culture is often a difficult problem in itself. Various systems of comparison have been developed, such as a consideration of what are termed "diagnostic traits" or complexes of traits. However, the most perfect comparison is obviously one which is based on as many different traits as possible, and in any consideration of trait identities it is by far most worthwhile to compare every single trait which may be uncovered. Once cultures have been established it is possible to point out which of these traits are really of importance in designating one culture as distinct from another.

After archaeological objects have been secured and studied, the problem of how the information contained in them may best be presented to fulfill the requirements we have just outlined confronts the archaeologist. Any final presentation of data attempted on the artifact level must, as the previous discussion has indicated, be capable of considerable flexibility, and it must attempt to show the point, both in time and space, where a particular trait first appears, as well as its persistence in time, its evolution, and the directions of its spread. Any final system must also be able to show both divergence and convergence, or combination, of traits and complexes, both as regards area and time, before their relationships can be interpreted.

A simple method by which such characters may be represented, at least figuratively, is a group of cases containing a series of drawers. Each case is made to represent a prescribed geographical area with its complex of traits, and each comparable drawer a predetermined time period. Artifacts are placed in their appropriate drawers and cases, as collected. By simply pulling out all the lower or earlier drawers, and successively later ones, it is then possible to trace the development and spread of any desired trait, complex, or culture.

Up to this point, though aims and some methods have been discussed, nothing has been said about the actual means by which chronologies, or series of sequential events, are determined and established. In problems of chronology building certain definite methods have been found of the utmost use to archaeologists. Many of these methods have been borrowed from other sciences; some few have been developed by the archaeologist alone.

Geology and *palaeontology* may sometimes be a distinct aid to the archaeologist in determining chronology. This has been particularly fruitful in certain old world fields, and in this country paleontology has played a part in demonstrating the contemporaneity of fossil animals and Paleo-Indian finds throughout the Southwest. Geology, particularly in recent depositional studies, has been of considerable aid in estimating the age of archaeological deposits. This has been especially useful in the dating of the Cochise finds, in southern Arizona and New Mexico, as well as certain deposits in Texas and other Southwestern states.

Palynology, a branch of botany, which deals with the spores of ancient, often fossil, plants has become a subject of much interest to archaeologists and an aid to them. By identifying the species of plants which grew in an area from the spores, a good idea of past ecology may be obtained. Once the sequence of environmental changes is worked out, these may be correlated to other data, and a series established in specific regions which in a general way is usable for dating purposes. Cultural evolution is often linked with environmental change, so that by seriation the interplay of culture and environment may be demonstrated. Much interest has recently developed in this problem with the result that competent palynologists are in considerable demand.

Distributional studies may be of value in reconstructing chronologies only in the most general manner, and then only if it be admitted that peripheral sites are of later periods than those of comparable culture nearer the center. Distribution studies, however, are of the greatest importance in other work, particularly in the bounding of the area of a culture.

Typology, though often a great aid in chronology building, must be regarded with considerable suspicion. Typology consists merely of arranging a series of objects in some definite order, usually from simplest to most complex, on the basis of their physical characteristics alone. In such studies as ceramics it is often possible to construct a long series showing many variants, and where it is found by other methods that one end of the sequence is earlier than the other, a chronology may be established. On the basis of simplicity or primitiveness alone, it is impossible to be certain which is the earliest, for any trait or even cultures may "devolve" or degrade, as well as evolve or advance. Typological studies have their most immediate value in the separation and identification of various types within any series.

As has already been mentioned, *stratigraphy* has been, and still is, the backbone of any archaeological work when problems of chronology are concerned. Although stratigraphy alone cannot give absolute dates, it can, and often does, result in very accurate and sometimes very microscopic relative chronologies. Not only is stratigraphy applicable to studies of trash mounds but it is equally of use wherever two separable horizons are discernible. Superimposed structures with their attendant culture may be separated and studied stratigraphically and even natural soil deposits may be defined and studied by this method.

Though stratigraphy is dependent upon the distinction of various layers in an accumulation, these layers do not necessarily have to be natural ones. Thus two types of stratigraphy are possible: what might be called *natural stratigraphy,* where already naturally formed distinct layers are present; and what might be termed *artificial stratigraphy,* where, in the absence of natural divisions, layers of a standard and convenient size are arbitrarily determined and blocked off, and the material from each of these is treated as though it came from a natural layer. This method may often be preferable to dealing with the natural strata, for natural strata may occur for reasons of no significance to the archaeologist, whereas if artificial layers or blocks of sufficiently small size are used, natural distinc-

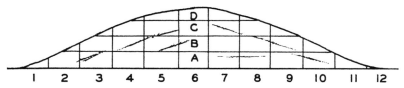

Fig. 10. A diagrammatic example of how a vertical face in the side of a trench through a trash mound is marked off in blocks for artificial stratigraphic study. From a base line half-meter sections are measured up and lettered progressively. These are divided into blocks one meter long, which are numbered. Sections are removed from the face to a depth of half a meter. Any other size block may of course be used, as dictated by the problems to be solved. In this manner any specific block may be referred to, such as layer C, section 5, or simply C5.

tions may later become apparent in them. Any natural stratigraphy present may also be utilized with the artificial strata, to complete the possible distinctions. The accompanying diagram illustrates the manner in which a section through a trash mound may be artificially split into strata and sections, with their accompanying specific designations, so that artifacts recovered from any part of the mound may be relocated in their eventual study and evaluation.

In many stratigraphic studies great quantities of artifacts, particularly broken pottery fragments or "sherds," are recovered. After these have been typologically classified they are counted from each section and tabulated in relative abundance of occurrence on a large chart. An examination of this chart then shows in what section of the mound any specific type was most abundant in relation to all the others, and in this manner it is possible to reconstruct the order of building of the mound, or other accumulation, which is being studied. It is by such a combined statistical-stratigraphic method that most archaeological chronologies are built.

Data secured from a study of *annual deposits,* of various sorts, are another source of chronology building. In the Southwest the greatest single source of chronological data has proved to be actual dates as derived from tree-ring studies. Before the development of this method all estimates of time in archaeology were based on such indefinite methods as relative weathering, geology, or stratigraphy, and none of them resulted in very accurate guesses of the age of ruins or cultures. With the development of tree rings, and the first actual prehistoric dates, these earlier estimates have, in general, been cut in half, or less. As much more is to be said concerning tree-ring dating in a later chapter the subject will not be discussed further here. Only one word of caution is perhaps necessary. The correlation of tree-ring dates with culture is often much more difficult than is generally realized, so that it is only after many dates have been ascertained and much study of culture has been accomplished that any dating is to be relied upon for specific details.

Glacial varves have been successfully counted back to several thousand years, but these are not available for study in the Southwest. Some similar work in dating has been attempted in the counting of what are apparently annual accumulations, or rings, in stalactites formed in caves, but situations where these are found covering or associated with culture are rare.

Chemistry and *physics* have produced a whole series of methods for the relative, or relatively specific, determination of the age of various materials from archaeological sites. The most generally utilized is that of carbon 14 dating. Radioactive carbon dating is based on the fact that all living things absorb radioactive energy that was ultimately derived from outer space, though in very minute amounts. It was demonstrated that the amount of energy received on the earth had reached a state of balance with the decay, or radiation, of the energy already there, and once this factor was established, and the rate of decay of radioactive carbon 14 was determined, the age of once living things could be determined by the amount of radiation still taking place from the carbon 14 in them.

Dr. W. F. Libby, the developer of this dating technique, not only had to demonstrate the equilibrium of radio energy on the earth, but he had to develop laboratory equipment sufficiently delicate to measure the small amounts of energy radiated from the carbon 14 of once living things. He also had to perfect means of concentrating the carbon 14, and had to determine its half life. This he finally established as 5,718 years. By half life it is meant that in this period one-half of the energy of the C 14 is lost through radiation, and in the next equal period, if no more is added, as in the case of a piece of charred wood, or bone or shell, which is buried, one-half of the remainder is lost. Thus by measuring the amount of radiation from the concentrated C 14 of a once living organism it is possible to tell within rather reasonable limits how long ago it lived.

The first radiocarbon dates were secured by Libby, while at the University of Chicago, in 1949. Since that time he and his associates have dated a large number of archaeological and geological sites and specimens. Other laboratories, using these techniques, have sprung up throughout the world, so that C 14 dating is being widely employed. At present most of these laboratories can date specimens as old as 30,000 or 40,000 years, and some seem to be able to get still older dates. The results are usually expressed with a probable margin of error indicated, so they are not absolute dates in the sense of tree-ring dates, but they are relatively exact, and particularly when applied to time spans of a few thousand years they are relatively quite exact. Radiocarbon dating has thus been a tremendous boon to archaeology, especially in dating earlier remains, and in areas where tree-ring dates have not been available.

A considerable variety of material may be used for C 14 dating, though the most easily usable is probably wood or charcoal derived from wood, as from ancient fireplaces. Bone and shell have been dated with more or less success, and even earths which contain considerable carbon, such as old habitation areas, have been used. The archaeologist should take some care, both in the collection of the specimen and its storage, to prevent any possible recent contamination.

Another technique which gave much promise of success is *thermoluminescence*. It is based on the fact that the atoms of which minerals are composed are slightly rearranged when the minerals are slowly heated. Through time they gradually come back to their original state, but if they are subsequently very suddenly heated they quickly go back into place and in so doing throw off light. The intensity of this light indicates how long ago they were heated. Several technical difficulties have arisen in the application of this method. The material has to be finely ground and prepared, it has to be very suddenly highly heated, and the means of measurement of the light emitted has to be very exact. It has appealed to archaeologists because pottery can be dated by this means, as can fireplace clays from earlier horizons. Controlled tests which have been made indicate it is relatively accurate, but the difficulties of building and operating the equipment have led to at least temporary abandonment of the project.

Fluorine tests have been used to show the relative age, or contemporaneity, of buried bones. Bones which have been buried for some time in the earth absorb a certain very small amount of fluorine, and by measuring it their age may be determined in relation to other bones buried in the same deposits. This method was used to prove the Piltdown find in England a hoax, but there is no reason why it cannot be applied equally well in this country. Similar chemical tests of other contaminants may be applied to specific problems of archaeological dating.

Under peculiar circumstances *documents* may be of some aid in establishing chronology in prehistoric periods, particularly in archaeological investigations of European cultures. In the Southwest, documents are of little value, for they either apply only to that period designated as historic, having been written by early European explorers, or are nonexistent, for to date no native Indian writing has been found here. It is possible, of course, that some of the pictographs which are so common in the Southwest may some day be successfully translated and found to be a sort of writing, but so far what little work has been done on these objects indicates that they are simply clan or other symbols and have no true connection with writing. Should these eventually be translated, somewhat in the manner of the stelae of the Maya Indians, they would be of the greatest value in chronology building. Typologically they may now be classified in the manner of pottery types, and thus are some indication of a chronology, though as yet not a very complete or specific one.

Probably the most generally used method of archaeologists everywhere is what is here termed seriation. *Seriation* may be defined as the correlation of various series. By this it is meant that as various series are worked out they may be checked against each other, to build eventually a much more complete chronology. If pottery typologies, house typologies, basketry, and sandal typologies are worked out and correlated with annual deposits, stratigraphy, and perhaps the chronologies indicated through geological and palaeontological studies, and if everywhere in this correlation there is no difficulty in making comparisons, then the final chronology has just that much more likelihood of being authentic.

The scientist is at all times looking for every check to substantiate, or even refute, his findings. For this reason it is his problem to examine every available bit of information before he gives a final decision. It is this combination of all sources of chronological data that is seriation.

One of the most fruitful sources of correlation, or cross dating of series, is the finding of trade objects in various sites. As a rule trade pieces appear to have been rapidly moved from one region to another, so that any lag in their travels is more or less negligible. Certain outstanding types of pottery were widely traded throughout the Southwest, and these have become almost the equivalent of key fossils in dating from one section to another. An example of such a type is what has been called, in general, St. Johns Polychrome. This beautiful orange-base pottery, though made in the Little Colorado River drainage area, was traded as far south as Mexico, throughout the entire desert, mountain, and plateau areas, and is one of the best dating types in regions where no tree-ring dates may be secured.

Once typologies of various objects have been worked out and dated, either exactly or relatively, they may, by correlation with associated materials, in turn date them, and so spread until large areas have finally been dated. It is somewhat in this manner that much of the Southwest has finally been relegated to dates in our own calendar and a chronology of absolute dates of culture established, so that the first step is taken in the creation of history from prehistory. As has been repeatedly suggested, the interpretation of relationships represents the final step.

Sources and Additional References

Davis, Jerome. An Introduction to Sociology, D. C. Heath and Co., Boston, 1927. (Book 3, Part 4, of this compiled series deals with culture from the standpoint of the sociologist.)

Dixon, Ronald. * The Building of Culture, Charles Scribner's Sons, New York City, 1928. (Very good discussion of traits and trait complexes with many examples of the principle of diffusion.)

Johnson, Frederick. Radiocarbon Dating, *American Antiquity*, Vol. 17, No. 1, Part 2, 1951, Society for American Archaeology, Salt Lake City, Utah.

Rice, Stuart, ed. Methods in Social Science, University of Chicago Press, 1931. (The chapter on the archaeological methods employed by Nelson is an excellent and worthwhile discussion of methods, in fact, the source from which the methods discussed here were taken.)

Wissler, Clark. The American Indian, Oxford University Press, New York City, 1917. (Discussion of culture traits, areas, and diffusion, as applied to the American Indian.)

———. Man and Culture, T. Y. Crowell Co., New York City, 1917. (Further discussion of culture, culture traits, etc.)

IV

Classification

One of the most difficult problems in any science is the establishment of a workable classification, or division of the study into various parts, that these parts may more readily be examined and compared. As any such divisions must of necessity have artificial delimitations, it is possible to construct classes on various bases. In any study of peoples three factors must be taken into consideration: time, space, and culture, or more specifically the temporal, spacial, and cultural factors. As most of our work in archaeology in recent years has been an attempt to establish cultural chronologies in various sections of the Southwest, the prevailing tendencies have been to stress the temporal in a classification, and then to point out its application, through correlations, to various other geographical regions.

In 1927 a group of archaeologists met in conference at Pecos, New Mexico, with the hope that through an interchange of ideas by various field workers some more organized sequential classification of Southwestern archaeology could be effected. A general cultural classification was quickly proposed, which, in its completed form, was briefly summarized by A. V. Kidder, and presented in *Science* in 1927. This classification, based solely on material derived from the plateau section of the Southwest, originally was intended as a simple division of the evolutionary sequence of culture as represented in this section into identifiable parts. It was solely a cultural classification, made up of culture stages which in the most general manner formed a sequential development, and was not intended as a division of Southwestern pre-history into time periods.

Since 1927 various modifications and additions have been made to the original classification as it has been applied by different workers. The terms and the order of divisions have persisted, but there has been a tendency for each individual to add to or modify the classification according to his own particular needs. The increasing importance which pottery has assumed in archaeological studies in the Southwest has led to placing more stress on this one trait by many people. In fact, it has become the popular determining criterion for stages.

The classification as presented below has been revised from the original as summarized by Kidder in *Science,* Vol. 66, No. 1716, by the addition of features which the writer has found most useful. These additions, largely consisting of pottery types and characteristics, are included as an aid to ready correlations with other classifications. They are also useful in correlating reports of field work which were published before the more general adoption of the Pecos terms.

The Pecos Classification as Somewhat Revised by Usage

Basket Maker I or Early Basket Maker. A postulated stage, pre-agricultural, yet adumbrating later developments.

Basket Maker II or Basket Maker. The agricultural, atlatl-using, non-pottery-making stage, as described in many publications.

Basket Maker III or Late Basket Maker or Post Basket Maker. The pit- or slab-house-building, pottery-making stage (the three Basket Maker stages were characterized by a long-headed population which did not practice skull deformation). Pottery is characterized in general by coarse lines, simple designs, many basket designs, and some crude life forms, generally a relatively coarse paste, and globular forms.

Pueblo I or Proto-Pueblo. The first stage during which cranial deformation was practiced, vessel neck corrugation was introduced, and villages composed of rectangular rooms of true masonry were developed (in some areas). It was generally agreed that the term pre-Pueblo, hitherto sometimes applied to this period, should be discontinued. Introduction of slips on pottery, burnishing, designs characterized in general by very fine lines, attached dots, and high triangles in the black-on-white types.

Pueblo II. The stage marked by widespread geographical extension of life in small villages; corrugation, often of elaborate technique, extended over the whole surface of cooking vessels. Black-on-white pottery types characterized in general by simple designs in wide lines, long flattened triangles with occasional attached dots, and rudimentary interlocking frets.

Pueblo III or Great Period. The stage of large communities, great development of the arts, and growth of intensive local specialization. The first introduction of polychrome types of pottery and a general marked decrease in the importance of corrugated types.

Pueblo IV or Protohistoric. The stage characterized by constriction of the area occupied; by the gradual disappearance of corrugated wares; and, in general, by decline from the preceding cultural peak. In many instances the implied cultural decline is not strictly true. Widespread use of polychrome pottery and the introduction of glazed paints.

Pueblo V or Historic. The period from A.D. 1600 to the present.

In 1935 Roberts suggested some slight modifications of the terms proposed in the original Pecos classification. These have subsequently been employed by many Southwestern archaeologists, are therefore to be found established in the literature, and so are presented herein. Roberts considered his proposal as no more than a slight revision of terminology in which he dropped the numerals of the original system. He was also attempting to eliminate any implications of a rigid chronology.

ROBERTS REVISION OF THE PECOS CLASSIFICATION

Basket Maker. To designate the stage formerly known as Basket Maker II, or Classic Basket Maker.

Modified Basket Maker. To replace Basket Maker III, Late Basket Maker, or Post Basket Maker. This would indicate it was essentially Basket Maker though somewhat changed in form, a valid concept.

Developmental Pueblo. This term would supplant both Pueblo I and Pueblo II, incorporating them under one heading. This suggestion resulted from the apparent fact that one or the other was absent in some sections.

Great Pueblo. An alternate title for Pueblo III.

Regressive Pueblo. To replace Pueblo IV. This term may be somewhat misleading, for it is now felt that Pueblo IV was not a period of regression.

Historic Pueblo. Proposed as an alternate in the original classification, and probably preferable to Pueblo V.

Byron Cummings developed and used a system of house types as the basis of a classification with some implications of chronology. Subsequent work has indicated that house types vary so areally that in specific instances any chronological order in relation to specific time may be questioned. As a purely house-type classification it has some use, and so is included in this book.

THE CUMMINGS CLASSIFICATION

I. *Archaic Period.* A period designed to cover the early, postulated, nomadic group.
   A. Brush Shelters in Caves. Used caves for homes, in which they had only nests so built no true homes, although caches, some slab-lined, were abundant.
   B. Brush Shelters in Open. Homes apparently of same type, and caches definitely of type above.
II. *Early Pueblo Period* (pithouses).
   A. Circular Pithouse Period. Houses circular and sunken, with walls of dirt, clay-plastered, or reinforced with stone, and roofs either flat or dome-shaped.
   B. Transitional Stage. Houses of semirectangular rooms with distinctly rounded corners.
   C. Rectangular Pithouse Period. Houses rectangular and sunken, walls of dirt, clay-plastered, or reinforced with stones, and flat-roofed.
III. *Late Pueblo Period* (surface structures).
   A. Small House Structures. Single structures built near each other, usually

of not more than two rooms joined, in an irregular group with no plaza, and apparently no associated kivas.

B. Unit-Type Villages. Houses and rooms joined in various shapes such as L, D; they may or may not be two stories high, with a plaza, often partly surrounded with rooms, in which is generally found a kiva.

C. Rambling Villages. Small units of houses which are not arranged in compact masses or in predetermined orientation.

D. Compact Villages. Community houses, or one building group composed of many rooms. Examples of this type are Pueblo Bonito, Betatakin, and Kiet Siel. This division may be further subdivided, on the basis of geographical locations, as follows:

1. Cliff Pueblos.
2. Mesa Pueblos.
3. Valley Pueblos.

E. Compounds. The type of structure found in the Upper and Middle Gila regions. These are composed of irregular masses of rooms of odd shape, enclosed within a surrounding wall.

Balcony House in the Mesa Verde is chiefly of interest because of the presence of a balcony at the level of the second-story floor. It is to the right in this picture.

A group of Midwestern archaeologists, feeling the need for a classificatory scheme for the cultures they were unearthing, met and finally formulated what subsequently became known as the McKern system. Objectivity of the classification was the main aim, and a second desirable feature was the broad applicability of the scheme. Although in general use much earlier it was formally reported by McKern in 1939, and has been used by many Midwestern archaeologists to the present. It is unlimitedly expandable, and although originally no implications of geographic location or chronological position were admitted, these have accrued as a natural result of application to specific problems through the years.

The McKern system groups likes and separates differences on various levels of comparison. This is accomplished by noting the total traits of a group, and stressing what are regarded as diagnostic traits. The smallest unit is the focus, the next largest the aspect, then the phase, and finally the pattern. There is an additional very valuable concept associated with this classification, the component. A component is a manifestation of a culture as represented at a single site, so that two or more components may be represented at a site. The system may be briefly identified somewhat as follows, although for fuller details the references listed at the end of the chapter should be consulted.

THE McKERN OR MIDWESTERN CLASSIFICATION

I. *Focus.* A group of communities with a preponderant majority of traits in common. Thus a number of individual sites might well constitute a focus, if these sites are much more alike in total traits than they are different.

II. *Aspect.* Foci are grouped together as an aspect, if they are found to share an approximate majority of determinant traits.

III. *Phase.* Aspects may be grouped together under the heading of a phase, if they have a significant, but minor, number of determinant traits in common. A phase is thus a cultural grouping of considerable scope.

IV. *Pattern* (previously termed "basic culture"). This is a group of phases which are classed together because they have in common only fundamental, or essential, determinant traits. This is also the largest category of the system.

The *component* should be added to this list, as the manifestation of a particular focus at a specific site.

At about the same time H. S. Gladwin, at Gila Pueblo, proposed another system of classification. It is an arrangement of roots, stems, branches, and phases, which are cumulative from smallest to largest categories, and most clearly show the affinities and derivations of any portion of the Southwest at various periods. The Gladwin system embodies the three necessary elements to any archaeological work: culture, time, and place, and as represented in chart form shows the derivation, or genetic relationships, of each of the phases through time.

The terms of the Gladwin system are descriptive of the general nature of the various categories, except for phases. The roots are the largest groupings from which several stems are usually indicated as diverging.

The stems are still major cultural groupings which split into a number of geographic branches. The phases are the smallest units included in the classification, and generally consist of several individual sites, or portions of sites which are enough alike that they can readily be grouped together. It is the phases which are arranged on a grid pattern of geographic area and time, the other categories being used to show the assumed genetic relationships between them. The functioning of any system can best be understood by an examination of specific application. Therefore reference to *Medallion Paper 15*, or any of the Gila Pueblo reports since 1934, will greatly aid in visualizing the working of this scheme.

THE GLADWIN CLASSIFICATION

  I. *Phase.* The smallest unit in the system. This is a group of individual sites which show much detailed similarity. They are generally restricted to one geographic area and a limited time span.
 II. *Branch.* These are groupings of phases which are obviously culturally related. In general they occupy specific geographic areas, but may include a more extended time span.
III. *Stem.* These are considerably larger groups of more distantly related cultures. There are some implications of geographic grouping.
 IV. *Root.* These are the broadest groupings of cultures in the Southwest, and might be considered somewhat comparable to basic cultures as previously suggested.

In applying and evaluating this scheme Colton has suggested that two alterations could profitably be made in it. The addition of the concept of the component would be useful in detailed archaeological work, for in many instances several phases may be found in one site. In view of the fact that the McKern system has employed the term "phase" for a much larger category, and to prevent confusion by archaeologists working in both areas, he has proposed that the Gladwin term "phase " be dropped and the McKern term "focus" be substituted for it. There is of course much to recommend this view.

One final criticism has been leveled at the Gladwin system. This is the use of linguistic names for some of the roots. Since it is as yet impossible to prove that any prehistoric cultural stream, with the exception of the Pueblo, is directly ancestral to any modern group, it has been repeatedly proposed that these terms be changed, particularly "Yuman Root."

Actually the series of units in the Gladwin system and those in the McKern, or Midwestern, system are much alike. Both consist of units based on cultural similarities and differences, which are derived from individual traits, and both have a series of categories running from small to increasingly large, wherein several of the smaller units go to make up the next largest. It is in interpretation, and associated implications of time, area, and interrelationships, that the Gladwin system is basically different. With the suggested modifications the Gladwin system would probably represent the most useful and perhaps the final form of a classification where detailed comparisons are necessary. It has proven useful to the Southwestern specialist, but, because of its very advantage to him (its detailed complexity), it cannot be the medium of comparison for the beginning student.

Soon after Hohokam culture was established as that culture character-istic of the desert section, Gila Pueblo proposed dividing it into a series of broad sequential divisions. As in the Pecos classification, these divi-sions have been correlated with dates, although in this case the dates are derived not through direct tree-ring datings but by trade pottery types which have been dated elsewhere, or by other methods of seriation. Phases make up local subdivisions of the larger groupings to serve as more de-tailed bases of study. These stages have been called "periods" in the pub-lications of Gila Pueblo, but they are actually stages of culture to which dates have been correlated. For the purposes of this book these broader period, or stage, classifications will be found most useful. The six period names are characterized by pottery types and other associated culture traits, so that in general they may be easily identified.

MAJOR STAGES OF THE HOHOKAM CLASSIFICATION

   VI. Modern Period—A.D. 1700–1900
    V. Recent Period—A.D. 1450–1700
   IV. Classic Period—A.D. 1200–1450
  III. Sedentary Period—A.D. 900–1200
   II. Colonial Period—A.D. 500–900
    I. Pioneer Period—200 B.C.–A.D. 500

In 1955 Wheat suggested a much simplified division of the Mogollon culture into sequential periods. These, beginning with the earliest, are Mogollon 1 to 5, and he has correlated the various regional divisions with these periods. Mogollon 1 includes the Pine Lawn of the Pine Lawn area, the Pine Lawn and Georgetown phases of the Mimbres area, the Penasco and Dos Cabezas of the San Simon branch, Hilltop as a later portion in the Forestdale area, and early Circle Prairie in the Black River area. His Mogollon 2 includes later Pine Lawn in the Pine Lawn area, San Lorenzo in the Mimbres area, Pinaleno in the San Simon area, Cottonwood in the Forestdale area, and late Circle Prairie in the Black River area. Mogollon 3 includes the San Francisco for the Pine Lawn, Mimbres, and Black River areas, the Galiuro in the San Simon, and Forestdale in the Forest-dale area. Mogollon 4 is Three Circle for the Black River, Pine Lawn, and Mimbres areas, Cerros for the San Simon, and middle Corduroy for the

Forestdale area. Mogollon 5 includes Reserve for the Pine Lawn and Black River areas, Mangus for the Mimbres area, Encinas for the San Simon, and late Corduroy for the Forestdale area.

This classification is an effort to equate the various stages of culture found in the several regions where Mogollon occurs, and to assign dates to them. It is the simplified kind of classification that should be most useful to students, but as may be seen from the above there is some overlapping of terms for various time periods in different regions. The classification in the Mimbres and Pine Lawn valley areas of Pine Lawn,

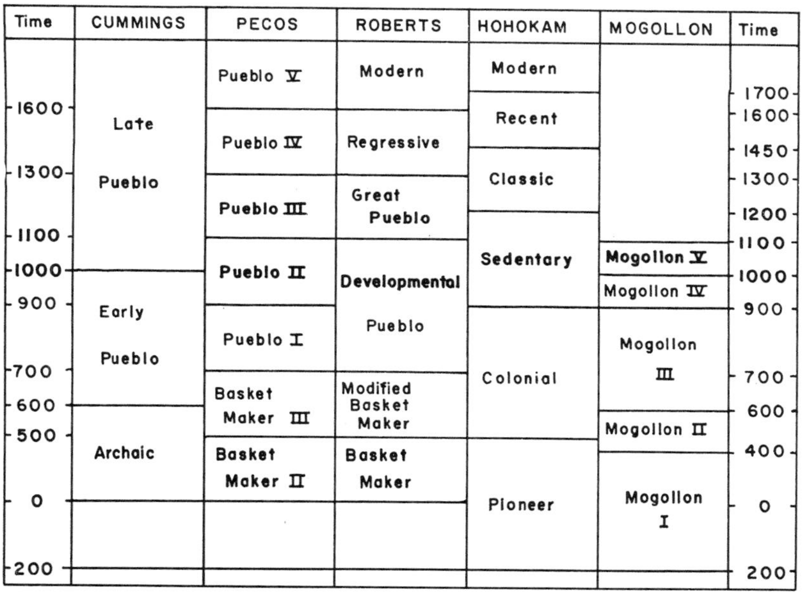

Time	CUMMINGS	PECOS	ROBERTS	HOHOKAM	MOGOLLON	Time
		Pueblo V	Modern	Modern		1700
1600	Late			Recent		1600
		Pueblo IV	Regressive			1450
1300	Pueblo		Great	Classic		1300
		Pueblo III	Pueblo			1200
1100						1100
1000		Pueblo II	Developmental	Sedentary	Mogollon V	1000
900	Early				Mogollon IV	900
		Pueblo I	Pueblo		Mogollon III	
700	Pueblo			Colonial		700
600		Basket Maker III	Modified Basket Maker			600
500					Mogollon II	
	Archaic	Basket Maker II	Basket Maker			400
0				Pioneer	Mogollon I	0
200						200

Fig. 11. A correlation, in the most general way, of the various classifications discussed herein, with dates indicating wherein they fall temporarily. The Pecos classification was proposed in 1927, the Roberts modification in 1935, the Hohokam classification by Gladwin in 1936, and the Mogollon scheme by Wheat in 1955.

Georgetown, San Francisco, Three Circle, and Reserve, with implications of chronology from earliest to latest, is perhaps better known and more generally referred to. Only time will tell which system will be most used.

Since the inception of Southwestern archaeology a number of different classifications have been advanced at various times by different individuals, each of which has been based on a combination of traits and to which other data have accrued as necessity demanded. With the passing of time and an increasingly more complete knowledge of the various culture stages, these classifications have had to be altered to fit the newer conditions.

Always they have been of two types: those of complicated detail, which are the bases upon which advanced research is accomplished; and those of a much more general nature, which have served to introduce beginning students to the subject. As it is this second class which most nearly fulfills the requirements of this book, it is these simpler schemes with which we will be concerned herein.

The present tendency to trace pottery types as a diagnostic of culture stages is an outgrowth of the recognition of the extreme sensitivity of pottery to change. Probably more than any other culture trait, pottery has been found to reflect minute temporal and areal differences, though at the same time carrying broad design similarities widely throughout the Southwest. Thus many more advanced research workers have come to regard pottery types as the best diagnostic of the various phases of the Pecos classification, particularly when it has become necessary to subdivide its stages further, so that when speaking of Pueblo III, for instance, what is frequently really meant is a certain combination of ceramic types.

However, it has been found that though any one trait, such as pottery, does follow a definite sequence in a particular region, other traits may not consistently correlate to it. This is true when house types and pottery types have been compared from two regions, an excellent example being Chaco Canyon and the Flagstaff area. In Chaco Canyon a general Pueblo II type of pottery is associated with pueblos, but near Flagstaff it is found with single-room pithouses.

As the ultimate purpose of the Southwestern archaeologist is to build history backward into unknown periods, and as history must be based as nearly as possible on time development, a chronology based purely on pottery will not always prove entirely correct when other traits are added to it. Even some pottery types lag regionally, or are not introduced quite so early in one section as another.

The classifications which have just been discussed are the main ones which have been used in the past or are still being used by Southwestern archaeologists. They cover the main stages of cultural evolution from the beginning of the introduction of pottery, or in some areas before, to the present time. If they are compared one to another it will be seen that they do not quite agree in time, or that some overlap with others. Some years ago it was learned that in the Flagstaff area it took about 200 years for culture to evolve to a state where it was clearly different, and as a result these 200-year periods have served more or less as the basis of such evolutionary schemes during the past several years.

The time break between the Archaic and Early Pueblo of the Cummings classification has been found generally to be between about A.D.

550 and 600, and the break between Early Pueblo and Late Pueblo at about A.D. 1000. The Pecos classification has been found to break fairly well at the 200-year periods up to Pueblo IV, which is 300 years long if the date of A.D. 1600 is accepted as the beginning of the Historic period, and although Basket Maker II seems to end generally about A.D. 500, the beginning date has not even yet been firmly fixed. Since the Roberts classification is simply a modification of the Pecos classification it is more or less equivalent, though there has been an increasing tendency to speak of early and late divisions of many of his stages. It is the Hohokam classification which seems to show the most radical variation from the others. The Pioneer stage, like that of the early Mogollon culture, started about 200 B.C. and lasted to perhaps A.D. 500. The Colonial seems to equate fairly well with Basket Maker III and Pueblo I. The Sedentary lasted from about A.D. 900 to 1200, the Classic from about 1200 to 1450, the Recent from about 1450 to perhaps 1600, and a Modern period has been suggested from A.D. 1600 to the present. It is thus possible not only to equate these various classificatory schemes but to arrange them in a time sequence which is at least generally acceptable.

Throughout this discussion two important factors have been repeatedly referred to. These are the three dimensional variations which must occur in any consideration of culture in relation to space and time. Of all possible bases of correlation only one remains constant, though indefinitely expandable or divisible, and that of course is time. This has been arbitrarily set in definite divisions, with which we are all commonly accustomed to correlate events, so that an ideal classification would be one based solely on this element.

Until about 1935 absolute dates which could be correlated with archaeological events covered only about two-thirds of the more recent archaeological stages of northern Arizona, making it impractical to attempt a classification based primarily upon time. The extension of the chronology and the securing of many additional dates has made possible the dating by tree rings of all major culture stages now well recognized and thoroughly characterized in the plateau area. Carbon 14 dates have supplemented datings in areas where tree-ring–datable material was not to be found, and has given relatively accurate dates of the earlier stages of the Southwest which cannot as yet be dated by tree rings. As a result, from this point on arbitrarily chosen time periods will be set up and used as the basis of discussion, and to these established periods culture developments from various areas will be correlated. The latter part of this book will be devoted to a discussion of culture as based on these time periods.

In the following list of periods an attempt has been made, in the most general possible manner, to indicate roughly the nature of the culture which existed at the time stated. It is impossible to give more than an indication of culture, for there was certainly considerable regional variation at the same time. Although these suggested characterizations will only be casually referred to in later chapters, they might be of some immediate value in fixing in mind a picture of culture evolution in the Southwest.

About 10,000 B.C.—*Ancient Period.* These are the people who were primarily hunters.

10,000 to 5000 B.C.—*Hunter Period.* Some of the more eastern of these people were still hunters, but many of those of Desert culture derivation were gathering and collecting with some hunting. It has been called Hunter period for all were hunting for their food, or at least searching for it.

5000 to 200 B.C.—*Collector Period.* During this period people were collecting and gathering more than they were hunting. Corn had appeared in the Southwest, but does not seem to have been a major part of the economy.

200 B.C. to A.D. 1—*Exploitation Period.* During this period people were exploiting their limited environments much more fully, were developing agricultural activities, were making the first pottery, and were beginning to settle more permanently in specific regions.

A.D. 1 to 500—*Founder Period.* It was during this period that the basic characteristics of many cultures were being founded; for instance Hohokam, Mogollon, and Basket Maker were all developed during this time.

A.D. 500 to 700—*Settlement Period.* During this period many different groups were becoming much more settled in their respective areas, and developing typical and distinct regional cultures.

A.D. 700 to 900—*Adjustment Period.* This was in many ways a period of adjustment in many regions of the Southwest. Widespread changes because of influences between areas was being effected.

A.D. 900 to 1100—*Dissemination Period.* This was a time when many cultures were vigorously expanding and spreading into new areas. Pueblo and Hohokam cultures were particularly vigorous now, and the Sinagua and Patayan areas were developing, as was the Rio Grande.

A.D. 1100 to 1300—*Classic Period.* This was the classic development in the Anasazi area for prehistoric people, although later cultures did not decline here. Many innovations may be seen now in several areas and cultures.

A.D. 1300 to 1600—*Culminant Period.* This was the period during which many cultures culminated. Anasazi particularly reached a sort of culmination. Hohokam and Mogollon had passed their peaks in the Southwest. The Rio Grande was reaching new heights of development.

A.D. 1600 to 1900—*Historic Period.* As implied this is the period when Indian tribal groups are known from historic accounts.

1900 to the present—*Modern Period.* This latest period has been called the Modern period because many Indian tribes in the Southwest have suffered radical cultural changes during the past half-century.

In evaluating any such scheme as that presented above it must not be forgotten that as one goes back in time the archaeological record becomes increasingly blurred, and that specific dating is more and more difficult. Thus the earlier periods, even though they may be dated by a number of carbon 14 dates, are probably less to be trusted than later periods. Even

Time	Period	Mogollon	Hohokam	Anasazi	Salado	Sinagua	Patayan	Rio Grande
1900	Modern		Pima Papago	Pueblo Ⅴ			Havasupai Walapai	Modern Pueblos
1600	Historic			Pueblo Ⅴ				Historic Pueblo
1300	Culminant			Pueblo Ⅳ	Polychrome	Clear Creek		Classic Pueblo
1100	Classic	Tularosa Reserve	Classic Soho	Pueblo Ⅲ	Polychrome B/W ?	Turkey Hill Elden		Coalition
900	Dissemination	Three Circle	Sedentary Santan	Pueblo Ⅱ.Ⅲ	B/W ?	Padre Angell Winona	Cataract	Development
700	Adjustment	San Francisco	Colonial Santa Cruz	Pueblo I		Rio de Flag Sunset	Nylier	Development
500	Settlement	Georgetown	Colonial Gila Butte	Basket Maker Ⅲ		Cinder Park	Pre-Pottery	Basket Maker Ⅲ
0	Founder	Pine Lawn	Pioneer Snaketown Sweetwater	Basket Maker Ⅱ			?	
200	Exploitation	Pine Lawn	Estrella Vahki	B.M. I ? Cochise				
5,000	Collector	Pre-Pottery Cochise		Cochise				
10,000	Hunter	Cochise Folsom etc.		L.Colorado				
	Ancient	Sandia etc.						

Fig. 12. Chart showing the periods and period names suggested herein, with correlation to cultural manifestations in various areas of the Southwest. The earliest evidences of man here have been included under the heading of "Mogollon" to save space. This table will be found useful, in a general way, in the interpretation of the relationships of later discussions in this book.

after the time of Christ some of the earlier periods are relatively poorly dated, and it is not until about A.D. 700 or even later that the tree-ring dates and culture correlations may be relied upon most fully.

Sources and Additional References

Cole, Fay-Cooper, and Thorne Deuel. Rediscovering Illinois, University of Chicago Press, 1937. (Gives a more complete discussion of the McKern classification as well as an example of the actual application to archaeology.)

Colton, Harold S. Prehistoric Culture Units and Their Relationships in Northern Arizona, Bulletin 17, 1939, Museum of Northern Arizona, Flagstaff. (Discussion of various classifications and revision of the Gladwin system.)

Gladwin, H. S. * A Method for the Designation of Cultures and Their Variations, Medallion Paper 15, 1934, Gila Pueblo, Globe, Arizona. (The Gladwin classification explained and illustrated. For more recent examples of the method see later reports of Gila Pueblo listed in the general bibliography.)

Kidder, Alfred Vincent. * Southwestern Archaeological Conference, *Science,* Vol. 66, No. 1716, 1927, New York City. (Summary of the Pecos classification as first outlined by Kidder, Roberts, and Morris.)

McKern, W. C. The Midwestern Taxonomic Method as an Aid to Archaeological Culture Study, *American Antiquity,* Vol. 4, No. 4, 1939, Society for American Archaeology, Salt Lake City, Utah. (Complete statement of the so-called McKern classification.)

Roberts, Frank H. H., Jr. A Survey of Southwestern Archaeology, *American Anthropologist,* Vol. 37, No. 1, 1935, Menasha, Wisconsin. (On p. 32 there is a statement of Roberts' revision of the Pecos classification.)

Wheat, Joe Ben. Mogollon Culture Prior to A.D. 1000, *American Antiquity,* Vol. 20, No. 4, Part 2, 1955, Society for American Archaeology, Salt Lake City, Utah. (The Wheat system of classifying and dating early Mogollon culture.)

V

Dendrochronology

At a small archaeological conference at Gila Pueblo (April 16-18, 1931), it was decided that the establishment of a chronology of Southwestern archaeological periods should be based on: first, tree-ring dating; second, stratigraphy; third, cross dating; and last, intensive analysis. This places dendrochronology, or a chronology built up as a result of the study of tree rings, as the most desirable of all means of establishing a series. Such a decision is wholly justified, for although the more recently developed method of carbon 14 dating has made it possible to date approximately many sites in the Southwest and elsewhere, these are not absolute dates, but are expressed with an estimated margin of probable error. Thus, only by tree-ring dating may individual ruins be absolutely dated to within the year, and sometimes the season, in which they were built. The duration of occupancy may often also be determined, with the various periods of building activity or repairs, and the approximate time of abandonment or destruction.

A. E. Douglass, an astronomer at the University of Arizona, conceived the idea of tracing climatic factors in tree growth in the arid Southwest, with the hope that sunspot activity affecting climate would in turn be reflected in the growth of trees. With a purely climatic objective in mind he first seriously began work on the yellow pines of the Flagstaff and Prescott areas in January, 1904. For this study he chose recently dead or still growing trees, and starting with outer known yearly rings was able to count back some 500 years. After counting several of these sections he soon realized that certain yearly rings were always of a definite relative size, as compared to the preceding and following rings. With recognition of this simple fact it was possible to carry the characteristic ring sequence in his head, and to date early portions of the series by recognizable characteristic ring sequences, even though the date of the outer ring of the specimen being studied was not known.

His next field investigation was the giant sequoias of California, where, with the same direct comparison method, he succeeded in building a sequence of over 3,000 years which was based on some 35 specimens. The results of this work disclosed that, although the trees of Arizona and California showed certain similarities, they were not identical in individual ring characteristics.

It soon became apparent that in order to extend the yellow pine record it would be necessary to find older sources of material. At about this time Wissler offered to send for examination quantities of wood gathered from prehistoric ruins in the Southwest. This offer was promptly accepted. The direct comparison method was also used in a study of this material, and it was found that the various prehistoric specimens correlated with each other as readily as had the historic ones.

With this encouragement Douglass began work on the yellow pine in earnest and in 1919, in a letter to Wissler, outlined the bridge method of "cross dating." This was based on the recognition that characteristic ring sequences of as little as 30 or 40 years were never exactly duplicated by the trees, and that certain short sequences might be relied upon in crossing or correlating two specimens, although subsequent dating has made

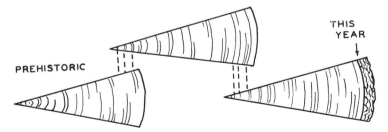

Fig. 13. Diagrammatic example of the bridge method of chronology building. The pie-shaped section to the right was cut in this year, and carries a ring sequence back to early historic times. By correlating these inner rings with the outer ones of the center piece the series is carried back to prehistoric times. The second bridging, or "cross dating," then gives true dates to the third specimen, which is from a prehistoric ruin.

less use of these "signatures" and more use of cross reference of series of rings and cross dating of groups of related beams. Thus Douglass found it was only necessary to correlate the inside rings of one specimen with the outside rings of another slightly older, and so build up a long chronology of fragments or individual pieces. By this system various independent records were established which had not, as yet, been connected to the later material bearing absolute dates.

Through the medium of lectures and publications, interest in the study of tree rings became widespread, and Neil M. Judd, who at that time was working at Pueblo Bonito under the auspices of the National Geographic Society, sent Douglass quantities of beams from that site. His work on this material was so satisfying to the society that funds were later secured from them to carry on the field and laboratory research.

In the spring and summer of 1928 Douglass secured the services of Hargrave, then a student at the University of Arizona, who, in an attempt to bridge the existing gap between the prehistoric chronologies and the earliest absolute dated series, collected beams from the Hopi towns. However, the dating of this early material was not accomplished until the following summer (1929), when another National Geographic expedition headed by Hargrave and Haury undertook excavation at Pinedale and Sholow ruins. Here a charcoal beam was uncovered which brought the two long sequences together by bridging the gap between them, and a great many of the large pueblos in the Southwest were assigned to dates in our own calendar. At the same time a continuous absolute chronology was carried back to A.D. 700. Among the great ruins at once dated were Pueblo Bonito, Aztec, Mesa Verde, Betatakin, Kiet Siel, Kokopnyama, Kinteel, Wupatki, Sholow, Pinedale, and about 30 others.

In the fall of 1930 Douglass gave his first course in dendrochronology to a group of students at the University of Arizona. This course has subsequently been given many times either by himself or by others with the result that a large group of tree-ring students have been instructed in tree-ring dating. These students, scattered throughout the Southwest, during the 1930's succeeded in dating a large number of additional ruins. Although Douglass began his study of tree rings as an aid to climatic studies, and though tree rings have materially contributed to climatic knowledge, their chief contribution has been in the dating of prehistoric ruins. As has already been pointed out, it was necessary early in tree-ring work to turn to archaeology as an aid to the extension of chronology, and in so doing many ruins incidentally were dated. With a realization of the value of such studies to archaeology, the archaeologists quickly looked to it for aid. Many of the archaeological students whom Douglass trained in tree-ring work turned to it to solve their archaeological problems in various portions of the Southwest, although few, if any, of this original group are now actively engaged in tree-ring studies.

During this period of pioneer work in dating Gila Pueblo, the Laboratory of Anthropology, the University of New Mexico, the Museum of Northern Arizona, and the University of Arizona were all actively engaged in dating sites. Most recently the only institution still making a major effort to do tree-ring studies, and to secure dates, is the Laboratory of Tree-Ring Research at the University of Arizona. So many dates have been determined for archaeological sites, altogether more than 800, that it has become impossible to keep track of them all. In an attempt to keep somewhat abreast of these developments in tree-ring work, a publication, the *Tree Ring Bulletin*, was established in the summer of 1934, wherein it was hoped all dates from ruins would eventually appear.

Much of the effort of Douglass and the various other early workers in the field was directed to an extension of the chronology before A.D 700. Quantities of material gathered by Earl Morris, and others, in the four corners district (Arizona, New Mexico, Colorado, and Utah) were in the possession of Douglass and had enabled him to build a chronology of several hundred years, but it was not crossed into the dated series which ended at A.D 700. Hawley, working with beams from Chetro Ketl, succeeded in extending the chronology to about A.D. 645, and the Museum of Northern Arizona added a few years to this, but still did not succeed in bridging the gap. It was not until March, 1935, that a charcoal fragment, this time a split plank, collected by the Museum of Northern Arizona near Flagstaff, succeeded in definitely bridging the gap. This brought in the earlier series from northeastern Arizona, and once more extended the chronology, now well into the first century A.D. The tree-ring series for the Southwest has since been further extended and now goes back to 59 B.C.

With this accomplishment all the major culture stages which had been recognized in northern Arizona were dated, making possible the outline of study, based upon actual dates, which will be followed in this book.

Since 1952 the activities of the Laboratory of Tree-Ring Research have been directed primarily to three kinds of dating efforts: the review and rechecking of dates which have been secured in the past, the securing of much larger series of dates from sites already dated, and the dating of additional sites which are currently being excavated. An example of this latter kind of dating is the securing of the first prehistoric tree-ring dates from Mexico, by dating the Casas Grandes site in 1963. The Casas Grandes dates were secured by developing a new procedure at the University of Arizona for adapting standardizing processes to electronic computer techniques. This is a very promising new method, and may in the future make possible the dating of sites which it has not been possible to date in the past.

The importance and possibilities of tree-ring dating can be grasped only when something of the methods and materials employed is understood. Many trees, such as the yellow pine, annually add one ring of growth. Growth begins shortly after the flow of sap in the spring with large thin-walled cells which in section are light yellowish in color. This cell growth continues throughout the summer, but as colder weather in the fall approaches the cells become smaller and heavier-walled, until at last growth stops with the retreat of the sap, and a reddish smooth line is formed at the outside of the ring. This cellular growth, falling between the smooth regular line formed by the outside edges of the harder fall growth, represents one annual ring.

In the semi-arid Southwest, and with trees growing under normal or average conditions, seldom, if ever, is there sufficient rainfall to enable the tree to enjoy its maximum possible growth. When an unusually dry season occurs, all or most of the trees in a given area will show small, or perhaps microscopic, rings for that year. The reverse, of course, is true in an unusually wet season. As the small rings are most striking, abundant, and consistent in this section of the country, they are used as guide or determining rings, and the tree-ring chronology, as already mentioned, has been built up on a notation of their occurrence.

Early in his work on cross dating ruins Dr. Douglass, realizing that some mechanical aid in recalling relative ring size would be of the greatest help in dating ruins, developed the short plot. This consists of a narrow strip of graph paper upon which each vertical line represents a year, every ten being indicated with a date written upon the slip. At each yearly ring that is noticeably minute, a long vertical line representing the ring is drawn down from the upper edge of the strip. Rings of varying size are depicted by lines of different lengths, the longest line for the smallest ring, very large rings being indicated by a *B* in their proper position.

When a new undated specimen is being studied, in which a date cannot readily be recognized by memory, a plot is made of its characteristics from the inside (or from left to right), to its last ring on the outside. This short record, with the piece number attached, is then slid along the main composite or key plot until it matches. A second review of the specimen may then be undertaken to check with the other dated pieces covering this time section, and if it closely matches the records represented by them it is obviously dated. Usually, by double checking, a date is established beyond any question of doubt, as is indicated by the two cuts showing dating by short plots in operation. It must be remembered that over a considerable period of years at no point has the record ever been found to duplicate itself.

Certain kinds of wood are much more adaptable to dating purposes than others. Probably the most generally dated is Douglas fir, since it has been found to be quite widespread in ruins in the Southwest, and the rings are regular in circumference and usually very well marked. Yellow pine has been found to be almost equally valuable, for it is very widespread and the

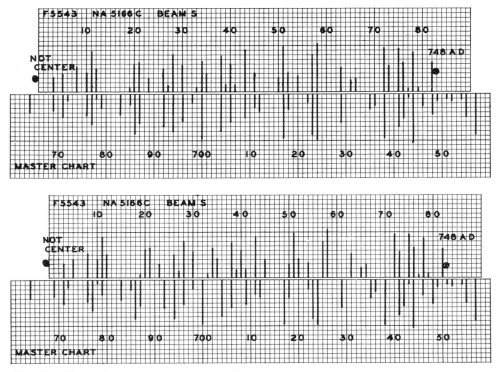

Fig. 14. Example of cross dating by short plots. The master chart is a compilation of a large series of specimens, noting their most distinctive characters. The specimen plot above, in the upper figure, has been moved along the master chart until the two records match, thus giving a date, in this case A.D. 748, as the outside ring of the specimen record. The lower example shows the specimen plot shifted right two years, destroying the correlation. Thus a characteristic beam may be dated with absolute certainty at one point on the master chart and nowhere else.

rings are also uniform in circumference and relatively well contrasted. Piñon has been found to be more generally datable than was originally believed to be the case, particularly when in a site with other types of wood which may be readily dated. Piñon rings are much fainter than those of fir or even pine. Juniper, although it is widely distributed in many parts of the Southwest, was not generally used by prehistoric builders where straighter and better poles, such as pine, could be obtained, but does occur in abundance in some sites. It is seldom found to be datable, and may be characterized as having an eccentric center and hairlike, almost microscopic, rings, with probably many absent. Cottonwood, because of the large and uniform size of the rings, has been found to be of no dating value, and oak and walnut have also been found to be of little or no use. Sage-

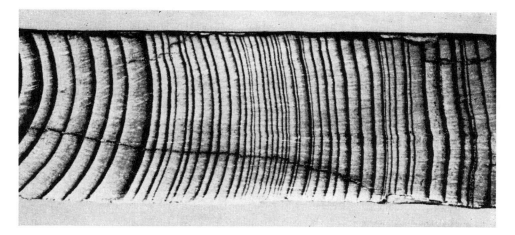

Fig. 15. Section of a tubular boring from a prehistoric Douglas fir beam. The small rings are the dry period late in the thirteenth century. It is the small, irregularly spaced rings which are the most distinctive and form the basis of tree-ring dating.

brush is datable, however, and some have good long ring records, but its dating value lies largely in charcoal from fireplaces.

At first it was felt by Douglass that it was necessary to have full sections of preserved beams which represented long sequences before it was possible to date specimens accurately. Full sections were considered necessary in order that the entire ring circuit might be studied to locate traces of rings which were absent from one part of the section or another, and to give more definite data on double rings (two rings grown in one season, one of which is false). However, with increasing familiarity with the various sections of the chronology, it was found that lost rings could be readily accounted for, and that doubles could generally be recognized with some ease. The result was that radial sections were entirely datable, and further investigation showed charcoal was equally valuable. This immediately opened a much larger field for dating operations, including all those sites in the open where wood would not survive but where burning preserved charred beams or portions of beams.

Various methods for the field collection of tree-ring material were soon evolved. It was 'a simple matter to saw a full section from one end of a preserved wood beam, in a cliff dwelling or other sheltered section, which was loose in collapsed roofs. For a huge log it was often simpler to choose one portion of the radius and make a V-shaped cut in one end from the side to past the center, thus removing a long triangular strip which might easily be prepared and read. But for peculiar situations, such as beams still supporting roofs in standing dwellings, Douglass evolved a tube with a

Fig. 16. One of the rare specimens of juniper which gives a characteristic and easily dated record. It is from Kiet Siel Ruin in Tsegi Canyon, northern Arizona.

set of saw teeth on one end and bit head fastened to the other. This implement, operated in a common brace, will remove a core from beams which cannot otherwise be collected. At best this method is long and tedious, and almost never can the core be broken off and removed whole.

Within the last few years the development of portable power-driven borers of this sort has made it possible to take large numbers of cores from beams in sites with both a minimum of labor and a minimum of disruption to the sites.

Charcoal, on the other hand, because of its very fragile nature, must be prepared in the field by quite different methods. Most charcoal which is found buried in damp earth will crack when it is exposed to the air and allowed to dry too rapidly. Therefore it must be carefully removed from the earth and allowed to dry at least partly in the shade. So far the best preservative which has been found is a solution of gasoline and paraffin, in which the charcoal, which has been more or less dried, is placed until it stops bubbling, when it is removed and set out in the shade to dry fully. The gasoline tends to carry the paraffin into the charcoal during immersion, and to drive out the water, after which the gasoline evaporates, leaving the charcoal impregnated with paraffin, which acts as a binding material. In dealing with very fragile and thin charcoal planks, or similar material, it is necessary to uncover one side and coat it with a thick shellac which is allowed to dry; the specimen is then carefully turned over and coated on the other side, before it may be handled. This is also true of semirotted wood. In handling exceptionally fragile specimens it is often possible to slip a piece of thin wood or cardboard under the charcoal after shellacking one side and then to tie the specimen to the board with string. All specimens should be carefully wrapped in cotton, tagged, and stored in boxes for transportation from the field. Extreme care is necessary in the collection of such material, as charcoal is prone to shell off from the outside, and it is the outside date that is most important for archaeological purposes.

A careful tagging and noting of the actual location of the specimen in the ruin, its attitude in relation to other beams, and similar information are absolutely necessary at the time of collection. If time is not taken to note fully the relation of the beam to its surroundings, the date which may later be derived from it will be of little or no archaeological significance.

A charred post in situ in a pithouse. It has been wrapped with string to prevent deterioration upon exposure.

The preparation of wood for dating in the laboratory consists of shaving down a sectional surface with a safety razor blade. A new sharp blade has been found to give a better, clearer, more readable surface than any other easily accessible instrument. The cut should preferably be at a slight angle to the true section of the piece, to reflect light best. As an aid to bringing out rings for reading a small quantity of kerosene may be applied to the surface with a daub. In preparing specimens for display, or even in reading some sections, the surface may be ground down and polished with fine sandpaper, and the finish may best be preserved with a coat or more of flexible collodion. Recent developments of new high-speed sanding machines and better abrasives have made the use of such equipment, when it is available and when numbers of beams must be prepared for study, almost as effective as the best razor technique. Such equipment is now in extensive use at the Laboratory of Tree-Ring Research in Tucson.

The best surface in charcoal is that which results by simply breaking the specimen across the grain. When first broken in this manner the rings stand out in very clearly defined relief, but much handling or continual reference to the record results in a dimming of this surface and the necessity of a new break. In some specimens, particularly where the rings are relatively large or distinct, a new razor blade may be relied upon to prepare a surface, but as the charred cell structure is very brittle it tends in any event to blur the record somewhat. Very fragile specimens may be further strengthened at this time by partially embedding in a block of plaster, coating with shellac or some hard wax, wrapping in gauze, and tying with an abundance of string, or by any similar method. Very fragile pieces of wood may be treated in much the same way.

Not every piece of wood or charcoal shows ring characters which permit dating. Studies undertaken by dendrochronologists indicate that certain locations are decidedly unfavorable to the formation of datable sequences whereas certain others are favorable. Trees which grow on steep slopes, narrow hilltops, or in very rocky soil, where runoff is rapid and soil water sparse, are inclined to show supersensitive records with many rings absent in years when no growth took place in the stem of the tree. Others growing near the bottoms of valleys or on the banks of streams or in springs or similar spots have such an abundant permanent supply of water that their rings are all more of a size, and thus are called "complacent" or "uniform," and are undatable. The ideally situated tree is one growing in good soil conditions, with runoff but not too steep a slope, so that most of the water which falls is utilized. For such a tree the record is sensitive, with few or no rings lost, and yet the rings have sufficient character or variation in width to make them easily datable.

The number of rings included in the specimen is obviously important in determining its datability. Unless unusually strong and easily recognizable ring groupings are present, sequences of less than 25 or 30 years are undatable. A really excellent piece will cover anywhere from 60 to 200 years, with an average ring size which is easily discernible under a six-power lens. Branches of trees are often difficult to date, as rings are inclined to be absent or double. Charcoal fragments, which were probably largely branches and small bushes and trees, and were used as firewood before being thrown into trash heaps as coals, too often are so far from actual outsides that they are not of much real value to the archaeologist. These fragments have been partially consumed as firewood before they have formed charcoal and have been thrown out, but they should all be saved, for some have been found to give good cutting dates and therefore shed light on the time of occupation of the site, not just the time of construction.

All tree-ring specimens which are collected at a site in the field should be sent to the laboratory, for much valuable information may be gained from them. The kind of wood may be identified from the charcoal pieces

A pithouse excavated by the Museum of Northern Arizona in the Flagstaff area. Charred beams have been cleaned off and left in place on the floor at the south end of the structure. The entrance is shown in the upper left.

even of fire sweepings, and a careful notation of the wood types will give much valuable information concerning the ecological conditions under which the pueblo existed. Frequently the brush, sticks, and splints included beneath the plaster and above the beams in rooms have aided in characterizing the types of flora prevailing at the time of occupation of the site. Sometimes a gradual stripping of the cover and lowering of the water table are well reflected in the slow dying of the trees, as indicated by the steady shrinking of the rings of all the trees collected at a site.

It is, however, in the archaeological interpretation of a list of dates derived from a ruin that the most can be learned of its occupation, and care in the profuse and proper taking of field notes is most particularly appreciated. As is true with many other problems, good common sense is here of the utmost value. A typical group of dates as derived from the beams of one room in a cliff dwelling where 14 excellent beams, all dated, have been preserved will illustrate this point. One date shows as A.D. 1145, two as 1173, and eight as 1174, with one each at 1176, 1179, and 1182. If they are listed horizontally, with their number of occurrences above, they will look like this (for present purposes it may be assumed that all of these dates are cutting dates, that is, that they are the actual dates when the beams were cut):

1	2	8	1	1	1
1145	1173	1174	1176	1179	1182

Although this is an ideally arranged situation it is nevertheless somewhat as may be expected in actual practice. Sometimes all beams in a room have been found to give the same date; in some rooms even more widely scattered dates than these are found.

The date 1145 probably represents the reuse of a beam from an earlier structure, from which it has been robbed, as it occurs entirely alone. The two beams from 1173 may have been surplus left over for a year from other building activities in the ruin, or they may have been cut the year before and stored for later use or to wait for seasoning of the wood. The eight beams at 1174 represent the building date of the ruin, or at least the cutting date of the beams when the builder had the plans in mind, for it is possible, of course, that the beams were seasoned for a year or two, after the Hopi method of today, before the building was constructed. The three following dates, because they stand alone, undoubtedly represent repairs made in the structure after it was built and during its occupation, the last date certainly coming near, that is, within four or five years, of the time at which this room was finally abandoned. Had it been occupied much longer the time period recognized between these repairs indicates that others would have been made. Thus it may be estimated, with considerable accuracy, that this room was occupied from 1174 to a short time after 1182, probably no later than 1186 or 1187.

An additional example, this time taken from actual dating experience at Kiet Siel Ruin, in Tsegi Canyon, may be of value. The first group of dates is simply 20 dates as secured from the ruin, without any attempt at organization or interpretation. They range in time from A.D. 1116 to 1284, and although they tend to group numerically in the vicinity of 1274 they still tell little. In the first column is the specimen number and in the second the date of the piece.

F.	DATE	F.	DATE
3161	1116	3114	1274
3124	1154	3118	1274
3164	1258	3135	1274
3108	1262	3144	1274
3152	1269	3183	1274
3138	1275	3112	1274
3192	1274	3113	1275
3106	1273	3116	1275
3119	1274	3117	1275
3139	1273	3111	1284

If, however, the dates are listed by rooms, as encountered in the ruin, they become more significant:

ROOM	DATE
12	1116
14	1154 (These are 11 dates from shakes in the roof)
6	1273
7	1269, 1274, 1274
13	1274
Storage	1274, 1274
8	1274, 1274, 1275, 1275
3	1274, 1275
15	1275
Beams found loose in rubbish	1258, 1263, 1273, 1284

With the data so arranged little skill in interpretation is required, for now a map of the ruin may be drawn and the dates may be placed in the rooms so that the order of construction of the pueblo may be seen.

Even more may be gained by a notation of the location of the various dates in the room. If the main central horizontal supporting beam gives a date of 1174 it is certain that the room was not built before that year, for it could not have been replaced after it was supporting all the other beams. The same would be true of the four main vertical support posts of the roof in a pithouse which were found to date the same year. Certain features which were added subsequently to the building of the room may easily be determined, such as the addition or enlargement of a ventilator in a pithouse.

So far, by the process outlined above, only a building date has been arrived at, but archaeologists are interested in dating as much of the associated culture as possible. Any material found resting on the floor of a room, such as pottery, basketry, clothing, jewelry, and other artifacts, must of course be assigned to the time of the last date, or shortly following it, as these were the articles in use at the time of its abandonment. In the first room outlined above, the ten-year period of occupation would show no change in materials being used, but if the period were to be extended to 200 years, as is indicated in some sites, radical changes would be expected. When a long period of occupation is indicated recourse must be made to the debris piles, where stratigraphic studies will indicate the changes of culture that took place. By an application of the seriation methods an approximate dating of these changes may be accomplished.

In applying tree-ring dating to archaeology other possible confusing situations must be considered. First, it is not entirely impossible that extensive robbing of older structures might throw correlations of dates and culture far off. Assuming that the removal of all cover, including trees, had eventually led to the abandonment of a region, and that 50 or 100 years later it was reoccupied, if no sizable trees were then at hand but many beams were still to be found in nearby ruins, it is entirely conceivable that these beams might have been reused. This might give a very wide and haphazard distribution of dates and form an exceedingly confusing problem. Such a situation is somewhat indicated at Wupatki.

In the same way it is likely that because one site was chosen for occupation it was chosen again by later people, who, seeing it occupied by a ruin with many beams and fine building stones, merely cleared away the debris and utilized at least part of it in building their own homes. Or, again, part of the site might have been allowed to fall into disuse, much like the Hopi towns of today, and later a house might have been built on the site of a much older one, the beams and stones of the earlier structure being utilized.

Almost from the beginning of dating of archaeological sites through tree rings various individuals have raised the question of the possibility of the use of dead trees for beams, in preference to the cutting of live ones. This is exceedingly unlikely in the light of the tools the prehistoric Indians had at their disposal. Stone axes would be a poor implement with which to fell a dead tree. However, in the rare total absence of live trees, it must be admitted that they might have been used.

The dating of charcoal or wood fragments from trash heaps, to correlate with the stratigraphy found there, has been undertaken by several individuals. Because many of the pieces will be likely to be small brush or branches, and because they are often far from an actual original outside, **true dates are very difficult** to obtain. Where there is a sufficient quantity of such material, as at the larger pueblo ruins, it can most profitably be utilized. Hawley, in her work on Chetro Ketl, employed this method to the fullest extent.

Little has been said thus far about the determining of actual outside or cutting dates, or more properly "bark dates." If the bark is still on the piece there is no doubt that it represents the actual cutting date. If the outside ring extends completely around the beam and is everywhere unbroken, it may generally be assumed to be a bark date. In many specimens it is possible to identify the outside by the peculiar surface which is to be found when the bark is removed. But where weathering has obviously removed some of the outside a great deal of experience is required to estimate the amount which has been lost. With charcoal an absolutely accurate guess is impossible, and any estimate within five years is usually somewhat questionable when the outside of the piece is badly and irregularly shattered.

All these situations, and more, are not only possible but frequently encountered in the application of dendrochronology to archaeology. Quantities of dates, and many correlations with cultural materials, are needed before accurate dating may be done over the Southwest generally, but these many correlations are rapidly forthcoming. In all primitive structures in the Southwest beams were used extensively, and as they rotted in place, or broke under prolonged strain, they were replaced. In houses which were sheltered in caves the beams are often found in place, and those in the open which were destroyed with fire sometimes contain much charcoal. Both these sources have supplied huge quantities of material, much of which has been dated and much more of which will eventually be dated. However, the supply is limited, and great care should be exercised not only in the collection of such specimens but also in their preservation.

The dating of specimens is by no means a simple process. It requires a great deal of actual experience before any degree of certainty may be acquired.

Sources and Additional References

Bannister, Byrant. Tree-Ring Dating of Archaeological Sites in the Chaco Canyon Region, New Mexico, Ph.D. dissertation, University of Arizona, Tucson, 1959, University Microfilms Inc., L.C. Card No. MIC 60-584. (Discussion of the derivation and application of archaeological dates.)

————. The Interpretation of Tree-Ring Dates, *American Antiquity*, Vol. 27, No. 4, 1962, Society for American Archaeology, Salt Lake City, Utah. (Discussion of the application of tree-ring dates to problems of archaeology.)

————, ed. Andrew Ellicott Douglass, *Tree Ring Bulletin*, Vol. 24, Nos. 3-4, 1962, Tree Ring Society, University of Arizona, Tucson.

Douglass, A. E. Climatic Cycles and Tree Growth, *Carnegie Institution Publication 289*, 1928, Washington, D.C. (Technical paper.)

———. * The Secret of the Southwest Solved by Talkative Tree Rings, *National Geographic Magazine*, December, 1929, Washington, D.C. (One of the best popular descriptions of the tree-ring method available.)

———. * Dating Pueblo Bonito and Other Ruins of the Southwest, *Pueblo Bonito Series 1*, 1935, Contributed Technical Papers, National Geographic Society, Washington, D.C. (Excellent discussion of methods and a long series of dates, with fine illustrations.)

Glock, Waldo S. * Principles and Methods of Tree-Ring Analysis, *Carnegie Institution Publication 486*, 1937, Washington, D.C. (As the title suggests.)

Haury, Emil W. * Tree Rings—the Archaeologist's Time-Piece, *American Antiquity*, Vol. 1, No. 2, 1935, Society for American Archaeology, Salt Lake City, Utah. (Excellent discussion of the application of tree-ring dating to archaeology.)

———. HH-39: Recollections of a Dramatic Moment in Southwestern Archaeology, *Tree Ring Bulletin*, Vol. 24, Nos. 3-4, 1962, Tree Ring Society, University of Arizona, Tucson. (Department of the dating of prehistoric sites by bridging a major gap.)

McGinnies, W. G. * Dendrochronology, *Journal of Forestry*, Vol. 61, No. 1, 1963, Washington, D.C. (Tree-ring dating brought up to current status.)

McGregor, John C. Tree Ring Dating, *Museum Notes*, Vol. 3, No. 4, 1930, Museum of Northern Arizona, Flagstaff. (Popular and short discussion of tree-ring methods.)

Schulman, Edmund. Tree Rings and History in Western United States, *Economic Botany*, Vol. 8, No. 3, 1956, Lancaster, Pennsylvania. (A good article, as the title implies.)

———. * Dendroclimatic Changes in Semiarid America, Laboratory of Tree-Ring Research, University of Arizona, Tucson, 1956. (One of the best discussions of the history and problems of tree-ring dating, with examples of ring analysis and tree growths in various areas.)

Smiley, Terah L. A Summuary of Tree-Ring Dates from Some Southwestern Archaeological Sites, *University of Arizona Bulletin*, Vol. 22, No. 4, 1951, Tucson. (As the title implies.)

———. Geochronology, *University of Arizona Physical Science Bulletin 2*, 1955, Tucson. "Dendrochronology," with Bryant Bannister. (Good discussion of tree-ring studies.)

Smiley, Terah L., Stanley A. Stubbs, and Bryant Bannister. A Foundation for the Dating of Some Late Archaeological Sites in the Rio Grande Area, New Mexico: Based on Studies in Tree-Ring Methods and Pottery Analysis, *University of Arizona Bulletin*, Vol. 24, No. 3, 1953, Tucson. (As the title indicates, an example of the application of dating.)

Stallings, W. S., Jr. A Tree-Ring Chronology for the Rio Grande Drainage in Northern New Mexico, *Proceedings of the National Academy of Sciences*, Vol. 19, No. 9, 1933. (A series of dates secured from the Rio Grande area.)

———. Dating Prehistoric Ruins by Tree-Rings, *General Series Bulletin 8*, 1939, Laboratory of Anthropology, Santa Fe, New Mexico. (Brief and clear discussion of tree-ring dating.)

VI

Pottery

The value of pottery was recognized early in Southwestern archaeological work, for during most of the major periods of Southwestern prehistory it was widely made and used. With more careful recent ceramic studies, and the division of general groups of pottery into explicitly prescribed types, it has become increasingly important. Intensive research on pottery has indicated that, because of the following points, it is the present most generally useful trait.

1. Pottery once made and fired is practically *indestructible*.

2. In any site (of pottery-bearing periods) which was inhabited for more than a few years it is relatively *abundant*.

3. It was made throughout the entire Southwest during most periods of cultural development and is therefore *widespread*.

4. It reflects minute *changes* (which may constitute definite types, or subtypes) both temporally and spacially.

5. It is relatively *easy to collect, handle, store, and study*.

For these reasons, pottery has become the most valuable diagnostic of cultural change, the first step in reconstructing archaeological history. It is, also, certainly the most valuable trait in the application of the seriation method of cross dating, or in correlating individual sites or even total culture complexes.

POTTERY METHODS

The best introduction to a study of pottery and pottery techniques, since ancient methods of manufacture can be reconstructed from a study of finished products, is a review of methods employed by living potters in the same region. The Hopi Indians, surrounded on every side by the ruins of their ancestors, the Pueblo people, represent the best possible source of such information. It may be assumed that ancient pottery, which is identical to that of today, was produced by the same methods as those now in use. Even though not all prehistoric pottery is paralleled by identical modern types, at least some ancient methods may be reconstructed by a careful study of modern ones.

Although plain or undecorated pottery is now made on all the three Hopi mesas and in most of the Hopi towns, those who produce the finest painted pottery live on the first or east mesa. Many of these people are actually a Rio Grande Pueblo group, who have lived so long in the company of the Hopis that they have assimilated many Hopi traits.

Quarries, centuries old, are the source of the clays from which the pottery is made. Three types are collected: a hard, light gray clay, from which the body of the vessel is built; a finer white clay, which is often used as an outer coating or slip; and a yellow clay, which burns red, used as a slip or a paint. These types are carefully selected at the quarries and removed to the pueblo, where they are prepared for use.

The first operation is to break up and then grind the hard dried clay chunks into a fine powder. This is accomplished on a metate, or grinding stone, with a mano, or handstone. The clay is ground to a powder and sifted, usually by choosing a spot where a gentle breeze is blowing, perhaps a doorway, and dropping the powder from a height to a cloth spread on the floor below. The wind thus obligingly grades the material. Only the more finely ground is collected and stored in bags or baskets until it is to be used; the rest is reground and the process repeated.

When a sufficient quantity of clay is prepared it is placed in a vessel and water added until a rather sticky paste, of doughlike consistency, results. This is thoroughly mixed and kneaded to the exact plasticity required, then placed in a solid container and covered with a damp cloth, to be used as needed.

If a temper is required to keep the vessel from cracking during shrinking incidental to the drying process, rock ground in a metate, or sand collected from a wash, is added to and mixed with the powdered clay before moistening. In certain sections of the plateau, it was a prehistoric practice to grind up and add sherds (broken pieces of pottery) as a temper; in other regions such material as cinders, or in the desert sands containing mica, were used in the same manner.

For the actual construction of the vessel a quantity of clay sufficient to form the base is removed from the supply and placed in a basket or large sherd in front of the operator. This acts as a support upon which the work may subsequently be more easily turned for manipulation. With the hands, and accompanied by constant turning, the lump of clay is modeled into the form of the base of the vessel to be made. This usually consists of a very shallow bowl-shaped or disk-shaped piece, which, when it dries slightly, may be removed from the support and placed directly on the ground.

A thin gourd or wood scraper is often brought into play to size down the thick walls, and somewhat smooth them, by scraping away excess clay. Another mass of clay is removed from the supply and shaped into a thin rope, one-half inch or less in diameter. The end of the rope is pinched to one point on the rim of the base, where it adheres, and by progressive pinching is coiled spirally around the work upward to form a portion of the body of the vessel. This is known as the coiling and scraping process, and was widely used by potters in the Southwest.

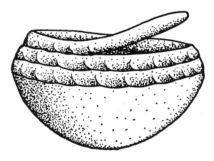

Fig. 17. Illustration of the method of modeling pottery by coiling. The base has been scraped smooth, while the coils, roughly pinched down, show at the top with the end of the rope of clay **free.**

The coils thus formed are allowed to dry slightly, when the scraper, usually dampened, is once more employed to thin down the sides and smooth the surface. By scraping only the inside at this stage, and leaving the outside of the vessel with pinched or indented coils, a type of decoration known as corrugation is made. Should this not be desired, the coils are first smoothed out by hand on both surfaces, and the vessel walls then rubbed down with a fragment of sandstone to the required thinness.

After a short period of drying to harden the clay of the body of the vessel, another coating of very fine clay may be added as a slip or wash. This is mixed with water, to about the consistency of heavy cream, and applied to the scraped surface with a rag or daub. After it has dried slightly it is polished vigorously with a fine-grained smooth-surfaced pebble to give a more or less high polish to the surface.

What is often termed a pseudo-slip may be created by simply wetting the surface of the clay and polishing with a pebble, without adding additional fine clay. This acts essentially in the same manner, by drawing the finer particles of the clay to the surface as a "float," and often cannot be told from a very thin true slip. Another short period of drying follows before the pigments of the design are applied.

Design paints are usually prepared in advance at considerable expenditure of effort, and stored until they will be used. The two most common pigments are derived from carbon and iron. The main source of carbon appears to be organic matter derived from plant juices. This, when fired, of course, carbonizes to a deep black. The iron is much more varied in results, for a slight trace of iron in clay will turn yellow or buff when fired in an oxidizing atmosphere, a higher content will be orange, and a considerable amount will fire red. An oxidizing atmosphere is one which contains sufficient oxygen, such as normal air, to oxidize the minerals of the paint during the firing process. A reducing firing atmosphere is one in which the gases which reach the pottery do not contain oxygen, and therefore cannot oxidize any minerals in the paint. As at least some traces of iron are to be found in almost all clays, only those which are pure kaolin, or are fired in a reducing atmosphere, will remain white or gray. As a result various combinations of buff, yellow, red, orange, and black form by far the largest part of the color decorations on pottery. By a careful selection

Two examples of Roosevelt Black-on-white pottery from near Roosevelt Lake. The bowl is very characteristic and shows the use of balanced solid and hatched areas as well as the common stepped element.

of the fine clay which forms the slip on the surface of a vessel, the uniform base color may be predetermined. The heavily pigmented surface slip appears to have been most typical of orange- and red-base colored vessels, and less so of the yellow and buff types.

Some iron is often present in carbon-black paint (a more common characteristic of certain areas) as well as traces in the slip of black-on-white pottery which has been fired in a reducing atmosphere. If such vessels are by any chance refired in an oxidizing atmosphere the carbon will tend to burn out, leaving the originally black paint red, and turning the white slip buff, or occasionally even yellow. Only in the Mimbres types does it appear that pottery was sometimes deliberately fired in such a manner as to oxidize parts of a vessel and reduce the rest, or to oxidize or reduce all.

Not only were carbon, derived from organic material, and iron used as pigments in decoration, but several other metals in mineral form were also used. Manganese, lead, and copper were the most common of these. Manganese appears in certain black-on-red types in the Flagstaff area, and copper and lead as a glaze paint on types from the Zuñi region.

Pigments are ground on a stone palette, where they are mixed with water to form a paste. They are applied directly to the surface of the vessel with a small fiber brush, apparently in predetermined patterns often of considerable complexity, with a surety of purpose which must be admired. Sections are first blocked out, and areas of solid pigment outlined before they are filled in. A second and even third coat may be applied if they are felt necessary.

After the vessel has been modeled to approximate shape, scraped to thickness and exact form, slipped, polished, and painted, it is put away in a shady spot to dry for several days. During drying any vessel shrinks considerably in size and, if it does not contain the proper kind and amount of tempering material, will often crack. Too rapid drying will also result in cracking, so that great care at this stage, as well as every other, must be exercised by the potter. At the time of firing the vessel must be completely dry, for any appreciable amount of water will cause steam to form internally, and sections to explode from the surface. For this reason, pottery is often given a slow drying near a fire just previous to its final baking.

Today the Hopis make use of dried blocks of sheep dung for fuel. The fire is started with wood, or other easily ignited material, and allowed to burn down to coals, manure is then piled about on this bed, and the pottery, carefully inverted, is stacked above it. Other chunks of fuel are then built up around, and finally over, the mound of pottery, being partly held in place by sheets of tin or large sherds. Much care must be exercised in piling pottery and in the distribution of fuel, so that pots are not touching each other on large enough areas to exclude the oxygen, or so that burning coals do not fall against the side of a vessel. The latter accident is a most common difficulty; it results in a reduced area surrounded by a carbon-black smudge, commonly referred to as a "smudge spot" or "fire cloud."

Although only one type of firing atmosphere is known and in general use today in Arizona, two appear to have been commonly employed prehistorically. Any atmosphere which contains even a small amount of oxygen during the firing process will be sufficient to produce oxidation of the iron pigments already described. This appears to have been by far the most widespread and common type of firing method throughout most of America, and certainly is the method typical of both the Hohokam and Mogollon people. However, in the plateau area, particularly among the earlier Pueblo people and the late Basket Makers, a reducing atmosphere was most commonly employed. The manner in which such an oxygen-free atmosphere may have been produced still remains somewhat of a mystery, for no vestige of what might have been considered a kiln has ever been discovered in the Southwest. Recent experimentation has indicated that a juniper-wood fire large enough to consume the oxygen in the vicinity of the vessel will produce such results, and it is felt that this may have been the method used. In certain sections of the plateau it is believed that some of the Pueblo people made use of coal in firing, and it is just possible that they placed live coals in pits dug into the ground, where small quantities of pottery were fired at a time while covered over with earth. By whatever method, it is certain that reduced pottery was made in the plateau and is typical of this section.

Unfortunately for the Indians, and perhaps fortunately for the archaeologist, a rather high percentage of loss attended pottery making. The manufacture of fine, thin, well-fired pottery is an extremely exacting process, for every step must be carefully carried out. The paste must be of the right type to fire well, it must be of the right consistency to model, if temper is needed it must be of the correct type to prevent cracking during the drying process, the vessels must be completely dried before firing, the paint permanent and well applied, and the firing so controlled as to prevent contact between vessels or with burning brands. Thus the art of pottery making is a highly skilled craft, and one may easily understand how an expert potter would be regarded with respect.

Prehistorically two distinct methods of pottery manufacture seem to have been in general use. In the plateau region it is possible that the earliest pottery was simply made by modeling the entire vessel from a mass with the hands alone. Though there is no indication that any other method was employed, neither is there any absolute proof that only modeling was used. Later, coiling apparently was introduced or, perhaps, even discovered, so that the first vessels showing this technique were coiled on the necks alone. This was followed by coiling most of the body of the vessel and scraping to size, as already described. It is an interesting and significant observation that all the Pueblo people made pottery in this manner, so far as is now known, and did most of their firing, until about A.D. 1300, in a reducing atmosphere.

The Hohokam people also formed their vessels by the coiling process, very much in the manner of the Pueblo group, though often using much larger ropes of clay for their coils, which were flattened down to form a greater area of the surface and body of the vessel. As the pot was formed it was further shaped and thinned by what is known as the paddle and anvil process. This required an anvil of stone or clay, which was held in one hand, and had a somewhat rounded upper surface, while a paddle, apparently of wood, was held in the other hand. The anvil was placed against the inside of the vessel, and the paddle was scraped over the outer surface, thereby thinning the clay of the wall to the desired thickness. This method may often be recognized in sherds by the presence of shallow anvil marks on the inside, particularly on those of large vessels which came from parts of the pot below the rim, for example, where they could not have been readily seen.

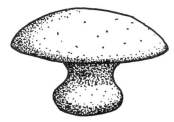

Fig. 18. Pottery anvil. These objects are of varying sizes and shapes, and are made of several materials including stone and pottery.

The Mogollon people apparently made use of the coiling and scraping method, possibly in some of their earliest types not scraping the outer surface but merely roughly rubbing it down. As a result the basic methods of pottery manufacture are of some aid in determining broad cultures in Arizona, and particularly in tracing influences from one of these groups to groups in other sections. In this manner it is possible to demonstrate Hohokam influence in the Flagstaff area, where some pottery types were made by the paddle and anvil method, although the coiling and scraping technique was also used.

TECHNICAL APPLICATION

In any ceramic effort in which individual pots are not produced in molds, and designs are not stamped or applied by transfer, individual variation is theoretically almost unlimited. Were it not for styles and modes, or vogues, no two pots, beyond the fact that they were containers, might be expected to be even similar. However, in examining large collections of pottery, although no two are identical, many are similar in general form, color combinations, and even broad design patterns.

There is a certain parallelism between pottery and human beings. Each individual is different, and is recognizable by minute characteristics of facial features, movement, stance, or voice. Sometimes because of outstanding combinations of these features an individual may be identified as a member of some particular family. The larger groups, such as races, are quite easily recognized. The same is true of pottery, for although a rare piece may defy identification, most may readily be placed in their proper broad classification.

Before any very detailed study may be made of prehistoric pottery, the various kinds must be divided into their proper categories and appropriately labeled. This means that they must be classified and named according to some scheme. At a conference held at Gila Pueblo in 1930 it was agreed by attending archaeologists that a standard form of naming would thereafter be followed in referring to newly determined pottery types. This name is made up of two parts, the first some geographic term, where the type has been found, followed by a descriptive name. For example, Black Mesa Black-on-white means that the type has been found in the Black Mesa area, and that it is black-on-white pottery. The various descriptive terms which were suggested at Gila Pueblo were: black-on-white, black-on-red, brown-on-yellow (now black-on-yellow), red-on-buff, polychrome, corrugated (both indented and plain), incised, slipped plain, and unslipped plain. These classes will still more or less identify most of the types known.

Although the term "type" is very loosely used in regard to pottery, a definite concept will be implied in this book from now on. A *type* is the smallest useful division of pottery which may be isolated and identified. The Museum of Northern Arizona has placed the further restriction on it that it must be of value in determining time or areal factors, or preferably both. This, then, is the unit in the system of classifying pottery below which no further division is possible, although at any time other types may be isolated from within one original type. There has been a recent tendency to group certain closely related examples together and refer to them as subtypes. In some instances, for specific limited purposes, this may be a useful concept. However, if they show cultural, areal, or time differences they should probably have the status of a type, but if they do not they had perhaps best be grouped under one general type heading. The largest division is a *ware,* which is a group of pottery types showing a majority of individual characters in common. This larger grouping has been introduced simply because it is an aid in dealing with obviously related types.

A third term, *series,* is also sometimes found useful. This implies that a number of types not only are related but they are actually genetically re-

Courtesy of the Arizona State Museum

Crushed storage jars found in a room at Point of Pines, Arizona. This is an unusual number, but storage pots are rather frequently found in storerooms in abandoned pueblos.

213204

lated. By genetically related it is meant, of course, that one developed from another, so that a time series has been produced. Thus one may speak of Tusayan Gray Ware, a part of which is the Tsegi Series, which is made up of Lino Gray, Lino Black-on-gray, Kana-a Gray, and several other types.

Still another ceramic concept has been found useful in specific kinds of studies. This is what Colton has called a *style,* which is a persistent combination of motifs and design elements which may be recognized as typical of certain pottery types. It is a decorative system, and may be found shared by more than one type but is usually limited to a type, and therefore may be one of the most readily recognized characteristics of it.

It has been suggested that a type is the smallest division that is possible, so long as it is a useful division. It is obvious to anyone who has made much study of ceramics that it is possible to subdivide pottery almost indefinitely, if individual sherds, or even vessels, are examined minutely and compared by the most extremely fine distinctions. From this it is apparent that the problem which confronts the working archaeologist is at just what point he will stop his study. At the present time it appears that a microscopic examination of masses of sherds is impossible and, in fact, does not yield a very great return to problems of the types that are now being investigated. For this reason, a macroscopic examination is what is most commonly relied upon, particularly for field and laboratory studies, where thousands of sherds are being examined and classified. The only mechanical aid normally employed is a relatively low-power hand lens, which is of use in identifying temper.

Microscopic studies, however, can be and often are exceedingly rewarding when dealing with specific detailed problems. It is therefore true in ceramic studies, as in every other phase of archaeology, that the method must be tailored to the problem. Through microscopic identification of types of temper, intercultural relationships may sometimes be demonstrated when other means are not successful, or minute studies of style trends may be the only way in which short periods of time may be identified. For these reasons any generalization as to the level of splitting in pottery studies can be applicable only in specific instances, and not generally.

The following criteria have been found to be most useful in establishing types. (1) The method of construction, whether coiled and scraped, or paddle and anvil. (2) Color of the clay in the body of the vessel. (3) The material, shape, and abundance of temper. (4) The nature of the fracture of the sherd, and its relative hardness. (5) The surface finish, such as polished, scraped, bumpy, corrugated, or otherwise altered. (6) The surface color and decoration. (7) When possible, distinctive characteristics of shape, or painted or other decoration. All this must be tempered by much actual experience and good sense, for here, as elsewhere, it is extremely easy to become so involved with the trees that one loses sight of the forest.

After handling great quantities of sherds, it is usually a simple matter for the individual worker to separate them, but it is an entirely different matter when an attempt is made to list these distinctions so that others may apply them with equal facility. Even the best of the most standardized descriptions are sometimes misleading, and for that reason it has been found generally advisable to build a sherd library of actual specimens, much like a study collection of fossils, for the aid of the student. Some time spent handling these collections will generally be of more permanent value than any amount of reading.

Early in this chapter the reasons why pottery is the best indicator of

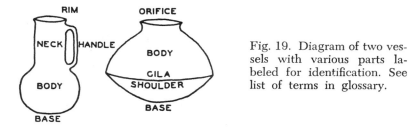

Fig. 19. Diagram of two vessels with various parts labeled for identification. See list of terms in glossary.

culture change were discussed; they may again be referred to as the reasons why pottery classification is desirable. Without definite classification, types cannot be isolated and readily referred to in later work. Once types are defined, time relations and geographic distributions may be worked out for them, and they become one of the archaeologist's most useful aids. It will be recalled that archaeology has been defined as the making of history from prehistory, and that the archaeologist is interested in the relationships of various events in their proper time and space context. Thus one of the basic problems of archaeology is tracing the origin and spread of traits. Pottery is certainly the best indicator of such relationships.

One of the most interesting problems is that of prehistoric trade, since pottery of certain types was made in restricted areas and at definite times. It is now becoming increasingly apparent that the actual point of manufacture of certain types may be much less widespread than was originally thought, it being possible that only a few families, or perhaps villages, made most, or all, of certain pottery types and traded them to surrounding areas.

Two types of pottery always have been commonly manufactured. One, a crude culinary or kitchen type, has been widely made by every people. These are the cook and storage pots of everyday use, usually of relatively large size, and seldom decorated. The other class is the table or ornamental type, almost invariably smaller, expertly finished, and usually highly ornamented. The culinary type was probably made locally by the people who used it, for large heavy vessels would have been difficult to transport over great distances. The finer vessels, because of their beauty and expert workmanship, as well as their usually smaller size, could be, and were, more widely traded. Because of this, trade relationships in ceramic studies are most profitably based on the decorated types, while information regarding human relationships may best be based on the study of culinary types. There has been a tendency to neglect this latter group, probably because of the relative ease of identification of the former. However, it is from the undecorated types that the most exact and vital information may be expected to come eventually.

There has apparently been a general misconception of the relative abundance of the decorated and undecorated pottery in the Southwest, particularly that from the earlier periods. Careful data taken from 33 sites in northern Arizona, mostly belonging to the Pueblo II culture stage and based on a great many sherds, show that the average amount of decorated pottery is only 7 per cent of the total in each site. This is a surprisingly small figure, but of the 33 sites only four had 20 per cent or more decorated. The large trash mound at Winona Village, just east of Flagstaff, which

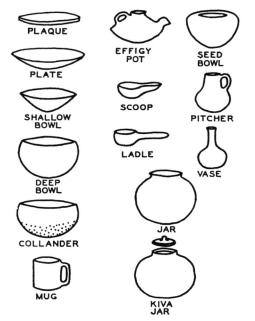

Fig. 20. Diagram of various pottery shapes. Terms will be found to vary with different individual writers so that these may be taken only as an indication of form names.

contained thousands of sherds, produced only 13 per cent of decorated types, while Tuzigoot Pueblo, a Pueblo IV site in the Verde valley, contained only 6 per cent.

If detailed study, such as chemical composition of paste or identification of minerals in the temper, is made, it might most profitably be directed more generally to the undecorated types. Such microscopic studies, although exceedingly difficult and slow to make, are, of course, of extreme value in indicating directions of trade. An examination of the early sherds from Snaketown Village, in the Middle Gila, showed that many of these sherds were made of the same material as those from the upper waters of this drainage area, thereby linking the early settlers in this area with the Mogollon culture to the east. This is the sort of information it is desirable to obtain as a definite step in historical reconstruction.

Much in the same manner, relative percentages of decorated and undecorated pottery from individual sites, once plotted, will indicate areas where certain types have been manufactured and the extent over which they have been traded. Such detailed studies have not been attempted as yet, for this type of information is probably not quite sufficiently complete to be conclusive. Without definite types none of this work could be accomplished.

Pottery is also the best known culture-trait indicator of time, for obviously constant experimentation was going forward in this medium. Designs, forms, and color combinations progressed rapidly, and taken as a whole they are relatively fine time division indicators, once they have been dated. The most accurately dated pottery is that derived from the plateau area, for it is here that the most abundant and readily dated beams are found. As the dating of sites, and so the dating of artifacts, has been discussed in a previous chapter, no attempt to review this matter will be undertaken here. In passing it might profitably be stated once more that the dating of even such abundant material as pottery from tree-ring dates is no simple matter, so that with few exceptions such dates must be considered little more than general indications of the period when the type was made and in use.

The list of dated pottery types given at the end of this chapter will be found most useful in later references, and when familiarity with these types is gained it will be possible to date individual sites by the types which are found on them. This can be done by a simple application of temporal seriation, often with considerable accuracy, and justifies learning at least a minimum number of the most common types.

Once pottery has been definitely named, dated, and placed as to region normally occupied, much use may be made of it. Reference has already been made to the information which may be gained from it as regards trade relations and culture associations. It is also possible, through cross finds of dated and traded pottery types, to assign at least approximate dates to sites which contain no datable beams. Much of the culture of the desert has been so dated, on the basis of trade pieces from the plateau. Not only is such dating useful over broad areas and between distinct cultures, but it is equally of value to dating in areas where dates are often found but individual sites do not happen to have datable material. This enables the archaeologist to fill in the gaps in his detailed time, geographic, and population studies more accurately, a phase of archaeology which is of utmost importance.

Larger classes of pottery, such as wares, are usually indicative of broader cultures. In a general way pottery containing mica temper is almost invariably derived from the desert area; that with sand, quite likely from the San Juan or Little Colorado area; crushed or prepared rock or sherd temper is most commonly found to be from the eastern San Juan or eastern Little Colorado section. Similar divisions may be made on the basis of the types of paints used or the methods of manufacture of the vessel.

In general it may be said that the Hohokam people made their pottery by the paddle and anvil method, that most of it contains mica or micaceous material, and that it was fired in an oxidizing atmosphere, and so is red-on-buff, buff, or tan. By comparison the Pueblo people made their pottery by the coiling and scraping process, tempered with sand, crushed rocks, ground sherds, or similar material, and fired largely in a reducing atmosphere, to produce a gray or white pottery. The Mogollon people built their pottery by coiling and rubbing down the surface, occasionally leaving a somewhat irregular surface finish, tempered largely with crushed rock, and fired in an oxidizing atmosphere, to produce a red and brown pottery.

Any study of Southwestern ceramics will be found filled with new and confusing terms. For this reason a brief glossary of ceramic terms in common use has been prepared, and will be found of considerable use by the reader.

Brief Glossary of Ceramic Terms in Common Use

Base. Portion of vessel upon which it naturally rests.

Body. Portion of vessel from base to neck.

Bowl. More or less hemispherical shallow vessel without neck.

Burnished. A more or less metallic surface luster, effected by rubbing the surface with a smooth object before firing.

Carbon paint. Black paint derived from carbonized organic material.

Ceramics. The art of making objects from fire-hardened earthy material.

Coiled neck. Vessel neck consisting of one continuous spiral of flattened clay coils.

Corrugations. Smoothed and flattened but distinct coils of clay.

Design elements. Not discussed here as they are taken up in their proper place under various pottery types where they may best be illustrated by diagrams.

Effigy. Any vessel fashioned after a living object.

Firing. Process of baking clay by fire.

Glaze. A glassy surface coating applied to pottery.

Globular. More or less spherical in body form.

Handle. Portion intended to be gripped in the hand or by the fingers.

Incised. Removal of a portion of the clay surface of a vessel, in lines, by means of a hard instrument before firing.

Indented corrugations. Finger-marked coils of clay on the surface of a vessel.

Iron-carbon paint. Paint containing some iron pigment, as well as carbon.

Ladle. Dipper-shaped vessel.

Leg. Any long and comparatively slender projection which supports the body.

Lid. Any cover purposely designed to close an orifice.

Lug. Knoblike projection not large enough to be gripped in the hand. Often perforated.

Monochrome. Pottery of only one color.

Neck. Portion of vessel from point where line of body turns toward the vertical to the rim.

Neck coils. Rings of flattened clay coils about the neck of a vessel.

Olla. Vessel with a globular body and a short neck.

Paste. Material from which a pottery vessel is formed.

Pitcher. Vessel with cylindrical body, and more or less tall straight neck.

Polished. Pottery surface smoothed by rubbing before firing.

Polychrome. Pottery decorated with three or more colors.

Pottery. A fire-hardened clay object.

Rim. Thickness of vessel wall at edge of orifice.

Scraped. Pottery surface which has been rubbed over with a blunt instrument before firing, thus removing some of the paste and leaving a slightly striated texture.

Sherd (or shard). Fragment of a broken pottery vessel.

Slip. External layer of clay, usually pigmented and visible, covering pottery. (*Wash* sometimes used as a synonym.)

Smoothed. Pottery surface which has been rubbed, but not polished or burnished, before firing.

Temper. Nonplastic material added to the clay in making pottery. (Usually angular, and often visible.)

Vessel. Any container (in this discussion made of pottery).

DATED POTTERY TYPES

The most useful means of determining the age of a pottery-bearing site is by dated pottery types. In the Southwest a number of the pottery types have been more or less accurately dated, and these, serving somewhat in the sense of time-marker fossils, may be used to tell when a site was occupied. Tree-ring dates are of course the most accurate means of establishing just when a site was built, or occupied, but such dates usually are not available until after excavation, and then only if material datable by the tree-ring method is found. The less exact carbon 14 dates also require usable material, and usually a lapse of some months before a date, or dates, may be secured by the laboratory. A site with some abundance of pottery may be dated, often with considerable accuracy, by simply walking over it, noting the types found, and bracketing, or seriating, their dates.

In many areas there are certain key types which are most useful, and if they, and their dates, are learned, the age of the site may readily be determined. An accuracy of 50 years in the occupancy of a site is usually readily possible, and in some cases 25-year periods, or even less, may be determined. An example of this technique of dating might do more to illustrate how it is done than any amount of descriptive discussion.

If a site in the Flagstaff area is found which has Black Mesa Black-on-white pottery, which dates at A.D. 875 to 1130, and Flagstaff Black-on-white, which dates between A.D. 1100 and 1275, it may be assumed that it was occupied between A.D. 1100 and 1130. This does not mean that it could not have been occupied earlier, and even later, but it must have been occupied during this time. If no St. Johns Polychrome is found, which began at A.D. 1175 and lasted to about 1300, it could not have been occupied as late as 1175. If it also lacks any Deadmans Black-on-red pottery, which dates from about A.D. 775 to 1065, then it could not have been occupied as early as A.D. 1065. The maximum possible range of occupation, in this simple example, would have been between A.D. 1065 and 1175, and the certain period of occupation sometime between A.D. 1100 and 1130.

This technique of bracket dating can be applied to most areas of the Southwest, for many pottery types have been dated either directly or indirectly. Some pottery, such as the red-on-buff of the Hohokam culture, has only been approximately dated by association with pottery traded from areas where it had been accurately dated.

The dates in the accompanying list are presented in two groups. The first is those which have been dated more or less directly by dendrochronology and are therefore the most accurate. The second list is made up of those types which have been dated by seriation with other dated types, and perhaps carbon 14 dates, and some tree-ring dates, which cannot be directly related to the pottery types. Both lists are equally useful, but the first is believed to be slighly more accurate.

These lists of dated pottery types will be found, by the student or practicing archaeologist, to be one of the most valuable and generally useful sections of this book. Familiarity with the types found in an area will facilitate an understanding of the prehistory of that area. Besides this it is a great satisfaction for one to be able to tell the age of a site, almost at once, by the pottery type found on it.

DATED POTTERY TYPES

Dated directly by tree-ring dates

NAME	SPAN	PERIOD OF ABUNDANCE
Arboles Black-on-white	900-1050	950-1000
Arboles Gray	900-1050	950-1000
Bancos Black-on-white	900-1000	900-1000
Betatakin Black-on-white	1200-1300	1250-1300
Black Mesa Black-on-white	875-1130	1000-1100
Chaco Black-on-white	1050-1125	1050-1125
Coconino Gray	865-890	865-890
Deadmans Black-on-red	775-1065	850-1000
Flagstaff Black-on-white	1100-1275	1100-1200
Floyd Black-on-gray	775-940	800-900
Fourmile Polychrome	1325-1400	1325-1400
Galisteo Black-on-white	1300-1400	?
Gallina Black-on-white	1000-1275	?
Gallup Black-on-white	1000-1125	1000-1125
Holbrook Black-on-white	900-1130	1075-1130
Kana-a Black-on-white	725-950	800-900
Kana-a Gray	760-900	760-900
Kayenta Black-on-white	1250-1300	1250-1300
Kayenta Polychrome	1200-1300	1265-1285
Lino Black-on-gray	575-875	610-800
Lino Gray	575-875	600-800
Los Pinos Brown	100-200	?
Medicine Gray	890-1060	890-1000
Moenkopi Corrugated	1075-1300	1075-1285
Piedra Black-on-white	850-975	850-950
Piedra Gray	850-975	850-950
Pinedale Black-on-red	1275-1325	?
Pinedale Polychrome	1275-1350	?
Red Mesa Black-on-white	850-1050	?
Reserve Black-on-white	950-1125	?
Rio de Flag Brown	775-1065	800-1000
Rosa Black-on-white	700-950	700-850
Rosa Gray	700-950	700-850
Santa Fe Black-on-white	1200-1350	1250-1350
St. Johns Polychrome	1175-1300	1200-1275
Sunset Red	1065-1200	1075-1140
Tusayan Black-on-white	1200-1300	1250-1300
Tusayan Corrugated	950-1275	1050-1150
Walnut Black-on-white	1065-1250	1150-1200
Winona Brown	1075-1200	1075-1125
Wupatki Black-on-white	1200-1300	1250-1300

Dated Pottery Types

Dated by seriation

NAME	SPAN	PERIOD OF ABUNDANCE
Adamana Brown	early 300's	
Alma Neck Banded	600-700-950	
Buff Black-on-red	850-1000±	?
Chaco Black-on-white	1070-1130	?
Citadel Polychrome	1115-1200	1115-1180
Deadmans Black-on-gray	900-1115	960-1100
Deadmans Fugitive Red	775-1150	850-1150
Elden Corrugated	1085±-1200±	1100-1180
Forestdale Red	600-700 period	
Gila Plain	300-1350	300-1350
Gila Polychrome	1300±–post 1400	?
Gila Red	pre 1200–post 1400	?
Gila White-on-red	1200-1400 general period	
Jeddito Black-on-orange	1275±-1400	1300-1400
Jeddito Black-on-yellow	1300-1625	?
Kiet Siel Polychrome	1200-1300	?
Kowina Black-on-white	1200-1400	?
Lino Fugitive Red	575-775	?
McDonald Corrugated	1100-1300	1100-1200+
Mancos Black-on-white	900-1050	?
Medicine Black-on-red	1075-1125	?
Mesa Verde Black-on-white	1200-1300	?
Mogollon Red-on-brown	775-950	875-925
Pinto Polychrome	ca. 1200-1250	?
Puerco Black-on-red	1030-1175	1050-1125
Salado Red	1300-1400	?
San Francisco Red	750-950	750-950
Sholow Black-on-red	1050±-1200	?
Sikyatki Polychrome	1375-1625±	?
Sosi Black-on-white	1075-1200	
	(not well dated)	
Sombrito Brown	400-700 period	
Tonto Polychrome	1250±-1400	1300-1400
Tularosa Black-on-white	1100-1250	1100-1250
Tusayan Black-on-red	1050-1130	1050-1130
Tusayan Polychrome	1100-1300	1150-1275
Verde Black-on-gray	1050-1200 or 1300	?
Woodruff Red	600-700 period	

Sources and Additional References

Amsden, Charles Avery. An Analysis of Hohokam Pottery Design, *Medallion Paper 23*, 1936, Gila Pueblo, Globe, Arizona. (Data on Hohokam designs and design elements.)

Breternitz, David A. * Archaeological Interpretation of Tree Ring Specimens for Dating Southwestern Ceramic Styles, Ph.D. dissertation, University of Arizona, Tucson, 1963. (Most of the critical dated pottery types referred to herein.)

Colton, Harold S. The Reducing Atmosphere and Oxidizing Atmosphere in Prehistoric Southwestern Ceramics, *American Antiquity,* Vol. 4, No. 3, 1939, Society for American Archaeology, Salt Lake City, Utah. (Brief discussion of this subject.)

————. Primitive Pottery Firing Methods, *Museum Notes,* Vol. 11, No. 10, 1939, Museum of Northern Arizona, Flagstaff. (Discussion of Indian methods of firing pottery in the Southwest.)

————. * Potsherds, *Bulletin 25,* 1953, Museum of Northern Arizona, Flagstaff. (Best present brief discussion of the problems of Southwestern ceramic studies.)

Colton, Harold S., and Lyndon L. Hargrave. * Handbook of Northern Arizona Pottery Wares, *Bulletin 11,* 1937, Museum of Northern Arizona, Flagstaff. (Best source of information available on the pottery with which we are concerned. Most of the subjects discussed in this chapter are to be found here. Highly recommended, particularly the chapters by Colton, which are more general discussions.)

Gifford, E. W. Pottery-Making in the Southwest, *Publications in American Archaeology and Ethnology,* Vol. 23, No. 8, 1928, University of California Press, Berkeley. (Data on basic methods of pottery manufacture.)

Gladwin, Winifred and H. S. The Use of Potsherds in an Archaeological Survey of the Southwest, *Medallion Paper 2,* 1928, Gila Pueblo, Globe, Arizona. (Discussion of pottery classification and survey methods.)

————. A Method for the Designation of Southwestern Pottery Types, *Medallion Paper 7,* 1930, Gila Pueblo, Globe, Arizona. (Data concerning pottery designations.)

————. * Some Southwestern Pottery Types, Series I, *Medallion Paper 8,* 1930, Gila Pueblo, Globe, Arizona. (Data on the Gila Polychrome and Red series.)

————. * Some Southwestern Pottery Types, Series II, *Medallion Paper 10,* 1931, Gila Pueblo, Globe, Arizona. (Data on the red and black-on-white series, from the eastern Little Colorado area.)

————. * Some Southwestern Pottery Types, Series III, *Medallion Paper 13,* 1933, Gila Pueblo, Globe, Arizona. (Data on the red-on-buff and buff types, from the Gila area.)

Haury, Emil W. The Age of Lead Glaze Decorated Pottery in the Southwest, *American Anthropologist,* Vol. 34, No. 3, 1932, Menasha, Wisconsin. (Glaze pigments from the Zuñi region.)

————. * Some Southwestern Pottery Types, Series IV, *Medallion Paper 19,* 1936, Gila Pueblo, Globe, Arizona. (Descriptions of Mogollon and early Mimbres pottery types.)

Hawley, Florence M. Prehistoric Pottery Pigments in the Southwest, *American Anthropologist,* Vol. 31, No. 4, 1929, Menasha, Wisconsin. (Data on the chemical composition of pottery pigments.)

———. * Field Manual of Prehistoric Southwestern Pottery Types, *University of New Mexico Bulletin 291,* 1936, Albuquerque. (Best discussion of pottery types for eastern Arizona and New Mexico.)

Kidder, Alfred Vincent, and Anna O. Shepard. * The Pottery of Pecos, Vol. II, 1936, Department of Archaeology, Phillips Academy, Andover, Massachusetts, Yale University Press, New Haven, Connecticut. (The portion by Miss Shepard will be found of the most general value in explaining detailed laboratory methods of pottery study.)

McGregor, John C. How Some Important Northern Arizona Pottery Types Were Dated, *Bulletin 13,* 1938, Museum of Northern Arizona, Flagstaff. (Data on a few dated pottery types from northern Arizona.)

Sayles, E. B. Some Southwestern Pottery Types, Series V, *Medallion Paper 21,* 1936, Gila Pueblo, Globe, Arizona. (Pottery types from northern Mexico.)

Stallings, W. S., Jr. Notes on the Pueblo Culture in South Central New Mexico and in the Vicinity of El Paso, Texas, *American Anthropologist,* Vol. 34, No. 1, 1932, Menasha, Wisconsin. (Data on pottery types from southern New Mexico.)

PART TWO

DESCRIPTION OF CULTURES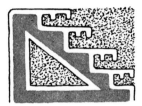

VII

The Early People

An introduction to the archaeological history of any American group should certainly be prefaced with a discussion of the theories of the origin of the Indian. To do justice to this subject it would be necessary to write a paper the dimensions of this entire book, but as the primary interest of this volume is Southwestern archaeology alone only a few of the most favorably considered theories will be mentioned.

To date no palaeontological evidence has come to light in America indicating the presence of any mammal forms, ancient or modern, which closely resemble man. Because of this the Old World has long been considered the probable home of the human race, and any inquiry into the origin of the American Indian is most concerned with the possible means by which man reached America, and at approximately what date.

Four routes have been open to human crossing from the Old to the New World in past time. Man might have come directly across the South Atlantic from Africa to South America, for it is here, across this ocean, that the two continents are closest together. This would have required boats of sufficient seaworthiness to have weathered a lengthy crossing, and as we now understand European prehistory such boats were not known at a very early date. The second possible route is directly across the South Pacific, but here again what information is available is opposed to any very early crossing. Although there are an abundance of islands dotting the Pacific Ocean, the eastern islands do not appear to have been occupied in great antiquity, probably not long before the time of Christ. Boats necessarily had to be developed before a complete crossing could have been effected, and again this would place the date far too late for the original peopling of America. The third possible route is across the north Atlantic, from northwestern Europe through Iceland, Greenland, and to our own northeast coast. The open water passages by this route are

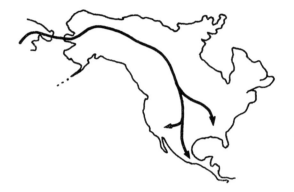

Fig. 21. Map illustrating the most commonly accepted idea of the route of migration of early man from Asia across Bering Strait into America. The main route probably was east of the Rocky Mountains, a branch entering the Southwest from the east.

relatively short, but still great enough so that substantial ships would have been required before a passage could have been made. The likelihood of travel across the ice during one of the glacial periods may probably be discounted, because of the difficulty of providing food for such a long trip. The fourth possibility is by far the most probable and the one which is enjoying the greatest popularity at the moment. This is a crossing from Asia to America through Bering Strait. At the present time this strait is so narrow that in proper atmospheric conditions it is possible to see land from either side, and geological evidence indicates that in prehistoric time it may have been much narrower. Under such conditions it would have been simple to cross on the ice from one continent to another, and to have made the passage before boats of any sort were invented.

Physically the American Indian is very closely related to the general Mongoloid type, thereby strengthening the theory of the Bering Strait route. However, careful studies have indicated that the historic eastern Indian shows more Caucasoid characters, lightly overlying the abundant Mongoloid, and that there is a slight trace of Negroid, or perhaps Australoid, in some of the modern Indians of South America. From this it is possible to postulate a relatively early migration of small numbers of Mongoloids from Asia to America which formed the main strain of the American Indian, followed by later, still smaller, groups of Caucasoids from the east, and Negroids from the south. The very strong Mongoloid characters in the west would suggest continued Asiatic movements into America at later dates, to strengthen further the already present Mongoloid elements.

If the Bering Strait passage is accepted as the earliest route into America, the next question of interest is how humans eventually reached the South-west. The most favored route is one through the northern, and non-mountainous, portion of Alaska, which turned south on the eastern slopes of the Rocky Mountains, one branch working southeastward into the Mississippi valley, another going through the western high plains into Mexico and thence into South America. It was a group of this latter branch which is believed to have swung farther west through lower country into the Southwest. A direct passage from Alaska down our west coast is felt to be highly improbable, for the present rugged nature of the country would have made such a route in early prehistoric times nearly, if not wholly, impossible.

The time at which man might have entered America appears to be still more doubtful. Archaeological history is very much like a long series of preserved periodicals which have been constantly in use. The earliest volumes are tattered and worn, portions lost, and others faded to the point where they are almost unreadable. The later chapters are more complete, the story clear and more easily read, and these volumes lie at the top of the pile where they may most easily be gotten at. Too, people who chose one location as the site of their homes will be followed by others who will choose the same location for the same reasons, obliterating or scattering the remains of the earlier residents.

It is for these reasons that the earliest chapters of archaeological history are difficult to determine with certainty, so that theory or possibilities must be relied upon until sufficient data make more accurate conclusions possible. Geologically it appears that a passage to America and a route down the east side of the Rocky Mountains may have been open between about 25,000 and 11,000 years ago, with a land bridge where Bering Strait now lies. This would have been a time of rigorous climate, so that any migrants to the New World would have had a hunting, and more or less arctic, type of culture. At something like 35,000 years ago there was also a land bridge, but the climate was quite cold. Between about 35,000 and 25,000 years ago the climate was milder, but the strait was some 20 miles across, and people would presumably have had to cross on the ice in the winter.

The earliest known relatively well-dated cultures, in what is herein defined as the Southwest, are some 13,000 years old. From about 10,000 years ago to the present there is much more abundant evidence of man in this area, with more or less continuous developments from one stage to the next. When it is remembered that there were still ice sheets to be found in the northern part of the Midwest 11,000 years ago there can no longer be any doubt that man existed in this country during the later stages of the ice age. Most, but not all, of these earliest sites have been found in the south, and Southwest, well outside of the ice areas.

ANCIENT STAGE—10,000 B.C. and Earlier

The earliest evidence of man in the Southwest is represented by what has been generally designated as the stage of big-game hunters. Most of the finds of this culture are what were kill sites, for they represent the places where large game animals were killed and apparently butchered. Because the projectile points are the most distinctive artifacts, these tools have been carefully studied, classified, and named. Most of the earliest projectile points are lanceolate in shape, lack any side or diagonal notching, and many have fluting, or shallow flakes struck from the base along the faces of the points. They also frequently have ground edges near or along the base, probably to prevent the lashing of the points to the shaft from being cut.

What may be the earliest type of projectile thus far found, though it has not been definitely proven to be oldest, is called *Sandia*. A characteristic is the presence of a shoulder on one side of this otherwise leaf-shaped projectile. It has been suggested that Sandia points may be divided into two subtypes. Type 1 has a rounded base and the cross section of the blade is lenticular. Type 2 has a stem with straight or parallel sides, a square base which may sometimes be slightly concave, and the blade has a cross section which is diamond-shaped. To date there is no definite evidence that these represent chronological types.

Sandia Cave, which lies at the north end of the Sandia Mountains in New Mexico, was originally dug by Hibben, and is a long tunnel-like limestone cave in which several clearly marked levels of occupation were found. There was an upper zone which had essentially modern remains in it, then a lime crust which sealed off the lower levels, under which there were Folsom types of artifacts. Below this was a water-deposited laminated layer of yellow ochre, and then a habitation layer with the typical Sandia points and extinct forms of horse, bison, camel, mastodon, and mammoth.

There has been much discussion as to the age of these materials, so that more recent work done here by Agogino, but as yet not published, is eagerly awaited and should shed much light on the date. A second site, the Lucy site, which was dug by Roosa, is also in New Mexico. This area consisted of old pond deposits, some of which have been subsequently blown away to expose the artifacts. Here Sandia points, Clovis points, and Folsom points were all found in association. Since this is believed to have been a kill site, the question has been raised as to whether or not they are all contemporary. In trenching Roosa found six Sandia points, the bases and lower edges of which were ground. Much has been made of the fact that the rounded-base Sandia points lack longitudinal fluting, but it has also been suggested that such a base does not lend itself to

Fig. 22. Map locating the various early sites referred to in the text. The Little Colorado finds are along the middle of the Little Colorado River, while Cochise finds are scattered over an area of Arizona and New Mexico but seem to be most common in the southern part.

long shallow flakes. One of the square-base Sandia points found at the Lucy site was fluted.

Coeval with the Sandia type, or nearly so, is another very widespread type of projectile point which has been named *Clovis*. This particular kind of point is also long and leaf-shaped, but has fluting on the faces from the base toward the point. The Clovis site, from which the name of this type was derived, has been worked in over a period of years since 1933 by a number of individuals. The first work done by Howard uncovered some flake knives, or scrapers, and snub-nosed scrapers associated with burned bison bones and charcoal. Cotter, digging in 1936 and 1937, found artifacts associated with mammoths, two of which were the fluted points which gave the name to the type. These were comparatively long blades, one slightly over four inches, the other just over three inches long, and were fluted about halfway up the face. During this work, and subsequently, bone tools were found with these stone points. These bone tools may have been projectile points as well.

Most of the Clovis-type points are large, tend to have concave bases, there is grinding of the edges on or toward the base, and the flaking is shallow and well executed. The general flaking is not as well controlled as that of the later Folsom types. It does not give the impression of the

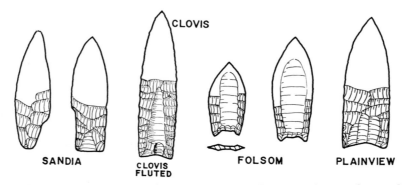

Fig. 23. The major early types of projectile points found in the Southwest, believed to represent a chronological series from left to right. Type 1 of the Sandia point is at the left, type 2 at the right. One of the type 2 points found at the Lucy site has a concave base and fluting. The Clovis type varies from one and a half to five inches long, with an average of about three inches. They are fluted, are fairly heavy points, and most have basal grinding. The Folsom points show remarkable craftsmanship, and vary from three-quarters of an inch to three inches long, with an average of about two inches. They have ears, generally basal grinding, prominent fluting, and fine marginal retouch. The Plainview type is illustrated by a general or schematic example. This type was formerly called Yuman. There is no fluting, but there are base flakes and ground bases. The largest are about three inches long.

ripple surface resulting from these paralled flakes that is so characteristic of Folsom and some later types. The suggestion has been made that these points, in their variations, all be classed as Llano complex, to distinguish them from other later types.

The Clovis site was located in a comparatively high area where there were apparently a number of lakes, and perhaps some stream beds. These attracted the animals which were slain with the Clovis points. Of much interest is the fact that these early hunters were also working bone into polished tools. With them were flake knives and scrapers, and simple flakes which might have been used in cutting up the animals. Despite the fact that the Clovis sites are mostly kill sites, a complex of tools has been found which gives us some idea of a general way of life, or a stage of culture.

In southeastern Arizona the Lehner site was excavated and reported by Haury. Here a total of 13 points were associated with the bones of mammoths, and there were also scrapers and other flake tools. The points are of the general Clovis fluted types, though they show a considerable range in size, and in most of the fluting the flakes are not as long as they are in many typical Clovis points. Although this is also a kill site, once again a tool complex was found.

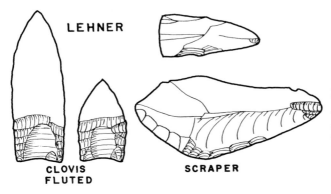

LEHNER

CLOVIS FLUTED   SCRAPER

Fig. 24. Diagram of artifact types found at the Lehner site in southeastern Arizona. The largest and smallest of the Clovis-type points are shown. The largest point is 97 millimeters long.

In the same general area Haury also found another similar kill site, called the Naco site. A total of eight points were associated with mammoth bones, and they too are of the general Clovis type. The largest here was 116 millimeters long, or some four and a half inches, and the typical fluting was also rather clearly present. The Naco site may be grouped with the Lehner site on the basis of the similar point types, and may be assumed as of somewhat comparable age.

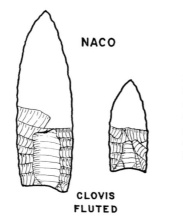

NACO

CLOVIS FLUTED

Fig. 25. Projectile points found at the Naco site in southeastern Arizona. They are of the Clovis fluted type, the largest of which is 116 millimeters long. The range of sizes is indicated by these two points.

Additional Clovis material has been found by Hester in the Portales, New Mexico, area, at the Blackwater Locality No. 1. Here he uncovered the skeletons of four mammoths and with them four stone tools. In working in this general area he found what is probably the best evidence to date of the chronological or superimposed position of Clovis and other later projectile point types. Altogether in this area he has collected more than 200 Clovis artifacts, a number of which are bone tools. One grinding stone, of the oval mano type, was found as well, and side scrapers, end scrapers, flake knives, and fleshers, once more constituting a complex of tool types.

Above the Clovis finds at this site was a layer which contained Folsom remains, thus demonstrating that in this instance, at least, Folsom was later than Clovis. Still higher were objects which have been identified as Portales projectile points, and these are of the general Plainview or what has been previously called the Yuman type. At the top of the series were Archaic materials. Broad surveys undertaken in this general area of eastern New Mexico located a number of similar early sites, and study of the kinds of flint used in the production of the Clovis points suggests that the people who used them ranged over a considerable area in securing the material from which they made their points.

From all of this it may be seen that there are a number of sites in the eastern part of the Southwest which were occupied primarily by hunters, though they probably also did some collecting and perhaps gathering of foods. The carbon 14 dates which have been secured from a number of these sites show that the Sandia and Clovis types of remains may be assigned to a period about 10,000 B.C., or earlier. The earlier such specific dates suggest that man existed in the Southwest perhaps 13,000 years ago.

One of the sites which was believed to have been the oldest in the Southwest proper was the Tule Lake site, originally reported by Harrington. Here carbon 14 dates of some 28,000 or 30,000 years ago were found, and in apparent association with them human-made artifacts. Most recently a much more careful and extensive re-examination of this area has been undertaken, with the result that the dating has been revised downward. This Tule Lake site, or rather a series of springs, was occupied by man some 13,500 years ago, but the evidence of human occupation extending back this far is very sparse, consisting of a few flakes, one scraper, and what are apparently bone tools, the latter being very simple pointed objects. Since water at this time was apparently limited to a series of springs it is assumed that both prehistoric animals and man used the springs, but ranged rather widely in the general area. Too little of material culture has been found here to make it possible to determine the real nature of the way of life of the people involved.

What may be older, equally old, or even possibly not of great antiquity is a series of thus far undated finds along the Little Colorado River in northern Arizona. Here, along the old terraces of the river, members of the Museum of Northern Arizona staff have found numbers of chipped stone artifacts which seem to have been associated with ancient campsites. None have been found actually in situ, but on these same terraces the bones of now extinct animals have been found as well. The sites are on the tops of hills eroded from the river-gravel terraces bordering the Little Colorado River and some of its tributaries, from about Cameron to the vicinity of Holbrook. No habitations were found but several hun-

Photo supplied by James J. Hester

The Blackwater Locality No. 1, near Portales, New Mexico. In the foreground are the bones of mammoths with which Clovis types of artifacts were found. In the background intermediate levels contained Folsom artifacts, while above them were Portales or Plainview artifacts and at the top Archaic artifacts.

dred stone artifacts have been collected. The sites are always at about the same altitude above the present river bed, among gravels which contain such workable materials as quartzite, chert, and agatized wood, in the form of water-washed boulders. Part of the industry was core, but chips were also utilized. The forms include hand axes, choppers, cutting edges, scrapers, some of which are keeled, and gouges. To date no points have been found which could definitely be associated with the other implements. All of the artifacts have been picked up from the surfaces of the hills, none embedded in them. Although all of these artifacts are of a rather primitive type, there is thus far no proof that they are of any great antiquity.

HUNTER STAGE—10,000 to 5000 B.C.

Hunter Culture

Probably the first truly convincing find of the association of human-made artifacts and extinct animals was that made near Folsom, New Mexico. Here several very characteristic flint points were uncovered in a quarry accompanying the bones of an extinct form of bison. These flints were subsequently named *Folsom* points, and this name has followed them wherever they have been found. Eighteen such points, many of them broken, were found at this quarry, and their relatively great number, and the fact that the tail bones of most of the bison were missing, led to the supposition that the animals had been slaughtered when they came down to drink at a water hole, and their hides, with the tails attached, removed.

The general interest which excavations at the original Folsom quarry aroused led Roberts to do several seasons' work at the Lindenmeier site near Fort Collins, Colorado. This site originally occupied an old valley bottom which contained bogs, springs, and marshes. These are believed to have attracted the same sort of extinct bison which were found at Folsom, as well as similar hunters. The large scattered campsite is now overlaid with accumulations of dirt up to 17 feet in depth, so that considerable labor was required to clear the area down to the original occupation level. No habitations have been found, although surface fires, split bones, hammerstones, the debris from chipping implements, and implements themselves were in some abundance. The points are of the typical Folsom type.

The Folsom projectile point is of such a characteristic form that once seen it can never be mistaken. On each side a large shallow flake has been struck from the base toward the point, so that in section it appears to be biconcave. Careful shallow parallel flaking, which gives a general ripple effect, shaped the edge to approximate outline, and some secondary chipping has made it quite exact. In fact all processes in the production of these points have been surprisingly well controlled. Two horns, usually distinct, are found at the corners of the base, and the greatest width is commonly forward of the center.

Besides the projectile points at the Lindenmeier site, there were also found snub-nosed scrapers, side scrapers, end scrapers, a variety of cutting edges, rough flake knives, large blades, drills, gravers, sandstone rubbing stones, and a few bone tools which probably are punches or awls. The stone industry was primarily flake, rarely core. Associated with these artifacts were the bones of extinct bison and camels.

A number of carbon 14 dates have been secured from Folsom sites, and although there is some indication that this type of culture may have lasted for some years, it has generally been assumed to date about 10,000 years ago. This was apparently primarily a hunting way of life, so it may be assigned to the general hunting pattern, in distinction to a gathering and collecting pattern.

Folsom types of points have been found very widely scattered throughout the high plains and in the Southwest to about the Arizona–New Mexico line. Recently the Chicago Natural History Museum has reported finding one Folsom site in eastern Arizona, about 20 miles east of St. Johns, but in general this culture does not seem to have expanded much west of the Rockies in the Southwest. Folsom and Folsom-like points have been found as far east as the east coast area, but they are far more abundant in the west.

It will be recalled that Folsom points were superimposed above Clovis points at the Blackwater site, and where they have been located in other sites they seem also to have been slightly more recent, or could not be distinguished stratigraphically. Thus by both carbon 14 dates and stratigraphy it is clear that the Folsom type is at least generally later than the Clovis point. Typologically it would also seem logical that such a sequence might be indicated, for the better-made and more fully fluted Folsom type appears to have been a natural evolution from the Clovis type.

Not all of the Folsom-type points are fluted, and this indicates that another logical evolutionary step may have been the production of leaf-shaped, ripple-flaked points which lacked fluting. This latter type has been called *Plainview*, but was formerly labeled Yuman. These are also more or less leaf-shaped, frequently have concave bases, and have very well-controlled parallel, or ripple-type, flaking. Carbon 14 dates from sites where points of this type have been found would suggest that they are later than Folsom, some of them having been made perhaps 5,000 years ago.

Many other specific instances of finds which are of this ancient Hunter stage of culture could be referred to in and around the Southwest, but reference to the list cited at the end of the chapter will add to them, and expand this subject. A typical example of evidences of early man in the Southwest is that of Burnet Cave near Carlsbad, New Mexico. Here Howard found, in the fill of the cave, bones and other material to a depth of about nine feet, with fire hearths, obviously human-made, to a depth of five feet eight inches. Bones, scattered throughout the fill, represent an extinct four-horned antelope, bison, California condor, horse, deer, sandhill crane, woodchuck, mountain sheep, camel, prairie falcon, and a musk-ox–like animal. Charcoal and ash layers occurred throughout the fill to a depth of over eight and a half feet, and in some places contained burned animal bones. At more than five feet a Folsom-like fluted point was found under a large stone, and was associated with bison and musk-ox bones and charcoal.

Desert Culture

At a time probably almost as early as that of the earliest Hunter cultures, which seem to have been more eastern in their distribution, the Desert culture was developed in the western part of the Southwest. In distinction to the Hunter group it was more oriented to gathering and collecting, and less directly to hunting. Although projectile points are found with it, particularly in the later developments, they are smaller and have notches, or are stemmed, and frequently have serrations.

In a general way characteristic features of the Desert culture seem to have been sparse populations in small, more or less migratory groups, who occupied caves and therein built grass beds. These people seem to have been seasonal gatherers who harvested small seeds and so rather fully exploited their natural environment. They made basketry, cordage, netting, matting, fur cloth, and used tump lines. The hunting implement was the atlatl, with pointed hardwood foreshafts and stone points. They also had flat curved wood clubs. By at least 7000 B.C. they had and used flat milling stones, presumably for grinding small seeds, and basin-type lower grinding stones. They had the fire drill, and most of their stone work was flaked by percussion chipping, with many scrapers, choppers, crude knives, and similar implements.

Since the Desert culture people made use of caves, many of the artifacts have been preserved that would not have survived in open sites, and as a result the perishable items listed above, such as basketry, have been found. It may be argued that the more eastern Hunter groups also had many of these items, but that since they are mostly found in either open sites or in caves where fragile artifacts were not preserved, we simply lack knowledge of them. If this is the case then the main differences between the two groups lie in the chipped and ground stone artifacts, and even those do not seem to be always entirely exclusive.

Although the Desert culture began certainly by about 9000 or 10,000 B.C. it might be considered as surviving as a way of life for longer or shorter periods in various parts of the Southwest. This kind of subsistence pattern was widely spread throughout the western basin and range country, in the earlier stages, coming about as far east as the Rio Grande valley. Here it seems to have overlapped at various times with the eastern Hunter groups, so that there was apparently a sort of shifting frontier in this area.

The typical Desert culture lasted as a clear-cut entity to about 2000 B.C., when certain agricultural products, particularly maize or corn, were introduced, and it became appreciably, though not radically, modified. By probably 200 or 300 B.C., with the addition of pottery and houses, Mogollon culture had developed from it, and at about this time, or at most not long after, Hohokam culture began its rise. The question then of just when the Desert culture must be considered no longer present, if it ever became extinct, is not as yet satisfactorily settled.

What was probably the second (after Folsom) case of well-authenticated early man in the Southwest was found in Gypsum Cave, in the southern tip of Nevada. Some rather mixed, but convincing, stratigraphy was worked out here. In the uppermost layers Harrington found evidences of Paiute occupation, in the second layer Pueblo culture, in the third Basket Maker

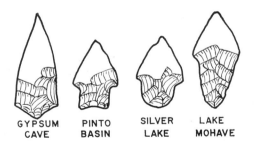

GYPSUM CAVE   PINTO BASIN   SILVER LAKE   LAKE MOHAVE

Fig. 26. Diagram of projectile point types from California and Nevada. These are all obviously dart points and not arrow points.

culture, and the fourth consisted of a layer containing only mountain sheep dung and remains. Below this were two layers of sloth dung, and below these, or eight feet from the surface, two fireplaces which were unquestionably built by human hands. This places the age of the fire builders at least as early as, if not earlier than, the sloth inhabitants of the cave, and the sloth is a now extinct mammal in North America. In this cave was a distinctive, somewhat diamond-shaped projectile point type which has become known as the Gypsum Cave type.

In 1926 Byron Cummings uncovered two human skeletons which were embedded in the side of Cienega Wash on the Empire Ranch, not far from Sonoita, Arizona. Both of these were obviously burials, for they were fully extended and placed approximately in a line. Unfortunately they were not accompanied by any burial offerings, which would serve as an aid to dating, but they were found covered by approximately 12 feet of stratified deposits. These deposits were made at a time when this area was an ancient lake bed, and therefore may have been several thousand years old. No detailed anthropological measurements have been published on this material.

In 1927 Cummings uncovered the skull, minus the lower jaw, of a mammoth in Sulphur Springs valley, not far from Bisbee, Arizona. The stratum in which the skull was found definitely overlies one in which there were groups of rubbing stones. These handstones are similar to later combination rubbing and hammerstones, for they are flattened on two sides and show slight indications of having been pounded on the edges. No other types of implements were found here, but the bones of other extinct animals, particularly bison, were subsequently found in the sides of the washes.

Gila Pueblo later became interested in tracing this culture in southeastern Arizona, and has succeeded in making many additional finds. It has been named Cochise culture after the fact that many of these finds have been made in the vicinity of ancient Lake Cochise, now of course long dried up and represented only by ancient beds. Sayles, who has done most of the work on this culture, has divided it into three sequential stages, the earliest the Sulphur Spring stage, next the Chiricahua stage, and finally the most recent, the San Pedro stage. Extinct animals have been found associated with the earliest, or Sulphur Spring, stage, that with which we are at present primarily concerned. The age of this stage has not been fully worked out as yet, but carbon 14 tests indicate it may date from about 6000 or 7000 B.C. to perhaps 4000 B.C. The associated artifacts consist of many flat milling stones and small handstones, a few percussion-flaked plano-convex implements, but no points or blades.

The following Chiricahua stage, which seems to date from about 4000 to perhaps 500 B.C., is characterized by the presence of larger, shallow, basin-type milling stones, handstones, biface percussion-flaked implements, and rare pressure-flaked projectile points which are probably intrusive. The final stage, the San Pedro, dates probably from about 500 B.C. to sometime shortly after the time of Christ. It may be characterized by the presence of a typical mortar and pestle, and by a preponderance of chipped implements, both plano-convex and biface, which are frequently retouched by pressure. Laterally notched projectile points, and knives, seem to be indigenous to this culture. Thus there is a good developmental sequence of Cochise culture which lasted for some 6,000 years in this portion of the Southwest.

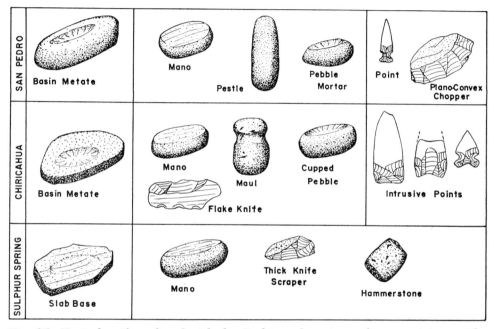

Fig. 27. Typical artifacts found with the Cochise culture in southeastern Arizona. The earliest Sulphur Spring stage dates about 8,000 to 6,000 years ago, and consists mostly of slab grinding stones and oval, more or less flat-sided manos, as well as hammerstones and some rough percussion-flaked tools. The Chiricahua stage dates probably from about 6,000 years ago to perhaps 500 B.C., and includes basin metates, mauls, and intrusive projectile points. The latest stage, the San Pedro, seems to date from about 500 B.C. to shortly after 1 A.D., and has mortars and pestles, various rough-flaked core tools and heavy flake tools, and projectile points.

Much more intensive and extensive work throughout the Southwest has shown that the Cochise culture is more widespread than was originally thought. It was at first believed to be limited to the southeastern portion of Arizona and the southwestern corner of New Mexico. It now has been found throughout most of western New Mexico and almost all of Arizona. Similar culture has been found to be even more widespread throughout the greater Southwest, and in various parts of the larger basin and range country.

One of the most interesting caves thus far explored in the Southwest is

Ventana Cave, in southern Arizona, which was dug by a University of Arizona group. The cave is in the side of a small butte, and in the back of it there was a seep spring so that it was annually used by Historic desert Indians as a place of shelter during the saguara fruit harvest period. A considerable and gradual accumulation of debris in this cave made it possible for Haury to designate several distinct layers.

At the bottom of the deepest part of the cave was a conglomerate deposit which contained two doubtful implements, both of basalt, one a crude scraper, the other a hammerstone. Above this was a volcanic debris layer, from which charcoal and a total of 90 stone artifacts came. One was a somewhat fluted, broken projectile point, suggestive of the Folsom type. The other tools were knives, scrapers, choppers, planes, hammerstones, and grinding stones. The complex suggests Folsom in a general way, and San Dieguito of the lower Colorado River, as defined by Rogers. The fauna includes dire wolf and tapir, but the rest of the mammals are like those Folsom man hunted. Above this, after a long period of erosion, was a deposit of red sand. This distinct stratum contained 54 stone objects, 21 of which were points. Some of these points, which tend to have somewhat square bases, are suggestive of Pinto points found in California. Other objects were knives, scrapers, and planes. In this stratum, and from here on, modern types of animals were found. Above this was a midden of some meters' total depth which could be divided into four recognizable culture stages. The lowest of the midden material contained many artifacts assignable to the Chiricahua stage of the Cochise, and both Pinto Basin and Gypsum Cave types of projectile points. Side and end scrapers and choppers were also found here. The next layer up contained projectile points and ground stone artifacts which were typical of the San Pedro stage of the Cochise culture. The points have lateral, or corner, notching. The next zone was the dry zone, and in it were found Hohokam artifacts of the Gila River type of Hohokam, and at the surface projectile points and other artifacts which may be assigned to the Papago Indians, who are found in this area today.

The main point of interest to us, here, is that the earlier deposits in this cave must date from the time period with which we are now concerned. There is evidence of man in the desert part of the Southwest at a time when now extinct types of animals roamed the area. A good estimate of a beginning date would be some 10,000 or 12,000 years ago, and if this continuing cultural sequence may be assigned to the Desert culture, then here again is evidence that it had a long history in the southern desert area.

In northern Utah, Danger Cave was dug by Jennings, and once more evidence was found of an early beginning of the Desert culture, certainly

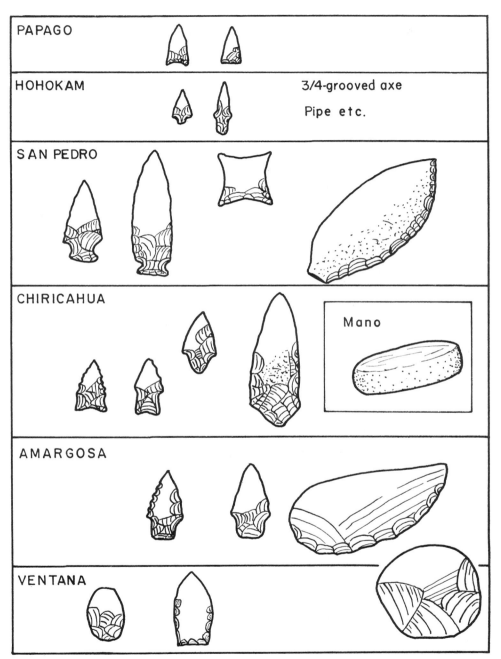

Fig. 28. The sequence of stone artifact types found at Ventana Cave in southern Arizona. With the possible exception of the earliest point these are all typical of the Desert culture. The mano is characteristic of the Cochise culture.

as old as Folsom, if not older. Carbon 14 dates derived from the cave show an age of some 11,000 years, or 9000 B.C. Since the cave was occupied for some time the dates are scattered over a span to about 2000 B.C. In the lowest level very simple projectile points were found, but in the overlying

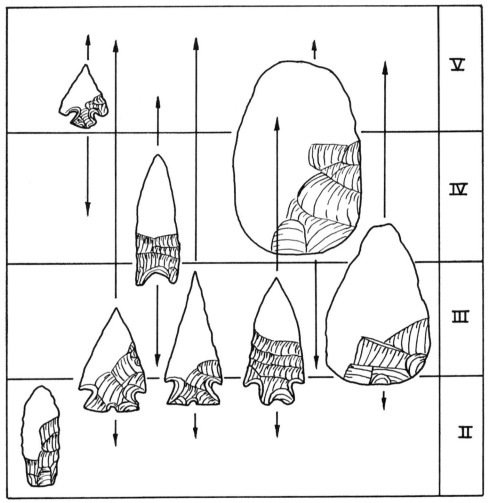

Fig. 29. Diagrams of artifact types found in Danger Cave in Utah. These are Desert culture points and show notching and stems. Lowest left point is 38 millimeters long.

layers more elaborate types occurred. Corner and base notching seems to have been typical of some of the earlier points from the bulk of the cave, and only in the uppermost levels were there smaller types. Scrapers of various sorts, and choppers and knives, also occurred. This cave, like Ventana Cave, gives a good sequence of local developments of projectile point types through some time span.

COLLECTOR STAGE—5000 to 200 B.C.

As has been suggested, the Hunter stage seems to have survived well into this period, at least in the eastern portion of the Southwest. Here the general Plainview type of point is most characteristic of the early portion of this period, and is found on a number of individual sites in eastern New Mexico and into the high plains. These are ripple-flaked points often with concave bases, and are some of the finest chipped projectile points made in this country. From present inadequate evidence it would seem possible that these cultures in the Southwest took on more and more of the sedentary agricultural way of life as time went on, and it was not until quite late, a millenium or so A.D., before they again shifted gradually to a more and more bison-hunting way of life.

These Plainview points, or points of Plano tradition, are comparable to the Archaic culture of the eastern portion of the United States, and have in fact been so called by some Southwestern workers. If it is remembered that they were formerly called Yuman, reference to the older literature will be more readily understandable.

Of the Desert culture, which may be assigned to this period, mention has already been made of the Chiricahua stage of the Cochise culture. Projectile points were more common in this stage, but the collecting and grinding of seeds undoubtedly still formed the main base of the way of life at this time. In fact, the presence of grinding stones and their basin metates is typical of all stages of the Cochise culture. The bulk of the material in the midden at Ventana Cave can also probably be assigned to this period, where Chiricahua Cochise artifacts were found. This is probably also true of the major portion of Danger Cave, where most of the projectile point types may perhaps be assigned to this general period.

Finds of Cochise culture, of the same general time span, have been very widespread throughout the Southwest. For instance Agogino has found Cochise-like culture at the San Jose sites on the middle Rio Grande. Carbon 14 dates on these sites are about 5000 B.C., although the fauna is modern, and the quantities of milling stones indicate a gathering type of economy. The culture is affiliated primarily with the Cochise complex, but there are also relations to Pinto Basin sites and to pre-ceramic sites along the middle Rio Grande valley. The Santa Ana pre-ceramic sites in Sandoval County, New Mexico, show a complex which may be related to both Chiricahua and San Pedro Cochise. They probably date from about 2000 B.C. to the time

of Christ. Somewhat similar pre-ceramic lithic sites have been reported
from the headwaters of the San Juan River, in the Navaho Reservoir area.
They seem to be related to Cochise culture as well, and perhaps to Pinto
Basin material, and are presumed to date in about this general period.

From these and other finds, the San Jose culture has been defined as
occupying an area in northwestern New Mexico, as indicated on the accompanying map. Most of the dates which have been assigned to it fall

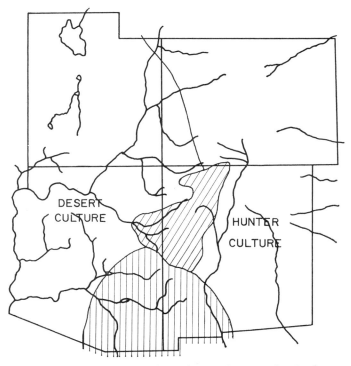

Fig. 30. In the most general way late Chiricahua and San Pedro Cochise, or pre-pottery
Mogollon, is shown on this map by the vertically hatched area. To the north is the
San Jose variant, which in many ways is intermediate between Cochise and Basket
Maker, and which is shown by diagonal hatching. The general area of Desert culture
and that of Hunter culture are also broadly indicated. As yet there is generally too
little specific data on these early sites to make specific outlining of areas possible.

between about 2500 and 250 B.C. These are seasonal sites, which are more
those of gatherers than hunters, though some hunting was practiced, and
therefore they all may be classed as of the Desert culture. In many respects they are intermediate between Cochise and Basket Maker. Other
such cultural and regional divisions of this early Desert culture will no
doubt be possible with additional work.

In California the Lake Mohave culture has been defined. Here artifacts and campsites were found scattered about the old beaches, most abundantly at those levels which were near, or slightly above, the highest point reached by the lake. The outlet of the basin in which the lake lay is now cut through 11 feet of solid granite, and it is assumed that the human occupation was before this channel had cut to its present depth. No metates have been found associated with this culture, although what are termed hammerstones, with more or less flat sides, might also have been used as rubbing stones. Other chipped artifacts are choppers, scrapers, some keeled, round scrapers, end and side scrapers, flake knives, gravers, and drills. Probably the most distinctive implements are rather broad projectile points which have been identified and divided into two obviously related groups, the Lake Mohave and the Silver Lake types. Some Yuman, or Plainview, and Folsom-like points have also been found here. Carbon 14 dates secured in the work at the Tule Lake or Springs site indicate that the Lake Mohave culture may be dated at some time about 3000 B.C. or slightly before. The typical Lake Mohave and Silver Lake points are stemmed rather than notched.

Somewhat later than the Lake Mohave culture in southern California is the Pinto Basin culture. This was found to be centered along the Pinto River, a stream which was apparently flowing during the same damp period. The date is probably about 3000 B.C. The campsites are located on the river terrace, all at nearly the same level, and extend for some six miles along the now dry stream. Fossil bones of both camel and horse come from this same area. Associated artifacts include bifacially flaked pointed blades, knives, scrapers of numerous types, incising tools, hammerstones, choppers, and grinding tools. The typical projectile point has a broad square stem which is most commonly concave on the base. Both these and the Lake Mohave points are broad short points, and it is quite likely that they were atlatl dart points.

The San Pedro stage of the Cochise culture, the last stage in this sequence, poses some problems which as yet have not been completely answered to the satisfaction of all archaeologists. The San Pedro has been defined in southeastern Arizona, and here it does not contain any pottery, even of the simplest kind, but the Carbon 14 dates which have been secured from it indicate that it existed from perhaps 200 or 300 B.C. to shortly after the time of Christ. In the major Mogollon area pottery was certainly present before the time of Christ, and may have been in use by this culture as early as about 300 B.C. Although houses are known from the San Pedro stage they are small, more or less rounded, rather shallow pits, with a step entrance on one side, and associated with undercut storage pits. Again by this time Mogollon culture had rather formalized house structures. The rest of the culture of the San Pedro stage is clearly a continuation and elaboration of that of the preceding Chiricahua stage, with both basin and slab metates and mortars, handstones and pestles, hammerstones, and various scrapers. Projectile points were more common, suggesting more dependence on hunting than had been the case previously, and are rather long and slender with broad side notches.

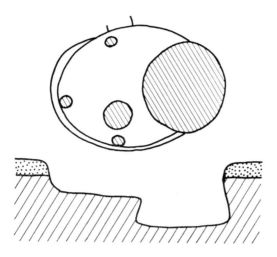

Fig. 31. A San Pedro Cochise "house," with a storage pit at the right, a step entrance at the top, and post holes. This may be the earliest type of structure found in the Southwest. It is a little over two meters wide.

With the addition of just two things the San Pedro stage of the Cochise culture would have to be considered a slight variant of the first Mogollon stage, the Pine Lawn. These two traits are pottery and burials, and of course the more formalized houses and kivas which distinguish the earliest Mogollon. There are other minor traits which also seem to change at this time, such as the greater use of stone and shell ornaments, bone tools, stone vessels and the stone slab palette, and projectile points which are somewhat broader and with corner notches. It is generally assumed that these various traits were introduced from Mexico, largely because no other better explanation of their source is as yet known. In any event it is apparent that in the Mogollon core area there were additions to the Cochise culture which made it become Mogollon, while in more peripheral areas it still maintained a Cochise character.

In the Wet Leggett site, in the Pine Lawn valley of New Mexico, milling stones, choppers, and scrapers were found which are strongly suggestive of the Cochise culture, but these may most probably be assigned to the Chiricahua stage. Here also the floor of a house was found which was like the San Pedro house reported by Sayles from farther south. The flaked tools were largely percussion-flaked, and the projectile points relatively small. Metates were open at one end and scoop-shaped, a trait which would definitely tend to tie this stage of Cochise to the Mogollon culture, despite the fact that Antevs has suggested a date for it of some 1,500 years B.C.

One of the most informative dry caves is Tularosa Cave, which was dug by Paul Martin for the Chicago Natural History Museum. Here a considerable depth of accumulated material gave a long chronology, beginning at about 2000 B.C. This cave, in its lowest part, dates about the same as Cordova Cave nearby, and the Wet Leggett site. The earliest remains may be related back to the Desert culture, and in fact are more nearly like Cochise than any other known group. Most typical early artifacts are the grinding stones used in the preparation of seeds, and chipped stone scrapers and choppers, all of which are also characteristic of Cochise.

Particular traits which were found in the pre-pottery levels of Tularosa Cave, and to some extent were shared by Cordova Cave, are the following. The basin type of metate predominated, although the slab type was present, and the manos were ovoid and of the one-hand type. Small metate-like grinding stones were also found. Chipped stone objects included flake knives, scrapers, choppers, and projectile points. There were also broad-base and flaring-base drills, and hammerstones, rubbing stones, and abrading stones. The points were corner-notched with an expanding stem and thin-based, although there were also some with small shallow lateral notches, slender lateral notches, slender lateral notches with an expanding base, and diagonal notches with down-raking barbs and an expanding convex base. Certainly the atlatl and, according to Martin, probably the bow and arrow were in use at this time. The atatl points had large lateral notches. Bunts were also used. Stubby bone awls and bone fleshers were found. Digging sticks were in use for cultivation, and most interesting of all, quantities of corn cobs were found. Other plants which were utilized were beans, squash, gourd, yucca pods, cacti, black walnuts, acorns, grass seeds, sunflower seeds, and desert primrose leaves. There were storage pits and grass beds but no evidence of house structures. Rope snares were used for securing small game. There were also flexible cradles and netted carrying bags. The fire drill was in use, and hearths were found. There was a wooden scoop. Baskets of the two-rod and bundle type predominated, but there were also bundle with rod core types and twined baskets, and there were leather bags. Fragments of moccasins were found, but the most typical footgear was wickerwork sandals. There were marine shell bracelets. Some use was made of gourd vessels as containers, and unfired pottery was very rare, but present.

As will be seen later, a number of these traits are shared with the earliest of the Basket Makers, and much might be made of these parallels. However, the similarities between the two groups may also be explained by the fact that they both developed from the early Desert culture, and that these traits are to be found in the Desert culture. In fact the pre-pottery levels of Tularosa Cave may be regarded as a rather late development of the

Desert culture, if it can be defined as including the use of some agricultural plants, such as corn and beans and squash. In any event the abundant materials preserved in this cave give us a good picture of the type of culture which prevailed just before the introduction of pottery into the Southwest.

Fig. 32. Wickerwork sandal of the type found in the pre-pottery horizon at Tularosa Cave. It was not limited to this stage alone, but was also found later. This is a two-warp type.

Although only some of the most striking examples of early man have been considered herein, much more information on this subject may be secured by reference to the list of publications at the end of this chapter. It is hoped that the framework presented will prove adequate, for those who may be interested, to add further details.

SUMMARY

In general throughout all of this time period, some 11,000 years, a simple way of life is represented which may be, in its broadest sense, referred to as the Early Man stage of culture in the Southwest. Whether the way of life was more oriented to hunting or to gathering, this long period was a time when man was attempting to make the most of his natural environment. Hunters, although they were primarily big-game hunters, were not solely hunters, so far as is now known, but gathered and collected as well. Gatherers were not solely gatherers and collectors, but hunted to some extent too. There are, however, two distinguishable general ways of life: the Big-Game Hunters, who are to be found mostly to the eastern part of the Southwest, and the Gatherers, or Desert culture people, who lived in the rest of the Southwest. The Hunters made large projectile points, many of them fluted; the Gatherers, when they had projectile points, made them shorter, broader, stemmed or notched on the sides, and many with serrated edges. The Hunters generally, though not totally, lacked grinding stones, while the Gatherers made a very considerable use of them, even at their earliest known appearance.

The question of just when the Desert culture may be regarded as ending is one which has not as yet been clearly defined. As has been suggested, it may be considered as having survived in some portions of the Southwest, notably the northern part, essentially to the present, if it is defined solely as a general subsistence pattern. If, however, it is regarded as ending with the introduction of occasional domesticated plants, then it must be terminated at about 2000 B.C. with the earliest introduction of corn into the Southwest. An alternative interpretation is that it may be viewed as having lasted until the first introduction of pottery, in which case it would have come to an end about 200 B.C. Perhaps this is not a really important, or pertinent, question, for the Desert culture may be considered a basic way of life which in some areas changed early to other means of subsistence and in others survived far longer. In any event it is clear-cut early, but as time goes on it becomes less and less distinct. In this sense it may be considered a basic culture from which others were derived.

It is not only possible but quite logical to divide this general long Early Man stage into three subdivisions. The first of these, from about 13,000 years ago to 10,000 B.C., saw the first known evidences of man in the Southwest. At this time the two ways of life seem to be most marked. The next period, that from about 10,000 B.C. to perhaps 5000 B.C., what has been called herein the Hunter period, saw the elaboration, or evolution, of these ways of life, and what appears to be a much fuller occupation of the Southwest. The two groups were still distinct, but each had developed more skillfully made artifacts and more diversified tools. Both were very much oriented to a dependence on their environment, and though some were occupying caves others seem not to have done so. In the last, the Collector period, that from about 5000 to 200 B.C., the greater emphasis in the Southwest seems to have centered in the development of the Desert culture. Some domesticated plants were introduced during the last part of this period, and the way was opened for the rapid and spectacular developments of later times. The stage was set, and the curtain was about to go up.

Sources and Additional References

Amsden, Charles. Man Hunting, *Masterkey*, Vol. 5, No. 2, July-August, 1931, Southwest Museum, Los Angeles, California. (Popular article on Early Man in America.)

Antevs, Ernst. Geological Dating of the Lehner Mammoth Site, *American Antiquity*, Vol. 25, No. 1, 1959, Society for American Archaeology, Salt Lake City, Utah. (As indicated by title.)

Botelho, George W. Pinto Basin Points in Utah, *American Antiquity*, Vol. 21, No. 2, 1955, Society for American Archaeology, Salt Lake City, Utah. (As indicated by title.)

Bryan, Kirk, and L. L. Ray. Geologic Antiquity of the Lindenmeier Site in Colorado, *Smithsonian Miscellaneous Collections*, Vol. 99, No. 2, 1940, Washington, D.C. (As indicated by title.)

Bryan, Kirk, and Joseph H. Toulouse, Jr. The San Jose Non-ceramic Culture and Its Relation to a Puebloan Culture in New Mexico, *American Antiquity*, Vol. 8, No. 3, 1943, Society for American Archaeology, Salt Lake City, Utah. (As indicated by title.)

Campbell, E. W. and W. H. The Pinto Basin Site, *Southwest Museum Paper 9*, 1935, Los Angeles, California. (The Desert culture Pinto Basin complex of California.)

Campbell, E. W. and W. H., Ernst Antevs, Charles Avery Amsden, J. A. Barbieri, and F. D. Bode. The Archaeology of Pleistocene Lake Mohave, *Southwest Museum Paper 11*, 1937, Los Angeles, California. (Report on Lake Mohave culture.)

Colton, Harold S. The Sinagua. A Summary of the Archaeology of the Region of Flagstaff, Arizona, *Bulletin 22*, 1946, Museum of Northern Arizona, Flagstaff. (Brief statement of the apparently early culture of the Little Colorado River valley.)

Dittert, Alfred E., Jr. Navajo Project Studies, I. Preliminary Archaeological Investigations in the Navajo Project Area of Northwestern New Mexico, *Papers in Anthropology 1*, 1958, Museum of New Mexico, Santa Fe. (The San Jose culture is discussed.)

Dittert, Alfred E., Jr., James J. Hester, and Frank W. Eddy. An Archaeological Survey of the Navajo Reservoir District, Northwestern New Mexico, *Monograph 23*, 1961, Museum of New Mexico, Santa Fe. (Discussion of the San Jose culture in this area.)

Harrington, M. R. * Gypsum Cave, Nevada, *Southwest Museum Paper 8*, 1933, Los Angeles, California. (Excellent report of Gypsum Cave and a summary of finds of Early Man in America.)

Haury, Emil W. * The Stratigraphy and Archaeology of Ventana Cave, Arizona, University of New Mexico Press, Albuquerque, 1950. (Detailed report of a Desert culture cave, and Cochise culture.)

―――. * Artifacts with Mammoth Remains, Naco, Arizona: Discovery of the Naco Mammoth and the Associated Projectile Points, *American Antiquity*, Vol. 19, No. 1, 1953, Society for American Archaeology, Salt Lake City, Utah. (As indicated by title.)

―――. Association of Fossil Fauna and Artifacts of the Sulphur Springs Stage, Cochise Culture, *American Antiquity*, Vol. 25, No. 4, 1960, Society for American Archaeology, Salt Lake City, Utah. (As indicated by title.)

Haury, Emil W., E. B. Sayles, and William W. Wasley. * The Lehner Mammoth Site, Southeastern Arizona, *American Antiquity*, Vol. 25, No. 1, 1959, Society for American Archaeology, Salt Lake City, Utah. (A Clovis kill site in Arizona.)

Hester, James J. * Blackwater Locality No. 1, a Stratified Paleo-Indian Site in Eastern New Mexico, Texas Memorial Museum, Fort Burgwin Research Center, in press. (Evidence of the chronological position of Clovis and Folsom cultures.)

Hibben, Frank C. Association of Man with Pleistocene Mammals in the Sandia
Mountains, New Mexico, *American Antiquity*, Vol. 2, No. 4, 1937, Society for
American Archaeology, Salt Lake City, Utah. (A preliminary report on the
Sandia Cave discoveries.)

Howard, Edgar B. Evidence of Early Man in North America, *Museum Journal*,
Vol. 24, Nos. 2-3, 1935, University Museum, University of Pennsylvania, Phila-
delphia. (General summary of the Early Man situation as well as reports on
Burnet Cave and the Clovis finds.)

Jennings, Jesse D. * Danger Cave, *Memoirs of the Society for American Archaeology*, No. 14, 1957, Salt Lake City, Utah. (Excellent report on a Desert
culture cave site in northern Utah.)

Martin, Paul S., John B. Rinaldo, and Ernst Antevs. Cochise and Mogollon Sites,
Pine Lawn Valley, Western New Mexico, *Fieldiana: Anthropology*, Vol. 38,
No. 1, 1949, Chicago Natural History Museum. (As indicated by title.)

Martin, Paul S., John B. Rinaldo, Elaine A. Bluhm, Hugh C. Cutler, and Roger
Grange, Jr. * Mogollon Cultural Continuity and Change: The Stratigraphic
Analysis of Tularosa and Cordova Caves, *Fieldiana: Anthropology*, Vol. 40,
1952, Chicago Natural History Museum. (The early occupation in these caves
is essentially Cochise culture.)

Mason, Ronald J. * The Paleo-Indian Tradition in Eastern North America, *Current Anthropology*, Vol. 3, No. 3, 1962, University of Chicago. (Excellent general recent summary of Early Man.)

Renaud, E. B. Prehistoric Flaked Points from Colorado and Neighboring Districts, *Proceedings of the Colorado Museum of Natural History*, Vol. 10, No. 2,
1931, Denver. (Report on Folsom and other early points.)

———. Yuma and Folsom Artifacts, *Proceedings of the Colorado Museum of
Natural History*, Vol. 11, No. 2, 1932, Denver. (Discussion of early flint types.)

———. The First Thousand Yuman-Folsom Artifacts, Department of Anthropology, University of Denver, Denver, Colorado, 1934. (Additional data on
the abundance and distribution of Folsom and Yuma points.)

Roberts, Frank H. H., Jr. * The Material Culture of Folsom Man as Revealed
at the Lindenmeier Site, *Southwestern Lore*, Vol. 2, No. 4, 1937, Gunnison,
Colorado. (Excellent short discussion of the general material traits thus far
known of the Folsom culture.)

Rogers, Malcolm J. San Dieguito Implements from the Terraces of the Rincon-
Pantano and Rillito Drainage System, *The Kiva*, Vol. 24, No. 1, 1958, University
of Arizona, Tucson. (Desert culture artifact complex.)

Roosa, William B. The Lucy Site in Central New Mexico, *American Antiquity*,
Vol. 21, No. 3, 1956, Society for American Archaeology, Salt Lake City, Utah.
(Report on Sandia points from a kill site.)

Sayles, E. B., and Ernst Antevs. * The Cochise Culture, *Medallion Paper 29*,
1941, Gila Pueblo, Globe, Arizona. (Best published report on the Cochise
culture.)

Sellards, E. H. * Early Man in America, a Study in Prehistory, University of Texas
Press, Austin, 1952. (Excellent summary to date, as indicated.)

Wormington, H. M. * Ancient Man in North America, *Popular Series 4*, 1957,
Denver Museum of Natural History, Denver, Colorado. (Good summary of
Early Man to the date of writing.)

VIII

Exploitation Period: 200 B.C. to A.D. 1

MOGOLLON

During the period from about 200 or 300 B.C. to the time of Christ the later part of San Pedro Cochise, if we may rely upon carbon 14 dates, flourished in certain parts of the Southwest, while in other more restricted areas the beginning of what must be considered Mogollon culture was established. The features which distinguish earliest Mogollon from latest Cochise are formalized and rather elaborate structures, and pottery. Burials also have been found, but earlier people must have disposed of their dead in some manner, so this is probably not an entirely new trait.

The lithic tools of the earliest Pine Lawn Mogollon are quite clearly a continuation of Cochise, with all of the forms of late Cochise present. Agricultural plants, including corn, beans, and squash, continued into Pine Lawn, and may have played a more important part in the economy of this stage than they had earlier. Haury has pointed out that the earliest use of domesticated plants in the Southwest was probably much like that of the wild plants they were already familiar with, and that it was not until about the time of Christ that the true potential of corn was realized with the development of more intensive agriculture. This led to the flowering of most of the major Southwestern cultures in the immediately succeeding years. Corn thus remained a very great potential but unrealized asset for some 2,000 years.

One of the most pertinent questions concerning the history of the Southwest is where agricultural plants and pottery came from. The general consensus of present opinion is that they were derived from the south, specifically from Mexico. This is based on the fact that dates from this area show that both pottery and agriculture were as early or earlier here than they are known to have occurred in the Southwest. The earliest known

Photograph courtesy Museum of New Mexico

A Los Pinos phase pithouse in the Navajo Reservoir district of New Mexico which dates between about A.D. 200 and 400. The house is inside a ring of cobbles and has an antechamber on the far side.

Mogollon pottery types are rather well made, indicating that at least the idea of ceramics was introduced from some outside source. Pithouses are also rather formalized when they first appear in this culture. More specifically the earliest pottery in the Southwest is, in the broadest way, suggestively similar to early pottery types from Mexico, particularly in the use of a red surface finish.

The accompanying map indicates the general area over which Mogollon culture of this period has been found to occur. As may be seen it is in the headwaters of the Gila and Salt rivers, lying across the present boundary between Arizona and New Mexico in what has been designated as the southern portion of the mountain area, and extends into the higher parts of the plateau to the north and the desert section to the south. This is an area of large valleys where agriculture would have been possible, and in general also includes some of the best game country of the Southwest. The central part of this region may be considered a sort of core area, so that as one goes outward from it more primitive, though contemporary, cultures are found.

This is the area over which San Francisco Red pottery occurred. As has been suggested it is a fairly sophisticated pottery type, as regards such

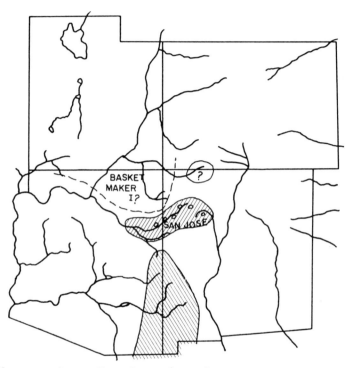

Fig. 33. The area of Mogollon, dating from about 200 or 300 B.C. to the time of Christ, is shown to the south by the hatched area shaded from upper right to lower left. The dating is based on carbon 14 dates from O Block Cave and Tularosa Cave. The area has been extended into the San Simon area of Arizona and on into Mexico on the assumption that the source of pottery, and possibly other traits, was Mexico. The later San Jose culture manifestation is shown to the north with hatching running from upper right to lower left. Basket Maker I is suggested as possibly occurring still farther north.

features as paste, shapes, thickness, and surface finish, and for these reasons it has been assumed that it must have been introduced from outside of this immediate area. Houses do not seem to have been consistent in pattern with the exception of the large kivas, for they have been found to vary throughout the several distinguishable areas. Although stone work in general is a continuation from the Cochise or pre-pottery levels, a few traits are added now, such as trough metates, more nearly rectangular manos, pipes, and more elaborate stone bowls. Thus, the innovations which distinguish early Mogollon from San Pedro Cochise are few.

As defined by the Chicago Natural History Museum, the Pine Lawn phase spans more than the period indicated herein, in fact it includes both the Exploitation and Founder periods. Since early versus later traits have generally not been distinguished, the problem of identifying the early traits is not always an easy or perhaps a reliable one.

The most complete list of traits has come from Tularosa and Cordova caves, because here perishable materials have been preserved. Houses, found in open sites of this stage, are large, more or less circular pithouses, with a short entrance area, a central post in many instances, and a firepit. Associated with each loosely knit village is at least one large structure, as much as 30 or 35 feet in diameter, which must be considered a ceremonial structure, or kiva. These kivas are present from the beginning of the Pine Lawn, and are therefore far earlier than similar ceremonial structures in the Anasazi.

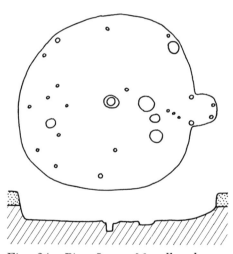

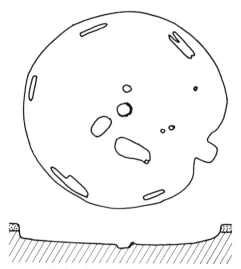

Fig. 34. Pine Lawn Mogollon houses are large; the greatest diameter of this one is 6.65 meters. There is a sloping entrance on the east, a central post and other scattered posts, and several rather shallow storage pits. Although these are not as deep as later Mogollon houses they are fairly deep, and are definitely pithouses. The roof was presumably flat and extended over the entrance.

Fig. 35. This large structure, 10.4 meters in greatest diameter, was probably a ceremonial structure, or kiva. There is a short entrance on the southeast side, a central firepit, and a number of storage pits. The shallow trenches around the periphery may have been floor drums used in dancing, a trait which is found in later kivas which are apparently derived from these early Mogollon prototypes.

The most common pottery types are Alma Plain, Alma Rough, and San Francisco Red. Alma Plain is the most abundant type, and forms most of the common culinary vessels throughout all Mogollon stages. The paste is coarse and brown, with rarely a gray core, and contains coarse heavy temper of heterogeneous material. The surface is unslipped, but often rubbed down with a tool. Interiors are poorly finished, and rarely smudged black. The surface color is buff through gray to red-brown. Shapes are bowls with rounded rims and jars, the jars far outnumbering the bowls. Alma Rough is like Alma Plain but the surface has been left rough.

Fig. 36. Shapes of typical Pine Lawn pottery. The two upper left are Alma Rough. The two lower left are Alma Plain. The two right examples are of San Francisco Red.

San Francisco Red is of particular interest because it appears to have been a type very basic to the Southwest. The paste has a core which is gray to brown and includes whitish angular particles as temper. The interiors are slipped and tool-polished, occasionally showing the marks of scraping through the slip. The exteriors are smoothed, or more rarely finger-dented, among later types, and sometimes coiled, or showing scoring, as though with grass stems. One of the most characteristic features of the surface is a sort of dimpling, almost certainly the result of coiling and rubbing over in polishing the outside of the vessel. The color of the slip is brown to a rich red. Forms are bowls, both shallow without curved sides and in later periods deeper, and small round-bodied jars. Seed-jar forms occur very rarely in later periods.

The earliest of these types may be distinguishable from later examples, for it has been suggested that two variants occur. Alma Rough, or Unpolished Brown, is similar to, and probably ancestral to, Alma Plain, but is thick, undecorated, never so well finished, and has coarser temper. Most common forms are hemispherical bowls and globular jars without necks. Polished Red is suggestive of, and perhaps ancestral to, San Francisco Red. It is also undecorated, has coarser paste and a less well-finished surface, and occurs most commonly as narrow-mouth jars and shallow bowls.

Some fragments of unfired pottery were found in deposits of this age, which lends some credence to the theory that clay lining of baskets may have been used for parching and not as a means of modeling unfired clay vessels. The same sort of unfired pottery has been found with Basket Maker II, and was at one time regarded as evidence for the beginning of pottery making in the Southwest. However, since the first known pottery is of sufficient sophistication to indicate that it had a preceding evolution elsewhere, this theory is less credible.

During the Pine Lawn stage food was the same as during the pre-pottery stage, with the use of simple agricultural plants, hunting, and undoubtedly some gathering. One of the striking features of the houses is the presence of sizable storage pits which were undoubtedly used for storing vegetable products. The digging stick continued from pre-pottery times throughout all Mogollon stages.

Ground stone tools consisted of metates of the basin, slab, and scoop types, in fact all of the various types which are typical of Mogollon. Manos were mostly of the ovoid one-hand type, although some were rectangular. There were pebble and boulder mortars, and of course pestles. Chipped stone tools consisted of scrapers and choppers, and various types of drills. The projectile points were a continuation of all previous types, so there is clear evidence of the use of the atlatl, and there is also good evidence of the use of the bow and arrow, at least by the later portion of this stage of culture. One of the distinctive features of Mogollon seems to have been the production of the notched bone awl, and these are found now, as are fleshers.

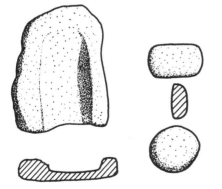

Fig. 37. Although slab and basin metates were still in use, the trough type open at one end appeared about now. Manos vary from almost circular to semirectangular.

Of ornaments, bracelets made from marine shells traded from the Gulf of California are typical. Whole olivella and cut shell beads and bone and stone pendants are also a part of this culture. Pipes were made of both stone and pottery and are of the long more or less cigar shape, or cloudblower form. Apparently reed cigarettes were sparingly used at this time, which raises the question of where they were used first, here in the Mogollon or in the Hohokam culture, where they are found to be very common later. Clay human figurines were also made.

Fig. 38. Simple stone bowls were a part of the Pine Lawn assemblage of stone objects. They usually lack decoration.

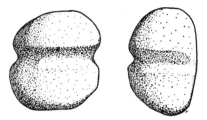

Fig. 39. Mauls are of two types. The left more rounded form with a full hafting groove may have been the earliest. The right three-quarter-grooved type is perhaps slightly later. Mauls are relatively abundant in Mogollon sites.

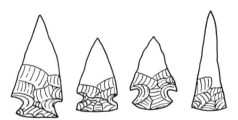

Fig. 40. Projectile points of Pine Lawn Mogollon. The most typical form is probably the third from the left. Corner notches are more common than lateral notches. At the right is a drill.

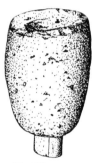

Fig. 41. The most typical stone pipe is cylindrical, and may have a short bone stem. Pipes begin here and are found throughout most Mogollon stages.

Flutes were present, and dice of both wood and bone were in use at this time, as they were earlier. Basketry was also of the same types as during the pre-pottery stage, but with the addition of flexible twined basketry as well. Matting was of both the twined and sewed types. Wickerwork sandals were the most common type, some with continuous outer warp and some with concentric warp. There were also some of leather. No moccasins were found from here on in the history of Mogollon. Other clothing consisted of twisted cord sashes and fur and feather blankets, a type of covering found throughout the history of the Anasazi and surviving today among the Hopi Indians.

Flexible cradles were also in use, and there were net carrying bags and a twined flexible carrying basket. Fire drills were present, and in use all through the various Mogollon stages. The dead were buried both in the trash and in subfloor pits in the houses. Burials were typically partly flexed rather than tightly so.

From the foregoing it may be seen that the first truly sedentary, agricultural, pottery-making, house-building culture in the Southwest was early Pine Lawn Mogollon. Just when this culture reached this stage is not as yet specifically established, but on present carbon 14 evidence it would appear to be pretty definitely between about 300 and 150 B.C. Between then and about the time of Christ most of the traits which have just been listed came into use, and the general pattern of the Mogollon culture was set. At this time it was not only the most culturally advanced group in the Southwest but it was also one of the most vigorous, for it was shortly to become the stimulus for the rapid development of other cultural groups.

EARLY PIONEER HOHOKAM

At a time not a great deal later than the earliest Pine Lawn stage of the Mogollon the Hohokam culture began to develop. In fact, as now understood there is much to indicate that this first Hohokam was so like the Mogollon that there are relatively few distinguishable traits. As has already been suggested, many contemporary Southwestern cultures are so similar in general character that minor distinctions must be rather assiduously hunted out to differentiate them, and such seems to be the case with the first Hohokam.

Although a historical sequence of events has been presented earlier herein, as they are believed to have developed, it must be borne in mind that actual information, as a result of archaeological work, is often secured in the opposite order. Late sites are usually dug first, so that the most information is acquired about them, and from this, earlier cultures are indicated and eventually investigated. Only when many data are at hand is it possible to reverse the order and write a history.

This has been true of the work in the Gila area, for here the large, still standing sites were the first to be worked. It was after a fairly good knowledge of these surface sites had been secured that earlier ones were investigated, for they consisted of much less impressive pithouses. Not until history had been carried well back into the pithouse stage was it realized that even these cultures were not the earliest, and members of the Gila Pueblo staff, who had been investigating the problem of the Hohokam, began a serious search for still earlier sites.

Of all the sites located in a widespread survey, Snaketown Village appeared the most likely to give a long sequence of development. This site, on the Gila River near Gila Butte not far from Chandler, Arizona, not only was of exceptional size but contained several huge trash mounds. It is trash mounds which generally give the most convincing stratigraphy in archaeological work, so these were quickly trenched in order to develop a sequence for this site. As digging progressed it became apparent that Snaketown was earlier than had been originally thought, and the Pioneer stage was defined.

In order to have a better understanding of the significance of the finds made at Snaketown the accompanying table has been prepared. Gila Pueblo referred to these divisions as periods, but herein they have generally been

PERIOD	SNAKETOWN	CASA GRANDE	TRADE POTTERY	DATES
				1400A.D.
CLASSIC		CIVANO		
				1325
	SOHO	SOHO		
				1200
SEDENTARY	SACATON		P.II. BLACK MESA B/W – KANA-A	1000
				900
COLONIAL	SANTA CRUZ		P.I. KANA-A B/W	
				700
	GILA BUTTE		B.M.III. LINO B/GRAY	
				500
PIONEER	SNAKETOWN			
				300
	SWEETWATER			
				200
	ESTRELLA			
				100
	VAHKI			
				I AD

Fig. 42. Chart illustrating the periods and phases of the Hohokam as found at Snaketown Village and at Casa Grande. Under the column headed "Trade Pottery" are listed the types which have been found intrusive at Snaketown. This chart is adapted from Haury, and the right-hand column gives his correlation with dates.

designated as stages, for they are certainly stages in the sequential development of this culture as based primarily on ceramic types, especially of the earliest stages. From this table it may be seen that the Pioneer stage, which has been defined essentially from this site alone, was divided into four substages. From earliest to latest they are Vahki, Estrella, Sweetwater, and Snaketown. These are followed by Colonial stages, then Sedentary, and in this general area by the Classic. It has even been suggested that the series might be carried on through a Decadent to a Historic stage here.

Like the Mogollon, the earliest stages of the Hohokam are the least accurately dated. In attempting to determine the age of the Pioneer culture various devices have been employed. Since tree-ring dates are presumably not possible at present, it has been necessary to turn to other means. Unfortunately, at the time Snaketown was dug carbon 14 dating was not developed, so it was not applied. No dated trade pottery from the north was in the Pioneer stage, but such pottery types were found from the Colonial stage on, so that these divisions could be rather accurately dated. By projection backward it was proposed that the Vahki stage of the Pioneer might have begun as long ago as about 300 B.C. Subsequent evidence would indicate that a more conservative time estimate could be as late as about the time of Christ, or at most a century or two before. Certain similarities between early Hohokam and Mogollon ceramics imply that it may have begun as much as two or perhaps even two and a half centuries B.C., but the definite dating must remain for the securing of adequate carbon 14 dates. On the accompanying chart the most conservative dating has been shown.

From our present viewpoint the most pertinent problem is the question of which came first, Mogollon or Hohokam. The preponderance of evidence, as of the moment, is that Mogollon, as defined by the first appearance of pottery, somewhat preceded Hohokam, but there is no assurance that still earlier Hohokam horizons will not eventually be uncovered. The duration of each of the Pioneer stages is of course somewhat speculative as well, but about the magnitude of those indicated on the chart may well be within reason.

Pioneer Hohokam culture, even in this earliest now recognized phase, is an already well-established culture, certainly indicating an ancestry somewhere. Previous to about A.D. 500 the Hohokam culture may be identified in general as a pottery-making, agricultural, shallow pithouse–building stage, all features which are also shared by the Mogollon of a comparable, or earlier, time. For these reasons it was shown in one of the earlier maps as an extension of the Mogollon culture into the desert area, and there is no present evidence to argue that such was not the case, although certain traits, as found at Ventana Cave, seem to show a local evolution of stone artifacts from Cochise.

Just what specific area the Pioneer Hohokam occupied is not clearly and fully known as yet. In the accompanying map it has been indicated as lying within the drainages of the Gila and Salt and extending somewhat southward, although there is slight evidence of Pioneer Hohokam in the

Verde valley. If the assumption that many of the traits which constituted this stage of culture were derived from Mexico is accepted, then it might be extended still farther south. In any event this map can be taken as only a general indication of the area which was probably occupied at this time.

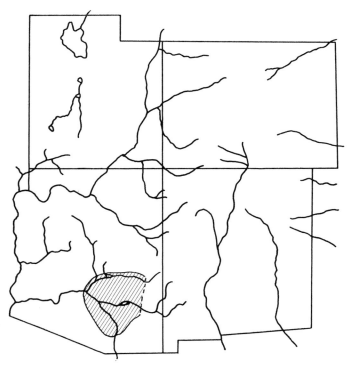

Fig. 43. Map showing, in a very general way, the area where it is assumed Pioneer Hohokam is probably to be found. The eastern edge remains uncertain and so is shown with a dotted line. The close relationship between early Hohokam and Mogollon has been demonstrated, but the line of demarcation between the two has not been defined as yet.

The phases, or stages, which may be assigned to the Exploitation period are the Vahki with comparative certainty, and probably also the Estrella. Only plain or undecorated pottery was found in the Vahki stage, and this not only is reminiscent of Pine Lawn Mogollon, but a careful analysis of the components of some of this plain pottery from both the Gila drainage and the Mogollon area indicated it was essentially identical. As will be seen shortly there are other general parallels between the two cultures.

Turning to an examination of the material traits of these early stages of culture, Haury has listed four pottery types which occur during Vahki and Estrella. In the Vahki stage there is Vahki Red and Vahki Plain. Vahki

Red seems to have developed from San Francisco Red, and so far it is known only from Snaketown. Vahki Plain seems to have been an ancestral form of Gila Plain, which in turn lasted to at least as late as A.D. 1350 in the Gila area. The pottery types which are found in the Estrella stage are Vahki Red, Gila Plain, and Estrella Red-on-gray. The type which is exclusive with the Vahki stage is Vahki Plain; that which distinguishes the Estrella stage is Estrella Red-on-gray.

Fig. 44. Shapes and designs of the pottery of the Hohokam Exploitation period. The upper four figures are Estrella Red-on-gray, and the designs to the right are of this type. The upper left-hand bowl in the lower diagrams of shape is Vahki Red, the lower left diagram is Vahki Plain, the other three are all Gila Plain.

Vahki Red is a most interesting type because it seems to be quite typical of the early reds of this culture. Though it is relatively rare, about 4 per cent of the total pottery of Snaketown, it was made locally as shown by temper studies. It is red-brown in color, slipped and polished, and was constructed by the paddle and anvil method. Mica flakes used as a tempering material occur in some abundance. They provide an easily recognizable distinction when comparing this type with its close relative, San Francisco Red, from the Mogollon area, which does not have mica temper. The forms are both bowls and jars, the former the more common.

Vahki Plain, the direct ancestor of Gila Plain, is as well made as any later forms of Gila Plain. Quantities of fine mica flakes were used as temper, and they show through on the surface, a very characteristic feature of Gila Plain. The color is brown to gray, with moderate polish. The forms are both bowls and jars, and this type forms 96 per cent of the pottery of the Vahki phase.

Gila Plain, which appears first during the Estrella stage, is one of the most widespread and long-lived types of the desert area. The color is gray to brown, often mottled outside and blackened (smudged) inside. There is no slip, so that the surface is slightly rough to the touch. The paste contains much coarse mica tempering, and, like all these types, it was made by the paddle and anvil process. There is a strong suggestion of similarity to Alma Plain of the Mogollon culture, which has led Haury to feel that they are related.

Estrella Red-on-gray, typical of only the Estrella phase, is the earliest painted pottery of this area, although it forms only about 2 per cent of the total pottery of this stage. The paint is on a light gray or brown background, often showing fire clouds, and is polished, sometimes after the painted design has been applied, to spread the paint slightly into the background. Designs consist of broad simple parallel lines, very crude or rudimentary hatching, no interlocking scrolls, and occasional small elements. As an additional design element coils on the outsides of bowls are often outlined by incising with a sharp pointed implement, or this incising is arranged in parallel lines to form simple geometric designs.

Bowls of Vahki Red, during this later period, were also incised on the outside in a similar manner, thus making it possible to distinguish this later type from the earlier Vahki stage examples which lacked this feature.

From this it may be seen that two kinds of pottery were made at the now known beginning of Hohokam, and that three types were in vogue by the Estrella stage. One is a red-surface type, the second is a plain undecorated group, and the last and latest is painted with red designs on a brown, buff, or gray background. This last class often has incised exteriors. Only the plain type survived into later times.

In the Pioneer stage horizon at Snaketown a great many clay human figurines were found. These may be grouped into two general classes, torsos and heads. The torsos are strongly suggestive of similar human figurines found in the Basket Maker culture of the plateau, and this latter group may well have taken the idea of modeling them from the Hohokam. The heads find no close parallel in the Southwest, but are very strongly suggestive of those typical of the Archaic horizon in the Valley of Mexico. Characteristically they are flattened, with a depressed back, slits for eyes and mouth, and a raised or pinched-up nose. Since they begin in the Vahki stage, and are at this time rather well done, it may be assumed that they were introduced from some outside culture, and again Mexico is the most logical source.

Dwellings are all of the pithouse type, and are relatively shallow in relation to their size. In fact some appear to have been houses which were

built in shallow pits rather than true pithouses in the sense that the earth
walls formed part of the structure. Of the earliest, or those few which may
at least tentatively be assigned to the Vahki stage, some are extraordinarily
large for a Southwestern pithouse, as much as about ten meters on a side.

HEADS   TORSOS

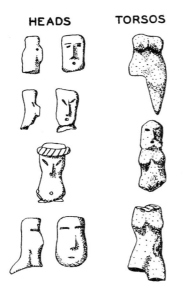

Fig. 45. Pioneer human figurines, heads and torsos. The
upper head is Snaketown,
the next lowest is Sweet-
water, the next both Sweetwater and Estrella, the lowest Vahki. The top two torsos
are both Sweetwater, and the
lowest is Vahki. The heads
particularly are reminiscent
of Mexican types.

Both in size and general arrangement they suggest some of the prehistoric
plains pithouses. The predominant form now seems to have been roughly
square, and in square footage, but not in shape, they are comparable to
the early Mogollon ceremonial structures. This fact has led Gladwin to
suggest that they well may have served a ceremonial function, and he has
further indicated that similar, though markedly smaller, more or less square
structures were the dwellings at this time. All follow a somewhat similar
pattern in that each possesses an entrance passageway, which was probably covered, and a firepit directly in front of it but within the structure.
The earliest houses had roofs which were supported by four posts set well
within the room, thus giving a central square top. Later, during the Snaketown stage, as will be seen, the support system changed, and the houses
became more elongated and with a tendency toward rounded ends. This
pattern seems to have prevailed subsequently.

The Estrella house, illustrated in the diagram of floor plans, also may
have been a ceremonial structure because of its size. It shows a surprising
number of support beams, a feature which apparently recurred in later
phases in the Tucson area. In this structure there is no definite arrangement
of roof supports, and in fact there are so many post holes that if they were

all utilized at one time it is hard to imagine how humans were able to occupy this room.

Over the supporting beams were laid cross sticks, bark, grass, or other material, and then a plaster cover. Viewed from the outside they probably

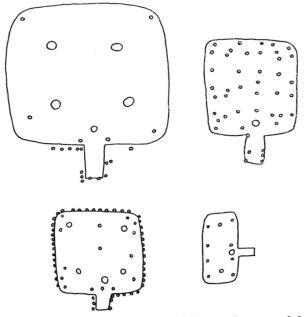

Fig. 46. House types of the Pioneer stage of Hohokam. The upper left figure is Vahki, the upper right Estrella, the lower left Sweetwater, and the lower right Snaketown. All are shallow pithouses, or houses built in slight pits. Fireplaces are near the entrances and the patterns of support posts are shown. All are drawn to approximately the same scale. The Vahki house is about 12 meters wide.

would have appeared more like mounds than dwellings, and from the inside they must have resembled a wood-lined cyclone cellar, or vegetable house.

One of the most consistent traits of the Hohokam, with very few exceptions, was the cremation of the dead, to the sorrow of the Southwestern archaeologist. Therefore it is not possible to give any data on the physical type of the river people. During all of the Pioneer stage bodies were cremated in fires which reduced them to small quantities of very badly burned and broken bones. These, with the equally fractured offerings of pottery, were buried in pits or trenches, which were dug through the looser topsoil into a hard layer of caliche or lime-impregnated earth. Throughout most Hohokam periods it was the custom to make burials in certain areas, so that once one is located others are almost certain to be found. No Estrella cremations were located at Snaketown, and burial offerings, such as stone objects, occurred mostly in the later Pioneer stages, the earlier Vahki offerings consisting almost wholly of broken pottery.

Stone culture of the early Pioneer stage is of interest because it was during this period that the foundation was being laid for the very fine stone work which was to follow. Although there were some vesicular basalt mortars and pestles they were certainly not the main grinding implements. For this purpose metates and manos were most generally used. The one-hand mano is the common type, and it had a convex grinding surface. Although only metate fragments were found from the earliest Pioneer stage it is quite probable that they were not markedly different from the open-end trough types that were typical from Sweetwater on. Corn was almost certainly grown by the Hohokam at this time, but just how important a part of the economy it formed is not known.

Stone palettes, used for the grinding of pigments, appear to have had their inception in the Vahki phase at the beginning of the Pioneer stage. The first forms are relatively small flat sandstone slabs, roughly rectangular in shape with rounded ends and corners and a flat grinding surface. From this developed, in the later stages of Pioneer, a more definitely rectangular form with a raised rim. A parallel has been drawn between these palettes and the assumed evolution of the metate, from flat slab to open end with raised sides.

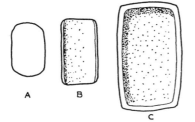

Fig. 47. Diagram of palette types of the Pioneer stage. A, a flat slab only, is the earliest type. B has a raised rim on the sides and strongly suggests the open-end type of metate. C is the latest type with a low raised rim about the entire edge.

No stone axes are known from the earliest Pioneer stages, but only from the Snaketown stage on, when they were apparently introduced to these people from some outside source.

Stone bowls were relatively abundant at this time, but none were ornamented with carved decorations. They are almost invariably inclined to be straight-sided, and are symmetrically made. This is, thus, the beginning of a tradition which later became one of the typical traits of the Hohokam culture.

Few arrow points have been found in this horizon, but enough occur to establish the use of the bow and arrow at this early date, a time almost comparable, if not actually so, with the occurrence of the bow and arrow in the Mogollon. These are light points of exact outline and careful work-manship. Heavier points, which have been considered knives or dart points, are somewhat more abundant and show much cruder flaking. Not enough of any of these have been secured to make it possible to establish character-istic types.

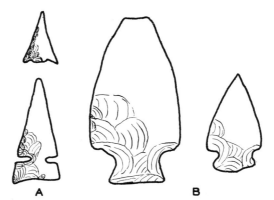

Fig. 48. Types of chipped stone points from the Pioneer stage. Those above A are fine, well-flaked points, probably arrow points. The ones above B are knives or dart points.

Because of the open nature of the Snaketown site, and in fact most of the sites in the desert area, no perishable material has been recovered from Pioneer horizons. Thus, nothing is known of cloth, basketry, sandals, and similar objects.

It might be added that such simple stone tools as hammerstones were found throughout these early stages, and whetstones were in the Vahki stage.

Ornaments at this time were relatively simple, but large bracelets, un-ornamented, were made from marine shells. Small disk shell beads were found in all of the Pioneer stages as well, and shells used as beads were found from the Estrella stage on. These consisted of such types as olivella and conus, all of which clearly show trade contacts to the Gulf of Cali-fornia. Incised bone tubes were also found from the Estrella stage on, with simple geometric designs.

From this it may be seen that even at the known beginning of Hohokam culture it was a relatively rich and quite distinctive complex. Many of the traits which later on became elaborated were now established. These people were occupying the major river basins in the desert area, and the way was open for them to become more fully rooted here and to develop their highly sedentary way of life.

BASKET MAKER I

Just what was going on in the plateau country to the north at this time is not known for sure. It has already been pointed out that later stages of Desert culture were found in this area, and it may be that an essentially Cochise way of life and type of culture survived here until Basket Maker II culture was established. It is hardly conceivable that this great area would not have been occupied at all, for certainly at least portions of it were inviting to man.

Scattered about in various parts of the plateau, sites have been located in the open which consist of village refuse materials but which lack pottery. Mostly they are indicated by the presence of chips of stone, scrapers and choppers, and generally a few projectile points. In the Cohonina area, for instance, there are several such sites known which appear to have been short-time campsites, for they lack any depth of accumulations. The projectile points found on them are not materially different from later types, but they lack the more elaborate evidences of permanent settlement and later cultures.

Perhaps these sites, the late Desert culture and the pre-pottery campsites, might be grouped together under the general heading of Basket Maker I, a stage postulated in the original Pecos classification to cover just such a general type of thing. In any event much more work and two kinds of information must be gathered before they can be definitely allocated to their proper niche in Southwestern prehistory. A number of these small sites must be adequately excavated and their contents classified; and sufficient carbon 14 dates must eventually be secured from them to demonstrate their age clearly. In the meantime all that can be done is to note their presence.

On the map for Mogollon (Fig. 33) the later survivals of the San Jose culture have been indicated. These also might be considered a sort of broad Basket Maker I. They are local developments, some of which may be traced back to far earlier beginnings. Possible Basket Maker I has been shown still farther north.

SUMMARY

One of the most difficult problems at present is that of determining the relative ages of the early stages of these cultural groups. It must certainly be admitted that this general Exploitation period is not well dated, and the culture stages at this time are not clearly defined. Only many more dates, derived presumably by carbon 14, and hopefully by an extension of the tree-ring series, will give definite answers to the many questions of age which may now be raised.

One of the most pertinent problems is just where the Estrella stage should be placed, here in this period, or later. The presence of decorated pottery in it, and the lack of such a type in early Pine Lawn, obviously raises the question of contemporaneity. It thus may well be that Estrella is later than early Pine Lawn, and should be so listed.

The house forms of Mogollon, in the central area of this culture at this time, seem to be predominantly circular, while the few known Hohokam structures are quite square. The presence in both of very large structures raises the question of whether or not these represent special ceremonial structures and not houses. There are apparently smaller, somewhat similar structures found in both at this time, and these latter may well have been the homes of the people. As house types are examined from east to west, or from clearly Mogollon to clearly Hohokam, they tend to blend, so that there is a zone where they are not clearly different.

In general the Hohokam seem to have been slightly more sophisticated in their stone work than the Mogollon. Perhaps even at this early date additional stimulus was being received by the Hohokam from Mexico, but if so it does not appear to have been very marked.

Mogollon culture was about to begin a rather wide spreading outward, to contact and influence the cultural development of other people. This was less true of the Hohokam, who were soon to become much more definitely tied to the soil, and so remained more localized. There was some early interchange of influence between Mogollon and Hohokam, but there was less evidence of Hohokam influence on other groups, particularly those to the north.

The two groups may be clearly identified at about this time in their home centers, but they do tend to intergrade to some extent, and as a result rather minor traits must be relied upon to distinguish them. In general these features are house shapes, and emphasis and elaboration of certain objects, particularly by the Hohokam. These differences are not so much of kind as of degree: Hohokam, for instance, made better or more elaborate stone work.

Sources and Additional References

Gladwin, H. S. Excavations at Snaketown II, Comparisons and Theories, *Medallion Paper 26*, 1937, Gila Pueblo, Globe, Arizona. (A most fruitful source of information on general problems relating to the Pioneer Hohokam stage.)

————. Excavations at Snaketown IV, Reviews and Conclusions, *Medallion Paper 38,* 1948, Gila Pueblo, Globe, Arizona. (Revision of the data reported previously for the Hohokam. Particular attention is called to the house-type revision.)

Gladwin, H. S., Emil W. Haury, E. B. Sayles, and Nora Gladwin. * Excavations at Snaketown, Material Culture, *Medallion Paper 25,* 1937, Gila Pueblo, Globe, Arizona. (Main present source of the material culture of the Pioneer stage. All of the illustrations have been taken from this work. To any serious student of the Hohokam it should serve as the basic work of reference.)

Jennings, Jesse D. The American Southwest: A Problem in Cultural Isolation, in Seminars in Archaeology: 1955, *American Antiquity,* Vol. 22, No. 2, Part 2, Society for American Archaelogy, Salt Lake City, Utah. (Discussion of the general nature of early Mogollon and Hohokam.)

Martin, Paul S. The SU Site, Excavations at a Mogollon Village, Western New Mexico, *Anthropological Series,* Vol. 32, No. 1, 1940, Field Museum of Natural History, Chicago. (First of three reports on the SU site, an early Mogollon village.)

————. The SU Site, Excavations at a Mogollon Village, Western New Mexico. Second Season, *Anthropological Series,* Vol. 32, No. 2, 1941, Field Museum of Natural History, Chicago. (As indicated by title.)

Martin, Paul S., and John B. Rinaldo. The SU Site, Excavations at a Mogollon Village, Western New Mexico, *Anthropological Series,* Vol. 32, No. 3, 1947, Field Museum of Natural History, Chicago. (As indicated by title.)

Martin, Paul S., John B. Rinaldo, and Ernst Antevs. Cochise and Mogollon Sites, Pine Lawn Valley, Western New Mexico, *Fieldiana: Anthropology,* Vol. 38, No. 1, 1949, Chicago Natural History Museum. (Excellent discussion of early Pine Lawn culture in the Pine Lawn area.)

Martin, Paul S., John B. Rinaldo, Elaine A. Bluhm, Hugh C. Cutler, and Roger Grange, Jr. * Mogollon Cultural Continuity and Change: The Stratigraphic Analysis of Tularosa and Cordova Caves, *Fieldiana: Anthropology,* Vol. 40, 1952, Chicago Natural History Museum. (Best general summary of this culture stage.)

Wheat, Joe Ben. * Mogollon Culture Prior to A.D. 1000, *American Antiquity,* Vol. 20, No. 4, Part 2, 1955, Society for American Archaeology, Salt Lake City, Utah. (Excellent summary and correlation of early Mogollon history, brought up to 1955.)

IX

Founder Period: A.D. 1 to 500

MOGOLLON

Almost from the very beginning of Mogollon culture certain characteristics were established which define it. Before this the Desert tradition had introduced agriculture into this area, and it continued and was presumably further developed. Brown and red pottery was typical, and was coiled and scraped, slipped, smudged, and polished. Large structures, assumed to be ceremonial in function, were found from the beginning of Mogollon, and were definitely earlier than those of the Anasazi. Somewhat later neck-coiled and textured pottery developed, again before similar types were found in the Anasazi. Sizable villages also characterize early Mogollon, of 10 to 30 houses located on ridges or high mesa and butte tops, but generally not on main routes of travel. Burials were made in pits both inside and outside of houses, and were flexed. These people collected and hunted as well as made some use of corn and bean agriculture. Stone tools were mostly a continuation of those of the later Cochise stages.

On this general base the later Mogollon culture was built, and it does not seem to have evolved as rapidly as some other cultural groups. It was, however, apparently a way of life which continued to influence the development of other people with which it came in contact, particularly to the north.

Reference to the accompanying map will show that Mogollon culture was spreading out from what may be considered the core area at this time, with extensions to the north, northwest, and even somewhat to the east. In the preceding period it was possible to identify the San Simon, Mimbres, and Pine Lawn branches, and during this period the Forestdale and Black River branches were added. The San Simon branch lies largely in Arizona to the southwest; the Mimbres branch to the east of it; and the Pine Lawn branch to the north, in the headwaters of the San Francisco River. The Black River branch lies to the west of the Pine Lawn branch in Arizona, and the Forestdale branch is in Arizona to the north. Thus it is possible to differentiate several identifiable branches at this time, each of which has certain more or less diagnostic traits.

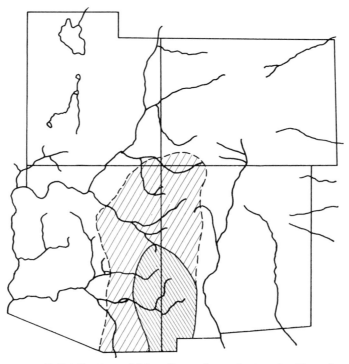

Fig. 49. The area of distribution of Mogollon culture during the Founder period, from the time of Christ to roughly A.D. 500. The area of fine hatching is the central area where the most typical culture of this time is to be found; the coarser hatching indicates the area of maximum spread and influence, as based primarily on the distribution of pottery types. It is also possible to speak of a northern and southern division, the southern with the first decorated pottery, the northern lacking it and having only plain types.

With the beginning of the first painted decorated pottery, it is apparent that two broad divisions of Mogollon culture may be made. To the south and west painted pottery is a part of the ceramic complex, while to the north and northwest plain pottery, often red or reddish and sometimes smudged, is found.

The most interesting new pottery type is Dos Cabezas Red-on-brown, which is an index type for the Dos Cabezas phase of the San Simon branch. The question of its derivation is not settled, for it may have been an outgrowth of either Alma Plain or San Francisco Red. The exterior is slipped red but not polished, and the interior has red designs consisting of broad lines and rectilinear patterns. The forms are deep hemispherical bowls, the decoration is on the interior, and it has been smoothed over after it was painted on the surface so that the edges of the lines fade somewhat into the background. The designs are most commonly broad chevron patterns and triangles pendant from the rim.

The question which is immediately raised is that of the relationship between this earliest painted Mogollon pottery and the first painted Hohokam pottery. Similar systems of design layout were apparently used, and the method of polishing over the decoration was the same. Typologically, and in general conception, the two are thus essentially identical, and there must have been some relationship between them. It will be recalled that Estrella Red-on-gray was placed in the preceding period when the Hohokam was discussed, but it should also be remembered that some question of the justification of this dating was raised. Since there is little doubt that the two types are related, the question remains as to which was earliest, and what gave rise to them. The dates of these stages are not exact enough to make possible specific determination of which was first. The similarity would suggest contemporaneity, and there is the probability that they at least overlapped somewhat in time. As to the stimulus which gave rise to them, the geographic location of the branches in which they are found, to the south and west, would clearly indicate that this practice came from the south. In fact decorated types did not occur in the north for some time.

The two other Mogollon pottery types of this period were Alma Plain and San Francisco Red. With variations in the preference of shapes they continued throughout the life of the Mogollon, and so might be considered diagnostic of it. Clearly related but variant types are to be found in the several branches at this time, and it may even be argued that such types as Rio de Flag Brown of the Flagstaff area were somehow derived from early Mogollon or similar Hohokam influences.

Almost from the beginning the way in which Mogollon pottery was finished was quite different from the Hohokam, and in fact this may be used to distinguish the two. Mogollon pottery was made by coiling and then was smoothed to final shape by scraping, or simply rubbing over the surface with a pebble or other polisher. This gave it a characteristic dimpled surface appearance, and this peculiar dimpling may be regarded as evidence of relationship wherever it is found, for it was not typical of other cultural groups. The Hohokam, on the other hand, almost from the beginning of pottery making coiled their pottery, and in the case of the larger jars finished them by the use of the paddle and anvil process. The anvil was used inside the vessel, and the paddle outside, to thin and give surface

Fig. 50. Pottery of the Founder period. The left-hand column is plain types, the central column is red types, and the upper right bowl is Dos Cabezas Red-on-brown, as is the design below it. This is the earliest type of decorated Mogollon pottery. The red paint is slightly blurred into the background.

finish to the pottery. This resulted in large shallow depressions on the inside, which may frequently be seen and may generally be felt in the cross section of a sherd. Not only did these techniques start almost at the beginning of pottery making in each culture, but they persisted throughout their history.

No clear-cut distinctions in Mogollon houses of this period have been made. In general they tend to be rather deep, and use has been made of the side of the excavation as an integral part of the structure, in distinction to Hohokam houses. They also have sloping entrances, which were covered, from the outside surface of the ground to the floor, and firepits in the rooms. Storage pits within the structures seem to have still been characteristic.

The method of disposal of the dead was by inhumation. The bodies were generally loosely flexed and buried in trash mounds, in storage pits, or in the open.

The physical type of the Mogollon has been a question of some interest, for Haury reports an examination made by Woodbury of the skeletal material found at Mogollon and Harris villages as quite distinctive. Although they are probably not quite as early as the period under discussion they may give some idea of the general type involved. Woodbury has classified these people as closer to a Caddoan group than to any other, and has characterized them as having low vaults and undeformed round heads. Other individuals from these sites are of the general Pueblo type. The sample is not large nor widespread, and may not therefore be typical of the Mogollon as a whole. A series of burials from the SU site all are unlike the Woodbury type, and very similar to the general Pueblo type as regards form, but were either not deformed posteriorly or very slightly so. Although too little work has been done on these people to make it possible to characterize them, the small amount of material measured to date indicates they were not like the Basket Makers of a comparable time.

In all sites of this period two types of metates have been found. One is the basin type, an apparent holdover from the earlier slab type of pre-pottery days, and the second a slab type open at only one end. This latter form has a lineal grinding face which resulted in raised parallel sides. The mano types seem to be similar to those already described from the preceding period.

Axes were lacking, but both full-grooved and three-quarter-grooved mauls are found. These continued with little or no change through the entire history of Mogollon.

Ornaments do not seem to have changed during this period, and projectile points are the same, or essentially so. The most common type of point is still that with diagonal notches which is rather broad in relation to its length. Perishable materials have already been discussed in general, and they also had not changed in any marked way. Feather and fur robes were clearly a part of this culture, but as has been indicated probably began slightly earlier.

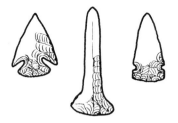

Fig. 51. The most common chipped point is that to the left. It is short and wide with diagonal notches. The drill is winged, or has an expanding base. The third point is heavier and not so well chipped.

Hunting implements were apparently still both the bow and arrow and the atlatl, the latter of which will be more fully discussed under the Basket Maker heading, as will several other types of artifacts. Food continued to be the same rather broad group of plants, the only change of particular interest being the beginning of an increase in the amount of 8-row corn over the previously more abundant 12- and 14-row varieties. This prob-

ably was an adaptation to the peculiar ecology of this part of the Southwest rather than a new import of corn types.

Bone and horn objects were also little if any altered. The bone awl with
the notch on the side, as indicated in the accompanying illustration, was
typical not only now but during the previous period and throughout most
subsequent Mogollon stages. In fact it seems to be more or less typical
of Mogollon culture wherever it is found.

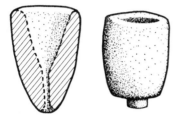

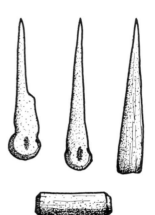

Fig. 52. Mogollon stone and clay pipes
are of two types. That to the left was
made in one piece, as is shown by the
cross sectional diagram. This type was
found at Mogollon Village. The one to
the right is of two pieces, a bowl and a
bone stem.

Fig. 53. The most distinctive bone implement is the notched bone awl as in the
upper left. The central illustration is of
the straight-edge split type, and at the
right is a pointed splinter. The bone tube
at the bottom is not decorated.

No particular ceremonial objects are known from this period. Large
structures which must probably be considered ceremonial in nature have
already been noted, and are still characteristic.

In general, culture now may be considered simply a continuation of the
preceding stage, with no marked additions or subtractions. The major difference as presently understood is to be found in the pottery types, which
are thus diagnostic of these stages. Painted pottery certainly had appeared
by now, particularly in the southern portion of the range, and in many
ways is reminiscent of the earliest Hohokam painted pottery. Both of these
types show a certain amount of careless smudging which occurred during
firing. Pottery which was deliberately smudged on the interior was found
in the northern portion of the Mogollon range, and soon after became the
most common form in this area. The real elaboration of surface manipulations in ceramics had not yet begun, but was soon to appear. All of the
Mogollon pottery may easily be distinguished from the contemporary

Hohokam pottery by the fact that the latter was made by the paddle and anvil process and the former was not.

Perhaps the most interesting feature of this Mogollon period was the spreading out of its influence over a comparatively wide area. This is particularly noticeable to the north and northwest, where, as has already been suggested, it took on some slight local variations. An example is the Bluff site, in the Forestdale valley, which has given dates in the vicinity of A.D. 300. The houses here are circular to rectangular, the latter often with entrances, and there are large circular structures which were probably ceremonial. The pottery is smudged on the interior, and includes both Forestdale Smudged and Woodruff Smudged. Forestdale Smudged has quartz sand temper, a smudged interior which sometimes spills over to the outside, a lustrous black interior finish, no slip, and a brown to reddish exterior. The form is limited to bowls.

In the Petrified Forest the Flattop site also has somewhat brownish pottery. Here the houses are more or less circular, many of them slab-lined, and sometimes with entrances. The native pottery is Adamana Brown, which has coarse sand temper, and tends to be from gray to red on the outer surface. Forms are dominantly jars and bowls, but there are some ladles, and many of the jars are globular. There is some question as to the method of manufacture employed, but it may have been paddle and anvil, thus raising the possibility that this particular type was ultimately derived from the Hohokam and not the Mogollon. However, the houses look more Mogollon than Hohokam, and the pottery is of the general brownish type most commonly thought of as Mogollon-derived.

From the foregoing it would appear that it was at this time, and immediately following, that Mogollon was at its most vigorous. It was beginning to come into contact with other people, and was soon to exert certain rather significant influences on them.

HOHOKAM

The later phases of Pioneer Hohokam, the Sweetwater and Snaketown, are simply evolutions from the earlier Pioneer phases. The general area which was occupied by this culture has not been more specifically defined, so that the previous map may be considered an indication of where it is found, but little more. The things which are diagnostic of this period are pottery, houses, and axes, with the production of other more and more elaborate objects, most of which were a part of the preceding period. Stone work, especially, shows a greater sophistication and imagination in production.

All of the pottery types which were found in the preceding period continue during this one, with the exception of the decorated type, Estrella Red-on-gray. The first of the new types, that diagnostic of the Sweetwater phase, is Sweetwater Red-on-gray. It is a red painted design on a gray to light brown surface which has been smoothed. Exterior coils are also incised with a sharp tool, to form a deep V-shaped groove, and are occasionally painted over with lines from the rim down. Definite hatching, some of which is rather fine and regular, is a marked style which distinctly separates it from the preceding type. It will be recalled that the earliest decorated

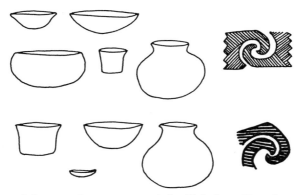

Fig. 54. Shapes and designs characteristic of the Hohokam Founder period. The upper five diagrams and design are all of Snaketown Red-on-buff. The lower four figures and design are all of Sweetwater Red-on-gray. The smallest diagram is that of a scoop.

Hohokam pottery consisted of simple designs in broad lines. As time went on these broad lines became narrower, and they were generally more carefully applied. See Fig. 44 for this evolution.

Snaketown Red-on-buff, the diagnostic type of the Snaketown phase, has a red painted design on a buff to gray surface which has been polished but not slipped. The background of this type is lighter, tending to be more buff than brown, and so distinguishable from that of the earlier types. More than half of the bowl exteriors are incised with very fine, regular, deep scratches. The outer surface also has a simple painted line. Very fine regular hatching is characteristic of this type, to distinguish it from the preceding.

Clay figurines are still a typical feature of the Hohokam, and those of the Founder period are not markedly different from earlier examples. Reference to the illustration in the preceding chapter will show this slight evolution. Both heads and torsos were still being made, the heads with hollow backs and the torsos somewhat suggestive of Basket Maker types.

Dwellings were all pithouses, in that they were constructed in shallow pits. During the Founder period, the predominant shape of the dwelling seems to have become more rectangular, but they had the covered entrance passageway, the firepit in front of the entrance, and a superstructure as already described. During the Snaketown stage the primary roof-support pattern, at least in some cases, changed from four posts to two on the central line. This led to the use of a ridge pole, and a framework somewhat like that shown in the accompanying illustration. This type of construction continued from the Founder period on, and as will be seen the major alterations which were effected concerned the nature and shape of the entrance. Large, presumably ceremonial structures were still being constructed, at least during the Sweetwater stage, but also there were somewhat smaller dwellings.

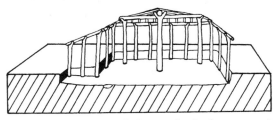

Fig. 55. Diagrammatic representation of the method of construction of a Snaketown-type pithouse. The framework only is shown here, the outer covering having been removed.

The main grinding implements of this period were metates and manos. The one-hand mano is the most common type, but some are obviously long enough to have been used with two hands. Although the corners are inclined to be rounded the manos are in general rectangular and were more or less brick-shaped, wearing down into thinner slabs after long use. The most typical metate is open at both ends, with relatively high sides and a slightly concave section both laterally and longitudinally. Into this fits the rectangular mano which was rubbed back and forth through the trough of the metate to grind the grain or other material. Even the outsides of these metates are rather formally shaped, and they are in fact quite definitely superior to the earlier basin-shaped milling tools. Corn was certainly available to the Hohokam, and a considerable dependence must have been placed upon it by now.

Stone palettes, used for the grinding of pigments, went through an evolution during the Pioneer stage. In the Snaketown stage there was a low raised rim around the outside of the grinding face, and although the sides and ends were slightly convex they were almost rectangular in plan. This marks the beginning of a rather long evolution and elaboration in the production of these objects.

The stone axe of the Founder period is represented first in the Snaketown stage, and is already a remarkably well-made tool. It is three-quartergrooved, long-bitted, and has very distinctive raised ridges around the groove. They are not only distinctive but on the whole they are excep-

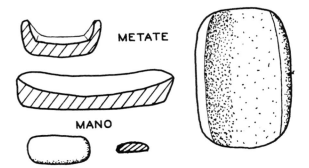

METATE

MANO

Fig. 56. Diagram illustrating metate and mano types. The right-hand figure is a vertical view of a metate, the two left figures are cross and longitudinal sections. The two lower figures are a vertical view and section of a typical mano.

Fig. 57. Type of stone axe characteristic of the Snaketown stage of the Pioneer Hohokam.

tionally well made and finished. Since they seem to appear suddenly, and are of this distinctive form, it may be assumed that they had a previous simpler evolution elsewhere. No mauls have been found with material of this period.

Stone bowls were relatively abundant, and are almost invariably inclined to be straight-sided and symmetrically made. Only during the Snaketown stage were they decorated, and then with relatively simple incised lines in straight geometric patterns. A very marked increase in the excellence of all stone work is noted now.

A few crude animal effigies, mostly of vesicular basalt, have been found which could be assigned to this period. In the last, or Snaketown, phase, a mica schist stone knife with serrated edges and attached shaft which had been carved out of one piece, as well as a carved slate resembling a curved wooden club, were found. These are exceptionally well-made objects and perhaps were originally designed for some sort of ceremonial purposes. A very well-made stone dipper is also of this stage.

Probably the most interesting object of this sort is a small human statuette, made of granite, also from the Snaketown phase. It was carved in the full round, and though not expertly done is rather well made. The figure is in a squatting position with a shallow bowl resting on the lap.

Projectile points have already been described for the Pioneer stage, and not enough have been found to make it possible to determine trends or preferences within this cultural stage. Both arrows and the atlatl seem to have been in use at this time, judging from the types of points found. If the carved stone mentioned above is a representation of a curved wooden club, this could be added to the list of weapons.

In shell ornaments whole shells continued to be used as beads, and shell bracelets were made. Apparently a few shell bracelets were carved with comparatively simple purely geometric designs, but they were not so elaborate as later examples. A certain amount of cutout shell, in the form of pendants, occurred now; some are simple silhouettes of animals.

As has been suggested, foods must have included corn (and probably also beans and squash), for the Mogollon culture certainly had it far earlier and there is much to suggest early contacts between the two groups.

Carved bone tubes were also made at this time, some with animals incised on them.

Ceremonial objects, except for the possible use of very large structures for this purpose, are not otherwise indicated.

In summary, pottery is probably the greatest aid in identifying stages of the Founder Hohokam period. Sweetwater Red-on-gray and Snaketown Red-on-buff are the two best indicators of this period. Other earlier types survive into and often through this time.

Houses seem still to have been represented both by large, perhaps ceremonial, structures, and smaller domiciles. Toward the end of this period houses became more rectangular, but all were built in relatively shallow pits. The fact that they are pithouses does not distinguish them, for all true Hohokam houses were pithouses. This generalization is likewise true of the disposal of the dead, for cremation was still practiced, and the remains were disposed of in pits and trenches, a trait which carried over into the next stage.

Of stone objects the most distinctive seems to have been the axe, with its markedly raised ridges about the three-quarter groove. The long slender bit and careful workmanship were carried over into later times. The stone palettes are also distinctive: rectangular with somewhat rounded ends and corners, and in their latest occurrence with slightly raised rims.

BASKET MAKER II

The cultures which are characteristic of the desert and mountain sections of the Southwest have been characterized, so that now the plateau remains to be examined. The earliest stage definitely recognized in the plateau is the Basket Maker. The name, it will be recalled, was derived from the fact that early excavators noted that certain burials found in the caves did not contain pottery but had a good many very fine baskets. Since that time much work has been done on this culture by Cummings, Kidder, Guernsey, Morris, Roberts, and others. These men have succeeded in contributing significant information to give a clear picure of just what pure Basket Maker was.

In the preceding chapter the question was raised as to whether or not certain remains in the plateau should be considered Basket Maker I, but no clear decision was reached. If Basket Maker I remains somewhat elusive, Basket Maker II is certainly well understood. Because many of the remains of this culture are found in dry caves, perishable materials have been preserved, so that there is a fairly complete list of traits. Almost certainly it has its roots back into what has been herein called the Desert culture, so that in this sense it has a very respectable antiquity. Also, if the relation-

Museum of Northern Arizona photo

One of the many caves in the plateau area which was occupied by people of the Basket Maker culture. The Basket Maker medicine bundle, pictured separately, was found here.

ships suggested throughout this book may be accepted it is the only true Basket Maker culture thus far clearly represented, for by the latter part of the next period it had apparently received a considerable series of influences from outside and was in a state of transition to what later became known as Pueblo.

A large series of dates have now been secured from this period in the plateau area, and it is clear that this culture began sometime within at least the first century A.D. The greatest difficulty has arisen in the problem of correlating dates and culture once they have been secured, for these people, as will soon be shown, apparently did not build definite houses over

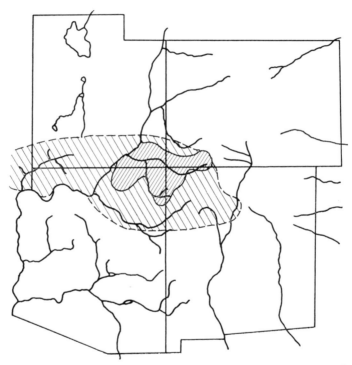

Fig. 58. Map roughly indicating the area of greatest concentration and the extent of Basket Maker culture during the Founder period. The area of greatest concentration is confined to the San Juan and is found particularly in the washes draining into it from the north. The area of maximum spread is probably much greater than that indicated, and even this is far from densely populated.

much of their range. The end date seems to be more solidly established than the beginning date.

Basket Maker II has been identified in the Pecos classification as the "agricultural, atlatl-using, non-pottery-making stage, as described in many publications." This brief statement is still useful in identifying this stage.

From the accompanying map, it may be seen that the heart of this culture is mostly confined to the San Juan drainage. Cummings has suggested Grand Gulch, Utah, one of the larger washes draining south into the San Juan River, as the one locality where the most characteristic Basket Maker II material has been found. If this be true it might be considered somewhat in the nature of a type area within the core area. Other places where it has been uncovered in a more or less pure state, by Cummings and other investigators, are Cottonwood Wash, Utah, the Monument Valley region of both Arizona and Utah, the Tsegi Canyons, the Cariso and Lukachukai mountains, Canyon de Chelly and Canyon del Muerto, and the adjoining country of northwestern New Mexico.

The map also indicates that sites, possibly less typical, have been found as far as southern Nevada, southwestern Utah, the White Mountains of Arizona, and over a relatively large area in northwestern New Mexico. Suggestions of a Basket Maker–like culture have come from even farther afield, including the Mississippi valley, Chihuahua, Mexico, and western Texas.

As true native pottery is essentially absent during this period in this area it is possible to turn immediately to a discussion of house remains. The first Basket Maker II houses which were found were those dug by Morris in the Durango, Colorado, area. The roughly circular single-room dwellings were up to 25 feet or more in diameter. The clay floors were shal-

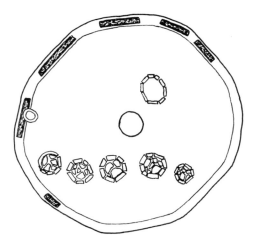

Fig. 59. Diagram of one of the houses found in the Durango, Colorado, area which is of this period and Basket Maker II culture. It is circular, has cists sunk into the floor, a central firepit, and walls built of logs laid horizontally. Maximum diameter is over nine meters.

low and saucer-shaped, with a firepit at or near the center. Characteristically there were a number of storage bins, which could be grouped into four kinds; large, deep, jug-shaped pits, slab-lined pits, slab-lined pits surmounted by above-floor mud domes, and mud domes entirely above floor level.

The floors turned up at the sides of the pithouse excavation and ended against horizontal logs. Above these, also horizontal, were pieces of wood of various sorts overlapping and interlacing, with mud used to fill the interstices and to chink and point up the structure. The wall supported a cribbed roof, so that no interior roof supports were needed. No walls were found standing high enough to indicate entrances. Many of these houses were burned and tree-ring dates were secured from them, mostly falling in the second and third centuries A.D.

Morris has suggested that although similar structures are not known from much of the rest of the area occupied by this culture it is quite possible that they may have been in vogue, for they are anything but obvious. In the Navaho Reservoir area in the Los Pinos phase, which dates from about the time of Christ to perhaps A.D. 400, though they clustered mostly in the A.D. 100 to 200 range, a total of 24 sites were found which contained from 1 to 11 structures. They were generally located on knolls. These houses are also large circular houses which are not really pithouses. The earliest houses lack cobble rings around them, and actually contain the most pottery; the late houses have rings of cobbles surrounding them, and some have antechambers, apparently the earliest known from the Southwest. Some unfired vegetable-tempered pseudo-pottery was found here, and a few sherds and vessels of the very rare Los Pinos Brown. This type has sand temper, and was almost certainly derived from the Mogollon area, either directly or indirectly. It will be recalled that brown and red types of pottery date earlier in the Mogollon. Thus, the earliest known houses in the plateau come from southwestern Colorado and northwestern New Mexico.

In the rest of the area no true houses have thus far been found, but this may mostly be the result of excavations of this period being largely confined to caves. Almost all of these caves are in the San Juan drainage. This led to the original assumption that these people were shallow-cave dwellers, but the more recent finds of houses have raised the question of whether or not they lived mostly in the open and used the caves only seasonally when in search of wild foods and for storing them.

Cummings in his class lectures described two kinds of shelters that he found here. The occupants seem to have scooped out a shallow depression in the back of the cave and lined it with leaves, shredded cedar bark, or similar material. A windbreak of piled-up rocks or poles leaned against the back wall and perhaps covered with skins or blankets completed these "nests." Such a shelter can hardly be called a home, and the idea that there were more substantial structures elsewhere is very appealing.

Although the occupants of the caves do not seem to have had true houses in them they certainly did construct some very excellent caches, or storage pits. Cists are essentially circular in form and were dug into the loose fill of the caves, or in the bottoms of canyons in the open. Those which are in loose material are almost invariably lined with rocks to hold back the slop-

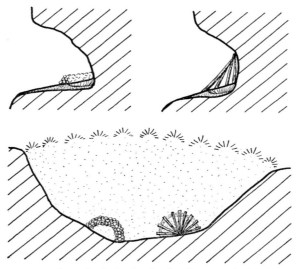

Fig. 60. Nests were sometimes built in the back of a cave behind a windbreak of rocks or poles, somewhat like those indicated above. It is always possible, of course, that such structures really are the work of later people.

ing sides. Some are also paved with a flagging of flat rocks, although others are simply clay-lined. The average is from three to five or six feet in diameter and eighteen inches to two feet deep.

These cists were primarily used for storage bins, for from them quantities of cached materials have been removed. The method of roofing varied from covering with one large flat slab of stone to poles laid across the top, covered by brush, and then by sand. The fact that most of these pits have been carefully covered and that many of them now contain stored materials would suggest that, for at least part of the time, the owners were away from the caves in which the materials were found. The economy of the Basket Makers was about equally divided between hunting and agriculture. As a result it is likely that treasured articles, grain, and seed foods were cached here while the owners were away hunting, and at least occasionally never returned for. A secondary use to which cists were often put was the reception of burials, for many fine mummies have been secured from them.

Surprisingly enough the physical type of pure Basket Makers is not well known. Hooton lists a series of San Juan Basket Makers in his report, "The Skeletal Remains of Pecos," but he does not state whether they are Basket Maker II or III and does not give the number of the series measured. Although many skulls and mummies have been found, no serious study seems

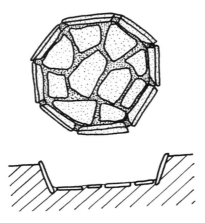

Fig. 61. Cists, such as the one pictured above, are typical of this culture. Some are slab-lined, others have plastered clay walls and floor, but all are more or less circular.

to have been made of these people. Of two things we may be fairly certain. None of the skulls show any flattening of the posterior portion, possibly the result of the use of a soft covered cradle in infancy, and many of the skulls are long in relation to their width. In many the top of the skull

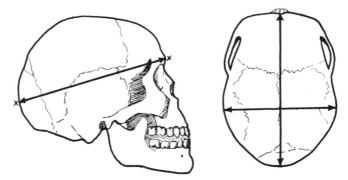

Fig. 62. The true Basket Maker skull appears to be long-headed, though not markedly so, as in the illustration. The heavy lines indicate the position and direction of the length and breadth measurements used in determining whether a skull is long, medium, or broad-headed.

also seems to show a slight peak or ridged effect, and although the eyebrow ridges and other processes are more marked than in later Pueblo types, the bones themselves are not heavy. As to the exact nature of the rest of the body bones there seems to be some disagreement in the writings of the authorities who have mentioned them, some suggesting they are heavier than those of the Pueblo people. Adult males seem to have been of fairly good size, one mummy which the writer has seen being nearly six feet long.

Burials are always flexed, sometimes tightly so, and are occasionally wrapped in a robe. Over the head of the body a large flat basket is almost

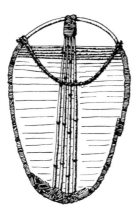

Fig. 63. Cradles are more or less flexible and made of light materials such as the one above of reeds. They were covered with shredded juniper bark or tanned mountain sheep skins to form a pad so that the back of the skull was never deformed.

invariably found, and with many a new pair of sandals was included. As has been suggested, many burials are in stone-lined cists, and it is possible that the small size of the cist led to the custom of flexing, in which the knees are drawn up to the chest and the arms are usually extended at the side.

Cradles are of considerable interest, for they are definitely of a type different from those used by the Pueblo people. A typical cradle consisted of a more or less oval frame upon which were lashed cross reeds to make it firm but still somewhat flexible. Over this was placed a padding of shredded juniper bark, mountain sheep skin, or some similar soft material. In the example pictured, a human-hair rope tie is shown. Others have been found in which the backing seems to have been made of cord netting. It is assumed that the soft cradle permitted a normal development of the back of the skull, whereas the Pueblo baby board, which was at least in some examples firm, did not, and so deformed the posterior of the head of these later people.

Metates and manos continue older types and seem to have been relatively rare, although corn was grown. The prevailing type has the flattened surface ground to an oval depression. It is assumed that this was a result of a circular or oval motion in grinding, as compared to the lineal movement of the later types. Manos are either rounded or oval. Corn was certainly ground on these implements as well as acorns and some of the more compact berries and seeds which were collected.

Probably the most interesting stone objects are the points, which are relatively large but many of which are beautifully flaked and shaped. They were made mostly by percussion, although some secondary pressure flaking was used. Because of their size and more or less uniform shape, it is assumed that they were atlatl dart points and not arrow points. Many have diagonal side notches for securing them to the atlatl dart foreshaft; some apparently do not. Larger blades are assumed to have been knives. Atlatl points seem to vary from about one and a quarter to one and half inches long, while knives are sometimes twice that length. They are made of chert, chalcedony, and other fine-grained rocks.

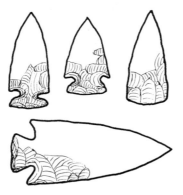

Fig. 64. Both points and knives are illustrated above. The points are atlatl dart points and are larger and heavier than most Southwestern arrow points. Larger knives, like the above, appear to have been rare.

Basketry is outstanding. In any group in which there is very little or no pottery some such industry as basketry usually is of magnified importance. These people seem to have expended most of their artistic effort on basketry and fiber fabrics such as bags and sandals. With the development of pottery by later groups there was a shift of emphasis to that medium. Baskets were made in two weaves. By far the most elaborate forms were produced by the coiled technique. This was the building up of the container from the center of the base by a growing spiral coil which was continually sewed to the one just below. Two rods were included in the coil to give the vessel stiffness, also a bundle of grass or other fibrous material, which gave the coil bulk and formed a mass through which the splint could be sewed. The second technique was twining, in which radiating rods formed the basis and about which other splints or rods were intertwined. This formed a coarser container and was used for the larger and cruder baskets.

Basket forms are very distinctive, the most common being the large shallow traylike baskets. These are from 3 to 4 inches deep and from 12 to 24 inches in diameter. Bowl-shaped baskets, with a tendency to flattened bottoms, are more rare. Decoration was effected by dyeing the sewing splints either black or red before they were included in the basket, thus giving three colors, black, white, and red. Water-carrying baskets were made with an almost pointed bottom and were covered with pitch. These are somewhat suggestive of Paiute forms. The carrying basket included in the illustration was either very rare or did not occur this early. The twilled weave was apparently not in use before Pueblo culture became well established.

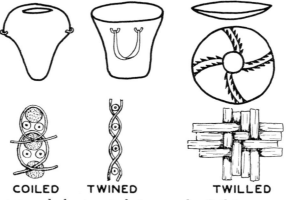

COILED   TWINED   TWILLED

Fig. 65. Baskets are made by two techniques only. Coil types are of two rods and bundle, with the sewing splints passing through the underlying bundle. Certain baskets were also made by the twine technique. No twilled baskets are known from this period or culture. The upper left figure is a pitch-covered coiled water basket. The loop ties are of human-hair cord. The right figure is the typical large shallow basket with design. The central upper figure, a carrying basket with tump strap, may not have been typically Basket Maker, for the specimen pictured is a Pueblo I example. The twilled weave was probably introduced sometime near A.D. 700.

Sandals are probably one of the most distinctive traits of these people. At this time all the sandals made were square across the toes. Some had a fringe of buckskin or shredded juniper bark at the toe. Even now there appear to have been two general classes of sandals, one of a very fine weave and made of cords, the other of a coarser weave made of partly shredded or whole leaves. The yucca plant furnished the material from which they were made, as it has a very tough leaf with long fibers extending from the tip of the leaf down into the roots. To secure these fibers the plants were collected by being cut off at the root, then allowed to decompose partly while moist, and finally were beaten, probably between two pieces of wood, to crush off the softer tissues and leave the long tough fibers. From this material, and apocynum, a plant related to milkweed, cords often of two strands and sometimes in two colors were twisted. The cords were then woven into various objects, one of which was the better class of sandal.

Ties were of two distinct types. The most common seems to have been one in which a loop for the toes and another for the heel formed the base, with variations over the arch of the foot. Another type had a series of cord loops around the edge of the sole across which various ties were attached over the foot. No other decoration was found on these sandals.

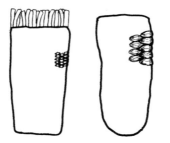

Fig. 66. Basket Maker II sandals all have a more or less square toe. Some have a buckskin or fiber fringe; others do not. Both fine twined weaves and coarser weaves appear to have been typical, the coarse probably for general wear.

Another feature of Basket Maker culture seems to have been the manufacture of cloth bags. These were woven in twined weave, and many have a colored woven-in design. Bags are all inclined to be somewhat larger at the bottom than the top. This technique of producing a clothlike fabric definitely antedated the vertical or true loom in this section.

Shredded cedar-bark bags were also produced. The bark was shredded and grouped into long bundles or rolls which were either woven together or tied together by cords to produce a sort of rectangular, blanket-shaped, heavy pad. The ends were then turned back to meet in the middle and were

Fig. 67. Bags made of fiber cord are typical of this culture. They are made by a twisted twine weave which starts at the bottom of the center of the bag. Some are plain but others have a colored woven-in design. The detail of weave to the right is what is known as "coil without foundation," and is a technique by which other articles were made, and at later dates.

fastened along the side. This produced an envelope open down the middle of the top, to some extent suggesting the hide storage bag or "trunk" of Historic plains Indians. These bags were used for the storage of such large objects as corn on the cob and were often placed in cists. Mats of shredded cedar bark, whole yucca leaves, or even reeds were made in the simple over-and-under weave and used as floor or house coverings.

The only fabrics at this time which approached cloth in weave, appearance, and form were feather and fur robes. These were made by splitting soft feathers down the vane, or cutting rabbit or other fur into strips, and winding them about fiber cords. The method by which this was done is shown in the accompanying illustration. One strip was lapped under and over the other to continue the winding. These fur- or feather-incased cords were then placed parallel to each other and in contact and tied together by twined cross cords. This produced a heavy but very warm blanket or robe which appeared as a solid mass but was quite open. The Hopi and Paiute Indians still make similar fur blankets.

Such blankets were apparently necessary because of the comparatively small amount of clothing worn by these people. Besides sandals and blankets the only piece of clothing worn by the men was a G-string. This was made of yucca fibers looped over and attached to a cord. The cord went around the waist and the fiber mass was drawn down between the legs and up the back to be looped over the cord. Women supplemented sandals and blankets with a short skirt of fibers which was suspended from a cord around the waist. One very complex leather moccasin is also of Basket Maker age, although it was foreign to this culture.

Fig. 68. Robes were made by twisting split feathers or strips of fur around a cord and then tying this together with twined stringers. The upper figure shows the method of twisting a fur strip, the lower a detail of how the strips were held together. This resulted in a soft and very warm blanket.

Fig. 69. Skin bags, as the above, are typical. They are skins of small animals tied at the mouth.

Not only were woven bags made, but skin bags formed from the whole skins of small animals were used. These were made by skinning the animal forward from the back legs to the nose, and tying or otherwise closing the mouth, eye, and foreleg openings. Apparently small objects were kept in these bags, particularly collections of odd-shaped stones and ceremonial articles.

Of the few weapons known and used by these people, the atlatl and atlatl dart seem to have been the principal hunting and defensive tool. The accompanying diagram illustrates both these objects. The atlatal dart was a light spear five to six feet long and about half an inch in diameter, and was made of two parts. The foreshaft was a cigar-shaped short section of hardwood which had the attached stone point at one end and was somewhat pointed at the other. The shaft was of a lighter wood with a small hollow or pith center and conical holes drilled at both ends. The foreshaft fitted into the front end and apparently was made detachable. The butt was for the reception of the prong on the atlatal. Feathers seem to have been generally used but were not carefully applied, for although three were most common two or four were sometimes used, but apparently at other times none.

The atlatl was a flat, slender, flexible piece of hardwood, the purpose of which was simply to act as a lever to extend the arm during the cast. The upper surface was flat, the lower slightly convex. The handle was shaped at one end, which ended with two loops, usually of leather, through which the fingers were inserted. At the other end, on the upper surface, was a groove which terminated with a small point flush with the surface. This was to engage the butt of the dart. On the underside small stones called atlatl weights were sometimes lashed. These are assumed to have been charms, for they could have served no useful purpose. The atlatl illustrated has two such stones.

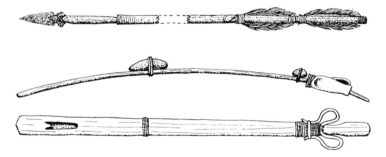

Fig. 70. The top illustration shows an atlatl dart with the mid-portion removed. It consists of a feathered shaft and a short hardwood foreshaft with the point. This is really a light feathered spear. The atlatl shown in side and top view is a flexible throwing board which acts on the principle of the lever to lengthen the arm. This specimen has two weights, or charms, attached to its underside.

In throwing the dart the atlatl was gripped in the hand with the flat side upward over the shoulder. The first and second fingers were hooked through the loops and used to steady the board. The butt of the dart was placed in the groove against the point, and the shaft steadied with the thumb and third finger. The cast was made overhand by releasing the dart during the foreward throw. Such hunting devices have had a widespread distribution throughout the world but as compared to even a moderately effective bow and arrow are rather poor implements. The aim is not so accurate as with the bow, nor is the range so great, although the shocking power with the heavier atlatl dart was probably more.

Grooved clubs are also a characteristic feature of this culture. They are made of wood and are about three feet long. Four longitudinal grooves incised into each side extend from the handle to the top. These lines are always broken at one place in their length. It has generally been accepted that they were used as rabbit sticks, in a manner to be described later, but in a conversation with the writer Mr. Amsden suggested that they might also have been used as fending sticks in conjunction with the atlatl. They are similar to such sticks used for this purpose elsewhere.

Food is represented by a great variety of animals, some of which were relatively large. Deer and mountain sheep were commonly killed, and all the small rodents were trapped. Some very ingenious nets and snares were devised for this purpose, one being the purse type. Large nets suggesting tennis nets, made of cords, were probably used to catch rabbits which were driven into them. Human hairs were also made into snares for birds. Vegetable food was also varied, apparently consisting of every edible seed and nut, as well as berries. Agriculture consisted only of corn, squash, beans, and possibly the sunflower. Corn was of the yellow flint variety, and the ears, by later standards, were very small, almost what a Midwestern farmer would call "nubbins." No stone hoes were known in this area; the wooden agricultural implements developed at this time seem to have carried

Fig. 71. Basket Maker and Pueblo agricultural implements are digging and cultivating sticks as in the illustration. Some have straight points and crooked or straight handles; others have blades. The former were probably for planting, the latter for loosening the soil.

through all subsequent periods and cultures in the plateau. Pointed sticks, some with crooked handles, were used in planting and perhaps in breaking the soil. Sticks with flattened blades, as in the illustration, were also used to loosen the soil, and possibly for weeding. However, agriculture was not a basic industry to these people, their efforts apparently being about equally divided between hunting and farming. The only domesticated animals were

the dog and perhaps the turkey, which was certainly domesticated in the
following period.

Ornaments, though not greatly varied, are distinctive. Stone beads of
both globular and elongated forms are typical. They are made of hard stone,

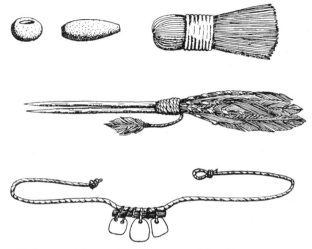

Fig. 72. Basket Maker people made great use of feathers as ornaments. The central
figure is probably a feather hairpin. The two upper left illustrations are stone beads,
the right a grass-stem hairbrush. The lower necklace is of the short choker type with
a loop and toggle tie, and is very characteristic of these people.

some of granite, and are highly polished and drilled. Acorn cups and a
variety of small hard seeds were also drilled and strung. However, the most
distinctive ornaments seem to have been feathers. These were sometimes
attached to strings which were apparently tied to the hair, or were fastened
to sticks bound together to suggest combs. Some combs in the succeeding
period were made by tying several pointed sticks together like high Spanish-
type combs and were ornamented with beads or other objects. The short
choker-type cord necklace is also typical. It was only long enough to go
around the neck, and was fastened in the back by a loop and toggle. Most
of these had ornaments, such as pendants, tied to only a short section of the
front portion. Although not ornaments, hairbrushes made of grass stems
bundled and tied together might be mentioned at this time. Such objects
are still in use by the Hopi Indians.

Cylindrical pipes of both stone and clay are very characteristic. They
are long and slender, or short and squat, as in the illustration. Stone pipes
were often made of slate, banded or plain, and were drilled from both ends.
Occasionally a bone tube was added to short forms, but the long slender
straight pipe seems to have been most typical. Many of these objects were

finely made and polished, and apparently they were prized possessions of the Basket Maker people, for they were often buried with the dead.

Bone implements seem to have been much less abundant than at other times or in other cultures. The awl appears to have been most commonly of

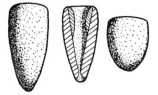

Fig. 73. Straight stone and clay pipes are very common to this group. Some are longer and more slender than others, and a few have bone stems as already described and pictured.

the short type pictured, or made of a splinter of bone sharpened at one end and perhaps spatula-shaped at the other. Split deer metatarsals, with the head left, were either rare or lacking. Bone tubes, used as beads, and bone tube whistles, often of bird bones, were made at this time. The whistle carries over to modern Hopi Indians in much the same form. Bone dice were also a distinctive trait. These are small oval or rounded-end fragments of polished bone which have varying numbers of incised lines crossing their faces. It has been suggested that they are gaming implements because of their similarity to bone dice used by the Pueblo Indians in gambling games today.

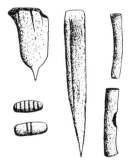

Fig. 74. Bone awls do not appear to have been made of split deer metatarsals. Bone dice with incised lines and bone tubes and whistles are all typical.

Fig. 75. The wooden doll figured is reported by Guernsey. It may represent a pre-pottery figurine effort of these people.

Guernsey reports the finding of a small wooden doll, as shown in the illustration. As no pottery was known to these people they could not make fired-clay human figurines, and this may perhaps represent the same idea expressed in wood. Probably it was made as a plaything for a child.

In summary an unusual list of characters are found to be typical. The area occupied is primarily the San Juan drainage, most of the known sites being located in the deep box canyons so characteristic of this section, though others are in the open. Simple, relatively large, circular houses are known from the eastern part of the area, and shelters or windbreaks which may have belonged to this culture have been found in caves. Stone-lined circular cists are typical, and were used for burials or as storage caches. The physical type is at least in part long-headed, approaching medium-headed, and is never deformed posteriorly. A flexible oval cradle covered with shredded bark or other padding was used. The metate has an oval grinding face, never a lineal one. Points are atlatl dart points, longer, broader, and heavier than later arrow points. Stone knives, larger than these points, are rare. The most typical basket is the large, flat, traylike basket which usually accompanied burials and was placed over the head. Other deeper and more bowl-shaped baskets are rarer. Sandals are one of the best diagnostic traits of this period: they are always square-toed, sometimes fringed. Bags were made in the twined weave. Robes, probably of both feather and fur, were made by tying together wrapped cords into the form of a blanket. Skin bags were also made of the whole skins of small animals. The atlatl and atlatl dart are characteristic, as is the grooved club. Food consisted of wild plants and animals and a small variety of yellow flint corn. Ornaments may be characterized by the profuse use of feathers. These occur attached to combs or to cords. Large round and drop-shaped stone beads are very characteristic, in fact one of the diagnostics of these people. Tubular stone and clay pipes are almost equally characteristic, as are bone dice. Seed beads of various sorts are also important.

Of this long and impressive list certain features may be considered distinctive of the Basket Maker II stage of culture. Probably the most distinctive are the square-toed sandals and the stone beads. To these may be added the undeformed skull, flexed burials in cists, and the use of the atlatl and atlatl dart. Not only does positive evidence help to identify this group but the definite lack of certain other features is equally important. Pottery is very rarely present, never in sun-dried form, and the bow and arrow is absent, as is cotton.

SUMMARY

During the Founder period decorated pottery was made by both Mogollon and Hohokam, but very little if any true pottery was made, insofar as is now known, by typical Basket Maker II. The decorated pottery was in comparatively simple designs, often at first only wide lines in chevron patterns, in red-on-brown and red-on-buff colors. Some plain brown pottery was found to be rather widespread in the Southwest, throughout much of western New Mexico and into northern Arizona. The question remains as to whether or not these occasional vessels were made locally or were traded to these areas from the Mogollon or Hohokam. Both scraping and polishing and paddle and anvil methods of finishing were used on these vessels, so that much still must be done to determine their specific origins.

At the beginning of this period the decorated pottery of both Mogollon and Hohokam was similar in design, and even somewhat alike in form, but toward the end of the period the two ceramic traditions became more distinct. In the area between typical river Hohokam and the characteristic Mogollon intergrades in pottery types began to appear, and this same variation is indicated in house types.

Houses were found in all major areas and in each of the cultures at this time. Mogollon and Basket Maker houses were essentially circular in general plan, but the Hohokam houses were rectangular, and late in the period began to have more rounded ends. Most were pithouses, or at least houses built in pits of varying depths. In general the Mogollon houses were deeper than those of the Hohokam, and from what little is now known of Basket Maker houses they varied considerably in depth. Large structures, which may well have been ceremonial, were definitely a part of the Mogollon, and may have been Hohokam. So little is known of Basket Maker houses of this period that it is not possible to be sure whether or not kivas were present. In the following period they were found.

Both Mogollon and Basket Maker traits may generally be traced back to their origins in the earlier Desert culture, and in stone work to the Cochise or Cochise-like cultures. Many traits are thus shared. Hohokam also showed Desert culture beginnings, but even now was including elaborations not found in the Mogollon or Basket Maker. Many of these advancements, and they are particularly apparent in stone work, pottery designs, and structures, probably were derived from Mexico. Earlier Mexican influences are indicated with the introduction of agriculture and pottery, so this is a continuation of this process, or a second wave of such stimuli.

Much information is available for this period in the caves occupied by both the Basket Makers and the Mogollons, and this has made possible a much fuller idea of the traits of these people than of the Hohokam. It is in these very things that the two show many parallels. Probably if such objects were also known from Hohokam even more similarities would be evident.

Thus the further back in the tracing of these cultures one is able to go the more alike they seem. This may be partly a result of the fact that earlier cultures, and so artifacts, were simpler than later ones, or, as has

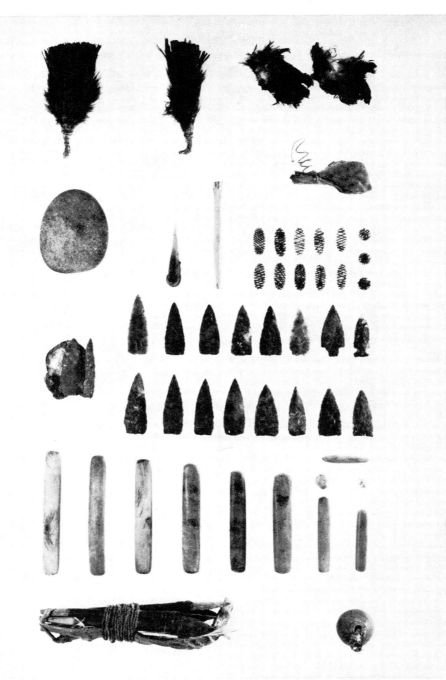

Museum of Northern Arizona photo

Contents of an early Basket Maker medicine bundle. Note the bone dice, the feather ornaments, and the atlatl dart foreshafts tied together with a string.

been suggested, it may be because they sprang from a general way of life which has been called the Desert culture. The more recent these cultures become the more differences are to be found in them, and this again is only what might be expected as a result of some regionalization and slight isolation. They were each beginning to develop localized and so somewhat independent ways of life, and this will be seen to be emphasized more and more as time goes on.

It is the beginning of these differences in various areas which has led to the suggestion that such regionalizations should be somehow recognized and specified. Haury, in the work at Ventana Cave, became aware that there were differences between the river Hohokam and those of the drier areas away from the rivers. To distinguish these two groups he has proposed that the river people be called the riverine or typical Hohokam, and that the others be called the Hohokam of Papagueria.

Di Peso, in his work in the area around Dragoon, sees another distinguishable segment of this general development which he has proposed be called Ootam. This includes some of the intermediate cultural developments previously referred to, and is thus both culturally and geographically identifiable.

Both of these are usable and perhaps quite valuable concepts, and we will see other similar suggestions of cultural groupings and designations in other areas slightly later. Examples are divisions within the Patayan of the Colorado River culture area, and such cultural segments as Sinagua and perhaps Salado. These are all valid and useful, depending on the degree of detail which is being considered at the moment. For our purposes they need only be noted at this point.

At about this time agriculture became much more important in the way of life of all of these people. Although corn had been known for about 2,000 years, as has been mentioned, it was treated much as other wild plant foods were treated, and it was not until it became more intensively cultivated that there was a real cultural stimulation in the Southwest. After it assumed greater importance in these groups they enjoyed a sort of cultural explosion, and the way was open for them to develop very rapidly in subsequent periods.

Sources and Additional References

Amsden, Charles Avery. The Ancient Basketmakers, *Masterkey*, Vol. 12, No. 6, November and following, 1938, Southwest Museum, Los Angeles, California.
———. Prehistoric Southwesterners from Basketmaker to Pueblo, Southwest Museum, Los Angeles, California, 1949. (Basket Maker culture described.)

Danson, Edward Bridge. An Archaeological Survey of West Central New Mexico and East Central Arizona, *Papers of the Peabody Museum of American Archaeology and Ethnology*, Vol. 44, No. 1, 1957, Harvard University, Cambridge, Massachusetts. (Distributions of cultures and the various regions are pointed out herein.)

Dittert, Alfred E., Jr., James J. Hester, and Frank W. Eddy. An Archaeological Survey of the Navajo Reservoir District, Northwestern New Mexico, *Monograph 23*, 1961, Museum of New Mexico, Santa Fe. (Description of Los Pinos phase houses in this area.)

Eddy, Frank W., and Beth L. Dickey. Excavations at Los Pinos Sites in the Navajo Reservoir District, *Papers in Anthropology 4*, 1961, Museum of New Mexico, Santa Fe. (Report on a Basket Maker II site in this area, which is related to the Durango sites in Colorado.)

Gladwin, H. S. Excavations at Snaketown II, Comparisons and Theories, *Medallion Paper 26*, 1937, Gila Pueblo, Globe, Arizona. (As indicated by title.)

————. Excavations at Snaketown IV, Reviews and Conclusions, *Medallion Paper 38*, 1948, Gila Pueblo, Globe, Arizona. (Re-evaluation of the Hohokam culture at Snaketown.)

Gladwin, H. S., Emil W. Haury, E. B. Sayles, and Nora Gladwin. * Excavations at Snaketown, Material Culture, *Medallion Paper 25*, 1937, Gila Pueblo, Globe, Arizona. (The most complete discussion of Hohokam culture of this period.)

Guernsey, Samuel J. * Explorations in Northeastern Arizona, *Papers of the Peabody Museum of American Archaeology and Ethnology*, Vol. 12, No. 1, 1931, Harvard University, Cambridge, Massachusetts. (Discussion of Basket Maker culture.)

Guernsey, Samuel J., and Alfred Vincent Kidder. * Basket Maker Caves of Northeastern Arizona, *Papers of the Peabody Museum of American Archaeology and Ethnology*, Vol. 8, No. 2, 1921, Harvard University, Cambridge, Massachusetts. (The above two papers are basic to the problem of Basket Maker II.)

Haury, Emil W. * The Mogollon Culture of Southwestern New Mexico, *Medallion Paper 20*, 1936, Gila Pueblo, Globe, Arizona. (Original identification of the various divisions of Mogollon culture.)

Haury, Emil W., and E. B. Sayles. An Early Pit House Village of the Mogollon Culture, Forestdale Valley, Arizona, *University of Arizona Social Science Bulletin 16*, 1947, Tucson. (The Bluff site, a northwestern extension of the Mogollon culture at this time.)

Kidder, Alfred Vincent. An Introduction to the Study of Southwestern Archaeology, Phillips Academy, Andover, Massachusetts, 1924. (Basket Makers are discussed under the heading of "Sites Without Pottery [Basket Maker].")

Kidder, Alfred Vincent, and Samuel J. Guernsey. * Archaeological Explorations in Northeastern Arizona, *Bulletin 65*, 1919, Bureau of American Ethnology, Washington, D.C. (Fine source of data on Basket Maker culture from the western portion of the San Juan.)

Martin, Paul S., John B. Rinaldo, Elaine A. Bluhm, Hugh C. Cutler, and Roger Grange, Jr. * Mogollon Cultural Continuity and Change: The Stratigraphic Analysis of Tularosa and Cordova Caves, *Fieldiana: Anthropology*, Vol. 40, 1952, Chicago Natural History Museum. (Best statement of general Mogollon culture of this period.)

Morris, Earl H. * Archaeological Studies in the La Plata District, Southwestern Colorado and Northwestern New Mexico, *Carnegie Institution Publication 519,* 1939, Washington, D.C. (Read particularly the introduction for a discussion of the Basket Maker culture of the four corners area.)

————. Basketmaker II Dwellings Near Durango, Colorado, *Tree Ring Bulletin,* Vol. 15, No. 4, 1949, Tree Ring Society, University of Arizona, Tucson. (As indicated by title.)

Morris, Earl H., and Robert F. Burgh. Anasazi Basketry, Basket Maker II Through Pueblo III: A Study Based on Specimens from the San Juan River Country, *Carnegie Institution Publication 533,* 1941, Washington, D.C. (Thorough description of Basket Maker baskets.)

————. Basketmaker II Sites Near Durango, Colorado, *Carnegie Institution Publication 604,* 1954, Washington, D.C. (As indicated by title.)

Nusbaum, Jesse L. A Basket Maker Cave in Kane County, Utah, with notes on artifacts by A. V. Kidder and S. J. Guernsey, *Miscellaneous Paper 29,* 1922, Museum of the American Indian, Heye Foundation, New York City. (Report of a site which is far to the west but much of the culture of which is typical Basket Maker.)

Sayles, E. B. The San Simon Branch, Excavations at Cave Creek and in the San Simon Valley. I. Material Culture, *Medallion Paper 34,* 1945, Gila Pueblo, Globe, Arizona. (Description of the Penasco phase in this area.)

Wendorf, Fred. Archaeological Studies in the Petrified Forest National Monument, *Bulletin 27,* 1953, Museum of Northern Arizona, Flagstaff. (The Flattop site is of this period in this part of northern Arizona.)

Wheat, Joe Ben. * Mogollon Culture Prior to A.D. 1000, *American Antiquity,* Vol. 20, No. 4, Part 2, 1955, Society for American Archaeology, Salt Lake City, Utah. (Characterization of the various branches of Mogollon culture at this time.)

X

Settlement Period: A.D. 500 to 700

MOGOLLON

The distribution of Mogollon culture of the Settlement period is not greatly different from that of the preceding Founder period. The core area is a little larger, and the maximum extension to the north, east, and west is perhaps a little more. A number of sites to the northeast and northwest of the core area had what appear to be Mogollon-derived pottery types. As will be seen by reference to the Basket Maker map, much of the same area is included in this Mogollon distribution, so there is definite overlapping of the two cultures. The same is true with Hohokam on the west, in which direction various degrees of intergradation are found.

It will be suggested that this intrusion of relatively early Mogollon culture into the Basket Maker area was responsible in large part for the alterations which took place in Basket Maker III at this time. In any event there can be little doubt that the two groups were in contact with each other. Many of the modifications of Basket Maker culture were the addition of the kinds of things which had already been established as a part of Mogollon, such as pottery and house forms, and even the large ceremonial structure, or kiva. All in all this was a period of considerable intermingling of influences.

The extension to the south into Mexico has been shown, for surveys in northern Mexico indicate that Mogollon culture definitely extends some distance in this direction. It is not fully understood just how far it goes and exactly what the nature of sites of this period were. One reason why it is assumed that it must have had a considerable southward extension is that many Mogollon traits were derived from Mexico, and these must have traveled upward through northern Mexico to reach the Southwest proper.

Pottery shows relatively minor variations and additions to what was made before. The forms are perhaps a little more varied, and the deco-

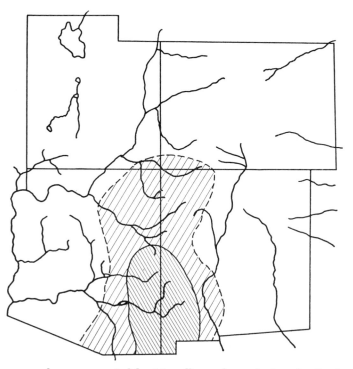

Fig. 76. The general area occupied by Mogollon culture during the Settlement period. Comparison to the other maps at this same time will show that there is considerable overlapping. This is because all areas where a substantial quantity of Mogollon pottery has been found have been included within the broader extent of this culture.

rated types seem to have slightly more elaborate designs. They are not, however, as elaborate as those of the Hohokam at a comparable period. San Francisco Red and Alma Plain continued to be made, and were by far the most abundant pottery of this period. Variations of Alma Plain included neck coiling and some texturing, and the smudging of the interiors of plain types was relatively common in the north. Decorated pottery seems to have been limited to bowl forms.

Alma Neck Banded and Alma Scored are forms of Alma Plain with the same heterogeneous angular and rounded temper. Alma Plain has an unslipped surface, sometimes polished with a tool inside and usually outside, and rare smudging in bowl interiors which may not be intentional. Alma Neck Banded is distinguished by broad coils, averaging about one centimeter wide at the neck, and from two to six in number. The coils are flat, laid up with a slight overlap and very rarely indented with the finger. The coils were frequently polished over, and sometimes almost obliterated, which gives the neck a somewhat fluted appearance. Just when within the period this type of pottery was made is not quite clear, but it was almost certainly earlier than similar neck banding in the Anasazi, and probably some years previous to neck banding among the Patayan. This was the beginning, then, of a technique which became popular in other areas later. At first this type was limited to jar forms, although later it included pitchers as well.

Fig. 77. Shapes of Mogollon pottery found during the Settlement period. The upper left-hand figure is the only decorated form. The bowl below it is San Francisco Red, and the bottom one is plain. The left-hand jar is red, the two lower jars are plain forms, and the upper right is Alma Neck Banded, the only form known.

The decorated pottery which may probably be assigned to this period is San Lorenzo Red-on-brown. The temper is predominantly white angular particles and some rare quartz grains which are rounded. The exteriors are usually rough and dimpled, as a result of pressing the coils down with the fingers and polishing over them. The interiors of bowls are scraped until smooth, then polished, but they are never slipped. The paint is a reddish brown, and of the same type as the slip used on the exteriors. The painted lines are blurred on the edges as a result of rubbing the surface after it was decorated. The designs, all geometric, are poorly executed, with variable-width lines and overlapping corners. The interiors of bowls were often broken up into four equal quadrants and the same simple design painted on each. Only lines and triangles were used.

In many respects this pottery is reminiscent of the presumably earlier Dos Cabezas Red-on-brown. The fact that it is limited only to bowls, the general elements and layout of the design, and the habit of blurring the painted design slightly into the background are all similar. That they are related or derived types can hardly be doubted.

Houses are still pithouses, are relatively deep with long entrances, and are more or less circular in plan. The structures found by Haury at Mogollon Village and the Harris site have a fireplace in the floor near the entrance and a central support post. There are secondary posts around the outside of the structure. Some of these houses tend to be flattened on the side toward the entrance, and they are of two sizes, large, suggesting ceremonial use, and smaller, probably habitations. This general type of structure seems to have been typical of this culture and at about this time period over at least part of the area occupied by the Mogollon.

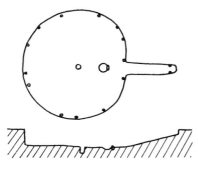

Fig. 78. A general diagram of the type of structure found in Mogollon culture at this time. Note particularly the central support post, the firepit near the entrance, the general round shape, and the long entrance.

Unfortunately archaeologists have made divisions within the various cultural streams, as phases or foci, which do not exactly correlate in time between these groups. This is partly a result of the accident of the order of excavation, wherein one segment is defined and others compared to it, and partly because each different culture did not change at the same time but had an independent, or somewhat independent, evolution. This is true of all three of the major groups now being discussed. Added to this is the fact that as work goes on in each culture definitions of the phases or foci are sharpened, and from time to time the duration of any given stage is redefined. Since the Anasazi sequence of the plateau area was the first to be dated by tree-ring methods, and so was the first culture and area where stages could be quite accurately assigned to time periods, the chronology developed here has been used for correlation with the other groups.

For these reasons, and because not too many dates have been secured even yet for Mogollon in many areas, the culture now under discussion cannot be placed exactly within the time span allotted to the Settlement period. There is little doubt, however, that it falls somewhere within this time span, for sufficient dates have been secured, either by direct tree-ring dating or cross finds of dated pottery types, to make such a correlation possible.

The materials preserved in Tularosa and Cordova caves have greatly expanded the list of artifacts which now may be ascribed to this culture stage. Many of the stone artifacts continue with little or no alteration, but some of the perishable items do show change or additions, and many indicate parallels with those of the Basket Maker III stage in the north.

Basin, slab, and scoop metates are all found, and the manos are mostly definitely one-hand, either round or oval in plan. There are a few pebble mortars, some made of boulders, and plain stone bowls continue. Points are rather slender with lateral notches and expanding stems, or are diagonally notched. Atlatls and darts, and bows and arrows, are both indicated. There are fewer flake knives, and flanged drills decrease in numbers. There are also, of course, blade scrapers and choppers. Basketry is of the two-rod and bundle, the half-rod and bundle, and the bundle types in coiled examples. The coil without foundation weave is found now as well. Twilled and twined matting was made, as well as the fur and feather robes which have been seen before. Both plaited sandals and multiple-warp sandals were made, and leather bags continued. Other clothing consisted of string aprons for the women. There were also flexible cradles and net carrying bags, and the burden strap, or tump line, was in use.

A partly flexed burial uncovered by the Museum of Northern Arizona near Flagstaff. This is the usual Mogollon method of burial. In a more tightly flexed position the knees would be drawn up almost to the chin.

In food habits there seems to have been a tendency at Tularosa and Cordova caves for a greater dependence on the gathering of wild plants than had been the case earlier. Eight- and ten-row corn was replacing the types of higher numbers. In ornaments whole shell beads were still being used, as were the other shell objects. Stone and pottery pipes were made, and reed cigarettes were commonly in use by this period. There were also both human and animal figurines. Painted sticks were rare but present, and the reed tube was found from this point on in this culture. Plain bone awls increased, and bone fleshers were made.

A few examples of unfired pottery were found in the work in the caves. This was apparently originally a lining of baskets, and may have been used for parching. Reference to the discussion of Basket Maker III will show the parallel in this trait.

In general Mogollon culture now shows less in the way of innovations than the other two groups which are about to be discussed. One has the impression that it was a very vigorous early culture which somehow failed to alter and develop as rapidly as other groups. Perhaps the geographic location in the mountain section had something to do with this apparent lack of progress, or perhaps the fact that it already had many of the traits that others were acquiring at about this time makes it appear more retarded by comparison than it actually was.

In summary most of the pottery types continue to be made, but with the addition of texturing in the otherwise plain types, such as the roughening of the surface in Alma Rough, and the coiling of the necks in Alma Neck Banded. The decorated pottery is very simply ornamented, with designs that seem to be more like earlier examples from the southwestern portion of this area than more advanced types. In fact the entire matter of what now appear to be lags in the correlation of general design styles is difficult to explain. It has been seen that quite possibly Hohokam had about the earliest decorated pottery, then in the western part of the Mogollon area similar styles appear, and finally the same styles are found farther east, more in the heart of the Mogollon country. If this be true these very simple design styles lagged considerably in diffusing over a relatively small area, and is one of the few cases where such a lag is apparent in the Southwest.

In other traits only relatively minor features are added to or modified from earlier types. The many parallels which will be seen with Basket Maker III have led some to postulate that the two were actually the same, and so to doubt the validity of Mogollon. However, enough distinctive traits will be noted to separate definitely these two cultures.

HOHOKAM

In the preceding chapters the most outstanding traits of Pioneer Hohokam have been briefly reviewed as illustrated by the finds made at Snaketown. Since it is the only site of this stage of culture which has thus far been rather completely dug and fully reported, it must be relied on for information concerning Pioneer Hohokam culture. As it was an unusually large village, even for the Hohokam, it undoubtedly assumed a position in this prehistoric group somewhat comparable to that held by one of the larger cities in our own culture. It is in such dense metropolitan areas that the leading craftsmen are concentrated and so the majority of out-standing art objects produced. As a result the picture obtained from this site is probably not quite typical of that prevailing in the average small village of this area and time.

Three Colonial Hohokam sites have been dug and reported on, thus probably giving a much broader and perhaps truer picture than that of the Pioneer stage. A large portion of Snaketown was found to be of this culture, and because it is most meticulously reported will serve as a basis of comparison and characterization. Since so few sites of either Pioneer or Colonial Hohokam have been dug so far, additional work will probably modify what is now known concerning them.

The Colonial stage has been divided into two phases which are based on cultural distinctions and represent temporal horizons. Although these two phases are distinct they are in many ways not so well marked as comparable periods in Pueblo culture. The earliest, or Gila Butte, has been dated from about A.D. 500 to 700, and is the one with which we are primarily concerned here. The later or Santa Cruz phase lasted from about A.D. 700 to 900.

As tree-ring dates are wholly lacking in the desert area, dates applied to this section must be derived from well-dated northern pottery types which have been traded to these people. Not only have Basket Maker III and Pueblo I sherds been found at Snaketown but the same types were also found at the Roosevelt and Grewe sites, which are also Colonial. The two most common of these traded types are Lino Black-on-gray and Kana-a Black-on-white, the dates of which have been listed in the dated pottery types in the pottery chapter. From these several checks it is pos-sible to assign convincing dates to these two phases.

The accompanying map is an effort to indicate, at least approximately, the range of Colonial Hohokam culture. The data from which it was made were secured by Gila Pueblo from a widespread sherd survey in the des-ert area, and the relative percentages of the sherds which were diagnostic of culture stages were carefully plotted. These charts were then compiled into a series of maps which include most of the sites diagnostic of these stages. This, and other maps in this book, have subsequently been some-what modified as a result of further surveys, and through interviews with many of the individuals at work in this area. The fine-hatched portion is that which contains the most typical sites of this stage; the outer area is simply intended to give a general idea of the maximum limits to which marked influence succeeded in spreading. It may be seen that the Colonial culture lies in the Middle Gila, centering on the Gila and Salt rivers, and extends only slightly farther west than their junction. Even at present it is not possible to distinguish the geographic distribution of the two branches concerned, for they are apparently in about the same area, and thus only one map has been prepared of the entire Colonial stage.

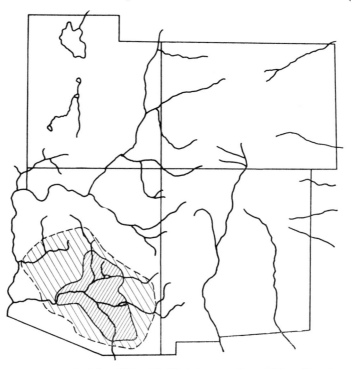

Fig. 79. The area occupied by Colonial Hohokam culture. No effort has been made to distinguish between Gila Butte, which falls in the Settlement period, and the later Santa Cruz phase. It will be noted that though the center of the area is along the rivers, the most extensive evidence of this culture is much wider, going almost to the Colorado River to the west and up the Verde. These people were essentially tied to the rivers at this time.

Hohokam culture at about this time appears much more stabilized than during the Pioneer stage and it developed a more distinctive general character. The alterations which are apparent at about A.D. 500 and immediately following are great, probably somewhat comparable to those changes from Basket Maker to Peublo in the north. Mexican influence is clearly indicated at this time in several specific traits, and this must have been a rather close contact. Not only did the arts become more standardized but also Hohokam influence, even at this relatively early date, appears to have been spreading widely to other areas.

Pottery here, as well as elsewhere in the Southwest, is one of the best indicators of culture. As has already been stated, Gila Plain carries through all Hohokam stages in some abundance from its first appearance in the Estrella phase of the Pioneer stage. Beside Gila Plain, Gila Butte Red-on-buff is characteristic of the Gila Butte phase of the Colonial stage.

Gila Butte Red-on-buff is of particular interest in that it is probably somewhat transitional between the decorated Pioneer types and the later well-standardized Colonial types. It was made by the paddle and anvil process, but the surfaces are smoothed, the first wash or slip being applied to this type. The color is buff, although fire clouds are common, a fact which tends to darken the otherwise light color. Forms are bowls, possibly the most outstanding character being the tendency to flaring rims, jars, scoops, plates, and pedestal vessels. Although hatching still appears, the most characteristic feature of the designs of this period is the greater abundance of small repeated elements and short parallel lines, often as a fringe. Shallow incising into the plastic clay of the surface with a blunt instrument is also very characteristic of the outsides of bowls and jars. Red lines were frequently drawn slanting downward from the rims over the incised parallel lines on the outsides of bowls.

Fig. 80. Gila Butte phase Hohokam pottery forms and designs. All of the forms left of the design elements are decorated, as is the upper jar to the right. The two bowls and the other jar to the right are plain. Scrolls and small, much-repeated design elements like those shown are typical of the pottery of this period.

Clay figurines were found only at Snaketown, where enough occurred to establish a type for this period. Both heads and torsos were still being made. The Gila Butte type seems to be characterized by the presence of incised eyebrows.

There is some question as to the exact house type of this period, but some houses were elongate rectangular pit structures, sometimes with rounded ends, and characteristically with rounded corners. Although houses of this general stage are quite large, those at the Roosevelt site averaging about 12 by 20 feet, they are relatively shallow, usually from one to two feet deep. In general Hohokam houses were built in pits, rather than utilizing part of the side wall of the pit itself. A sunken en-

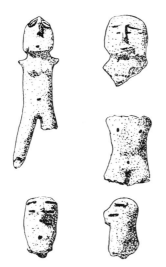

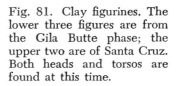

Fig. 81. Clay figurines. The lower three figures are from the Gila Butte phase; the upper two are of Santa Cruz. Both heads and torsos are found at this time.

tranceway gave access to the level of the floor at one of the long sides, and directly in front of this was the firepit. The low two-post gabled type of roof was apparently still generally used, and the sides of the dwelling were enclosed with a "wattlework" wall of reeds which was probably plastered over.

One of the most striking and interesting features of this entire culture is the presence of what have been definitely identified as ball courts. Several have been more or less excavated, and a number are known throughout the desert country. The ball court found at Snaketown is a large and imposing structure, and it has so many striking features that there is no doubt as to its identification. A playing floor was excavated into the caliche of the original ground surface to a depth of some four or five feet, and the dirt removed was piled around the periphery to form a wall probably not less than 15 and possibly 18 feet or more high. In the exact center of the floor a stone marker was embedded. The floor, 56.25 meters long and 18.75 meters wide, is in the form of a long oval with almost parallel sides and more or less rounded ends. Although the side walls form a steep angle with the floor the ends rise gradually to a cleared area which terminates with a low artificial wall.

The original ball court at Snaketown was built during the Gila Butte phase but was altered twice, once during the Santa Cruz phase and again

apparently at its end. This would place the building of the court sometime before A.D. 700 and the final alteration near A.D. 900.

The aboriginal ball game, played in similar courts, is best known from
Central America, where Spanish accounts of the Maya game of "Pok-ta-

Fig. 82. The large ball court found at
Snaketown. The floor of this structure is
56.25 meters long and 18.75 meters
wide. It was probably between 15 and
18 feet deep at the time it was in use.
1 locates the center marker, 2 the end
markers, 3 the raised cleared end areas,
and 4 the raised portions delimiting the
end areas. A game like "Pok-ta-pok" was
played in it.

pok" are fairly complete. It was played with a solid native rubber ball
for points which were scored by striking the ball through rings set vertically into the sides of the court. The player could use only parts of the
body other than the hands or feet. Similar accounts come from Mexico,
but here no definite ball courts are known, although they are found as

Courtesy of the Arizona State Museum

The large ball court at Snaketown half excavated. The playing floor and the side walls
are apparent, and some idea of the size of the structure and the height of the walls
may be gained by reference to the figures.

far south as South America. It is an odd fact that the only prehistoric rubber ball known from this entire region comes from the desert section of Arizona.

The amount of labor which the construction of such a court as this represents, when the primitive implements with which the work was accomplished are recalled, certainly indicates such an exceptional social organization and direction as to warrant admiration. This is paralleled only by the construction, during the next period, of extensive irrigation ditches which carried water for several miles from the main streams to agricultural terraces below the villages.

The universal Hohokam practice of cremation leaves no data as to the physical type of these Indians. Burials consisted of the cremated bones of individuals together with the fire-broken and often somewhat melted objects burned with the bodies, which were collected and deposited in a shallow depression in the caliche hardpan beneath the soil fill. It will be recalled that the characteristic method of disposal of the charred bones during the Pioneer stage was in trenches instead of in individual pits.

Stone implements are abundant, very characteristic, and well made. Metates are of the trough shape, open at both ends, and usually long and slender. Some are carefully shaped on the outside to conform to the grinding surface, others are only crudely shaped, or perhaps not shaped at all, on the outside. Manos are of the block type, some being exceptionally well made.

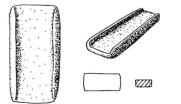

Fig. 83. Long slender metates with raised sides and block- or brick-shaped manos are typical of this period.

Fig. 84. Stone palette with a raised rim bearing longitudinal incised lines and with a groove around the outside edge. It is made of slate.

Palettes had by now become much more standardized than during the preceding period, and had evolved into such a highly conventionalized form that they no longer bore any real resemblance to metates. They are characteristically made of slate, carefully worked down to a thin rectangular slab with a low raised rim about the periphery. The rim generally bears incised lines, usually not deeply cut, which form a design parallel to the edge. These objects are characteristic of the Hohokam culture of the desert area. The use to which they were put remained problematical until Haury uncovered some with the remains of pigments still adhering to them. The labor necessary to produce such a palette would suggest a purpose other than strict utility.

Stone bowls were also much more elaborate than those of the Pioneer stage. They are more carefully made and finished with both incised and some raised designs. The best of these objects were produced during the following period.

Another most interesting feature of the Hohokam of this time are stone disks which served as bases for mosaics of plates cut from pyrite crystals. These mosaic plaques are almost identical with pyrite mosaics known to have been in use in Mexico, and are in fact one of the best indications of contact with, or at least influence from, Mexican cultures. The base of the plaque is a thin smoothed sandstone slab, slightly rounded or beveled at the edges and drilled with one or two holes as a method of attachment. One flat surface is covered with the pyrite crystal mosaic, so arranged and joined that the individual pieces present a smooth flat surface which is essentially metallic and suggests a mirror. It is also quite possible that lignite buttons from the later Pueblo culture in the plateau are an attempt to produce similar mirrors.

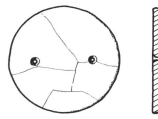

Fig. 85. Stone base of a mosaic pyrite mirror. These are characteristically Mexican objects.

Fig. 86. Stone axes, though well made, are not so striking as Pioneer types. They are shorter and lack the raised ridges around the groove.

The stone axe differs markedly from the Pioneer type in that the raised ridge bordering the groove is lacking. It is also characteristically shorter in the bit, and altogether more stocky. The only type is the three-quarter-grooved axe. It is made of volcanic rock and is well finished. Mauls do not seem to have been used, but hammerstones are relatively abundant.

During this period the projectile points were well made, were long and slender, or comparatively so, and had a tendency toward serrated edges. The stem was short and there were slight wings on the sides at the base as a result of the diagonal notches which formed the stem.

Little is known regarding the hunting implements of these people, except that they had and used the bow and arrow, since the small light points must have been used on an arrow.

Ornaments were most striking and well made, and probably more than anything else the Hohokam people excelled in carving shell. Most outstanding of such work were the bracelets, many of which were carved in relief, and a few were cut out by carving so deeply as to cut through the shell. Designs are geometric, many simply of incised lines, but others represent conventionalized life forms. Disk and tubular shell beads were common, the former occasionally being double-lobed. Olivella shells were used as beads simply by grinding off the end and stringing, or grinding down further and using much as a disk bead. Olivella shells were also strung when only the spire was broken off, and conus shells were drilled in the spire portion to form pendants. Occasionally other flat whole shells were drilled near the beak portion and used as pendants.

Fig. 87. Carved shell bracelet. This frog decoration is an example of one of the simplest of these carved shell ornaments, many being much more complex. The Hohokam people excelled in shell carving.

Disk stone beads and stone pendants were manufactured in some abundance and in various forms. Most of the pendants were flat or silhouette representations of various animals. Turquoise inlays, mostly rectangular or square, were apparently made even as early as the Pioneer stage. Painting was practiced both on shell and stone ornaments, but was used rather sparingly.

Bone objects are less abundant and striking than shell. Apparently bone beads are lacking in this culture, and bone awls are certainly not common, the few known being predominantly of the pointed sliver type. It was not until the succeeding period that much use of bone and horn seems to have been made.

In summary it has been shown that the area occupied by the Hohokam at this period is much better known than that of the preceding period, and many more sites have been located. Pottery is rather characteristic, the most outstanding feature probably being designs, wherein the profuse use of small repeated elements is noteworthy. The most distinctive form is the flaring-rim bowl, as well as the pedestal plate. Figurines are probably more definitely standardized, although certainly little if any better made. The incised eyebrows are the most consistent characteristic.

Pithouses are relatively shallow, long structures, with rounded corners, or ends, and an entranceway on one of the long sides. The large ball

court, which Haury has named the "Snaketown type," is a most outstanding architectural feature. In stone objects the craftsmanship is better and
the forms are more varied. Stone palettes are typical, and stone bowls are
more ornate. The pyrite mirror is distinctive. Carved shell shows much
variety and imagination, and is very skillfully made.

Many features of this period of the Hohokam are found to reflect certain Mexican or Central American influences. Most striking identities are
the mirrors. Ball courts also certainly show some relationship to the south,
probably having been derived from this quarter. Trade relations of so
richly endowed a site as Snaketown were probably widespread, and it
may have been by this medium that some of these traits reached the
Hohokam.

BASKET MAKER III

In the preceding chapter Basket Maker II culture has been identified
as the earliest well-defined stage represented in the plateau. Basket Maker
III in many ways appears to have been an evolution of this culture, attain-
ing a slightly higher level in most traits and with the introduction of a
few new and distinctive characters. Almost certainly most of these traits
came from people with whom the Basket Makers were in contact. As a
result, before the end of this period radical changes were under way which
became much more intensified during following times.

This period and culture may be dated with much more accuracy than
the preceding, for a great many more tree-ring dates have been secured.
The earliest definite dates from a Basket Maker III house have been secured and reported by Morris. The earliest of these are near the end of the
fifth century, specifically A.D. 475. Although the beginning date of 500 remains somewhat vague, the end date of about A.D. 700 is much better established. Certainly in many areas by this time a Pueblo I type of culture had
evolved. There is some evidence that this period could with profit be split
in half, the earlier portion being confined to those people who did not have
pottery and the latter half to those who did.

The Pecos classification has defined this culture as the "pit- or slab-
house-building, pottery-making stage," and to this is added the following:
"Pottery is characterized in general by coarse lines, simple designs, many
basket designs, and some crude life forms, generally a relatively coarse
paste, and globular forms."

The area which it occupied is to be seen on the accompanying map,
where it becomes immediately apparent that an eastward extension has
taken place. The southern extension which includes the Little Colorado
valley did not have a very dense population except along the several large

washes draining southwestward out of the Hopi country. The area of maximum occupation is marked by very few sites, and these are probably not quite typical Basket Maker. In no section, however, was a very dense population found, for the nature of the economy prevented large settlements.

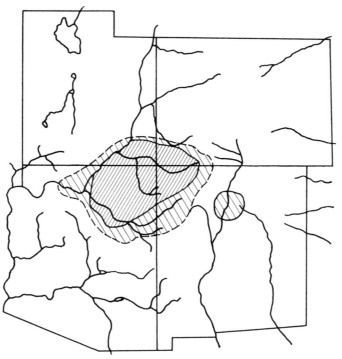

Fig. 88. Area of greatest spread and concentration of Basket Maker III culture. The most typical and abundant sites are still found in the San Juan drainage, but a few people of this culture had spread down to include the Little Colorado valley. There also seems to have been a slight shift to the east.

The earliest houses appear to have been a natural evolution of the houses and cists of the preceding period, for many of them are actually little more than elaborated large cists with roofs. They are circular, or roughly so, some egg-shaped in plan, and range from one to five feet deep and from nine to twenty-five feet in diameter. In soil which would permit, the walls were clay-plastered, while in looser soil they were slab-lined, occasionally the floor being slab-covered as well. Houses of this type have been found both in caves and in the open, and in these forms range from Navaho Canyon through the San Juan to Chaco Canyon on the east. Firepits are usually near the center, and occasionally small slab-lined storage bins are on one side.

The main distinctions which may be drawn in this type of house lie in the methods of roofing. Cummings has described in his classes an arrangement of small poles set about the periphery of the house which were drawn together and tied in the center of the roof. An opening was left on one side,

One of the late Basket Maker circular slab-lined pithouses found by the Museum of Northern Arizona near Grand Falls on the Little Colorado River. This structure has a floor ridge radiating from the firepit.

and the poles were covered with mats or brush and finally plastered over. A second much more characteristic type apparently was the four-post arrangement, in which the posts were set into the floor in the form of a square. These supported the roof beams, against which side poles were leaned from the edge of the excavation. The poles were then covered with brush or matting, and the whole plastered over. The result was a house rectangular and flat at the top, but with a circular ground plan. A third type of roof was formed by placing the four support beams on a small shelf or banquette and pointing them in to meet in the center. This would have resulted in a quadrilateral pyramid effect.

To the east, at Shabik'eshchee Village in Chaco Canyon, Roberts found circular and almost rectangular pithouses with quadrilateral post arrangements, but with two extraordinary features. On the floor of several of these rooms were low ridges of clay which led from the firepit, near the center, to the walls diagonally through the front corner posts. Morris reports essentially the same arrangement from his work in the four corners area. Roberts also found several definite entrances, some slab-lined, a few of which expanded into a small antechamber or an alcove-like second room.

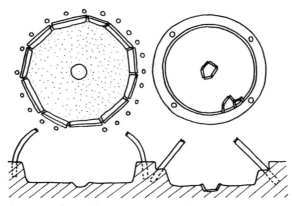

Fig. 89. More or less circular pithouses are typical of Basket Maker III culture. Some are slab-lined, others only clay-lined. Two types of roofing are found: those in which poles are set on the rim and bent over to meet in the middle, and four posts either set vertically in the floor or slanting in from a bench on the sides. Some of these houses are egg-shaped or oval.

At Kiatuthlanna circular pithouses had somewhat similar features, but there the entrances were replaced by ventilators. At Grand Falls, on the Little Colorado River, the writer found late houses with the floor ridge and entrance.

Thus the house type at this time seems to have been very varied regionally. In the western San Juan proper, houses are circular and rarely have the peculiar features that are found to the east or southeast, although the floor ridge was found in the Kayenta area. Even though these sites apparently fall late in the period they are much more elaborate than those of the west and lend weight to the feeling held by the writer that the new influence came from that direction.

Another site, Alkali Ridge, in southeastern Utah, is probably a more or less intermediate culture between Basket Maker III and Pueblo I. It was dug by J. O. Brew for the Peabody Museum. Houses are like those of Chaco Canyon, having floor ridges and ventilators or alcoves. In form they are both round and almost rectangular. Of even more interest is the presence of a red-on-orange or brown pottery, called Abajo, which to the writer strongly suggests Mogollon ceramic influence. The same type of site has been reported by Morris. Houses are the same, with antechamber and floor ridges, and the storage rooms in a block behind these houses are identical. Latest types show the use of some of these storage rooms as living rooms.

The cultural instability and unrest, which was even then evident, probably resulted in the marked changes between Basket Maker and Pueblo culture.

At, or slightly before, the beginning of this period sun-dried clay vessels were being produced by the Basket Maker people. Although a true and

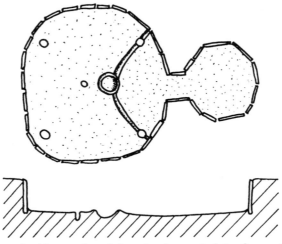

Fig. 90. The type of pithouse found late in the period in the eastern San Juan and Little Colorado areas. The house is circular but tends to the rectangular, has a raised clay ridge leading from the firepit to the sides, and in many cases an "annex" entrance.

rather fine pottery was made by both the Hohokam and Mogollon people at an even earlier date in southern Arizona, every step in the natural evolution of pottery making is known from this section and culture. The earliest vessels were produced by lining a basket with clay and carrying it up above the rim. Sometimes large clay luglike handles were modeled on the rim portion. Crushed juniper bark was included in the clay to prevent it from cracking during drying, and the natural shrinkage of the clay permitted its being removed from the basket. It was assumed that the idea of including vegetal matter in the clay was derived from the use of such material in the clay linings and "bricks" used in house construction. Soon grass stems were substituted for shredded bark, and at about this time it appears that firing was used as a method of making the pottery more substantial. The next step was the substitution of sand grains for grass stems, and a much better and thinner pottery resulted.

It has already been suggested that this type of unfired pottery may have been used as parching trays, and may not in fact have been the first groping steps in the production of pottery, since it has several times been found in association with true fired pottery. Morris displayed at the science meetings in Flagstaff a basket-impressed sun-dried vessel and a larger fired brown vessel of what is obviously a Mogollon type. Both came from a Basket Maker burial. In his more recent report he has further mentioned and described this association of Basket Maker types with what is obviously Mogollon pottery, most probably San Francisco Red, or derived types. This indicates that at least in the eastern part of the area these two people had come in casual contact before the making of definite pottery in the north. From this contact the idea of pottery making probably preceded exact knowledge of the technique, so that experimentation, aided from time to time by additional specific information, may have given rise to the sequence already described.

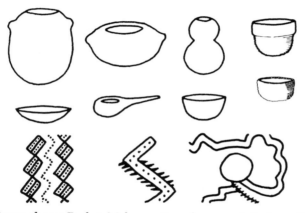

Fig. 91. This figure shows Basket Maker pottery forms and designs. Forms tend to be globular. The upper right figure is a sun-dried clay vessel modeled in a basket shown just below. Design elements are unattached dots and coarse lines.

Two types of pottery were produced by the Basket Makers, Lino Gray and Lino Black-on-gray. Lino Gray, very likely the first type, is of a hard, coarse, gray paste with sand temper. Fracture is irregular, and the sand grains protrude beyond the surface, in many pieces showing fine lines radiating from the grains. The forms are all globular, strongly suggesting baskets and gourds or other life forms. It is interesting to note that this type and its companion are the only pottery types in the Southwest with true spouts, for some gourd-shaped ladles have hollow, pointed handles which are open at the tip. Lug handles, placed above the center of the vessel and perforated vertically as though for the insertion of a handle, are common. Forms are rounded jars, some with a second globular neck, flatter jars suggesting seed jars of later periods, double-lobed small jars, and both deep and shallow bowls.

Lino Black-on-gray seems to have been a slightly later development which was decorated with a black design. Forms and the scraped rough surface finish are the same, although painted surfaces were more carefully finished. Designs are both geometric and life forms, the former apparently in many cases having been taken directly from basket or other fabric decorations. The most common elements are coarse lines, approximating an eighth of an inch in width, and unattached dots. Short crossed lines, slightly suggesting pendant triangles, and points occur. Life designs, all crudely executed, vary from human to unidentifiable forms.

Several other types of allied gray and black-on-gray pottery have been identified from other sections. One division into east and west may now be made on the basis of pigments. Those of the west have a carbon paint which does not turn red in an oxidizing atmosphere. The eastern types have an iron paint which does turn red. Certainly an even more careful examination of all these types would be profitable.

Associated with this pottery is a very small amount of finely made black-on-red. Although this is a widespread type its point of origin is not definitely known. Because it is entirely foreign to the rather well-controlled reducing atmosphere of the Basket Maker types, it is assumed to have been introduced in small amounts from some other area.

Two other interesting objects of clay were made at this time. One is a small human figurine, always female, which tends to suggest at least indirect contact with the Hohokam. It is decorated with punched and incised designs, as in the accompanying illustration. The other object is also made of clay but is conical and has a hollow base. As the use to which it could

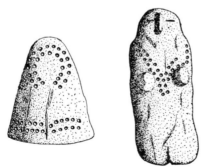

Fig. 92. Both human figurines and conical clay objects are found in Basket Maker III sites. Apparently all figurines are female, and both kinds of objects are decorated with punched dots and sometimes incised lines.

have been put remains problematical, it often has been called ceremonial. The ceremonial class has been a most useful category to the archaeologist, for those objects whose use he cannot definitely identify are often pigeonholed here.

The physical type of these people, like that of the preceding group, has never been carefully determined. One fact alone remains clear: none of the crania show definite posterior deformation, and the cradles are of the same soft type. The head form seems to vary from long to medium, particularly in the eastern San Juan, where Morris reports the finding of undeformed broad-headed individuals of this culture stage. Burials are generally the same, although at one place, again in the eastern San Juan, crypts were undercut in the solid stone bottoms of the caves for the reception of bodies. Actually this is not a far cry from the usual cist burial.

Metates and manos changed from those with an oval depression to the lineal type. These are essentially of a trough shape, and in the east are open at only one end. Block-type manos aré by far the most common form. It is possible that some of the oval metates may have survived in the western San Juan. Mauls, both full-grooved and three-quarter-grooved, also occur. The most common type to the west is the full-grooved rounded form, while to the east the three-quarter-grooved type is more common.

Chipped points and blades are essentially as described and pictured for the preceding period, for the atlatl and dart still survived. However, almost at the end of this time, or sometime between about A.D. 650 and 700, the bow and arrow was introduced into the eastern section. At an even earlier time Morris reports that the resident Basket Maker people were in contact with bow and arrow–using people, for he found one individual in Canyon del Muerto with an arrow still in her body. The arrival of the bow and arrow is definitely proved by the finding of arrow butts which had grooves instead of the usual drilled hole in the end, thus indicating that they had received a string instead of the prong on the atlatl. What few points have been found that might have been used on arrows are larger and coarser than most later types and suggest atlatl points. In general workmanship they are similar to the Mogollon type.

Basketry is the same as that of the preceding period, both as to form and decoration. There are probably more of the smaller and deeper baskets, but the shallow traylike baskets were also sparingly made. Possibly the first plaited types were introduced at this time. These were formed by cutting off the narrow-leaf yucca plant at the base and interweaving the leaves to produce a small narrow baglike container with a returned and tied-down rim. This type seems to have lasted sporadically into later periods, a situation which may occur in any trait, for once an object becomes established it may recur at any subsequent period.

Besides pottery, the most characteristic feature of this culture stage is the manufacture both of very fine sandals and of tump straps. Two classes of sandals were again made, those which were for everyday wear, and much finer dress sandals. The finer ones are of particular interest, for they are the most distinctive. Instead of being square-toed they have a crescent portion left out of the toe, and so are called "crescent-toed." This was probably a result of suspension of the warp threads on a loop instead of a bar. The heels are commonly bent up and tied together. In the most elaborate forms the upper surface is divided into three zones. The toe portion carries a band with geometric designs in colors across the ball of the foot. The central section has a longitudinal ribbed pattern, and the heel either no pattern or a second band of colors in designs. The under surface has a geometric raised design not unlike the tread on an automobile tire, and perhaps for somewhat the same reason. Life in the cliffs meant that good footing was a necessity.

Sandals of this class are woven from very fine cords of yucca or apocynum fibers in an over-and-under weave. They are made double so that the colored design does not extend through to the under surface. The raised design was formed by placing a tuft of fibers under the filler cords as they were woven. These sandals are really amazing examples of weaving, and once seen can never be mistaken for other types.

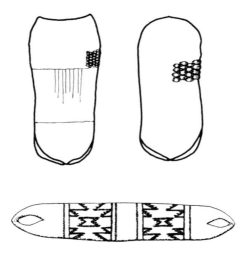

Fig. 93. Crescent-toed sandals appear at this time. They are very finely woven, often with color designs on the top and raised patterns on the bottom. Coarser sandals were also made. The tump strap shown below is twined-woven and has a color design in a geometric pattern. These are very characteristic Basket Maker III traits.

Tump straps are an American device by which heavy burdens were carried on the back, suspended from the head. Basket Maker tump straps were woven from cords, like the sandals, and often had similar geometric color designs. Two loops, one at each end, formed a base to which ropes were attached, and which in turn were attached to the burden. The load was raised to the back and the tump strap placed high across the forehead. By leaning forward the burden was supported by the back above the hips, but the strap prevented it from sliding off. In difficult climbing, such as negotiating hand holes pecked into the side of a vertical cliff, the hands were left free. The amount of preparation and effort which went into the

making of these objects and sandals is impressive, and the best were undoubtedly highly valued by the makers.

Bags were still made, as were both feather and fur robes. Parts of the
robes were often of feathers while other portions of the same article were
made of fur. Skin bags were also still used, apparently. As has already been
mentioned, the atlatl and atlatl dart were certainly in use until about the
end of the period, when the bow and arrow was introduced. Digging
sticks remained definitely the same.

Ornaments show little change, particularly as regards the survival of
feathers. The large stone beads do not seem to have been made in such
abundance, and shell beads were much more common. Olivella shells were
particularly popular, being simply broken or ground off at the end for
stringing. Turquoise was established in the east by this time, for beads
and pendants of this material have been found.

Pipes are very characteristic and show little change, although the form
seems to have been more commonly cigar-shaped than stockier. Bone shows
little change, with the possible exception of awls, many of which are now
of the split metatarsal type with half of the head of the bone left intact.
These forms are inclined to be longer than earlier types. Bone tubes and
whistles were still rather common.

Fig. 94. Awls of the long split
metatarsal type appear at this time.

In the earlier portion of this period the food of these people was very
similar to that of the preceding group, but toward the end changes may
be noted. Turkeys were certainly domesticated at this time, for definite
evidence such as enclosures and masses of manure have been found in the
caves occupied by Basket Maker III people. Almost at the end of the period
the type of corn seems to have changed from the small yellow flint variety
to larger ears, some of which have variegated colors.

By way of summary only a relatively few features are found to be typical
of these people when they are compared to Basket Maker II. Essentially
circular pithouses became widespread, and although they show what may
be an eastern and western variation they are all of one general pattern.
Probably the best diagnostic is pottery, although it was made most abundantly during only the latter half of the period. Unfired clay vessels are
an aid in dating the earlier portion. The skull is still undeformed, although
apparently undergoing change to a broader type. Elaborate crescent-toed
sandals are an excellent criterion of this group, and show involved techniques of weaving in color and raised patterns. Other traits remain about
the same as in the preceding period. The difficulty of identifying charac-

teristic traits of each period will increase as more recent time is reached, for, as has been many times suggested, much material carried over and cultural influences from other groups became more marked.

Near the end of this period several changes from pure Basket Maker culture were already under way. Because many of these seem to have taken place to the south and east of the main Basket Maker culture area, it is logical to assume that the influence responsible for them came from this direction. In the southern portion of the mountain section Mogollon culture, which appears to have been quite strong at a very early date, was noted. Many of the characters which have been mentioned bear a Mogollon stamp, a fact which has led some archaeologists to suggest that influence has been from the Basket Maker and Pueblo people to the Mogollon instead of the reverse. The fact that Mogollon antedates Basket Maker would imply that the main influence was to the north, although some characters must have been exchanged.

This has led to the suggestion that Mogollon or at least a Mogollon-like culture was responsible for the development of pottery in the plateau. Houses also probably had their main impetus from this source, and certain stone artifacts such as the point types probably came from here. Perhaps even the later physical type was a Mogollon–Basket Maker cross.

The economy of Basket Maker III was not predominantly agricultural, but about equally divided with hunting. The atlatl and dart were used, and a great variety of traps and snares were employed. Turkeys were domesticated. Interest in arts was primarily centered in weaving fabrics of fibers other than cotton, and some surprising results were archieved. Baskets, sandals, bags, and tump straps are all characteristic and well made. Feather and fur robes were produced, and great use was made of shredded cedar bark, both for bags and mats. Skins were tanned and utilized in a variety of ways. Human hair was widely used as rope as well as tied on baskets, with the result that many of the women kept their hair cut short, as shown by the mummies which have been recovered. Thus the first bobbed-hair American flappers are of some antiquity. Much use was made of feathers as ornaments, although other objects like stone and shell were also used. Beautiful highly prized cylindrical stone pipes were made. Bone whistles were used. Circular cists, or caches alone, were first characteristic, and later circular pithouses were widely made.

Certain people living in this area today show similarities of culture to the Basket Makers, as has been pointed out. The Paiute are apparently very close in many of their traits. The house is somewhat similar, excellent coiled basketry is made, skin blankets are woven, and the economy is similar. Early Navaho culture, without European influence, suggests Basket

Maker. Houses were usually circular and somewhat excavated. Basketry was made by coiling, and a crude, open-mouth, pointed-bottom pot was the only ceramic effort. Economy was similar; only the larger use of hides would be a distinction. As a result the writer has considered the possibility that a few of the supposed Basket Maker sites, particularly on the periphery of the area, might actually be the remains of early Piaute, Navaho, or similar people.

NEW MEXICO AND THE RIO GRANDE

Little has thus far been said about the prehistory of New Mexico, and now might be an appropriate time to make a quick review of this area before discussing what is found here during this period. In northern and eastern New Mexico it will be recalled that the Clovis or Llano complex prevailed at about 13,000 or 12,000 B.C. About 10,000 years ago the Folsom culture was found here. The Portales complex, made up of such things as Eden, Scottsbluff, and Milnesand, existed probably from about 9,000 to 7,000 years ago with suggestions of survivals to as recently as about 6,000 years ago.

In the southern and central part of the Rio Grande valley is late Cochise, and a later evolution from it might be considered a sort of Basket Maker I stage, if such a stage is to be recognized. In the north and east at this time there was a general stage of hunters and gatherers which is as yet not well defined.

In the preceding period the Durango and Los Pinos phase sites and culture have been identified as being found in north and northeastern New Mexico. They consist of circular houses, some with antechambers, and lacking native pottery but having some unfired clay vessels. There are also a few sherds of simple brown pottery, presumably traded in to these groups, which is undoubtedly related to the general brown pottery development to the south.

Between about A.D. 400 and 700 a cultural development occurred in northern New Mexico, as indicated in the accompanying map, which has been called Sambrito. This culture stage has not yet been fully reported on, but it is characterized by the presence of Sambrito Brown pottery, a type made locally. It has sand temper, is of simple more or less globular forms, and as might be expected is reminiscent of some Mogollon brown types, as well as some Basket Maker III forms. Villages are located on bench areas and consist of from 1 to 20 houses. The typical house is small and circular and lacks the cobblestone rings found in some other earlier structures in northern New Mexico. Although most of the chipped stone tools are percussion-flaked, some pressure flaking was used. Metates are of the open-end trough type, the basin type having gone out of vogue. Ground and polished bone tools are common. The atlatl was the main hunting implement.

In the Zuñi-Acoma area, and from there south into the mountains, a Basket Maker II–like culture prevailed which in some of its traits is remi-

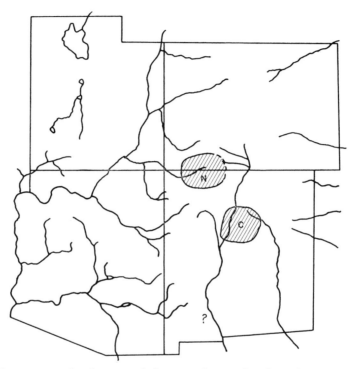

Fig. 95. The picture of cultures and their areal spread in New Mexico is not as clear at this time as it is in some other regions of the Southwest. In the area marked N, to the north, Sambrito Brown pottery is found in sufficient abundance to establish it as a type. Brown pottery is also found in the central area, and in the south Mogollon was in sway, with other brown pottery spread over a considerable area.

niscent of the San Jose culture, and which may therefore be at least in part derived from this source. It will be seen that such regional variations will be found with increasing frequency in various parts of the Southwest as time goes on.

In the middle, or central, Rio Grande there are also sites which have brown pottery that may be assigned to this same general time period, again as indicated on the accompanying map, but these have not been fully reported in the literature. In the lower Rio Grande valley Mogollon culture pretty definitely spread from the west into this area. Pottery which is probably of this period has been collected from a number of sites here, and some excavation has been undertaken, but again it is not fully reported.

There was thus, in New Mexico, a brown pottery stage of about this time which was very widespread. It is generally not well defined or reported, but because it forms a more or less continuous distribution from the south to the north it must have all been related. As one looks for a stimulus for these types, Mogollon, with a much earlier development of brown pottery types, is the logical source. It has already been suggested that Mogollon in turn probably derived its stimulus from the south in Mexico, so that this wave of brown pottery making likely swept northward from Mexico, gradually spreading, either by trade or example, throughout this portion of the Southwest.

SUMMARY

To summarize and compare the cultures which existed at this time in the Southwest, the Mogollon, at least as indicated by the presence of Mogollon or Mogollon-derived pottery types, was spreading out rather widely to the north. It was apparently also influencing the various cultures with which it came in contact. Decorated pottery was being made by the Mogollons, as it was by the Hohokam, and the vessels were coiled and scraped and polished. A characteristic feature is the presence of dimples on the outsides of many of the vessels. In other traits it does not seem to have been progressing as rapidly as the Hohokam.

The Hohokam were becoming more and more tied to the soil, and were limited to the larger river valleys of the Gila and Salt. Irrigation was either started or was about to develop, and with it the people were to become even more fixed in one site location, and so progressively sedentary. During this time period there was a good deal of very direct and continued influence from Mexico. Traits which are obviously shared are ball courts and mirrors, and less certainly figurines. Pottery designs are also found to have a good many parallels, and it may well be that Mexico was the source of many of these. Ground stone was enjoying a considerable stimulus that would continue throughout subsequent periods. This trait was another typical Mexican one as well. Shallow pithouses were still being made, and would continue as typical of the Hohokam culture. Another very characteristic habit of these people was the formation of definite trash mounds, some of which grew to considerable size.

In the northern plateau portion of the Southwest, Basket Maker III was a period of considerable change. Pithouses were widespread and of varied types in the several regions, and in fact all of the methods of construction found in subsequent periods were developed and in use by this time. The first truly native pottery was being made, and it was fired in a reducing atmosphere in distinction to the pottery of the other areas and cultures. It is quite likely that the idea of pottery making originally came from the Mogollon, for some of the plain brown pottery of this culture was found in the northern area even before the local people were making any fired vessels. To a lesser extent Hohokam may have influenced pottery making, but it does not seem to have had as direct contacts as that of the Mogollon. The first Basket Maker pottery was of simple forms, tending to be more or less globular, and copying life forms such as gourds. Designs on the first decorated pottery were taken from those previously used on basketry, or were life forms, many of which are difficult to identify. These people produced some very fine work in fabrics, especially sandals, tump straps, and bags, but no cotton fibers were apparently available to them. The distribution of this culture was rather more extensive than that of the preceding

Pictographs of this sort are found widely distributed throughout the Southwest.

period, and it was overlapped in almost all of its range by Mogollon culture or a Mogollon-like expansion outward from the center.

Throughout much of New Mexico brown types of pottery are found. These are probably derived from Mogollon, or from the same source where Mogollon secured its ceramic influences. Unfortunately not too complete reports are available on this material, but will probably soon be forthcoming.

Of all of these cultures Hohokam was by far the most vigorous, with a very marked indigenous development which was soon to see even more striking additions. It is quite clear that many of the stimuli which led to this rapid development came from Mexico, and would continue to come for some time. Hohokam was already restricted, but since at such sites as Snaketown it had even now reached a rather high level of development, it probably had influence on other more far-flung cultures, through trade or as a result of visitors. Mogollon was spreading wide, or at least sending out strong influences in ceramics to others, but it was not particularly altering internally. Later, when Pueblo culture developed to the north and spread southward, Mogollon began to show considerable modification. Apparently there were not as direct, or as vigorous, Mexican influences on the Mogollon now as there were on the Hohokam.

Basket Maker II remained a more or less stable culture for what appears to have been a considerable length of time. During the Settlement period, with the development of Basket Maker III, a considerable number of innovations appeared. Houses, though occurring earlier, became widespread, pottery was made, and possibly new agricultural plants were introduced. It was a backward culture compared to Mogollon, and lagged considerably behind the developments of Hohokam. It has been suggested that it was a result of the contacts with Mogollon, and perhaps less directly with Hohokam, that rather marked alterations came about. This must thus be considered somewhat in the nature of a transition period, as was the next, when further alterations resulted in still more marked revisions in the general culture, to give rise to what has been called Pueblo.

One of the most obvious processes which can be seen in operation at this time is the effect one cultural group had on another. Isolation does not seem to have been effective anywhere in the Southwest, and influences from the south, which had begun much earlier, continued. The story of the Southwest is thus one of interrelationships throughout most, if not all, of its history.

Two examples of the kinds of problems which arise when cultural influences are found to intermingle will be sufficient here to give some idea of the difficulties confronting the archaeologist. In the Petrified Forest area at the Twin Butte site, Wendorf found a culture which is comparable in time to Basket Maker III of the plateau area, but which differed in some rather marked respects. Most of the houses were circular and slab-lined, but there were deep storage cists with them, and there was also a large circular structure with a bench and a sloping entrance which must have been ceremonial. The slab-lined structures are reminiscent of Basket Maker, but the kiva is suggestive of Mogollon. Two kinds of pottery were found here, Forestdale and Woodruff.

Forestdale Plain, which is like Woodruff Brown, is sand-tempered, unsmudged, unslipped, and brown. Besides Forestdale Plain there are varieties called Forestdale Smudged and Forestdale Red. Woodruff Red is sand-tempered, red-slipped, and occurs in both bowls and jars. These types are scraped, are gray and brown in color, and although they typically have sand temper some varieties have crushed-rock temper. All of these brown types are very suggestive of the general Mogollon pottery, and this writer is inclined to so consider them.

In the immediate Flagstaff area the Cinder Park focus has been identified and is considered by Colton to be assignable to the earliest Sinagua culture in this area. Houses are pithouses, 13 to 17 feet in diameter, either circular or rectangular with rounded corners, and have long sloping entrances and roof poles which leaned in from the periphery to the center. These are very like some of the Basket Maker houses of farther north and east. Subsequent work on another Cinder Park site has unearthed rectangular pithouses and a large circular kiva. This again looks more like Mogollon than Basket Maker, for kivas are known to be early in the Mogollon culture. The associated native pottery is what has been called Rio de Flag Brown. In many characteristics this type is very suggestive of Alma Plain. The temper is volcanic sand and feldspar crystals, the color varies from brown-gray to black, there are often fire clouds, and it is made in the form of bowls, jars, jugs, and even ladles. One of the real problems connected with it is that it seems to have been finished by the paddle and anvil process, in distinction to the Mogollon method of finishing pottery by scraping and rubbing. In many traits it shows similarities to Mogollon, but in others, particularly the finish, it looks Hohokam. In no respects does it really suggest Basket Maker. Whether or not this represents the beginning of the Sinagua culture here depends entirely on how Sinagua is defined.

Both of these cultures obviously represent mixtures of influences, and a similar situation can probably be demonstrated in many areas, particularly at this time, when stimuli were being spread widely throughout the Southwest.

Sources and Additional References

Amsden, Charles Avery. An Analysis of Hohokam Pottery Design, *Medallion Paper 23*, 1936, Gila Pueblo, Globe, Arizona. (Review and summary of Hohokam design elements and combinations.)

Brew, J. O. Archaeology of Alkali Ridge, Southeastern Utah, *Papers of the Peabody Museum of American Archaeology and Ethnology,* Vol. 21, 1946, Harvard University, Cambridge, Massachusetts. (This site is largely Pueblo I, but there is some slight evidence that it may have begun in Basket Maker III. It is in many ways very distinctive.)

Colton, Harold S. The Sinagua. A Summary of the Archaeology of the Region of Flagstaff, Arizona, *Bulletin 22,* 1946, Museum of Northern Arizona, Flagstaff. (See the discussion of the Cinder Park focus.)

Danson, Edward Bridge. An Archaeological Survey of West Central New Mexico and East Central Arizona, *Papers of the Peabody Museum of American Archaeology and Ethnology,* Vol. 44, No. 1, 1957, Harvard University, Cambridge, Massachusetts. (Distribution and interrelationships of cultures in this area are shown.)

Dittert, Alfred E., Jr., Frank W. Eddy, and Beth L. Dickey. Evidences of Early Ceramic Phases in the Navajo Reservoir District, *El Palacio,* Vol. 70, Nos. 1-2, 1963, Museum of New Mexico, Santa Fe. (Very brief report on both the Los Pinos and Sambrito phases, the latter of which is pertinent here.)

Gladwin, Winifred and H. S. The Red-on-Buff Culture of the Gila Basin, *Medallion Paper 3,* 1929, Gila Pueblo, Globe, Arizona. (This early summary of Hohokam culture in the central area is of value in placing the general culture and Colonial in relation to it.)

———. Some Southwestern Pottery Types, Series III, *Medallion Paper 13,* 1933, Gila Pueblo, Globe, Arizona. (Review of the red-on-buff pottery types of the Gila, including Colonial types.)

Gladwin, H. S., Emil W. Haury, E. B. Sayles, and Nora Gladwin. * Excavations at Snaketown, Material Culture, *Medallion Paper 25,* 1937, Gila Pueblo, Globe, Arizona. (Contains the most detailed description of a rich Colonial Hohokam site thus far excavated and reported.)

Guernsey, Samuel J. * Explorations in Northeastern Arizona, *Papers of the Peabody Museum of American Archaeology and Ethnology,* Vol. 12, No. 1, 1931, Harvard University, Cambridge, Massachusetts. (Best general discussion and summary of the Basket Makers of the San Juan area.)

Haury, Emil W. * Roosevelt: 9-6, a Hohokam Site of the Colonial Period, *Medallion Paper 11,* 1932, Gila Pueblo, Globe, Arizona. (Excellent discussion and report on a Colonial Hohokam site.)

———. Some Southwestern Pottery Types, Series IV, *Medallion Paper 19,* 1936, Gila Pueblo, Globe, Arizona. (Description of the several Mogollon types of pottery.)

———. * The Mogollon Culture of Southwestern New Mexico, *Medallion Paper 20,* 1936, Gila Pueblo, Globe, Arizona. (Original definition of the Mogollon culture.)

Kidder, Alfred Vincent. An Introduction to the Study of Southwestern Archaeology, Phillips Academy, Andover, Massachusetts, 1924. (Basket Maker III culture is briefly discussed under the heading of "Sites with Crude Pottery [Post–Basket Maker].")

Kidder, Alfred Vincent, and Samuel J. Guernsey. * Archaeological Explorations in Northeastern Arizona, *Bulletin 65,* 1919, Bureau of American Ethnology, Washington, D.C. (Excellent source of Basket Maker culture if the material reported is sorted in the light of recent terminology.)

Martin, Paul S., John B. Rinaldo, Elaine A. Bluhm, Hugh C. Cutler, and Roger
   Grange, Jr. * Mogollon Cultural Continunity and Change: The Stratigraphic
   Analysis of Tularosa and Cordova Caves, *Fieldiana: Anthropology,* Vol. 40,
   1952, Chicago Natural History Museum. (Excellent reference for the more
   perishable objects of this culture and time.)
Morris, Earl H. The Beginnings of Pottery Making in the San Juan Area; Unfired
   Prototypes, and the Wares of the Earliest Ceramic Periods, *Anthropological
   Papers,* Vol. 28, Part II, 1927, American Museum of Natural History, New
   York City. (Discussion of the pottery sequence from unfired types to true
   pottery.)
————. Archaeological Studies in the La Plata District, Southwestern Colorado
   and Northwestern New Mexico, *Carnegie Institution Publication 519,* 1939,
   Washington, D.C. (See particularly the introduction for a good summary of
   the archaeology of this period in this area.)
Roberts, Frank H. H., Jr. * Shabik'eshchee Village, a Late Basket Maker Site
   in the Chaco Canyon, New Mexico, *Bulletin 92,* 1929, Bureau of American
   Ethnology, Washington, D.C. (Characterization of late Basket Maker III in
   the east.)
————. The Ruins at Kiatuthlanna, Eastern Arizona, *Bulletin 100,* 1931, Bureau
   of American Ethnology, Washington, D.C. (A late Basket Maker site in the
   Little Colorado area.)
Sayles, E. B. The San Simon Branch, Excavations at Cave Creek and in the San
   Simon Valley. I. Material Culture, *Medallion Paper 34,* 1945, Gila Pueblo,
   Globe, Arizona. (Description of the culture of this area at this time.)
Wendorf, Fred. Archaeological Studies in the Petrified Forest National Monu-
   ment, *Bulletin 27,* 1953, Museum of Northern Arizona, Flagstaff. (See the dis-
   cussion of the Twin Butte site, which is of this period.)
Wheat, Joe Ben. * Mogollon Culture Prior to A.D. 1000, *American Antiquity,* Vol.
   20, No. 4, Part 2, 1955, Society for American Archaeology, Salt Lake City,
   Utah. (General description and correlation of the various branches.)
Woodward, Arthur. The Grewe Site, *Occasional Paper 1,* 1931, Los Angeles
   Museum of History, Science, and Art, Los Angeles, California. (Mimeographed
   preliminary report on the work at the Grewe site, containing a great deal of
   very valuable information.)

XI

Adjustment Period: A.D. 700 to 900

MOGOLLON

During this period Mogollon culture is best represented in the central area by the San Francisco stage. The area over which Mogollon may be considered to have existed is indicated on the accompanying map. The central area is shown as extending south into Mexico, and has been drawn west to the juncture of the Santa Cruz and Gila rivers. Actually in the western portion of this section there is much intergrading at this time with Hohokam, so that a variant of the Mogollon was developed here, as shown by the publications of the Amerind Foundation. To the northwest Mogollon was still to some extent represented as far as the Flagstaff area, if the ceramic types and certain other features are admitted as being derived from this culture. In the far north it was now being taken over by local developments which could no longer be considered primarily Mogollon, for the Pueblo culture was beginning to evolve in this quarter.

In general this was the time when the broad-line and narrow-line red-on-brown pottery spread throughout the central area, and lesser amounts are found in the northern peripheral area. Other traits went with the ceramics, and often can be ascribed to Mogollon on the basis of priority there. There are tree-ring dates for sites in the Mimbres, Pine Lawn, and Forestdale branches, so that it is more accurately dated than previous periods. The extension to the west of the core area is based on the concept that the Ootam were a southwestern branch of the Mogollon, a theory which is debatable. More is to be said on this subject.

Pottery and house types have perhaps been most fully worked out for this period and culture, as is the case with most other areas and times. Probably the most typical pottery is Mogollon Red-on-brown, but of the decorated types San Lorenzo Red-on-brown and Three Circle Red-on-white are also found in the core area. Other types are simply continua-

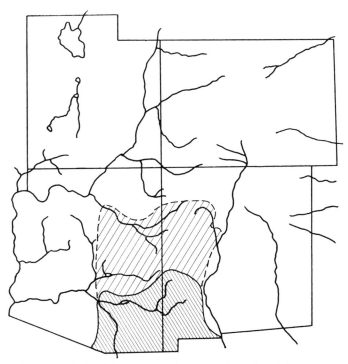

Fig. 96. Distribution of the Mogollon culture during the Adjustment period. Note particularly the westward expansion of the core area and its southern extension. This is assuming that Ootam is related to Mogollon.

tions of earlier pottery, or elaborations of the plain and textured examples. San Francisco Red is still present, Alma Plain and Alma Rough decrease, Alma Neck Banded and Alma Scored increase, Alma Incised is a variant of Alma Plain, and Reserve Smudged is a more northern type. Trade pottery is the typical Pueblo I type of the north, and particularly of the eastern portion of the Pueblo area.

Mogollon Red-on-brown, though never of great abundance, is probably the most typical Mogollon type with a painted decoration. The paste is light gray to reddish brown, and the temper is white angular particles and some rounded sand grains. The interiors are both unslipped and slipped. When a slip is used it is frequently so light that the scrape marks of finishing show through it, and is of a somewhat pinkish to brown color.

Exteriors are slightly indented, so that they have a large dimpled effect, are polished, and sometimes show tool marks parallel to the rim. Fire clouds are not uncommon. Decoration is in a reddish brown pigment which was commonly polished over before firing, so that the edges of the lines are slightly blurred into the background of the slip. Designs cover the insides of bowls, the outsides of jars, and are purely rectilinear in type. Lines in general are finer than those of previous decorated types.

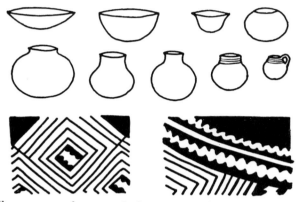

Fig. 97. Mogollon pottery forms and designs. Bowls and jars were both made, as well as the rare pitcher with a handle. The design shown at the left is from Mogollon Red-on-brown; that at the right is Three Circle Red-on-white.

Three Circle Red-on-white seems to be more or less contemporaneous with Mogollon Red-on-brown. The paste is dark to light brown, and the temper is heterogeneous fine material with only a few larger particles. The surface is scraped and then slipped with a chalky white slip, which sometimes crackles when fired to form many fine crossing lines. Bowl exteriors are only roughly finished, a few having a reddish brown slip or, more rarely and apparently late, corrugations. Forms are both bowls and jars. Bowls have flaring rims, or are the deep hemispherical type, but occur in only about the proportion of six to one. Decorations are in the same red-brown paint as Mogollon Red-on-brown, a few being blurred by polishing before firing, the rest not. Designs are carried to the rim. This type apparently enjoyed only a short life, and was never very plentiful.

Designs of both Mogollon Red-on-brown and Three Circle Red-on-white are composed primarily of fairly coarse lines and massed areas of color with serrated edges. All the design elements are rectilinear, and the area upon which the design is applied is characteristically divided into four equal sections, on the bowls by drawing a cross through the center of the vessel. This quadrant division of design is also found on other types in the plateau and the Upper Gila and Salt areas at slightly later times.

The plain, textured, and neck-coiled types have either already been described or are self-explanatory. In general it seems that various manipulations of the surface of the pottery are more early and more common in the Mogollon than in other cultures and areas now.

Characteristic of the San Francisco phase were rectangular houses with rounded corners 12 to 18 feet long and relatively deep. In this type there was a central post with additional posts near or on the walls. In some houses two secondary posts were located on the central line. A firepit was still in the same relative location, and a long sloping entrance was located on one of the long sides. Other houses were rectangular and somewhat shallower, with a central post, four corner posts, and two additional posts on the long axis. In some cases cache pits were within the house. In the Mogollon and Harris sites there were distinctive undercut storage pits outside of the houses. Other perhaps slightly later houses at the Harris village were rectangular with more nearly square corners, and were shallower and smaller, being only 8 to 15 feet long. Four corner posts were typical features, with a fifth post on the center line near the back wall. Large, often circular structures were almost certainly ceremonial in nature, for only one or two were found in each village.

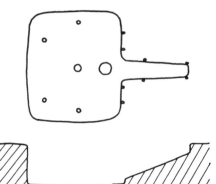

Fig. 98. Houses are rectangular with rounded corners and still have the large central post, but also have two others on the central line and supplementary posts. The entrance and firepit arrangement is much the same.

What is obvious from this brief description of houses is that they now vary regionally. Some are quite deep, others more shallow, some have rounded corners, others do not, and the number and arrangement of the roof-support posts vary as well. In general, however, the typical structure was a pithouse, relatively deep, with a long entrance passageway. There was a firepit near the entrance, and the roof was either flat or nearly so.

Regarding the physical type, it has already been pointed out that too little data is available to make definite generalizations possible. The disposal of the dead remained essentially as previously.

In other material traits pipes were decreasing, but reed cigarettes became more common in Tularosa and Cordova caves. In general Mogollon pipes tend to be more stocky than Basket Maker ones. Animal and human figurines were present, as well as cornucopia objects made of clay. The human figurines and cornucopia objects are very reminiscent of Basket Maker examples. Morris has suggested the clay cornucopia-shaped objects may be miniature copies of carrying baskets.

Basin metates were rare, while the scoop type was common, and rectangular manos were the most abundant although some oval forms did persist. Mortars and pestles decreased. Hoes were present. Points were small with shallow lateral or diagonal notches. The atlatl was apparently still in use, but about to go out of style. Flake knives decreased in abundance, but scrapers and choppers were still in common use. Drills were decreasing, but there were some broad-base ones.

Ornaments included tube beads and whole shell beads as previously noted. Feathers were used as ornaments, and there were still fur cloth robes. Most interesting is the fact that the cradle was now a rigid type, a trait which seems to find a parallel in the Anasazi at about the same time.

Basketry was mostly of the two-rod and bundle type, although there were examples of the bundle with rod core, bundle, and half-rod and

Fig. 99. One of the plaited, more or less square-toed sandals which become more common at this time in Mogollon culture. They are presumably somewhat later in Pueblo culture.

bundle. Probably late in this period the twilled-ring shallow basket appeared, another trait which seems to have been in use by the Anasazi as well. There was twilled matting, and cotton and bast fiber cloth made in a simple over-and-under weave. There was also bast fiber twined fabric. Wickerwork sandals were still common, and plaited, more or less square-toed sandals seem to have been introduced about now. All previously described types survived.

As has been stated the atlatl was apparently still in use in this culture, but the bow and arrow was also well known, in fact a quiver was found. One of the more interesting features of this culture was the introduction of miniature bows and arrows, possibly ceremonial in nature. There were also painted sticks. Food was the same as in the preceding period, but as has been noted the corn type was changing from larger numbers of rows to fewer, the most common now being eight or ten rows.

The notched bone awl persisted as a characteristic feature of this culture. A wood spoon which may be assigned to this time was found in the caves.

Unfired pottery seems to have increased, a trait which raises serious doubts that it was a prototype of the fired pottery in the north. It has been suggested that these vessels may have served as parching trays.

Photograph courtesy Museum of New Mexico

A Rosa phase pithouse in the Navajo Reservoir district which dates about A.D. 800. The firepit, deflector, and ventilator are in a line, and there are four post holes and a storage bin in the far wall.

By way of summary it is the pottery which exhibits the most typical and distinctive series of traits of the Mogollon during the Adjustment period. There is much variety in the types produced, with various manipulations of the surface as a means of decoration. The painted types are either red-on-brown or red-on-white, a variant of the brown with the addition of a white slip. Designs are relatively simple, but more complex than earlier styles, with filled-in areas. In the north many of the vessels still typically had smudged interiors.

Houses, though varied by areas, were dominantly based on the pithouse concept, with sloping entrances and deep rather than shallow. Roof supports showed considerable variety, but the central post seems to have been a more or less common principle. Storage pits were characteristically outside, but there were some in the houses.

Other traits show some additions or modifications and some deletions. Several individual objects are reminiscent of Basket Maker, but others are suggestive of Pueblo. The hard cradle is an example of this latter type. As has been suggested several times, it is believed that both Mogollon and Anasazi had their roots back in the early Desert culture, so the parallels in many traits might well be expected. If Hohokam culture had been as well preserved in dry cave sites it is quite probable that many perishable items would have been found to be shared among all three.

HOHOKAM

The Hohokam culture which occupied the Gila and Salt river valleys during the period from about A.D. 700 to 900 was the Santa Cruz phase. Reference to the Hohokam map for the Settlement period will indicate approximately the area which was occupied at this time. It will be noted that the main center was pretty much limited to the river valleys, for the culture of the Papagueria was slightly different, and has been distinguished by Haury and others. Many of the traits of the river Hohokam, such as extensive irrigation projects, were lacking in Papagueria, and the pottery in many cases was sufficiently different to be distinguishable. Some of the decorated types, particularly slightly later, tended to have a smudged background which gave them a more or less red-on-gray appearance.

Pottery is of course still the most distinctive single trait, and three identifiable types have been assigned to this stage. Gila Plain continued through this time, and can now be distinguished only by the addition of a few more varied forms. As did all Hohokam pottery, it contained mica as a noticeable part of the temper, so that it may easily be separated from other types not made in the desert.

Santa Cruz Buff, though rare at Snaketown, is a type which is distinctive largely because of its exceptional thinness of vessel wall, its lightly washed and smoothed surface, and its manufacture in the form only of small jars with handles. Handled jars are not typical of Hohokam, but this type, as determined by careful analysis of paste and temper, was made by these people. Because of its relative rarity it is only mentioned.

Santa Cruz Red-on-buff is the identifying type of the Santa Cruz phase or focus. As was true of the other types of the Hohokam it was made by the paddle and anvil process, with careful smoothing on the decorated surface, which had a light slip. It had as a part of the temper small flakes of mica, which was probably secured with the desert sands used in the paste. The color is buff with a pinkish tendency. The flaring-rim bowl is a characteristic form, but even rectangular vessels occur. Heavy-walled vessels are of this type, as well as of others, and apparently are characteristic only of Hohokam culture. It has been suggested they were used somewhat as incense burners, for many show traces of carbon on the insides. Jars, plates, scoops, ladles, and even beakers are all characteristic. Small repeated elements are probably the most outstanding feature of design, with some negative painting wherein the buff of the background shows through the red of the paint as the main design element. Jars with wide flaring mouths and flaring-rim bowls are the most typical forms.

Pottery figurines, as will be recalled, were found only at Snaketown, and those of the Santa Cruz type most commonly appear to have had the

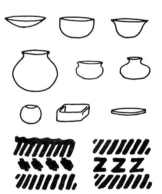

Fig. 100. Hohokam pottery forms and designs of this period. The designs shown are only some of those in use. Pedestal vessels were still made, and heavy-walled vessels are a part of this culture, although not shown. The most common decorated form is the flaring-rim bowl and the wide-mouth jar.

"coffee bean" eye. A small bean-shaped mass of clay was added to the face to form the eye, and then was incised to indicate the lids. These types are strongly reminiscent of certain Archaic forms from the Valley of Mexico.

Houses are elongate rectangular structures built in a pit, sometimes with rounded ends, and characteristically with rounded corners. Although they are quite large, as much as 12 by 20 feet, they are relatively shallow, usually not more than one or two feet deep. A sunken entranceway gave access to the level of the room on one of the long sides, and directly in front of this, in the floor, was the firepit. The main roof support consisted of two upright posts on the long axis of the room, although smaller secondary post holes were found around the periphery of the floor. Thus the low-gabled type of roof was the rule, and the sides of the dwelling were enclosed with a wattlework of reeds which was probably plastered over. In all major characters these houses were very similar to late Pioneer types.

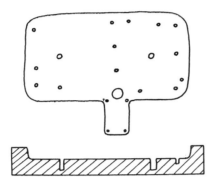

Fig. 101. Plan and section of a typical house. It is relatively shallow, rather long and slender, has rounded corners and sometimes rounded ends, a roofed entrance on one of the long sides with a firepit directly in front of it, and two main support posts.

These people also sometimes made use of what appear to have been outdoor brush kitchens, similar to those in use by the Pima and Papago Indians today. This "shade" structure is a most efficient and useful feature in a climate as extreme as that of southern Arizona, for it consisted largely of a roof supported on poles under which cooking and other activities could be accomplished in hot weather. Somewhat similar structures will be noted for the Cohonina culture in the northern part of the state.

Circular and conical pits have also been found which gave every evidence of the use of fire, for they were filled with fire-blackened and broken boulders. Several theories have been advanced concerning the use of these pits, the most favorable of which seems to be either that they were for cooking or that cholla fruit was roasted in them, much as the Pimas and Papagos are now doing.

Ball courts certainly carried over into this period, and in fact the large court at Snaketown was modified at this time. The creation of such a large structure is paralleled only by the construction of extensive irrigation ditches. At Snaketown one such ditch is known to belong to this stage. Although originally it appeared to be of great width, excavation revealed that it was a relatively narrow and steep-sided ditch. The very arid nature of the country predetermined the use of irrigation in this area, as soon as any considerable population settled in any restricted region. Conversely the establishment of irrigated fields would probably tend to draw additional individuals to the village, so that such a large site as Snake-town might result. Some of these ditches carried water for several miles to the agricultural fields below the villages.

As has been suggested in the preceding period, stone implements were very abundant, very characteristic, and well made. Metates and manos seemed unchanged, but palettes had become much more elaborate. Although the rims were still primarily decorated with incised designs, some were found at Snaketown which had additional ornaments in the form of tabs carved on the ends. Sometimes these were animals, but more commonly they were simply circles. Rarely, raised patterns were carved on the rim, and a few palettes in the form of animal silhouettes or diamond shapes were found.

Fig. 102. Carved stone jars of this period may have simple incised designs or figures such as the rattlesnake in half round. The bottom stone vessel is an animal figure with a hollowed-out basin in its back. Stone carving had already surpassed the best efforts of the inhabitants of the plateau area, even during later periods.

Some of the stone bowls were also much more elaborate than those of the preceding period. Some had raised designs of snakes, frogs, or even humans. In the entire Southwest such objects were equaled only by those made during the Sedentary Hohokam stage, so that the Hohokam people certainly may be considered stone workers of excellence. Besides conventional bowls ornamented with relief figures there were occasional small animal statuettes, in the full round, and with basins in their backs. These effigy vessels undoubtedly represent only an elaboration of the bowl form.

Axes were still of the shorter type, and mauls do not seem to have been used, but hammerstones are relatively abundant, as they were through all periods. They are made of some hard material, such as quartzite, most specimens having apparently been shaped largely by use, and as a result vary from spherical forms to irregularly shaped ovals.

The Hohokam people not only produced remarkable ground and carved stone objects, but they also excelled in chipped stone. Probably the most characteristic features of the projectile points are their long slender shape and the presence of deliberately and carefully formed serrations, particularly near the base and along the central portion of the blade. Occasionally these serrations assume the shape of barbs. Chipping throughout the point is well controlled, so that they are very symmetrical. Both obsidian and chert were used. Small-neck bases and concave wide bases with ears are characteristic, and less abundantly triangular notched points occur. The practical identity of the simpler of these types with some of those in the Flagstaff area is a striking feature. Heavy projectile points and knife blades are quite rare. In general these are the finest projectile points produced anywhere in the Southwest at any time.

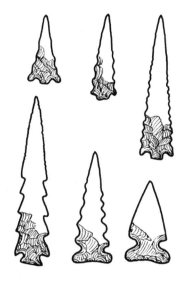

Fig. 103. Points, such as the above, are long, slender, and exceptionally well made, with careful secondary chipping which produced marked and even serrations along the edges.

Unfortunately basketry was not found directly preserved in any of the sites of this stage thus far excavated, although at Roosevelt impressions of a coiled basket were found on the inside of a pot, and at Snaketown fragments of what appear to have been a sandal were uncovered. Charred bits of yucca-leaf matting were also uncovered. The lack of such material, of course, does not mean that it was not produced, for the open nature of the sites would make its preservation most unlikely unless it was carbonized. It may well be that this culture was richly endowed with perishable items.

Charred cotton seeds in a small bowl were found at one site of this period. This seems to indicate that these people had and raised cotton, and if they did it is logical to assume that they wove it into fabrics. This is probably about as early evidence of cotton agriculture on the plateau as is known, and may actually have occurred slightly earlier.

As to hunting implements, the use of the bow and arrow is indicated.

The small fragile projectile points already described must have been arrow points, for, as has been suggested before, all known atlatl dart points are heavier and more coarsely chipped.

Charred corn which dates from the Colonial stage was in the Snaketown site, a fact which is certainly not surprising, but no squash or beans were found. This again does not mean they were not present and in use. Animal bones showed a marked increase in the use of small rodents over larger mammals as compared to the Pioneer stage. In fact Haury suggests that the relation of abundance of corn, rodent remains, and the development of irrigation is marked.

Probably as much as anything else, the Hohokam people of this time excelled in the carving of shell. The carved bracelets were outstanding, many of them being in relief, and a few were cut out, or cut through. One carved bracelet was found with a figure similar to the plumed-serpent

Pictograph found in the Gila area. This style is commonly called a sun symbol.

design of Mexican art. Some are quite lifelike carvings of animals. Small rings were also often carved, and shell was worked into pendants of various shapes, some in such life patterns as birds. Fragments of cut shell were used in mosaic work, many representing elaborate small figures. Shell beads were of the types already described.

In summary certain elaborations and additions to Hohokam culture may be seen at this time. Carving in general was far better than previously, and this Mexican-like trait became a typical feature of this culture. Pottery shows only minor variations of form and design, and houses, even when compared to the latest Pioneer types, were not in any way radically different. Probably the most important developments were the construction, or at least remodeling and use, of the large ball courts and the building of extensive irrigation ditches. This required the cooperation, planning, and direction of a number of individuals. Irrigation also tied the people to the land at one spot, for it represented a considerable investment of time and effort. Other features of this culture during this period are more in the nature of refinements and elaborations than introductions.

Many features are found to reflect Mexican or Central American influences. The mirrors have already been pointed out for the preceding period. The snake motif in shell carving and on stone bowls is suggestive of Mexico. Ball courts are also definitely allied to the south. Even pottery forms and designs show some influences from this direction. Taken as a group it thus becomes clear that Mexico was either directly or indirectly, through trade contacts, exerting a considerable influence on the Hohokam now. In general Hohokam looks more and more like a distantly related or peripheral area of the Mexican cultures.

PUEBLO I

Pueblo I culture has been characterized in the Pecos classification as: "The first stage during which cranial deformation was practiced, vessel neck corrugation was introduced, and villages composed of rectangular rooms of true masonry were developed (in some areas)." To this might be added the introduction of slips, high polishing, designs characterized in general by extremely fine lines, attached dots, and high triangles in the black-on-white types. It is well to keep in mind the fact that in such a definition, largely based on pottery types, none of the pottery designated as diagnostic of a period or culture suddenly appeared in full bloom. Actually, gradual pottery gradations took place from Basket Maker III through Pueblo I to Pueblo II. As a result the pottery types described in detail are simply the most distinctive for each group and time period.

The area occupied by most typical Pueblo I culture is not greatly changed from that of Basket Maker III. The main expansion of the core area was a probable extension southward into the White Mountains and westward through the Flagstaff area to the south rim of the Grand Canyon proper. The maximum expansion has purposely been left ample, although there is at present some doubt that it actually spread as far west as shown, and the southeastward extension into the Rio Grande valley might be contested to some extent. Pottery types found in these areas suggest Pueblo I, though they are not identical with it in the core area. By this method it may be suggested that rather wide contacts and perhaps influence existed at this time.

Of the stages in Pueblo culture, least is known of Pueblo I. Regional variations appear to have been very common as regards both house and pottery types, and almost every site of this culture shows evidence of Basket Maker or Pueblo II occupation as well. This general mixture has made it very difficult to separate true Pueblo I from the other manifestations, and has suggested the possibility that this is actually a relatively short stage (if a true culture stage at all) which at most represents a period of change or readjustment and stabilizing of culture from the Basket Maker complex.

At present the time period seems to be fairly well established from a number of sites scattered throughout the plateau area. Any site which is found to date after about A.D. 700 contains neck-coiled pottery, probably the best single Pueblo I diagnostic. The end is very well and accurately dated, at least in the Flagstaff section. Neck corrugations are found to become indented at about A.D. 890, and by 900 definite Pueblo II black-on-white types were established here. As a result the duration of this stage of culture over most of the plateau may roughly be stated as from A.D. 700 to 900.

Specific places where Pueblo I sites are well represented are the Navaho Springs district of the Rio Puerco, Komar Springs in the upper Jeddito valley, along the Polacca Wash, and in the Moenkopi Wash and the Hopi country. The upper or eastern San Juan also has some very typical and interesting sites of this culture stage, as does the southeastern core area shown on the map.

Certain pottery types of this period are very characteristic and easily identified. The chief plain or cooking pottery held more tenaciously to the globular shapes already described as characteristic of the preceding period. The utensils are gray, both in paste and surface color, and contain coarse sand temper. Some forms appear not to have had any decoration and so are at present indistinguishable from Lino Gray. Further study of these types will probably make distinctions possible on the basis of shapes, but so far this study has not been comprehensively attempted.

The most common utilitarian type is Kana-a Gray. The body of these vessels is always undecorated, but the neck is made up of flattened coils. It has been suggested that the body was modeled after the manner of Lino Gray, but that the necessity of restricting the neck led to the development of coiling in this portion of the vessel. It is possible to make a distinction in the manner by which the coils were produced. In one type the coils are simple circles of clay which were made and applied in a unit before they were flattened to the coils below. These might be

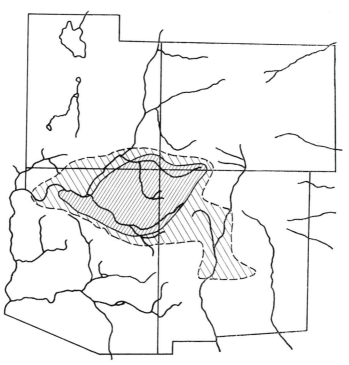

Fig. 104. Area of Pueblo I culture. The fine hatching is that portion where the most typical culture of this period is found, and shows a slight extension of that of Basket Maker III. The area of greatest expansion may be debated, but Pueblo I types of pottery are found here.

termed "neck coils." The second type was the construction of the neck by a continual spiral of clay, which begins at the base and works gradually upward to the rim. This type might be termed "coiled necks." It is further felt by some that this represents an evolutionary development of the coiling technique in this area, the former type appearing first. The writer, however, remains to be convinced on this matter. Forms are either jars or pitchers with the first true handles.

The second common type of pottery is Kana-a Black-on-white. This is the first true black-on-white pottery to appear on the plateau and shows the first common use of massed black areas in decoration, the effect being achieved by outlining the geometric patterns and filling them in solidly with black. The paste is gray and contains sand temper. Decorated surfaces are scraped down and characteristically polished with a smooth pebble before firing. Some are apparently covered with a true slip; others have only been polished while damp to produce a semblance of a true slip. The outsides of bowls, or other undecorated surfaces, are often only scraped and left somewhat rough. Forms are bowls, usually with more or less steep sides, relatively large jars with a tendency to sloping necks, seed jars, and small pitchers.

Designs are characteristic and formalized for the first time as regards elements. All true Kana-a Black-on-white types have geometric designs made up of very fine lines, high triangles, and attached dots. These may be combined into several patterns, two of which are shown in the accompanying illustration. Of these the right-hand design was possibly slightly earlier, and in fact somewhat suggests elements found on bas-

Fig. 105. Pottery designs and forms of the most characteristic types of this period. Forms still tend to be globular. Neck coils are most typical, and are diagnostic of this culture and period.

kets. The surface is white, sometimes almost as white as paper, and designs are in a clear, more or less lustrous, black paint. Execution is on the whole good, though a careless overlapping of the fine lines is very typical.

Variations of this general description of the black-on-white pottery of this period are found in the several areas of Pueblo culture. Several specific types have been defined in the eastern portion of the area. Kiatuthlanna Black-on-white is well known; it is polished on the decorated surfaces, has a white slip, and clear black designs which include waved hatched elements as well as the solid triangles, fine lines, and dots. Gladwin has also defined White Mound Black-on-white, which is sand-tempered, has no slip, is more gray than white in color, and has solid triangles, fine lines, and dots as elements of the decoration. In distinction to this he has further defined Red Mesa Black-on-white, which has a clear white slip. It is of particular interest that associated with all of these types in the eastern portion of the Pueblo area there are polished red vessels.

The introduction of any new medium of art expression characteristically leads a people through a period of groping before techniques become standardized. As regards designs this period of trial seems to have been largely confined to Basket Maker III times, for by now it was standardized. Methods of manufacture appear to have been developing, as illustrated by both neck coils and the tendency to globular as well as more formal shapes. Thus Pueblo I people were apparently still much interested in ceramics and were seriously struggling with the problems of this medium.

So few black-on-red types of this period have been found, either in sherds or whole vessels, and so little study has been made of them that they can only be mentioned here. The paint is a lustrous black on a clear red slip. What few designs of this type have been examined by the writer seem to contain many of the elements of the preceding black-on-gray types. It does not yet occur in sufficient abundance to be considered a typical Pueblo pottery.

One of the most interesting pottery types of this time is Abajo Red-on-orange, which was found by Brew on Alkali Ridge in southeastern Utah. It was constructed by coiling and fired in an oxidizing atmosphere. The temper is sand and rock fragments. There is no slip, but the surface is smoothed, and the design is in red through various plum colors to almost black. The designs are suggestive of Basket Maker and Pueblo basket designs, and are like La Plata and Bluff Black-on-red pottery. There are also some parallels with Pueblo I examples from the Piedra region and Dragoon Red-on-brown pottery from southeastern Arizona.

This type is mentioned in some detail because it is so out of place with the other pottery of this general area and time. The fact that it is oxidized and red-on-orange suggests the impetus, for it may have come from outside the general area of Pueblo I culture—perhaps, as is implied above, from the Mogollon region. Were it not for the presence of comparatively small amounts of black-on-red types in all of this area it would be even more striking. Just how and why such oxidized types are found throughout this region is not as yet fully understood, but when it is remembered that brown pottery of considerably earlier date its found here perhaps it is not too surprising. These brown types are generally related, in the broadest way, to Mogollon influences.

This raises the natural question of why and how the Pueblo people developed the distinctive technique of firing by a reducing atmosphere. If they acquired knowledge of pottery making from the Mogollon or Hohokam groups it might be assumed that they would also secure specific firing information and produce brown and red types. As they did not do this, at least to any extent, it is quite likely that they learned of pottery before they were sufficiently in contact with either of these groups to learn exact methods. Such an idea is strengthened by the finding of what is obviously a trade pot in a Basket Maker burial in the four corners area. Individual experimentation in firing led to the use of a reducing atmosphere. As no specific information is to be had on actual firing methods the most that may be said is that in the plateau area a knowledge of pottery preceded definite knowledge of how it was manufactured.

By way of a final comment it might be mentioned that in the eastern San Juan and Little Colorado areas the black-on-white pottery, which is found in the company of neck-corrugated vessels, shows a more Basket Maker III cast, as regards designs, than does that to the west. There is also a difference in black paints, which contained more iron in the east than in the west. This peculiar ceramic mixture has led to much difficulty in determining and correlating definite culture stages in the two areas.

Although house types of the preceding period show considerable variation, those of the present are even more varied. They range from pithouses to surface structures, and are sometimes combined in the same site. Some of the surface rooms were even apparently made with fairly good masonry.

Probably the most interesting general structures were those found in southeastern Utah and southwestern Colorado and reported by Brew and Morris respectively. The accompanying illustration is a segment of a site from the La Plata district as reported by Morris. There are long lines of contiguous surface storage rooms, a part of which are enlarged and are apparently living rooms. Inside of these, and separated from them, are pithouses, which Morris has suggested are proto-kivas. Since he assigns this site to late Basket Maker III and Pueblo I they are of particular interest to us, for they may be the earliest massed arrangements of surface rooms found anywhere in the Southwest. Essentially the same situation existed at Alkali Ridge, where one village contained up to 300 rooms. The pithouses are of the type with ridges on the floor. This general village arrangement is probably the ancestor of the unit type of pueblo which developed shortly later and which then had a definite kiva associated with it.

In the area immediately south of the four corners, in the Chaco branch, Gladwin defined three phases, all of which fall in this period. He feels they show an evolution through time, and there can be little doubt that the structures do show such a development. The White Mound phase has structures much like those reported by Morris and Brew, but less pretentious, with pit structures and blocks of storage rooms associated. The Kiatuthlanna phase was largely defined by pottery types, but the Red

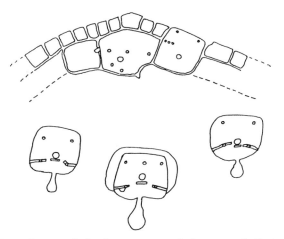

Fig. 106. A portion of one of the larger sites of this period. It is made up of both surface and pit structures, and was reported by Morris in the La Plata district.

Mesa phase, which dates later in the period, had blocks of house units and pretty definite kivas. The associated culture is still essentially Pueblo I, and the dates are in the ninth century A.D. Here, then, the series may be shown evolving typologically to the unit type of structure, so that it was just one step to the larger pueblos of the succeeding time.

Villages of the earlier type are found extending westward through the immediate San Juan drainage, and they appear to have survived as an important architectural feature for some time. This apparently rapid development of surface rooms in some areas might well explain the report by Guernsey of circular slab-lined rooms in loosely organized groups at Sa-a-kim Village. A quick transition from this type through the rectangular pit form to the surface structure would account for his also finding associated square-cornered rooms above ground. These were of adobe and stone masonry, and were roughly grouped into communities, both in the open and in caves. A somewhat comparable situation was reported by Roberts in the Piedra River area. Here he found pithouses singly, and roughly grouped into small units about what appears to have been a kiva. They are very shallow, almost surface rooms, and contained corner posts. The kiva-like structures are very suggestive of pithouses, and are of circular form, but with four posts supporting the roof.

In the western San Juan area Cummings considered the rectangular pit-house to be the most characteristic house of this period. Guernsey describes the house as varying from rectangular slab-lined pithouses to surface masonry rooms. Both are probably correct, for this was certainly a

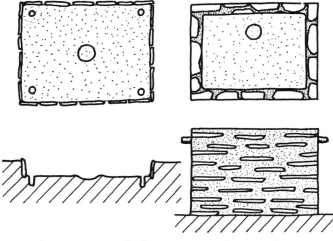

Fig. 107. Rectangular structures which are nearing the typical masonry of later stages vary from slab-lined shallow pithouses to surface structures as shown. The type of masonry shown is few rocks and much adobe clay, and though found most typically in the western San Juan may be a stage in the evolution of stone masonry.

period of transition, when many traits were rapidly changing, and it is most likely that some surface structures were being made in this western section. In the Hopi country, the Colorado River drainage area, and perhaps parts of the western San Juan, rectangular pithouses lasted quite late, but in other portions of the plateau, as has been indicated, they seem to have either been lacking or of very short duration between circular pit-houses and surface structures.

Not only were pithouses and surface structures being produced but various methods of wall construction were being tested. Wattlework walls were rather common, rocks were used either sparingly with much clay or more as definite walls, and even adobe "turtle backs" were being employed. Thus the entire matter of structures seems clearly to have been in a state of experimentation and transition.

The Pueblo I physical type has nowhere been reported in detail. Apparently all skulls were deformed posteriorly. Guernsey describes the skeleton as light-framed.

Although burials are extremely rare, the few that have been recovered are flexed. This corresponds to the earlier types of burials in the plateau area. They occur in caves, in rubbish heaps, and very rarely under the floors of rooms. The scarcity of material of this age and pure culture makes generalized statements regarding both physical type and burial customs none too reliable.

Pueblo I metates seem to have been of two closely allied types. By far the more common is made of a rather flat slab of stone with a depressed lineal grinding face open at only one end. The accompanying illustration shows such a flat sandstone metate. These are found in the eastern San Juan, locally throughout the Little Colorado area, and sporadically in the west. The second type is the trough-shaped metate open at both ends. This is found over much the same area, though more sparingly, and seems to have been most common in the west. Manos are of the block type.

Fig. 108. The flat-slab sandstone type of metate pictured seems to have been the most typical of this period. It is usually open at only one end, and has a lineal grinding surface.

Mauls are found to be relatively abundant in sites of this age. They are predominantly of the full-grooved type, although some three-quarter-grooved forms appear. As these have already been described they will not be reviewed. Axes are characteristically of the full-grooved type. Quite a few are roughly chipped and show little grinding even on the cutting edge, but have a notch on each side for hafting. Ground forms, though rarer, are much more perfectly made and are like the types already described. All have relatively short bits.

Points are well made and well shaped. Flaking is predominantly finished by pressure, with the result that the edges are much better controlled. The side notch is typical, and long, slender, delicate points are not uncommon. All are much lighter in weight, and most are smaller than atlatl dart points, although it is certainly conceivable that either might be larger or smaller than the other.

Baskets continued in much the same forms, weaves, and designs as those made previously. Guernsey reports finding an unusually fine carrying basket which had high triangles in red and black bands as an element of the design. Some analogy might be drawn between this example and the prevailing pottery decorations.

The true yucca ring basket was the main basketry contribution of this period. It was made by plaiting or twilling yucca leaves together into a shallow bowl-shaped mat. The ends of the leaves were then brought up inside a wooden ring, turned down over the outside, and tied. This resulted in a shallow basket which could be used as a sieve, and is identical in every way to similar baskets made today by the Hopi Indians.

The development of the ring basket and its steady increase in popularity paralleled the rise of pottery. At the same time the larger of the coiled baskets decreased in number. This was perhaps the natural result of the substitution of one type of container for another, for with the development of ceramics, baskets, which were more tedious to construct, would have become less popular than pottery.

Besides the types already mentioned, rush and reed mats were extensively made and used. These were abundant throughout all succeeding periods, being sometimes used as floor-coverings, roof coverings, or even as storage-pit linings. Crushed cedar-bark mats and bags do not seem to have survived.

Practically nothing is known about sandals. Guernsey pictures and describes one sandal with a rounded toe which he believes to be Pueblo I. It is quite likely that the finer woven types of the preceding period survived, at least to a slight extent. The weave of the one specimen pictured is twined.

Fig. 109. Sandal type pictured by Guernsey, which he feels is Pueblo I.

Knowledge of cloth fabrics from Pueblo I is as limited as that of other perishable materials. Cotton was certainly introduced at this time, as fragments of cotton cloth have been found by several investigators. The question of the derivation of Southwestern cotton has been raised many times but never satisfactorily answered. A wild cotton grows in the southern part of the state, and it is possible that domestic cotton was derived from it. The fact that the Hohokam people are known to have had cotton at a slightly earlier date would indicate that the Pueblo groups derived this material already domesticated from them. By now corn had become much more varied.

Regarding hunting implements the only definite knowledge is that the bow and arrow replaced the atlatl and dart. The substitution took place late in the preceding period and had apparently become definitely established. Other hunting implements are not known, unless awls and the axe may be so classed.

Foods also are little known. As has been suggested, corn of several varieties was grown, and squash and beans were common. It is also quite likely that the turkey was still domesticated by at least those groups actually in the San Juan area, for turkey remains are found abundantly in later periods there.

Ornaments are not well known. Feathers undoubtedly still played an important part in decoration, but beads were more common and better made. Many are smaller than those of the preceding stage. A much greater use of turquoise was characteristic at least of the eastern part of the area.

In summary only a few traits are known to be distinctive of this stage of culture. Probably the most distinctive single trait is the corrugated-neck jar. Associated with this in more or less amounts is found the Kana-a style of decoration, with very fine lines, attached dots, and high triangles. Regionally other black-on-white types show styles of design more nearly approaching Basket Maker III. The house varied greatly in the several regions, so that no one form may be said to be typical. The metate is of two types, the most important innovation of which is the establishment of a definite lineal grinding surface, often open only at one end. Other cultural material is too mixed with that of other stages or too little known to draw sweeping conclusions.

One other question should be discussed before going on to later periods. The traits constituting Basket Maker culture have already been summarized and form a long and impressive list. Certain traditions of artistic and utilitarian endeavor have been pointed out, particularly in weaving. Gourds hung in nets and baskets formed the main container group, and fabrics of many sorts were manufactured. Houses were at best unimpressive habitations. Pueblo culture saw a shift of interest in all these respects. Houses almost immediately became much elaborated and moved up to the surface of the ground. Stone masonry soon became a most characteristic trait. Pottery developed to such an extent that it began to replace other containers and formed a new avenue of artistic expression. Baskets were still made, but in far less numbers. The introduction of cotton as a fiber suitable for weaving made possible certain soft cloth fabrics that were not known previously, and the use of human hair or yucca and apocynum fibers became less. The bow and arrow, becoming a more efficient weapon for hunting and warfare, widened the sphere of such activities, and the substantial house made life possible in any area and under almost any condition. This is well illustrated by the fact that almost no Pueblo I sites have been found in caves.

THE COLORADO RIVER

To the west of the Anasazi area at this time, along the Colorado River, is a culture which Colton has defined as the Patayan. That it is distinctly different from the Pueblo cannot be doubted, but that it is related to it in its earliest portion is equally certain. The most extensive surveys and evaluations of the Colorado River region have been undertaken by Schroeder, who has suggested various terms to identify portions of this area culturally. One of the most interesting proposals he has made is that all of the cultures which developed from west of the Mogollon Rim and to the Colorado River might be called Hakataya. This would include what other archaeologists would consider to be quite different kinds of development, but there is much to recommend his attitude. He would derive this cultural evolution, over this wide area, originally from the Desert culture, which it has already been suggested goes back to ancient beginnings. Since it is impossible in a work of this sort to evaluate the validity of such a contention, our main attention will be directed to the identification of the cultural divisions in this western area.

Schroeder has suggested that only the northern development on the Colorado River be called Patayan. This would include the Cerbat branch on the west and the Cohonina on the east. The cultures found in the rest of the river, from its mouth to the dam, he would call Laguish. That they may be separated into two identifiable divisions is quite apparent.

It has already been suggested that very early cultures developed in the desert section of the lower portion of this area, and that something which bridged the gap to this period must be assumed. The culture which Rogers has called Yuman I probably fulfills this requirement, at least to some extent. Schroeder has suggested that a branch which he has called the Palo Verde existed at this time in the lowest part of the river valley. North of it is what he feels was a westward extension of the Hohokam culture, and in fact Gila Pueblo has found some red-on-buff pottery of this period here. Between here and the Cerbat branch so little is known that it is impossible to suggest just what may have existed.

In the big bend area of the Colorado River the Cerbat branch was in existence. The pottery in relation to that of the Cohonina, to the east, is more brownish rather than primarily gray. In fact there is a graduation from more gray pottery in the east to more brown in the west, suggesting poorer control of firing methods in the west. This pottery includes both jars and bowls, and most of it has some mica in the temper. The structures are indicated by rock outlines. Further definition of this culture must await more complete survey and excavation.

To the east, roughly in the area south of the Grand Canyon, and west to include Mount Floyd, is the Cohonina culture. It is at present the best

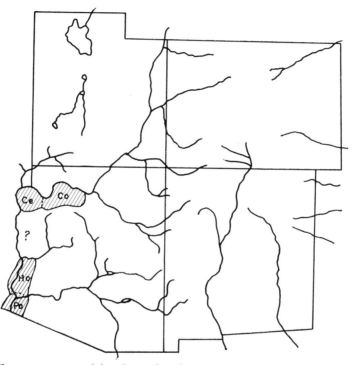

Fig. 110. The area occupied by the Colorado River cultures at this time. In the north are the Cerbat branch on the west and the Cohonina on the east. At the mouth of the river is the Palo Verde branch and above it a westward extension of Hohokam. What lies between the Cerbat and this is still not fully enough known to define.

known of any of these groups because of more excavation and perhaps even more thorough survey. The pottery types which are found here include Deadmans Gray and Deadmans Fugitive Red, in the plain types. These are found in both bowls and jars, and the paste, temper, and method of construction are the same, the only difference being the use of a fugitive red on the outsides of the red jars and rare bowls. The paste is sandy and the temper includes some very small flakes of mica.

The decorated pottery of this period and area has been identified as Floyd Black-on-gray and a variant which is the same but with a fugitive red outside. Forms are dominantly bowls, which are rather deep and hemispherical. Much of this pottery is indistinguishable, in gross examination, from Kana-a Black-on-white, for it is often almost white, the decorated surface is well polished, and the designs are essentially identical. The relationship between the two cannot be questioned. There is, however, an almost total lack of Kana-a Gray pottery here, so that neck coils are not found. They do occur quite commonly in the succeeding period on Deadmans Gray. The main distinguishing feature between Kana-a Black-on-white and Floyd Black-on-gray is the minute mica flakes found in the latter and lacking in the former. It has also been assumed that Patayan pottery was made by the paddle and anvil method.

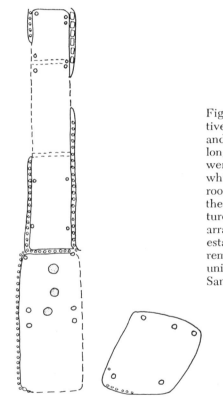

Fig. 111. The most distinctive house type of this time and Cohonina area is the long series of rooms which were surface, and one of which served as the living room. To the south end on the east there is a pit structure. Enough of this general arrangement were found to establish it as a type. It is reminiscent of similar long units found in the eastern San Juan at this time.

Houses in this area are very interesting. In the eastern portion of the Cohonina area a circular pithouse, shallow and very like similar pithouses in the western San Juan, was found. In it were sherds which were definitely Kana-a Black-on-white. In the western part of this area, however, there were quite different structures. Probably the most distinctive was a long series of rooms, very slightly excavated or not at all. The smaller of these were storage rooms, but the larger was a living area. At the south end, to the east in each case, a definite fairly rectangular pit structure was found.

These units are in a very general way reminiscent of the contemporary structures of the eastern San Juan. The most interesting fact of their construction is that they were built by sinking posts into the ground and building a substantial flat roof on top of them. Poles were then set on top of the ground and extended to this roof, withes were interwoven between them, and the whole plastered over. This resulted in a wattle and daub wall. Just what function the pit structure to the east had is unknown, but it is tempting to suggest that it may have been ceremonial in nature. What fire areas were found were in the larger, more substantial rooms, and they were not constructed basins but rather just areas.

The weather in this section of the Southwest is mild over much of the year, but does get cold in the winter, so that another allied concept seems to have been the shade. This was just a roof under which work could be done in hot weather, and on top of which it was carried out during cooler periods. Another type of structure, which has been called a patio house,

A large Cohonina surface structure during excavation. Note the standing clay wall to the left with the post holes in it. The strings are used in locating features and mapping.

began at this time, but was so much more typical later that the description of it will be deferred. It is quite likely that the so-called forts of the Cohonina culture were a development from this early long house type.

In stone tools metates were of both the basin and scoop types, the latter being by far the most typical. Manos were more or less of the block type, and hammerstones and polishing stones were relatively abundant. Chipped stone points, as shown in the accompanying diagram, were very well made, and often had small serrations on the edges. They are slightly suggestive

Fig. 112. Typical projectile points of this period are long and slender and have serrations. The drill was also a part of this culture.

of contemporary Hohokam points but are not so ornate, and they lack the large barbs. The stems are formed by small corner notches. Another type is a simple triangular point, which was generally not quite so well flaked. Expanded stemmed drills are also found.

One of the striking features of this culture throughout its existence is the virtual lack of any ornaments. Axes also seem to have been very rare, despite the fact that the Hohokam made considerable use of them.

Data concerning perishable material for this area is completely lacking, for no dry caves have been dug, although at least one is known. No direct data is at hand concerning food, but it has been assumed by the writer that these people had corn, because of the presence of many metates and manos, and that they did considerable hunting and preparing of hides. With respect to their ceremonial life there is no direct data either, unless the presence of pit structures associated with the long structures may be so regarded. In the following period there is some slight indication that sweat baths may have been in use.

In summary it may be said that the culture of the entire Colorado River, from the Grand Canyon to its mouth, is sufficiently different from that of other areas to justify setting it apart. Relationships and influences seem to be rather widespread, but the basis of this way of life is probably rooted far back in time. This is an area where more research would be well rewarded. As is the case in most areas where excavation has been undertaken, distinctive houses have been found. Pottery is the second identifying trait, and it is sufficiently distinctive to set this section off as different from others.

OOTAM

In the area where Mogollon and Hohokam cultures are shown by the maps to be overlapping, a distinctive mixture of these two cultures may be seen. Di Peso has suggested that this constitutes a distinguishable entity which he has called the Ootam. The Amerind Foundation of Dragoon has done considerable work in this section and has succeeded in defining a long series of stages, the earliest of which appear to date at about this time.

Two sites, the Gleeson site and the earliest part of the Tres Alamos site, are good examples of the nature of this culture. At the Gleeson site there seems to have been a peculiar, or at least distinctive, mixture of Mogollon and Hohokam cultures. Mogollon traits have been identified by Tuthill as burials, pit ovens, bone tool types, and figurines. Traits he assigns to Hohokam are houses, the general level of the economy, shell work, figurines, pottery, and stone work. Here he found 9 cremations and 102 inhumations, all flexed. Stone axes are of the three-quarter-grooved type. There are palettes and shell bracelets, some like Hohokam types, and painted bone tubes. Bone awls lack the notch typical of Mogollon.

The native pottery has been identified as Dragoon Red-on-brown. It is tempered with sand and light angular chunks, but otherwise seems to be a specialized Hohokam type. Trade pottery was found here from the Mogollon-Mimbres area to the east, the Trincheras culture to the south and southwest, and the Hohokam to the west. In general Tuthill is inclined to feel that this represents a special phase of the Hohokam rather than Mogollon.

The earliest phase at the Tres Alamos site, the Cascabel, may perhaps more definitely be assigned to this period, for it is believed to date from about A.D. 700 to 900. Houses are pithouses, and the typical red-on-brown pottery is unslipped on the exterior and slipped on the interior. This phase also has both cremations and inhumations, and at least in later stages pithouses which were built into groups with compound walls. Some of the pithouses are square or rectangular, and deep, with entrances like those of Mogollon, and some have more rounded ends and stepped entrances like slightly later Hohokam. Although no stratigraphy was found here, the trash mounds on the site were shallow and of one phase only.

The kind of intergradation which is found in these sites, and others in this area, is probably a condition which prevailed much more widely than is at present commonly recognized. Wherever sufficiently intensive work is undertaken similar situations seem to be uncovered. A somewhat comparable condition will be pointed out later for the Flagstaff area, where shortly a considerable admixture of cultures will be seen.

THE RIO GRANDE

From the accompanying map it may be seen that the occupation of the Rio Grande valley was centered in the central portion. There can be little doubt that other areas were also occupied, but not a great deal is known, or at least published, concerning them. In the south there was apparently still brown pottery, and small sites over a considerable area. In the central portion the main local pottery type seems to have been San Marcial Black-on-white. Here, and to the north, there are Lino Gray and variants of this type, and apparently some Kana-a.

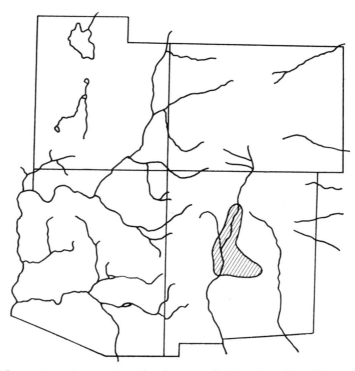

Fig. 113. The main concentration of culture in the Rio Grande valley seems to have been about the area indicated on this map. There can be little doubt that a larger area was occupied, but present evidence is not sufficient to make the drawing of lines of maximum spread possible.

In the northern part of the Rio Grande the sites contemporary with Pueblo I, and hence of this period, are small and slightly more numerous than those of Basket Maker III. The northern extension is about that indicated on the map, or to the mouth of the Chama River. Sites here contain Kana-a Gray and Alma Neck Banded as well as Kiatuthlanna Black-on-white. Occasionally sherds of La Plata Black-on-red and Abajo Red-on-orange are found.

The general lack of sites of this period in the northern Rio Grande has led Wendorf to raise the question of whether or not the Athabascans had entered this portion of the Southwest by now. The abundance of sites of this period to the immediate north and west, and the strikingly high development of architecture there, would seem to indicate that something was keeping these people out of the northern Rio Grande valley.

In the southern portion of the Rio Grande valley the Jornada branch of the Mogollon culture had its beginning by at least about this time. It is typified by the presence of the brown pottery types noted above.

Courtesy of the Arizona State Museum

Examples of both extended and semiflexed burials. These lack offerings, but many burials include pots and other articles.

SUMMARY

By way of comparison a brief examination of the various maps of this period will show how cultures tend to overlap areally. There is a clear intermingling of Hohokam and Mogollon in southern Arizona. The Mogollon and Anasazi continue to overlap to a considerable extent, as shown by the presence of Mogollon pottery types, or derived forms, in the Pueblo country. The Mogollon also spread toward and perhaps into the lower Rio Grande area in the south, and Anasazi clearly spread into the northern Rio Grande area, beginning what amounted to a long period of Pueblo dominance of this region. Similar intergradations of culture may be seen in the Cibola-Chaco-Acoma area, where pottery types and even house types show considerable variation.

Ceramics typical of the various cultures are more clear-cut now, yet Mogollon and Hohokam pottery types seem to intergrade somewhat in the area occupied by the Ootam. Designs, and probably also forms, were widely borrowed from one culture to another, and it will be seen that in immediately subsequent periods more design borrowing was practiced. However, certain general characteristics stamp the pottery of each of these major cultures. Mogollon pottery was scraped and then polished, often resulting in a marked dimpled effect on the outsides of vessels, it was oxidized so that reds were now typical of this group, and smudging was very characteristic in the north part of the Mogollon range. Hohokam pottery was finished by the paddle and anvil process, was fired in an oxidizing atmosphere so that buffs were typical, and contained mica as a part of the temper in greater or lesser amounts. Anasazi pottery was scraped and polished, and the most typical was fired in a reducing atmosphere to produce white and gray types. The black-on-white types had become more formalized in design, but varied significantly by regions. Black-on-red types had become a part of this culture, and the distinctive Abajo Black-on-orange of the northeast was being made.

Structures were equally varied at this time. The area of the greatest architectural advance was the four corners. Here architectural types ranged from pithouses to surface or near surface units with what have often been called proto-kivas. The blocks of rooms included both storage units and living quarters, and were built in almost every conceivable manner from adobe blocks through wattle and daub walls to the use of stone. Toward the end of the period many of these units strongly suggest the unit type of proto-pueblo, and some were even combined into larger assemblages totaling some 300 rooms. In the Cohonina area, far to the west, other long units of rooms were also associated with pit structures on the south and east.

They too showed varying methods of construction from wattle and daub to stone. In much of the rest of the Anasazi area pithouses seem to have been the most common type of dwelling, and this was also true of the Mogollon area and the Hohokam. Ceremonial chambers or kivas were a part of the Mogollon culture, and the Hohokam had large ball courts, which probably had at least some ceremonial or religious significance.

In all of these cultures the most striking advance was made by the Hohokam. Here Mexican influence had become more intensified, and a rapid development of arts and crafts took place. Irrigation was also certainly established, and agriculture must have become even more important to their way of life. The next greatest advance took place in the Anasazi culture in the plateau area. This was really a time period rather than a culture stage, for it was a period of transition from what might be considered a Basket Maker way of life to Pueblo. The stage was set for a very rapid florescence which was to take place during the next period. Many traits were widely diffused now through these various cultures, although each somehow managed to give each culture an individual stamp of its own.

It would seem that Mogollon culture was still exerting a considerable influence on Anasazi culture to the north. The Hohokam, with their more advanced state, were certainly having some effect on the development of Mogollon culture, and apparently less direct effect on the developing Pueblo culture to the north. On the west Patayan culture seems at this stage in our knowledge to have had a quite independent cast, but it too was certainly being influenced to some extent by the Anasazi, and probably to a lesser extent by the Hohokam. The use of the brush shade or outdoor kitchen is a point in case.

Some areas seem to have been rather sparsely settled, particularly the northern Rio Grande, as has been noted. Certain regions were also showing a very rapid development, while others were quite backward. The higher country around Flagstaff is a case of peripheral or retarded culture. Now Mogollon was certainly not advancing as rapidly as either Hohokam or Anasazi, although it appears that Mogollon was the original stimulus of both of these cultures and areas. Thus there was a shift of leadership to the four corners and the desert areas.

The most important region to an understanding of the development of the Southwest from now on was that section stretching from the four corners in the north south into Mexico. Here things were already beginning to happen on a rather grand scale, and they would continue to do so. As one goes outward from this center the cultures are found to vary considerably, and in general to be less vigorous.

From this point on Pueblo culture was destined to have a very rapid rise, and to radiate outward to influence other areas and cultures. Hohokam culture was soon to reach a peak and begin a decline, or at least to show less advance. Mogollon culture had already lost its initial vigor. This was then a period of comparatively great change, and general stimulus and unrest in the Southwest. In many areas populations were on the increase, and this was to reach a peak in the following period.

Sources and Additional References

Beals, Ralph L., G. W. Brainerd, and Watson Smith. Archaeological Studies in Northeastern Arizona, *Publications in American Archaeology and Ethnology,* Vol. 44, No. 1, 1945, University of California Press, Berkeley. (Includes some Pueblo I sites and pottery.)

Brew, J. O. * Archaeology of Alkali Ridge, Southeastern Utah, *Papers of the Peabody Museum of American Archaeology and Ethnology,* Vol. 21, 1946, Harvard University, Cambridge, Massachusetts. (One of the largest Pueblo I sites thus far dug and reported, and a most interesting one.)

Colton, Harold S. The Patayan Problem in the Colorado River Valley, *Southwestern Journal of Anthropology,* Vol. 1, No. 1, 1945, University of New Mexico Press, Albuquerque. (The argument for the Patayan as a root in the Colorado River area.)

Danson, Edward Bridge. An Archaeological Survey of West Central New Mexico and East Central Arizona, *Papers of the Peabody Museum of American Archaeology and Ethnology,* Vol. 44, No. 1, 1957, Harvard University, Cambridge, Massachusetts. (Discussion of the distribution and nature of the various cultures in this area.)

Fulton, W. S., and Carr Tuthill. An Archaeological Site Near Gleeson, Arizona, No. 1, 1940, the Amerind Foundation, Inc., Dragoon, Arizona. (An example of the Ootam culture in southeastern Arizona at this time.)

Gladwin, H. S. The Chaco Branch, Excavations at White Mound and in the Red Mesa Valley, *Medallion Paper 33,* 1945, Gila Pueblo, Globe, Arizona. (Report on the sites and culture of this period of the Chaco branch.)

Gladwin, H. S., Emil W. Haury, E. B. Sayles, and Nora Gladwin. * Excavations at Snaketown, Material Culture, *Medallion Paper 25,* 1937, Gila Pueblo, Globe, Arizona. (The most complete report on a Hohokam site including this period.)

Guernsey, Samuel J. * Explorations in Northeastern Arizona, *Papers of the Peabody Museum of American Archaeology and Ethnology,* Vol. 12, No. 1, 1931, Harvard University, Cambridge, Massachusetts. (Consult the tabulated lists at the end of this paper.)

Haury, Emil W. * Roosevelt: 9-6, a Hohokam Site of the Colonial Period, *Medallion Paper 11,* 1932, Gila Pueblo, Globe, Arizona. (Excellent report on a Colonial site.)

———. * The Mogollon Culture of Southwestern New Mexico, *Medallion Paper 20,* 1936, Gila Pueblo, Globe, Arizona. (Original definition of Mogollon.)

Kidder, Alfred Vincent. An Introduction to the Study of Southwestern Archaeology, Phillips Academy, Andover, Massachusetts, 1924. (Pueblo I culture is discussed under the heading of "Sites with Less Developed Pottery [Pre-Pueblo].")

Kidder, Alfred Vincent, and Samuel J. Guernsey. Archaeological Explorations in Northeastern Arizona, *Bulletin 65*, 1919, Bureau of American Ethnology, Washington, D.C. (Pueblo I culture is treated herein.)

Martin, Paul S., John B. Rinaldo, Elaine A. Bluhm, Hugh C. Cutler, and Roger Grange, Jr. * Mogollon Cultural Continuity and Change: The Stratigraphic Analysis of Tularosa and Cordova Caves, *Fieldiana: Anthropology*, Vol. 40, 1952, Chicago Natural History Museum. (Major reference for the perishable materials of this period.)

Martin, Paul S., and Elizabeth S. Willis. Anasazi Painted Pottery in Field Museum of Natural History, *Anthropology Memoir 5*, 1940, Field Museum of Natural History, Chicago. (Examples of Pueblo I pottery types.)

Morris, Earl H. * Archaeological Studies in the La Plata District, Southwestern Colorado and Northwestern New Mexico, *Carnegie Institution Publication 519*, 1939, Washington, D.C. (See particularly "Site 23" and the introduction for a discussion of Pueblo I.)

Roberts, Frank H. H., Jr. * Early Pueblo Ruins in the Piedra District, Southwestern Colorado, *Bulletin 96*, 1930, Bureau of American Ethnology, Washington, D.C. (Discussion of the eastern phase of this culture, showing surface houses of several rooms.)

————. * The Ruins at Kiatuthlanna, Eastern Arizona, *Bulletin 100*, 1931, Bureau of American Ethnology, Washington, D.C. (Contains a discussion of Pueblo I material found in the pithouses.)

Rogers, Malcolm J. * An Outline of Yuman Prehistory, *Southwestern Journal of Anthropology*, Vol. 1, No. 2, 1945, University of New Mexico Press, Albuquerque. (Excellent statement of Yuman prehistory with the definitions of Yuman I, II, and III.)

Schroeder, Albert H. The Hakataya Cultural Tradition. Facts and Comments, *American Antiquity*, Vol. 23, No. 2, Part 1, 1957, Society for American Archaeology, Salt Lake City, Utah. (Definition and discussion of the Hakataya.)

————. The Hohokam, Sinagua and the Hakataya, *Archives of Archaeology*, No. 5, 1960 (on 4 microcards), Society for American Archaeology and the University of Wisconsin Press, Madison. (Statement of the Hakataya as defined by Schroeder, and the nature and relationship of the various divisions within it.)

Tuthill, Carr. The Tres Alamos Site on the San Pedro River, Southeastern Arizona, No. 4, 1947, the Amerind Foundation, Inc., Dragoon, Arizona. (Example of a site intermediate between Hohokam and Mogollon at about this time.)

Wendorf, Fred. A Reconstruction of Northern Rio Grande Prehistory, *American Anthropologist*, Vol. 56, No. 2, Part 1, 1954, Menasha, Wisconsin. (Brief statement of this period for the northern Rio Grande.)

Wheat, Joe Ben. * Mogollon Culture Prior to A.D. 1000, *American Antiquity*, Vol. 20, No. 4, Part 2, 1955, Society for American Archaeology, Salt Lake City, Utah. (The various branches defined and correlated, with approximate dates.)

Woodward, Arthur. The Grewe site, *Occasional Paper 1*, 1931, Los Angeles Museum of History, Science, and Art, Los Angeles, California. (Contains a good deal of information about a Colonial site.)

XII

Dissemination Period: A.D. 900 to 1100

MOGOLLON

The extent of area occupied by Mogollon culture of this period is entirely dependent on how Mogollon is defined. If it includes all those sites which contain pottery that shows relationships back into earlier stages of this culture then it extends over a considerable area. If, on the other hand, it is limited to what could only be considered the most typical sites it would have to be restricted, being limited to a much more southern extent.

The accompanying map has been prepared to show the maximum extent which may be considered Mogollon rather than the minimum. A line has been drawn which separates the northeastern from the southwestern portion, to indicate the area dominated by the expanding Pueblo culture to the north, and that mixed with Hohokam on the south and west. Reference to the contemporary maps of Pueblo and Hohokam cultures will show that these two clearly overlap the Mogollon, and this intermingling of the three has resulted in the blurring of what may be considered typical Mogollon.

In the core area two phases date at about this time, though they are probably not limited to the period indicated. These are the Three Circle and Reserve phases. In the Mimbres area the Mangus phase is late, and in the Forestdale area the Cerros and Encinas have been allocated to this time by Wheat. He has also assigned the Corduroy phase in the Forestdale area to this time. Thus there are several distinct divisions of Mogollon now, and each has identifying features, many of which are combinations of traits from outlying areas.

In general this seems to have been a time of abrupt change in the Gila and Salt river basins, and traits from this area spread into the Mogollon branches, particularly to the south. There was a similar southward expansion of Pueblo culture, and this resulted in many modifications of pottery

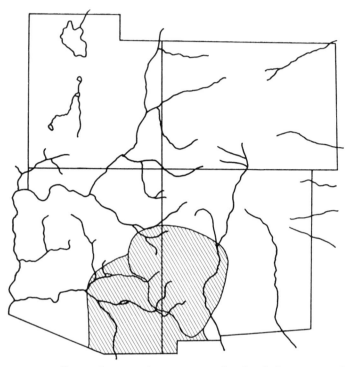

Fig. 114. Mogollon culture at this time may be divided into a northern or northeastern and southern or southwestern section. To the north by at least A.D. 1000 Pueblo culture was beginning to exert a considerable influence on it as shown by house types and pottery. The southern extension into Mexico shows continued relations in this direction.

and house types to the north. Since this is a period of blending of these cultures, as time goes on it becomes increasingly difficult to define and trace the limits of Mogollon culture. The northward blending seems to have been largely with the Chaco and Cibola branches, and in fact both Martin and Rinaldo are firm in their conviction that Mogollon developed into Zuñi culture as it continued to evolve in this area. After about A.D. 900 the brown ceramic complex spread to the Jornada branch on the east.

The southward extension into Mexico is very definitely indicated at this time. Studies made by Di Peso at Casas Grandes, and in the vicinity of this settlement, show that red-on-brown pottery had an early existence in this part of northern Mexico. Recently derived tree-ring dates from

Casas Grandes itself extend from the ninth century to as late as perhaps
A.D. 1400, or show a span of some 500 years or more. Thus Mogollon, as
such, was clearly related to the south rather early, and it apparently gradually contracted in this direction as time went on. This was partly induced
by the vigorous expansion of the Pueblo culture from now on.

Fig. 115. Pottery of this period includes a great deal of regional variation, both as
regards shapes and designs. The right-hand column of forms are all decorated types,
and the two examples of design are of northern related black-on-white pottery. Corrugated types, some indented and some not, were common. A few vessels were corrugated all over, and with plain corrugations and indented corrugations in patterns.
The scoop seems to have been derived more from the Hohokam than from the north.

Pottery, as well as house types, shows considerable regional variation.
A good deal of textured pottery, or that with manipulation of the surface
in various ways, is found, particularly in the central portion of the area
occupied. Neck coils are fairly abundant, and especially in the north there
are vessels with over-all corrugations. Some of these latter have indented
corrugations in bands or forming geometric patterns. Forms also vary by
regions, those in the north showing types suggestive of the developing
Pueblo shapes, while those in the southwest include scoops, more reminiscent of the Hohokam.

Decorated pottery is also considerably varied, the most striking feature
of which is the common occurrence of solid and hatched balanced areas,
as shown in the accompanying illustration. There is a definite relationship
in decorated design styles with the Chaco Canyon area to the northeast,
and the question of just where this style of design developed first may be
raised.

By this time Alma Plain and San Francisco Red were becoming much more rare, but such types as Reserve Smudged, Reserve Black-on-white, Reserve Indented Corrugated, and incised corrugated were more common, at least in the latter part of this period and in the Mimbres or central area. Trade types include a considerable variety, but Puerco Black-on-white and Mimbres Black-on-white were found here as well as the plain types.

This period may be divided rather logically into an earlier and a later segment, the latter showing more marked influence from the Anasazi, and this is particularly apparent in the decorated pottery. In the San Simon branch, to the southwest, two types are found. The earliest of these, Cerros Black-on-white, is a variant of Three Circle Red-on-white, which has already been discussed. It has a white slip with a red painted design, and occurs in the forms of both jars and bowls. The design includes such elements as curvilinear lines, for the first time, scrolls and squiggles, and similar features. The perhaps somewhat later Encinas Red-on-brown is a red or purplish paint on a brown background. The designs are both curvilinear and rectangular, and include the use of small repeated elements. The edges of the painting are slightly blurred into the background, a feature we have already seen as typical of many of the Mogollon pottery types.

In the Mimbres area Three Circle Black-on-white undoubtedly survived into the early part of this period. Later Mimbres Bold Face Black-on-white came into being. This latter type was probably much influenced in its development by the Pueblo culture from the north. The paste is gray, the temper coarse and angular and predominantly soft, although some quartz sand is found. Interiors of bowls are smoothed and have a chalky white polished slip, while exteriors are unslipped and gray to brown in color. Decoration varies between black and a chocolate brown. Execution of design is better than in preceding types, and there are new elements such as scrolls and wavy hatching lines. Shapes are bowls, jars, seed jars, and pitchers. This type precedes Mimbres Classic Black-on-white.

In the Reserve phase there is Reserve Black-on-white. The temper is angular and opaque and is probably at least in part crushed sherds. The core is white or gray, the vessels are slipped and polished, and the paint is mineral black. As may be seen from the examples of design a considerable use was made of balanced triangular solid and hatched areas. The most common form is the pitcher, but jars and bowls were also made. It has been suggested that this type is an early form of Tularosa Black-on-white, and that it is related to Puerco Black-on-white. It may be distinguished from Tularosa because the Tularosa hatching is finer and better controlled.

To the south and east the Capitan and Mesilla phases have been identified as belonging to the Jornada branch and being assignable to the
Mogollon culture. The main distinguishing feature of this area is the abundant presence of El Paso Brown pottery, and relatively late the occurrence of some El Paso Polychrome.

When houses are considered, equally varied types are found. Before
about A.D. 1000 pithouses were more common, but after this date, particularly in the central and northern portions, surface multiroom structures
prevailed. A typical pithouse of the Three Circle phase is illustrated. It
was rectangular, had a sloping entrance passage, firepit near the entrance,
and four corner posts. Others had four corner posts and sometimes others
on the central axis. This type is obviously a continuation of preceding
pithouses which have been seen to be typical of the earlier evolution of
Mogollon.

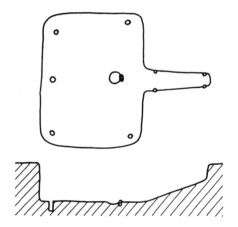

Fig. 116. The house of the
Three Circle phase is more
distinctly rectangular with
nearly square corners. Four
corner posts and another
near the back wall are characteristic. Note the long entrance and the firepit with a
rock on the front edge which
acts as a slight deflector to
fresh air drafts.

At Point of Pines, the Black River branch of the Mogollon is represented
by Nantack Village. It consists of 11 semisubterranean pithouses and a
kiva. The pithouses are rectangular and have lateral entrances. Ceramics
are similar to Three Circle Mogollon. The main village seems to have been
occupied between about A.D. 900 and 1100, although there were scattered
farm houses to perhaps as late as A.D. 1275.

Farther north, or at later times, there are multiroom surface structures.
These vary from a few rooms to a good many, and most of them have
associated kivas. The types of wall construction vary from flat rocks laid
up in a minimum of mortar, to boulders, to adobe or even wattle and
daub walls. Kivas are of considerable interest at this time, one reported
by Bluhm being particularly so. To the west of it was a small surface
masonry pueblo of eight or ten rooms. The kiva is a comparatively large

structure 26 by 32 feet on a side, and has a long sloping entrance. There are three supporting posts on the central line, two nearer the entrance, a fireplace near the entrance, masonry walls, and what appear to be floor drums. These are long shallow depressions which it is assumed were covered with boards so that when they were stamped on they gave forth a hollow booming sound. Such drums have been found rather widely distributed in structures which may mostly be ascribed to Mogollon or Mogollon-derived cultures. Just where and how they originated is uncertain, but even earlier ones have been found in large rectangular kivas with much-rounded corners and sides southeast of Flagstaff. There is a suggestion of similarity with the present-day Hopi use of a resounding board in the snake dance.

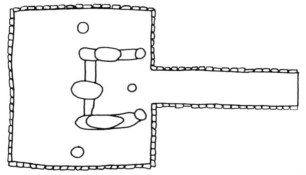

Fig. 117. Kiva with resonators, or floor drums, found in the Mogollon culture of this time. Note the strong resemblance in shape of this structure to slightly earlier house types.

In regard to associated traits, most carry on from earlier stages with comparatively little change. In Tularosa and Cordova caves Martin found that bows were present, and arrows had been found much earlier. It will be recalled that house types were introduced at about A.D. 1000 from the Pueblo culture into this general area, and the black-on-white pottery and indented corrugated pottery came in from the same source at about the same time. Though houses were lacking in the caves many other artifacts were found, including pottery.

Plaited sandals were by now the most common type, some with the scuff toe. The string apron was also present. While pipes were found to decrease in number, reed cigarettes increased, and these latter were shared with the Hohokam. The three-quarter-grooved axe was present, but was probably introduced from the Hohokam, the full-grooved axe being the more likely native type. Metates were the slab and scoop types, some open at both ends. Manos were typically rectangular, and many were worn down until they became beveled. There were also pebble mortars and pestles. There were no atlatls in use at this time, so far as is known, and the points were mostly small and diagonally notched. Flake knives and scrapers were common, though blades were lacking. Drills also seem to have decreased in number, but hoes increased. There were clay animal figurines and miniature bows and arrows, both of which may have been ceremonial. Rigid cradles were exclusive. Notched awls were also still apparently typical.

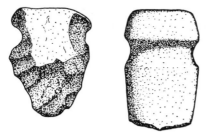

Fig. 118. Probably the most typical axe was full-grooved, although three-quarter axes were found. These are from the Harris and Starkweather sites.

Basketry was mostly of the half-rod and bundle type in coiled weaves, and the twilled-ring basket was common. Twilled matting was also abundant, and there was cloth of both cotton and bast fibers, and netting. Food was the same as that of the previous phase and period. Ornaments consisted of shell bracelets, and bone tube and shell beads. One trait which seems to have appeared about now in this culture is the grooved arrowshaft straightener. Another trait, which had an earlier beginning but survived into this period, was painted wood tablets, the use of which is not definitely known.

In general summary of the later development of the Mogollon culture it is possible to divide it into a more northern and a southern section, and into two temporal divisions which break at about A.D. 1000. Pueblo culture was having a very real influence on the development of the pottery and house types to the north at and after this date. To roughly this time the more typical pithouses of Mogollon prevailed, and the pottery of brown and red types was the most common. After this date the shift in these traits was remarkably swift, with the introduction of surface house structures, often of considerable size, and the local manufacture of Pueblo pottery types.

That portion of the culture which may be considered to be native shows no radical or marked innovations, unless they can be accounted for by outside introduction. Thus the original vigor of the Mogollon seems to have been more or less exhausted, and it was receptive to the changes which came from the pueblos now so rapidly developing to the north. On the west the Hohokam was still exerting a good deal of influence on the development of the southern Mogollon, with continued intergradations between these two groups in this southern area. In various villages in-humations and cremations are found together, and even architectural types seem to have been in some ways intermediate between the two cultures. The Amerind Foundation has done considerable work in this area and on this problem.

From this time on Mogollon culture seems to have been retracting south-ward, as a distinct entity, and to have been found more in northern Mexico than in the Southwest proper. Casas Grandes, which lasted to perhaps as late as the fifteenth century, might be considered as a related center of much higher development. Although it had a long and very vigorous his-tory, in many ways it has a Mogollon-like cast, or perhaps it would be more proper to suggest that Mogollon had a somewhat Casas Grandes cast. In any event, after about this period Mogollon was gone as a dis-tinct and vigorous culture in the Southwest.

HOHOKAM

The evolution of Hohokam culture from its earliest known beginning would apear to have followed a more or less uniformly progressive course from the Vahki phase to about the end of the Colonial, or perhaps into the Sedentary stage. Just what represents the peak of Hohokam culture is still somewhat a matter of debate, but it has become increasingly ap-parent in the last few years that the Classic stage is not actually the highest culture. Probably it was achieved in the Sedentary, for at this time many traits, particularly arts, reached about their highest develop-ment.

Although a great many sites of Sedentary Hohokam culture are known, and though many of them have been examined and a few dug, the only truly systematic review of the material culture of these people is found in the Snaketown reports. The latest occupation at this site is Sedentary as shown by the Sacaton phase. Gladwin has pointed out that, to the east in the vicinity of Casa Grande, another phase, possibly shorter and nearer the end of the period, is represented. This he has called Santan. However, it is from this one site that the majority of our information comes.

Because of the abundance of trade types of pottery from the plateau country to the north which is found in the Gila drainage it is possible to assign quite accurate dates to this stage. Very recently evidences of Hoho-kam occupation and culture influence have been definitely uncovered in the Flagstaff area, where the associated Pueblo pottery and actual tree-ring dates contributed substantiating evidence to this dating. The Seden-

tary stage has been found to correlate rather well with the Pueblo II
stage of culture, so that dates of A.D. 900 to 1100 may be applied with
some assurance to both areas. There is some question as to the final date
of the Sedentary stage, and it may have lasted as late as about A.D. 1200,
but it was certainly existing at the earlier date of A.D. 1100.

From the accompanying map it may be seen that the region occupied
by Sedentary Hohokam people is much like that of Colonial times. Perhaps
there is a slight tendency for the area of purest and most abundant sites
to be more concentrated in the vicinity of the two main streams, and there
is some evidence that, with the exception of the northward extension toward Flagstaff, the tendency was for a restriction of outlying sites.

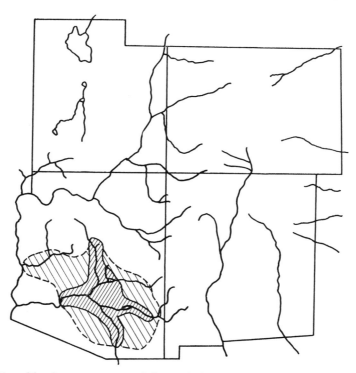

Fig. 119. Roughly the area occupied by Hohokam culture at this time. The core area
is limited to the main river valleys, and the maximum expansion is slightly less than
previously. Note particularly the extension up the Verde valley to the north.

Pottery of the Sedentary stage shows several marked changes from that
of the preceding periods, particularly as regards form and decoration. Scoring and incising as a decoration is practically absent, and the rare flaring-
rim bowl is larger and deeper than the Colonial form. A marked Gila
shoulder has developed, often lying well below the center of the vessel.

Tripod and tetrapod vessels are still present, as are rectangular and other eccentric forms. Probably the most striking characteristic of this stage is the prevalence of very large vessels, some of the jars holding as much as 30 gallons, and even many of the bowls being of exceptional size. Although small elements still occur as contributing parts of the design, they are usually incorporated as a portion of the complex fabricated decoration. Panels are common, and in their general pattern they suggest fabrics, many being remarkably well laid out in the space they occupy.

Specific pottery types which occur at this time are Gila Plain, Sacaton Buff, Sacaton Red, and Sacaton Red-on-buff. In the Santan phase, Santan Red occurs with a smudged interior and a brilliant red-slipped exterior. Sacaton Buff, though not very abundant, is a light buff-slipped pottery which otherwise is like Sacaton Red-on-buff. Sacaton Red-on-buff and all other Gila types were made by the paddle and anvil method, the insides of jars occasionally showing distinct anvil marks. There is a light buff slip which often forms a poor base for the iron oxide of the painted design. The surface is smoothed but not polished, much of it giving the appearance of being porous because of the small holes which it often contains. Designs are in band patterns, panels, and a great variety of other arrangements. Panels and hatching are very characteristic, and a

Fig. 120. Decorated and plain pottery forms and designs. The marked Gila shoulder and the prevalence of geometric designs often blocked out into rectangular areas are very typical. Heavy-walled vessels also seem to be quite characteristic of this period.

few negative designs occur. Interlocking rectangular and curved scrolls also appear very typical. Forms are bowls and jars, as illustrated in the diagram.

Sacaton Red is a heavily slipped, reddish brown pottery, polished inside and smoothed outside. Typologically it is not closely related to the buff and red-on-buff types characteristic of the Hohokam and thus suggests some outside derivation. Since there are red types known from the Flagstaff area at at least a comparable time, if not earlier, it has been suggested that this might have been the source of these Gila Red types. It is made of native clays, however, and has much mica temper, which often shows through the surface slip. Although the type is very rare it is possible to suggest that forms are almost wholly bowls.

Besides pottery, clay human figurines were found in the Sedentary horizon at Snaketown. They are represented only by heads which show

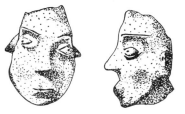

Fig. 121. Human figurines consist solely of heads. They were apparently modeled about a stick so that they have a vertical hollow depression in their backs. They seem to show an attempt at personal characterization.

impressions of cord-wrapped fiber bundles on the back, as though the body of the figurine was at this time made of fibers instead of clay. Modeling of these objects was very much better than modeling of earlier times, many specimens suggesting a definite attempt to reproduce actual individual characters. Colonial features such as incised eyebrows carried over, but the eyelids are now uniformly outlined and the nose is modeled into much more of a human nose shape.

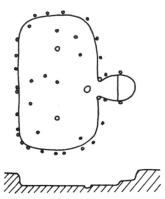

Fig. 122. The Sedentary pithouse is strongly suggestive of the Colonial type in that it is relatively long, slender, and shallow and has rounded ends. The arrangement of the firepit and two posts on the center line is also like this type. Only the entrance is markedly different, for it is inclined to be oval and contains a step. This house is about eight meters long by four and a half wide, with an entrance about two meters long. A similar house was found near Flagstaff showing a definite Hohokam influence there.

Houses are very suggestive in general outline of those of the Colonial stage, being relatively long shallow structures with a firepit in front of the entrance and two main posts set on the long axis of the floor. The roof appears to have been gabled but almost flat, much like present-day Pima houses. Supplementary posts, possibly as braces, were scattered about the floor, a feature which seems to have been more or less typical of Hohokam houses in periods following the Pioneer stage. A series of post holes occasionally found outside the walls suggests side-wall support posts and gives strength to the feeling that the side walls were much like those of Pima structures. The most distinctive feature appears to be an oval or egg-shaped entrance area, which contained a step between the level of the ground outside and the floor of the room. In general, Gladwin is inclined to feel that they are simply somewhat more comfortable and better-made homes than earlier types.

Ball courts survived into this stage but showed a distinct change from the earlier very large and parallel-sided forms. These structures are much

Courtesy of the Arizona State Museum

A typical later Hohokam house, showing the enlarged entrance in the foreground and the post pattern within and around the floor. Note also the rounded ends or corners. These are at most quite shallow structures.

smaller and more oval in shape, with very restricted end passages which flare to small flat areas on the old ground surfaces outside the walls. The central marker and two end markers are typically present, and in the small court at Snaketown two post holes were also found between these features. This court had a floor length of 22.7 meters and a width of 10.6 meters, or a length about twice that of its width. They were not so deep as the Snaketown type, having walls probably only eight to ten feet high. Several courts of this type are known throughout the Gila area, so that Haury has suggested the name "Casa Grande type" for them. One of the most striking features of these courts is the degree of exactness with which they have been planned and executed. The center marker is invariably located within at least a few centimeters of the exact center of the floor area, and the end markers are usually almost as accurately placed. The general outline is quite uniform, and the angle of the walls consistent in comparable parts of the structure. For this reason it has been suggested that these primitive people had some sort of measuring device which gave more accurate results than those produced by pacing.

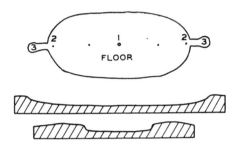

Fig. 123. The ball court characteristic of the Sedentary period is much smaller than the Snaketown type. Haury has called it the Casa Grande type. The form is more markedly oval, and the end passages and areas are quite small (3). The center marker is present (1), and the end markers (2) are usually found. The length of the small court at Snaketown was 22.7 meters and its width was 10.6 meters. The embankments were undoubtedly not so high, probably at most eight or ten feet.

A second engineering feat of some consequence was the large-scale construction of irrigation ditches. Casual excavation in ditches in various parts of the Gila led to the conclusion that they were much larger than they actually were found to be at Snaketown. Here the Sedentary ditch was only about a meter wide and deep in the actual excavated portion, though much deeper and higher when the material which had been removed from the excavation and piled on the side was considered. Thus the size of the ditches is not so impressive as the extensive systems of ditches which were produced to put large tracts under cultivation. It is the obvious evidence of coherent social organization and direction that is indicated by such undertakings as the ditches and ball courts that warrants admiration of the Hohokam people. Ditches were probably built by digging ahead of the flow of water, which would help to loosen the soil. Even so, the amount of

Fig. 124. Cross section of a Sedentary irrigation ditch as found at Snaketown. The actual ditch excavated was much smaller than had been supposed, being a meter or less wide and deep.

effort necessary to produce many miles of canals was tremendous with the only available digging tools stone or wood implements and baskets.

The prevailing type of disposal of the dead was still by cremation, only a few inhumations of this period having been uncovered. These were in such fragile condition that it was impossible to determine a general physical type from them. The inhumations were extended with the head toward the east and appear to have been accompanied with relatively few, or no, offerings. The burned bones of cremations were collected, along with

A Hohokam type of cremation in which the charred bones and ashes were placed in the lower jar and the bowl inverted over it before being buried. Note the bowl has been "killed" with a hole in the bottom.

pottery and other artifacts which had been placed on the fire, and buried in a shallow pit in the caliche, or placed in a jar and buried. In some instances the body was apparently burned in the pit, quantities of wood ashes, as well as other objects which had been in the fire, being simply left in the pit and covered over. It was from such sources that many of the finest artifacts found at Snaketown were recovered.

Ground stone implements of the Sedentary stage as a whole show only minor differences from those of the Colonial. Metates are of the open-end, raised-side type, though apparently not quite so long and slender as those of the preceding stage. Manos are essentially the same, being predominantly of the rectangular block shape; a few are so long as to suggest that they were used by two hands instead of one. Palettes are essentially the same as Colonial types, and are of slate with raised, decorated rims and some carved, ornamented ends.

Axes appear to be very much like the preceding type, with a three-quarter groove and rounded hammer head. They are longer and more slender than Colonial types but do not show the raised rim or the extreme length of the Pioneer axe. Grooved hammerstones are known but suggest axes which have been broken off on the bit end and reshaped to hammers. Stone bowls were still being made and are obviously a continuation or survival of the earlier types. Several are highly decorated with carved animals; on the whole they appear to be slightly more ornate. Large animal and bird figurines of stone with depressions in their backs were also still being made.

One hoe was found at the Snaketown site. It consisted of a thin slab of sandstone which showed obvious wear along one side. This is of particular interest for it has long been assumed that the stone hoe was the

Fig. 125. The sedentary stone axe is very suggestive of the Colonial although apparently tending to be slightly longer and more slender.

Fig. 126. Stone rings made of vesicular basalt were found to occur during this period at Snaketown. Some were grooved, as in the illustration.

typical cultivation implement of the desert section, as opposed to the digging stick of the north. Many stone hoes are known from the Upper Gila area, but they appear to have been less abundant in the Middle section.

Several small stone rings carved from vesicular basalt were also found at Snaketown. These objects are known from the Flagstaff area of northern Arizona, and their possible use has long been a subject of speculation. Actually, they closely resemble stone doughnuts, a few examples being grooved as in the accompanying illustration. It has been suggested that they were used somehow in a game, or perhaps were some sort of symbol or marker. It is interesting to note that 23 of these objects were found at Snaketown, a sufficient number to indicate that they are Hohokam in origin.

Points of this stage are exceptionally well made and as might be expected show some eccentric variations. The illustration gives examples of the most outstanding types. The long slender serrated-edge point is apparently the most common, and certainly the most expertly made. Over 600 of these were found at Snaketown Village. The technique of chipping was so well controlled that they are almost unbelievably slender and fine. In some examples the serrations approach backward-tilted barbs. The most extreme specimen, to the right in the diagram, shows one of the several eccentric forms produced at this time, perhaps a natural outgrowth of the barblike serrations on some of the long slender points. The two central points are obviously of a distinctly different type, the upper one suggesting some of those produced during the Colonial stage and the lower being similar in general outline to points made during the Pioneer stage. Although this last type is relatively less abundant it appears to be quite typical.

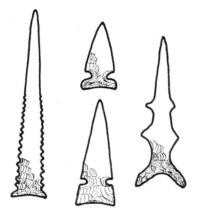

Fig. 127. Sedentary points are very suggestive of Colonial types. The long slender serrated edge is characteristic. The right-hand example is an extreme type almost suggesting a barb. The two central examples are obvious developments of the Colonial laterally notched types.

Perishable objects are almost as rare from this period as preceding times, so that no information is obtained on basketry or sandals. However, one fragment of cotton cloth which was recovered proved to be sufficiently preserved so that it could be studied. This was an exceedingly fine textile, very suggestive of similar woven fabrics found in the Verde valley to the north. At first glance it has the appearance of drawn work or very fine buttonhole work, for small circular openings are arranged in two parallel lines. Detailed examination proves that this effect was produced during weaving, and not subsequently, and that the weft or filler threads were used to draw the warp threads apart, thus leaving the holes. It is unfortunate that so much of this fine material has been lost, for the few suggestions of textiles from this part of the Southwest are truly remarkable.

Concerning hunting implements, there is very little information beyond the indication, from the small size of the points, that the bow and arrow was the main weapon. Foods also show little variation from those already mentioned.

Ornaments of this time are, as a whole, very similar to those of the preceding stage, although perhaps slightly more ornate. Shell carving is of the same type, but a new and striking technique of shell ornamentation was introduced. This consisted of the etching away of a portion of the surface of the shell to produce a design, a technique which required the understanding of a resist and the reduction action of some acid. Both geometric and life forms were produced on shell by this method. Though not abundant, shell etching is well authenticated by several specimens from sites other than Snaketown, as well as five specimens found at that site. Although shells were occasionally painted by people of this culture, none of the etched specimens show evidences of having been painted. Shell pendants, rings, and bracelets, both carved and uncarved, seem to have been more numerous during this time than at any previous period.

Stone beads of various forms, such as flat disks, button shapes, and pendants, seem to have been very common as well, and stone ear and nose buttons occurred. These last appear to have been typically Hohokam, at least in relation to the rest of the Southwest. None of these ornaments are of sufficiently distinctive character or number to warrant detailed discussion in a review of this nature.

Bone awls were much more abundant and varied than during preceding times. Not only were splinters of bone sharpened at one end used as awls, but the heads of the natural bone were often left as handles and the shafts pointed. Carved bone handles were also found on implements suggesting awls or daggers. These handles, although not elaborate, were, as a result of the carving, sufficiently roughened to give a better hand hold than the ordinary smooth bone surface would have afforded. Painted antler fragments decorated in black and red in geometric designs were found in a cremation. Bone tubes, ornamented with incised geometric and life form designs, were made at this time as well.

Probably the most interesting small objects found at Snaketown were a group of cast copper bells. A total of 28 were found together, all on the floor of one room where they had fallen at the time the house burned. An analysis of their material indicates they were made of Southwestern copper and not imported from Mexico or the Lake Superior region. All these bells are quite uniform in size and form, are small for Southwestern bells, and have a definite pear shape. The resonator is rounded at the bottom, is slit, and contained a loose pebble or copper fragment clapper cast in the bell. They were undoubtedly produced by the *cire perdue* or lost wax method, and they may possibly represent the earliest bells known from the Southwest. Certainly most other bells are much larger, more rounded, and appear to come from slightly later horizons.

With this review of the material culture of the Sedentary Hohokam people, it is now possible to summarize their most distinctive traits. Pottery probably forms the best single criterion for this stage, particularly Sacaton Red-on-buff. Forms are jars which have very short necks, with the rims sharply returned upon themselves, and the prevalence of a marked Gila shoulder. Great size seems to have been a distinctive feature of bowls as

Fig. 128. In one room at Snaketown several cast copper bells were found. They are of a type almost identical with bells made in Mexico. A stone or copper clapper was cast inside. The example pictured was about two centimeters long.

well as jars. In other forms less marked distinctions are found. Designs are typically geometric, with a strong suggestion of fabric patterns and containing many interlocking, curved, and rectangular scrolls. Human figurines of pottery consist solely of heads, which were apparently placed on fiber bodies and are an obvious attempt at real individual representation.

The distinctive feature of the house is a stepped entranceway, although farther east some walls with upright pole supports seem to have developed in the form of compounds. The ball court is of the small or Casa Grande type, very carefully made, and of a specific pattern which seems to have been widely copied. Irrigation ditches were abundant and, though not great in cross section, extensive.

Stone axes appear to have been slightly longer and more slender, and other stone objects, though not distinctive in form or design, were on the whole better made. This is also true of shell, wherein a new process, namely etching, was evolved as a means of decoration. The arrow points are remarkably well made, the best of any period in the Southwest so far as the writer has been able to learn. Exceedingly long and slender types are characteristic, with abundant, even, regular serrations on their edges for the base two-thirds of their length. Copper bells, almost identical with bells from Mexico in technique of manufacture and general form, were found at this time. They were made by the lost wax method and are distinguishable from later types in that they are much smaller and definitely pear-shaped.

In this chapter the Sedentary culture has been considered as primarily illustrated by the classic Snaketown site in the middle portion of the Gila area. Actually regional differentiation is known in other sections, notably those of the Upper Gila area and in the vicinity of Tucson. As an example of such variation, house types and cremation jars found near Tucson on the Santa Cruz differ considerably from those reported from Snaketown.

Probably a somewhat misleading impression has therefore been given as to the simplicity and regional uniformity of the Hohokam culture throughout its history. For instance, at Gila Bend what probably is a temple mound has been found and excavated by Wasley. It is plastered over, truncated, and more or less rectangular, and presumably had some sort of ceremonial structure built on its top. The general concept is very suggestive of temple mounds found in Mexico and Central America. Therefore, perhaps too much reliance has been made on the Snaketown reports in compiling this section, but they are by far the most complete and well-organized general data available.

PUEBLO II AND III

In the preceding chapter it has been shown that a good deal is known concerning the Adjustment period and Pueblo I culture. Even more is known about the cultures which flourished during this, the Dissemination period. Accurate dates have been secured from a large series of sites of this time and from all major divisions of the plateau area, so that culture variations are abundantly dated. With more certainty than for any preceding period it is therefore possible to state that the beginning was A.D. 900 and the end 1100.

An examination of the accompanying map will indicate the extent of the area occupied during this period. The area of greatest concentration is now the largest and the most continuous of any time in the plateau. The entire plateau was covered by a large number of individual houses or villages so that the total population has been estimated as the greatest of any time in this section. A comparison with the map of the preceding period will indicate the extent of this expansion. The area of maximum spread is also much greater than that of the preceding period, and possibly of any succeeding period. Strong influence went south through the mountain section, eastward into the Rio Grande drainage, north into central Utah, and west through Nevada to California. Such an expansion is indicated by the presence of pottery types obviously traded from the central area of concentration, and it may be assumed that with these trades went other influences.

Cultural variation in the several regions of the plateau is marked, probably the two extremes being found in the Flagstaff area to the southwest and the Chaco Canyon area to the northeast. As will be shown shortly, house types vary from one-room pithouses to multistory, multiroom pueblos, and general culture from a Pueblo II to a Pueblo III stage. The most rapid development in the plateau certainly took place in the eastern San Juan, so that for at least 400 years the people occupying this section were actually the leaders of Pueblo development.

Pueblo II has been defined by the Pecos classification as a widespread geographical expansion of life in small villages, introduction of corrugated pottery often elaborate and with designs over the whole surface of cooking vessels—and to this has been added Black-on-white pottery characterized

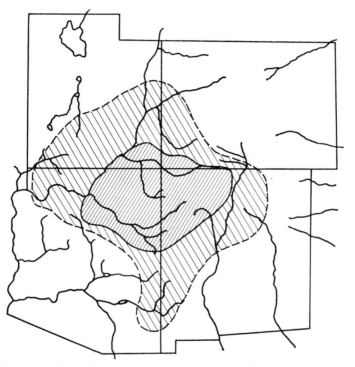

Fig. 129. The area of Pueblo culture occupied during the Dissemination period. The area of concentration is greatly expanded from the preceding, and in fact is the largest of any time in Pueblo development. The area of sites showing traces of this culture may have been even greater than that indicated.

in general by simple designs in wide lines, long flattened triangles, rudimentary interlocking frets, and occasional attached dots. Pueblo III culture has been defined as the classic period of large communities, great development of arts, and local specialization, the first important introduction of polychrome wares into pottery, and in many cases the best pottery produced during any period, with a general marked decrease in the importance of corrugated wares.

From these definitions it is obvious that an attempt was made to inject a definite time relationship into this classification, but as has been pointed out by several writers it cannot be so applied to this period in the plateau. Culture is far too variable to be classed as the same, or even closely similar, from the Flagstaff and Chaco Canyon areas, and other less striking and gradual variations of traits may be found between these two sections. As the discussion progresses it will be possible to point out certain consistent uniformities. At present it is probably sufficient to suggest that the most

General view of Pueblo Bonito. The D shape is apparent. Walls are standing to a height of four stories. The great kiva and the many smaller kivas may be seen.

commonly consistent single trait appears to have been the production of cooking vessels which were covered completely on the outside with corrugations often forming indented geometric patterns. Certainly polychrome pottery was not definitely introduced now, and with equal certainty such a site as Pueblo Bonito gives every evidence of having reached a stage of culture of large communities, great development of the arts, and local specialization.

Since one of the first prehistoric sites to be dated accurately was Pueblo Bonito, and since the culture found at this site had been recognized as Pueblo III, it was with considerable surprise that the Museum of Northern Arizona finally succeeded in dating single-room pithouses as of almost identical time and duration. Once the validity of this dating had been demonstrated it became obvious that culture variation was extraordinarily great, and many archaeologists have since been working in an effort to explain this discrepancy. Two things are obvious. First, Chaco Canyon was

definitely the cultural leader at this time. Second, the influences responsible for regional variations in rate of cultural evolution did not all come
from the same source.

Of all traits the most consistent and diagnostic time indicator is corrugated pottery. This pottery was apparently evolved as a means of decoration on the utility types. The earliest form is a medium-sized large-mouth
jar, in which indented corrugations form a band only in the neck portion.
This is obviously an evolution from the neck-coiled type of the preceding
period, in which the end of the thumb was used to pinch the coils together
at regular intervals. The indentations characteristically show thumbnail
marks, and are large, deep, and regular, invariably slanting diagonally.
Almost immediately the idea of corrugating the entire surface of the vessel
seems to be have been developed, so that the same types of large coils and
deep indentations were produced. This type dates sometime near A.D. 885.
See the upper left-hand figure in the illustration and the lower left-hand
detail of coils.

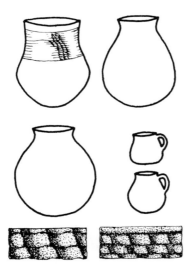

Fig. 130. The most distinctive pottery is the corrugated, which is deeply and
evenly indented, sometimes
in geometric patterns. The
upper left figure is the earliest indented corrugated
form, a detail of which is
shown to the lower left. It
has large deep diagonal indentations. The other forms
and the lower right detail are
typical of Tusayan Corru-
gated.

By 900 the technique of indented coiling had been much improved
by the use of smaller bands and offsetting of the fingernail marks. Coils still
covered the entire pot, with the exception of a large flattened band which
formed the rim. Smooth bands were also sometimes left to form geometric
patterns, particularly triangles. Forms with this style of decoration are jars,
pitchers, and rarely bowls, the insides of which have a black-on-white
design.

The most abundant type is Tusayan Corrugated. The paste is gray and
has relatively coarse angular sand temper. The inside was scraped but never

slipped; the outside is completely covered with small, deep, regular corrugations. Because these pots were used primarily for cooking, the outside was often coated with a layer of carbon, so that they are occasionally described in the literature as black. Through the western part of the Hopi country, the Flagstaff and Tsegi areas, temper is sand as described; to the east, a greater use was made of prepared angular light fragments as a tempering material. This latter type is found throughout the eastern San Juan and down the Little Colorado River to about the vicinity of Winslow.

Various writers have suggested that indented corrugations were made not only as a form of decoration but also to serve a definite utilitarian purpose by increasing the surface of the outside in relation to that of the inside of the vessel. This, it is felt, would gather heat over a large area and concentrate it in a much smaller area on the inside of the pot, thus making the contents cook more rapidly than in a vessel with a plain surface. In the opinion of the writer this credits the makers with more reasoning intelligence than they probably possessed in such a matter.

In the western portion of the area under consideration Black Mesa Black-on-white assumes an almost equal importance in dating. Although this specific type was relatively restricted in manufacture it was widely traded, and the style of design was very generally used. The time of duration was from A.D. 875 to about 1130. The paste is gray with sand temper. Vessels are covered with a white slip, and a clear black carbon

Fig. 131. One of the most typical and best-dated types is Black Mesa Black-on-white. The forms are bowls, jars, and pitchers as shown above. Two variations of designs are shown. The upper is perhaps an earlier form.

paint was used in the decoration. The insides of jars and the outsides of bowls are scraped and sometimes not slipped. In the order of abundance the common shapes are bowls, jars, pitchers, and ladles. Designs are always relatively simple, characteristically occurring in zones or bands.

The elements are lines about a quarter of an inch wide, low triangles with dots on the long side, and occasional dots on the lines. The prevailing style of decoration was to use ribbonlike lines in simple design patterns.

So far all pottery types which have been described in detail from the plateau area were fired in a reducing atmosphere. Now two black-on-red types occur in sufficient abundance to warrant detailed descriptions. The first of these is Deadmans Black-on-red. The paste is yellow, often containing a carbon streak, and is predominantly tempered with angular sand. Surfaces are well polished and slipped a bright red. The paint is a manganese type, producing a clear black sometimes grading to a dark purplish color. In the order of importance forms are bowls, seed jars, jars or jugs, and ladles. A distinctive feature is that decoration is often polished over before firing so that it is slightly blurred into the slip. It will be recalled that some of the Mogollon and Hohokam types were also treated in this manner. Design elements are coarse lines, wide or ribbonlike lines, and triangles. These are also very suggestive of the Mogollon. This type began by 775 and lasted to about A.D. 1065.

Tusayan Black-on-red is the second type. It also has a yellow-orange paste, but the temper is made up of soft, light, angular inclusions. It is usually well polished, the outer surfaces of bowls being sometimes slightly lumpy, and is slipped with a bright red slip. Designs, formed with manganese black paint, were applied in narrow and wide lines and hatched areas. Hatching is a markedly new feature in this area. Dates are roughly from A.D. 1050 to 1130.

Although a great many other pottery types are known and described from this period it is impossible to discuss them in detail here. An abundant literature will be found on this subject by those who are interested in following it further. In the Wingate phase, which is located in eastern Arizona and western New Mexico, and which dates about A.D. 900 to 1100, Gallup Black-on-white and Wingate Black-on-white pottery is found. It has a chalky white slip and a black design with the abundant use of hatched elements. The forms are mostly bowls and pitchers. With this pottery are houses of the unit type with associated kivas. It is from this earlier material that the Chaco culture developed which culminated in such sites as Pueblo Bonito.

In the Chaco Canyon area proper corrugated types are so similar to those already discussed that they need not be described except by noting that the lower left-hand figure in the accompanying illustration shows the most common form. Black-on-red rarely occurs, and is mostly Wingate Black-on-red. It is therefore in Chaco Black-on-white that the most outstanding characters are found. This type has a gray paste and light, angular, prepared temper. The vessels are scraped, and some bowl exteriors are not completely slipped. The surface is rubbed relatively smooth and covered with a paper-white slip. Decoration is in a black iron-carbon pigment, which sometimes oxidizes to a red or brown upon secondary or accidental firing. Both forms and designs are very distinctive. The most common forms are bowls with sloping sides and pointed rims, pitchers with small bodies and high necks, vases with small horizontal handles or

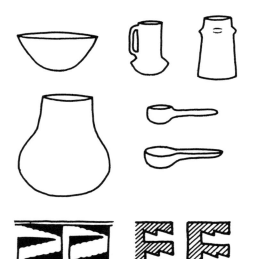

Fig. 132. Chaco Black-on-white pottery is equally distinctive both in form and design. Bowls have pointed rims and sloping sides. High-neck pitchers and vases are characteristic. The bat wing and fine hatched elements are also typical designs.

lugs, and ladles with open handles. Designs may be characterized by a use of fine lines, particularly in hatched areas, where the surrounding lines are characteristically much heavier. Low triangles with serrated edges, called "bat wings," are also a common element, as are wide bands along the rims of bowls. On a whole the pottery is well made, but the slip gives the appearance of being delicate or impermanent and is often light. The dates are A.D. 1070 to 1130.

House types show equal or greater variation. The simplest type is found in the Flagstaff area, and for that reason the discussion of houses will begin here. The most characteristic house is a deep rectangular pithouse which has four corner posts, a central firepit, ladder entrance, and a ventilator. These structures are relatively deep and in certain features suggest Mogollon influence. Those found in forested areas were lined with wood, as in the accompanying illustration. Probably the most outstanding feature is the use of split planks as a wall lining, and split shakes in many as a roof cover under the clay. Just how the logs were split with primitive tools remains a question, for they were formed by splitting the log across the rings, or from the outside to the center, and not parallel to the surface along the rings. So many of these houses have been dug and reported in the vicinity of Flagstaff that almost all variations are known.

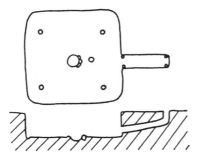

Fig. 133. The Flagstaff type of pithouse is relatively simple. It is rectangular with four corner posts, central firepit, ladder post, and ventilator.

The deep wooden pithouse gradually gave way to an equally deep masonry-lined structure in this section. Associated with this latter type are small surface masonry rooms, three or four grouped together, which were probably granaries. Sometime shortly after A.D. 1100 it seems to have altered to the small unit type of surface structure. From this time on the pueblo prevailed.

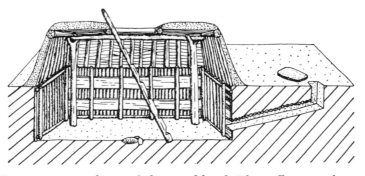

Fig. 134. Reconstruction of one of the wood-lined, Flagstaff-type pithouses. The entrance hatchway also served as a smoke hole, and the ventilator could be blocked outside with a stone. Poles, split planks, and shakes were all used as lining and roofing materials.

A few miles east of Flagstaff, at Heiser Spring near the Little Colorado River, three small surface rooms and a kiva-like pit structure were excavated by the Museum of Northern Arizona. The pithouse is obviously of the most interest. It is relatively deep, oval in form, with a banquette or bench, and a small platform on one side. Floor features include four support posts, a ventilator, deflector, firepit and floor opening in line, and a base rest for a ladder through the roof hatchway. It is felt that this kiva-like room actually was the dwelling while the surface rooms were utilized for storage only. Similar structures are found in Tsegi Canyon at a slightly later date, about A.D. 1130, and are believed to have served the same purpose.

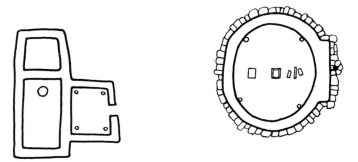

Fig. 135. At Heiser Springs, near Wupatki National Monument, a sunken kiva-like house was found associated with three small surface rooms. It is felt this structure was the main dwelling. It had four support posts, a banquette, a platform, ventilator, central firepit, and ladder entrance, all features strongly suggesting the formal kiva of the east.

If such an arrangement actually is a pithouse and three surface granaries, it is surprising that it should have been oval in form when all other pithouses in this section are rectangular. It is also surprising to find it in such close proximity to the rectangular pithouse type described above. The obvious answer is that even at this time distinct ethnic groups had become sufficiently established over most of the plateau so that two slightly different cultures existed close together and contemporaneously. In the western San Juan similar structures are known to have existed to as late as A.D. 1130 and this site is probably a southern extension of this type. There is, however, always the slight possibility that such a structure is actually a local ceremonial form, and hence primarily a kiva. Farther to the east, in the center of the Hopi country, present evidence indicates that houses were masonry-lined pithouses with either a D or rectangular outline.

It will be recalled that in discussing the Pueblo culture of the Adjustment period proto-kivas and masses of surface rooms were seen in the eastern portion of the San Juan. Similar blocks of rooms, with associated pithouses or ceremonial structures, were found in the central San Juan during this Dissemination period. They are so similar in general concept and execution that they must have been derived from this more eastern source. In fact they seem to last even into later periods.

On going farther northeast, into the Mesa Verde section of southwestern Colorado, one of the most interesting house types is found. This has been described and pictured by Prudden, and named the Small House. The main dwelling is a small, compact, one-story unit of surface dwelling rooms. The masonry is excellent, in fact much of it is true masonry in the sense that the walls are narrow and the stone blocks extend through from one side to the other. The blocks are also carefully chosen and somewhat shaped, forecasting the remarkable stone work of the succeeding period here. Associated with these small dwelling units are found definite subsurface kivas.

The kiva is relatively small, 12 to 15 feet in diameter, and is circular except for a platform on one side. The wall is lined with a bench or ban-

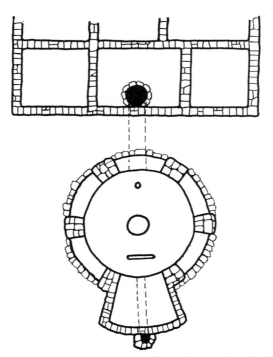

Fig. 136. In the Mesa Verde area structures like this are found. The house is a small unit, never over one story high. The kiva typically has a banquette, pilasters, platform, ventilator, deflector, firepit, "sipapu," and sometimes a passage leading to one of the rooms of the house. This is Pruden's unit type of house.

quette upon which rest six or eight stone pilasters. These pilasters supported the roof, which was formed by placing poles across them from one to another. Additional poles were placed across the angles thus formed until a dome-shaped roof was constructed. Important floor features consist of a ventilator extending under the platform, a deflector, central fire-pit, "sipapu" hole in the floor, and in some a second underground entrance connecting with one of the dwelling rooms. The sipapu, found in some historic kivas, is regarded as a symbol representing the mythical opening into the underworld through which the ancestors are supposed to have reached this world. This type of kiva is very similar to the later type in the Mesa Verde region.

To the south, in that area lying between the Little Colorado, Zuñi, and Puerco rivers, Roberts has reported a medium-sized surface pueblo struc-ture of about 45 rooms and 4 kivas. This site apparently belongs to this time for ceramic characters would seem to be related both to Deadmans and to Chaco style in black-on-white types, and corrugated pots are of this age. The site is of particular interest because it appears to have been made up of relatively small, more or less square blocks of rooms, each in-cluding one kiva. The walls of the earlier section, although above ground, were made of adobe; those of the later portion were made of rock. The earlier kivas are inclined to a D shape, but those of the later sections are definitely round. To the writer this site forms the link between the unit-type house of the Mesa Verde area and the huge pueblos of Chaco Canyon.

Beyond any question the most impressive site in the entire Southwest at this time was Pueblo Bonito. Not only is it the largest masonry struc-ture made to this date, but it was obviously planned and executed as a definite unit. The earliest portion was in much the same form as the final completed structure. The presence of a great many circular kivas as well as a few extraordinarily large kivas is of particular interest.

Although Pueblo Bonito is the largest pueblo in this group there are many more similar pueblos nearby. Architecturally these sites are note-worthy because of their size, not only as regards the pueblo as a whole, but also in the extraordinary thickness of the walls and the size of the rooms. The walls of all structures are filled with rubble on their interiors and with carefully coursed and shaped sandstone blocks on their exteriors. The typical pueblo surrounds a court, with the highest stories at the back, which form a blank wall, and with a line of one-story rooms cutting off the fourth side. The total height of rooms at the back is usually three or four stories. Within the court are the kivas, always one great kiva and usually several other smaller ones.

The kivas are of two types. The great kivas are circular in form and from 40 to 60 feet in diameter. A wide masonry bench encircles the room, and in the center is a raised fireplace, on either side of which are two sunken masonry-lined rooms. The roof was primarily supported by four large pillars near the center. On the north side is a stairway cutting through the banquette from the floor to a large room on the ground level, and surrounding the structure are a series of surface rooms.

The smaller kivas seldom exceed 25 feet in diameter. A banquette supporting six pilasters runs around the wall. On the south a ventilator opens to the outside and runs under the floor to near the firepit. To the west of the firepit is often found a single small masonry vault.

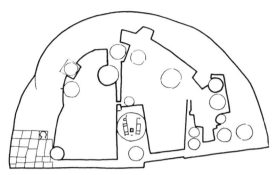

Fig. 137. Pueblo Bonito was unquestionably the most outstanding site of this time. The illustration is only a rough outline of the block of rooms, the relative sizes of the rooms being indicated in the lower left-hand corner. Position of kivas is indicated by the roughly sketched circles, with some details only in the largest.

Though there are several of these large pueblo ruins in the Chaco Canyon area there are also a great number of smaller, more isolated sites of comparable age. These smaller sites would roughly correspond to the suburban villages clustered about our own great cities. Some of these sites are in themselves relatively large, but many of them are only of one or two rooms. The smaller ones probably represent the agricultural peasants who through choice or necessity repaired to more remote regions. The amount of food necessary to support life in one of the large villages must have been considerable, and it is thus equally possible that during certain seasons a part of the population removed to the smaller sites to grow the required foodstuffs.

Pueblo Bonito has been accurately dated by a large number of beams as existing between A.D. 919 and 1130. The first is such an early date that one is inclined to wonder if most of the site was not built late in the period. Information as to the location of dated beams, however, shows that a large part was built in the tenth century, and that the plan originally begun was simply further carried out and expanded. As a result one must admit that multiroom and multistory pueblos, with highly formalized masonry and the wide use of horizontal beams supported by walls, were well known at this time. It is for this reason that the previous suggestion has been made that masonry developed in this eastern section.

The great sites of Chaco Canyon seem to have been about as far advanced in other culture traits as they were architecturally. For the construction of such large and well-planned villages it would have been necessary to have a compact, functional, and well-directed social organization. Other objects appear to have been comparably developed, so that a high specialization of arts and crafts must have been the rule.

It is the opinion of the writer that cultural evolution naturally progresses, with population increase, to the point where individual specialization is inevitable. In small scattered communities this is impossible, for there is no outlet for specialized industries. In such circumstances each individual must produce all or most of the objects used by his own family. With population increases, and clustering in large communities, such an outlet is available, and specialization results. Such a population increase, localization of population, and specialization in arts had obviously taken place by this time in the Chaco area. Probably next in this respect was the Mesa Verde section and those areas in the headwaters of the San Juan lying north and east of the four corners.

Although the physical type has nowhere been described in detail it was substantially broad-headed. Deformation of the skull was practically universal and appears in many individuals to have been very marked. Almost invariably this deformation is not well centered on the back of the head, but is slightly to one side or the other.

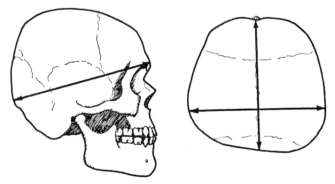

Fig. 138. The Pueblo physical type is definitely deformed posteriorly, as in the above illustration. The skull pictured is an extreme example of deformation, and is practically as wide as it is long.

The base of the cradle is similar to that of the Basket Maker type already described and pictured, which was covered with reed or leaf matting. The head of the infant appears to have often been supported on a hard block which thus deformed the skull during its growth. Another type was made of two boards tied together upon which the child was strapped. For the first type at least the descriptive term of hard cradle is somewhat misleading, for the cradle was firm but within itself not hard, except for the head rest. Burials of Pueblo II culture and of this time have been found near Grand Falls on the Little Colorado River with the head resting on a hard rock, suggesting that it had served as a sleeping support. If such objects were in general use they would account for the radically deformed skulls which are so typical.

From very incomplete data it would appear that the typical burial was flexed and placed on one side or the other. Burials are most commonly found in refuse heaps or similar locations where digging was relatively easy.

Metates, like those of the preceding period, were of two types. The eastern form is the scoop-shaped metate, open only at one end; the western form was mostly trough-shaped. As has been pointed out, these two types overlap and are mixed together in the San Juan and Little Colorado areas. At about the end of this period flat slabs appear to have been introduced, or developed, which were fitted into boxes formed by setting three flat stones on edge around the grinding stone. The block type of mano is by far the most typical and common, although some triangular or wedge-shaped manos are found.

Axes, not particularly abundant, are of two types. The full-grooved axe was possibly made in some areas to about this date but was never anywhere very abundant. The three-quarter-grooved axe was by now quite well established in the plateau area, in all sections with the possible exception of the middle and lower portions of the immediate San Juan River. Mauls are of both full-grooved and three-quarter-grooved types.

Sometime during this period large circular or rectangular lignite buttons appeared in the Pueblo culture. Such a button is illustrated (Fig. 141). The closest parallel is in the pyrite mirrors of the Hohokam culture, and it is quite possible that they were derived from this source. As pyrite was not easily accessible in this northern area, or was not used by these people for other objects, it is likely that they would substitute the black shiny material and make similarly shaped and highly polished buttons. Strength is lent to this theory by the recent finding of strong Hohokam influences of this date in the Flagstaff area at Winona Village.

Arrow points, although somewhat varied, are predominantly triangular in form. Both lateral and corner notches are characteristic. In the Flagstaff area a long slender point with distinctly serrated edges may probably be ascribed to the Patayan culture, although it is very similar to the slender Hohokam point. The more triangular point with side notches is also found here though less commonly. A similar heavier point is found in the Tsegi area, while the corner-notched type is reported from the Puerco section.

Basketry is represented by the two types already described. The twilled yucca ring basket was now well established. Coiled baskets are not abun-

Fig 139. Arrow points were typically triangular. The two end forms are from the Flagstaff area, that at the left possibly being Patayan. The two central forms are from the east.

dantly reported, although they must have been relatively common. Those specimens which the writer has examined are of the two-rod and bundle type, with stitches which are not split. This is the type already declared typical of the Basket Makers, and in fact the same forms, with the exception of the large flat basket, were made. Light matting of reeds or leaves was common, although the thick Basket Maker type of matting is apparently lacking.

Because of the open nature of most of the sites of this period sandals are completely unknown from any area other than Chaco Canyon. Here several examples were found which are of the rounded-toe and notched-toe types characteristic of Pueblo III culture. As these will be described in some detail in the next chapter they will not be discussed here.

Unfortunately almost nothing is known of cloth fabrics. Fragments have been recovered which probably are of this age, but no very large pieces are reported. From them it is possible to suggest that quite large fabrics were woven, and if they were, they would certainly have required a true vertical loom. Diagonal weaving was known, and red and black were both used with white to produce color combinations. The beater pictured herewith was probably used in beating out the bulk cotton to separate the seeds from the fibers, and to orient the fibers.

Hunting implements are restricted to the bow and arrow. The arrow is of particular interest because, like the atlatl dart, it was made in two pieces. The main part of the shaft was a light reed, which was plugged in the notched end. To this end were attached three feathers to aid in directing flight. The other end was left hollow, and into it was fitted the hardwood foreshaft, which was pointed and often shouldered. The stone point was attached to the foreshaft. Arrows are much shorter and lighter than atlatl darts. The bow is relatively short and poorly made, the example illustrated being typical. The rabbit stick also appears to have been in use. This is a flattened bent stick, somewhat suggestive of the Australian boomerang, which was sailed after a fleeing rabbit to strike it down from behind. Such sticks are in use by Hopi Indians today.

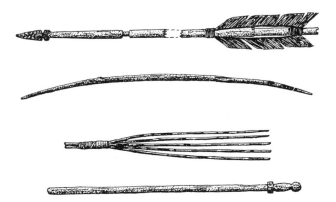

Fig. 140. The arrow at this time was made of a reed with a hardwood foreshaft, and characteristically had three feathers, as in the above illustration. The bow was short and relatively simple. The obvious beaterlike implement, made of five sticks tied together, was possibly used in flailing cotton. The wand pictured at the bottom is from Pueblo Bonito and has been considered ceremonial.

So few specific data concerning foods are available that it is impossible to speak with authority on this matter. Certainly corn, beans, and squash were all grown and eaten. Turkeys were probably still domesticated in some areas. Animal foods included a large variety, although an even greater use seems to have been made of smaller rodents.

Ornaments are of special interest. Stone carving of such ornaments as pendants reached a high level, particularly in the Chaco area. The use of inlays, especially turquoise, became equally prominent now. The finest examples of both these styles of work come from Pueblo Bonito, where the two objects pictured were found. Fine disk stone and shell beads were also made in some abundance, and larger similar clay beads are not uncommon. Shell pendants are not distinctive, but carved stone pendants, often in the form of animals or birds, are strikingly well done. From both Chaco Canyon and the Flagstaff area copper bells are reported, but most likely these were imported rather than made locally. Pipes are of the tubular form, and at least in some localities are of the short-stemmed type.

Bone and horn objects are about the same as those already described. They consist largely of awls, fleshers, and similar tools. Tubular bone beads do not appear to have been characteristic.

Ceremonial objects are not well known. At Pueblo Bonito certain slender wooden staffs are assumed to have been made for such ceremonial purposes, but the relegating of such objects to the ceremonial category is at best somewhat uncertain.

In summary it is possible to point out certain features which are typi-

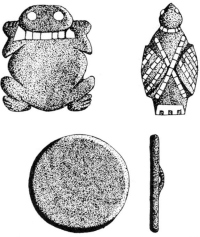

Fig. 141. Stone ornaments become elaborate at this time. The two upper figures are examples of stone carving and turquoise inlay from Pueblo Bonito. The bottom figure is one of the lignite buttons found in the Tsegi country. It is probably a local copy of one of the pyrite mirrors of the Hohokam culture.

cal of this period. Of these the most outstanding, and the best time indicator, is the over-all indented corrugated pot, in which deep identations, sometimes in patterns, are characteristic. Black-on-red pottery for the first time has become important in Pueblo culture and was undoubtedly made by these people as well as their white and gray reduced types. Black-on-white pottery may be characterized by the introduction of the fine hatching in the east and north, and by a common use of wide lines and low flat triangles in simple designs. Physically, the head is consistently deformed posteriorly and is mostly broad. Points are predominantly triangular in shape and commonly side- or corner-notched. Houses are the most varied of all traits, running the gamut from rectangular pithouses to multistory and multiroom pueblos. The kiva was well developed and formalized with a series of distinctive features, some being of extraordinary size. No polychrome pottery was typical of this period.

A few further suggestions might be made by way of a series of summary comments. Masonry and associated architectural features seem to have developed first in the east, or perhaps the four corners area. The largest houses, as well as the largest kivas, were first known here. These influences extended west through the San Juan and Little Colorado rivers. Many other influences may be demonstrated. Hohokam people extended the sphere of their culture first into the Flagstaff section and then apparently northward as far as the San Juan region. Mogollon traits certainly reached the Chaco area to the north, for in this section several Mogollon-like pottery types were known. It is the further feeling of the writer that this culture carried many traits to these people which are now ascribed to Hohokam influence. Mogollon traits also went west through the Puerco and Little Colorado rivers to about Flagstaff. As a result of the sudden blending of these many influences, radical changes and rapid cultural rises in local areas were effected. The center and greatest development lay to the east, probably in Chaco Canyon. Many traits emanated from there to other regions, although in such places as the vicinity of Flagstaff some culture traits remained relatively primitive.

The speed of evolution of Pueblo architecture is still amazing. Although all necessary architectural features were known by people with Basket Maker and Pueblo I types of culture, a full-blown architecture appeared very suddenly at about A.D. 900. The most logical source for the stimulus which gave rise to this development may have been Mexico, for the Casas Grandes site was well established by this time. There were almost certainly contacts between the two regions.

In general the culture which flourished in the plateau was widespread. It also appears to have had much influence on that of other areas. Trade was widely established, and contacts must have extended through south and central Utah to southern Nevada and on into California, as well as into southern Arizona and southern New Mexico. From such information it is possible to state that this was certainly a period of dissemination, but it was also a period of very rapid blossoming of Pueblo culture. Even in the backward Flagstaff area the way was paved for a striking development during the next period.

SINAGUA

The Sinagua culture, which is found in the northern part of Arizona, generally to the south and east of Flagstaff in its more picturesque stages, was originally defined and delimited by Colton, and named by him. The name is from the Spanish *sin* (without) and *agua* (water), for this is now a comparatively dry area. It is defined by a series of plain pottery types, the only ceramics certainly made by these people, although it is possible that later in their history they made copies of Pueblo pottery, particularly in the southern portion of their range.

There is no doubt as to the mid-portion of this culture, for it is clearly distinctive, but the beginning and end dates may be debated, and are dependent on the definition of Sinagua. Colton begins it with the appearance of Rio de Flag Brown pottery in the immediate Flagstaff area, which

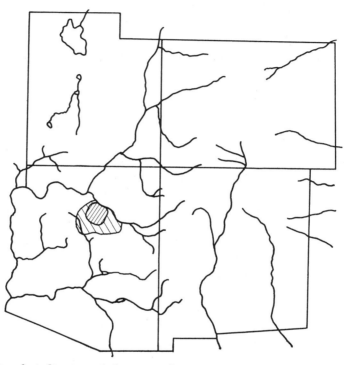

Fig. 142. Rough indication of the area of Sinagua culture during the Dissemination period. The fine hatching is the section covered by Sunset cinders from the eruption of the volcano east of Flagstaff.

occurred first in about the eighth century A.D. This is an interesting type in that it is very like Alma Plain of the Mogollon in most respects, but was made, or finished, by the paddle and anvil process. It has angular temper, is brown or dark gray if the surface has been sooted through use, and occurs most typically as large, or comparatively large, jars. In this earliest period houses are shallow, or surface, and have wooden superstructures.

The progression of the native-made pottery then went through an evolution of a number of plain types: Angell Brown, Youngs Brown, Winona Brown. These types were also finished by the paddle and anvil process, and were fired in an oxidizing atmosphere. The temper of all this pottery is angular light inclusions, and it is relatively abundant and thus easily recognized. Late in this period Sunset Red pottery developed, which has a certain amount of fine black volcanic cinders used as temper and is thus also readily identifiable. The outer surface is smoothed, is typically a brick red, often with fire clouds, and the inner surface is characteristically smudged. Bowls, jars, scoops, and pitchers were all made. The forms of all this pottery show considerable variation, including the Gila shoulder and scoop forms, both features found in the Hohokam types to the south.

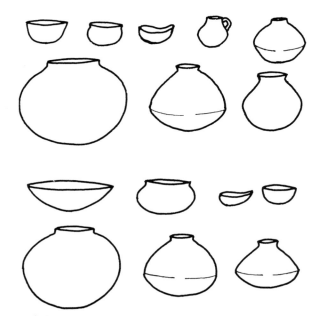

Fig. 143. Shapes of the most common undecorated pottery of the Sinagua. The upper group is Sunset Red, the lower is Winona Brown. The similarity in shapes is obvious. Note the presence of the Gila shoulder in many of these vessels.

There can be no doubt that the Sinagua pottery of this Dissemination period was influenced from several sources. It has already been pointed out that the earlier Rio de Flag Brown is very suggestive of Alma Plain, and such contemporary types as Winona Smudged and Winona Corrugated, with their very fine temper and paste, dimpled surface finish, and corrugations which are small and even and sometimes partly polished over, are very reminiscent of Mogollon types found farther to the east and south. The method of finish, and even some of the forms, are so like Hohokam pottery that its influence must also be admitted. Finally the abundance of trade pottery from the Pueblo culture, and its eventual duplication locally, adds the third major group which contributed to this ceramic development.

The house types are in many ways even more varied than the pottery types. In the immediate area east of Flagstaff the most common houses are wood-lined pithouses with an entrance through the smokehole-hatchway and a ventilator. Others lack ventilators but have alcoves. There are stone-lined structures, which are apparently pithouses, and with associated blocks of surface storage rooms. In some areas there are definite kivas, even as early as the preceding period, and in other portions of this Sinagua region there are kivas with surface masonry rooms. Even quite clearly pueblo architecture is found developing at such sites as Wupatki Pueblo.

The Sinagua culture has been divided into a considerable number of distinguishable foci, based on house types and the pottery which is found associated with them. This peculiar and varied combination of traits seems to have been the result of the geographic location of the Sinagua, and was certainly greatly stimulated or exaggerated by the eruption of Sunset Crater. This small volcano, now some thousand feet high, erupted sometime in the tenth or eleventh century and spread a layer of cinders over a considerable portion of this section of northern Arizona. The cinders, acting as a mulch to conserve moisture, made the growing of crops a very simple matter and so attracted people from widely dispersed areas. People of Hohokam culture came from the Verde valley, Mogollon people were attracted from the south and east, and Pueblo culture, if not actual people, came in from the north.

This admixture of cultural backgrounds gave rise to a very colorful florescence of the Sinagua. Many of the more outstanding traits were introduced from these various sources and blended here. As time went on and the cinders blew into dunes, so that they no longer formed an even covering of the rich clay soils, the people began to move away, to the south, the southwest, and even to the east. This is an exceedingly interesting cultural amalgamation and stimulus. A very rapid local rise in culture took place, which reached a peak at about this time, then in later periods a disintegration, or at least regression from this peak, may be seen. In itself the Sinagua represents a most unusual opportunity for the study of cultural dynamics.

Some of the pithouses found near Flagstaff are very suggestive of Mogollon, as are the early kivas known in the southern part of the area. Some of the pottery types are also strongly reminiscent of the Mogollon in that they are brown or red and have a more or less dimpled surface, or some have fine corrugations, unlike that of the Pueblo culture. Hohokam traits are indicated by houses with rounded ends and side entrances, and there are definite copies of red-on-buff pottery which was made locally. The pottery in general was made by the paddle and anvil process, a trait typical of the Hohokam.

The most abundant decorated pottery was derived from the Pueblo culture, most of which was made in the southern part of the Pueblo area. Both sand and crushed angular inclusions were used as temper. The most typical and abundant pottery was Black Mesa Black-on-white with its

Museum of Northern Arizona photo

A pithouse of the Sinagua culture found near Flagstaff, Arizona. Note the central fire-pit, the four-post support for the roof, and the ventilator or entrance passage on the east side shown in the foreground. Tree-ring dates from this fairly deep pithouse indicate it was occupied during the ninth century A.D.

characteristic ribbonlike, comparatively simple designs. Holbrook Black-on-white was introduced from the east, and may be distinguished by the angular white temper.

One of the most interesting architectural features of the Sinagua culture is small oval ball courts, which are in all major features almost identical to the smaller courts of the Hohokam. The one illustrated was found at Winona Village east of Flagstaff and may have been one of the earliest in the Sinagua culture, dating from the latter part of the eleventh century. They are found in numbers, and although they came in comparatively late apparently rapidly expanded throughout this area and culture.

The only stone-lined court is the one at Wupatki National Monument northeast of Flagstaff. All are of about the same size, some 90 feet long and about half that wide. The floor is essentially level, and the walls are slanted slightly back as they rise from the floor. At the ends the walls slant back more sharply, and there are raised areas at the ends which also are flattened. There is always a center marker in almost the exact center of the floor, so that it would seem they were laid out by some measuring device. The walls, judging from the amount of fill and standing height, were probably about nine feet tall. Since they are practically identical to the Hohokam type, and were preceded in the Hohokam area by larger courts, it may certainly be assumed that they were introduced as a trait from this culture and from the south.

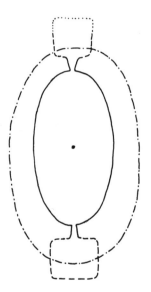

Fig. 144. Plan of the small ball court found at Winona Village in northern Arizona. It is apparently one of the earliest Sinagua ball courts. It is 94 feet long by 48 feet wide at the floor, and the walls may have been about 9 feet tall originally. The walls are almost vertical at the sides and more flaring near the ends. The center marker rock is in almost the exact center of the floor. The dash and dot line indicates the crest of the ridge as originally found, the dashes are the margins at the ends, and the dotted line is postulated.

Burials consisted of both cremations and inhumations, the latter being typically extended and lying on the back. Cremations were mostly gathered up and put into jars and buried in more or less localized areas, sometimes in the trash mounds. The most common area of cremation was the Winona Village region, where, it is also worthy of note, the most definite evidence of Hohokam culture traits were found.

Metates are mostly of the trough type, open at both ends, and the typical mano is the block two-hand type. Three-quarter-grooved axes are common, and grooved arrow-shaft smoothers are definitely a Sinagua trait, particularly in its later stages. Small stone cylinders of vesicular basalt were also relatively abundant in this culture. Pottery disks, many perforated, are typical.

The most outstanding traits during the florescence of this culture were the ornaments and ceremonial objects. Both shell and stone were used extensively, and some very fine ornaments were produced. Nose plugs and lip plugs were relatively common, and were frequently made of red

National Park Service photo

Wupatki Pueblo is a Sinagua site located northeast of Flagstaff, Arizona. It was built along a ridge in two units, and has a large circular room, presumably ceremonial, and a stone-lined ball court associated with it.

argilite, and the nose plugs not infrequently had turquoise buttons attached to them with lac. Lac was used as a plastic base for the modeling of very elaborate inlay pendants and other objects, in which turquoise was conspicuous. Shell was used for bracelets and pendants, and although they were not carved as the more elaborate Hohokam specimens were, they were comparatively common. Shell was also occasionally painted, but no etched examples have been found.

Perhaps the most interesting ceremonial objects were sticks with hands and deer feet carved on one end. These seem to have been rather widely distributed, and were used in a ceremony in which a sort of sword-swallowing display played a part. Other such sticks had turquoise and stone inlays on them.

Points were typically rather long triangles, many with small lateral notches, and not a few with concave bases. They were light in weight and very well flaked.

Perishable materials included twilled matting and coiled baskets of several varieties. Cotton cloth was also apparently common, at least late. Such other tools as weaving battens and sticks of wood have been found. The most common bone object was the awl, which occurred in some abundance in most Sinagua sites.

Hunting implements were the bow and arrow. Foods included corn, beans, squash, gourd, and mescal fibers which were chewed. The dog and the turkey were definitely domesticated, and parrots, no doubt introduced from Mexico, were kept.

In general this is a strikingly rich cultural florescence as now known for this area and time. It is best defined by the plain pottery types, which were locally made in some abundance. Structures were varied, and in at least some instances included the kiva. Ornaments are outstanding and varied. Many of the traits clearly show derivations from the Hohokam and perhaps to a lesser degree Mogollon. Pueblo obviously also contributed much to this cultural development, and pottery was traded from the Pueblo to the Sinagua in some quantity. The rapid rise of this culture to a peak can be related to the eruption of Sunset Crater, and its decline in this immediate area may be related to the blowing away of the cinder cover.

A rather large area was covered by the Sinagua, and it is an obvious and distinct culture, at least at its peak. Colton would have it extend through a very long span of time, from the late eighth century to the fourteenth or fifteenth century A.D. Schroeder would include it in the eastern portion of his Hakataya area, and so relate it westward. It will be suggested that in its later manifestation it was at least in part the source of some Hopi developments, or was clearly related to Hopi culture.

PATAYAN

The area occupied by the Patayan culture was larger now than it had been in the preceding period, or at least more is known of it in a larger area. The Prescott and the Amacava branches are rather well defined, the Agua Fria branch is added, and the northern Cerbat and Cohonina have been much more fully explored. Of all of these branches the most in detail is probably known of the Cohonina. The next greatest amount of information is now at hand concerning the Prescott and Cerbat branches. The extent of all of these groups is somewhat dependent on how they are defined, so that the accompanying map may be considered more a general indication of their extent and boundaries than any clear-cut demarcation. Dotted lines are used to divide the Cohonina from the Cerbat, and the

Prescott from the Amacava, for each grades, at least ceramically, into the other.

The Cohonina culture has been found to extend roughly from Kingman to north of Flagstaff and from the Grand Canyon south almost to highway

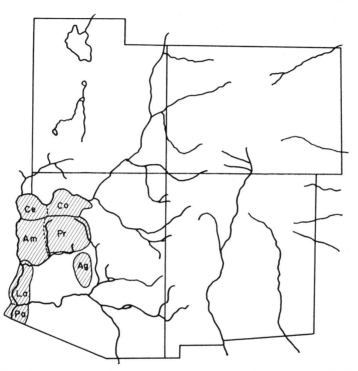

Fig. 145. Distribution of the Patayan culture units at this time. Ce is Cerbat; Co is Cohonina; Am is Amacava; Pr is Prescott; La is La Paz; Ag is Agua Fria; Pa is Palo Verde. The most detail is known of the northern branches.

66. Pottery is the San Francisco Mountain Gray Ware, and is made up of Deadmans Gray, Deadmans Black-on-gray, and Deadman's Fugitive Red. All are made by the paddle and anvil process, as are other pottery types of the Patayan area, and they are tempered with sand and small amounts of very tiny flakes of mica which often show on the surface. They are generally well smoothed, if they are decorated, and the design is in a carbon-black paint and consists of rather fine lines, attached dots, low triangles, and simple scrolls. The design shown in the accompanying illustration is typical.

The most interesting Cohonina pottery is the fugitive red. Mostly this was made in the form of jars, and the paste and temper are the same as the Deadmans Gray pottery. The outside, however, was covered with a red paint which is now often quite fugitive, that is, it may be removed by vigorous scrubbing. This red paint must have been available to the Cohonina in some abundance, for quantities of this type of pottery were made

Fig. 146. Common pottery forms and design of San Francisco Mountain Gray Ware. The central figure is a typical Deadmans Fugitive Red form. The design is a Deadmans Black-on-gray style.

and traded rather widely, particularly to the Sinagua to the east. Sometimes the outsides of black-on-gray bowls were painted red as well as the jars. The Havasupai Indians today have a mine located in a cave in the Grand Canyon from which they secure this red paint, and they have developed a brisk trade in it to the Hopi Indians and others.

The house types are very varied, including surface shades, pithouses from oval to rectangular, patio houses, proto-forts, and even what must

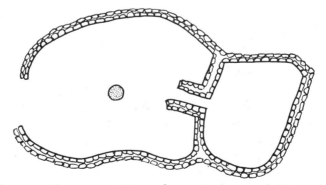

Fig. 147. Diagrammatic representation of a patio house of this period. The living room is to the right; the patio, to the left or west, contains a firepit. The masonry was poorly constructed and consisted only of low walls, the upper portion of which was wood. This type of structure would have been most useful in an area with a comparatively warm climate.

be considered surface pueblo-like units. Probably the most distinctive form is the patio house, in which a living room was attached to a wall which surrounded an open patio. In the area north of Williams the house portions of this combination did not have fireplaces, but fire areas were found in the patio. If masonry was used it did not rise more than a foot or two and the upper portion was made of wood by putting poles into the rock walls, intertwining withes in them, and covering the whole with clay. In some instances the house might be a shallow pithouse with an attached surface room which served as the patio.

The surface shade type of structure has already been described in connection with the preceding period. Pithouses are not particularly distinctive, though they vary considerably in outline, some being small and oval or egg-shaped, others almost rectangular. The so-called proto-forts are more interesting and warrant further comment. Mostly they consist of one large room with only one entrance which is built up to some height with stone walls. These walls are outlined on the outer and inner surfaces with rocks and filled between with earth and perhaps rubble. Posts were

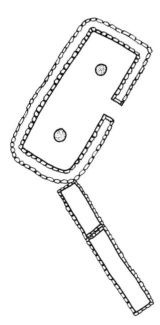

Fig. 148. One of the long structures which is suggestive of the more compact forts. The large room is 38 by 14 feet inside, and the two smaller rooms are 38 by about 5 feet. If the long narrow rooms were attached to the long side of the large room the result would be a typical fort. Note the fireplaces in the center of the large room.

presumably set into them and the upper portion built in the way already described. Some long narrow rooms, presumably storage rooms, were then frequently associated with this larger structure, as shown in the accompanying illustration. The well-known forts which occur in the Patayan culture, particularly in peripheral areas, are similar, but the long rooms have been attached to the long sides of the larger structures, and there is generally no outer doorway, entrance presumably being from the roof.

The final type of house is what might be considered a sort of unit-type pueblo, but lacking any kiva. These were also made in the lower portion with rock walls, and the upper was no doubt wood. Various combinations of these several house types may be found together in more or less of a unit. Shades were frequently found with other structures, and there is some evidence that sweat baths may have been used by these people, although this evidence is certainly not at present conclusive.

A typical Cohonina settlement could hardly be called a village, for individual houses were scattered over a wide area. Trash mounds, as such, were not a part of this culture, and if anything characterizes these settlements it is the variety and lack of standardization of the structures or of the general settlement plan. There is nothing comparable to the compact villages of the Pueblo culture at this time.

Stone work is not elaborate nor very varied. The metate is of the trough type, usually open at both ends but sometimes open at only one end. This

Fig. 149. Metates are either trough-shaped and open at both ends or open at one end like this example, depending entirely on the extent of use and whether they were reversed during wear.

latter condition was apparently the result of not turning the metate end for end during the grinding process. Manos are of the block type, and most are rather well shaped and of the two-hand variety, although one-hand types were also used. One of the most striking lacks of this entire area and culture is stone axes, for although these people made considerable use of wood, axes are essentially lacking.

Burials are very rare indeed, only three having thus far been found which might be considered Cohonina. For this reason it has been suggested that cremation was probably used, the bones being scattered broadcast so that none have been located.

Two other very striking absences are typical of these people. They do not seem to have left any bones in their trash accumulations, or made much use of bone in the production of tools. Only a relatively few bone awls are known, and these are not particularly elaborate, but they do have fine points, suggesting their use in sewing hides or weaving fine baskets. The other marked lack is in the use of ornaments, practically none of which have been found in this culture. It is a very interesting and striking fact that the Havasupai today do not make much use of ornaments, in comparison to other Indians living in the Southwest.

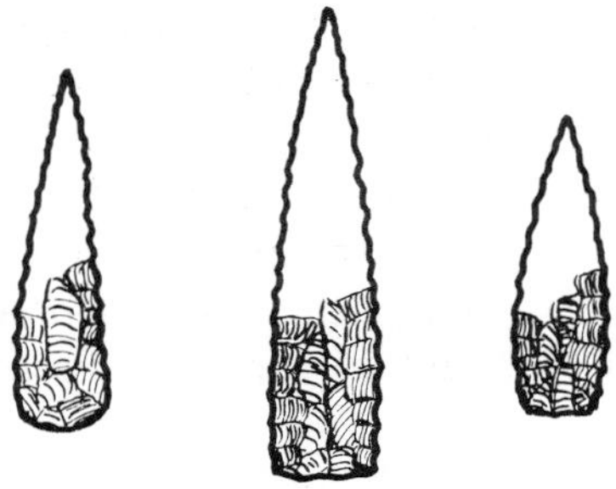

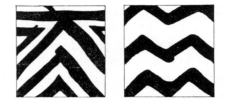

Fig. 150. The only type of point which is believed to be typical of the Cohonina at this time is long and slender and with fine serrated edges. Other types occur as well.

Fig. 151. Simple, crudely executed designs typical of Verde Black-on-gray pottery. This is a dull black paint on a gray base.

The projectile point types include one distinctive form, which is long and slender and serrated on the edges. Other types were used, but this particular form was found in all of the Sinagua structures of this period which have been excavated. There can be little doubt that it was used on an arrow and shot from a bow.

The Prescott branch extends west from Prescott where it grades into the Amacava, a line which has not as yet been too well defined. The pottery was fired in an uncontrolled atmosphere, so that it varies in color from gray to brown, with the most reduced gray types to the east and the more oxidized examples to the west. The same situation prevails between the Cohonina on the east and the Cerbat to the west. There was also more mica temper used in the pottery made to the east than to the west. As has been stated, all of the pottery was made by the paddle and anvil process, and that of the Prescott area has been defined as belonging to the Prescott Gray Ware. The most distinctive type is Verde Black-on-gray, which has rather coarse temper with a considerable amount of mica, is found both in the form of jars and some bowls, and is decorated with a carbon-black paint. The designs are rather crudely drawn, consisting mostly of chevron patterns, and since the black does not contrast well with the gray of the background it is not a very distinctive or outstanding type. The accompanying illustration shows typical examples of the design. Sometimes even the inner portion of the necks of jars had simple designs on them.

The houses were shallow rectangular pithouses with rounded corners, and forts seem to have been built and used here as well. Later on, rectangular masonry pueblos were built, and with them were small, shallow, oval, rock-outlined structures, the use of which is not as yet definitely known.

The disposal of the dead is unknown, like that of the Cohonina. Metates are of both the trough and basin types. Pottery anvils, scrapers, choppers, and projectile points constitute most of the types of artifacts thus far known. The points, at least shortly later, were simple triangles with concave bases.

In general it may be said that both the Cohonina and the Prescott branches showed considerable influence from, or at least parallels with, the Pueblo culture on the east. This is particularly true of the early Cohonina pottery types, as has already been pointed out, and of the later Prescott pueblo structures.

The Cerbat branch is west of the Grand Wash cliffs and to and including the big bend of the Colorado River. The pottery is oxidized and paddle and anvil and may be assigned to the Tizon Brown Ware group. As has been several times indicated it is more brown in the west, and as it is traced east shows more reducing and so more gray examples. The people of this culture occupied mostly rock shelters at this time, although later they occasionally built U-shaped jacal houses. Metates are slab types with shallow oval grinding surfaces.

The Amacava, which it will be recalled was assigned to the Laguish stem, extends along the Colorado River from about Hoover Dam south to Parker. Most of the sites which have been located here are apparently temporary campsites, and little is known concerning the definite types of houses used. The pottery is paddle and anvil, and has been grouped together under the general heading of Lower Colorado Buff Ware. Metates seem to have been of the slab type, which were ground all over.

In the southern portion of the Patayan area Rogers' Yuman II was certainly in vogue at least sometime during this period. He describes the structures as circular and domed with brush walls and mentions that these people also camped in caves. The metate is the flat rectangular-shaped slab, and the mano is of the rectangular-shaped single- and two-hand types. Jewelry was in use here, with beads and pendants made of shell. The pottery was made by the paddle and anvil process, and included such forms as jars, bowls, and scoops. He also suggests that disposal of the dead was by cremation with the ashes ungathered.

From all of this it may be seen that the Patayan culture throughout all of its range shows considerable variation now. In the north the tendency is for the ceramics to be reduced, but as one goes west they become more and more oxidized. The most widespread single trait is the uniform finishing of the pottery by the paddle and anvil process. Houses are very varied, and if there is one trait which is shared it is that they do not follow standardized patterns of production. Other artifacts are limited in variety and numbers. The virtual lack of any use of ornaments in the Cohonina is a striking trait, as is the lack of bones in these sites. In the present state of our knowledge the gradations which are found between the various identifiable groups is more apparent than any clear-cut boundaries which may exist between them. Here is obviously a considerable area, and important cultural development, where much more work needs to be done.

NORTHERN PERIPHERY

The prehistory of the northern part of the Southwest, that in Utah, goes back to the Desert culture, for as late as A.D. 400 there are a conspicuous number of Desert culture traits still apparent, and in fact many of them persist into Historic periods. By about A.D. 800 the distinctive northern

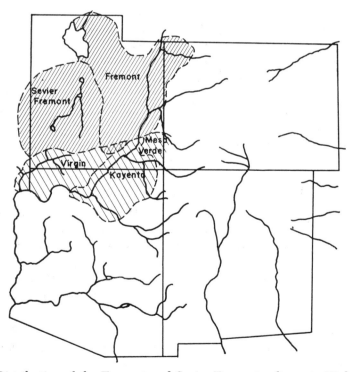

Fig. 152. Distribution of the Fremont and Sevier Fremont cultures in Utah. The Sevier Fremont shows the most Anasazi influences. To the south are the Virgin, Mesa Verde, and Kayenta cultures which are Anasazi.

culture pattern was established, and it survived as a more or less clear-cut entity until about A.D. 1150 or 1200, when it disappeared and was replaced by nomadic groups whose way of life was again more like that of the earlier Desert culture.

The Anasaszi culture extends into the southeastern portion of Utah, where both Kayenta and Mesa Verde are represented much as they are found in the heart of their areas. To the west, as is shown on the accompanying map, and north of the Grand Canyon, is found what some have regarded as the Virgin branch. Others are disinclined to recognize it as a distinct culture. Here some distinguishable pottery types have been isolated, perhaps the most unusual one with olivine temper.

To the north are two somewhat different cultural groups, the Fremont and the Sevier Fremont cultures. These were certainly both well established at this time. The Fremont, to the east, seems to have been the most distinctive of the two, while the Sevier Fremont, to the west, shows more Pueblo traits.

The Fremont culture is distinguished by locally made plain pottery types, and the use of calcite as a temper, as well as by other traits. There was apparently a considerable use of wild plant foods and hunting by these people, but at the same time they had corn of high row numbers. They had trough metates, and more or less rectangular one-hand manos. Structures were made of both adobe and masonry, but they continued to use caves and overhanging shelters as well. They hunted with the bow and arrow, and had stone drills. Smooth stone balls were a feature of the Fremont culture as was the use of rectangular bone gaming pieces. Other traits were figurines, tubular pipes, some basin milling stones, matting, triangular corner- or side-notched points, some very good coiled basketry, and moccasins.

Almost all of these traits are not exclusive of the Fremont culture, but find individual parallels with other groups. It is in the combination of traits that the distinctive culture results. In general comparison to the contemporary Anasazi to the south it is not as high a culture, but is one which was well adapted to the way of life pursued in this more northern region. Many features are reminiscent of Basket Maker III, so that it is a variant of the Anasazi in some respects, but that it is distinguishable is equally apparent.

The Sevier Fremont culture to the west is illustrated by such sites as Beaver, Garrison, Paragonah, Willard, Ephraim, Grantville, and Warren. It was the most modified by the Anasazi, far more than the Fremont culture. Its roots also go back to the early Desert culture, and it disappeared by the time Pueblo IV had developed in the Anasazi area. Ute and Paiute culture seems to have been the modern derivation of this group. There is thus a gap in the history of this area between the last of the Anasazi at about A.D. 1300, or a little later, and the first records of the Utes in A.D. 1776.

THE RIO GRANDE

The Rio Grande may be divided into what might be considered a northern, a central, and a southern section. On the accompanying map the northern portion has been indicated with a T to designate the Taos area, the central section, which extends well north in the western portion, has no designation, and the southern portion has a J to indicate the Jornada branch. Of these the Jornada branch has already been mentioned in the discussion of the Mogollon culture, for it has been assigned to the Mogollon by Lehmer. It is distinguished by the presence of brown pottery and relatively simple structures.

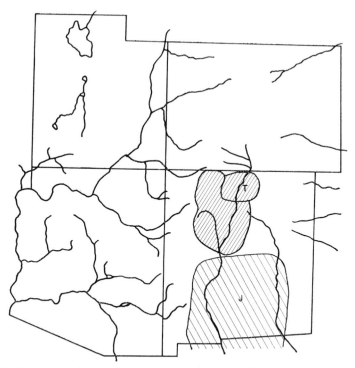

Fig. 153. Cultures which are found in the Rio Grande valley at this time may be divided into a northern and a southern section. In the north are the Pueblo-derived and Anasazi cultures, while to the south is the Jornada branch of the Mogollon. The area with a T is the Taos section, which may be distinguished from the rest of this northern area.

In the middle valley there are two pottery types which are found to be derived from the west but are established in the Rio Grande. The most typical of these is the Socorro Black-on-white type. The temper is fine sand and some crushed dark inclusions. The paste is fine and gray, and there is a thin white float matching the paste. The designs are in black iron paint, and the hatching and other elements are very well executed. Forms are jars and bowls.

Associated with this type is Los Lunas Smudged, which is related to the Mogollon-derived types of the south and west. The paste is soft and friable and the temper is sand. The outside has very well-made fine coils either over the whole body or just the upper part. The forms are bowls.

As in other parts of the Southwest a considerable number of phases have been worked out here beginning with the Rosa phase, which terminated at about the start of this period. Going north it is possible to trace this culture into the Chimney Rock phase, through the Piedra and Arboles phases, while to the south the Gallina phase is of this period. By about A.D. 1330 farther south this development is known as the Jemez phase. In general in this book phases have not been specifically referred to, but similar sequences and regional cultural manifestations are known almost throughout the Southwest.

Apparently most of the cultural stimulus for this area came more or less directly from the Anasazi to the north and west. Architecture, however, in the Rio Grande valley proper, was largely based on adobe construction rather than the masonry or selected rocks which was being used in the eastern Anasazi area. Pithouses were still in vogue.

In the northern part of the Rio Grande two types of pottery were also typical. Kwahe'e Black-on-white was made with crushed pottery temper and has a thin wash but no true slip. It is related to Escavada Black-on-white but is more crudely made. The second type of decorated pottery found here is Taos Black-on-white. The temper is mostly sand and it is considered by Hawley to be a form of Escavada Black-on-white. With it is a plain type with smoothed surface and incised decorations. Both Kwahe'e and Taos Black-on-white seem to have developed relatively late in the period.

At about the end of this period a distinctive culture began to develop in the Gobernador and Largo drainage areas to the west of the Taos area. Pottery types, some of which do not look particularly Southwestern, and peculiar round towers distinguish this culture, but since they are most typical of the following period they will be discussed there.

One of the most interesting features of this period in the Rio Grande valley is that there was a significant increase in the number of pueblos, and in fact this same population explosion is apparent over most of the Southwest. In the northern part of the valley the area of occupation was extended to the Canadian on the east and beyond Taos on the north. The sites now range from small 10- to 12-room pueblos to fairly large communities of over a hundred rooms. They have kivas associated with them, the larger pueblos typically with several kivas. The pueblos have adobe wall construction, and tend to be of rather small cell-like rooms. The kivas are semisubterranean and are circular in outline but lack many of the features considered typical of the more western Anasazi examples. There are no benches, pilasters, deflectors, or southern recesses in any of these northern structures.

Burial was flexed inhumation. Artifacts included chipped stone axes with polished bits and notches for hafting, not the full- or three-quarter-grooved axes polished all over which have been seen in other cultures. Mauls were full-grooved. Pipes were of both clay and stone and were simple tubular and elbow types. Metates were both full-trough, open at both ends, and the scoop type closed at one end. There were also basin-type milling stones. Manos were grooved for the fingers on the sides and with a single grinding surface. There were a few bone awls which were not distinctive but had gradually tapering points. Ornaments consisted of shell bracelets and turquoise beads and pendants. The shell bracelets were of glycemeris and therefore must have been traded some distance from the Gulf of California.

There can be little doubt that the Rio Grande cultures in the central and northern portions were variants from the Anasazi culture, which by now had reached rather high levels of development farther west. In fact pottery types can be traced from the native locally made Rio Grande types through intermediate types to those which have already been mentioned as typical of the eastern Chaco area. As has been suggested, the Rio Grande Anasazi primarily used coursed adobe to construct their pueblos, and the kiva types were quite different from those of the Chaco. Also the San Juan Anasazi kivas had banquettes, pilasters, and a recess over the ventilator, all of which the Rio Grande kivas lacked. Neck-banded and plain gray culinary pottery seems to have lasted much longer in the Rio Grande than it did in the San Juan area. The occurrence of incised pottery is not, however, a survival of earlier Anasazi types, and may find its closest parallel with pottery from the plains.

SUMMARY

In summary of the Dissemination period two points are immediately obvious. First, at this time there was a population explosion in the Southwest, which resulted in the widespread extension of Southwestern cultures. Almost certainly not only were there more people living here than at any other time, but there must have been more sites, for most of them were not as large as they tended to become later. Second, the leadership of cultural development had definitely shifted away from the Mogollon so that the two outstanding groups were the Hohokam and the Pueblo.

Sedentary Hohokam culture was feeling a considerable influence from Mexico, and many more things were introduced, or older introductions either persisted or were further developed. Pottery was much more varied

An extended inhumation found near Flagstaff, Arizona. One pot had been included with the body as an offering. The numbers refer to the site and the number of the burial, in this case site N.A. 2131, burial 1.

in forms and the designs were much more elaborate. The typical house was still a very shallow pithouse and with a stepped entrance. The small ball court was now in use, and irrigation projects had been undertaken on some scale. Stone work was very well made, and projectile points were truly remarkable. The people in such villages as Snaketown were becoming very thoroughly tied to the soil, and highly sedentary. Within the desert area there were cultural variations which had become apparent by now, and intergradations to the Mogollon are particularly apparent to the east.

This cultural mixture between Hohokam and Mogollon is well illustrated in such sites as the Gleeson site, east of Tombstone in southeastern Arizona. Here Mogollon traits are represented by inhumations, pit ovens, and bone tools, while Hohokam traits are houses, though not exclusively so, the general economy, pottery, though it too is in some senses intermediate, and the extensive use of shell and figurines. Actually the development of this culture in this area is of sufficient distinction to warrant a separate division and designation.

Mogollon culture, on the other hand, had not so markedly changed from what it had been before. Pottery included a number of coiled types which were rather remarkably well made, and black-on-white pottery was being introduced from the north. This was the beginning of a considerable influence from this quarter which was to have a marked effect on the future development of Mogollon culture. Although the area occupied was relatively large, there seems to have been a shift to the south into Mexico, or the connections in this direction were strengthened. Structures continued to include pithouses, although surface pueblo units were appearing to the north, and kivas were still a definite part of this complex. One rather striking trait was the presence of what appear to have been floor drums in these ceremonial structures.

Anasazi culture was well on its way with the development of Pueblo in the northern part of the Southwest, and expanded over a very wide area. Ceramics particularly enjoyed a great florescence, with a profusion of local types developed. Two general styles are of widespread occurrence: over-all indented corrugated vessels, and two kinds of black-on-white. The first of these is the Black Mesa style which is made up of rather broad ribbonlike lines in comparatively simple patterns, and the second is the development of hatching balanced with solid areas, particularly in the Chaco and Puerco regions. In general the first of these may be considered western and the second eastern. Also paint types now were carbon in the west and iron base in the east.

Architecture was exceedingly varied, from deep wood-lined pithouses in the Flagstaff area to huge multistory and multiroom pueblos in Chaco Canyon. The kiva also became quite formalized, with a banquette, pilasters, deflector, ventilator, a platform area above the ventilator, and in most cases a sipapu. The area of highest Pueblo development was the eastern San Juan, and it was closely seconded by the Puerco. Thus the rapid rise of Pueblo culture took place in the four corners area and to the south of it.

Other outstanding traits were the production of rather fine inlaid mosaic jewelry, and the increasing dependence on agriculture as a basic way of life. Only in the development of the pueblo style of architecture and possibly in pottery did the Pueblo people outshine the Hohokam.

In the Flagstaff area the eruption of Sunset Crater led to the development of the rather striking Sinagua culture, or at least to its florescence. The only pottery types which are native are plain and are brown and red, but they were rather well made. Clear evidence may be seen of influences from the Hohokam which spread up the Verde valley and introduced such things as ball courts at this time, Pueblo influence from the northeast, and to a lesser degree Mogollon influence in house types and some ceramics. The pottery, for instance, was made by the paddle and anvil process, and some forms are very suggestive of Hohokam types, but the red may have been stimulated by the Mogollon.

Farther west in the Patayan area the Cohonina culture had developed certain distinctive traits. Pottery was copied after Anasazi types and was reduced in contrast to that for most of the rest of this culture region. Houses were varied and included such exotic forms as forts and patio houses, as well as pithouses and surface shades. Some of the most interesting features of this culture are its lacks, such as the paucity of bones of any kind, the lack of interest in jewelry, and the fact that no convincing evidence has as yet been uncovered as to how they disposed of their dead.

As one goes farther west pottery firing becomes less well controlled and more and more oxidized, until at the Colorado River it is quite red or brown. Structures and other traits are not as well known from the rest of this area as from the Cohonina, but in the Cerbat some have been explored and in the Prescott branch others have been dug. The Prescott branch seems to show more direct relationships with the Pueblo culture than even the Cohonina did.

In the northern periphery, in Utah, Anasazi culture spread well into the southern part of the state. Both the Kayenta and Mesa Verde branches encroached from the southeast, and in the southwest the Virgin culture north of the Grand Canyon is generally conceded to be Pueblo with only local variations. Farther north in Utah the Sevier Fremont is to the west and shows many more Anasazi characters than the Fremont culture to the east. This latter has its roots far back in the Desert culture, and although it developed agriculture and made pottery, it also depended to a considerable extent on hunting and gathering. In almost all respects it may be considered as being peripheral to the major cultural developments of the Southwest. These people had a few distinctive traits, such as figurines of characteristic types, moccasins, and distinctive square bone dice.

Cultures in the Rio Grande again show Anasazi relations, and are distinctive mostly on rather minor traits. Pottery types are different only in detail from those to the west, and architecture is not so elaborate. Houses were made of adobe walls rather than stone, and kivas lacked many of the typical features of those of Chaco Canyon. In the southern portion of the Rio Grande the Jornada branch of the Mogollon occurred, and was marked by the presence of much brown pottery.

By examining the various maps in this chapter it may be seen that many of these cultures spread out into and overlapped with other cultures. Hohokam went up the Verde valley and reached the Flagstaff area in some strength. Anasazi spread out into and mingled with Mogollon. Even with all of this intermingling, individual areas showed distinct traits which on the whole mark them off more or less clearly from other areas.

This was thus a time of great stimulus in the Southwest, one which was to precede a period when some even more interesting developments were to take place. Culture was now developing at a rapid rate, and although a good deal of this stimulus may be accounted for by way of Mexico, all was not from outside. There was a good deal of internal development which had already taken place, and more was soon to come.

Sources and Additional References

Amsden, Charles Avery. An Analysis of Hohokam Pottery Design, *Medallion Paper 23*, 1936, Gila Pueblo, Globe, Arizona. (Very worthwhile summary review of Hohokam design elements and combinations, with evaluation of their relationships.)

Bartlett, Katharine. Material Culture of Pueblo II in the San Francisco Mountains, Arizona, *Bulletin 7*, 1934, Museum of Northern Arizona, Flagstaff. (Much of the material reported here is of the Patayan culture.)

Beals, Ralph L., G. W. Brainerd, and Watson Smith. Archaeological Studies in Northeast Arizona, *Publications in American Archaeology and Ethnology*, Vol. 44, No. 1, 1945, University of California Press, Berkeley. (A number of sites of this period are reported herein from the western San Juan area.)

Bluhm, Elaine A. The Sawmill Site, a Reserve Phase Village, Pine Lawn Valley, Western New Mexico, *Fieldiana: Anthropology*, Vol. 47, No. 1, 1957, Chicago Natural History Museum. (Discussion of the small pueblo with a kiva with floor drums.)

Colton, Harold S. Winona and Ridge Ruin, Part II. Technology and Taxonomy of the Pottery, *Bulletin 19*, 1941, Museum of Northern Arizona, Flagstaff. (The pottery of Winona and Ridge Ruin in detail.)

————. A Revision of the Date of the Eruption of Sunset Crater, *Southwestern Journal of Anthropology*, Vol. 1, No. 3, 1945, University of New Mexico Press, Albuquerque.

————. * The Sinagua. A Summary of the Archaeology of the Region of Flagstaff, Arizona, *Bulletin 22*, 1946, Museum of Northern Arizona, Flagstaff. (Best statement of the Sinagua to date.)

Colton, Harold S., and Lyndon L. Hargrave. Pueblo II in the San Francisco Mountains, Arizona, and Pueblo II Houses in the San Francisco Mountains, Arizona, *Bulletin 4*, 1933, Museum of Northern Arizona, Flagstaff. (Much of this material is also of the Patayan culture, but other portions deal with Pueblo culture.)

————. * Handbook of Northern Arizona Pottery Wares, *Bulletin 11*, 1937, Museum of Northern Arizona, Flagstaff. (Detailed discussion of general ceramic problems as well as of the types mentioned in this chapter.)

Danson, Edward Bridge. An Archaeological Survey of West Central New Mexico and East Central Arizona, *Papers of the Peabody Museum of American Archaeology and Ethnology*, Vol. 44, No. 1, 1957, Harvard University, Cambridge, Massachusetts. (Compares the cultures at this time, and points out the abandonment of some of the mountain area at the end of this period.)

Euler, Robert C. Archaeological Problems in Western and Northwestern Arizona, 1962, *Plateau*, Vol. 35, No. 3, 1963, Museum of Northern Arizona, Flagstaff. (Brief discussion of the Virgin, Cohonina, Cerbat, Prescott, and Amacava branches.)

Euler, Robert C., and Henry F. Dobyns. Excavations West of Prescott, Arizona, *Plateau*, Vol. 34, No. 3, 1962, Museum of Northern Arizona, Flagstaff. (Report on work in the Prescott branch.)

Fulton, W. S., and Carr Tuthill. An Archaeological Site Near Gleeson, Arizona, No. 1, 1940, the Amerind Foundation, Inc., Dragoon, Arizona. (An example of the intergradation of Hohokam with Mogollon culture at this time in southeastern Arizona.)

Gladwin, H. S. * Excavations at Snaketown II, Comparisons and Theories, *Medallion Paper 26*, 1937, Gila Pueblo, Globe, Arizona. (Much information on general problems relating to the Hohokam.)

Gladwin, H. S., Emil W. Haury, E. B. Sayles, and Nora Gladwin. * Excavations at Snaketown, Material Culture, *Medallion Paper 25*, 1937, Gila Pueblo, Globe, Arizona. (Represents the only comprehensive review of Sedentary Hohokam.)

Gladwin, Winifred and H. S. The Red-on-Buff Culture of the Gila Basin, *Medallion Paper 3*, 1929, Gila Pueblo, Globe, Arizona. (Early summary of Hohokam culture in the Middle Gila area.)

————. The Red-on-Buff Culture of the Papagueria, *Medallion Paper 4*, 1930, Gila Pueblo, Globe, Arizona. (Early review of Hohokam culture in the south central portion of the area.)

————. The Western Range of the Red-on-Buff Culture, *Medallion Paper 5*, 1930, Gila Pueblo, Globe, Arizona. (General and early review of western Hohokam culture.)

————. Some Southwestern Pottery Types, Series III, *Medallion Paper 13*, 1933, Gila Pueblo, Globe, Arizona. (Excellent review of characteristic red-on-buff pottery types from the Colonial period on.)

————. The Eastern Range of the Red-on-Buff Culture, *Medallion Paper 16*, 1935, Gila Pueblo, Globe, Arizona. (Very good discussion of the eastern variant of the Hohokam culture.)

Guernsey, Samuel J. * Explorations in Northeastern Arizona, *Papers of the Peabody Museum of American Archaeology and Ethnology*, Vol. 12, No. 1, 1931, Harvard University, Cambridge, Massachusetts. (See particularly the chapter dealing with Pueblo II and the table of summarized characters at the end of the book.)

Harlan, T. P. A Sequence of Ruins in the Flagstaff Area Dated by Tree-Rings, Master's thesis, University of Arizona, Tucson, 1962. (Source of many of the dates referred to herein.)

Hawley, Florence M. The Significance of the Dated Prehistory of Chetro Ketl, Chaco Canyon, New Mexico, *University of New Mexico Bulletin*, Monograph Series, Vol. 1, No. 1, 1934, Albuquerque. (Report of a Chaco Canyon site comparable to Pueblo Bonito.)

Jennings, Jesse D. The American Southwest: A Problem in Cultural Isolation, in Seminars in Archaeology: 1955, *American Antiquity*, Vol. 32, No. 2, Part 2, 1955, Society for American Archaeology, Salt Lake City, Utah. (Distinction of the Fremont and Sevier Fremont cultures.)

Judd, Neil M. The Material Culture of Pueblo Bonito, *Smithsonian Miscellaneous Collections*, Vol. 123, 1954, Washington, D.C. (This site was constructed during the Dissemination period.)

Kidder, Alfred Vincent. An Introduction to the Study of Southwestern Archaeology, Phillips Academy, Andover, Massachusetts, 1924. (This material is discussed on the basis of culture and not time but may be separated with some consideration.)

Kidder, Alfred Vincent, and Samuel J. Guernsey. * Archaeological Explorations in Northeastern Arizona, *Bulletin 65*, 1919, Bureau of American Ethnology, Washington, D.C. (Pueblo culture is not clearly separated here by periods but includes some of this age.)

Lehmer, Donald J. The Jornada Branch of the Mogollon, *University of Arizona Social Science Bulletin 17*, 1948, Tucson. (Southeastern Mogollon at this time.)

Martin, Paul S., and John B. Rinaldo. Turkey Foot Ridge Site, a Mogollon Village, Pine Lawn Valley, Western New Mexico, *Fieldiana: Anthropology*, Vol. 38, No. 2, 1950, Chicago Natural History Museum. (A site dating early in this period.)

———. Sites of the Reserve Phase, Pine Lawn Valley, Western New Mexico, *Fieldiana: Anthropology*, Vol. 38, No. 3, 1950, Chicago Natural History Museum. (Discussion of this period with pottery illustrations.)

Martin, Paul S., John B. Rinaldo, Elaine A. Bluhm, Hugh C. Cutler, and Roger Grange, Jr. * Mogollon Cultural Continuity and Change: The Stratigraphic Analysis of Tularosa and Cordova Caves, *Fieldiana: Anthropology*, Vol. 40, 1952, Chicago Natural History Museum. (Perishable items and a good characterization of this period.)

Martin, Paul S., and Elizabeth S. Willis. Anasazi Painted Pottery in Field Museum of Natural History, *Anthropology Memoir 5*, 1940, Field Museum of Natural History, Chicago. (Some pottery of this period is illustrated.)

McGregor, John C. * Winona and Ridge Ruin, Part 1: Architecture and Material Culture, *Bulletin 18*, 1941, Museum of Northern Arizona, Flagstaff. (Detailed report of a number of Sinagua sites.)

———. Burial of an Early American Magician, *Proceedings of the American Philosophical Society*, Vol. 86, No. 2, 1943, Philadelphia. (Description of a remarkable collection of Sinagua artifacts found with one burial.)

———. * The Cohonina Culture of Northwestern Arizona, University of Illinois Press, Urbana, 1951. (Best present report on excavated Cohonina sites.)

Morris, Earl H., and Robert F. Burgh. Anasazi Basketry, Basketmaker II Through
  Pueblo III: A Study Based on Specimens from the San Juan River Country,
  Carnegie Institution Publication 533, 1941, Washington, D.C. (Basketry types
  of this period for the Anasazi.)

Pepper, George H. Pueblo Bonito, *Anthropological Papers*, Vol. 27, 1920, American Museum of Natural History, New York City. (The fine plates in this
  report will give a good idea of the culture traits found here. Detailed descriptions make reading of this volume tiresome for the beginning student.)

Roberts, Frank H. H., Jr. * The Ruins at Kiatuthlanna, Eastern Arizona, *Bulletin
  100*, 1931, Bureau of American Ethnology, Washington, D.C. (The portion of
  this report which deals with the culture from the surface pueblo is of this
  date.)

Rogers, Malcolm J. An Outline of Yuman Prehistory, *Southwestern Journal of
  Anthropology*, Vol. 1, No. 2, 1945, University of New Mexico Press, Albuquer-
  que. (Brief statement of the chronological development of the lower Colorado
  River area cultures.)

Sayles, E. B. The San Simon Branch, Excavations at Cave Creek and in the San
  Simon Valley. I. Material Culture, *Medallion Paper 34*, 1945, Gila Pueblo,
  Globe, Arizona. (Discussion of the Cerros and Encinas phases.)

Schroeder, Albert H. * The Hakataya Cultural Tradition. Facts and Comments,
  American Antiquity, Vol. 23, No. 2, Part 1, 1957, Society for American Archaeology, Salt Lake City, Utah. (As indicated by title.)

————. * The Hohokam, Sinagua and the Hakataya, *Archives of Archaeology*,
  No. 5, 1960 (on 4 microcards), Society for American Archaeology and the
  University of Wisconsin Press, Madison. (Detailed discussion of the Sinagua
  in relation to the Hakataya.)

————. The Pre-eruptive and Post-eruptive Sinagua Patterns, *Plateau*, Vol. 34,
  No. 2, 1961, Museum of Northern Arizona, Flagstaff. (Very good brief characterization of his views of the Sinagua.)

————. An Archaeological Survey of the Painted Rocks Reservoir, Western
  Arizona, *The Kiva*, Vol. 27, No. 1, 1961, University of Arizona, Tucson. (As
  indicated by title.)

————. * The Archaeological Excavations at Willow Beach, Arizona, 1950, *University of Utah Archaeological Paper 50*, 1961, Salt Lake City. (Sites in western Arizona of some time span and Cerbat culture.)

Taylor, Dee C. The Garrison Site, *University of Utah Anthropological Paper 16*,
  1954, Salt Lake City.

Wasley, William W. A Hohokam Platform Mound at the Gatlin Site, Gila Bend,
  Arizona, *American Antiquity*, Vol. 26, No. 2, 1960, Society for American Archaeology, Salt Lake City, Utah. (As indicated by title.)

Wheat, Joe Ben. * Mogollon Culture Prior to A.D. 1000, *American Antiquity*, Vol.
  20, No. 4, Part 2, 1955, Society for American Archaeology, Salt Lake City,
  Utah. (Good comparative statement across the field for this period.)

Wormington, H. M. A Reappraisal of the Fremont Culture, *Proceedings of the
  Denver Museum of Natural History*, No. 1, 1955, Denver, Colorado. (The most
  complete discussion of the characteristics of the Fremont culture.)

XIII

Classic Period: A.D. 1100 to 1300

PUEBLO III

Much definite information has been obtained concerning the culture which flourished in the plateau area during the Classic period. This specific knowledge includes a wide geographical range and the entire time. span represented. Large sites were flourishing throughout much of the plateau, and are therefore impressive and easily located. They contained quantities of "loot," to reward quickly the efforts of the archaeologist. Douglass was also able, early in his work on tree rings, to establish dates for most of these sites, and thus directed a good deal of popular interest to them. Subsequently almost all other sites of similar age which have been dug were dated, so that it is undoubtedly the most accurately dated of all Southwestern periods.

As a result it is possible to speak of a late and an early phase of the culture of this time, in most sections. The early phase existed from A.D. 1100 or 1130 to about 1200 and is the less understood of the two, although there is a good deal of specific information concerning it. The late phase existed from 1200 to 1300, in most sections, and is widely and fairly well understood.

Dating of the beginning of this period has been firmly established in the western portion of the area by the abandonment of the Black Mesa Black-on-white type of pottery and the introduction of polychrome types. In other sections the beginning date may be determined by similar ceramic changes, one of which is the deterioration and decrease in abundance of corrugated types. The end of the period is marked by the drought, which has been established by Douglass and repeatedly referred to by others.

This period, from A.D. 1276 to 1298, saw little rainfall over the northern part of the Southwest; in fact the drought left a marked record in the ring growth of trees in practically all sections. That it was extremely disastrous to the aboriginal population, particularly of the plateau area, is proved by the abandonment of the entire eastern San Juan and the area to the north. Probably it represented a sort of last tribulation of accumulating difficulties, for there is evidence of earlier droughts of some consequence, and nomadic invaders may well have been entering this area by this time. A shift of population is found to have taken place about A.D. 1300 to the south and east, a direction in which Pueblo contacts had already been established. Movements were to areas where a sufficient water supply was assured in dry time. Such locations were the southern end of the Black Mesa, now occupied by the Hopi Indians, the mountain section of the state, the Zuñi area, and a large portion of the immediate Rio Grande valley.

From the accompanying map it is apparent that the area of greatest concentration and purest culture had been reduced. Fewer sites were occupied, but they were much larger on the whole than those of the previous period. One point must be kept in mind when examining this map: the occupation of the Rio Grande is not included. It would thus be possible to extend the area much farther east, as has been indicated by the outline of maximum diffusion. There was also a southward extension of Pueblo culture, which, although it became modified almost immediately, penetrated well into the Upper Gila drainage area. As it has been designated the Salado culture, it will be discussed more fully under this heading.

Probably most striking is the decrease in the area of maximum expansion. The direction of movement seems to have shifted slightly, with more emphasis on expansion to the east and south than to the north and west. Extension of influence and trade also seems to have been greatly reduced to the north and west, and to have shown a considerable spurt to the south and to a lesser extent to the east. The purest Pueblo culture is certainly to be found now lingering only in the immediate San Juan area, as Mogollon culture had already established a strong influence in the eastern portion, and Hohokam culture a similar influence in the south and west.

One of the most interesting problems of this period is the explanation of the increase in size and decrease in number of the sites. Several suggestions have been made in an effort to account for this fact. One is that the natural cultural evolution of the people would result in the compaction of the population. A second suggestion has often been made, that the press of enemies required the building of large pueblos for protection.

As far as the writer has ever been able to see, there is no real evidence of warring in the plateau at this time. Compared to the many skeletons found with arrow heads still embedded in the bones in the Mississippi valley, skeletons from the Southwest with such evidences of warfare are

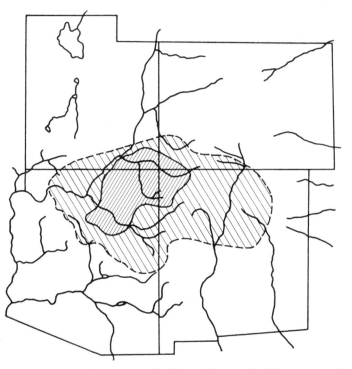

Fig. 154. Map indicating the extent of culture during the Classic period. No attempt has been made to include Rio Grande or early Salado cultures in this map. Both the area of greatest concentration and of maximum expansion are reduced, if these associated outlying cultures are omitted. It has been particularly reduced from the north and west. Fewer but larger sites were characteristic at this time.

extremely rare. Most pueblos are also found upon careful examination to be anything but deliberately formed forts. Actually they are probably mostly an outgrowth of a realization that by grouping rooms the number of walls required is greatly reduced. This is well illustrated by the utilization of large blocks of rocks and the curving back walls of caves for the same purpose. From all present definite information it would appear that the Navahos existed as a serious threat to the Pueblo people only at a much later date. There is some indication that certain intervillage "squabbling" did take place, however, for some few sites are found which were definitely fortified. These almost invariably are the outposts lying at the edges of culture areas, and very likely they represent contacts between two more or less unfriendly ethnic groups. In other instances local failures of crops probably resulted in raids on neighboring groups, which have left indications of sporadic fighting. Such evidences do not appear to be universal even in any one small section.

From the essential bibliography included at the end of this chapter it may be seen that there is considerable literature dealing with the culture of this period. Most of these reports are an exposition of the regional variations from the general Pueblo culture pattern which existed. For this reason no serious attempt will be made to present a detailed discussion of each variation. As there was actually a great deal of overlapping or blurring of local cultures an almost infinite number of regional variations might be pointed out. Since such microscopic division is impracticable, small sections will be lumped and only the most outstanding characters of the major divisions discussed. To the writer four such major divisions are apparent. These are: (1) that area lying between Flagstaff and the western San Juan; (2) the Hopi country, including the Hopi Washes, the Little Colorado River throughout its central section, and the Puerco drainage; (3) the Mesa Verde section of the eastern San Juan; (4) the Zuñi area of the upper Little Colorado River in the White Mountains and eastward into the Zuñi River region near the state line.

As pottery and house types give the most definite information concerning regional variations of culture, the characteristic features of these two traits will be discussed first by the sections outlined. After this a general discussion of the other material culture traits will be presented.

Sometime near A.D. 1100 Moenkopi Corrugated pottery began to develop from Tusayan Corrugated. In all features of paste, temper, and finish the two types are exactly alike; they differ only in the manner of production of the corrugations. Moenkopi corrugations are less well marked in all features than Tusayan. The coils are wider and flatter, the indentations farther apart, less deep, and irregularly spaced. In some instances they are so poorly formed that a second glance is required to realize that the surface is indented corrugated. Vessel shapes are similar to Tusayan, except that they are possibly more inclined to be squat and globular, particularly the pitchers. The evolution from one type to another was not sudden, so that many intermediate forms are found, and in some areas, such as the central San Juan, Tusayan seems to have survived later along with Moenkopi. The general impression is inevitable that care was not exercised in the manufacture of such vessels. More carefully corrugated types were in vogue to the southeast, but these were oxidized and red or brown instead of the gray of the Pueblo types. Moenkopi Corrugated was widespread, and in most instances is a good indicator of this period, for it lasted to about A.D. 1300.

The first definite area to be discussed is that which seems to have centered somewhere in the Moenkopi Wash. Influences were extended both north to the western San Juan and south to the Flagstaff area. As a great many pottery types have been identified from this section it is more profitable to speak of styles of design in the black-on-white types than to refer to them specifically. The Tusayan style of design is diagnostic of the early portion of this period here. It is typically composed of rectangular blocks forming the pattern, which are made up of zigzag lines and

Fig. 155. Outline of the most common vessel shapes and detail of the Moenkopi Corrugated pottery type. It serves as an indicator of this period.

Fig. 156. Vessel forms and the Tusayan style of design on black-on-white pottery types. This style is indicative of this period, beginning in the early portion by about 1150 but lasting in some types as late as perhaps 1300.

opposed triangles as illustrated in the lower portion of the illustration. In some pieces the central line is omitted and the opposed triangles are exaggerated. Large hatched scrolls, as shown in the same illustration, are also found to be typical, particularly on large vessels such as storage jars. The forms are predominantly bowls and jars as shown, but large jars with small mouths also occur. The temper is sand, or white fragments, the paste gray with a white slip and a black paint forming the design. A feature which appears to be characteristic of some of the many types with this design is an outflaring rim with a marked angular interior shoulder. This style seems to have existed most abundantly from about A.D. 1150 to sometime after 1200, perhaps as late as 1300 in some types.

At about the same time Tusayan Polychrome was evolved as the first polychrome pottery to achieve popularity in this section of the plateau.

This type was a direct development from Tusayan Black-on-red, through Citadel Polychrome. The paste, finish, paint, and even some of the designs are similar to the former type, with the exception of the red slip which was applied only as a form of wide-line design outlined with black. This left the orange paste without a slip forming the background of the red and black design. The temper is prepared soft angular material, and the surface is carefully smoothed. The forms are bowls, ladles, and perhaps jars. The bowls have straight sides, often with slightly flaring rims, and small strap handles placed just below the rim and parallel to it. The interior is decorated with red lines outlined with black on an orange background, the exterior with broad bands or wide lines of red on the unslipped orange surface. This type of pottery began about A.D. 1100 and lasted to about 1300.

Fig. 157. Forms and simple style of design found on Tusayan Polychrome. This is the earliest polychrome type which became popular in the plateau area. The background is orange, the hatched portion red, and the black line black. In associated types it existed from about A.D. 1100 to 1300.

In the latter portion of the period a very striking black-on-white pottery developed. The finest type which has this style of decoration is Kayenta Black-on-white. The paste is gray to white and contains fine sand temper, so fine in fact as to be almost invisible to the naked eye. The surface is slipped white and has a clear carbon-black paint. True Kayenta Black-on-white is well fired and gives off almost a metallic ring when struck. The style of decoration is very striking and was widely copied in other types. It is so applied as to appear a black background with white lines forming the design. This style has been variously termed "negative," "mosquito bar," and "massed black." Forms are bowls with straight sides and horizontal strap handles, ladles of the bowl and handle variety, and a distinctive large jar. This has a flattened area below the neck and a tendency to a rounded Gila shoulder lower on the body. It is one of the most striking types of jars produced in the Southwest in any period. Although less formalized styles of this type of decoration were being produced by about A.D. 1200, the most highly developed forms do not seem to have appeared until almost 1275.

At about 1265 another type was produced in the Tsegi or northern portion of this area. It is Kayenta Polychrome, and is exactly like Tusayan Polychrome in every particular except that the black line is in turn outlined with a fine white line. Forms are bowls, as described for Tusayan Polychrome, ladles of the bowl and handle variety, and small jars or pitchers.

Moenkopi Corrugated is found associated with all these types and so is probably one of the best time indicators of this period in the western area.

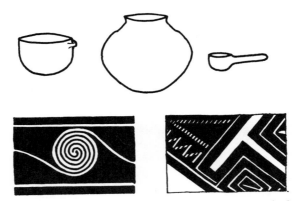

Fig. 158. Vessel forms and styles of design found on Kayenta Black-on-white pottery. These styles of design are indicative of the latter portion of this period, from about A.D. 1250 to 1300. Less well-executed copies of the negative motif were made on other types.

In the earliest portion Tusayan Corrugated occurs in small amounts, and Tusayan Black-on-red in slightly greater numbers. Because of this overlapping of types it is necessary to consider ceramic complexes in dating individual sites in which beams are not secured.

House types to the north, in the central and western San Juan, are greatly varied throughout all of this time span. There was much use of wattle and daub or jacal construction in building walls, but not all structures were surface. Pithouses survived well to the end of this period, particularly in the Kayenta area, and many of them, as well as some of the surface structures, had a firepit near the door and upright stone slabs, like wings, set on each side of it. This is reminiscent of the earlier floor ridges seen in the pithouses found farther east, but they are considerably later, surviving to about A.D. 1300. They are also higher. The pithouses occurred singly or were combined with surface structures in lines or in units. This strange combination of house types, though defying understanding now, may eventually be explained if and when other social customs may be related to them and specific derivations traced.

Most of the kivas found in these sites are circular, some with surrounding benches and usually with a platform on the southeast. Characteristically they had a ventilator running under the platform, a deflector, a firepit, and then a stone-lined recess in the floor, all in a line. Some of the kivas are rectangular, and they may be found in the same sites as the circular kivas, a feature which will be noted for sites in the Tsegi area.

The house unit pattern is most interesting, for in many ways it is very reminiscent of much earlier arrangements to the east. These consist of

An example of the wattle and daub type of construction used for some walls in Betatakin Pueblo. A tied brush fence was first built and then plastered with adobe. This is probably a very early type of wall.

lines of contiguous rooms arranged along a wall and alternating with living rooms and flagstone-floored storage rooms. The living rooms are easily identified because of the presence of firepits. They are usually found on ridges or mesa tops and suggest defensive arrangements, for the walls are commonly large heavy walls. They may occur in several lines crossing the mesa top, or in various patterns, and incorporated with them may be one or several kivas. There is no real evidence that they were for defense, and in fact in at least one case there was a suggestion that they might be terraces, for runoff from a higher terrace was ditched into it. Whatever the real meaning of these distinctive structures the type is well established for this area, for a number of them have been found, although not yet fully reported in print. The relationship to such an earlier site as Alkali Ridge seems clear.

In the Moenkopi and Flagstaff areas pueblos are also of masonry and as a rule are of moderate size. All of the kivas are rectangular and more or less underground. Wupatki Pueblo is a fine type site of this section and time. It is a medium-sized pueblo, with two units of closely massed rooms above ground and several rectangular, only slightly sunken kivas. The masonry is of sandstone blocks, chosen for form but not carefully shaped to fit, and set into a mass of mortar from both sides of the wall. The core of such masonry is filled with a quantity of clay and small stones.

Late sites to the north have both circular and rectangular kivas. At Kiet Siel, in the Tsegi Canyon system, circular kivas occur, while at Betatakin, about eight or nine miles away, only surface rooms which might have served as kivas are found. Other interesting architectural features in these sites are wattle and daub walls, walls made of turtle backs, small doorways closed with an inset stone slab, and loom ties in rooms. To the south in the Flagstaff area, only rectangular underground kivas are found. These are masonry-lined and have a ventilator leading out one of the long sides, but no other kiva features. A typical site in this southern portion is Turkey Hill Pueblo; to the north, Kiet Siel and Betatakin, both in the Tsegi system, could serve as types.

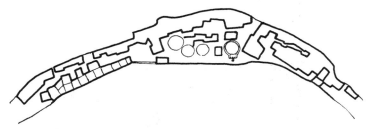

Fig. 159. Rough sketch plan of the house blocks of Kiet Siel Pueblo. It is the largest cliff pueblo in this section. Relative room sizes are indicated to the lower left. Circular kivas with bench and platform are found here. The masonry is much cruder than that to the east.

In the second area, that of the Puerco, Little Colorado, Hopi country, three new pottery types are found. Tularosa Black-on-white is the first and most interesting. The dates, although not so accurately established, are from 1100 to 1250. For the present no attempt at division of this type will be made, although Gladwin has pointed out that three regional distinctions may be seen, the Puerco, Roosevelt, and true Tularosa Black-on-white types. These three types will be combined under one general descriptive term and called Tularosa, for this name is best established in the literature. The importance of this broad group lies in the fact that it is part of what might be considered the earliest Salado culture, which by now had begun to penetrate the mountain section south of the plateau. Originating in the Little Colorado, it reached the Upper Gila area and spread throughout most of the headwaters of the Gila and Salt streams. The paste is gray to white, with crushed or prepared angular temper fragments. The surface is covered with a white slip and decorated with a black iron-carbon paint which may locally burn brown or red. It was made by the coiling and scraping process, and was fired in a reducing atmosphere although some examples are found which have been in part oxidized, apparently almost always by an accidental secondary firing.

Both designs and forms are very characteristic features of this type. Designs are either purely rectilinear or a combination of rectilinear and curvilinear elements. There is a tendency for solid and hatched areas to be balanced, as in the design illustrations in the accompanying figure.

Fig. 160. Forms and styles of decoration of Tularosa Black-on-white pottery. Designs consist of balanced solid and hatched elements, with long fine parallel lines in the hatching. Typical forms are shown. Bowls have sloping sides. Pitchers are globular, often with animal figurine handles, some of full figures, others with only protruding heads.

Fine hatching was widely used, in which the hatch lines are drawn parallel to the long axis of the area to be filled in. Once the design elements and combinations are thoroughly in mind, this general pattern may be very easily recognized wherever it is found. Since it is most striking its probable derivation is of some interest. The abundance of fine hatching points first to the Chaco Canyon as a basic source of at least part of the design. Next would be features derived from the Mesa Verde, such as the opposed stepped triangles. The third source would be the west, where rectangles and triangles are most prevalent. From this it is apparent that the pattern was derived from a combination of elements and ideas secured from several sources, but the use of balanced solid and hatched elements goes back into the preceding period with such pottery as Escavada Black-on-white and allied types. These styles and elements of design were carried into later types and further elaborated.

Forms are bowls with distinctly sloping sides, suggestive of Chaco Canyon, ladles of the bowl and handle variety, and pitchers with animal figurine handles. The bodies of pitchers tend to be squat and very rounded, with relatively constricted necks. Effigy handles are either simply heads of animals, as in the lower left-hand example in the accompanying figure, or of full round animals spanning from the neck to the body, as in the lower right-hand figure. So far as the writer is aware, such handles are confined solely to this general kind of pottery.

Farther west, in the central Hopi country, Jeddito Black-on-orange made its appearance. This type dates later, from about A.D. 1275 to 1400. It is the first of a long series of Hopi orange or yellow types, and marks a definite shift in interest from pottery largely produced in a reducing atmosphere to that fired in an oxidizing one. Temper consists of angular prepared fragments and a slight amount of sand. Paste is light brick red to orange, and there is no slip. The pigment of the design is manganese; apparently it was often applied lightly, and it fires black varying to a reddish brown. Forms are bowls, ladles, and rarely jars. The designs are found on the insides of bowls and ladles and the outsides of jars; they consist of hatched and solid elements. A characteristic feature is the presence of a broad "life line" just below the rim on bowls. A similarity both in form and in design to the next type to be described indicates some connection between the two.

To the south and east St. Johns Polychrome had developed by about A.D. 1175 and became very important between then and about A.D. 1300. The paste varies from gray to brown and contains angular prepared fragments of temper. Vessels were produced by coiling and scraping and were slipped with a heavy bright red-orange slip. The only form known is hemispherical bowls, which are so named because the greatest diameter is found below the rim. Rims are invariably beveled inward. Black designs, both geometric and curvilinear, occur only on the interiors. Many of them are so very suggestive of the Tularosa style of design that they may be definitely ascribed to the same source. On the outer surface a zone below the rim is decorated with a wide rectilinear band or by repeated small geometric elements in white paint. Thus three colors, orange, black, and white, are present, and the pottery is classed as polychrome. This is one of the most pleasing types of pottery ever produced in the plateau area. Not only may it be appreciated today but it was equally appreciated then, for it was one of the most widely traded types ever produced. Wherever sites of any size or duration are found which date between about A.D. 1175 and 1300, fragments of St. Johns Polychrome are almost certain to occur. Such evidences of trade have been traced as far south as Mexico, both in the Rio Grande and the Gila and Salt drainages, and they have been found in all sites throughout the plateau area.

Fig. 161. Form and styles of design of St. Johns Polychrome. The lower design, black on the orange-red base, is found on the inside of the bowl. The upper design is a white band on the outside below the rim, the shaded area of which is the orange slip. This bowl shape is typical and has a rim which is beveled inward. It was very popular and widely traded.

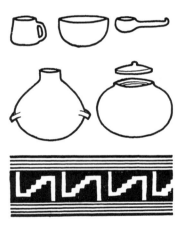

Fig. 162. Mesa Verde Black-on-white forms and designs. The stepped element and framing lines are typical. Forms such as the kiva jar in the lower right are outstanding. The down-raking handles on the jar, the mug, and the upturned tip of the ladle handle are equally distinctive.

House types in this section appear to be relatively small pueblos of surface, masonry, rectangular rooms. Throughout the Hopi country present evidence indicates the presence of sunken, masonry, D-shaped kivas.

Turning next to the four corners, the Mesa Verde culture may be seen to have succeeded in overshadowing Chaco Canyon culture by this time. The most outstanding pottery type is Mesa Verde Black-on-white. The paste is gray to white and contains angular fragments of temper. The slip is a distinctive pearly gray-white, with a depth of luster which often gives one the feeling of being able to peer slightly into it. The paint is carbon black; the design characteristically occurs in bands or zones with parallel framing lines above and below, and the geometric elements are often so arranged as to give a slight suggestion of the Kayenta negative style of execution. Opposed stepped triangles, as illustrated, are a very common element. Bowls uniformly have square rims, as is often true of other forms, and are decorated with large dots or dashes or both. Forms of this type are very characteristic and distinctive. The kiva jar is round-bodied and has the only true pottery lid ever produced in the Southwest. Had vessels of this sort been made with spouts and a handle they would have looked very much like teapots. Relatively large jars were produced, with down-raking handles located below the center of the body. They are globular in form and have small necks. Mugs with vertical handles, strongly suggesting beer mugs, are also very characteristic. Bowls have straight sides and square rims, and ladles are of the bowl and handle variety but with the tip of the handle most commonly turned up. This type dates from about A.D. 1200 to 1300.

In the Chinlee and Chaco Canyon areas Mesa Verde styles of decoration and forms appear to have been combined with the preceding Chaco Canyon types to produce a hybrid characteristic of neither. In the Puerco area it has already been suggested that Tularosa Black-on-white was such a cross, and in New Mexico other types seem to have developed in a similar way. From these ceramic indications, and other characters such as masonry types, it is possible to suggest that Mesa Verde influences were moving outward from its center to modify the developments in Chaco Canyon and other bordering areas. Thus the cultural leadership of the plateau changed now from Chaco Canyon to Mesa Verde. Marked influence also spread east into the Rio Grande drainage, there to build upon Chaco characters.

In this discussion of pottery only the most diagnostic styles of design and the most outstanding types have been mentioned. However, it must be recalled that a great many specific pottery types were being produced. Not only was regional variation at its maximum throughout the plateau, but also Pueblo culture was spreading from the plateau into many other areas.

The finest stone masonry in the Southwest was produced in the Mesa Verde at this time. Individual blocks were carefully shaped and laid with very little mortar, and at most only slight chinking. To square ends and flatten surfaces the blocks were shaped by pecking, so that the surface of the stone is often distinctively dimpled. So far as the writer is able to learn this is also the only area where solid rock walls were produced. By this is meant that individual stones often extended from one surface to another, so that no core of rubble or clay was used. As a result the walls were usually thin, and most of the rooms were relatively small and irregular in shape. This is particularly characteristic of the large pueblos located in the caves of the Mesa Verde area proper. Kidder has pointed out that they give the appearance of having been started in a modest way and then added to as necessity demanded.

Probably one of the most typical features of these sites is the presence in every pueblo of one or more round, oval, D-shaped, or rectangular tower. These are usually called watch towers as they are located in such a way as to command the approaches to the pueblo, and are often loop-holed. Kivas are abundant and very characteristic. They are as round as it was possible to build them and average about 13 feet in diameter. They are always underground or, where close bedrock was encountered, excavated as far as possible, a retaining wall being built around them and the intervening space filled with earth. A narrow bench with six masonry pilasters encircles the room, thus forming six equal-length segments, the southernmost of which is widened to form a platform. A ventilator leads under this southern recess to the floor. Beyond it is a masonry or wattle-work screen or deflector, beyond this a firepit, and still farther in a straight line a sipapu three or four inches in diameter. This type appears to have been strictly adhered to.

By far the best-known sites in this section are those of the latter portion of the period, as represented by the several large cliff dwellings included in Mesa Verde Park. Of these, Cliff Palace is the largest and probably the best known. Lowry Pueblo, in southwestern Colorado, is an example of an earlier site which shows a mixture of Mesa Verde and Chaco cultures. Aztec Ruin and several of the large sites in the Chaco Canyon show similar mixtures of culture, or replacement by Mesa Verde, most of them dating well before the end of the period.

In the fourth area to be considered, that which has been designated Zuñi, one very distinctive pottery type, Pinedale Polychrome, developed late in the period. The dates are from about A.D. 1275 to 1350. The paste is gray and the temper is normally ground-up potsherds. It is covered by a heavy red to orange-red slip which has been well smoothed. Designs are in either a thin dull black paint or the earliest true glaze paints to be used in the Southwest. The glaze paints are often so thick as to be slightly raised above the surface of the vessel. Designs, both purely geometric and conventionalized, show a definite outgrowth from Tularosa and St. Johns Polychrome types. Vessel forms are hemispherical bowls and much more rarely jars. The interiors of bowls have a black design on the red-orange slip, while the exteriors bear a black design outlined with a thin chalky white line.

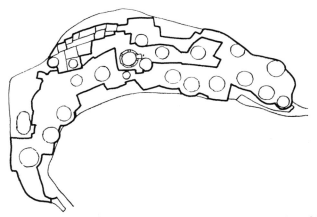

Fig. 163. Rough outline plan of Cliff Palace. The heavy lines outline blocks of rooms, which are shown in relative size in the upper left portion. Kiva positions are shown by circles, only one of which has been completed. Irregularly shaped rooms are typical.

This type is the first of a series of specialized types developed in this area which made a considerable use of glaze paints. They were still further evolved during the next period in the true Zuñi area farther east. Its derivation may be traced by design elements and color combinations back through St. Johns Polychrome, from which the color ideas were certainly derived, to Tularosa Black-on-white, from which many of the elements came.

In the Zuñi area proper there are large multiroom pueblos, some of two or even more stories, with enclosed courts or plazas in many. In the living rooms there are slab-lined firepits and flat metates in slab boxes as well as some wall niches. Definite storage rooms may be distinguished from living rooms. The kivas are circular with benches, and some with platforms. They each have a ventilator passage, a deflector, a firepit, an ash pit, and a sipapu all in line. These smaller kivas may be in front of units of rooms or embodied within them. In each village there is usually a great circular kiva, which has a surrounding bench and four posts for support.

Slightly farther south, in what has become known as the Pine Lawn area, there are both large and smaller pueblos built of either boulders or coursed sandstone rocks, depending primarily upon the availability of materials. Plazas and courts are a common feature of these sites, and in some instances there are walls surrounding the pueblos, a feature which still farther south became the compounds of the Upper Gila and Salt. Associated with these pueblos are great kivas which are rectangular with

Spruce Tree House in the Mesa Verde is one of the more spectacular sites in this park. Note particularly the ladder extending through the roof of the circular kiva in the left foreground.

a ramp entrance. They are usually not deep in relation to their size, and although they lack many of the typical floor features of kivas farther north they do have a firepit and a deflector. At the Mineral Creek site, which dates early in this period, a large circular kiva was found which seems to have had floor drums, a trait which was noted for the preceding period here, and may be a hallmark of the Mogollon.

At Point of Pines, between about A.D. 1250 and 1275, there seems to have been an actual migration of people from the Anasazi to the north. There is much to suggest that this northern stimulus might have come from the Kayenta branch of the Anasazi.

In both of these areas Tularosa Black-on-white pottery is typical, while in the northern portion Chaco Black-on-white and St. Johns Polychrome are found, and in the southern area there is Reserve Black-on-white and

Gila Corrugated. The presence of this last corrugated type tends to tie this region with the Upper Gila as does the general plan of the pueblos.

The variations found in masonry in these several regions have been pointed out, and now it might be well briefly to summarize the types represented. Masonry of the western San Juan is relatively poor. Here thin slabs of odd-shaped sandstone were laid in abundant clay mortar, acting as much as a binder to hold the wall together as for the main support of the wall. The best masonry type is in the Mesa Verde section of the eastern San Juan, where true masonry was built; blocks are carefully shaped, often by pecking, and laid in very little mortar. An intermediate type is found throughout most of the Hopi country and upper Little Colorado area, although it is inclined to be largely of the western San Juan type. In the mountain areas, including that section around Flagstaff, still cruder masonry walls were made of boulders.

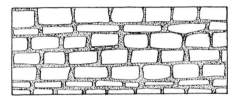

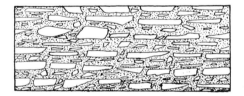

Fig. 164. Comparison of masonry types from Mesa Verde (upper) and western San Juan (lower) areas. Mesa Verde blocks are shaped and have little clay mortar and few spalls. The western San Juan type is of very irregular blocks with much clay mortar and many spalls.

Physically the Pueblo people of this period are much the same as those of the preceding period. The skull is broad or round, and deformed posteriorly, often to one side. The frame is light. As has been pointed out, skull deformation was probably accomplished not primarily by the use of a hard cradle board, but by a hard head rest upon which the head of the infant was placed. As a result cradles may now be disposed of by simply stating that they also are similar to the types described.

It has been the common assumption of most of the excavators in large sites that they have not located the main burial plots of the inhabitants, for they have felt that more should have been recovered than are usually found. Perhaps the people buried their dead in widely scattered individual spots, like the Navahos today, so that no definite burial ground was used. However, it is quite likely that a fair percentage of burials have been found, and that the excavators have been inclined to assume a larger population than actually existed. Burials have been located in trash heaps, under the floors of rooms, and in sealed and abandoned rooms. In fact inhumation was practiced in almost any spot where digging was relatively easy. The bodies are generally flexed in the western San Juan; in the eastern either flexed or straight. To the southwest many are straight in that area in which Hohokam influence appears to have penetrated.

Cremation is occasionally found in widely scattered sites. It was practiced in the Flagstaff area in certain cultures flourishing at this time, and it occurred as far north as the western San Juan. Fewkes reports evidences

National Park Service photo

Aztec is one of the more northern of the large pueblos. In the foreground is the great circular kiva which has been restored. As may be seen, the masonry in this site is very well done.

of cremation in the Mesa Verde section, and it probably also was occasionally practiced to the southeast. As this is a basic culture trait, one associated with religious ideas and teachings, it is felt to be a strong indication of actual culture contact, perhaps even of movements of people.

It is a satisfying fact that it is found only in such sections and at such times in the plateau as would suggest some remote Hohokam characters. As cremation was a universal Hohokam habit it may be taken as basically of this origin, although it must be admitted that under unusual circumstances an individual in any culture might have been cremated.

Both metates and manos show considerable variation. During the earlier portion of this period in certain sections, particularly to the southwest, high-sided metates open at both ends seem to have been in general use. To the east, and in the San Juan drainage, scoop-shaped shallow metates open at only one end were more common. Later these were widely replaced by a flat sandstone slab set into a box. This type was a permanent fixture of the dwelling, as the upright box slabs were set into the floor and the metate stone set into the box in a bed of mortar. Manos varied from the plain block type to grooved or triangular forms. The triangular form was evolved by wear from the block type.

Axes are predominantly of the three-quarter-grooved type, the only full-grooved forms occurring in the San Juan area. Although they are not so long and slender as the finest examples from the Gila, they are very well made. Both from the distribution and from the materials of which these axes are made it is quite likely that they were traded into the plateau from the south, and not made locally. Full-grooved mauls are still quite common. Other ground stone implements show considerable variation, both in form and use, suggesting rasps, saws, and an abundance of various abraders. Polished stone mirrors were also still being made, at least in the western San Juan area, in both rectangular and circular forms.

Fig. 165. Arrow points are still predominantly triangular in this area, both with and without side notches. The winged drill, shown in the center, is also typical.

Arrow points, as a rule, are not found abundantly in any sites of this period, at least as judged by Midwestern or other standards. Certainly such hunting implements did not assume the importance that might be expected of them. Although the actual point type appears from the scanty published descriptions to be varied between regions, the predominating form is still essentially triangular. Laterally notched types are widely distributed, and triangular points without notches, as illustrated in the accompanying diagram, are not uncommon in the Tsegi area. Winged drills, as illustrated, are also relatively common. They are square or triangular in cross section and obviously were held in the hand for boring. A close similarity to Midwestern types is suggested. Knife points are common, are usually more coarsely chipped than arrow points, and are often set into wooden or bone handles. They are not as a rule large blades, and many might possibly be considered arrow points of unusual size. Where obsidian was available this material was used for points, chert being more commonly utilized in the manufacture of knives. Large sharp fragments of chert and obsidian were also used as cutting tools, judging from the abundance of such implements found in every site.

Apparently without exception wherever sites of this age are seriously excavated, evidences of yucca ring baskets are found. From this it may be considered the most characteristic basket of this time. Coiled baskets, although possibly not so abundant as in earlier sites, are represented. They are of the usual two-rod and bundle variety in most sections, although at Pueblo Bonito three-rod baskets have been reported, and Judd mentions a one-rod basket from his work north of the Colorado River. The shapes seem to have been about as reported from previous times. Rush matting was probably very common and is often found covering the floors of excavated rooms. It was made in quite large mats and had a definite selvage or edge.

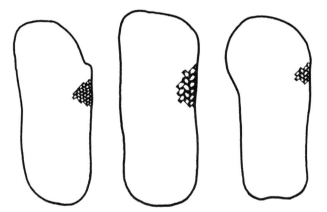

Fig. 166. The most common sandal is made of split or whole yucca leaves in a twilled weave. The notched-toe form to the left is the most diagnostic of this period. Other forms tend to be either rounded or square-toed.

Sandals are well known and are, at least in some types, very characteristic. The most typical is that with a notched toe, as shown to the left in the accompanying illustration. The most striking feature of the sandals is that they are predominantly of the twilled weave, of split or unsplit yucca leaves. As twilled weaving in yucca and reeds was very common, it may be assumed that this style of mat and sandal making had become popular in preference to the twined weaves of the Basket Maker stages. The notch for the toe is on the outside of the foot, in the area of the small toe, definite rights and lefts having been made. Other sandals of the same weave have more rounded or somewhat pointed toes, and squared toes. The ends of the leaves, often shredded, were left on the underside of the sandal to give it a thick sole and to act as padding. Only fine weaves have been illustrated, although a great many coarse examples have been found. Some twined-woven sandals in very coarse weaves were also made. The notched-toe sandals from Pueblo Bonito are of particular interest in establishing a date and region for their origin.

Cloth fabrics seem to have reached a very high development, and although they maintained about the same status during the next two periods, even the finest appear, if anything, to have been only slightly better. Fur blankets assumed an important status in the clothing of these people, as might well be expected for they are still made by Hopi Indians. However, the most striking fabric development was the rise in abundance and varieties of forms and weaves of cotton cloth. The presence of large cotton blankets, some of several feet, required the use of a large loom, almost certainly a complex upright loom comparable to that of the Hopi or Navaho Indians today. Only narrow strips of fabric could have been produced on the horizontal or slanted belt loom, and to make larger pieces it was necessary to sew several of these strips together. Because the large fabrics were made in one piece it is assumed that the vertical loom was used.

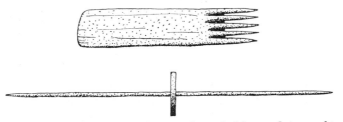

Fig. 167. The upper object is a wooden comb probably used in packing down the filler or weft threads in weaving cloth. The lower is a spindle, complete with whorl, which was used in spinning or twisting fibers to make yarn or thread for weaving.

As has been suggested, variations in both form and weave are exceptional. Some of the most interesting fabrics were produced in the coil without foundation weave from yarn made of cotton fibers. They were made into shawls, caps, and leggings which were worn above sandals or more rarely attached to them. One very exceptional shirt found at Poncho

House was made of four pieces sewed together to form the front, back, and sleeves, with a slit for the head. As this poncho is like the Mexican and Central American type in use today it may possibly show contacts in this direction. Yarns were colored red, brown, black, and white, and were woven in all important weaves known by later weavers in this area, including the straight over-and-under and the twilled. A loose warm cloth was made with a slightly twisted filler or weft, and a heavier canvaslike cloth of a tightly twisted weft and warp. Sometimes the heavier cloth was painted with a pigment in designs after it had been woven. Tye dying was also known at this time, as one fragment of green dyed cloth from the Tsegi country shows. This had a green-blue background with parallel rows of white dots with green centers.

Rawhide and dressed buckskin were manufactured into a number of articles of clothing and dress. They included relatively large robes and moccasins. Nowhere, however, were they very abundant.

Hunting implements were little different from those already described as typical of the earlier periods. The bow and arrow was certainly still the main hunting weapon, and the use of the rabbit stick became much more common. Snares and nets were also abundant and in general use for the capture of both animals and birds. The presence of large rabbit nets made of yucca-fiber cord in a true netting weave, and suggesting very long tennis nets, is probably a survival from Basket Maker culture.

Ornaments had become generally diversified and abundant. A considerable use was made of turquoise, particularly in the east. Inlays appear to have been quite common, and beads of all sizes from one-half inch in diameter to microscopic were made of jet, hematite, lignite, turquoise, shell, stone, and clay in abundance. Turquoise was generally used for beads, pendants, and inlays. Shell was most commonly used for pendants, rings, and bracelets. Stone was used for beads, pendants, and occasional rings. None of these objects were so elaborately carved or so well made as those from the Hohokam culture. Olivella shell beads were still very popular, for they could simply be cut or ground off at the end and strung. Abalone shell was also used rarely for pendants because of its unusual color. The black buttons, either in squares or circular disks, which were highly polished and average about two and a half inches in diameter, were common throughout the San Juan area. These have already been compared to the pyrite mirrors of the Hohokam.

Pipes were widespread although not anywhere very abundant. The most common form was the straight or tubular pipe of stone or clay, as already described. Elbow pipes were rarer, although they did occur; they are somewhat suggestive of the elbow pipes of the plains and mounds regions to the east. Stone pipes were carefully made, well polished, and seldom decorated.

Probably a greater variety of ceremonial objects is found now than from any preceding period in the plateau. The most common is a small leather or cloth bag which contains a collection of pebbles and other queerly formed objects. This is probably a medicine bag. Besides such trinkets there is a great variety of wooden objects, such as crooked and painted sticks, bundles of intertwined twigs in the form of complex crosses, and human and bird effigies. Odd-shaped stones were also occasionally painted. Strikingly enough, the most varied collection of such objects has come from the western San Juan region.

This circular kiva found at Cliff Palace is typical of the Mesa Verde. Characteristic features are the small size, banquette, pilasters, bench ventilator, deflector, and firepit.

In summarizing the Classic period probably the most outstanding characteristic could be stated as a general high level of all traits. This balance of its various components is one of the features which marks a rather highly developed culture. Variations in ceramic and house types have been pointed out for four regions of the plateau. These are the western area from about Flagstaff north to the western San Juan; the Hopi country including the Puerco, Little Colorado, and Hopi Washes; the eastern San Juan area comprising the Mesa Verde–Chaco sections; and the Zuñi area in the upper waters of the Little Colorado River and including the Zuñi River.

The introduction of polychrome pottery is a feature of this period, for three important types of polychrome appeared. To the west Tusayan and Kayenta Polychrome developed. In the central section St. Johns Polychrome had an early rise to enjoy great popularity. From this and to the southeast, Pinedale Polychrome developed, the first pottery in the Southwest with a true glaze paint and the direct ancestor of the later Zuñi types. Black-on-white pottery also reached a high level, both in designs and forms. Tularosa Black-on-white, developing in the Little Colorado, began its expansion south to establish the Salado culture and to carry with it later polychrome types. Mesa Verde Black-on-white developed a very formalized design and outstanding shapes, in most areas considerably overshadowing Chaco types. To the west, throughout the Hopi country and as far as Flagstaff and the Tsegi Canyons, early Tusayan and later Kayenta styles of design were developed.

Masonry shows considerable variation in technique and excellence of construction. The best was in the four corners area, where blocks were carefully shaped and coursed in thin walls and small rooms. To the west, irregular rocks were laid in abundant clay mortar, with much chinking with small spalls. Intermediate types are found to the south and perhaps in the center. The most elaborate and formalized kivas are in the east, where all the features of the Mesa Verde type are present. This kiva was distributed down the San Juan to the Tsegi with only slight changes. The rectangular underground kiva is most typical of the southwestern part of the area, while incomplete evidence would indicate that the D-shaped kiva was most characteristic in the Hopi country.

Other cultural material is not particularly outstanding. The box metate was definitely established at this time and became the dominant form in later periods. Arrow points were predominantly triangular in shape and had either side notches or none. Sandals were flat and made in the twilled weave, the most typical form being the side-notched type. Weaving of cotton fibers became an important industry, and the presence of a large vertical loom is indicated. Beads were highly evolved, with many very minute types in a variety of materials. Ceremonial objects were equally varied.

Diagnostic features of this period consist largely of definite pottery types, masonry, local kiva forms, and the notched-toe sandal. A great deal of detailed information has been acquired about this culture and these times. Perhaps it is a result of this information that many regional variations are apparent and certain definite diagnostics are not so obvious as in those sections and times about which less is known.

The Classic period is well dated both in its beginning and at its end— the beginning probably best in the western and eastern sections, the end by the great drought of the late thirteenth century. This drought was one of the great catastrophes in the history of Pueblo development and probably was the main contributing factor to the abandonment of the entire San Juan drainage at about A.D. 1300.

CLASSIC HOHOKAM

Classic Hohokam is undoubtedly the most interesting of any of the Hohokam periods, for it was at this time that a new culture, the Salado, was beginning to impress itself on the Hohokam people. In general that part of the culture which represents a pure Hohokam group was simply an evolutionary continuance of the preceding stage, the Sedentary. In fact

Gila Polychrome types of pottery found in a burial in the Roosevelt area. These are one of the best indicators of Salado culture.

by the latter part of Sedentary time it would seem that early Salado people had already exerted a certain mild influence on the Hohokam inhabitants of the Middle Gila area, particularly in such matters as the multiroom surface structures which appeared about then. This influence was carried over to the Classic period, becoming gradually stronger to about A.D. 1300. At this time Salado people themselves entered the Middle Gila and actually mingled with the Hohokam residents, a remarkable example of the peaceful combining of two culturally different groups in single communities.

Because of the intermingling of these two groups any discussion of the culture of Classic Hohokam is difficult. In many respects the two people remained distinct, but it is more than likely that in others they mutually influenced each other to produce a variety of new trait combinations which are actually characteristic of neither. Although a considerable amount of excavation has been done in sites of this late period, much was done before it was realized that two groups had mingled. As a result it is very difficult to determine from early reports what traits belong to either culture. The most comprehensive evaluation has probably been made by Gladwin.

To assign a beginning date to this period is a relatively simple matter, for the end of the Sedentary has been established as about A.D. 1100. The abundance of trade pottery in early Classic sites, which was derived from areas where tree-ring dates may be applied with some assurance, corroborates this date. It is in the question of the end date that difficulty is encountered. Gladwin and Haury have suggested that the Classic period lasted to at least A.D. 1400, and certainly Salado culture had removed from the Middle Gila area by about that time, although it may have lasted in the east as late as A.D. 1450. The problem revolves about the question of how long the Hohokam people retained their distinctive character after their association with the Salado people, and before they apparently disappeared from the scene as a distinct archaeological group, or modified their culture and moved into the Papagueria area. The approximate date of A.D. 1350 which has been suggested for this event appeals to the writer, although Gladwin still feels that they may have survived into modern times in certain sections of the desert area with only a perishable culture. Thus the end date of the Classic Hohokam period is much less certain than the beginning. Trade pottery from such sites as Gila Pueblo, which has been dated by tree rings, would indicate an end date sometime between A.D. 1350 and 1400.

Gila Pueblo has suggested that there are two phases making up Classic Hohokam. The earliest of these, the Soho phase, is dated as about A.D. 1100 to 1300, although the present feeling is that it may be somewhat later, while the latest or Civano phase existed from 1300 on to the end of the period of occupation, or, as has been suggested above, to about A.D. 1400. It is the Civano phase which shows such an abundance of Salado characters, and in fact it probably consisted largely of that culture.

The region occupied by people of Classic Hohokam culture is illustrated by the accompanying map. From this it is immediately obvious that the area of greatest concentration has been so reduced as to include only that section at and immediately above the junction of the Gila and Salt rivers. The area of maximum distribution also is greatly reduced, probably with its main extension southward along the Santa Cruz River to include Tucson. An examination of the two similar maps for the Colonial and the Sedentary periods clearly illustrates the continual shrinkage of the area occupied from about A.D. 500 on. An analogous situation is found in the plateau from a period of maximum expansion at about A.D. 1000 to the greatly restricted area occupied by the Pueblo people today.

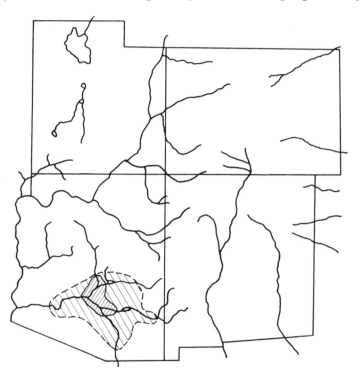

Fig. 168. Generalized map showing the area of concentration and greatest distribution of Classic Hohokam culture. This, and the other Hohokam maps, have been derived from Gila Pueblo publications and modified as a result of discussions with workers in this field. The area is considerably reduced from that of the preceding period.

That this culture was still quite virile and that the people were congenial to their neighbors is amply illustrated by the many types of trade pottery found in relative abundance in ruins of the Classic period in the Middle Gila. Pottery types from all over the desert area of the Southwest are commonly found in these Middle Gila sites. A surprising number were also traded to them from the Pueblo area. There is some evidence that two important commodities went north in exchange. These are fine cotton fabrics and shell. The evidence for shell is probably the stronger, for quantities of marine shells from the Gulf of California are found in the plateau country, and it is quite likely that much of this material traveled through the hands of the Hohokam people. Some of the finest cotton fabrics produced in the Southwest have come from the Gila drainage area. An extraordinarily fine piece was found at Snaketown, and the Tonto cliff dwellings and Verde valley salt mines have produced others. Such contacts, once definitely established with the north by about A.D. 1000, must have continued to the end of Hohokam culture.

Pottery characteristic of the Classic period is Gila Plain, Gila Red, and Casa Grande Red-on-buff. Besides these native Hohokam types, two Salado types, Gila Polychrome and Tonto Polychrome, were made in the Middle Gila area at this time. Gila Plain has already been described in detail. Gila Red is of considerable interest, for although it arrived ahead of the actual Salado people it has many suggestive Salado characteristics. The paste is porous, often with conspicuous mica temper, and was made by the paddle and anvil process. Forms are jars, bowls, some quite large, pitchers, and an abundance of eccentric animal or plant effigies. Two distinctive features characterize this pottery: the insides are smudged black and are either polished or dull, and the exteriors have definite parallel striations—a characteristic which has often given rise to the term "onion skin" in describing this type. The striations are obviously deliberately placed to form a sort of decoration, for they radiate from one or two focal points. This character is a distinction from similar types of other regions. The exterior of Gila Red bears a bright red slip, usually with fire clouds which mar its otherwise beautiful surface.

Casa Grande Red-on-buff is the last of the red-on-buff types produced in the Gila area and is not abundant in comparison with the other types found in Classic sites. Probably the most distinctive feature is the jars, all of which have the vertical necks of the preceding period. They were made by the paddle and anvil method, the surfaces smoothed, sometimes almost to a polish. The surface color is a light buff and the decoration an iron red. Certainly the most common form is the large jar, or olla, with a vertical neck, and often holding upwards of 30 gallons. Bowls occur but rarely. The decoration seems to have been a continuation of the preceding period with much use of paneling and a suggestion of fabric designs. The use of negative painting seems to have become highly developed, particularly in scrolls and frets. Although the Gila shoulder is retained it is in modified form, and there is a tendency for jar bodies to be nearly globular.

As Gila and Tonto Polychrome will be discussed under the heading of Salado culture, it is only necessary to mention that they are black and white on red in color, and in peculiarities of forms suggest some relation to Gila Red.

House types are interesting because they show considerable variation and much influence from outside. As has already been suggested, there

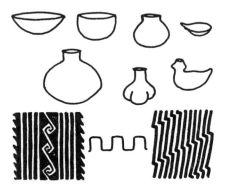

Fig. 169. Classic pottery forms and designs of both red-on-buff and Gila Red types. The animal and plant forms are found in Gila Red. The Gila shoulder is much less marked on jars, which are still large.

was a tendency during Sedentary times for houses to emerge from the ground and become surface structures. This was probably a culture trait derived from the southward- and eastward-moving Salado people, who had by now occupied most of the mountainous portions of the Upper Gila area. These people brought with them most of the architectural features of the pueblo which they had secured from the plateau area to the north where the true pueblo type of house had already been evolved. It is quite possible that the eastern Hohokam, coming in contact with the "Salado-ans," copied their type of house and then passed only the idea of this type of structure on to their relatives to the west.

Probably one of the most interesting early Classic sites showing this influence was dug near Tucson, under the direction of Dr. Cummings, by the Arizona State Museum. This site proved to be a series of rectangular pithouses with step entrances very similar to those already described as typical of the Sedentary stage in the Middle Gila Basin. However, in some places the houses were found to have been placed with the ends within a foot or two of each other, thus leaving a wall of earth between. Some of these walls had subsequently collapsed and been repaired by rebuilding the wall of rocks and clay, probably marking the introduction of masonry in this area. The groups of two or three contiguous pithouses, several such units of which formed the site, were connected by a wall which continued around the entire point of the ridge upon which they lay. This arrangement is very suggestive of the compound.

The next step in the architectural development of this section was the introduction of surface houses, an excellent example of which is found at

Sacaton 9:6. Here Gladwin has reported a structure strongly suggesting the pueblo compound type of dwelling produced by the Salado people, but made of adobe walls instead of rock masonry. Probably the most interesting feature of this site is that the walls contained posts set vertically into the center of the adobe to act as a primary support for the rest. Interwoven between the spaced posts was small brush, a type of wall somewhat suggesting present-day Pima construction. As a result of this interior strengthening the walls were very thin, possibly eight inches, and so never could have supported more than one story. Long and irregularly shaped

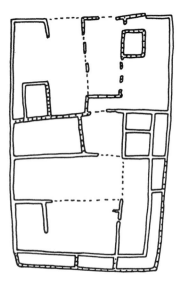

Fig. 170. Generalized plan of a house found by Gladwin at Sacaton 9:6, and belonging to this period. The walls without dots are solid adobe; those with dots are poles covered with a layer of adobe. Both types have relatively thin walls and are built entirely above ground. After Gladwin, 1929, p. 33.

rooms were previously used by these people in this area, a feature which carried over into the later heavy adobe-walled compounds. This type of construction is believed to have belonged to the earlier or Santan phase.

It was during the Classic period that irrigation reached its greatest development in the Gila, ditches apparently being larger and watering greater areas than at any other time. Estimates of the number of acres under cultivation approach present-day figures in the sections in which old irrigation was practiced. In fact many of the ditches used by the prehistoric people have simply been cleaned out and incorporated in modern systems. Apparently cross profiles of these ditches were very similar to, though perhaps slightly larger than, those already discussed.

Although some inhumations have been found in the Classic period, it is doubtful whether they belong to Hohokam or Salado people, as it was not uncommon for both polychrome and red-on-buff pottery to be buried with an individual. However, the characteristic method of disposal of the dead still seems to have been by cremation. During the Soho phase in the Middle Gila area the cremated bones were most often placed in a jar, less commonly under an overturned pot, under a mass of broken sherds, or in association with several vessels. To the east, in the vicinity of Bylas, the Arizona State Museum has uncovered several cremations placed in large jars each covered with a bowl. These may belong to the end of the preceding period, but the vessels might be either red-on-buff or polychrome. In several cases one was polychrome while the other was red-on-buff, thus showing that the two people were in contact at this time, and so suggesting the Classic period.

The stone implements appear to be very much like those of the preceding period. Metates and manos are about the same, and mortars formed in bedrock were also used. Stone palettes are definitely lacking, but the stone axe is well made and of the rather long, slender, three-quarter-grooved type. Mirrors and carved stone bowls were not made at this time. Points, surprisingly enough, are rather scarce, possibly even more so than in preceding periods. Perishable materials such as basketry, sandals, and cloth fabrics are either lacking from the sites known to have been dug or are unreported by the workers. Hunting implements are represented only by arrow points.

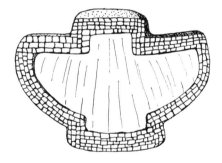

Fig. 171. Pink shell ornament with blue turquoise mosaic found in the Casa Grande National Monument. This may be either Hohokam or Salado, but it represents a high type of ornament of this period.

Figurines were apparently no longer made, but various forms of jewelry survived. One of the best examples comes from Casa Grande, where a pink shell bird-shaped object with a border of inlaid turquoise was found. Unfortunately it is impossible to be absolutely certain which group was responsible for the production of such things, for turquoise inlaying was practiced by both the Hohokam and Pueblo people in much earlier times. Cutout shell pendants in animal forms also seem to have been made at this time. Very little or nothing is known of bone and horn.

In summarizing the traits of the Soho phase Gladwin lists the following: pottery jars had vertical cylindrical necks, decorated in patterns of straight lines, and Gila Red came into general use; houses were sometimes contiguous, but of only one story. These traits he also considers characteristic of the Civano phase, but would add the following traits of Salado culture: multistory, heavy-walled, adobe houses; Gila and Tonto Polychrome pottery; inhumation; compounds; the hoe; the arrow straightener.

Thus, in summary, we may only point to pottery types and house types as characteristic of this period. The most striking pottery feature is the vertical-neck olla, second the presence of lifelike forms, particularly in Gila Red Ware, and polychrome types. True Hohokam houses were either similar to preceding types, were wholly surface and quite perishable struc-

Courtesy of the Arizona State Museum

A human cremation as found at Point of Pines, Arizona. The cremated bones were gathered up, placed in a bowl, and another bowl inverted over them before they were buried.

tures, or were surface compoundlike structures and were never more than one story high. These latter are probably an outgrowth of influence from the Salado people.

Allusions have been made to differences in various areas at this time, and it might be well to mention very briefly two slight but noticeable culture variations in two marginal regions. In the Santa Cruz area, to the south of the central section, and in the vicinity of Tucson, red-on-buff bowls commonly had a geometric band design below and parallel to the rim. Still more characteristically the insides of these bowls were often smudged to a dark gray or black color, which gives the appearance of a red-on-black pottery. To the east, in the mountain region, the section with which the Salado people may be associated, compounds more nearly approach the conventional pueblo, and the walls are made of boulder masonry instead of puddled adobe.

Such regional variation, although it has not been stressed, is apparent in the culture of the Hohokam almost from its known inception in the Gila drainage. This has made it possible for workers at Gila Pueblo to set up several phases as subdivisions of the general culture. Too little is known in detail concerning most of these to discuss them very fully, and it has been felt that the student would be more confused than aided by such detail.

THE DRAGOON AREA

In the southeastern part of Arizona the Amerind Foundation has done a good deal of work in defining the Ootam and the local cultural variations. Di Peso has postulated a series of influences which he believes are responsible for the distinctive cultural manifestation found here, ranging from Mogollon and Hohokam through Anasazi and Mexican influences to Spanish. The Tanque Verde phase occurred in the Tucson area and to the southeast at this time, and is distinctive because of the smudging of red-on-buff pottery to give it the appearance of red-on-black or gray. Other types are represented by the survival of red-on-brown and red, which now seems to be more related to Gila Red than to the Mogollon reds.

Houses are particularly interesting, for although pithouses apparently survived to the early part of this period, compounds, or compoundlike arrangements, came in. Houses were contiguous, and were connected with a wall which surrounded a courtyard or courtyards. Some walls had posts incorporated in them, and the rooms were built on mounds which were the result of the collapse of previous structures. The use of surrounding walls suggests defense, and gives credence to the idea proposed by Gladwin that Athabascans were putting pressure on all of these people from here north into the Anasazi area.

Both inhumations and cremations are found, and the mixture of traits makes the separation of cultural derivations difficult. Many of the artifacts are related to or derived from the Hohokam, particularly in the earlier part of this period. Slate palettes, carved and etched shell, serrated-

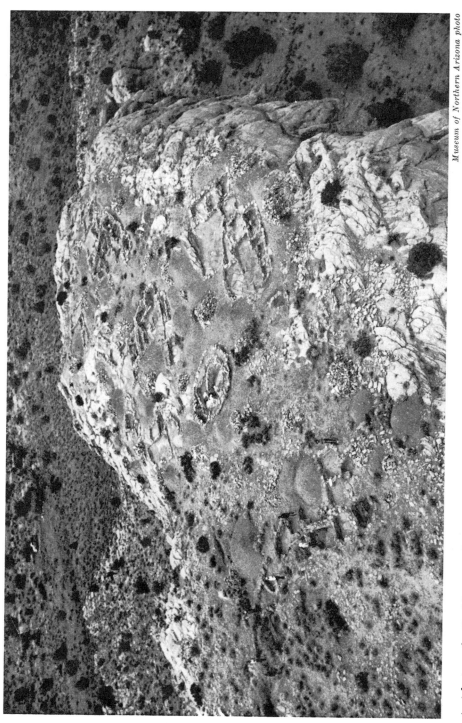

Aerial view of a Pueblo site under excavation in the San Juan drainage. It is on top of a small mesa which could be easily defended. Note particularly the blocks of rooms, the kiva in the central area, and the standing masonry walls.

edge projectile points, and even small ball courts are found. Cremations may be in jars with a bowl turned upside down over them. Somewhat later Mexican-like spindle whorls, overlap manos, and an abundance of striated but unsmudged red pottery suggest Mexican derivation to Di Peso. Thus there is in this area a cultural variant somewhat comparable to the Sinagua to the north, which was also the result of the mixture of several cultural stimuli. It has been rather fully characterized by the extensive and intensive work of the Amerind Foundation.

Di Peso has pointed out that the typical Hohokam is confined to the river valleys, where extensive irrigation was practiced, whereas the culture in the Dragoon area was in the foothills and on lesser outwash fans and did not make such use of irrigation. He feels this culture, which is truly a desert culture, may be referred to the Ootam, and that the ceramics were derived from the Mogollon, but that Hohokam traits and more definite Mexican traits were introduced.

There are apparently no plain ware pottery stages in this area, the earliest having painted pottery. There are red-on-brown and fairly early red-on-buff pots which are found together in various combinations for some time. The ceramic complex then modifies to Papago pottery, and eventually becomes simply plain red.

At the time under discussion Anasazi influences filter into this area, and also other traits come in from the south and west. This includes striated or "onion skin" red pottery, the modeled spindle whorl, and puddled adobe construction. The people who came down from the north made their own types of pottery, including polychromes, and then they seem to have left, or to have been absorbed, and the local people made the same kind of pottery, but of native materials which can be distinguished. Even stone-lined rectangular structures, which were probably ceremonial, are found here. There were also trade relations with, and probably influences from, the Casas Grandes area in Mexico, for this was a flourishing town and community.

MOGOLLON

One of the problems which constantly confronts archaeologists is just when in the course of amalgamation of cultures one ceases to be recognizable and it alters into another kind of thing. Such is the case in what might be considered the later stages of Mogollon, for after about A.D. 1000 or 1100 Pueblo influence became so marked in much of what had been considered Mogollon territory that it can hardly be called typical Mogollon. However, the Mogollon roots, or what might be considered the underlying Mogollon traditions, survived in some aspects of this culture to much later dates. The brown pottery types, for example, survived latest in the central and southern area, and for this reason many Southwestern archaeologists consider that as time went on Mogollon moved more and more to the south, into northern Mexico, and eventually essentially out of Arizona and New Mexico.

In the northern part of what had been the Mogollon range by this time the pueblos which are represented showed more and more of a Zuñi cast, and it is believed by Martin, and others, that it eventually contributed directly to the development of the later historic Zuñi. In the far southern part of the range it reached a sort of culmination in the well-known early Mimbres culture, and farther east into the Jornada branch of what has been called the El Paso phase. Between these two sections of marked cultural differences there are many distinctive cultural groups, that of the Point of Pines area, which enjoyed a development over a long period of years, and such other regions as the Sierra Anchas.

By now pithouses had generally given way to pueblos, and in many areas definite kivas were found associated with them. Kivas seem to be lacking in the far south, but elsewhere they were of some size, were rectangular, at least in the central area, and had sloping entrances and sometimes floor drums. The actual pueblo structures were constructed of a variety of materials, varying from much use of adobe walls, through pole and adobe construction, walls of river boulders, and finally walls made of selected rectangular or semirectangular blocks.

Pottery was equally varied by regions. The plain pottery types still were often reddish or brown, and one of the most typical was a considerable variety of very well-made corrugated types, which occurred abundantly in the Upper Gila area and were to a somewhat lesser extent more widespread. These included plain and indented corrugations in patterns, the coils being very small and even in many examples, sometimes slightly polished over, generally in brown or reddish types and frequently with smudged and polished interiors. If any single group might be considered typical of Mogollon at this time it is these pottery types.

Polychrome pottery was introduced into this area, or local varieties developed, as well. One of the most widespread trade polychrome types is St. Johns Polychrome, which was so popular that it is found in almost all sites of this general period. Although it was apparently originated and manufactured to the north, in the upper Little Colorado River area it is found as far south as Mexico.

Two other traits which seem to have been fairly widespread were the use of arrow-shaft straighteners, or polishers, and the presence of small pottery animal figurines. The former usually had only grooves in the face of the stone block through which the shaft was presumably passed, but in some cases a ridge was formed at right angles to the groove or grooves. The animal figurines are relatively simple, with short peglike legs, ears, and tails. They are not limited to this immediate area but are also found in other cultures, such as the Sinagua to the west.

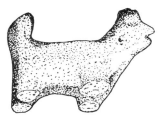

Fig. 172. Small clay animal figurine from the Stark-weather site.

In the Reserve area the Chicago Natural History Museum has excavated a number of sites which are of this period, and from which it is possible to gather a good picture of what the culture was like. Slightly farther west the University of Arizona work at Point of Pines has shed additional light on this period. In general these sites show a mixture of underlying Mogollon influences and additions from the Anasazi, which were often built on locally to give them a definite individual stamp.

Structures are surface pueblos, many of only one story but sometimes of more. Kivas are characteristically found associated with them, and are typically rectangular, often with a sloping entrance to one side, and sometimes in earlier types with floor drums. As has been suggested masonry types vary considerably, dependent on area and availability of materials. In the case of some well-preserved cave structures, roofing methods are clearly shown, with posts, main beams, secondary shakes or other filler used, and brush and clay roofs.

Metates may be either in bins in the rooms or of the open-end types. Manos vary from simple rectangular slabs to the wedge or beveled shapes which result from pressure on alternate edges of the mano in grinding. They are often long and of the two-hand type. Flakers, choppers, flake knives, and other simple stone tools persist from earlier times. In general, projectile points tend to be triangular, often with lateral notches, but sometimes with corner notches. They are small arrow points. Grooved axes, most typically of the three-quarter-grooved type, are common, and mauls are still found. Stone hoes are also apparently a part of this culture. Some rectangular stone vessels were made and used, and a few were painted.

Shell objects were abundant, particularly shell bracelets, and some were carved in simple designs. Painting was practiced as an additional decorative element on some of the stone objects, such as stone bowls and stone slabs. This was a trait which was again shared with other areas and cultures, such as the Sinagua.

The economy was based firmly on agriculture by now, though a variety of animals were hunted and collected.

In general summary the various phases which might be loosely grouped together on the basis of geographical distribution and the fact that they share certain ceramic traditions, and even broad house-type similarities, do seem to show many shared traits but specific differences. Architecture is of the pueblo type, but with varied construction materials. Kivas are rectangular, those at Point of Pines with a bench along one long side, those in the north with floor drums at least early. Sloping side entrances are common. They are generally found in patio areas surrounded more or less by rooms, though restrictions of location may prevent this arrangement. Pueblos vary from a few rooms to more than a hundred, and from one story to two or perhaps more. Outside doorways may or may not be present.

Stone work does not show any marked or exclusive traits, and in general is not as good as that of the earlier Hohokam. The bow and arrow was in general use, and points are small and triangular and often with side notches. Metates vary from the bin to the trough type, and manos are rectangular and frequently two-hand. Painted stone altar slabs are found in some phases, such as the Pinedale.

The most distinctive traits are found in the pottery types, of which the most widespread is well-made corrugated and smudged brown pottery which may be grouped under the general term of Upper Gila Corrugated. In the north are the basic brown pottery types which are derived from the earlier Mogollon stages plus such additional types as Tularosa White-on-red, and various polychromes and black-on-red types. There are some Zuñi glazes in this area, plus such local types as Four Mile Polychrome and St. Johns Polychrome. It has been suggested by Martin and his co-workers that this northern area ties into the developing Zuñi culture, with the polychrome pottery and the presence of full-grooved axes and other traits.

Farther south there are even more abundant and varied indented and plain corrugated pottery types. Such decorated pottery as Pinedale Black-on-white, Pinedale Polychrome, Pinedale Black-on-red, Pinto Black-on-red, and Pinto Polychrome are found.

This was thus a time when regional variation was becoming marked throughout what had been the Mogollon culture area. In several instances phases which were in existence now can be traced to Historic or proto-Historic cultures, particularly to the north. Mogollon as a vigorous and easily identified entity had essentially ceased to exist. It was modified locally by other groups, but most markedly by the vigorously expanding Pueblo culture of the north.

Toward the end of this period certain considerable portions of the Mogollon culture area was abandoned. Southern Mogollon seems to have remained in this section, and to have extended on southward into Mexico, but central Mogollon may have moved northward as part of Pueblo cul-

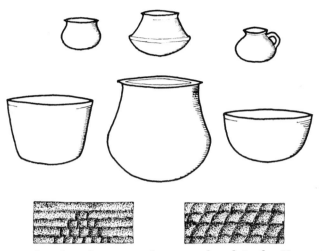

Fig. 173. Forms and styles of corrugated pottery found in the Upper Gila area. The lower left figure shows partial indentations to form designs on the outsides of the bowls. The lower right is the type of over-all indented corrugated found on large jars such as that in the lower center. There is a tendency toward shoulders and large mouths in jars and large deep bowls. The interiors of bowls are smudged black and often highly burnished.

ture. It may be that some of the traits which these people brought north with them affected the later development of Pueblo culture. In a sense they were simply moving back home, for they had by now taken on more and more of the Pueblo way of life and traits.

Repeated reference has been made to the Jornada branch of the Mogollon as that development which took place in the southern part of New Mexico, but no detailed characterization of it has been undertaken. It might therefore be profitable to do so briefly at this point.

Lehmar, in reporting on it, has divided it into four sequential phases: the Hueco, which dates pre A.D. 900, the Mesilla, which dates from about 900 to 1100, the Dona Ana, which dates from 1100 to 1200, and the El Paso, which dates from about 1200 to 1400. The first of these has its roots well back in the Cochise, and therefore may be tied to the Desert culture. It is represented mostly by cave deposits, and architecture is unknown, though there may have been some storage cists. Basketry is mostly of the two-rod and bundle type, twilled and twined mats were made, there was netting, two-warp sandals, and some suggestion that cotton may have been known and in use. The atlatl and the fending stick were the common hunting implements, and bow fire drills and planting sticks were in use. Corn of the 12-row type and squash were grown. The people were long-headed. Stone tools consisted of choppers, leaf-shaped blades, drills, knives, points of a variety of types, and core scrapers. Metates, manos, and mortars were all used. The people hunted deer and small game and used snares and nets.

In the Mesilla phase houses were both rectangular with side entrance passages and circular with roof entrances. The most abundant pottery was El Paso Brown, and rare painted examples foreshadow El Paso Polychrome. Trade pottery was Mogollon types, Mimbres Black-on-white, Bold Face, and Classic. Conical clay pipes were made. Ornaments included shell beads and bracelets, and turquoise was used. Points were fine and thin and with straight or concave bases. The bone awl was of the splinter type. Manos were round to oval and metates were basin, flat, and trough types. Mortars and pestles were both in use. Burials were flexed.

In the Dona Ana phase pithouses survive in some areas but also adobe-walled surface structures are found, which consist of massed rooms. The pottery is El Paso Brown and El Paso Polychrome, as well as Mimbres and Chupadero Black-on-white and St. Johns Polychrome.

In the El Paso phase houses are adobe-walled surface structures, built around plazas or in blocks. In the south, adobe blocks built along the south walls have been called "altars." The pottery is El Paso Polychrome, which has black and red designs on the brown background, and St. Johns Polychrome and Chupadero Black-on-white as trade. The same artifacts continue but additions are the trough metate with less of the basin type, fewer mortars and pestles, the arrow-shaft polisher and straightener, axes, palettes, copper bells, animal effigies, stone balls, and reel-shaped objects. It is thus obvious that at this time there were many contacts with outside groups.

The area in which these phases of the Jornada branch are found is in the southern Rio Grande valley and extending into Mexico. As may be seen by reference to the various maps in which it is shown, it is somewhat of a pear-shaped area. In general, as has been repeatedly stated, the diagnostic trait is the presence of brown pottery, which is found through all phases.

MIMBRES

Mimbres is one of the most distinctive cultures found in the Southwest, largely because of the remarkable designs on its pottery. The area which it occupied is southwestern New Mexico, spreading northward into the Upper Gila drainage, extending on the south to the Mexican line, on the east from the Mimbres valley (from which the name is derived), to the west across the Arizona line. Mimbres culture begins before this period, but reaches a sort of peak probably in the early portion of the period.

Ceramically, and in other traits, it is possible to trace this development back into earlier Mogollon stages. The pottery styles may probably be related ultimately to the Tularosa or Roosevelt Black-on-white types, and house styles also show early relationships to Mogollon pithouses, but then develop definite surface structures.

A large site excavated by the Arizona State Museum in the Santa Cruz drainage area near Tucson. The heavy adobe walls superimposed on older ruined structures are typical here.

The two most typical pottery types are Mimbres Bold Face and Classic Mimbres Black-on-white. Present evidence indicates that Mimbres Bold Face Black-on-white is the earlier of the two, but it is found in most of the sites which have been excavated with Mimbres Black-on-white as well. It has thus been possible to suggest two divisions of Mimbres, the earlier stage associated with the Bold Face pottery, and the later with the Classic pottery.

In the earlier phase houses are one-story above-ground pueblos in which the walls are made of river boulders laid in much mortar. In this respect they suggest some of the compoundlike pueblos of the Salado culture of the Gila and Salt areas. Some of the rooms have been partly excavated into the ground, but most are surface. Associated with these pueblos are large ceremonial rooms, rectangular in shape and at least semisubterranean, with long entrance passages. They are therefore suggestive of Mogollon kivas. Some seem to have had ventilator shafts.

The pottery is Mimbres Bold Face Black-on-white, Classic Mimbres Black-on-white in lesser amounts, or lacking, and Mimbres Corrugated. In many of these sites there is also Alma Plain and perhaps some San Francisco Red. The Bold Face type is so named because the design is in general boldly executed, and in most cases is not so expertly painted as the later Classic pottery. Typical design elements are somewhat balanced hatched and solid masses, in which the hatching often runs the long way of the area covered, and which by the standards of other areas is very well drawn, often appearing as though marked off with a ruler. The Mimbres Corrugated pottery is clearly related to Upper Gila Corrugated types, is well made with fine corrugations which are not infrequently indented to form patterns, and the interiors of vessels are characteristically smudged.

Metates are trough types which have one closed end or are open at both ends, and apparently varied from types not fully shaped on the outside to those which were so finished. The manos are of the block type and are usually carefully shaped. Hoes are found as a part of this culture, and this trait might conceivably be related to Hohokam. Axes are of both the three-quarter- and full-grooved types with the three-quarter being the most common. There are some carved stone vessels, and mortars and pestles. Projectile points are both laterally and diagonally notched. There are also, of course, scrapers. Pipes are tubular and of both stone and clay. Awls are both plain and notched. Much use was made of shell, in the form of bracelets, pendants, and other ornaments. These people also seem to have been excellent craftsmen in the manufacture of both shell and stone beads, and apparently made them in some abundance.

Burials are flexed inhumations, and there is typically occipital flattening of the skull. The later Classic phase does not show radically different physical types.

In the Classic stage, which dates in the early portion of the period under discussion, the same pottery types are found, with greater abundance of the Classic Mimbres Black-on-white. This is the pottery which so distinguishes the Mimbres culture. Two styles of decoration are commonly found, one purely geometric, the other including some most fascinating highly conventionalized life forms as in the accompanying illustration. These animals, including on some occasions man, are usually in the centers of the bottoms of bowls and surrounded by geometric designs. In every specimen the execution is remarkably exact, in fact the drawing is far superior to that of any other period or area of the Southwest. This pottery was primarily fired in a reducing atmosphere, to produce a good black-on-white, but in some instances it was oxidized, when the colors became red on light brown on cream, a most pleasing combination. It is all surprisingly attractive.

Fig. 174. Classic Mimbres Black-on-white pottery shapes and designs. The bowl is by far the most common decorated form. The associated coil types are well made and usually fine coils. The execution of designs is remarkable, and the use of animal figures in the bottoms of many bowls is quite typical. Geometric designs are a combination of solid and hatched areas, the hatching of very fine lines and expertly drawn.

Mimbres Black-on-white pottery has a paste which is friable and not strong, and it is black through gray to a reddish color. The temper consists of a relatively large amount of fine quartz sand, with occasionally black sand, and even magnetite and some mica. The designs have been described above as exceptionally well done, but it might be added that the brush work is fine and straight and very regular. A heavy white or cream slip was added to the surface of this pottery type both outside and inside and the surface was smoothed.

Another pottery type found in the Mimbres area is a polychrome which is yellow, red, and black on white. Classic Mimbres Black-on-white is, however, the dominant type, and Mimbres Bold Face Black-on-white is dying out at this time.

Houses are still pueblo-type structures and the walls are made of river boulders, but with a more sparing use of mortar, and many of the walls were plastered over. In general the buildings are larger, and although they are still one-story they were built around a courtyard plan. They generally lack outside doors, so that they must have been entered from the roof. The kivas are the same, rectangular with sloping side entrances. The stone, bone, and shell work are all similar, as are burials.

Unfortunately, the work done and reported in this area was undertaken before specific phases had been identified and isolated. Therefore there is little attempt to separate materials which might actually have been of aid in making smaller distinctions of time and culture. The need for additional work is thus clearly indicated.

By the first half of the thirteenth century Mimbres culture was gone, and even earlier it had disappeared in the southern part of the area occupied. In the southern and western part of the area there is some evidence of people from other areas moving in and briefly occupying the Mimbres country. However, none of these latter people seem to have stayed long, and this section soon became totally unoccupied, unless sporadically by essentially nomadic groups.

To the south, in the 1200's, several other phases have been isolated but not fully reported. The El Paso phase, for instance, is apparently a distinctive one. In some cases pueblos were built of adobe and arranged around plazas or courts. Since these have not been adequately reported no attempt will be made to discuss them further.

In summary the most distinctive trait of the Mimbres culture is the excellent pottery which was made by these people. The designs on this pottery are the most outstanding of any in the Southwest. Ultimate derivation seems to have been out of earlier Mogollon, but with Pueblo influences. There is some slight suggestion of relations to Hohokam, but they do not seem to have been strong, and such cultures as the Salado, with which Mimbres came in contact to the north, may have played some part in shaping its destiny. The vigorous and developing culture of Casas Grandes, to the south in Mexico, may also have played a much more significant part in its history than is now commonly recognized, but more intensive work in both areas and cultures and direct comparisons will be necessary before the true extent of such influence can be demonstrated.

SALADO (BRANCH)

Reference has been made to the Salado as a southern extension of the Anasazi into the Gila-Salt drainages in the desert area and in the western portion of the mountain section. Although a good deal of work has been done on it the most recent definitive report is that by Steen and others on the Tonto cliff dwellings. Most of the reports which deal with Salado material culture have included it with other artifacts without any attempt at distinguishing what is Salado and what is not, since the traits in most of these sites are much mixed. Thus, although the distinguishing features are well known, many details concerning the associated traits are not clearly understood. Actually Salado probably represents another cultural mixture of Anasazi, Mogollon, and Hohokam.

The origin of the Salado culture in the Little Colorado area of the plateau has already been implied, because of the presence of such plateau pottery types as Wingate Black-on-red and St. Johns Polychrome, and its southward spread into the Gila drainage indicated. It might be well at this point to mention that there are two allied, but separable, ceramic complexes which are associated with this single prolonged southward movement of culture. The first of these was in full swing at about A.D. 1100, and is identified by black-on-white pottery. The second, coming somewhat later, was well established by about A.D. 1250, and is identified by polychrome pottery. The Salado culture lasted to about A.D. 1450 in the Gila drainage, before it was dissipated, the latest manifestation of the polychrome pottery being found to the east and the south. During the major Salado occupation of the Gila, general Pueblo characters are found in both pottery and house types. Other features which may be considered more or less diagnostic are extended inhumation, possibly much use of basketry, the manufacture of large cotton blankets, and fine stone and shell work.

Steen feels that the Salado culture may be identified solely by the presence of the polychrome pottery, and therefore limits it to this later period, and that other traits are derived from other cultures. He also believes, as this writer does, that an actual migration of people into the Gila Basin took place at this time. Not all other archaeologists agree with this view, particularly Schroeder, who holds that the modifications of local cultures were a result of influences rather than migration.

On the accompanying map no effort has been made to separate the early from the late ceramic complexes, so that both are included. As a result a comparatively large area is covered by this total culture in the Gila and Salt river drainages. When it is remembered that a period of at least 350 years is represented, the extent of the area becomes more understandable. From this map it is apparent that the Salado culture primarily occurred in the mountain section, but spread both west and south into the desert to include at least sporadically the entire Upper Gila area. This culture might be very easily subdivided into several smaller divisions, on the basis of temporal and areal distinctions, as Gladwin has already indicated. Certainly the desert and main mountain sections are distinguishable, as well as an early and late phase of both, and the mountain section could be divided into a northern, central, and southeastern portion. However, the lack of detailed published information makes such minute divisions impracticable.

By now it has become apparent that two of the most important periods in Southwestern archaeology were about A.D. 1100 and 1300. Both these dates mark radical cultural upsets in the plateau and desert areas and are strongly reflected in the history of Salado culture. It has already been pointed out that its beginning was in the upper Little Colorado area, and

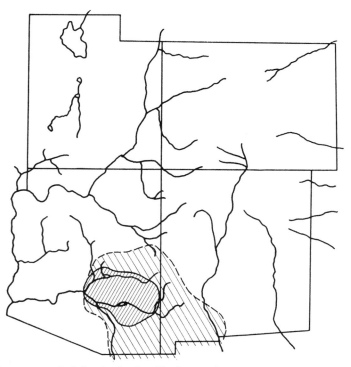

Fig. 175. Area occupied by both the black-on-white and the polychrome phases of the Salado culture. The area of greatest concentration lies in the Gila and Salt drainages above their junction. The black-on-white phase was more in the mountain section while the polychrome phase was more widespread. The area of maximum expansion goes south into Mexico during the polychrome phase.

suggested that it started a serious expansion southward by about A.D. 1100. The next period of expansion was most marked at about A.D. 1300, when the abandonment of the San Juan gave a strong impetus to this southward movement. Although it was a vigorous culture it appears to have mixed quietly with both Hohokam and Mogollon, which had passed their peak by this time and were ready for the acceptance of new ideas and perhaps new blood.

Several pottery types are characteristic of the Salado culture. Tularosa Black-on-white as a distinctive type has already been described. As Gladwin has pointed out, and as has been suggested here, it is probably subdivisible into Puerco and Roosevelt, distinctive but definitely associated types. Gila Red is very characteristic, as are Pinto, Gila, and Tonto Polychromes. Upper Gila Corrugated is most commonly found associated with the black-on-white types in the headwaters of the Gila and Salt rivers, and Salado Corrugated with the polychrome sites. Several other types of pottery also occur in this complex, but as they are now felt to be of less importance they will not be discussed.

Roosevelt Black-on-white differs from Tularosa Black-on-white not in general arrangement of design or forms but in several easily overlooked particulars. Bowls are much smaller and tend to be relatively thicker-walled, and they have a very small horizontal strap handle or perforated lug on one side. Pitcher handles tend to be made of straps instead of animal figurines or animal heads. Duck bowls, such as the right-hand figure in the accompanying illustration, are quite common. The bases of jars or

Fig. 176. Forms of Roosevelt Black-on-white pottery, a variety of Tularosa Black-on-white. Bowls and duck canteens are less common than jars, and the jar handles are strap rather than animal figurine, as are those of true Tularosa, but the designs are similar.

pitchers are marked by a horizontal black band terminating the design, which viewed from the bottom appears like a circle. Tularosa is the same, but the bottom line terminating the design, when viewed from below, commonly suggests a roughly formed five-sided star.

One of the most interesting pottery types associated with this complex is Gila Red. This type has been dated from about A.D. 1200 to post 1400. Work at Winona Village, just east of Flagstaff, has shown that Sunset Red and similar types had an origin slightly earlier than A.D. 1100. As these types are definitely related to Gila Red, as has been pointed out by Gladwin and others, it is quite possible that Gila Red had its origin in the Flagstaff area and spread south, changing slightly as it went as a result of different techniques and materials. Strong Hohokam influence is apparent at Winona Village, and it is possible, of course, that the concept of a red type might have been introduced from the south.

Gila Red was made by the paddle and anvil process, and fired in an oxidizing atmosphere. The paste is red to buff or gray, and contains water-worn sand temper with some mica. The outside is slipped with a bright red slip, sometimes shading to an orange tint, which is marked with polishing streaks. These streaks are often so prominent that the type has been referred to as "onion skin." They begin either at one focus, usually the center of the base, and extend outward to the rim, or pass across the bottom of the vessel from two foci on the rim. Forms are very varied, including bowls, plates, jars, ladles, and a great variety of eccentric and life forms. Jars characteristically have a Gila shoulder, sometimes very marked, and many of them have a high cylindrical neck, as in the central upper example in the accompanying figure. Bowls are of both shallow and deep hemispherical shape, but occasionally are rectangular or oval. One of the most characteristic forms is the scoop.

Fig. 177. Forms of Gila Red pottery. The scoop is typical, as is the high-neck jar. The Gila shoulder is common in jars. Effigy canteens in bird or other life forms are not uncommon. This type characteristically has the "onion skin" surface finish caused by smoothing striations.

In the Upper Gila or mountain area, a general class of very fine corrugated pottery was being made, probably sometime between about A.D. 1100 and 1200. It has been referred to as Upper Gila Corrugated. Its origin appears to have been associated most directly with Mogollon development, and so should not properly be included here, but by now a strong Pueblo influence, through the Salado culture, was being felt by the Mogollon, and this type was most likely a result of this mixture. The pottery was made by coiling and was fired in an oxidizing atmosphere. The paste is fine and hard, gray to brown in color, and contains fine temper, mostly sand. The walls are exceptionally thin for corrugated pottery. Forms are bowls and jars with rare small pitchers. Bowls are smudged black on the interiors and often highly burnished. The exteriors have exceptionally narrow and even corrugations, commonly covering the entire surface, but sometimes confined to the neck portion. In large jars indentations cover the entire surface, but in bowls they sometimes form only a portion of the corrugations, thus creating a design. (See the lower left illustration in Fig. 173.) There is a tendency to shoulders in jars and flattened bases in bowls, as well as large mouths on jars and pitchers. Bowls are deep, even in relation to their large size. This type probably represents about the finest corrugated pottery.

Somewhere in the upper Little Colorado or White Mountain area polychrome pottery developed and spread. As soon as it had moved into the Gila and Salt river drainages it took on a distinctive character of its own. The first of these southern types is Pinto Polychrome, which has generally been roughly dated as between about A.D. 1200 and 1250. Vessels are fired in an oxidizing atmosphere. The paste is medium to coarse and red to gray in color, with sand temper containing some mica. It is on the whole crumbly and relatively poor. The only forms are bowls, the exteriors of which are covered with a reddish slip. The interiors have a thin white to cream slip, upon which the dull black design was applied. There is no decoration on the exteriors. Designs are often very suggestive of Tularosa Black-on-white, and contain balanced solid and hatched elements. The most distinctive feature of this type is that the design extends to the rim, without a separating white space or framing black line.

Fig. 178. Forms and designs of polychrome types. The lower left design is found on Pinto Polychrome, the earliest of the group. It suggests a Tularosa style. The lower right is Gila Polychrome, which has a broad black band above the design and below the rim. The upper design is Tonto Polychrome, in which red forms part of the background. Typical forms are shown.

The second type in this series is Gila Polychrome. It has been dated at between A.D. 1300 and post 1400, but the range is somewhat uncertain. It is often typically associated with the third type in sites as well as with Pinto Polychrome. In most respects it is like Pinto, but jars and effigies were made as well as bowls, and the design is different. Bowls are still the most common form. Bowl interiors are slipped white and have a black design, the most characteristic feature of which is the presence of a broad black line separating the main portion of the design from the rim of the vessel. This line, often referred to as a "life line," is generally broken at one point in its circuit. Jars contain a white-slipped background with the same broad upper black line, and a red slip applied above and below the decorated zone. Designs are largely made up of massed black elements, such as tapering triangles or coarse serrations on wide lines. Detailed studies suggest that this pottery was made in many local areas.

The third type is Tonto Polychrome, which has been dated as existing in abundance at about A.D. 1400. It seems to have occurred by about A.D. 1250 and to have lasted to about A.D. 1450 over much of the area occupied by the Salado culture. In such characters as paste, firing, and form it is like both Pinto and Gila Polychrome. The forms are bowls, jars, vases, and some eccentric shapes. Some of these vessels, particularly bowls and jars, are exceptionally large. In this type the white slip of the background has a black and red design so arranged that the red appears to be the base although it was applied last. (See Fig. 178.) Bowls have all three colors on both the insides and outsides. The black designs in most characters are similar to those of Gila Polychrome.

Gila and Tonto Polychrome are typologically and geographically so similar that Steen has proposed that the term Tonto be dropped and both varieties be referred to as Gila Polychrome. Haury, on the other hand, believes there is a slight temporal difference and that therefore they should be separated. In any event the concept and even execution of design is very similar in these two types. The polychromes were made by the coiling and scraping method as distinct from the paddle and anvil method of finishing Gila Red and such allied types as Tonto Red and Roosevelt Red.

All these three types were made in varied and interesting forms, many of which are similar to those of Gila Red. Some of the vessels are carefully shaped, but others are markedly irregular. Bowls are both hemispherical and with outflaring rims. Vases with very tall slender necks and globular bodies are common. Jars are, on the whole, relatively small, although some unusually large examples have been found. Life forms, such as squash or duck canteens, are not uncommon, and such peculiar flat-bottom jars as that shown in the upper right corner of the figure occur.

One other common type of pottery remains to be identified. This is Salado Corrugated, which has been roughly dated as existing between about A.D. 1150 and 1250. It seems to have accompanied the earlier of the polychrome types. It was fired in an oxidizing atmosphere and is made of a medium to coarse red or brown paste, with sand temper and some mica.

The forms are bowls, jars, and eccentrics. The outsides of both bowls and jars are corrugated with indented oblique marks. The corrugations are often mostly obliterated by smoothing. The outsides of vessels are red to a purplish color, and the interior is always smudged black. Occasionally a chalky white design was applied to the outside, in narrow lines with pendant dots or triangles. The paste is so poor and friable that this is a relatively poor type of corrugated pottery, especially in comparison with the fine Upper Gila Corrugated already mentioned.

As has several times been stated, Salado culture may be defined in either of two ways. Steen would confine it to the later polychrome pottery phase only, but the writer, along with Gladwin and others, would include the earlier black-on-white phase as well. Also Steen would be inclined to limit it somewhat to the Gila and Salt drainages and consider it as one geographical unit, while the writer has chosen to consider it as occupying portions of two adjacent physiographic provinces, the western part of the mountain area and the eastern part of the desert section. Much may be said for the Steen contention, and only time and much more excavation on this problem will give definitive answers to this question. The identification of Salado house types, and some of the associated traits, is dependent on just how the culture is defined.

The general house type of Salado seems to have been more influenced by Pueblo culture than Hohokam, for the most typical Hohokam house is a pithouse. It is quite probable that architectural concepts came to the Salado by way of the Mogollon, which by now was strongly influenced in much of its culture by Pueblo. The compound type of structure seems to have developed here and to have been the most typical general structural plan of the Salado, although cliff dwellings and pueblo-like masses of rooms were built in some areas.

A pueblo might be defined as a mass of rooms completely or partially surrounding one or more courts, often with a wall closing the open end, or sides. A compound, on the other hand, is a surrounding wall within which scattered clusters of rooms are found.

During the earlier period, that in which Tularosa or Roosevelt Black-on-white pottery, and perhaps Pinto Polychrome, is found, a common structural type is the simple compoundlike arrangement in which groups of rooms, either very shallow pits or surface houses, are connected by a wall. This general type has already been discussed. Farther to the east, and north, in the mountain section, more nearly true pueblos are found. Masonry consisted of both sandstone blocks and boulders set into mortar, so that most of the walls were comparatively massive. Few of these sites are large, and kivas do not seem to have been a part of the Salado culture.

Slightly later, during the Gila and Tonto Polychrome stage, in the Gila area proper, small pueblo-like masses of rooms were located inside of surrounding compound walls. As stones were at a premium in the sandy desert section adobe clay was used for the construction of these massive walls. The classic compound site of this period in this area is, of course, Compound A at Casa Grande. The central structure within the compound is four stories high, and the walls are as much as four feet thick. Many theories have been advanced as to the method of construction of these heavy walls, even the suggestion that movable forms were used for the pouring of adobe. However, it is certain that they were made in sections, which were built up of puddled clay with a rounded top and straight sides, and allowed to harden before the next section was added. Casa Grande is so well known through many written descriptions that there is no need for further details here.

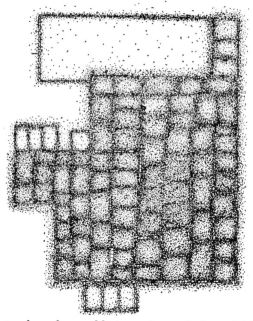

Fig. 179. Approximate plan of a pueblo-type site made from field survey notes in the Roosevelt Lake area. Essential features are the mass of rooms and the court. Masonry is of water-worn river boulders set into abundant clay mortar.

By the time the polychrome invasion had gotten well under way, larger, more massive pueblo sites were being built in the eastern mountain section. One such site near Roosevelt Lake has walls made of river boulders set in an abundance of clay. The main portion of the site is constructed of

massed rooms, mostly one story high, but there is evidence of a few of two
or more stories. A long narrow court is indicated at the north end of the
site. In the Roosevelt Lake area other sites are of the compound type, as
is indicated by three compounds found on the old Meddler Ranch. Three
trash mounds are associated with them. Each of these compounds consists
of a surrounding wall enclosing rooms. At the time of the location of this
site no excavation had been undertaken so that only the general sketch plan
of the outline could be recorded. The point which is being made here is
that even in the mountain section not all structures were alike, and although
there may be a time difference between these pueblo-type sites and the
compoundlike ones, the two types are both found here.

Fig. 180. Rough sketch plan from field notes of a site consisting of three compounds
on the old Meddler Ranch in the Roosevelt Lake area. This type of structure is typical
of Salado sites in the Middle Gila area, and is probably best represented by Compound
A at Casa Grande.

The history of the Salado culture may thus be identified as two southward pushes of Pueblo influence, if it is not limited to the later phase as
Steen does. The first of these had Roosevelt and Tularosa Black-on-white
pottery, and occupied smaller sites than did the later thrust. At about this
time, or slightly later, the first of the polychrome pottery types appeared,
in association with Gila Red and Salado Corrugated. The house type was
larger and distinctly Puebloan in the eastern or mountain section, but to
the west, in the Gila and Salt drainages proper, it was of the adobe compound type. At Roosevelt transitions between these two house types may
be seen. Pinto Polychrome appears definitely to predate the later types,
and there is some question as to the validity of separating Gila Poly-

chrome and Tonto Polychrome and some justification of the argument that they had best be grouped together under the single heading of Gila Polychrome. By about A.D. 1400 the Salado culture of the Gila area began to break up, and eventually the people making up this culture either were absorbed by other groups or so modified their way of life that their descendants cannot be determined with certainty. Gila Polychrome, however, persisted perhaps for many years, and seems to have spread farther south.

The physical type was essentially Pueblo, with round deformed heads and comparatively light-boned frames. Burials were either semiflexed or extended, and were often placed within or beneath trash mounds or in houses. In some sections and periods quantities of grave goods were interred with the bodies.

Metates are of the high-sided trough shape, and manos are rectangular and ground on one side. The stone axe is uniformly of the three-quarter-grooved type, and is usually well made. Mauls are relatively abundant and are of the full-grooved type, at least to the east. Points are triangular and similar to those of the plateau and desert at this time. Some are long and slender and with a tendency to serrations; others have straight sides and lateral notches.

Although most of the excavated sites have been in the open, where perishable material is seldom found, it is quite likely that basketry was an important product of this group. In the north some sites of about this age, and perhaps of this or a related culture, contained painted baskets. A great deal of matting was used on the floor and it was woven in a variety of patterns. Probably cotton cloth was well developed and in wide use by these people, for a large series of such articles have been found at the Tonto cliff dwellings. In fact one of the more important products may have been weaving in a variety of patterns. Some of these cotton blankets are of some size and clearly indicate the use of the vertical loom.

Knowledge of hunting implements is not very exact, although the bow and arrow was certainly common. It is quite likely that other Pueblo hunting implements accompanied the complex south. Foods were also similar to those of the Pueblo people to the north, although irrigation was resorted to in the desert section. Cultivated foods found at the Tonto cliff dwellings included corn, pumpkins, squash, kidney beans, tepary beans, lima beans, jack beans, amaranth, gourds, and of course cotton. Lac and pine pitch were used. Reed cigarettes were a part of this culture, perhaps originating in the Mogollon and spreading to the Hohokam and so to the Salado as well. Not only was cotton used in fabrics but yucca fibers were woven, as well as the hair of bighorn sheep or goats. A great variety of wild plants were also used, including acorns, agave or mescal, various cactus fruits, hackberry, juniper, mesquite beans, walnut, wild grapes, and yucca.

Ornaments were another product of this group. Quantities of very fine and excellently made stone beads have been found in many sites of this culture, some of which are practically microscopic, and drilled and ground with precision. Shell was also worked into pendants and other articles, perhaps as an influence from the Hohokam. Plain shell pendants or bracelets are abundant, many often being found in one grave.

These people were also workers in stone, and produced some outstanding stone bowls, or dishes. One such was made of a light green, fine-grained stone and was carved in perfect proportions. It was a long, shallow, rectangular vessel with slight knobs at the corners as though for grasping in the hands. Such fine objects were probably somehow connected with ceremonial practices, for they are much too ornate for ordinary use. Bone and horn objects, so far as the writer is aware, are very similar to those of the Pueblo culture. Awls are relatively common, and do not appear to show any distinctive variations from those already described.

The sandals which have been found, particularly those from the Tonto cliff dwellings, are more or less square-toed and are plaited.

In summary only a few characteristics of this culture seem to be distinctive. The most outstanding single trait is the polychrome pottery types. Compounds may probably also be considered a part of this culture, though perhaps not exclusively so, if their definition is not limited to the more elaborate later examples. Good stone and shell work, basketry, matting, and very outstanding cotton cloth may be shared with, or perhaps even derived from, Hohokam.

Salado culture seems to have had two sources. The earlier black-on-white pottery and general culture came from the Puerco–Little Colorado area, and appears to have been ultimately associated with the Mogollon culture to the east at this time. The second influence is marked by polychrome pottery, which had its inception in the mountain area in or just south of the upper reaches of the Little Colorado River drainage, and seems to have spread out into and become associated with the Hohokam. Gila Red pottery may have originated near Flagstaff, in the Sinagua branch, as indicated by work done at Winona Village, where many characters are shared with Salado. Other sites to the east, as reported by Hough, also have some Salado traits and complexes, some even having Gila Polychrome pottery. The Salado culture undoubtedly received most of its influence from Pueblo, but with Mogollon character, and in turn influenced later Mogollon. After about A.D. 1400, or at the latest 1450, Salado was gone from the Gila and Salt river valleys proper, and probably moved east, and particularly south, to combine with Mogollon derivatives in this direction.

Not all investigators are inclined to group both the black-on-white and the polychrome stages as Salado, but to limit it only to the latter. Certainly the polychrome stage is by far the most distinctive, but this writer is still inclined to group them both as Salado, for they both show Pueblo or northern derivations and southward extensions.

PATAYAN

As may be seen from the accompanying map, what has been called the Patayan culture is represented in about the same areas and by the same regional groups as during the preceding period. To the north there is evi-

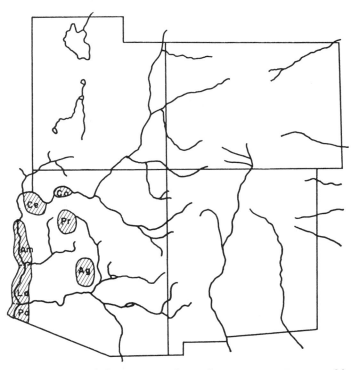

Fig. 181. Major divisions of the Patayan from about A.D. 1100 to roughly 1300. Co is Cohonina; Ce is Cerbat; Pr is Prescott; Ag is Agua Fria; Am is Amacava; La is La Paz; Pa is Palo Verde. Information supplied by Schroeder.

dence that some of the local groups were shifting about and perhaps occupying smaller areas than they had occupied previously.

The Cohonina culture has been directly traced by actual excavation only to about A.D. 1150, after which time just what became of these people is open to debate. There is a strong suggestion that the area they occupied was much reduced, to a concentration in Havasu Canyon and perhaps the area immediately about its headwaters on the plateau. It is further maintained by Schwartz that they continued in a direct line into the Historic Havasupai in this area. This theory is not acceptable to Euler and others, who maintain that the Cerbat branch expanded to the east, occupied the area of the Cohonina, and so developed into the Pai.

Cohonina ceramics are still basically the San Francisco Mountain Gray Ware, made by the paddle and anvil method, and largely fired in a reducing atmosphere, at least in the early portion of this period. Structures are also very varied, including forts, or fortlike architecture, as well as shades, patio houses, and irregular surface structures. Metates are typically the trough shape open at both ends, and the manos are more or less rectangular and quite often of some size.

As has been suggested, comparatively little is known of the later part of this period. It is quite clear that in ceramics there were many parallels with, or influences from, the Pueblo culture. It has been pointed out that some of the structures are very reminiscent of the small unit-type pueblo. In pottery the greatest similarity is found in earlier types.

The question of the disposal of the dead by the Cohonina is regarded by this writer as still being unresolved. There is a general lack of definite information on this subject, which has led to the assumption that cremation was the usual practice. A few inhumations have been located and it has therefore been argued that this was the method of disposal of the dead. It should be recalled, however, that in any culture the general pattern of custom may not be adhered to in rare instances, so that three inhumations do not constitute clear-cut evidence of a custom. Certainly many more bodies had to be disposed of than these few.

In regard to the Cerbat culture it has already been stated that Euler feels by about A.D. 1150 this group expanded eastward to displace the Cohonina. He further holds that they subsequently developed into the Pai, Walapai, and Havasupai. Rock shelters were the typical structures occupied by these people. The diagnostic pottery is the Tizon Brown Ware, which was made by the paddle and anvil method and was essentially oxidized. Metates are flat slabs with shallow oval grinding areas, and the manos are on the whole smaller than those of the Sinagua. In general the pottery was less well controlled in firing even than that of the Cohonina, and had more oxidized results.

The Prescott culture is perhaps less well understood than the Cerbat. The beginning date and the end date, and final disposition of this somewhat distinctive manifestation, is quite unknown. It seems to have been most vigorous between about A.D. 900 and 1200, but only much more intensive and extensive surveying and excavation will make clear what happened to it after about this latter date. The diagnostic pottery is the Prescott Gray Ware, which was made by the paddle and anvil process and in the east was quite typically reduced and so gray and black on gray. Farther west the control was less certain and more oxidizing is found. It will be recalled that this same trend was noted farther north in the Cohonina and Cerbat. The typical structure in this area was the pueblo, but apparently totally lacking kivas. There were also some "forts," or what seem to have been specially· constructed buildings which might easily have been defended on occasion. There is considerable Pueblo influence on this culture as well, particularly in architecture, and to a lesser extent in ceramics.

What became of the Prescott culture is not as yet known, and as has just been stated the end date has not been determined. It occupied what is now essentially the Yavapai area, and so it has been suggested that these prehistoric people eventually became Historic Yavapai.

The Amacava culture is marked by temporary campsites, mostly indicated solely by sherd areas. Little detailed work in the way of excavation has been done here, or at least reported, but it does seem that it extends into the Historic period and is clearly related to the modern-day Yuman-speaking groups. The pottery, including a number of types, particularly Pyramid Gray, is of the Lower Colorado River Bluff Ware, and is oxidized and made by the paddle and anvil process. Rogers has noted that trailside shrines are found here, and that they extend back into the pre-pottery horizons. Since this is a fairly warm area it is quite likely that any structures which were built were more or less perishable. Schroeder feels that by A.D. 1150 this culture went south to about Needles, and that it later developed into the Historic Mohavi.

Along the lower Colorado River area the La Paz and the Palo Verde stages are found. These are also comparatively little understood, and not well reported. Certainly part of these cultures may be assigned to Rogers' Yuman II. They have been most clearly distinguished by Schroeder. The pottery was made by the paddle and anvil method, and was oxidized. Structures were circular and brush-covered, and caves were occupied as well as campsites. The metate type is a flat slab ground more or less all over, and tends to be rectangular. Jewelry was used, consisting mostly of shells from the gulf, and in distinction to the lack of Cohonina jewelry. Arrows seem to have been tipped with hardwood foreshafts, since stone points are doubtful. Cremations were practiced in this area and these cultures.

The Agua Fria is also not well known, although it had sites constructed of stone, but according to Schroeder it too developed into the Historic Yuman.

In general summary it is quite clear that much is still to be learned about the cultures which are found in this general area at this time and continuing into the Historic period. What is specifically known through excavation concerns only the earlier portion. Certain areas were apparently re-

Fig. 182. Yuman II pottery shapes. After Rogers.

stricted in occupation, or people withdrew from them at this time. The question of the relationship of the Cerbat and the Cohonina is not conclusively settled, nor is the disposal of the dead of the Cohonina. All of the cultural subdivisions of the Patayan need further definition through excavation and extensive and intensive survey, to bridge them more clearly from this period to the Historic groups now found in this general area.

The concept of the Hakataya, as put forth by Schroeder, might be reviewed at this point. It will be recalled that he has held that it is possible to group many of the cultures found in western Arizona under this general heading, at least during the earlier stages of some of them. He feels that Hakataya has roots back in Rogers' Pinto, or Amagosa, and may in fact be traced even farther back to the general Desert culture.

He would include everything at the beginning of ceramics from the Mogollon Rim west to the Colorado River under this general heading. Pioneer Hohokam would be a part of the Hakataya, as would the Sinagua culture before the eruption of Sunset Crater. The Hakataya also includes the Amacava, Cerbat, Prescott, and Cohonina branches. Major traits which in general distinguish this broad complex are square jacal and roundish stone-outlined architectural features, uncontrolled gray or brown paddle and anvil–made ceramics, cremations, and mortars and pestles. This complex appears to be basic to all of the cultures of the Yuman Root on the lower Colorado River and in western and central Arizona in ceramic times only, as well perhaps as those of the California desert and the northern portions of Lower California. Reference to Rogers will disclose that he has also allied the lower Colorado River cultures with those of California.

SINAGUA

The Sinagua culture in north central Arizona between A.D. 1100 and 1300 is distinguishable largely by the presence of characteristic plain red pottery. In most, but not all, traits it was dominated by a strong Pueblo flavor. On the basis of ceramics and other traits it may be divided into an early and a later stage, as is also true with many of the other cultures at this time, but these are minor divisions and do not warrant particular consideration herein.

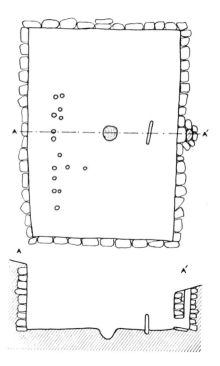

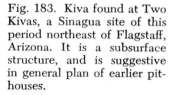

Fig. 183. Kiva found at Two Kivas, a Sinagua site of this period northeast of Flagstaff, Arizona. It is a subsurface structure, and is suggestive in general plan of earlier pithouses.

Structures were surface rooms massed in the general pueblo pattern, and some had rectangular subsurface kivas which were reminiscent of earlier pithouse dwellings, while others seem to have lacked them entirely. Masonry was of available materials, sandstone or limestone slabs or basalt boulders. In some cases the walls were very well constructed, with two finished surfaces filled between with rubble, and occasionally the courses were chinked with small spalls.

The area occupied was in the vicinity of Flagstaff, including the cinder fall from Sunset Crater, and from there south and east into the canyon country of this portion of the plateau. Many well-known sites were constructed and occupied during this period, including Wupatki National Monument, the Ridge Ruin, Two Kivas, Turkey Hill Pueblo, and Elden Pueblo just east of Flagstaff on highway 66. At Wupatki there is both a masonry-lined ball court and a large circular masonry structure which also probably served some ceremonial function.

Two related pottery types are most distinctive and most abundant: Sunset Red and Turkey Hill Red. Sunset Red may easily be distinguished by the fact that it contains greater or lesser amounts of fine black cinders from the Sunset eruption. It is hard, well-fired, and well-made pottery, which was manufactured by the paddle and anvil process, and so often shows striations on the outside and anvil marks inside. It is typically smudged inside, and a bright brick red outside. The outside frequently has fire clouds, where bits of fuel falling against it during the firing process resulted in areas being reduced to gray or turned black. The forms are both jars, some with handles, and bowls. This pottery was made in some quantity and is often found associated with burials.

Turkey Hill Red, which is perhaps a little more abundant late in this period, differs largely in that it has a heavy red slip which is generally well polished, and the temper rarely includes some cinders but is more typically angular light-colored fragments.

The decorated pottery was either traded from the Pueblo culture area or was made locally more or less as copies of Anasazi types. Walnut Black-on-white and Holbrook Black-on-white are found in such quantities that they almost certainly were made locally.

Spindle whorls, modeled of clay, are a part of this culture. Another typical pottery artifact is the rather abundant presence of both perforated and unperforated sherd disks. These are usually quite circular and are ground on the edges. There has been much speculation as to how they were used; one was found with a thong through the hole which was held in place by a knot.

Arrow points are simple triangular points with lateral notches, many very expertly made from large flakes and not a few from petrified wood or other attractive materials. Arrow-shaft straighteners also seem to have been a typical part of this culture, some with just a transverse groove, but others with a raised ridge at right angles to the groove. Manos are of the block type, some with finger grooves on the sides, others worn down more to a somewhat triangular shape in cross section. Metates vary from occasional scoop-shaped forms to trough types open at both ends, and flat slabs, the latter most commonly of fine-grained sandstone. Small stone balls and square blocks of stone were made for some unknown purpose. Occasional stone figures of animals were also sculptured. A large number of small stone cylinders, mostly made of vesicular basalt, are usually found in sites of this culture.

Bone awls were common, some with heads made of the end of the bone, others simply of splinters. Bone chisels were also found.

These people manufactured much jewelry, some of which was quite outstanding. One trait was the use of nose plugs, in the septum of the nose, and these varied from short straight rods to larger curved ornaments which were commonly made of red argilite. A few of these ornamental objects had buttons of turquoise fastened to the ends of the argilite with lac.

Turquoise, stone, and shell were all used in inlays, some set in a background of modeled lac. Pointed sticks with hands and feet carved on their ends were clearly ceremonial in nature, in fact the specific ceremony in which they were used has been identified as Hopi. Shell was extensively used for ornaments, some cut into pendants. Shell bracelets were typical, and beads were of the simple disk type or sometimes double-lobed. Pendants of conus shell were quite typical.

As is the case with many archaeological sites, the Sinagua people located their small villages at strategic spots. They were near springs, or at least not far from available water, where land for agriculture was readily accessible, and where fuel and building material were to be had in the form of timber. There is some indication that the ecology has changed somewhat in at least part of the area they occupied. For example, there was probably a shallow lake not far from the Ridge Ruin where none is to be found today, for the old lake bed is still apparent and many fish were eaten by these people since quantities of fish bones were found in this site.

By way of summary the early portion of this period probably represents about the peak of Sinagua culture. It was at this time that their best work in art was done, as shown especially in the fine turquoise jewelry they produced. A considerable area was occupied, and although there may have been slightly less population than in the earlier period when these people were living in smaller, more scattered sites, they were now occupying larger pueblos. They were still apparently maintaining strong trade relations with the Hohokam to the south, from whom they were presumably getting shell and perhaps other raw materials, and with the Pueblo people to the northeast. Their cultural traditions show roots which may be traced back into the earlier Mogollon.

By now regional variation was beginning to be apparent in the Sinagua culture, so that as one looks at sites from various portions of the large area they occupied, differences become apparent. As has been mentioned, one ceremony which was in use by the Sinagua at this time may be traced to the Historic Hopi. There is some evidence that the Hopi Snake Clan may have come from this area and this culture. Thus they may be related, at least in part, to the Historic Hopi Indians.

THE GALLINA PHASE

One of the interesting manifestations in the Southwest at this time is the Largo-Gallina phase. It is located in a relatively restricted area, including the Largo and Gallina drainages in northwestern New Mexico. Two features are worthy of note concerning it: the common occurrence of towers which were apparently dwellings, and a type of plain pottery which was apparently locally developed but the general shape of which has led to comparisons with Navaho pottery and forms found to the east in the plains.

Among others two distinctive types of pottery are found in this area. The first is Gallina Black-on-gray, which has fine monogeneous paste and fine grit temper. It was manufactured by coiling and scraping, and was fired in a reducing atmosphere. The paint is a carbon paint and the surface color is gray. The forms are bowls and jars, the latter of which tend to have sharply restricted necks, and there is on some the suggestion of a shoulder. Although the bases sometimes are quite restricted, since they were probably started in baskets, the actual base is usually more or less flattened. Designs are simple patterns of comparatively narrow lines and

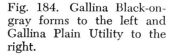

Fig. 184. Gallina Black-on-gray forms to the left and Gallina Plain Utility to the right.

hatching, none of which is as well executed, or as complex, as contemporary pottery farther west.

The other type is what Hibben has named Gallina Plain Utility. It too is gray, and the temper sometimes includes large quartz pebbles, occasionally almost as large as the thickness of the wall of the vessel. This pottery was made by the paddle and anvil method, and was also fired in a reducing atmosphere. In some cases the coiling on the neck has not been smoothed down and is still apparent. The mouths are wide, the necks are sharply restricted, and most of the vessels are elongate and have quite pointed bases.

In gross outline these forms are suggestive of both the plain Navaho cook pot and other vessels from the high plains. Actually it would now seem that it is possible to trace even the development of this form to earlier and more full-bodied types without the necessity of deriving it from outside the immediate area. Navaho pottery is commonly decorated with a raised appliqué design in the neck and rim area, and so does not actually resemble this type, except in general shape. Also it now appears that the Navahos did not get into this section until a much later date.

In the same area both Mera and Hibben found a few sherds of cord-impressed pottery. Much interest originally centered in them, for they are quite foreign to the Southwest, but now it is known that they occur not far to the northeast in the high plains, thus apparently indicating trade contacts in this direction.

Gallina Plain pottery, another type defined by Hibben, is grit-tempered and finished by the paddle and anvil process on at least the bases and the lower portions of the larger vessels. Thus there are two methods of manufacture represented in the construction of pottery in this area.

The masonry is relatively good, with the stones set into clay mortar and plastered over on the inside. Structures are surface, and some are so tall that they must be considered towers. Many of these are round and apparently were entered from the roof, suggesting that they were built for defense. In fact there is evidence that some of the occupants were attacked and destroyed in these towers and left there. One of the most typical features of all these houses, whether they are rectangular lower units or towers, is the presence of a ventilator shaft. In front of the ventilator opening in the floor is a fire basin and almost walling off this portion of the room is a line of above-floor bins. Several of the houses excavated by Hibben had murals painted on the walls, which usually consisted of comparatively simple designs.

Other traits which are distinctive are elbow pipes with projecting feet, which do not seem to find exact parallels in other areas. The stone axe is side-notched and has a third notch in the base, or the end opposite that which is used to cut, and a narrow cutting edge. The arrow-shaft straightener is made with a ridge which has notches in it over which the arrow was presumably straightened. Hibben also pictures some large flaked-stone knives which have lateral notches near the middle of the blade.

From this, while it may be seen that the Gallina phase is distinctive, it is not so much of a misfit in the general scheme of the Southwest as it had at one time been assumed to be. Relationships with the plains are rather those of trade than direct influence, and the apparent parallel of pottery shape with the Navaho is more a matter of fortuitous happenstance than any direct relation. It is·true that while both the use of the paddle and anvil and the scraping and polishing method of pottery manufacture is not a common circumstance, it is not unique. The habit of building towers as habitations may have developed locally, or possibly resulted from the need for defense.

THE RIO GRANDE

During the period from A.D. 1100 to about 1300 there was a movement of people eastward into the Rio Grande valley and the concentration of populations in larger and larger pueblos. The local cultures took on more

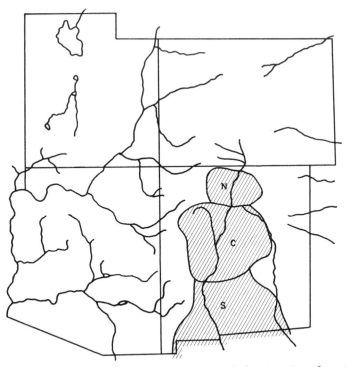

Fig. 185. Three geographic and cultural divisions of the Rio Grande valley are now possible. N, the northern section, has Santa Fe and Wiyo Black-on-white pottery types. C, the central section, has Socorro and Chupadero Black-on-white pottery types. S, the southern area, is characterized by the presence of Jornada Brown pottery. Variations in architecture and other traits help identify each of these areas further.

and more distinctive color, and the way was being set for the typical Rio Grande developments of the succeeding periods.

As is indicated by the map it is possible to divide the valley into three more or less distinguishable areas. In the southern portion Jornada Brown pottery is typical, is rather widespread, and is a continuation of earlier brown pottery types. It also survived into later brown pottery types, and moved farther southward in succeeding periods. In the central area Socorro and Chupadero Black-on-white pottery is typical, and these also have their roots back in previous types and extend into later types. In the northern area Santa Fe and Wiyo Black-on-white pottery is most typical, and in fact is diagnostic of developing cultures here.

Turning to the ceramics of the central area first, Socorro Black-on-white has already been described as occurring in the preceding period. It survives into the present period, apparently with little change. The culture of the area occupied by this pottery type now shifted more to the east. To the northwest, north of Grants, it grades into more truly Chacoan types, but in general it all is reminiscent of Chaco. The paste is gray, with a fine temper, has a thin white or gray slip, and has somewhat the appearance of a mat finish. The design is in a good black, grading to a reddish brown color, so that it obviously contains iron, and there is much use of a very fine hatching of excellent draftsmanship.

Chupadero Black-on-white is most concentrated from the Rio Grande east to about Santa Rosa. In several respects it is strongly reminiscent of Socorro Black-on-white, particularly as regards the use of solid and hatched areas. The undecorated surfaces are crudely finished by being brushed or scraped. Designs are in black grading to red-brown. The paste is a fine well-fired gray, and the temper is fine gray particles of stone and crushed potsherds. Forms are flat-bottom bowls with thin black-top rims, jars with flaring rims, and pitchers with rope handles. This type, which is later than Socorro Black-on-white, spans from late in this period into the succeeding one, or from about A.D. 1150 to perhaps as late as 1650.

In the northern area Santa Fe Black-on-white is perhaps most characteristic of this general period. The paste is gray and rather soft, and the temper is coarse sand, sherds, and volcanic tuff. The undecorated surface is rough and poorly finished and the decorated is lightly slipped and not well smoothed. Panel decorations which extend to the rim are typical and hatched triangular figures are common. The forms are bowls. There is obvious influence in this type, from Gallina and Kwahe's Black-on-white types. It is most typical of the latter half of this period and extends into the beginning of the following period.

Wiyo Black-on-white is found only late in this period and again extends into the early stages of the succeeding period. It seems to have clearly been derived from Santa Fe Black-on-white. The clay is a soft brown, and the temper is very fine crushed tuff. Interiors of bowls are slipped with a thin slip of the same color as the paste and the paint is a carbon black. Designs are bold, lines are broad, and there is characteristically a top framing line. Forms are bowls.

A large adobe-walled New Mexico pueblo which was excavated by members of the Laboratory of Anthropology staff.

Typical structures are pueblos of massed rooms, often with a court or plaza, and made by either coursed adobe sometimes set on a base line of rocks, or of rock walls set in a rather abundant clay mortar. Some of these are relatively large communities of over 100 rooms. A few jacal-type single structures have been found as well. The most typical kiva seems to have been subterranean and circular. Kiva walls were often made of adobe, sometimes with poles incorporated in them for reinforcement. Typically there is a circular clay-lined firepit and ash pit, a ventilator opening to the east, and a movable slab damper. Kiva shapes and types seem to have varied by areas and within sites. Some are rectangular, some are above ground, and some have been designated "corner kivas" by Kidder, such as those he uncovered at Forked Lightning Ruin. These latter types are built into the room blocks.

Kivas in the Rio Grande lack certain features which are typical of those of the western Pueblo area, such as benches, pilasters, and deflectors. This, combined with the difference in shape and the fact that some are subsurface while others are surface, constitutes considerable variation.

Other traits which may be assigned to this period and which are found in the central area, but particularly in the northern section, are chipped stone axes notched for hafting, some with ground bits, and full-grooved mauls. There are also ridged arrow-shaft straighteners. Pipes are either simple tubes or elbow shapes, of both clay and stone, the latter usually not of right angles. Projectile points are small, obviously now arrow points, triangular, and with either diagonal corner notches or lateral notches. Ornaments include both beads and pendants made of turquoise, and shell bracelets, which seem to have had a long history of popularity.

Both milling stones with two-hand grinders and metates were in use. The early metate was troughed and open at both ends or closed at one end. The manos frequently had finger grooves for grasping. Later the flat slab metate appeared and became dominant, and with it are frequently found two-hand manos which are triangular in cross section. There are relatively few bone awls from this time. Burials seem to have been dominantly flexed.

Although only decorated pottery types have been described from this central and northern area, culinary pottery was relatively abundant. Indented corrugated jars were typical of this time, in many of which the corrugations had been more or less smoothed over, particularly toward the end of the period. These are of a number of individual types. Just at about the end of this period the first of the glaze-painted pottery types begin to appear, possibly introduced from the west where they were beginning to develop, but since they are most typical of the succeeding period they will be described there.

A considerable number of sites in this area and of this general period have been excavated, and not a few reported. For example, Pindi Pueblo seems to have begun its existence at about the end of this time and to have survived well into the succeeding period. For this reason no attempt has been made to discuss the culture of this area in more detail, and the reader is referred to the somewhat more extensive bibliography listed herewith for additional and more specific information.

The southern part of the Rio Grande valley was occupied from about A.D. 1100 to perhaps as late as 1450. Surveys and limited excavation, centering in the El Paso vicinity, have located sherd areas and some house remains. The sites along the Rio Grande proper are mostly indicated by sherd areas alone, whereas other areas have house remains as well. These consist of tanks, basins, natural springs, and points where travelers apparently stopped, for here are found sherd accumulations and pictographs.

As has already been stated, the dominant pottery type is the Mogollon-related or -derived Jornada Brown, but other decorated types, both as trade and as native productions, occur. Chupadero Black-on-white, which has been described above, is found in this area. It will be recalled that it has been related in decoration to Socorro Black-on-white, so this style of design, with similar black-on-whites, has a considerable distribution. A second pottery type is El Paso Polychrome. It has a coarse paste with sand and carbon inclusions as temper, and is slipped brown. Bowl interiors have a black and red design, while exteriors are plain brown, though they may be either slipped or unslipped. There is also a heavy plain type which is brick red and contains much sand temper. Mimbres Black-on-white was a very common trade type. Pottery from the Casas Grandes area in northern Mexico is also found intruded into this section to some extent, and in fact the relationships between the Mogollon and the Casas Grandes area are now known to extend back for a considerable period.

Although the El Paso area may be considered to represent a distinct cultural entity, it is quite clear that the decorated pottery is derived from both the Mogollon and Anasazi cultures. To the east, campsites with the same general ceramic complex were located in the open, often in sand dunes, where fireplaces were found but no evidence of structures.

In general summary of the Rio Grande area there is clear evidence of a suddenly expanding population. Larger sites were far more abundant than they had been previously, and even some of the main culture traits are suggestive of the western Pueblo area. Mesa Verde styles of pottery design are very pronounced late in the period, and in fact have led some to suggest that quite possibly people of Mesa Verde–Chaco derivation were moving eastward into the Rio Grande. In other local ceramics designs may be traced back through earlier forms and ultimately to a Chaco influence. In general there can be little doubt that at about this time, and certainly in the near future, there was a considerable shift of population center from the west to the east. From this time on the northern portion of the Rio Grande valley probably had more inhabitants than were to be found to the west.

Typical structures were pueblos of massed rooms, and built either of adobe walls or rock walls, or combinations of both in the same sites. Some jacal-like structures may be assigned to this period, at least one of which, at Pindi Pueblo, had a four-post support arrangement. Kivas differed from those to the west in that they lacked certain features, such as benches, pilasters, and deflectors. They varied in shape from circular to rectangular and from subsurface to surface types, even sometimes in the same pueblo. The corner kivas which were embodied in part of the pueblo structures have been identified and named as a distinctive type by Kidder. Posts were sometimes used in the adobe walls of the kivas.

Other artifacts show only minor variations from those which have already been described as typical of the west. Metates were both trough in

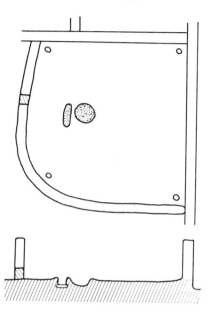

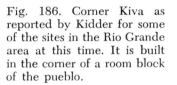

Fig. 186. Corner Kiva as reported by Kidder for some of the sites in the Rio Grande area at this time. It is built in the corner of a room block of the pueblo.

the early portion of the period and flat slab later, the latter with some large manos which are triangular in cross section. Some axes were chipped and notched for hafting and some had ground-down cutting edges. Pipes were both tubular and of the elbow type but of obtuse angles rather than right angles between the bowl and stem. Considerable use was made of turquoise in jewelry, and shell was also present. Burials were typically flexed, and the backs of the skulls were characteristically flattened.

In general this period is the beginning of a marked and rapid rise of the Pueblo culture in the Rio Grande area. Certain traits also developed which became progressively elaborated through subsequent time. Such is the case of the pipes, for instance, which from now on were more elaborately made. Stone figurines of animals, and several other traits, began to take on a more local caste, and the distinctive New Mexico Pueblo culture developed.

SUMMARY

In general the Classic period is well named, for many of the individual Southwestern cultural manifestations reached a rather high level of development. Subsequently some seem to have deteriorated, such as was the probable case of the Hohokam, while others simply elaborated on the general culture which had been developed by this time, as seems to have been the case with the Pueblo culture.

Certain broad similarities, or generally shared traits, are thus to be found over considerable areas of the Southwest. Pueblo architecture was widespread, in fact in one form or another the dominant type of structure. Projectile points were arrow points, and were small, lightly made, triangular in general outline, and mostly side-notched though not always so. The first general appearance and popular occurrence of polychrome pottery took place, late in the period, as did the first use of glaze pigments for the decoration of pottery. It is interesting that the idea of the use of a glaze slip, which would have made the vessel waterproof, was never developed in prehistoric times in the Southwest. Metates were becoming broader, sometimes were enclosed in bins, and the two-hand mano was much more prevalent. Grooved axes were now widespread, and ridged arrow-shaft straighteners were found particularly throughout the eastern half of the area. Cotton fabrics seem to have been rather widely produced. All of these traits were, at most, simply elaborated on throughout subsequent time.

The Pueblo culture in the northern portion of the Southwest had reached a rather high level in all traits, a condition which might well be taken as an indication of an advanced cultural attainment. Four areas have been considered as showing considerable variations and so are distinguishable. Of these the most outstanding area in many ways was still the four corners section, wherein superior architecture and even very good ceramics are found. In the earlier Chaco Canyon culture, and the later Mesa Verde, large settlements and many well-made artifacts attest to the superiority of this area. The western San Juan and the Hopi country are less spectacular, and the Zuñi area is probably slightly so.

Pottery in general reached a rather high level of perfection now in the Pueblo culture as well, with probably the best-made and best-fired pottery ever produced in the Southwest being Kayenta Black-on-white. The development of the polychrome pottery of this culture and time was also impressive, particularly the St. Johns Polychrome, which enjoyed a very widespread popularity. In the upper Little Colorado and in the Zuñi area there was the first use of glaze paints on pottery.

As has been suggested, by far the best masonry is now found in the four corners area, particularly that of the Mesa Verde area and culture. Also the most outstanding kivas are found, since all of the features which are thought of as being typical of kivas were developed here: the banquette, pilasters, platform, ventilator, deflector combination. Circular kivas are typical of the eastern part of the area, while rectangular ones seem to have been developing in the west. The great kiva of the Zuñi area and of Chaco Canyon was circular.

The box metate was becoming popular for the first time, with a flat grinding slab and a long two-hand mano. Weaving was varied and often of exceptional quality, with cotton the most popular material used.

Just at the end of this period the great drought, probably in combination with other factors, contributed to the abandonment of all of the eastern San Juan drainage. It has been suggested that some of the occupants of the eastern part of this area moved farther eastward into the Rio Grande valley, while others to the west and in the central part moved south to join with what later became the Hopi Indians.

Hohokam culture in southern Arizona was undergoing some rather drastic changes. Distinctive red-on-buff pottery was made in the form of jars with vertical cylindrical necks, and there was also the widespread production of Gila Red. Houses, though apparently pithouses survived, were sometimes contiguous but never more than one story high. In some cases they seem to have been joined by a wall which surrounded them or formed a compoundlike arrangement.

Salado culture was in contact with the Hohokam and was apparently strongly influencing it. Compounds, as such, appear for the first time in the Hohokam area, and the Salado people apparently lived peacefully with the Hohokam. In the Dragoon area further modifications were being made on Hohokam culture, so that here too there seems to have been a continuing combination of Anasazi influences, perhaps mostly through Salado. As a result, both house types and ceramics are found to vary from that of the typical Hohokam.

Mogollon culture by now had definitely lost its clear-cut identity, and particularly in the north was becoming more and more influenced by Pueblo culture. Pueblo architectural ideas were pretty definitely infiltrating the Mogollon culture, and although most kivas were rectangular, and often had long sloping entrances, other architectural features were definitely Pueblo. The main traits which retained Mogollon stamps were the various types of locally produced pottery. This is particularly true of the corrugated types, most of which were brown, and many of which were exceptionally well made and of fine even corrugations. The smudging of the interiors of bowls was also characteristic.

As Mogollon culture as a vigorous entity was waning in the major portion of the Southwest it seems to have maintained its contacts to the south, and to have gradually withdrawn in this direction. It now would appear that there were early, and persisting, contacts between Mogollon and the Casas Grandes area in northern Mexico.

In the southeastern part of New Mexico the Mimbres culture reached its peak early in the period. The most distinctive feature of Mimbres is the production of pottery with superior geometric and naturalistic designs. This black-on-white or red-on-cream pottery is of such remarkable execution that it stands out as the finest ever produced in the Southwest. Some

A doorway in one of the rooms in Kiet Siel Pueblo. A flat slab was fitted into the recessed shoulder.

of the figures of animals are a pure delight. The architecture is of the general pueblo pattern, masses of rooms combined into a large block and apparently not over one story in height. By A.D. 1300 the Mimbres area had been abandoned by the Mimbres people.

Salado culture, which began its development during this period, is clearly related to, or derived from, Pueblo culture. The question in fact may be raised as to whether or not it is a distinct culture, instead of a modification of Pueblo with a southern extension. Herein it has been suggested that both the earlier black-on-white and the later polychrome pottery constitute aspects of this culture, despite the fact that Steen argues that only the polychrome stage is really Salado. Thus it is primarily on pottery types that Salado has been isolated and defined. There is some question as to whether or not the compound is really a development from the pueblo concept, despite the fact that compounds grade into more pueblo-like arrangements as they are traced east.

Two sources have been suggested for the ceramic complex which has identified Salado. The earlier black-on-white pottery is pretty clearly related to similar types in the Puerco and Little Colorado areas. The later polychrome types may well have had their genesis in the mountain section farther to the south.

The Patayan seems to have been both a distinctive general way of life, and so a distinctive culture, and to have been confined to a specific geographical region. As has been shown, boundaries between the various divisions of Patayan have not been clearly defined, and this will require much more detailed work for they grade gradually into one another. The concept of the Hakataya, as proposed by Schroeder, has some justification, although his inclusion of other early cultures may not be so readily acceptable.

The Sinagua culture reached a peak early in this period in the area south of Flagstaff, and although it survived into later periods was not so spectacular. The distinctive feature of the Sinagua is again the plain locally made pottery. This was made by the paddle and anvil process, and is brown. The decorated pottery is either borrowed from or copied after Pueblo pottery. It has been pointed out that early Sinagua was developed from a combination of all of the three major cultural groups, the Mogollon, Hohokam, and Anasazi. By this time Mogollon was exerting comparatively little influence on it, but both Anasazi, in the form of Pueblo, and Hohokam were still very evident as indicated by continued trade. By now, too, Sinagua was beginning to show much regional variation, as were most other cultures.

One of the many distinguishable cultural divisions is that found in the Gallina area of northwestern New Mexico. Pottery with pointed bottoms is striking. Architecture was also unusual with the presence of round towers which were apparently used as homes.

As has been pointed out, the central and northern parts of the Rio Grande valley were now rapidly developing. There has been a suggestion made that perhaps some of the population of the Mesa Verde area actually moved east and settled in the valley, and there seems to have been some justification for such a view. Pottery was locally made, and of distinguishable types, but had its genesis either in earlier westward related types or was influenced from the west. This is particularly apparent in the black-on-white types as regards design elements, combinations, and even layouts.

The typical masonry structure was the pueblo, but adobe walls were often substituted for the stone walls of farther west. Kivas were variable, and generally different from those of the west, lacking certain characteristic western features. Some were round, some rectangular, and either subsurface or surface structures. Others were even integral portions of the pueblos. In most other traits the Rio Grande pueblos were much like their neighbors to the west.

From all of this it may be seen that during the Classic period there was a certain rather widespread unity of the general level of cultural attainment. Many things were now shared broadly throughout the Southwest. At the same time there was considerable regional diversity, especially in ceramic traditions and in architectural details. This diversity is particularly apparent in the peripheral areas, the Patayan, the Durango, and even the Rio Grande.

Sources and Additional References

Adams, William Y. and Nettie K. An Inventory of Prehistoric Sites on the Lower San Juan River, Utah, *Bulletin 31*, 1959, Museum of Northern Arizona, Flagstaff. (Discussion of the Kayenta and Mesa Verde sites in the main gorge of the San Juan River.)

Amsden, Charles Avery. An Analysis of Hohokam Pottery Design, *Medallion Paper 23*, 1936, Gila Pueblo, Globe, Arizona. (Comparative data on Hohokam pottery designs.)

Bartlett, Katharine. Material Culture of Pueblo II in the San Francisco Mountains, Arizona, *Bulletin 7*, 1934, Museum of Northern Arizona, Flagstaff. (Much of the material included in this report may be assigned to the Patayan culture.)

Beals, Ralph L., G. W. Brainerd, and Watson Smith. Archaeological Studies in Northeast Arizona, *Publications in American Archaeology and Ethnology,* Vol. 44, No. 1, 1945, University of California Press, Berkeley. (Pueblo III sites in the western San Juan.)

Bradfield, Wesley. Cameron Creek Village, a Site in the Mimbres Area in Grant County, New Mexico, School of American Research, Santa Fe, New Mexico, 1929. (Detailed account of sites excavated in the Mimbres area, with many fine illustrations of Classic Mimbres pottery and other types.)

Caywood, Louis R., and Edward H. Spicer. Tuzigoot, the Excavation and Repair of a Ruin on the Verde River Near Clarkdale, Arizona, Field Division of Education, National Park Service, Berkeley, California, 1935. (Includes material found in the Verde River, which is only casually mentioned in this chapter.)

Colton, Harold S. * Prehistoric Culture Units and Their Relationships in Northern Arizona, *Bulletin 17*, 1939, Museum of Northern Arizona, Flagstaff. (Contains a short but good discussion of Patayan culture.)

———. Pottery Types of the Southwest, *Ceramic Series 3D*, 1958, Museum of Northern Arizona, Flagstaff. (Descriptions of many of the pottery types and wares defined by Schroeder which are found in the Patayan area.)

Cosgrove, C. B. and H. S. The Swarts Ruin, *Papers of the Peabody Museum of American Archaeology and Ethnology,* Vol. 15, No. 1, 1932, Harvard University, Cambridge, Massachusetts. (Detailed report of this site with many fine illustrations of associated cultural material including Mimbres pottery.)

Danson, Edward Bridge. An Archaeological Survey of West Central New Mexico and East Central Arizona, *Papers of the Peabody Museum of American Archaeology and Ethnology*, Vol. 44, No. 1, 1957, Harvard University, Cambridge, Massachusetts. (Excellent summary of the archaeology of the southeastern portion of this area.)

Di Peso, Charles C. The Babocomari Village Site on the Babocomari River, Southeastern Arizona, No. 5, 1951, the Amerind Foundation, Inc., Dragoon, Arizona. (Description of a village which dates late in this period and has a surrounding wall.)

——. The Reeve Ruin of Southeastern Arizona, No. 8, 1958, the Amerind Foundation, Inc., Dragoon, Arizona. (Summary and evaluation of the archaeology in this area from this period on to the historic Spanish contact.)

Euler, Robert C. Archaeological Problems in Western and Northwestern Arizona, 1962, *Plateau*, Vol. 35, No. 3, 1963, Museum of Northern Arizona, Flagstaff. (Discussion of the various Patayan branches and what needs to be done to explore them further.)

Euler, Robert C., and Henry F. Dobyns. Excavations West of Prescott, Arizona, *Plateau*, Vol. 34, No. 3, 1962, Museum of Northern Arizona, Flagstaff. (Prescott branch sites of this period.)

Ezell, Paul H. Is There a Hohokam-Pima Culture Continuum? *American Antiquity*, Vol. 29, No. 1, 1963, Society for American Archaeology, Salt Lake City, Utah. (This writer concludes that there is such a continuum.)

Fewkes, Jesse Walter. * Casa Grande, Arizona, *Twenty-eighth Annual Report*, 1912, Bureau of American Ethnology, Washington, D.C. (Excellent and well-illustrated report on the Casa Grande ruins and material derived from this site.)

——. Designs on Prehistoric Pottery from the Mimbres Valley, New Mexico, *Smithsonian Miscellaneous Collections*, Vol. 76, No. 6, 1924, Washington, D.C. (A series of fine illustrations of Classic Mimbres pottery.)

——. Additional Designs on Prehistoric Mimbres Pottery, *Smithsonian Miscellaneous Collections*, Vol. 76, No. 8, 1924, Washington, D.C. (A large series of fine illustrations of Classic Mimbres pottery.)

Gladwin, H. S. Excavations at Casa Grande, Arizona, *Southwest Museum Paper 2*, 1928, Los Angeles, California. (Report on work at Casa Grande which includes the Salado culture and its first recognition.)

Gladwin, Winifred and H. S. * The Red-on-Buff Culture of the Gila Basin, *Medallion Paper 3*, 1929, Gila Pueblo, Globe, Arizona. (Good early general discussion of the Hohokam of the Gila Basin.)

——. The Red-on-Buff Culture of the Papagueria, *Medallion Paper 4*, 1930, Gila Pueblo, Globe, Arizona. (Basic discussion of the southern variant of the Middle Gila Basin.)

——. The Western Range of the Red-on-Buff Culture, *Medallion Paper 5*, 1930, Gila Pueblo, Globe, Arizona. (Brief discussion of the Hohokam archaeology of the Lower Gila area.)

——. * Some Southwestern Pottery Types, Series I, *Medallion Paper 8*, 1930, Gila Pueblo, Globe, Arizona. (Original and basic descriptions of polychrome and red types from the Gila.)

————. Some Southwestern Pottery Types, Series II, *Medallion Paper 10,* 1931, Gila Pueblo, Globe, Arizona. (Detailed descriptions of the black-on-white pottery types of the Salado culture.)

————. * Some Southwestern Pottery Types, Series III, *Medallion Paper 13,* 1933, Gila Pueblo, Globe, Arizona. (Basic descriptions and discussions of Hohokam Red-on-buff types of pottery.)

————. A Method for the Designation of Cultures and Their Variations, *Medallion Paper 15,* 1934, Gila Pueblo, Globe, Arizona. (Discussion and charts showing the relationship of the cultures considered in this chapter as well as others.)

————. The Eastern Range of the Red-on-Buff Culture, *Medallion Paper 16,* 1935, Gila Pueblo, Globe, Arizona. (Contains valuable maps showing the distribution of sites of these cultures.)

Gladwin, H. S., Emil W. Haury, E. B. Sayles, and Nora Gladwin. * Excavations at Snaketown, Material Culture, *Medallion Paper 25,* 1937, Gila Pueblo, Globe, Arizona. (The discussion of Hohokam culture in this volume by Gladwin will be found most useful in clarifying the Classic Hohokam culture.)

Guernsey, Samuel J. * Explorations in Northeastern Arizona, *Papers of the Peabody Museum of American Archaeology and Ethnology,* Vol. 12, No. 1, 1931, Harvard University, Cambridge, Massachusetts. (Data on sites and culture of the San Juan area.)

Hargrave, Lyndon L. Results of a Study of the Cohonina Branch of the Patayan Culture in 1938, *Museum Notes,* Vol. 11, No. 6, 1938, Museum of Northern Arizona, Flagstaff. (Report and evaluation of the Cohonina branch of the Patayan culture.)

Haury, Emil W. Minute Beads from Prehistoric Pueblos, *American Anthropologist,* Vol. 33, No. 1, 1931, Menasha, Wisconsin. (Detailed discussion of beads from Pueblo sites.)

————. Kivas of the Tusayan Ruin, Grand Canyon, Arizona, *Medallion Paper 9,* 1931, Gila Pueblo, Globe, Arizona. (Description of an excavated site in the Grand Canyon area.)

————. The Canyon Creek Ruin and the Cliff Dwellings of the Sierra Ancha, *Medallion Paper 14,* 1934, Gila Pueblo, Globe, Arizona. (Fine description of sites and the material culture from this area.)

————. Excavations in the Forestdale Valley, East-Central Arizona, *University of Arizona Social Science Bulletin 12,* 1940, Tucson. (Sites of this period in the Forestdale area.)

————. The Excavation of Los Muertos and Neighboring Ruins in the Salt River Valley, Southern Arizona, *Papers of the Peabody Museum of American Archaeology and Ethnology,* Vol. 24, No. 1, 1945, Harvard University, Cambridge, Massachusetts. (Important sites in the Salt River of this period.)

————. Painted Cave, Northeastern Arizona, No. 3, 1945, the Amerind Foundation, Inc., Dragoon, Arizona. (Report of Basket Maker III and Pueblo III at this site, where quantities of fabrics and other artifacts were found.)

Haury, Emil W., and Lyndon L. Hargrave. * Recently Dated Pueblo Ruins in Arizona, *Smithsonian Miscellaneous Collections,* Vol. 82, No. 11, 1931, Washington, D.C. (Report of sites in the Zuñi and Hopi areas.)

Hewett, Edgar L. Antiquities of the Jemez Plateau, New Mexico, *Bulletin 32,* 1906, Bureau of American Ethnology, Washington, D.C. (As indicated by title.)

Hibben, Frank C. The Gallina Phase, *American Antiquity*, Vol. 4, No. 2, 1938, Society for American Archaeology, Salt Lake City, Utah.

———. The Gallina Architectural Forms, *American Antiquity*, Vol. 13, No. 1, 1948, Society for American Archaeology, Salt Lake City, Utah.

———. The Pottery of the Gallina Complex, *American Antiquity*, Vol. 14, No. 3, 1949, Society for American Archaeology, Salt Lake City, Utah.

Hough, Walter. Archaeological Field Work in Northeastern Arizona. The Museum Gates Expedition of 1901, Smithsonian Institution, Washington, D.C., 1903. (Descriptions of Salado traits and sites found in the northern portion of the Salado area.)

Judd, Neil M. Archaeological Observations North of the Rio Colorado, *Bulletin 82*, 1926, Bureau of American Ethnology, Washington, D.C. (Report on several sites in this area.)

———. * The Excavation and Repair of Betatakin, *Smithsonian Institution Publication 2828*, 1930, Washington, D.C. (Detailed report of this site in the Tsegi Canyon area.)

Kidder, Alfred Vincent. An Introduction to the Study of Southwestern Archaeology, Phillips Academy, Andover, Massachusetts, 1924. (The section in this book dealing with the prehistoric Puebloans is still an excellent description of this period.)

———. Pecos, New Mexico: Archaeological Notes, *Papers of the Peabody Foundation*, Vol. 5, 1958, Phillips Academy, Andover, Massachusetts. (Forked Lightning Ruin definitely belongs to this period.)

Kidder, Alfred Vincent, and Samuel J. Guernsey. * Archaeological Explorations in Northeastern Arizona, *Bulletin 65*, 1919, Bureau of American Ethnology, Washington, D.C. (Contains excellent reports on San Juan sites of this period.)

Lehmer, Donald J. The Jornada Branch of the Mogollon, *University of Arizona Social Science Bulletin 17*, 1948, Tucson. (As indicated by title.)

Martin, Paul S. Lowry Ruin in Southwestern Colorado, *Anthropological Series*, Vol. 23, No. 1, 1936, Field Museum of Natural History, Chicago. (Report on an early Classic site in this area.)

———. Archaeological Work in the Ackmen-Lowry Area, Southwestern Colorado, 1937, *Anthropological Series*, Vol. 23, No. 2, 1938, Field Museum of Natural History, Chicago. (Report of the general archaeology of this section.)

Martin, Paul S., and John B. Rinaldo. Excavations in the Upper Little Colorado Drainage, Eastern Arizona, *Fieldiana: Anthropology*, Vol. 51, No. 1, 1960, Chicago Natural History Museum. (Site 31 is of this period.)

Martin, Paul S., John B. Rinaldo, and Eloise R. Barter. Late Mogollon Communities, Four Sites of the Tularosa Phase, Western New Mexico, *Fieldiana: Anthropology*, Vol. 49, No. 1, 1957, Chicago Natural History Museum. (As indicated by title.)

Martin, Paul S., John B. Rinaldo, Elaine A. Bluhm, and Hugh C. Cutler. Higgins Flat Pueblo, Western New Mexico, *Fieldiana: Anthropology*, Vol. 45, 1956, Chicago Natural History Museum. (A Mogollon Brown–dominated Tularosa phase site.)

Martin, Paul S., John B. Rinaldo, and William A. Longacre. Mineral Creek Site and Hooper Ranch Pueblo, Eastern Arizona, *Fieldiana: Anthropology*, Vol. 52, 1961, Chicago Natural History Museum. (Both of these sites fall within this period.)

Martin, Paul S., John B. Rinaldo, William A. Longacre, Constance Cronin, Leslie G. Freeman, Jr., and James Schoenwetter. Chapters in the Prehistory of Eastern Arizona, 1, *Fieldiana: Anthropology*, Vol. 53, 1962, Chicago Natural History Museum. (Several of the sites discussed fall within this period.)

Martin, Paul S., and Elizabeth S. Willis. Anasazi Painted Pottery in Field Museum of Natural History, *Anthropology Memoir 5*, 1940, Field Museum of Natural History, Chicago. (Some illustrations of the pottery types discussed herein.)

Mera, H. P. Chupadero Black on White, *Technical Series Bulletin 1*, 1931, Laboratory of Anthropology, Santa Fe, New Mexico.

———. Wares Ancestral to Tewa Polychrome, *Technical Series Bulletin 4*, 1932, Laboratory of Anthropology, Santa Fe, New Mexico.

———. Ceramic Clues to the Prehistory of North Central New Mexico, *Technical Series Bulletin 8*, 1935, Laboratory of Anthropology, Santa Fe, New Mexico.

———. Reconnaissance and Excavation in Southwestern New Mexico, *Memoirs of the American Anthropological Association*, No. 51, 1938, Lancaster, Pennsylvania. (As indicated by title.)

———. Some Aspects of the Largo Cultural Phase, Northern New Mexico, *American Antiquity*, Vol. 3, No. 3, 1938, Society for American Archaeology, Salt Lake City, Utah.

Morris, Earl H. * Archaeological Studies in the La Plata District, Southwestern Colorado and Northwestern New Mexico, *Carnegie Institution Publication 519*, 1939, Washington, D.C. (The discussion of both Chaco Canyon and Mesa Verde cultures found in the introduction is well worth reviewing.)

Morris, Earl H., and Robert F. Burgh. Anasazi Basketry, Basket Maker II Through Pueblo III: A Study Based on Specimens from the San Juan River Country, *Carnegie Institution Publication 533*, 1941, Washington, D.C. (Excellent data on and illustrations of basketry of this period.)

Nesbitt, Paul H. Starkweather Ruin, *Bulletin 6*, 1938, Logan Museum Publications in Anthropology, Beloit, Wisconsin. (A somewhat earlier site which shows the derivation of the Mimbres culture.)

Prudden, T. Mitchell. A Further Study of the Prehistoric Small House Ruins in the San Juan Watershed, *Memoirs of the American Anthropological Association*, Vol. 5, No. 1, 1918, Lancaster, Pennsylvania. (Includes illustrations and descriptions of the Mesa Verde kiva type.)

Rinaldo, John B. Foote Canyon Pueblo, Eastern Arizona, *Fieldiana: Anthropology*, Vol. 49, No. 2, 1959, Chicago Natural History Museum. (A small pueblo of this period on the Blue River in eastern Arizona.)

Rogers, Malcolm J. An Outline of Yuman Prehistory, *Southwestern Journal of Anthropology*, Vol. 1, No. 2, 1945, University of New Mexico Press, Albuquerque. (Discussion of Yuman I, II, and III.)

Sauer, Carl, and Donald Brand. Pueblo Sites in Southeastern Arizona, *Publications in Geography*, Vol. 3, No. 7, 1930, University of California Press, Berkeley. (Maps giving the distribution of the various components of the Salado culture.)

Schroeder, Albert H. The Hohokam, Sinagua and the Hakataya, *Archives of Archaeology*, No. 5, 1960 (on 4 microcards), Society for American Archaeology and the University of Wisconsin Press, Madison. (Best statement of the concept of the Hakataya by Schroeder, and definitions of the various divisions within it.)

Schwartz, Douglas W. Havasupai Prehistory: Thirteen Centuries of Cultural Development, Ph.D. dissertation, Yale University, New Haven, Connecticut, 1955. (As indicated by title.)

———. Demographic Changes in the Early Periods of Cohonina Prehistory, in Prehistoric Settlement Patterns, ed. by Gordon R. Willey, *Viking Fund Publications in Anthropology*, No. 23, 1956, New York City. (As indicated by title.)

———. Climatic Change and Culture History in the Grand Canyon Region, *American Anthropologist*, Vol. 22, No. 4, 1957, Menasha, Wisconsin. (Discussion of Cohonina development.)

Spicer, Edward H., and Louis R. Caywood. Two Pueblo Ruins in West Central Arizona, *University of Arizona Social Science Bulletin 10*, 1936, Tucson. (Report of two sites in the Prescott area which are only very briefly mentioned in this chapter.)

Stallings, W. S., Jr. Notes on the Pueblo Culture in South Central New Mexico and in the vicinity of El Paso, Texas, *American Anthropologist*, Vol. 34, No. 1, 1932, Menasha, Wisconsin. (As indicated by title.)

Steen, Charlie, Lloyd M. Pierson, Vorsila L. Bohrer, and Kate Peck Kent. * Archaeological Studies at Tonto National Monument, *Technical Series*, Vol. 2, 1962, Southwestern Monuments Association, Globe, Arizona. (Best recent general summary of the Salado problem.)

Stubbs, Stanley A., and W. S. Stallings, Jr. The Excavation of Pindi Pueblo, New Mexico, *Monographs of the School of American Research and the Laboratory of Anthropology*, No. 18, 1953, Santa Fe, New Mexico. (The early part of this site dates from this period.)

Toulouse, Joseph H., Jr., and Robert L. Stephenson. Excavations at Pueblo Prado, *Papers in Anthropology 2*, 1960, Museum of New Mexico, Santa Fe. (The early part of this site falls in this period.)

Tuthill, Carr. The Tres Alamos Site on the San Pedro River, Southeastern Arizona, No. 4, 1947, the Amerind Foundation, Inc., Dragoon, Arizona. (Some discussion of the archaeology of this period in the Tucson and Tres Alamos area at this time.)

Wendorf, Fred. A Report on the Excavation of a Small Ruin East of Point of Pines, East Central Arizona, *University of Arizona Social Science Bulletin 19*, 1950, Tucson. (The pithouses and culture of the Willow Creek phase belong to this period.)

———. *A Reconstruction of Northern Rio Grande Prehistory, *American Anthropologist*, Vol. 56, No. 2, Part 1, 1954, Menasha, Wisconsin. (Excellent summary statement of this period for the northern Rio Grande area.)

XIV

Culminant Period: A.D. 1300 to 1600

PUEBLO IV

The Culminant period is also one of the best-dated Southwestern periods, for it is marked at its beginning and end by specific events. The beginning date is the end of the great drought, a date which has been very accurately established as close to A.D. 1300. The end is that time at which Spanish customs began to make themselves seriously felt on Pueblo Indian culture. Although the date 1540 might be chosen, as the time when Coronado first came in contact with the Pueblo people, Spanish culture certainly did not much affect Pueblo Indians before about A.D. 1600. It is for this reason that 1600 has been chosen as the end of the Culminant period, or the last of the prehistoric periods in the Southwest. As will be seen from the following discussion, culture changes tend to fit these dates in most sections of the plateau with almost no overlapping.

With the abandonment of the eastern San Juan during or at the end of the great drought, movements were south into the Hopi and Zuñi areas and east into the Rio Grande and the intervening sections. This drift resulted in clusters of population, the densest portions forming several areas, three of which are sufficiently marked to warrant special discussion. These are the Hopi Washes north of the Little Colorado River, the extreme head-water portion of the Little Colorado River, and the Zuñi area. In the Rio Grande at this time many similar centers were forming. As permanent water appears to have been the primary determining factor in the choice of residence, other less well-known sections were also occupied. Many of the canyons draining the higher southern edge of the plateau had scat-

tered sites, as did the Verde River valley in its northern portion, an area
about Winslow, and the mountain section on both sides of the state line
between Arizona and New Mexico. There were even small Hopi sites scattered sparsely through the central San Juan, on its south side, and in the
vicinity of Navaho Mountain, and extending on into the succeeding period.

An examination of the accompanying map makes clear the nature of
this southern and eastward movement. At this time the total area of concentration was greatly reduced, as was also the total Pueblo population.
The attitude of southern migration led to the intermingling of both cul-

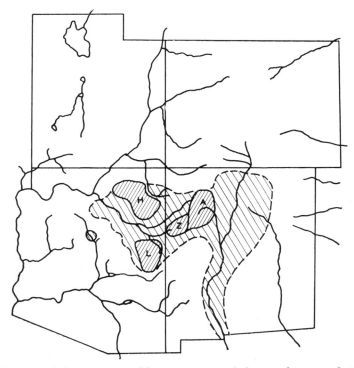

Fig. 187. Outline of the major Pueblo area occupied during this period. Four centers
of concentration are indicated. H is the Hopi area; Z is the Zuñi; L is the upper Little
Colorado; A is the Acoma. The eastern San Juan drainage was abandoned at this time,
and only scattered sites are found in the lower San Juan and the Navaho Mountain
area. Large sites are found widely scattered now. The southward extension formed one
portion of the Salado culture.

tures and people and gave rise to a modified Pueblo culture which is called
Salado. To the east, in the Rio Grande, the basis of culture had been laid
in early Basket Maker stages and was later modified by influences from
both the Chaco and Mesa Verde. Certainly by now it had taken on a distinctive cast of its own. As the Rio Grande is outside the area of this dis-

cussion, it will be confined to a consideration of the Hopi, upper Little Colorado, and Zuñi areas. Certain relationships of these areas may be pointed out now. Ceramically the Hopi area is distinct, and the upper Little Colorado, which might also be termed the western Zuñi area, and the Zuñi area are the closest. Architecturally, at least as concerns kiva types, the Hopi and upper Little Colorado are similar, and the Zuñi is distinct.

Beginning with the Hopi area for a detailed examination of pottery and house types, it is found that pottery fired in an oxidizing atmosphere had become the prevailing type. Some reduced black-on-white types were also being made, but these were certainly not predominant. This change in firing methods is of considerable importance and marks the serious acceptance of a series of yellow and orange pottery so characteristic of the Hopi Indians.

The ancestral form of the Hopi yellow series has been described in the preceding chapter. This was Jeddito Black-on-orange. From about 1300 on, the course sand temper found in this type was not included in the Hopi yellow types which became so common. This was probably the result of the adoption of a clay found in the Hopi Washes area which required no additional temper, as it already contained sufficient very fine sand grains.

A few of the most important decorated types which are characteristic of this period are Jeddito Black-on-yellow, Bidahochi Polychrome, Sikyatki Polychrome, and Awatobi Polychrome. Distinct but related types such as Jeddito Stippled and Jeddito Engraved should be mentioned also. All these form a closely related group, distinguishable largely on the basis of styles of decoration. The common utility pottery is also divisible into distinct types as based on the styles of ornamentation. The three most characteristic are Jeddito Plain, Jeddito Corrugated, and Jeddito Engraved.

Jeddito Black-on-yellow is obviously a direct outgrowth of the previous Jeddito Black-on-orange. The dates which have been assigned to it are about A.D. 1300 to 1625. It is therefore one of the best general diagnostics of the Culminant period, for it not only conforms to the span of dates suggested but also is relatively widespread in the plateau as a traded type. It was fired in an oxidizing atmosphere. The paste is hard, fine, yellow, and although it contains fine sand this sand is generally not visible to the eye. The surface is well smoothed by being compacted. The paints of the design are manganese, which fire black to brown. Designs are mostly geometric, but some life forms occur, such as that illustrated in the lower right-hand corner of the accompanying diagram. The forms are bowls, jars, and ladles, the most abundant of which are bowls. This is a strikingly beautiful, hard, golden yellow pottery, which enjoyed much popularity in the Southwest at this time.

Two related types, which occurred later in the period, must be considered next. The first of these, Jeddito Stippled, has been dated as from about A.D. 1350 to 1600. This type is exactly like Jeddito Black-on-yellow except that part of the design is produced by stippling or spattering black

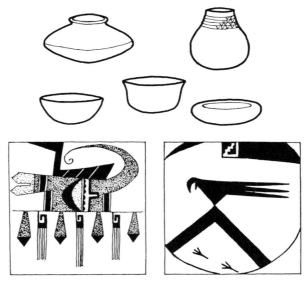

Fig. 188. Pottery forms and styles of design found in the Hopi area. There are both geometric and life designs. That at the lower left is a polychrome type in which the background is yellow, black is black, heavy shading red, and light shading lighter red. The lower right figure is found on Jeddito Black-on-yellow. The upper right form is Jeddito Corrugated.

paint onto the yellow background. The second type is Jeddito Engraved. It also is exactly like Jeddito Black-on-yellow but in portions of the black paint a pointed instrument was used to engrave fine lines through to the yellow background before firing. The dates assigned to this type are A.D. 1350 to 1600.

The second most important and certainly the most striking type is Sikyatki Polychrome. Dates assigned to it are A.D. 1375 to 1625. The paste and finish are the same as Jeddito Black-on-yellow, although in many specimens the surface has been even more carefully smoothed and polished. The difference in these two types lies in the nature of the decoration. Sikyatki Polychrome has a black and red decoration on the yellow background. Designs may be either purely geometric or life forms. This is an extraordinarily pleasing and beautiful pottery type, often occurring in such striking and unusual forms as the jar and bowl in the upper left and lower right corners of the illustration. It is the type which was revived, largely through the efforts of Nampeyo, in the early twentieth century, and has since become the most characteristic modern Hopi pottery.

Awatobi Polychrome, which existed from about A.D. 1400 to 1625, is a further elaboration of Sikyatki Polychrome. The paste, temper, finish, and color combinations are the same, but the two techniques of stippling and

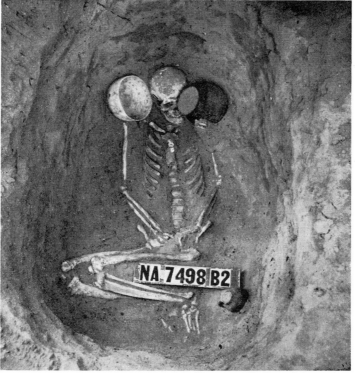

Museum of Northern Arizona photo

A typical semiflexed Pueblo burial. Pottery and other offerings are common in such burials.

engraving were both added to the design. The walls tend to be slightly thicker, and in at least some pots the execution is not quite so good as that of the previously described types. Vessel forms are all those pictured.

Probably one other type, Bidahochi Polychrome, should be mentioned. It has been tentatively dated as between about A.D. 1320 and 1400. The paste, temper, and forms are the same as Jeddito Black-on-yellow, and the designs are always geometric. One character alone marks it as distinctive. The black design is outlined with a fine white line. Forms are both bowls and jars, the jars being more common. This type does not appear ever to have been very abundant.

The common utility pottery, like that of the present Hopis, is made of a yellow or brown paste and has a coarse sand temper. Three types are known, Jeddito Plain, Jeddito Corrugated, and Jeddito Tooled. Jeddito Plain might be considered the basic type and the others variants of it. The paste is yellow through an orange to brown, as is the surface. The surface is not carefully rubbed and in fact is usually quite rough, simply being scraped down. Fire clouds and other blemishes are common. Forms are jars and flat platelike vessels. The upper right-hand vessel in the figure is of this type.

Forms of this entire group of pottery are distinctive. Flat bowls with incurved rims are radically new. Probably the most distinctive form is the jar, shown in the upper left of the illustration. It is very broad in relation to its height and has a marked shoulder or change of angle of the body. The flaring-rim bowl became very common late in the period, and the bowl with straight rim, as shown to the lower left, is most characteristic of earlier forms.

Sites of this period are of the general existing Hopi type as regards architecture. The earlier sites, or those which lack the later polychrome pottery types, have as a rule excellent masonry and generally cover about an acre of ground. Like the later sites they are formed in blocks of rooms grouped about one or more open plazas or patios. Later sites are much larger, covering as much as 10 or 12 acres, and often formed in rows of buildings with long plazas between. It is these larger sites which are so similar to modern Hopi villages.

Many well-known sites are excellent examples of this period. Oraibi, Shungopovi, Mishongnovi, Chucovi, Ash Heap Terrace, and Sikyatki are located on or about the Hopi mesas. In the Jeddito drainage are Awatobi, Kokopnyama, Chacpahu, Kawaiku, Little Ruins, Nesheptanga, and Hoyapi, in the Polacca Wash. Bidahochi, West Ruin, Homolovi Ruin 1 and 2, Cottonwood Ruin, and Chevalon are all excellent and well-known sites.

As has been suggested, the kivas of the Hopi country and the upper Little Colorado section are essentially alike. They are rectangular in form and average 10 to 12 feet wide and about 14 feet long. The distinguishing feature is a short banquette or bench at one end or side of the room which is set off in a niche about three feet deep. In some cases a narrower bench is found along the other sides of the structure. A ventilator usually extends under the platform to open onto the surface. There is often a deflector between the ventilator opening and the firepit. The floor is characteristically paved with stone flagging and often has loom holes in it, as shown in the illustration. Almost an invariable feature is the presence of one or more rectangular sandstone loom blocks.

In the upper Little Colorado section only one important new pottery type was produced at this time. During the preceding period Pinedale Polychrome had been evolved, and from this Fourmile Polychrome quickly developed. Vessel shapes are bowls and jars. The surface is covered with

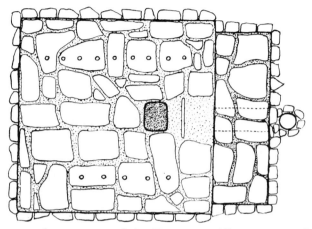

Fig. 189. Kiva type characteristic of the Hopi area. All are rectangular, have a short bench at one end, ventilator, deflector, and firepit. Some have narrow benches on the other sides. Many have loom holes in the flagstone floor.

a clear bright red slip on which designs are painted in black outlined in white. The black paint is a true glaze paint containing lead and copper; the white is chalky and not very tenacious. Both black and white are found on the insides and outsides of bowls. Designs are characteristically purely geometric. Jars have white painted necks, with simple repeated black elements, such as crosses, distributed about them. The remainder of the body of the jar is slipped red, and the black and white designs are confined between two horizontal black bands. The date has been tentatively assigned as between A.D. 1325 and 1400.

Present information indicates that no very long occupation of this area occurred. This appears to have been the latest pottery made here, although the closely related Zuñi types carried through to Historic times. As has already been indicated this type of pottery enjoyed an extension into the mountain section to the south.

Masonry seems to have been cruder than that of the preceding period, for unworked rocks were laid up with only a casual attempt at coursing, and walls were covered with a heavy plaster. The most typical sites of this area are Pinedale and Sholow ruins. The characteristic pueblo arrangement is a mass of room blocks surrounding a rectangular plaza. From present fragmentary evidence it would appear that they were seldom over one story in height.

In the eastern Zuñi area a great variety of pottery types was produced. They might be most broadly distinguished by the general use of glaze paints in several colors. Almost always the glaze pigment was poorly applied. Possibly because the pigment contained gritty masses, it was difficult to apply, and was often visibly piled on the surface of the pot. In many

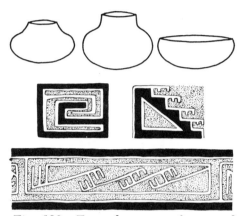

Fig. 190. Fourmile pottery forms and designs. Black is black, white is white, and shaded is red. The lower design is typical of the outsides of bowls; the upper ones are elements found on the insides.

Fig. 191. Forms and designs of Zuñi glaze types. Bowl forms from left to right are early to late, and are duplicated in the Rio Grande glazes. The upper band design is found on the outsides of bowls, the lower on the insides. Glaze paint tended to run and was not carefully applied.

specimens it appears to have run slightly. Had these people not been disturbed by the arrival of the Spaniards it is conceivable that they might have evolved the technique of slipping vessels with a glaze, and so have independently produced a waterproof pottery.

Pinnawa Black-on-red, Heshotauthla Polychrome, Pinnawa Polychrome, Adamana Polychrome, Wallace Polychrome, Hawikuh Glaze-on-white, and Arauca Polychrome are all types with glaze paints which may be ascribed to this general area and culture. Pinnawa Red-on-white is a nonglazed type which is also of this general series. The accompanying figure illustrates a variety of forms and shows two characteristic examples of interior and exterior decoration in glaze paint.

Masonry in this section is sandstone blocks set in adobe mortar, similar to that of the Hopi area. Houses are grouped into blocks about courts and they are of approximately the same size. Kivas, however, are markedly different, being most closely allied to the late Chaco Canyon and Mesa Verde circular structures. There are two types, both having narrow benches encircling the floor and both containing sunken rectangular chambers. Ventilators open to the outside and run under the floor to just in front of the firepit, instead of opening at the level of the floor at the side of the bench. This is a feature which was found in the Chaco type of circular kiva. The ventilator, deflector, firepit, and sipapu are all present, and usually form a straight line bisecting the structure. The two types differ only in that one has an expanding bench or platform on the side in which the ventilator is found. The smaller of the two averages only about 17 feet in diameter. The larger type is also circular but does not have the expanded bench. It varies from as little as 19 to as much as 55 feet in diameter. The masonry of both is well laid of coursed blocks.

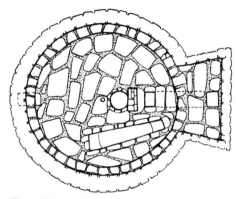

Fig. 192. The smaller of the circular Zuñi kiva types. These structures average about 17 feet in diameter. The distinguishing features are a platform on one side, a ventilator under the floor, a deflector, firepit, and sipapu. There is a narrow bench around the room.

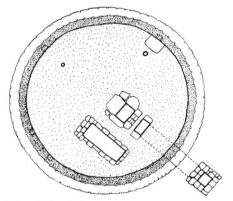

Fig. 193. The larger circular type of Zuñi kiva. This type lacks the platform but has all other features including a floor cist. The size varies from 19 to as much as 55 feet in diameter.

In general the culture of this period is very similar to that of the preceding. Certain techniques were elaborated and some crafts were more highly specialized, but all basic methods of manufacture were well known in earlier times.

Physically, individuals were light-framed and the skulls were deformed posteriorly. Burials vary locally between flexed and straight, and are found under the floors of rooms, in sealed rooms, or more commonly in definite burial plots. Both trash mounds and sand dunes were used as burial plots, and because the sand dunes were often not immediately within the confines of the village, such burials are rather difficult to locate.

Although a few trough-shaped metates are found the most common form seems to have been a flat grinding slab. These were mostly contained in mealing bins, as already described, but a few of them may have been used without bins. The most common mano was triangular in cross section. The axe in those sites which have been most carefully studied is the three-quarter-grooved type, although nowhere in the plateau do axes ever appear to have been very abundant. It is the feeling of the writer that the three-quarter-grooved axe was never made by any people living in the plateau, unless they were of Hohokam or Mogollon extraction. The very rare full-grooved axe was the most typical plateau type. Full-grooved mauls are very abundant and very well made. Hammerstones, of course, are very common. Mortars and pestles are rare but do occur in certain sections and sites, as do odd-shaped paint palettes.

So far as the writer is able to learn the predominant type of arrow point is the triangular form already described. The most widespread type appears to have a square base and lateral notches, although some with slightly concave bases and no notches occur.

One of the most characteristic features of this period is the presence of one or more loom blocks in almost every kiva excavated. Generally they are found in pairs. These blocks were used in the first stages of setting up a loom before it was raised from the horizontal to the vertical position. Poles were set into the shallow depressions in the blocks, and the other end was supported by niches in the side wall of the kiva. The warp threads were then wound between the two poles to space them properly before they were raised to the weaving position. These blocks, always made of sandstone, average about seven by eight or ten inches.

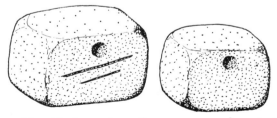

Fig. 194. Sandstone kiva blocks such as these are very characteristic of this period. They always contain one or more depressions for the reception of poles used in the first stages of setting up a loom. One or more are almost invariably found in kivas.

Surprisingly enough very little specific knowledge has been obtained concerning basketry. The yucca ring basket and coiled basketry must have been made, for these types have survived to the present. Sandals are also unknown to the literature, although matting has been commonly found.

Fabrics in the large open sites of the plateau were not preserved. However, from the salt mines in the Verde valley, a region just below the plateau, and in the mountain section some of the most exquisite fabric fragments from any period have been found. They are of interest because of their remarkably fine threads, the variation of color and weave shown, and their abundance. Probably the manufacture of cloth fabrics reached a very high level in the mountain section now, but it was also well developed in the plateau.

The use of the bow and arrow is definitely indicated by the presence of arrow points as well as by the fact that it was in use historically. The rabbit stick must also have been in use because of its survival. The stone knife was still common.

A box type of metate found in the Flagstaff area by the Museum of Northern Arizona. It is generally a relatively late type.

Although very little is known about foods in use at this time it is certain that corn was the staple. Animal bones which have been recovered from the various sites include a long list ranging from the larger mammals, such as mountain sheep, deer, elk, and antelope, to all the small rodents.

Ornaments show little change. The use of turquoise probably became more nearly universal. Wooden ear pendants, covered with turquoise mosaics, seem to have been very common.

Ceremonial artifacts are in no way different from those of the preceding Pueblo periods. Many of the kivas which have been excavated have murals painted on their walls, but this trait was also known from previous periods. Small stone animal figurines are not uncommon and are actually relatively abundant in the Rio Grande sites. Wooden staffs, wands, birds, and similar objects were probably made.

In sumary of this period only a few features are sufficiently characteristic to be worthy of special note. The end of the great drought marks the beginning date. The abandonment of the San Juan area, and the forming of three marked nuclei of populations with relatively uninhabited intervening areas, are an important feature. In the Hopi country pottery fired in an oxidizing atmosphere has yellow backgrounds and often polychrome designs. Large pueblos of several acres were characteristic. The plaza contained one or more rectangular kivas with a platform set in a niche at one end. In the upper Little Colorado area occupation was only for a short time during the early portion of this period. Houses were also in the form of pueblos, although smaller, and had essentially the same kind of kiva described for the Hopi area. Only one type of pottery, Fourmile Polychrome, is distinctive. This had a black glaze paint. In the Zuñi area, pueblos were also characteristic but the kiva type was round instead of rectangular. These kivas are of two types, those with enlarged platforms at one section of the bench, and those without. They are very strongly reminiscent of the Chaco Canyon and Mesa Verde types of earlier times. Material culture shows little variation from that of earlier periods and certainly did not make any radical departures from preceding types. Techniques in certain specialized industries became more involved, and local specializations took place. The period closed with the introduction of the first Spanish influence of any consequence, at about A.D. 1600.

THE RIO GRANDE

The same forces were at work on the Pueblo people of the Rio Grande as on those of the western pueblos in Arizona, so that there was a concentration in fewer but larger pueblos. There is some suggestion that actual migrations took place from the west to the east now, with the introduction of pottery types found in the west and other traits which may or may not be ascribed to such an influence. There was apparently, early in this period, a marked population increase in the Rio Grande valley, so that some of the largest pueblos ever found here, of hundreds of rooms, date shortly after A.D. 1300.

As may be seen from the accompanying map the northern part of the

Rio Grande valley was most thoroughly occupied, although there were scattered settlements down the valley as well. The Zuñi-Acoma area to the west was more or less distinct. In the northern part of the valley two divisions may be made, the biscuit ware pottery area to the north and what might be called the Pecos area farther south and east. In this area the glaze series of pottery types is distinctive, although both types were traded between these areas.

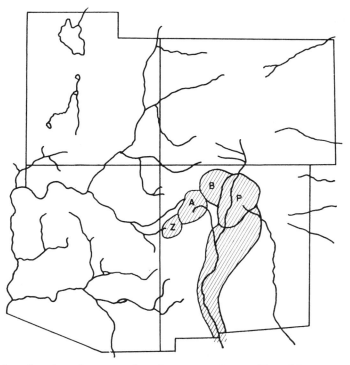

Fig. 195. Map showing the area of major occupation in New Mexico at this time. Z is the Zuñi area; A is the Acoma; B is the biscuit area of ceramics; P is the Pecos area of influence. Occupation in the rest of the valley was scattered.

Much regional differentiation is apparent, and it seems quite clear that the Historic cultural distinctions were being defined. Perhaps the most thoroughly reported site of this period is that of Pecos, on the eastern side of the Rio Grande pueblo area. Although Pecos Pueblo began its history much earlier it seems to have reached a peak of development during this period, and of course survived into the Historic period.

As has been suggested, toward the end of the preceding period Santa Fe Black-on-white had developed, and it was now being replaced by

Galisteo Black-on-white. In general the designs were still reminiscent of Mesa Verde pottery, and the paste and temper were the same, but there was commonly a crackled slip. In the north, masonry replaced some of the adobe construction, and some of the floors were slab-lined. Kivas seem to have been above ground and incorporated in the room blocks. In the area of Santa Fe adobe construction continued and kivas were also above ground and included in room blocks. They were oval or D-shaped, with ventilators on the east or south sides, adobe deflectors, and round clay-lined ash pits and firepits in the floor.

Burials were typically flexed in this early period. Other traits, or artifacts, do not seem to have been markedly different from the preceding types.

As this period developed certain rather marked alterations took place. Red-slipped and glaze-painted pottery, which was abundant at Zuñi apparently by about A.D. 1275, was widely traded to the northern Rio Grande area, where the local mat-painted black-on-whites were being made. These local types were such pottery as Wiyo, Pindi, and Poge Black-on-white. About A.D. 1325 to 1350 locally made glaze pottery with a red slip was made in the vicinity of Albuquerque, and begins the long glaze series found here.

It is particularly this sudden alteration in ceramic tradition which has suggested to some that an actual migration from the west took place now. Other traits have also been pointed to as possible introductions to the area, particularly rectangular kivas, which were certainly more typical in the Hopi area and to south of the Mogollon Rim in Arizona. It is quite likely that there were some migrants eastward, to continue the apparent movement of influences and perhaps people which was noted earlier, but it may be questioned that this was of any great magnitude.

As has just been mentioned, in the western part of New Mexico and eastern Arizona glaze paint designs were found on Zuñi and Little Colorado pottery, and this development was assuming a position of some importance. Actually the Zuñi-Acoma area ceramically was quite different than it was after the advent of Hawikuh. Hawikuh seems to have been intrusive in this area and to have brought in quite different ceramics, which changed the entire western New Mexico trend, and this in turn affected the development of the Rio Grande glazes.

As this influence spread eastward into the Rio Grande it was copied in the locally made types. They were derived in imitation of late St. Johns Glaze-polychrome, and seem to have had an early center south of Albuquerque. The styles of decoration were varied, but the paste contained crushed rock or sherd temper, and vessels had a red slip with dark glaze paint and a white mat paint. Sites which contain these types also had much more common black-on-white types.

From this developed the six well-known Rio Grande glaze types. The area occupied by these true Rio Grande glazes was that along the Rio Grande, and adjacent regions, from about San Marcial to Santa Fe. The series is essentially Pueblo IV in character, but existed into the Historic period. Styles of design and color combinations are so varied that it has been difficult to identify clear-cut types as based on multiple trait characters, and although a number of specific types have been named it was learned early that rim forms were the best diagnostic of the series. Reference to the accompanying diagram of rim forms and their sequential development will be helpful in understanding this series.

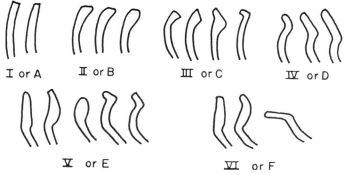

Fig. 196. Rim forms of the various types of glaze-painted pottery from the Rio Grande area. A to F were designations used by Mera, while I to VI were used by Kidder. Glazes started out well applied, but got progressively sloppier as time elapsed. The first are black-on-red, then black-on-yellow, then a variety of colors.

In a general way Glazes I and II and Biscuit A date in the 1300's; Biscuit B dates to the seventeenth century; Sankowi Black-on-cream extends up to the first of the eighteenth century; Glazes III and IV date from about A.D. 1400 to about 1500; and Glaze V dates in the vicinity of A.D. 1540. Glaze VI is more recent, and in fact dates sometime in the vicinity of A.D. 1600, when the glaze series began to degenerate, and this continued to about A.D. 1700, when the last of the glaze paints were used and after which time there was a return to mat paint. As has been mentioned, it is of interest that in the Southwest glazes were used only in designs, never as whole slips, and so did not serve to make the pottery impervious to water, as was the case in Europe and many other areas of the world.

As has been indicated, a number of other glaze types have been named from other areas. It was sometime between about A.D. 1325 and 1350 that the first red-slipped glaze-painted pottery was made near Albuquerque, and, as is indicated above, the other glaze types rapidly developed and spread into other more expanded areas. As this style of decoration became more widespread glazes were used on lighter backgrounds. Biscuit types A and B were made with a paste which suggested to Kidder the unfired biscuit stage of modern ceramics and hence the name. North of Santa Fe this biscuit pottery, with mat paint, prevailed.

General culinary pottery which was made during this period consisted of partly smeared-over or even mostly obliterated coiled pottery with the frequent addition of a micaceous wash. Less commonly such vessels had indented corrugations. This general style of the common cook pot was paralleled in the Hopi area, and similar things occurred also in the Zuñi-Acoma area.

Architecture consisted of fewer and very large pueblos, with masses of rooms arranged around courts or plazas. Both stone masonry and coursed adobe were used for walls, depending upon the specific area and the time. Kivas were circular and subterranean and had heavy deflectors which have been called altar deflectors. In the northern part of the area they were found in the plazas. All lacked pilasters and many of the other features found farther west.

In the area of Albuquerque both masonry and adobe were used in construction, but the kivas were rectangular and both subterranean and above ground. Some were incorporated in room blocks. They contained ventilators, ash pits and firepits, and deflectors. Some of those of coursed adobe had poles built into the walls for strengthening, and the roofs rested directly on the walls and were not supported by posts set into the floors or on pilasters.

Throughout the northern and central part of the Rio Grande all of the sites were large, permanent structures which must have housed a considerable population. There were even some great kivas, which are indicated by surface depressions, that were circular and had ventilators to the east and entrances on the west. Thus, as might be expected, at this time there is considerable variation found in architecture.

Most of the burials were flexed inhumations, though at Pecos late, perhaps in the Historic period, they were extended.

In general this was a period which might be characterized as a time of cultural florescence. All of the art and other forms continued into this period, and many of them were further elaborated on and developed. For this reason it has been termed the Culminant period. In the succeeding Historic period some of the native arts and crafts began to deteriorate, notably pottery, and others were modified after European types so that this is the last of the essentially unmodified stages.

Pipes now became much more ornately carved and finished, and animal figurines were common in stone. Bone tools were frequently carved. Pottery forms became much more varied and elaborated. Mural paintings were found, particularly in kivas, and are of varied subjects. Ornaments continued to be made in both shell and stone, and turquoise was commonly used.

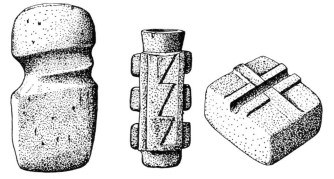

Fig. 197. Typical artifact types of this period in the Rio Grande valley as found at Pecos Pueblo by Kidder. Left is a spiral-grooved axe; center is an elaborately carved straight pipe; at the right is an arrow-shaft straightener. After Kidder.

In general summary it may be said that this period, particularly in its earliest part, was probably the one of highest cultural attainment and greatest population density in the Rio Grande. The same is true of the Hopi area, the upper Little Colorado, the upper Verde, the upper Salt, the Zuñi and White Mountain area, and south to Point of Pines in eastern

Fig. 198. Typical pottery forms of the Rio Grande area. The left column of bowls is early, the next later, the upper jar is a form typical of the Zuñi area to show how it differs from the Rio Grande shapes. The lower jars and the right column are Rio Grande forms.

Arizona. Even the Sierra Ancha region to the west and north of Point of Pines was occupied. After about. A.D. 1450 rather extensive areas were abandoned, particularly in central and eastern Arizona, and the Parajito Plateau and several other sections in New Mexico.

Ceramically two new trends developed: the emphasis on glaze paints used as designs on pottery, and the elaboration in varied forms. To the west in the Hopi country the emphasis placed on yellow pottery is equally marked. A distinctive trait of this time in the Rio Grande is the spiral-grooved axe, which was also found as an import at Awatovi in Arizona.

In general pueblos were large, and the walls were being built of coursed adobe, stone, and adobe and poles. Most of the adobe walls were set on stone bases in trenches. The rooms were generally relatively small, averaging perhaps nine or ten feet, and many of the inner partition walls were made of poles and adobe rather than something more substantial. Entrance was frequently from the roof, and ventilator openings were common. The lack of mealing bins suggests that many of these lower rooms may have been used primarily for storage, and the upper, now destroyed rooms served as living rooms. Kivas are commonly found in the plazas, and are most typically circular with plastered-over adobe walls. They contained ventilators, generally a sipapu, floor cists and wall niches, and many had murals painted on the walls. There were commonly loom holes in the floors and some were built above ground. There were also great kivas which were circular.

As has been repeatedly suggested, pottery showed a great variation in forms, including bowls, jars, eccentric forms of a number of kinds, and miniature pottery. Some of the sherds were worked into various forms, some even used as scrapers.

Pipes were tubular, or more rarely elbow. Both slab and basin metates were in use, and manos were rectangular, often with triangular sections. Stone bowls were made, and both grooved and notched axes, the spiral groove being quite distinctive. Mortars, abraders, and the already mentioned stone effigies of short-legged animals all are typical. Points are arrow points and are simple triangles, mostly with lateral notches.

Shell beads were made. Bone objects included tubes, flutes, awls, and rings. Burials were flexed or partly flexed, and were in trash areas or in rooms, or more rarely in other scattered spots.

By now the culture found in the several areas of New Mexico was indicative of that of modern groups, so that it is often possible to trace modern pueblos back into this period. Pottery has proven the best trait for such a genetic unraveling of the past. The several linguistic groupings which are found here today are indicated in these still prehistoric sites.

SINAGUA

By about A.D. 1300, or shortly thereafter, the Sinagua culture was expanding southward, and withdrawing from the northern part of the area it had formerly occupied. The sites in the vicinity of Flagstaff were either abandoned or being abandoned at this time, the last two well-known sites being Turkey Hill Pueblo and Elden Pueblo. Both of these were masonry pueblos constructed of boulder walls. There can be no doubt that they were copied after the pueblos which had been developed in the Anasazi area.

The sites which were occupied to the south were near the Mogollon Rim, generally on canyons draining southward to the desert, and they too were sizable pueblos, made of whatever available rocks were to be found. The Pollock site and Kinnikinnick Pueblo are good examples of Sinagua sites occupied shortly after A.D. 1300. Only the Pollock site has been extensively excavated, and it proved to be a moderately large pueblo in which there was a kiva of rather unusual details. It was rectangular, had a platform on the west with a wall on the edge of the platform, and an opening behind it to a room beyond. There was a bench on the north and south sides, and parts of the floor and the bench were covered with flat stone flagging. Two interior posts helped to support the roof, and there was a fire and ash pit on the central line. In general this type of kiva is reminiscent of the contemporary Pueblo kivas found to the north in the Hopi country.

Other well-known and somewhat later sites are Chaves Pass, to the east of Kinnikinnick and the Pollock site, and Tuzigoot, which is in the Verde valley near Clarkdale. Both of these sites are large pueblos as well, but only Tuzigoot has been excavated and reported. It is a mass of rooms lying along and adjacent to a ridge, and the walls are built of masonry. No definite kivas were found here, but one room which it was assumed might have been ceremonial was located in the middle of a block of other rooms.

The pottery which was made by people of Sinagua culture was the plain brown and reddish vessels which were used as the main culinary pottery. At the Pollock site there is evidence that some of the Pueblo pottery types were copied locally, for they are poor imitations of the northern examples. Most of the decorated pottery, however, was trade pottery, and came from the Pueblo culture to the north. At Tuzigoot a rather surprisingly high proportion of the pottery is derived directly from the Hopi country, and the same is apparently the case at Chaves Pass. These consist of the yellow and polychrome pottery types which were now popular with the Hopi Indians.

Certain other traits seem to have been characteristic of the waning stages of the Sinagua culture, though many may have been traded for to other peoples. Small animal figurines and even bird figurines were found at Tuzigoot. Jewelry still seems to have been an art of these people, and some good inlay pendants and other objects have been found. Beads were rather abundant at most of the sites dug, and even an engraved shell bracelet was found at Tuzigoot.

The feeling that the Sinagua was now in a state of cultural decline is more or less inescapable as one works with this period. The Pollock site showed actual deterioration in most of the artifacts which were produced there, and even the later masonry types were poorly executed and the burials had little in the way of grave offerings with them. The close relationship with the Pueblo culture, and the fact that a ceremony which has

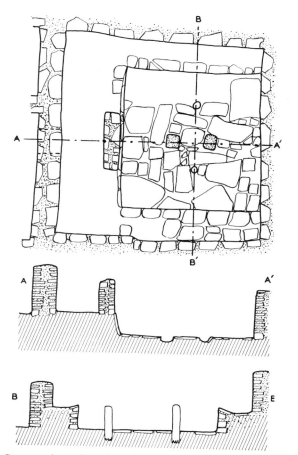

Fig. 199. A late Sinagua kiva found at the Pollock site southeast of Flagstaff, Arizona. It has a bench on two sides and a platform on the third. There is a masonry pillar on the edge of the platform and an opening through the wall behind it leading into one of the rooms of the pueblo. In general it is suggestive of Hopi kivas of this time.

been identified as Hopi was found in this culture, would suggest that at least some of these people moved northward and joined the Hopi Indians. Probably by about A.D. 1450 most of the large Sinagua sites had been abandoned. The question of the cause of this cultural deterioration has been raised, but so far little in the way of a concrete answer has been forthcoming. It is possible that the inroads of the more nomadic groups caused their way of life to collapse and made them move to the already larger and more secure Hopi pueblos for protection. A slight change in precipitation or

A late Sinagua burial found at the Pollock site. The large number of grave offerings are typical of such burials. The grave pit was covered with logs which, when they collapsed, disarrayed the bones and crushed many of the pots.

other environmental conditions may have made their chosen area of last occupation increasingly untenable. Whatever the reason they do not seem to have survived as a distinct entity later than well into this period.

SOUTHERN PUEBLO

It has already been suggested that in the upper Little Colorado River area Pueblo culture was well expanded and developed. Near Vernon, Arizona, Martin excavated Table Rock Pueblo, which is a mass of masonry rooms along a slight ridge. Associated with them are kivas which are rectangular, have a wide platform at one end, and a ventilator extending under the platform into the room. In general these are of the Hopi type of this same time. One of the kivas also had a slab-lined floor. The masonry of this pueblo is not outstanding, and it seems to have been one story high.

Ring-shaped slabs were used as hatchways. The pottery found was plain
brown and red, and Gila and Tonto Polychrome, Zuñi glaze types, Jeddito
Black-on-yellow, and Sityatki Polychrome. The Salado polychromes were
locally made of native paste. The site dates between about A.D. 1300 and
1450.

Courtesy of the Arizona State Museum

One of the rectangular kivas found at Point of Pines in Arizona. Note particularly the
ventilator, firepit, and end platform arrangement, and the stone flagging used in the
floor.

As one goes south from this area through the mountainous country near
the present boundary between Arizona and New Mexico, almost every
likely valley of any consequence had occupations of people, many of them
of this general period. The sites extend from the Little Colorado to the
Gila and Salt rivers, where they merge with what has been called the
Salado culture. Just where one cultural center or area of influence ends and

another may be said to begin is as yet somewhat uncertain. Throughout most of this area pottery with glaze paints became popular, though it was not universal in occurrence. There can be little question that it began in the north and spread south, and it remained most common in the north.

In the period just preceding that under discussion large pueblos are found in this southern area, varying from as few as perhaps 25 to as many as 100 rooms, arranged around a central court or plaza and containing at least one kiva. These kivas have a bench at one end, a ventilator shaft, frequently a deflector, and sometimes a sipapu. The pueblos are one story high and the walls are of coursed masonry. The pottery which is found at this time is Pinedale Black-on-white, Pinedale Polychrome, Pinedale Black-on-red, Pinto Black-on-red, and Pinto Polychrome.

Immediately following this, or during the time with which we are directly concerned, from about A.D. 1300 to 1400 or 1450, large pueblos flourished. Some of them in the mountain canyons were cliff dwellings, but others were in the open. They were built about plazas or courtyards and had the now familiar rectangular kiva, or kivas, in these courtyards. Typical pottery includes Fourmile Polychrome, Showlow Polychrome, Kinishba Polychrome, Kinishba Red, and as trade types Jeddito Black-on-yellow, Gila Polychrome, Gila Black-on-red, various early Zuñi glazes, and Cibique Polychrome. This is the Canyon Creek area and is essentially the complex with which we are already familiar farther north, though in differing proportions.

One of the better-known sites of this period is Gila Pueblo, which, though it started perhaps as early as A.D. 1200, was occupied to at least 1400. It consists of some 200 rooms and there is good evidence to assume that at least some were of two stories. Slabs were set at the foot of the walls just as they were at Point of Pines, to be mentioned later. Fireplaces were slab-lined fire boxes. There was the usual rectangular kiva which had a platform at one end. Ceramically this site looks more Salado than those farther north or west. Pottery types are Pinto Polychrome, Salado Redware, San Carlos Red-on-brown, and later Gila Polychrome, Gila Black-on-red, Fourmile Polychrome, and Pinedale Polychrome. There was also some Chihuahua Polychrome and Tucson Polychrome. Other traits are not particularly distinctive. There were stone hoes, some notched, a considerable array of jewelry of shell and stone, and some copper bells. Both extended burials and a few cremations were found.

Perhaps the most intensively and extensively explored small area is that of Point of Pines, where the University of Arizona has worked for several years. Here, in a wide and most congenial valley, were a number of sites spanning a considerable period of time, but terminating sometime between about A.D. 1400 and 1500. The part with which we are now concerned is the later occupation, that in the late fourteenth and fifteenth centuries. Massed pueblos were typical here as well, and were made of coursed masonry. Kivas were of the rectangular type already several times described.

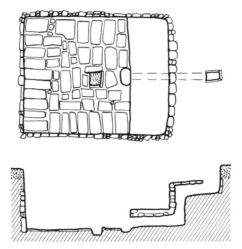

Fig. 200. Rectangular kiva found at Point of Pines in the Upper Gila area. Note the platform and the ventilator on the end, the firepit, and the flagstone floor.

with a bench at one end and a ventilator passage under it. Pottery types consist of a variety of corrugated styles, some of which are combinations of plain and indented corrugations, plain brown types, Kinishba Red, Fourmile Polychrome, Jeddito Black-on-yellow, the early Zuñi glazes, and Gila Polychrome.

A few words might be said about the native culinary pottery, which is quite distinctive. The paste of the various corrugated styles is rust to dark brown in color and usually carbon-streaked. Temper is abundant, of large angular fragments of tuff, and smaller amounts of sand and mica. The styles of corrugation range all of the way from neck corrugated to pattern indented and plain corrugated. The most common form is a large jar, though smaller jars do occur and occasionally bowls. The plain brown type has a brown paste usually carbon-streaked, and the temper is angular fragments of tuff and some mica which is often visible on the surface. This is fairly soft, crumbly pottery. The surface is usually rather well smoothed, and fire clouds are rare. Vessel shapes are bowls and jars, some quite large. Kinishba Red has a similar paste and temper, but there is a red slip on both the interiors and exteriors of bowls and the exteriors of jars. Forms are both bowls and jars. Another type, Kinishba Smudged, is the same but has a smudged interior. The Point of Pines variety of Fourmile Polychrome is like the typical Fourmile except that the paste is brown and the temper is angular tuff and some sand and mica. Bowls have a slip on both interiors and exteriors. The painted pigments are black and white, the black being dull, never glazed or lustrous. The designs differ slightly from typical Fourmile.

Fig. 201. Shapes of pottery types found at Point of Pines in the Upper Gila area. The left column is native corrugated types. The upper bowls in each of the central and right-hand columns are Kinishba Red. The two lower vessels in the central column are McDonald Corrugated. The bowl in the lower right-hand corner is Fourmile Polychrome. The two central vessels in the right-hand column are plain brown.

Other traits include metates open at both ends, or slab types, and rectangular manos, both one- and two-hand, some being triangular in cross section. Mortars and pestles were used. Axes are typically three-quarter-grooved, and there were also mauls. Arrow-shaft smoothers were relatively common. Arrow points seem to have been somewhat varied, being stemmed and diagonally and laterally notched. A flat stone slab which was painted probably to represent a mask was found. Bones were worked into awls, tubes, and even rings.

At Point of Pines it would seem that influences have been drawn from various cultures. The fact that there were some cremations might be interpreted as a Hohokam trait, and the rather good shell and bone work might be ascribed to the same source. The brown pottery, which seems to be basic to this area, might well be ascribed to the earlier Mogollon cultural influence. General architecture, with pueblos and rectangular kivas, and the painted pottery show definite connections to the north. For this reason it has been considered herein as a part of this southern extension of the Pueblo culture.

The question of whether or not it should be considered a part of the Salado culture is not answered. There is so much of an intergradation between all of the cultural manifestations in this part of the Southwest at this time that it will require the final reports on Point of Pines before it will be possible to make truly intelligent decisions concerning this point. The same sort of situation prevailed farther south, where the admixture of waning Hohokam and what may be a late Mogollon influence gave rise to something which, while distinctive, is not clear-cut, at least with the present status of our knowledge. In any event there was a strong development of culture, almost a local florescence, which took place in the mountain region along the line of the two states and from the headwaters of the Little Colorado on the north to the Gila and Salt on the south.

There was a general abandonment of this entire region sometime probably about A.D. 1450 to 1500. Just what caused a withdrawal from this apparently advantageous section is still in question. Agricultural practices had been developed to a high level, and the culture appears to have been healthy and the population flourishing. It is possible that the inroads of the Apaches caused their withdrawal to other areas, but if so there does not seem to have been any evidence of struggle or the widespread destruction of pueblos. Some were apparently abandoned hurriedly, for at Point of Pines rooms were found with what appear to be their equipment intact. Again much more extensive and intensive work must be done on this problem to give an adequate answer.

THE CULTURE IN THE DESERT

In the desert area of southeastern Arizona the native Hohokam culture was now coming under the strong influence of western Pueblo culture, possibly Salado, and was further being modified by Mexican influences. Mogollon cultural influences were so diluted that they are reflected only in certain ceramic and other tendencies that had their real stimulus much further back in time. The intergradation of culture in this area that was noted before continues, so that here is a more or less distinctive way of life.

In the Gila area proper the Civano phase, which dates from about A.D. 1300 to perhaps 1450, prevailed. Hohokam houses continued to be built and lived in, but pueblos, or compounds, of massive adobe and poured walls were also constructed. Probably the classic example of the typical compound is Compound A at Casa Grande. The walls are made of puddled adobe, without reinforcements, and reached as much as four stories high. The main house at Casa Grande has walls as much as four and a half feet thick at their base, which were constructed by building successive layers or blocks one above the other. Many of the rooms are very narrow and irregularly shaped. All of the main rooms are included in a high surrounding compound wall.

The peculiar shape of these smaller compound rooms, which would

National Park Service photo

The big house at Casa Grande in the Gila drainage originally stood some four stories tall and had walls of adobe more than four feet thick. It is located in Compound A in Casa Grande National Monument.

probably render them unfit as domiciles, has led to the suggestion that most of the actual houses of these people were of more perishable nature, and outside of the large adobe compounds. The already mentioned Hohokam-type houses may well have been the usual living structures. Some surface brush structures, somewhat suggesting Pima houses, have been found in this section, apparently associated with the compounds.

Pottery which is found in this area includes Gila Plain, Gila Red, Salt Plain, and Salt Red. Gila Polychrome is the most common Salado decorated type. Tonto Polychrome, if it is to be considered a definite type separate from Gila Polychrome, is late.

Most of the stone work is primarily utilitarian in nature. Metates seem to have been of the slab type. Shell is rare, in fact almost lacking, but turquoise inlay continues. Irrigation was apparently at its height, with one system of some 25 or 30 miles and one ditch about 15 miles long. It has been suggested that the expansion of ditches was necessary because of the accumulation of caliche in the soil, making old fields useless for agriculture and requiring progressive moving to new fields. Burials are mostly extended inhumations, with few cremations.

The question has of course been repeatedly raised as to just what happened to these Hohokam-Salado, or western Pueblo, people after about A.D. 1450, when the last direct evidence of their large settlements is found. Both Haury and Ezell have concluded that they eventually developed into the Historic Pima Indians in this general area, and there is certainly much to support such a view.

In the desert area, away from the major rivers, between about A.D. 1250 and 1400 the Sells phase flourished. There are a number of sites which may be assigned to this phase, actually more than 50, including Jackrabbit Village and Ash Hill. Houses were of wattle and daub construction and had rounded ends, with roof posts found near the corners. The doorway was to the east and there was a clay-lined firepit near the doorway. There were also massive adobe-walled enclosures which were filled in and formed raised platforms on top of which structures were built. It has been pointed out that similar pyramidal bases were found in Mexico. There were also large earth-walled enclosures with houses of the rounded-end type inside.

Pottery is Tanque Verde Red-on-brown, Sells Red, slipped and polished, Sells Plain, which is thick and nonmicaceous, and intrusives of Casa Grande Red-on-buff and rare Gila Polychrome. There is thus a distinguishable difference in the ceramic complex of these two areas, and this has led to the assumption that these people may have developed into the Papago of Historic times.

Other traits include top- and pulley-shaped spindle whorls, trough metates open at one or both ends, and loaf-shaped manos, the ends of which may overlap the metate slabs. Axes are of the three-quarter-grooved and both single- and double-bitted types. Mortars and pestles were in use, arrow-shaft polishers were common, there were stone hoes, palettes were still being made, and although there were rings, shell work was rare as compared to the elaborate shell work of earlier periods. Irrigation canals ran from the slopes of higher land to fields, and corn and beans were grown and were probably supplemented with some hunting. This is the desert branch of the Hohokam in Papagueria at this time as identified by Haury, or the Ootam of Di Peso.

On the San Pedro River northeast of Tucson, Di Peso has excavated the

Davis and Reeve ruins. Here there are house mounds and general pueblo or compound types of construction. Most interesting is the fact that rectangular kivas have been found at the Davis Ruin, which had a platform at one end and narrow benches on the two sides. This is so clearly a Pueblo trait that Pueblo influences cannot be doubted. Therefore Western Pueblo or Salado influences must be postulated, and according to Di Peso Mexican influences as well. The latter are such traits as the top-shaped spindle whorls and overlapping manos. At the Reeve Ruin pueblo-type architecture was also present, and such western Pueblo traits as arrow-shaft polishers and domesticated turkeys were found. Burials were also flexed. Thus in this region there is strong influence from the Pueblo culture to the north.

In the Tucson area proper there is the Tucson phase, which also dates from about A.D. 1300 to perhaps 1400 or 1450. A number of well-known sites belong to this phase, including University Ruin, the Hodges site, Tanque Verde, and Martinez Hill. The structures are of the pueblo type, of adobe, typically with posts incorporated in the walls. The adobe was laid up in courses some 20 centimeters thick and was plastered over. Occasionally some river stones were included in the walls. Compound walls surround these units.

The typical pottery is Tanque Verde Red-on-brown, with mica included in the paste, Tucson Polychrome, which has a red-slipped surface, and patterns in black outlined in a fugitive white. Designs are commonly polished over after being painted, a trait which harkens back to much earlier periods. Shapes are like Gila Polychrome bowls and jars. There are also Gila Polychrome, Gila Smudged, Sells Red, San Carlos Red, and San Carlos Red-on-brown. Thus another pottery complex may be identified in this immediate area, but the traded types tend to date these sites with others and to tie them together.

Metates are both of the trough and slab types and manos are rectangular. Mortars and pestles were used, as well as stone hoes and three-quarter-grooved axes. Both cremations and inhumations were practiced, and the physical type was broad-headed with occipital flattening.

Farther east, in the upper San Pedro valley south of Benson, Di Peso has excavated the Babocomari site. He has divided it into the earlier Huachuca phase and the later Babocomari phase. The date of the Babocomari phase is sometime about A.D. 1500 to 1650. The earlier phase had much trade pottery derived from the western Pueblo or Salado and the Hohokam, but the later phase lacked such trade pottery and had mostly Babocomari Polychrome and a native red pottery. From this it might be suggested that this site was receiving some influences from the Mexican sites in Chihuahua.

In architecture the earliest houses seem to have been larger and the later ones slightly smaller. The houses were early arranged around a circular court, but later were in block units with wing walls enclosing the blocks and forming closed plazas between the units. The pottery was made by the paddle and anvil process and consisted mostly of Babocomari Polychrome Plain and Smudged, the paste of which has mica temper. The polychrome was black and red on white. There were also plain brown types and some yellow to black examples with smudging.

Animal figurines were rare, but did occur, and modeled spindle whorls were of the Mexican type, though some disk types were used. The full-trough metate was not carefully shaped, and there were some slab types. The three-quarter-grooved axe was typical, as was the small-type arrow-shaft smoother, and there were hoes and fleshing knives. Few shells were used as ornaments, and there was no use of carving or overlay or inlay. The only domesticated animal seems to have been the dog. Cremation was almost wholly the method of disposal of the dead.

These people were primarily agriculturalists, though they also probably practiced some hunting and gathering. They planted in the river valleys, and possibly made some use of irrigation.

It has been suggested that the Apaches may have made some inroads on this culture and in this general area. If so they quite probably appeared sometime in the fifteenth century. What became of this culture historically is not clear, but Di Peso has suggested that it may be related to Papago.

In general summary two kinds of cultural environments may be identified: the river people, who are considered to be the typical Hohokam, and those who occupied the foothills and alluvial fans away from the immediate major river valleys. The latter have been identified by Haury as of the Papagueria, and by Di Peso as of the Ootam.

Culturally there is a continuation of the admixture and gradations which have been seen in the preceding period. The western Pueblo culture, or Salado, was exerting strong influence in the earlier part of this period, with the introduction of such traits as polychrome pottery, pueblos, kivas, inhumations, and perhaps the arrow-shaft polisher. This was mixed with or superimposed on the local Hohokam development. Certain strong Mogollon traits persisted, particularly in pottery, where the smoothing over of designs is an example, and the use of brown paste is perhaps also a trait. Di Peso has suggested that strong Mexican influences were now coming north, and there seems to be good evidence that such was the case. Thus this was not only an area of much mixture of culture but these cultures may be dissected and the fragments often defined as to source.

What became of these people still remains to be resolved. As has been seen in other areas, by about A.D. 1450 the record becomes much more evasive, and it is harder to trace developments. It was probable that the Athabascan- and Yuman-speaking groups were making themselves felt, and perhaps as a result of this the local cultures were forced either to move or to modify rather drastically their way of life. In general it does seem that prehistoric archaeological cultures did survive and develop into the cultures found historically in the general areas in which these people had been living.

SUMMARY

During the Culminant period, from A.D. 1300 to 1600, Pueblo culture was clearly the dominant culture of the Southwest. It reached a sort of florescence at this time, and although no markedly new traits were added, those which were already present were highly developed. The pueblo of massed rooms, often of two or even more stories, arranged in blocks around courtyards, or plazas, was the usual pattern. In these plazas kivas were found, and although the kivas varied in shape and even in whether they were underground or above ground, they generally had a ventilator, ash pit, and firepit arranged along a line. Not infrequently a sipapu was on this line as well.

In the west, with the ancestors of the Hopi Indians, the typical kiva was rectangular and had a platform at one end. It might or might not have benches on the sides. It was typically subterranean. This general type had a very wide distribution particularly to the south, where it is found associated with the western Pueblo culture. Rectangular kivas also are found in the Rio Grande area, along with circular ones, both of which might be either subterranean or surface. In the Zuñi area the typical kiva was circular, and the great circular kiva is found here, as well apparently as in some sites in the Rio Grande. Masonry was the usual type of wall construction to the west, but in the Rio Grande some walls were of coursed adobe, sometimes with poles incorporated in them. In the south adobe walls were also constructed, in some instances being poured, or packed into frames, to form heavy-walled structures.

Pottery in the Pueblo area is very characteristic and most diagnostic of the various cultural units. In the Hopi country the typical pottery was yellow, and although it might be polychrome or just black-on-yellow the paint was mat and not glazed. Culinary pottery was also yellow and contained coarse sand temper, sometimes being plain or more rarely corrugated in the neck area. In the Zuñi region the first of the glaze types had already been established with St. Johns Polychrome and Fourmile Polychrome. These were black and white on red or orange bases, and it was the black paint which was glazed. These were followed by a series of pottery types which had lighter-colored backgrounds and in which the glaze paint became very varied, including a sort of green color. Farther east, in the Rio Grande valley, mat-painted pottery began the period, but soon glazes which had been introduced apparently as trade were copied locally and the glaze series was developed. These vessels are most easily identified by rim forms, but individual types have been isolated and named. In some portions of the Rio Grande mat paints survived, and it was apparently from these latter that the Historic period mat paints were developed.

By this time it is quite obvious that the various cultures which were typical of the Historic period had been established. The Hopi culture was fixed much as it remains to the present. The Zuñi culture was well fixed in pattern, and the Acoma culture was similar to it. In the Rio Grande proper the various linguistic groups, and so cultural distinctions, had already been set, and the areas which they occupied at this time were not vastly different from those of today.

This northern cultural development clearly spilled over to the south and greatly influenced the history of the cultures in this area. Just what is western Pueblo and what might be called Salado is not clear. If Salado is defined only as the Gila Polychrome series, then other developments took place in the mountain area near the Gila and Salt. Point of Pines is such a case, where strong northern Pueblo influences are apparent. But even in this area there are also some suggestions of influences from other areas, particularly the Hohokam and to a lesser extent the Mogollon.

In the desert proper the vigor of Hohokam culture was definitely waning, and although some traits still persisted, such as house types and some pottery types, the Salado or western Pueblo culture was making strong inroads on it, and the way of life in this area was being vastly modified. Here it is possible to distinguish two patterns, that of the river valleys and that of the areas away from the rivers. The latter Di Peso has designated as Ootam. As these cultures are traced into later and later time they show more and more intergrading and intermingling. Mexican traits are seen in some of the later manifestations, and it is quite possible that there was some interaction culturally between this part of the Southwest and Casas Grandes in Chihuahua. Recently derived tree-ring dates from the Casas Grandes area show that Casas Grandes was occupied from the 800's to probably as late as at least A.D. 1400.

After about A.D. 1400, or at the latest 1450, many of these cultures began to disintegrate, or fade. Such was certainly the case of the Sinagua in northern Arizona. Here the same architectural features of the pueblo and the rectangular kiva are found, but ceramically and in many other traits the fine quality of earlier work was lacking. In any event, by about this same period it seems that this culture too had withdrawn or disappeared. It has been suggested that at least some of the Sinagua people must have joined the Hopi to the north.

The consolidation of the Pueblo culture into larger and fewer sites and the abandonment of the more southern areas have been ascribed by many to the influx of the Athabascans. Almost certainly they began their occupation of the Southwest before this period, but by now they may well have increased in numbers to the point where they became a very real menace to the more sedentary peoples. The Athabascan way of life was a nomadic or at least seminomadic existence predicated on hunting and gathering. The Athabascans were warriors, and in the later Historic period definitely preyed on the pueblos, so it may be assumed that they also did in this earlier period.

Farther to the west in the Patayan area the later history of the cultures is less well understood. In the north Schwartz has indicated that the Cohonina probably developed into the Havasupai. Whether this be true or not it is quite likely that the northern Patayan did develop into the Pai. In the southern part of the Colorado River valley Rogers has indicated his belief that the prehistoric cultures continued on into the Yuman-speaking tribes of this area today.

In general at this period it would then appear that much of the Historic pattern was already set in the greater part of the Southwest. By the middle of the period, or about A.D. 1400 to 1450, large areas were seemingly abandoned by the prehistoric peoples, many of whom had had roots far back into the past. There was at the same time a sort of general leveling out, or sharing, of many of the cultural traits of the Pueblo area, and the development of distinctive traits which characterized each of the subareas. This was also a time of what seems to have been considerable movement of people, or at least sudden population eruptions in certain areas. The New Mexico pueblos were greatly expanded. The people who had lived in the mountain area went somewhere, for there is little to suggest that they were killed off.

At this time certain minor innovations took place. In the Hopi culture the first use was made of coal as a fuel, and pottery was fired with it. This was probably as early as coal was used in western Europe, and it may actually have been even slightly earlier in the Southwest. In the Gila valley, early in this period, the most extensive irrigation systems were developed and used, but they seem to have been doomed because of the accumulation of caliche deposits in the soil. Among the Hopi Indians the men were weaving some very fine fabrics in cotton, and this art carried over to the present, where they continue to weave many of the ceremonial objects used by other Pueblo groups, notably the Zuñi. Thus this was in many ways the period of culmination of long cultural developments.

Sources and Additional References

Adams, William Y. and Nettie K. An Inventory of Prehistoric Sites on the Lower San Juan River, Utah, *Bulletin 31,* 1959, Museum of Northern Arizona, Flagstaff. (Indication of the occasional invasion of this area by later Hopis.)

Bartlett, Katharine. Prehistoric Pueblo Foods, *Museum Notes,* Vol. 4, No. 4, 1931, Museum of Northern Arizona, Flagstaff. (Data on and lists of Pueblo foods.)

Caywood, Louis R., and Edward H. Spicer. Tuzigoot, the Excavation and Repair of a Ruin on the Verde River Near Clarkdale, Arizona, Field Division of Education, National Park Service, Berkeley, California, 1935. (As indicated by title. This is a very late Sinagua site.)

Colton, Harold S. The Sinagua. A Summary of the Archaeology of the Region of Flagstaff, Arizona, *Bulletin 22,* 1946, Museum of Northern Arizona, Flagstaff. (Best statement of the history of the Sinagua to date.)

Colton, Harold S., and Lyndon L. Hargrave. * Handbook of Northern Arizona Pottery Wares, *Bulletin 11,* 1937, Museum of Northern Arizona, Flagstaff. (Detailed descriptions of pottery types mentioned in this chapter. The Zuñi glaze types mentioned but not discussed are reported in detail.)

Di Peso, Charles C. The Babocomari Village Site on the Babocomari River, Southeastern Arizona, No. 5, 1951, the Amerind Foundation, Inc., Dragoon, Arizona. (A village in this area which begins about A.D. 1250 to 1300 and extends into the Historic period.)

————. The Reeve Ruin of Southeastern Arizona, No. 8, 1958, the Amerind Foundation, Inc., Dragoon, Arizona. (This site dates in the vicinity of about A.D. 1300, and shows mixed culture.)

Dittert, Alfred E., Jr., James J. Hester, and Frank W. Eddy. An Archaeological Survey of the Navaho Reservoir District, Northwestern New Mexico, *Monograph 23,* 1961, Museum of New Mexico, Santa Fe. (Mentions the Navaho invasion of this area.)

Ezell, Paul H. Is There a Hohokam-Pima Culture Continuum? *American Antiquity,* Vol. 29, No. 1, 1963, Society for American Archaeology, Salt Lake City, Utah. (As indicated by title.)

Gladwin, Winifred and H. S. * Some Southwestern Pottery Types, Series II, *Medallion Paper 10,* 1931, Gila Pueblo, Globe, Arizona. (Detailed descriptions of Little Colorado pottery types discussed here.)

Hack, John T. The Changing Physical Environment of the Hopi Indians of Arizona, *Papers of the Peabody Museum of American Archaeology and Ethnology,* Vol. 35, No. 1, 1942, Harvard University, Cambridge, Massachusetts. (Best discussion of the environment of the Hopi country.)

Haury, Emil W. The Excavation of Los Muertos and Neighboring Ruins in the Salt River Valley, Southern Arizona, *Papers of the Peabody Museum of American Archaeology and Ethnology,* Vol. 24, No. 1, 1945, Harvard University, Cambridge, Massachusetts. (Excellent report of the culture found here, including many of the pottery types discussed.)

Haury, Emil W., and Lyndon L. Hargrave. * Recently Dated Pueblo Ruins in Arizona, *Smithsonian Miscellaneous Collections,* Vol. 82, No. 11, 1931, Washington, D.C. (Detailed descriptions of excavated sites in the Hopi and upper Little Colorado areas.)

Hodge, F. W. * Circular Kivas Near Hawikuh, New Mexico, *Contributions,* Vol. 7, No. 1, 1923, Museum of the American Indian, Heye Foundation, New York City. (Site excavated in the Zuñi area, and pottery series secured.)

Hough, Walter. Archaeological Field Work in Northeastern Arizona. The Museum Gates Expedition of 1901, Smithsonian Institution, Washington, D.C., 1903. (Much of the material described herein deals with this period.)

Kidder, Alfred Vincent. An Introduction to the Study of Southwestern Archaeology, Phillips Academy, Andover, Massachusetts, 1924. (Good discussion of Pueblo IV, and a discussion of the Historic period in New Mexico.)

————. * The Artifacts of Pecos, Phillips Academy, Andover, Massachusetts, 1932. (Very fine report on the artifacts of this period found at Pecos Pueblo.)

————. Pecos, New Mexico: Archaeological Notes, *Papers of the Peabody Foundation,* Vol. 5, 1958, Phillips Academy, Andover, Massachusetts. (Additional details on Pecos Pueblo, particularly kivas.)

Kidder, Alfred Vincent, and Charles Avery Amsden. The Pottery of Pecos, Vol. I, 1931, Phillips Academy, Andover, Massachusetts. (As indicated by title.)

Martin, Paul S., and John B. Rinaldo. Table Rock Pueblo, Arizona, *Fieldiana: Anthropology,* Vol. 51, No. 2, 1960, Chicago Natural History Museum. (A sizable pueblo with rectangular kivas which dates between about A.D. 1300 and 1450.)

Martin, Paul S., and Elizabeth S. Willis. Anasazi Painted Pottery in Field Museum of Natural History, *Anthropology Memoir 5,* 1940, Field Museum of Natural History, Chicago. (Some of the Rio Grande types are illustrated herein.)

Morris, Earl H. An Aboriginal Salt Mine at Camp Verde, Arizona, *Anthropological Papers,* Vol. 30, Part III, 1928, American Museum of Natural History, New York City. (Includes the fine fabrics found at this site.)

Reed, Erik K. The Distinctive Features and Distribution of the San Juan Anasazi Culture, *Southwestern Journal of Anthropology,* Vol. 2, No. 3, 1946, University of New Mexico Press, Albuquerque. (As indicated by title. The eastern expansion of this culture is indicated.)

————. East-Central Arizona Archaeology in Relation to the Western Pueblos, *Southwestern Journal of Anthropology,* Vol. 6, No. 2, 1950, University of New Mexico Press, Albuquerque. (An excellent brief comparison of these two archaeological areas.)

Roberts, Frank H. H., Jr. * The Village of the Great Kivas on the Zuni Reservation, New Mexico, *Bulletin 111,* 1932, Bureau of American Ethnology, Washington, D.C. (Description of a site excavated in the Zuñi area.)

Shepard, Anna O. Rio Grande Glaze Paint Ware. Contributions to American Anthropology and History, No. 39, *Carnegie Institution Publication 528*, 1942,
Washington, D.C. (The glaze-painted pottery analyzed.)

Smiley, Terah L. Four Late Prehistoric Kivas at Point of Pines, Arizona, *University of Arizona Social Science Bulletin 21*, 1952, Tucson. (As indicated by title.)

Smith, Watson. Kiva Mural Decorations at Awatovi and Kawaika-a; with a Survey
of Other Wall Paintings in the Pueblo Southwest, *Papers of the Peabody Museum of American Archaeology and Ethnology*, Vol. 37, 1952, Harvard University, Cambridge, Massachusetts. (As indicated by title.)

Stubbs, Stanley A., and W. S. Stallings, Jr. * The Excavation of Pindi Pueblo,
New Mexico, *Monographs of the School of American Research and the Laboratory of Anthropology*, No. 18, 1953, Santa Fe, New Mexico. (This site dates in
the late thirteenth and early fourteenth centuries.)

Toulouse, Joseph H., Jr., and Robert L. Stephenson. Excavations at Pueblo Prado,
Papers in Anthropology 2, 1960, Museum of New Mexico, Santa Fe. (Report
on a site dating between about A.D. 1200 and 1630.)

Wendorf, Fred. A Report on the Excavation of a Small Ruin East of Point of
Pines, East Central Arizona, *University of Arizona Social Science Bulletin 19*,
1950, Tucson. (Report on a site in this area dating from about A.D. 1350 to 1450.)

————. A Reconstruction of Northern Rio Grande Prehistory, *American Anthropologist*, Vol. 56, No. 2, Part 1, 1954, Menasha, Wisconsin. (Excellent brief
review of the northern Rio Grande.)

Woodbury, Richard B. Prehistoric Stone Implements of Northeastern Arizona,
Papers of the Peabody Museum of American Archaeology and Ethnology,
Vol. 34, 1954, Harvard University, Cambridge, Massachusetts. (Excellent cat-
alogue and summary of stone artifacts of this area.)

————. Prehistoric Agriculture at Point of Pines, Arizona, *Memoirs of the Society
for American Archaeology*, No. 17, 1961, Salt Lake City, Utah. (Discussion of
field plots, terraces, and other agricultural practices.)

XV

Historic Period

Although it is not the specific problem of this book to consider the Historic period, or that from A.D. 1600 on to the present, a few comments might be made to help orient the reader in regard to Historic tribes. The only areas occupied by ancient tribes in the plateau at this time were the Hopi and Zuñi sections, and the many pueblos of the northern Rio Grande were of course flourishing. Sites became larger and larger as the menace of the Navahos and Spanish raiders increased, and late in the period most of the sites in the open in the Hopi and Zuñi areas moved to the tops of mesas as a defense measure. Here they have remained ever since, although in the last few years there has been an increasing tendency among individuals to move down onto the flats again.

Ceramics among the Hopis deteriorated steadily from the beautiful Sikyatki and Awatovi polychromes, until the revival of the Sikyatki type by Nampeyo near the end of the period. The flaring-rim bowl became a common form, and styles of design similar to those in use by the Zuñi today were introduced. European forms were copied from Spanish vessels, but apparently they never became popular, except for water bottles and canteens. Utility types with coarse sand temper continued to be made in great quantities.

In the Rio Grande, glaze paint types IV, V, and VI were being made, although there was some late black-on-white pottery made locally as well. There were also some very striking new kinds of pottery such as Sankawi Black-on-cream, and beautifully made and finished polished red and polished black. European forms were occasionally copied here as well. Some

Majolica pottery is found in these Historic sites as well as the native-made types.

In the Hopi country the rectangular kiva with an end platform is still typical. In the Rio Grande, kivas are round, with upright slabs placed

Taos Pueblo is the most northeastern present-day pueblo. It is located in the northern part of the Rio Grande drainage and shows a few characters of plains and Spanish cultures. Note particularly the ovens.

around the base of the walls. They have a ventilator, deflector, and firepit in a line, and some have a sipapu. They are mostly subterranean, and are located in the plazas. Masonry pueblos in all areas are of one or two or more stories high, and many of the living rooms have built-in benches along one or more walls. There are commonly many storage bins, and frequently special storage rooms. Doorways lead directly into the plazas, and some of the rooms have stone flagging on the floors.

Certain Spanish influences, such as stairways, ovens, and chimneys, are apparent, but the general plan of the pueblo has remained essentially unchanged for centuries. It has mostly been since about A.D. 1900 that any significant alterations have been effected. Certain Hopi groups have split from the older conservative elements and established more European-style villages. Some still more radical individuals have built homes in the flats away from the mesas where agriculture is more profitable and more accessible.

Artifacts of the older types which have survived are slab metates and single- or double-hand manos. Early in the period, before metal objects were generally available, stone mauls and grooved axes were made, and they had stemmed and stemless points which were relatively poorly chipped, as well as snub-nosed scrapers. Objects made of shell were relatively rare.

Weaving among the Hopi remains one of the major arts of the men, although the Spanish introduction of wool instead of cotton caused a change in those articles not of a ceremonial nature. Metal working was also introduced either by the Spanish or Navahos, and such objects as rings, bracelets, earrings, bow guards, and similar ornaments are now made. Sheep herding has offered a new vocation to many individuals, as well as a permanent supply of meat, since sheep were introduced by the Spaniards.

In all basic respects the Pueblo Indians of today are living essentially the same life they were living 400 years ago, for they are perhaps the most culturally conservative Indians in this country. Their houses are the same, many of the objects of everyday use are the same, and their general economy is little changed. Only certain objects, such as those made of metal, are radically different.

It has been pointed out that during all of this period there was a pan-Pueblo way of life practiced by all of these Pueblo Indians. Certainly there was more that was shared than was specifically different among them, at least as regards material traits. Individual differences, as has already been pointed out, were minor, such as details of kivas or pottery type variations. In general they were peaceful individuals, and most of them prided themselves on this peaceful nature.

On the accompanying map a number of the Historic pueblos have been indicated by small triangles. By no means all of them are shown, but most of those which are still occupied are indicated. The general area of occupation of Pueblo culture in northern Arizona and New Mexico can easily be seen.

Surrounding the Hopi Indians in northern Arizona are the Navahos. These Athabascan-speaking people are very closely related to the Apaches, who occupy the more mountainous region to the south. Both were hunting, gathering, warlike groups early in their history, and they raided the more peaceful people with whom they came in contact. The polygamous Navahos raided the pueblos not only for food and other loot but for wives as well, and it is probable that the fine Navaho weaving, which is done by the women, was introduced as a result of this mixture. The Navahos and Apaches both still build less permanent homes than do the Puebloans, and in fact little usually remains to mark the early site of either a Navaho hogan or Apache gowa. Sheep were introduced to the Navaho and the women

and children own and herd them. The Apaches have become more cattlemen than sheepmen, and have recently developed some rather respectable
herds on their reservation lands.

Repeated mention has been made of the possible early inroads of nomadic warlike tribes in the Southwest. The Navahos were one of these

Fig. 202. The distribution of sites and tribes during the Historic period. The triangles
indicate the many pueblos which were occupied now, but not all have been included in
this map. The other tribal names indicate the general area in which each is found. The
Yuman-speaking group, for instance, includes several tribes, as does the Pai group.

tribes so it might be profitable to look briefly at their history as it is presently understood. The Navaho probably entered what is now New Mexico
about A.D. 1550 and settled first in the upper drainages of the San Juan
River. Earliest contacts with Pueblo groups were sporadic, but some Pueblo
traits, especially pottery, were accepted. After the reconquest that followed
the Pueblo Revolt in 1680, several Pueblo groups moved into the Gobernador district to escape the Spanish. There the Navahos and the Pueblo
people lived together, exchanging ideas and material cultural items. The
Navahos then took up many Pueblo traits, such as weaving, sand painting,
ceremonial forms, and items of social organization that are associated with

the Navaho today. The Navaho population, however, was not stable, and groups began to move south and west until all had left the Gobernador by A.D. 1775. It was not until slightly later that they occupied all of the area where they are now found.

Modern Navaho hogan. It is such houses as these which when in ruin and unaccompanied by European articles would somewhat suggest Basket Maker sites.

In the area to the north of the Grand Canyon the Ute and Paiute are found. They too have lived a more or less wandering, gathering, collecting, and hunting existence. Their history probably goes well back to at least the general Basket Maker type of existence, and perhaps may be traced further to the early Desert culture. They are the makers of good basketry, but are not noted for much else in the way of artifacts.

South of the Grand Canyon are the Pai: the Havasupai, the Walapai, and the Yavapai. It will be recalled that it has been suggested that these people are quite probably the descendants of the Cohonina, and so may have some antiquity. They were agriculturalists, but also extensively hunted and gathered, and produced some very good basketry. It is the Havasupai who now occupy the Havasu Canyon, a branch of the Grand Canyon, where they spend at least a part of their time. Traits which tend to link them with the past are little regard for personal jewelry, the lack of formalized ceremonials, the use of the sweat house, the manufacture of some simple pottery, and the construction of varied and casual housing.

In the lower part of the Colorado River various of the Yuman-speaking

groups are now found. It will be recalled that Rogers has suggested they
are descendants in this area of the local prehistoric populations. Their economy is largely agriculturally oriented and is based on the river environment. They, too, do not build substantial homes, and apparently not long

Walpi is the easternmost of the Hopi pueblos, and is a good example of present-day
Hopi villages. The tops of these mesas were easily defendable.

in the past maintained a somewhat mobile way of life in a restricted area.

Farther east the Pima and Papago Indians are found in the Gila, Salt,
and Santa Cruz valleys. Pima and Papago houses are not greatly different
from later Hohokam houses, being built of brush and poles and oval or
rounded at the ends. The widespread use of the shade is also a trait of
these people. Their pottery is red or black-on-red, and is suggestive of the
red pottery found here in prehistoric times, though not so well made. Their
economy is based on agriculture. It has been suggested that the Pima
Indians are descendants of the Hohokam proper, while the Papago and
perhaps other related groups are the descendants of the occupants of the
Papagueria or are the modern Ootam of Di Peso. Most recently Yaqui
Indians have been moving northward into southern Arizona from northern
Mexico.

Within the last very few years, particularly since the last war, many of
the Southwestern Indians have found employment away from their reser-
vations. The Navaho Indians, for instance, have taken jobs working on

railroads, where they have proved to be good workers. As a result many of them have been able to buy such modern luxuries as pickup trucks or passenger cars. They have also been increasingly thrown with individuals of European culture, so that their older, more conservative ways are being rather rapidly broken down or modified. This is true to more or less extent with all groups. The new highways through the Navaho and Hopi country are bringing increased numbers of tourists to them, with the inevitable result that their older cultural pattern is being further modified. Probably before too long it will be so altered that it will hardly be recognizable. Then the old way of life of the Southwestern Indian will be gone for ever.

Sources and Additional References

Jennings, Jesse D. The American Southwest: A Problem in Cultural Isolation, in Seminars in Archaeology: 1955, *American Antiquity*, Vol. 32, No. 2, Part 2, 1955, Society for American Archaeology, Salt Lake City, Utah. (See particularly the discussion of the unity of the Pueblo culture.)

Montgomery, Ross Gordon, Watson Smith, and J. O. Brew. Franciscan Awatovi, *Papers of the Peabody Museum of American Archaeology and Ethnology*, Vol. 36, 1949, Harvard University, Cambridge, Massachusetts. (Report on a Historic Awatovi pueblo in Arizona.)

Schroeder, Albert H. Navajo and Apache Relationships West of the Rio Grande, *El Palacio*, Vol. 70, No. 3, 1963, Museum of New Mexico, Sante Fe. (As indicated by title.)

XVI

Summary of Cultures

In the preceding chapters cultures have been compared at given times according to the periods set up early in this book. In such a presentation it is possible to see what was happening at various periods in the Southwest and to trace cultural developments at specific times. By so doing it becomes immediately apparent where and when innovations took place, but it does not make the tracing of the development of individual cultures through time a simple matter.

For this reason the present chapter has been included, for although a similar thing was done in the Introduction it is now possible to trace individual cultures, and culture traits, in far more detail. This makes it possible to understand more readily the evolutionary processes affecting each cultural or ethnic group.

From what has already been said, it has become apparent that not all of the problems of Southwestern prehistory have been answered. In fact as certain answers are achieved additional questions are automatically raised, so that there is a continued progression to a fuller understanding of just what took place. Many such new problems are raised in what might be considered core areas, or well-known cultures, but a considerable number concern cultures or areas which are not yet well understood.

Although the archaeological Southwest has perhaps been more intensively and extensively explored than any other comparable area, there are still many sections where only the most general work has been undertaken. The accompanying map has been prepared to give some idea, in the most general way, as to where the bulk of the work has been done and where relatively little has been accomplished.

Almost all of the Southwest has been more or less surveyed, but many of these surveys have, for one reason or another, been somewhat sketchy. Certainly much more intensive and extensive surveys are indicated for much of Utah, western Arizona, and eastern and southern New Mexico. Such work should be supplemented with at least a minimum of excavation, to indicate chronology and associated traits. The areas which have

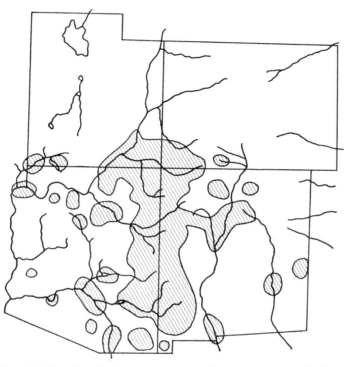

Fig. 203. The shaded or hatched areas represent those sections in which serious archae-ological work has been done, usually rather extensive or intensive excavation. The blank portions have been surveyed, generally on the surface alone, and do not include such intensive excavation, with a few very localized exceptions.

been most intensively explored are those which are shaded by hatching on the map. Here intensive survey has been accompanied by some excavation or even extensive excavation, so that much of the prehistory of these areas is known. However, in these sections of major work many problems still remain to be settled. Thus, although the prehistoric Southwest is well known its potential has by no means been exhausted, and it will no doubt continue to be the most productive area for the reconstruction of pre-history in the United States.

When this obvious lack of complete geographic and cultural evidence is borne in mind it is apparent that many of the bits of evidence presented herein are far from complete. For these reasons the maps which have been prepared and presented must be considered more general indications of areas occupied than exact boundaries between cultures at specific times. Also, as further data is amassed concerning presently well-known cultures, quite probably we will modify our ideas concerning them. This will most likely prove to be the case when it comes to comparisons between cultures. With all of these limitations in mind it is then feasible to turn to a characterization of the various streams of culture in the Southwest.

The earliest well-documented evidences of human occupation seem to date about 13,000 years ago. Carbon 14 dates have been secured from a number of sites which fall into about this period. Several of these sites are kill sites, where now extinct types of animals have been slain, but one or two are caves which were presumably occupied as temporary or sporadic shelters. Artifact complexes are quite limited, suggesting a simple way of life, but not necessarily proving that such was the case.

It now appears that at about this time there were two general, but basically different, ways of life practiced in the Southwest. One was primarily a hunting existence, which was no doubt augmented by some collecting and gathering but which seems to have been oriented largely to the securing of big-game animals, the mammoth and even bison. The second was just the reverse in emphasis, a largely gathering and collecting existence which was somewhat supplemented by hunting, perhaps of smaller animals.

Those individuals who were primarily hunters extended over a large area of the high plains and even the eastern part of the country, and westward to about the Arizona–New Mexico border. The gathering culture was more typical of the west, spreading throughout the northwest and south, even into northern Mexico, and east to a little beyond the state line just referred to.

Turning first to the people who were essentially hunters, the earliest period has been termed the Ancient stage. What may be the oldest type of artifact which may be associated with this stage is the Sandia type of point. Most of the Sandia points lack any fluting, but incipient fluting has been noted on a few that are of the square- or concave-base type. The Clovis points are typically fluted from the base partway up the blade. Both of these types are associated with large, now extinct mammals. With the Clovis types are found simple flake scrapers and also pointed bone tools which may be points as well.

On the terraces along the Little Colorado River certain very simple artifacts have been found. These may be of any age, but there is much to suggest they may also be of some antiquity. Unfortunately they have been found only on the surface and not in context.

The next stage, the Hunter stage, from about 10,000 to perhaps 5000 B.C., is characterized largely by more elaborately made projectile points, the Folsom points. They are smaller than the Clovis points on an average, and have fluting flakes which in typical forms extend most of the length of the sides. They also tend to be broader forward of the center, and to have ears on the base. Some Folsom points have been found which are not fluted. The animals with which they are most commonly associated are now extinct species of bison, which were apparently hunted in preference to other available animals. With them were flake scrapers and other simple core tools and a few pointed bone tools.

During the Collector stage, from about 5000 to perhaps locally as late as 200 B.C., the most typical projectile point of these Hunter people was what has been called the Plainview type. This general kind of point, with very fine ripple flaking on both faces, was formerly called the Yuman type. This is obviously related to the Folsom point in general form, but lacks the ears and the very large and long base flakes which give the fluting effect. Some basal flaking does occur but not single large shallow flakes. The animals which were most typically hunted at this time seem to have been essentially modern forms.

The second basic way of life was of about equal antiquity in the Southwest. It has been suggested that this general type of culture may be referred to as the Desert culture, and it is represented by a number of sites and shows even rather early a considerable variety within this broad pattern. Carbon 14 dates which have been secured are about 11,000 years ago, or around 9000 B.C. As a way of life it lasted to at least 2000 B.C., when corn first became known in the Southwest, or perhaps even later in some areas.

The Ancient stage is represented by such cave sites as Gypsum Cave, Ventana Cave, and Danger Cave. The earliest levels in these caves frequently show the association of now extinct mammals, and the artifacts are simple tools, flake and light core scrapers and choppers. There are also more or less leaf-shaped projectile points, but these do not seem to have been abundant. One open site which might be assigned to this period, with a carbon 14 date of about 13,500 years ago, is the Tule Springs site in Nevada. This was thought to have been much older, but recent work has dated it as of about this period. Little cultural material was found in it.

The Cochise culture begins a long and distinctive existence at about this time or perhaps a little later. Carbon 14 dates of the Sulphur Springs stage of the Cochise culture are about 6000 or 7000 B.C. and last to about 4000 B.C. This culture is found mostly in southeastern Arizona, and here is associated with extinct mammals, particularly mammoth and bison. The most typical stone tools are flat milling bases and relatively small, somewhat oval hand grinding stones with flat grinding faces. There are also some percussion-flaked plano-convex tools, but native projectile points seem to have been lacking.

During the Hunter period the Chiricahua stage of the Cochise culture flourished. Dates which have been secured suggest that it existed from about 4000 to 500 B.C. Typical artifacts are basin-type milling bases, hand-stones which are still one-hand and characteristically flat on the two grinding faces, some rather simple biface flake tools, and a few projectile points which seem to have been traded from other cultures.

In southeastern California the earlier Lake Mohave and slightly later Pinto Basin cultures are found. Dates secured from the Tule site suggest they date about 3000 B.C., or slightly earlier for the former, and somewhat post 3000 B.C. for the latter. They are characterized by typical shorter and broader projectile points, but the people still seem to have practiced largely a gathering way of life.

During the Collector period San Pedro Cochise existed in the Southwest, and there is some evidence that it was more widespread than the earlier stages. Although it has been dated as from about 500 B.C. to the time of Christ, or perhaps even to A.D. 200 locally, it is clearly a late stage of Cochise, and not Mogollon. Earlier, or by about 2000 B.C., corn was in use in Tularosa Cave in New Mexico. This raises the question of just when the change took place from Cochise to Mogollon, and whether corn was generally available to the several cultural groups at this time.

San Pedro Cochise includes the addition of mortars and pestles to the cultural complex, and chipped tools become much more abundant and varied. There are both plano-convex and biface tools and the use of pressure retouch is found on some of them. Projectile points are also present, and they are comparatively effective points with lateral notches. What are probably very simple irregularly shaped houses have been found in this San Pedro stage, and it would be very interesting to have exact dates of them to compare to the earliest Mogollon houses. The stone tool types of San Pedro carry over into the earliest Mogollon stages with little change, and if more formal houses are added to this list of traits, and pottery is also included, then it must be considered Mogollon.

The earliest Pine Lawn Mogollon is believed by Martin to date some 300 B.C., and it is quite probable that it does date at least 150 or 200 B.C., although carbon 14 has not produced dates of this degree of exactness.

This being the case it is very probable that some sites which must be considered Collector period sites, and some which are assignable to Mogollon, overlap in time. Just what the geographic and cultural relationship of these sites is has as yet not been sufficiently defined.

MOGOLLON

With the general introduction of agriculture, pottery, and more formalized houses into the Southwest, several streams of cultural development began to be formed. The earliest of these now seems to have been the Mogollon, which developed first in the general area of the upper Gila and Salt rivers and extended southward for an unknown distance into Mexico. As has just been stated, the stone tool types of later Cochise continued to be made in earliest Mogollon, but there were two additions which set these cultures apart. These were the manufacture of pottery and the building of more formalized houses. Agriculture, at least corn agriculture, had presumably already existed in this general area for some time.

The Exploitation period, that from about 200 or 300 B.C. to about the time of Christ, is most fully known for the Mogollon culture from the work done by the Chicago Natural History Museum in Tularosa Cave. Previous to this, and before 150 B.C., corn, beans, and squash were being raised. The atlatl was certainly in use, and the bow and arrow may have been known and used as well. Pseudo, or unfired, pottery was being made as basket liners, and may have been used as parching trays. Baskets were of the two-rod and bundle, bundle and rod core, and twined types. Moccasins were being worn as well as wickerwork sandals. There were netted carrying bags. Cradles were of the flexible back type. Ornaments included numbers of shell bracelets.

Lacking pottery, the question may be raised concerning this complex as to whether or not it was early Pine Lawn Mogollon or San Pedro Cochise. Despite the presence of certain traits such as agriculture, it may probably most logically be considered a part of Cochise.

The first true Mogollon is early Pine Lawn, with a time span of some 200 B.C. plus or minus perhaps as much as 100 years, to the time of Christ. Pottery at the very beginning of this period is relatively well made, and does not show the groping crudities that might be expected of the first efforts at ceramics. San Francisco Red is very typical and is sometimes well polished and quite red. Other types are Alma Plain and Alma Rough, neither of which are abundant. Pithouses are relatively large, are circular, have a central support post, and an entrance. Even larger structures are of the same general pattern but are considered to have been ceremonial structures, or kivas.

Metates were of the basin shape, slab and scoop types, and their accompanying manos were mostly ovoid and one-hand, though some tended to be rectangular. Mortars and pestles were also made. The atlatl was certainly in use, and there is good evidence that the bow and arrow was known at least by later in the period. Bone tools included the notched bone awl and fleshers. Shell bracelets were relatively common. Pipes of both stone and pottery were of the tubular or general cigar shape, and reed cigarettes were used. Basketry was very well made and included some flexible twined types as well as those already mentioned. Matting was present, and sandals were of the wickerwork weave. The digging stick was used in agriculture, and corn, beans, and squash were all raised.

In general this earliest Mogollon stage is quite clearly a development from late Cochise. The stone work is simply a continuation of Cochise types, and burials may also have been found in both. Agriculture, probably introduced from Mexico, had an earlier existence in this general area. The real additions are formalized houses and kivas, which were apparently forecast in late Cochise, and pottery, which may have been derived from Mexico as well.

During the Founder period, or that from about the time of Christ to perhaps A.D. 500, Mogollon culture became much more firmly entrenched in the Southwest. It also began to spread farther north, where it came in contact with the earliest Anasazi development, the Basket Maker II culture.

The first painted Mogollon pottery is found at this time, but only in the southwestern portion of the area occupied. This would suggest that it was possibly derived from Mexico, and that it may be related to the earliest Hohokam painted pottery which began at about this time. Dos Cabezas Red-on-brown has a broad-line type of decoration and the painted design has been rubbed over to spread it slightly into the background. This trait of polishing over the design remained a good diagnostic of Mogollon pottery for some time. Houses were deep pithouses, with relatively long sloping entrances, floor firepits, and storage pits within the rooms. Kivas were also still present, as they continued to be throughout the history of this culture. Flexed inhumation continued.

Metates are of both the basin and scoop types and manos are similar to previous forms. No axes have been found but there are both three-quarter- and full-grooved mauls. Ornaments are the same. Projectile points are similar, with diagonal notches, and are relatively broad in relation to their length. In some ways they are reminiscent of Woodland types from the Midwest and plains. Some perishable material is known, including feather and fur robes. Both the atlatl and the bow were in use. Food remained the same but with more 8-row corn and less of the 12- and 14-row types. The notched bone awl continued, and in fact is found as a typical part of this culture.

One of the things which is most apparent is that Mogollon does not show any marked changes but rather a gradual and more or less smooth evolution. Its influence was spreading out over a much wider area, and was coming in contact with other groups. At this time, and in the following period, it was probably about at the peak of its development as an unmodified culture.

Spruce Tree House, one of the cliff dwellings in the Mesa Verde.

During the Settlement period, from approximately A.D. 500 to 700, about the same distribution is found as during the previous period, including its extension southward into Mexico. Pottery innovations were Alma neck coiling and texturing and San Lorenzo Red-on-brown. The latter type is found only in the form of bowls, and the designs are rather poorly executed. Houses were more or less circular deep pithouses with long entrances and central support posts. The large size of some structures indicates they were kivas. Metates were similar to those of the preceding period, and mortars and stone bowls were also made and used, though they were not as well made as the best of the Hohokam examples. Flanged drills decreased in abundance, and points were of the expanding-stem or corner-notched type.

Basketry was of the two-rod and bundle, half-rod and bundle, and bundle coiled types. There was also some coil without foundation weaving, and twilled and twined mats. Sandals were plaited and of multiple warp. String aprons were worn by women. Shell beads were made. Pipes continued to be made, and were of both stone and pottery. Plain bone awls were common. Although agriculture persisted, the evidence from Tularosa and Cordova caves indicates that perhaps there was slightly greater use made of wild foods.

The parallels between individual Mogollon traits of this period and the contemporary Basket Maker culture have often been pointed out. This no doubt was partly a result of contact but may also have been the result of a common ancestry in the early Desert culture. It has been suggested that the earliest Mogollon was a vigorous culture, but it is already apparent that it did not rapidly change as it existed through time in any way comparable to the changes effected by the Anasazi to the north and the Hohokam to the west. This failure to alter in its later development sets it apart from the other cultures. Perhaps this is partly a result of its location in more or less mountainous sections of the Southwest where there was a ready supply of food, and where a degree of isolation existed.

The Adjustment period, from about A.D. 700 to 900, is characterized best by the San Francisco stage. There was somewhat of a withdrawal to the south of the area occupied. The decorated pottery is Mogollon Red-on-brown, San Lorenzo Red-on-brown, and Three Circle Red-on-white, all of which is characterized by rectilinear designs. There were also more of the textured types, such as Alma Scored and Neck Banded. To the north Reserve Smudged was being made. Typical structures are deep rectangular pithouses with rounded corners, fairly long passageways, and firepits. In fact houses show considerable variation in depth from deep to shallow or in the post-hole arrangements.

Metates were mostly scoop-shaped, and manos tended to be of the smaller one-hand variety. There were apparently some atlatls still in use, if the size of points may be taken as an indication, although the bow and arrow was certainly also present. Points have either lateral or diagonal notches. There were fewer pipes at this time, and animal and even some human figurines were made. Baskets were mostly of the two-rod and bundle type, and some twilled matting was made. Cotton cloth was clearly a part of this culture, and plaited square-toed and wickerwork sandals were made. The rigid cradle had replaced the flexible cradle. Unfired pottery seems to have been even more common than it was earlier, thus giving substance to the theory that it served as parching trays.

Some of the traits found at this time are reminiscent of Basket Maker III of the Anasazi culture, as has been noted previously, but others are suggestive of Pueblo I. The rigid cradle board falls within this latter category.

During the Dissemination period, or from about A.D. 900 to 1100, an increasing intergradation may be seen in the north with the Pueblo culture, which was becoming vigorous. This northern influence seems to have been derived largely from the Zuñi area rather than more to the west from the Hopi country, at least as concerns pottery. To the southwest there was a mixture with the Hohokam, which by now was also quite vigorous and had received additional stimulus from Mexico. In the center of the area, in what might be considered the purest Mogollon still surviving, the Three Circle and the Reserve phases are found.

In ceramics the use of balanced solid and hatched designs was very typical, and this came largely from the upper Little Colorado area. There was now much regional variation of pottery, with the survival and elaboration of corrugated types and the use of smudging, particularly in the north and central areas. In the early part of the period pithouses were found, but soon these gave way to multistory surface pueblos, especially in the north. Kivas became more formalized. Metates are slab, scoop, and even some trough shapes, and manos are typically rectangular in shape, some being worn down by use to a triangular cross section. The use of stone hoes also increased now. There is no evidence of the use of the atlatl, but arrow points are common and are small and diagonally notched. Another typical feature seems to have been the use of the grooved arrow-shaft polisher or straightener.

Cradles are of the rigid type. The most typical sandals are plaited, and string aprons persist. There are more reed cigarettes and less use made of stone or clay pipes. Baskets are both of the half-rod and bundle and the twilled-ring types, an obvious parallel with the Pueblo ring baskets. Netting was common, and cotton cloth was made. Ornaments consisted of shell bracelets, shell beads, and bone tubes.

By now Mogollon culture had lost its vigor and had changed from the source of new ideas and things to a borrower of such traits from other people. Pueblo culture in the north was so modifying Mogollon that it is no longer possible to be sure just what is Mogollon and what is actually largely Pueblo. A similar modification to the southwest was being effected with Hohokam.

In general summary of Mogollon it may be said that in its earliest manifestations in the Southwest it was a very vigorous and advanced culture.
Agriculture, houses, and pottery all began earlier here and in this culture
than they did elsewhere, or in other cultures, if our present evidences of
dating may be relied upon. Most traits therefore started at a rather high
level, but in a remarkable way they failed to be further modified and
developed. The roots of this culture may be traced back into Cochise, but
Mexican traits were apparently added.

The lack of trait modification is roughly indicated in the accompanying chart, which, when it is compared to those for the Anasazi and the
Hohokam, will make clear the stability of this culture over a comparatively long period. Toward the end of its development influences, particularly from the Pueblo culture, drastically modified it. This is especially
apparent in ceramics and architecture. Not only did Mogollon, or a Mogol-

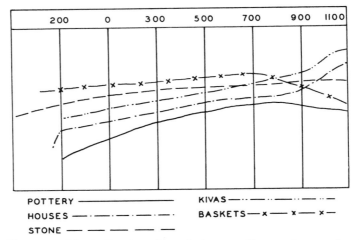

Fig. 204. Chart roughly indicating the relative excellence of several culture traits
typical of Mogollon through time. This is a purely subjective evaluation, and might be
modified by another individual, but it does tend to show two things, especially when
compared to similar charts prepared and presented for Hohokam and Anasazi cultures.
First, many of these traits begin very early, in comparison to other similar developments in the Southwest, and second, there is relatively little abrupt modification in most
traits or traditions. The sudden late upswing in houses and kivas was effected by Pueblo
influence.

lon-like culture, have the earliest agriculture found anywhere in the Southwest proper, but it also had the first structures which might be considered
purely ceremonial. It probably also had the first bows and arrows, yet
the atlatl seems to have been retained for a rather remarkably long time
after the bow was known.

Just at what point Mogollon as such ceases to exist is a subject which can be much debated. Certain traits seem to have persisted, such as textured pottery and oxidized pottery types, but others, such as the pithouse, were completely replaced. Probably the most logical assumption is simply that Mogollon was gradually overwhelmed by the developing Pueblo culture. In the opinion of this writer much must be ascribed to it in the early development of the Southwest, but it failed to respond to available stimulus as time went on and so eventually became overwhelmed by the very cultures it had helped to launch.

HOHOKAM

The date of the earliest known Hohokam is even less well documented than that of the earliest Mogollon. The major site which has been excavated and reported is Snaketown, and no carbon 14 dates were secured from it. However, there are certain very close parallels between the earliest manifestations in both these cultures, and it can hardly be doubted that they are related. Both seem to have developed more or less directly from Cochise, with the addition of pottery and formalized houses. But even at the beginning of Hohokam it seems to have been a relatively rich and quite distinctive culture.

The first well-identified Pioneer Hohokam stage is the Vahki, and it is possible that the Estrella might even be of almost the same age. These stages have been tentatively dated as sometime between about 200 B.C. and the time of Christ, or, if one is more conservative, from the time of Christ to perhaps A.D. 100 to 200. Ceramics are so similar to those of the early Mogollon, particularly the plain types, that it is very tempting to equate them in time. For this reason this part of Hohokam has been assigned to the Exploitation period.

The most abundant pottery is Vahki Plain and Vahki Red, the latter of which either developed from San Francisco Red or is clearly related to it, for in some individual sherds even similar paste and temper are found. In the Estrella stage both the plain types are found plus Estrella Red-on-gray, which has a red design on the insides of bowls and incising on the outsides. The question may thus be raised as to whether or not this is the earliest painted pottery found in the Southwest, earlier than that of the Mogollon, and it very possibly may be. Clay figurines are also found.

Structures are built in pits, are almost square with corner posts and a firepit and an entrance on one side, and some are very large. This huge size has led Gladwin to suggest that they may have served as ceremonial structures, and this suggestion has much to recommend it, for it will be recalled that kivas are found in the earliest Mogollon and the two cultures are obviously very close culturally.

One of the most typical features throughout the history of the Hohokam is the practice of cremation. Cremated bones were gathered up and placed in pits or trenches, with few if any artifacts.

Metates are of the open-end trough type, and manos are more or less rectangular and of the one-hand type. It is thus clear that these people had corn agriculture, although little in the way of agricultural products has been found in any Hohokam period. Simple mortars and pestles were also in use. Stone palettes began at about this time, but were either flat tablets or suggestive of metates. There were stone bowls, but they lacked carving. Shell bracelets and shell disk beads were made. The bow and arrow was clearly in use, as judged by the size of the propectile points, though some larger ones have been found which might have been atlatl dart points as well.

In most traits the Exploitation period of the Hohokam was not markedly different from that of the Mogollon. Certain individual traits are distinctive, and set the pattern for later developments. The use of cremation instead of inhumation is one, and the quality and diversity of shaped stone artifacts is another. Ceramically the differences are less marked at this time.

During the Founder Period, from about the time of Christ to perhaps A.D. 500, the Sweetwater and Snaketown stages are found, and these represent more or less an evolutionary continuation of the earlier stages. Perhaps more marked changes took place in some traits during the Snaketown than in earlier stages. Although the area of occupation is not fully defined, it is clear that in this period sites are located along the larger rivers, notably the Gila and Salt near their junction, and slightly upstream from this junction.

Pottery, houses, and axes all help to define this period, and though they are simply an elaboration of previous types they are distinctive. Stone working particularly became more important. Sacaton Red-on-gray pottery with the use of hatching as an element of design and incising of the coils on the outsides of bowls, and Snaketown Red-on-buff with no slip but a polished surface, are typical. Figurines were still being made. Houses were in pits, or were shallow pithouses, but more were rectangular than square. In the Snaketown stage there was a change from the four-post to the two-post support. Some very large structures were termed ceremonial by Gladwin.

The metates are of the trough type and the manos are of the one-hand block type. Palettes were still simple, but had raised rims. The Snaketown axe is very distinctive, being long and slender and having a raised ridge on each side of the three-quarter groove. Stone bowls in the Snaketown stage were much better shaped and sometimes decorated in incised lines. Bracelets were common, and some carving occurred now; whole shell beads were also abundant. There were even some cutout shell pendants.

In general Hohokam of this period still showed some rather close parallels with Mogollon. By the later Snaketown stage these parallels became less marked and Hohokam began to take on a more individual stamp. Perhaps Mexican influences were making themselves more clearly felt, for such traits as fine stone carving are certainly Mexican in derivation.

During the Settlement period, from about A.D. 500 to 700, the Gila Butte stage prevailed. The area occupied was still the Gila and Salt rivers in their central section but an expansion is indicated, particularly north up the Verde River. Gila Plain pottery was introduced, a type which became more and more abundant as time went on, and Gila Butte Red-on-buff, which may be characterized by the use of small repeated elements in the design, although some hatchings were still being used. Figurines were also made. Houses were more elongate, and in pits with rounded ends, or at least corners. There was an entrance on one long side, a firepit in front of it in the floor, and a two-post roof support which gave a slightly gabled effect. Perhaps one of the most striking architectural additions was the presence of large ball courts. These structures quite clearly are related to those of Mexico and must have been derived from this source.

Metates are of the long slender trough type, and palettes are more elaborate, with raised rims bearing incised designs. Stone bowls have both incised and raised designs, and are very well made. Another quite clearly Mexican trait is pyrite mirrors. Axes are of the three-quarter-grooved type, but are short and lack the raised edges around the groove. Points are definitely arrow points, are long and slender, and many have marked serrations on their edges. Shell carving reached a very high level, and inlays and disk stone beads were produced. Cremations were gathered up and placed in pits.

The most marked cultural alteration which may be seen is the very clear and rather abundant Mexican influence. Such things as ball courts and pyrite mirrors are so close identities that this relationship cannot be doubted. The question which may be raised is whether or not the ball courts took the place of earlier assumed ceremonial structures or kivas. In general this was a very rich culture.

The Adjustment period, from about A.D. 700 to 900, is best represented by the Santa Cruz phase. Distinctive pottery is Santa Cruz Red-on-buff, which has very abundant small repeated elements, and rarer negative painting. Some of the human pottery figurines have "coffee bean" eyes, a trait shared with Mexico. Houses are of the long type with rounded ends, side entrances, firepits, and two-post supports. They are from 12 to as much as 20 feet long, and are built in shallow pits. Shades were also in use at this time. Large ball courts still persisted.

Such large communites as Snaketown must have been almost entirely dependent on agriculture for an existence, and agriculture on a large scale would not have been possible in this arid area without irrigation. It is therefore quite probable that some form of irrigation existed previously, but by this period it is clearly present. Once extensive irrigation was developed, the people became more and more tied to the soil and even larger settlements developed.

Stone work included more elaborate palettes and stone bowls, the carving of which was often quite skillfully done. Projectile points are long and slender and with serrated edges, or sometimes even marked barbs. They are the best that were produced at any time anywhere in the Southwest. Shell carving was excellent, both in bracelets and in the use of mosaics. Both corn and cotton seeds have been found.

This was quite clearly a period of rather high Hohokam development in the arts and crafts. It is also a time when many clear-cut Mexican influences are to be seen. Carving in all media was excellent, and the working of both ground stone and chipped stone reached a high level.

The Dissemination period, from about A.D. 900 to 1100, may be characterized by the Sedentary Hohokam culture stage. The area occupied was perhaps slightly smaller than previously, and was still limited definitely to the main river valleys. In ceramics there was little use of scoring and incising, the presence of a rather marked Gila shoulder, the production of very large vessels, and tripod and other odd forms. Designs are often in panel arrangements suggesting fabric designs. Typical pottery is Sacaton Red-on-buff and Sacaton and Santan Red. Figurines consist of heads only.

Houses were in shallow pits, were rectangular with rounded ends, two-post supports, a firepit, and a very characteristic stepped entrance which sometimes was slightly enlarged. Small oval ball courts were of the Casa Grande type, and these spread northward into the Flagstaff area. Canals were much more extensive. Cremations were now placed in jars for interment. Ground stone continued about as previously, although some individually very fine work was done. Projectile points were very fine long points, some of which were barbed. Ornaments were outstanding with shell carving and even etching. There was some carved bone, and cast copper bells were made.

From this it is apparent that Mexican influences on the Hohokam were still being felt. Just how intensive and extensive they were is not clear, but they certainly were present.

The Classic period, from about A.D. 1100 to 1300 or perhaps slightly later, saw the arrival of the Sinagua culture in this area and its influence on Hohokam. The area of major occupation was now greatly reduced, being limited to the heart of the Gila and Salt rivers only. Hohokam pottery was Casa Grande Red-on-buff and the other plain types which have already been mentioned, particularly Gila Plain and Gila Red. The most distinctive form is the large jar with a vertical neck, and many of the designs include examples of negative painting. The houses were coming up out of the ground, and the first compoundlike structures are found. This was also the period of the greatest, that is, the most extensive and intensive, irrigation projects.

Just what became of the Hohokam may be debated. There is some evidence that at least part of them became modern-day Pimas, but in the southeastern portion of their area further modifications seem to have taken place and to have extended into the Historic period. Also just how much influence Salado culture had on the Hohokam is still not clear, for although these two people lived most congenially together it may be that Salado caused the eventual disintegration of at least some of Hohokam culture. Mexican influences do not seem to have been as strong at this time as they were previously.

In general summary certain things may be said about Hohokam with some certainty. The earliest stages were clearly related, in fact tied to, Mogollon. Rather early in the development of Hohokam clear Mexican influences are noted, and this stimulus continued until at least the Classic period. As a result some very fine work was done in carving of all sorts. Ball courts may have served the ceremonial needs of the people during most of their existence. Irrigation was developed rather early, and this tended to tie them firmly to the soil, but at the same time made possible a rather high level of artistic expression, and outlets for specialized products.

An attempt has been made to illustrate the rise and fall of various traits throughout the history of Hohokam. This has been presented in the accompanying chart. It must be remembered that this is a purely subjective evaluation of excellence, and so may be criticized, but it does show two general periods of rather high development, one between A.D. 700 and 900 and the other at about A.D. 1100, when most of the traits were at a rather high average. When this chart is compared to that of Mogollon it will be seen that it shows much more modification of traits than Mogollon did over possibly an even longer period. The beginning of this chart has been placed at about the time of Christ, perhaps too late for the present evidence, but this does not change the general information it contains. Hohokam was a very vigorous and important culture throughout most of its history in the Southwest.

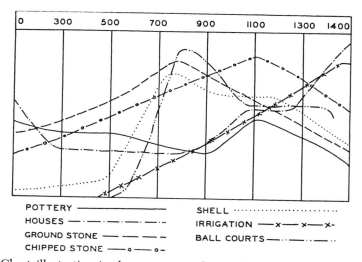

POTTERY ————————————   SHELL ·······························
HOUSES —·—·—·—·—·—·—·-   IRRIGATION —x—x—x-
GROUND STONE — —— —— —   BALL COURTS —··——··——··

Fig. 205. Chart illustrating in the most general way the relative development through time of several important Hohokam traits. Much criticism might be made of this method of presentation of such comparative data on the grounds that it is colored by individual choice, but it is useful in pointing out the periods of greatest change in a culture. There are two periods of marked cultural evolution represented, one between A.D. 700 and 900 and another at about A.D. 1100. Only two traits, houses and irrigation, rose toward the end of the Hohokam culture, and houses were probably influenced by Pueblo culture.

ANASAZI

Two distinguishable but chronologically related cultural manifestations flourished in the plateau area. The Basket Maker, the earliest of these, changed at about A.D. 700 to Pueblo. This change was occasioned by the introduction of a new group of people into the plateau, a group who mixed physically and culturally with the Basket Makers and so contributed to the production of the second distinctive culture. More specific information has been obtained on the development of these two groups than on any others in the Southwest.

Nowhere else has it been possible to assign an abundance of absolutely accurate dates to wholly prehistoric horizons. Tree-ring dating throughout the plateau has made it possible to date every cultural stage repre-

General view of Cliff Palace in the Mesa Verde. The typical excellent masonry is shown, as well as circular kivas and circular and square towers.

sented and to assign quite accurate duration dates to all periods with the possible exception of the earliest. To supplement tree-ring data an elaborate method of cross dating sites by ceramics has led to the assignment, in terms of our own calendar, of all the major sites which have been dug in this area. By the same method the dates of a great many unexcavated sites may be estimated with some accuracy.

Archaeological exploration and intensive excavation have been longer under way here than in either the mountain or the desert sections. Many thousands of dollars and the efforts of a large group of capable individuals have been directed to unraveling the history of the plateau. This was the area where the first sequence of cultural stages was pointed out, and the most detailed ceramic and other studies have been made.

Even though the plateau has been quite extensively surveyed and intensively excavated, many specific portions of this area remain comparatively unknown. Probably the most striking lack of detailed information is found in the entire central Hopi area in the earlier periods. This has been partly a matter of accident and partly due to the natural attraction of large sites for excavators, for the earlier periods represent generally quite unimpressive portions of its history.

The earliest culture in the plateau may be Basket Maker I, and there are some clues to the existence of such a stage, but these are not definite or conclusive in the north. The first well-represented period is the Founder period, and it has been most intensively examined in the San Juan drainage area. Not only has the immediate San Juan been investigated but the four corners area as well. Here, in the natural caves formed in the box canyons, a culture which is best represented by perishable materials is most completely preserved. As a result the Basket Maker II stage of culture, which probably flourished from about A.D. 200 or slightly earlier to 500, is best known from what may eventually be demonstrated to have been only a part of its range.

This true Basket Maker culture is quite distinctive, though it does show some traits which are shared with early Mogollon and others which seem to go far back into the early Desert culture pattern. Physically the people do not seem to be of so Mongoloid a cast as later groups, and possibly they had lighter and wavier hair and heavier bones than their successors. Their skulls were never deformed at the back, for they strapped their babies to cradles which had been padded with soft materials at the head.

Basketry was an important industry with this group, one of the most characteristic material traits being the use of large, shallow, coiled baskets which were often placed upside down over the heads of the dead. Pitched water baskets, carrying baskets, trinket baskets, and a variety of other forms were all made and used. Other containers were of gourd or squash, often hung in cord nets. Cotton was unknown, but a great deal of cordage was made from yucca and apocynum fibers, some of which was used in the manufacture of coil without foundation bags. Human-hair cord was also used for ties and other purposes, the women bobbing their hair to secure this material. Small whole animal skin pouches were characteristic. A warm and serviceable blanket was made from cords wrapped with feathers or fur to supplement the scanty clothing commonly worn. Sandals were of a coarse twined weave and square-toed, though sometimes with a toe fringe of buckskin.

The only substantial homes of this period which have been found are those from the eastern part of the range. These are circular pithouses with horizontally laid beams forming the sides of the houses. Farther to the west in the caves only the crudest windbreak shelters have been found. However, these latter people did have well-made cists or storage bins, which were sunken, circular, and often slab-lined. In these they stored food, hunting equipment, spare clothing, supplies, and other valuable articles, and often buried their dead.

Hunting equipage consisted of the atltal and atlatl dart. The dart was a light spear with a detachable hardwood foreshaft which was propelled with the atlatl, or throwing stick. Neither range nor accuracy was great, and in comparison with the bow and arrow it must have been a relatively ineffectual weapon. Large animals were hunted, but smaller animals were trapped in a great variety of most ingenious snares and nets. The economy was about equally divided between hunting and agriculture. Agricultural products consisted only of a small rounded-grain yellow flint corn as the staple, supplemented by squash and perhaps sunflower. A great variety of wild seeds and nuts were collected and eaten. Agricultural implements consisted of sticks, both pointed for planting and bladelike for weeding. This is in marked contrast to the use of the stone-blade hand hoe.

Ornaments were, as a whole, relatively simple. A great use was made of bright-colored feathers which were tied to the hair or on sticks which were worn in the hair. Wooden hair combs, sometimes decorated with beads or other objects, were also worn. Long cylindrical stone beads were characteristic, and pendants were not uncommon. The most distinctive feature was the choker type of necklace, which was fastened in the back with a toggle arrangement. Small ornate seed and shell beads were prized. Cylindrical or cigar-shaped stone pipes, very beautifully made of slate and other materials, are characteristic of this group.

Bone objects were dice, awls, and whistles. All three of these in one form or another persisted to much later periods.

The earliest pottery found in the northeastern portion of this area is Los Pinos Brown. Dating from about the time of Christ to A.D. 400, it seems to have been related primarily to Mogollon, and is not a truly Basket Maker pottery. The earliest true Basket Maker pottery is found to appear in the next period.

The life of these people must certainly have been seminomadic, for the type of economy would not have permitted a highly sedentary existence. Nowhere is any great population indicated, so that the mortality rate must have been high. The fact that caches are often found which contain quantities of valuable material suggests that they were in the habit of leaving a section and returning to it, and it is quite possible that one small band lived over a considerable area, to leave widespread but scattered indications of their presence. Withal their existence must have been difficult and precarious, for they occupied an inhospitable portion of the Southwest.

The next period, the Settlement period, that between about A.D. 500 and 700, shows a slightly higher cultural development in many ways. This stage, Basket Maker III, must have come in contact with a new invading group which effected certain drastic changes in the type of life before the end of the period. At the beginning, however, the general culture remained much the same. Circular or nearly circular houses became much more widespread. These were pithouses, some of which were slab-lined to hold back the loose soil, others of which were merely clay-lined in substantial soil. The method of roofing varied from poles set on the periphery of the hole and brought together at the top to form a dome to a four-post flat-roofed arangement. To the east some essentially circular pithouses show a second smaller chamber that might be termed an "annex."

Fabrics, though employing the same materials and techniques, show in some instances a further development. This is particularly marked in the production of fine crescent-toed sandals, the upper surface of which often has colored designs, the lower surface raised designs. Baskets, bags, and feather and fur blankets remained much the same.

Sun-dried pseudo-pottery vessels are found now as the liners of baskets. It has already been suggested they may have served as parching trays, but in this culture there is an evolution from the use of shredded cedar bark as temper through grass to sand. Soon these vessels were being fired, and a true pottery was being produced. The paste and surface color was gray; the sand temper showed through to the surface, which was only roughly smoothed; and the shapes were globular and copied after natural forms already in use. The only true spouts ever produced in the Southwest were made at this time.

Designs in a dull black paint were soon painted on the insides of bowls and the outsides of jars. In the beginning many of them were obviously copies of basket designs, but experimentation followed, and human and other unusual figures were produced. The elements most commonly used were coarse lines and unattached dots.

At about the same time crude human female figurines were modeled in clay. The eyes were slits, the nose a pinched-up mass of clay, and ornaments were indicated by punched decorations. Peculiar conical clay objects, of unknown use, were also made and ornamented in a similar manner.

The economy of this group was only slightly different from that of the preceding. Agriculture had become somewhat more complex, and larger types of corn were either developed or introduced. The production of houses made possible a more permanent form of life in the open and in areas which before had been inhospitable. An expansion of the area occupied may be noted, and probably a substantial increase in population took place.

Almost at the end of this period certain new features appear for the first time. In the east the physical type began to change slightly from a predominance of long-headed types to more rounded skulls, although the posterior was still not deformed. The bow and arrow made its first appearance. A very rare black-on-red type of pottery may probably also be ascribed to this same outside source, for it is better made and radically different in basic firing methods from that produced by the Basket Maker people.

In northwestern New Mexico the Sambrito culture was developed with Sambrito Brown pottery. Houses were circular pithouses and the metate was of the open-end trough type. The atlatl was in common use. In the central and southern Rio Grande valley brown pottery which seems to have been clearly derived from Mogollon predominated.

At about A.D. 700 certain further changes in culture became established. This marks the beginning of the development of the distinct Pueblo culture. The first period which has been isolated lasted from about A.D. 700 to 900 and is designated as a Pueblo I stage. It has been referred to as the Adjustment period, and it was certainly that, for a group with one set of well-established traditions found it necessary to adjust themselves to a new set of customs.

It has been suggested that this change was occasioned by the encroachment of new people who, mixing with the occupants, produced this new culture. To substantiate this claim several radical changes have been mentioned. The physical type was modified, and a hard cradle head support was introduced to flatten the back of the skull. The bow and arrow replaced the atlatl. Cotton was introduced. The coiling technique of pottery manufacture became widespread, and styles of decoration were formalized and standardized. The first masonry surface structures appeared and soon became highly evolved. Last, but perhaps of the utmost importance, at least at one site in southern Utah oxidized pottery was introduced in some abundance.

An attempt has been made to identify this invading group as basically of Mogollon culture. The earliest changes from Basket Maker took place in the eastern portion of the San Juan drainage. It was also here that the most rapid later developments are found. This section is geographically close to the Mogollon mountain area. The basic coiling technique was first employed by the Mogollon people, and they were also producing a well-made brown and red pottery when the Basket Makers were struggling with their first individual experiments. One definite Mogollon trade piece has been found in a Basket Maker site. Axes of any sort were very rare in the plateau during the earlier periods, and those which have been found are of a full-grooved type. Before A.D. 700 they were so rare as to be considered practically nonexistent, but after about this date they became more common. Types of axes found in the Mogollon and Pueblo areas are identical in the early periods of both. These are full-grooved and either chipped or ground to shape. Later the full-grooved axe became the only type characteristic of pure Pueblo culture. From this it is apparent that the contributing factor to the change of culture may well have been the introduction of Mogollon people to the plateau.

As very little detailed work has been done on pure Pueblo I sites, not a great deal is known about the material traits of this culture stage. Certainly the best-recognized single trait is pottery. Two types became general at this time. Jars were produced with flattened, but not indented, neck coils. This type is known as Kana-a-Gray. The paste and surface finish are similar to those of the previously discussed Basket Maker Lino Gray type. The second type is black-on-white, which is better made, and the decorated surface of which is universally more carefully prepared than the earlier black-on-gray Basket Maker type. Design elements of fine lines, attached dots, and high triangles were widely accepted. Forms were still predominantly globular but more varied than those of the preceding period. The first true handles were made now.

In the central portion of the Rio Grande valley San Marcel Black-on-white pottery was being made at this time. In the northern portion of the valley Anasazi pottery and architectural styles prevailed. In the south the brown pottery continued to predominate.

From this time on Pueblo culture enjoyed a steady rise. During the Dissemination period, from A.D. 900 to 1100, regional variation became much more marked, and both a general Pueblo II and Pueblo III stage of culture flourished in separate sections contemporaneously. Because of the greatly varied culture enjoyed in the several regions, and since this material has been discussed in a preceding chapter, no effort at a detailed review will be undertaken in this summary.

Certainly the cultural leader of the plateau was now Chaco Canyon. Here the greatest sites flourished, the most spectacular structures were built, and a specialization of the arts led to a very high local attainment. Elaborate jewelry, with much use of turquoise mosaics, and fine pottery were produced. Kivas became prominent and developed to great size. A very large population was concentrated in a small area.

Just to the north, in the Mesa Verde, but still in the general four corners region, smaller surface masonry structures were being built. Here the small kiva was highly elaborated with the banquette, pilaster, platform, ventilator, deflector, firepit, sipapu series of features. Masonry was remarkably well made, only a small amount of adobe mortar being used. Pottery, though not so fine as in the succeeding period, was well made.

In the lower San Juan both pithouses and surface masonry structures were in use. Masonry was of a small amount of rock and a greater proportion of adobe. Ceramics, though influenced both from the south and the east, were of a general southern type. South throughout the Little Colorado area and the Hopi country, houses were generally pit structures. The black-on-white pottery had a tendency to simple designs and the use of wide lines and low flat triangles. Throughout the entire plateau area the most common and characteristic general-utility pottery type was Tusayan Corrugated. This was a fine, evenly indented corrugated type which serves as one of the best widespread daters in ceramics.

In general this period represents a time when Pueblo culture was entrenching itself in the plateau. Traditions were being established which would mold its future course. Surface masonry structures were developed in practically all their characters, and specialization in the arts led to their rapid evolution. Population concentrations were as a result inevitable, and although this period had the greatest population of the plateau, it also marked the beginning of a decrease.

In the Rio Grande valley there was an increase in the number of pueblos at this time, and in the northern portion some of them were quite large, having as many as 100 rooms. The associated kivas were circular, and the most typical pottery was Kwahe'e Black-on-white and Taos Black-on-white. Most of the associated traits were parallel to those from the Pueblo culture farther west, so this simply represents an eastward extension of western Pueblo. In the central area Socorro and Escavada Black-on-white pottery was the most typical, but Los Lunas Smudged was also found. Here, even more if possible than in the north, Anasazi influence from the west was most obvious. Except for pottery the major difference is found in the type of walls which were built in the pueblos, for there was much greater use of coursed adobe in architectural construction. In the south, in the Jornada branch, brown pottery still continued to be made.

In the northern periphery, in Utah, the Fremont and the Sevier Fremont cultures were flourishing. The latter, more to the west, seems to show the greater Anasazi or Pueblo influence, and both have traits which suggest some relationships back to the early Desert culture. Along the Colorado River the Patayan culture was well established, and may be divided into a number of subcultures. Of these perhaps the best known is the Cohonina to the north, where reduced pottery was made as opposed to the more oxidized types farther west and south. In the vicinity of Flagstaff the Sinagua culture was well developed, and may be characterized by the manufacture of brown or red paddle and anvil–made pottery. In other traits it is much like Pueblo, as was the Cohonina.

The Classic period, from A.D. 1100 to 1300, was the time of general development and further refinement of these trends. Pueblo III culture was in full swing now, and the entire San Juan, Hopi, and Little Colorado areas were dotted with large pueblo sites. The attraction of these sites for excavators has led to a thorough understanding of this culture, and so a great many pottery types are well known. Not only did black-on-white and corrugated types continue to be made in even more refined form, but also the first polychrome types were produced. These were uniformly fired in an oxidizing atmosphere and were decorated with black, red, orange, and white colors.

Chaco Canyon culture had by now spread to other areas and taken on a complexion strongly tinctured by the cultures with which it came in contact. The Mesa Verde was at its height, and at this time evolved the outstanding square, round, and D-shaped towers which so definitely characterize it. In the western San Juan the large cliff dwellings and mesa pueblos which are so well known were flourishing. Throughout the Hopi country sizable pueblos had developed, and the first of the yellow pottery series made its appearance. In the upper Little Colorado area two types of distinctive pottery had evolved. The first of these, Tularosa Black-on-white, spread rapidly to the south and formed the vanguard of the Salado culture. The second, St. Johns Polychrome, became one of the most widely traded types ever produced in the plateau, and hence one of the best dating types in the Southwest. The first glaze-painted pottery also appeared at about the end of the period in this area as the ancestor of the later greatly varied Zuñi types.

No basic additions or alterations were made in the general culture during this period. Sites were on the whole larger and more imposing than previously, but they were not quite so large as those of the next period. Pottery types were highly developed and considerably diversified. A widespread manufacture of oxidized pottery marked an increasing interest in this method of firing. The specialization of industries which attended the creation of larger sites and population concentrations appears to have led to a greater interest in weaving. Sandals had by now changed to a preponderance of twilled forms, and the yucca ring basket became very common.

In all respects the culture of this period is relatively high. The populous sites show that conditions of life were satisfactory, and the lack of general defensive features would indicate that it was moderately peaceful. Populations tended to be concentrated in relatively small areas, at various times, with sections of sparse populations intervening. This was probably a result of the "human cycle," whereby an area was rendered unfit for residence after a certain period of human occupancy. These conditions were altered only at the end of the period by the great drought, and resulted in the abandonment of the San Juan drainage area.

The people who left the San Juan moved south to sections of more permanent water supplies, clustering during the following period in three areas. These have been designated as the Hopi Washes area, the upper Little Colorado area, and the Zuñi area. There were other settlements in the Verde valley and near Winslow. Certainly at this time there was also a considerable movement of people to the Rio Grande. This began the Culminant period, which lasted from about A.D. 1300 to 1600.

In the Hopi section large compact pueblos were being built which contained one or more courts or plazas, with rectangular kivas with a platform at only one end. The Hopi yellow pottery series had its development now, to culminate in the elaborate polychrome types produced near the end.

Occupation of the upper Little Colorado area was confined to the earlier portion of the period. Pueblos, though smaller than the Hopi type, were similar, and the kiva was suggestive of the Hopi type. A black and white on red pottery developed with a black glaze paint, and spread south into the upper drainage of the Salt River, but did not survive long.

In the Zuñi area pueblos were more suggestive of the Chaco Canyon types. Kivas were round instead of square, and some were of exceptional size. Pottery interest may be characterized as showing a marked preference for glaze types of paint, and a variety of color combinations was produced. However, glaze painting did not persist far into the Historic period.

In the northern and central Rio Grande valley large pueblos continued to be built, many of them of coursed adobe walls. The most striking pottery is that which has glaze paints used for decoration, and a considerable series of types have been worked out here based largely on rim forms, though color combinations, general vessel forms, and designs are also diagnostic. Kivas were mostly circular, though some corner kivas were built, and some were below or partly below ground while others were surface.

General culture showed almost no changes from that of the preceding period. All of the arts and crafts were carried on and perhaps further elaborated, but in general this time might well be considered a culmination of Pueblo history. By about A.D. 1600 Spanish culture was beginning to make itself felt in sufficient strength to color Indian culture. A substitution of certain articles of European manufacture quickly took place, and the purely Southwestern Indian began a very gradual metamorphosis.

During the Historic period, from A.D. 1600 to 1900, these gradual alterations accumulated. Fear of the Spaniards led to the location of pueblos on high mesas where they might more easily be defended, and here they still perch. The encroachment of raiding Navahos and lesser Apaches led to further entrenchment, and caused the conservative Hopi Indians to retain more of their former customs than many other Indian groups.

Two charts have been prepared in an effort to aid evaluation of the cultural history of the plateau area. The first of these shows the stages of culture found in each of the centers at various periods. The most complete series probably is found in the Hopi country, where the descendants of the earliest prehistoric Indians are still living. The shortest definite sequence of one culture in one area is in Chaco Canyon, where it was dispersed shortly after A.D. 1100. This fact may be readily explained, for a large population was concentrated within about 15 miles in a narrow canyon. The destruction of the cover led to the lowering of the ground water and the eventual necessity of abandonment. That it was later reoccupied after it had once more silted up is apparent by the superimposition of a Mesa Verde type of culture at Pueblo Bonito.

Periodic abandonment may be even better demonstrated in the Tsegi Canyon system, and shifts of population peaks may be shown between the Tsegi, Marsh Pass, Moenkopi and Wupatki areas. There were sudden and considerable population increases in the Tsegi Canyons in about 200-year cycles which culminated at A.D. 1300. Before this, A.D. 1100 saw a large population, as did the early portion of the tenth century. Alternating roughly with this, population increases may be noted in the Marsh Pass area, at the mouth of the Tsegi Canyon. This may best be accounted for by the erosion of the canyon, a result of the human cycle occasioned through occupation. This pulsation was felt as far south as the Wuptaki Monument area, where maxima were reached at about alternate periods.

The second chart is an effort to present, in the most general manner, a comparison of relative attainment of several traits developed in the plateau at various times. For this comparison pottery, houses, kivas, baskets, stone articles, sandals, and non-cotton fabrics have been considered. The

	HOPI COUNTRY	FLAG-STAFF	SAN JUAN	MESA VERDE	CHACO	ZUÑI
1900	P. Ⅴ.					P. Ⅴ.
1600						
	P. Ⅳ.					P. Ⅳ.
1300						
	P. Ⅲ.	P. Ⅲ.	P. Ⅲ.	P. Ⅲ.		P. Ⅲ.
1100						
	P. Ⅱ.	P. Ⅱ.	P. Ⅱ.	P. Ⅱ.	P. Ⅲ.	P. Ⅱ.
900						
	P. Ⅰ.	P. Ⅰ.	P. Ⅰ.	P. Ⅰ.	P.Ⅰ.& P.Ⅱ.	?
700						
	B.M.Ⅲ.		B.M.Ⅲ.	B.M.Ⅲ.	B.M.Ⅲ.	
500						
300			B.M.Ⅱ.			

Fig. 206. A table presenting the various sections of the plateau which have been discussed, and the culture stage represented in these sections at various periods. Lack of data may be a lack of knowledge and not an absolute absence, as in respect to the Basket Maker II stage, which may be much more widespread than indicated.

most interesting result is the obvious production of two peaks. One of these is reached at about A.D. 700 and the second sometime between about A.D. 1200 and 1400. It will also be noted that two distinct complexes of traits form these separate groups, the earliest of which is based on work in soft materials, the second in hard objects or materials. This shift in emphasis has been pointed out as a diagnostic of the two distinct cultures found in the plateau. At an intermediate period, around A.D. 900, these traits were crossing, and this is about the time designated as a period of cultural adjustment.

If this chart is compared to that of Hohokam culture, it will be seen that a somewhat similar situation existed in the two areas at about the same time. In the Hohokam the great period of change was slightly later but just as distinct, for two peaks were achieved in the traits considered. In general it may be assumed that the year A.D. 800 was one of considerable culture alteration throughout most of the Southwest. At this time traits were both rising and falling in both of these two major areas. When individual traits are compared in the two charts, considerable time variation of peaks may be noted. In almost every comparable feature the Hohokam is found to precede the Pueblo by several years.

If both of these charts are compared to that of Mogollon it will become

apparent that the latter did not show any of the marked alterations throughout its history that are so pronounced for the Hohokam and Anasazi. To
the writer this simply means that the Mogollon did not accept stimulus from
outside sources to the extent that these other groups did, and that it re-

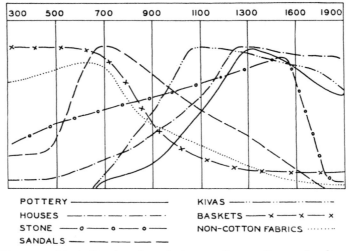

Fig. 207. Chart roughly indicating the relative excellence of several culture traits found
in the plateau at the time periods indicated. General trait combinations or traditions
have been chosen for this comparison. Two periods of marked alteration are indicated,
that at about A.D. 700 and from A.D. 1100 on to 1300 or perhaps slightly later. This is
admittedly a purely individual and subjective evaluation.

mained more self-satisfied and contained than the others. This impression may be somewhat false, for late in Mogollon history there was much
influence from Pueblo, but this stage has been considered as not primarily
Mogollon and so not listed with it. The relatively high level of Mogollon
culture at the beginning of its history is also apparent when compared to
the charts for the other two groups.

GENERAL SUMMARY

The later major cultural developments of each of the periods having now
been discussed in some detail, it is possible to examine and evaluate all
of them as a whole. Two points may be immediately made in such an
evaluation. First, there are at the most two cultural streams from which
most of the rest seem to have developed. Second, there are also two important disruptive periods in which cultures migrated widely and intermingled, and a third perhaps even earlier one.

The first quite basic influence which stands out in Southwestern archaeology is the Cochise culture, which may be considered a part of the early Desert culture. It is the first well-understood culture found in the Southwest proper. Present information indicates that the Cochise developed more or less directly into the Mogollon culture, which apparently was in its earliest portion a very strong culture with widespread influence on other people in the Southwest. Hohokam probably developed from this early Mogollon influence, but very quickly embellished it with features developed locally in the Gila area to give it a distinctive cast all its own. This Hohokam is the culture found to be distinctive of the desert area.

Mogollon also appears to have strongly influenced the cultural history of the plateau, not only early but continuously until it had in turn been over-shadowed by Pueblo development. Pueblo culture was most likely created by a combination of features taken from Basket Maker and Mogollon, but was fed by further influences from both Mogollon and Hohokam. At present it would seem that the Patayan culture also had its roots back in the early Desert culture, but was at least in part derived from or influenced by Hohokam culture.

If all this historical reconstruction is subsequently found to be accurate, the basic culture from which these groups sprang may be traced back to Cochise. From Cochise came Mogollon, which developed regionally to Hohokam and combined with the Basket Makers to produce Pueblo. From the work at Winona Village near Flagstaff it is clear that Hohokam also contributed to the later development of Pueblo culture. To the west Hoho-kam may also be shown to be related to the Patayan development.

Basket Maker would seem to have been the second distinctive cultural group in the Southwest. Although there are many similarities between Basket Maker and Mogollon it is the feeling of the writer that these are more the result of a common relationship back to the Desert culture, and a matter of environmental influence, than identities of people. It is quite likely that Basket Maker represents only a Southwestern variation of a basic widespread general culture in North America, although many more definite comparisons are needed before this postulation may be established.

From the Basket Maker Root in the plateau area grew the later northern developments. Combined with Mogollon and influenced by Hohokam it gave rise to Pueblo. This culture enjoyed a remarkable rise in importance, and soon was so strong that it spread into the desert section, as well as into the Rio Grande valley to the east.

From these two cultures, it is now felt, the rest grew. They did not de-velop alone, unmodified, in isolation, but almost certainly with many addi-tions gleaned from far and wide. Mexican influences have already been pointed out in typical Hohokam. Such contributions to Southwestern culture may now be demonstrated, and as other areas are more carefully studied more influences will probably be found.

Next to basic influences upon which culture has been built the archaeologist is interested in disruptive or important events whch have contributed to the history of the group being studied. When the nature and causes of such events are understood much of the functioning of human culture becomes clear. Two such periods of disruption may be indicated in the prehistory of the Southwest. For some time the nature and effects of the great drought have been known. This event contributed to the abandonment of the San Juan drainage area and lent strong impetus to the southern shift of people and culture which had already been under way.

In an effort to demonstrate the importance of this event better, a chart has been prepared. This is a graphic representation of the last dates found at a number of ruins. Only the period from A.D. 400 to 1500 has been chosen, for it is this span which covers most of the well-known archaeological history. Each vertical column represents a period of 50 years, and each column is the relative height of the number of sites which show an end date falling within this period. The fact that more dates have been secured from sites at the more recent end of this series should be kept in mind as it

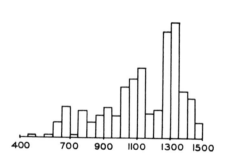

400   700   900   1100   1300 1500

Fig. 208. Chart showing the latest dates of sites which fall between A.D. 400 and 1500. The data from which this chart was built does not include all of the many presently dated sites, but it is felt that it gives some indication of the relative abundance of such dates at any given time. End dates have been grouped by 50-year periods, and the numbers indicated by the relative heights of the columns. The tallest column, from 1300 to 1350, represents 29 sites whose latest dates fall into this span. Two peaks may be noted, one at about A.D. 1100 and the other at about A.D. 1300.

is examined, for the columns are higher at the right than at the left of this chart.

In preparing the chart it was felt that the last dates at ruins would fall somewhere near the time of abandonment of the site, and that abandonment would indicate that the people were generally restless and moving about the country. These would also be periods of cultural disruption, for all factors sufficiently basic to cause population movements would be important enough to alter culture. Two such peaks may readily be noted in the chart. The first of these became marked at about A.D. 1000 and reached its peak at about A.D. 1100. The second is of shorter duration and is clearly confined to a time near A.D. 1300.

Probably conditions had become markedly unsettled before the great drought actually set in, but there can be little doubt that it was the deciding factor in large population shifts. The drought itself was likely somewhat in the nature of a last cause, the straw which broke the camel's back, and not the only motivating factor. Large sites were widely established at this time, particularly in the San Juan, and the human cycle, already explained, would have been well advanced in most of them. If this were true many natural resources, particularly underground water, would be locally almost exhausted, or at least in a critical state. Other factors not now well understood were also probably contributing elements. This period, however, is one of the most important that may be pointed out in Southwestern history.

As has been suggested, the earlier period seems to have had its origin about 1000 and to have reached its peak about A.D. 1100. Widespread causes which were behind this movement are much more difficult to explain. By A.D. 1000 Pueblo culture had begun its southward expansion in the form of the Salado branch. Present information, particularly that gleaned at Winona Village, indicates that this was not a one-directional culture advance, but was really an exchange. At this site reciprocal influences were certainly felt between the north and south. Here movements of people may be explained by the eruption of Sunset Crater, which, once the cinder mulch had been anchored above the old clay soil, formed an ideal agricultural area. In fact it had such great drawing powers that people flooded into this small area from all sides. It appears that here was one of the major gateways of exchange of ideas between the basic physiographic and cultural areas of the Southwest at this time. Too little information is had on other areas to point out similar influences.

The many sites now abandoned would certainly indicate that it was a period of general restlessness. Such a situation may best be explained by widespread contacts with other groups. It has already been indicated that expansion was taking place. Populations were increasing radically, and cultural development was very uneven regionally. All these factors probably combined to form the beginning of a unification of cultures and the creation of what is often referred to as a general Southwestern pattern. Regional variation certainly existed after this time, but it was not so marked as it had been previously. It is the cultures which existed after about A.D. 1100 that are generally thought of as truly Southwestern, for it was largely after this date that the pueblo, widespread pottery design similarities, elaborate weaving, and a great many other traits are to be found best represented.

Similar influences were at work in northern New Mexico. In fact the northern Rio Grande is in many respects parallel to the history of north-eastern Arizona, although in many others shows an apparent slight lag.

Such generalizations as those which have just been made are the aim of archaeology, though in much greater detail, and a broad historical picture is striven for by archaeologists. From such studies it is hoped that object lessons may be pointed out which will help us better to understand ourselves, and so to control more intelligently our own actions in the future.

General Bibliography

Anyone seriously interested in Southwestern archaeology should become familiar with the following periodicals.

American Antiquity, published by the Society for American Archaeology, and printed at Salt Lake City, Utah.

American Anthropologist, published by the American Anthropological Association, and printed at Menasha, Wisconsin.

Southwestern Lore, published by the Colorado Archaeological Society, at Boulder, Colorado.

Museum Notes, published by the Museum of Northern Arizona, at Flagstaff, Arizona.

Tree Ring Bulletin, published by the Tree Ring Society, at the University of Arizona, Tucson, Arizona.

Masterkey, published by the Southwest Museum, at Los Angeles, California.

El Palacio, published by the Museum of New Mexico, at Santa Fe, New Mexico.

Mesa Verde Notes, published by Mesa Verde National Park, at Mesa Verde, Colorado.

Southwestern Monuments Archaeological Supplements, published by Southwestern Monuments, at Globe, Arizona.

New Mexican Anthropologist, published by the Department of Anthropology of the University of New Mexico, at Albuquerque, New Mexico.

Southwestern Journal of Anthropology, published by the University of New Mexico Press, at Albuquerque, New Mexico.

In compiling the following list of reference books and papers an attempt has been made to include only those which the writer feels are of particular importance and are as a rule readily available in an anthropological library.

ABEL, LELAND J.
  1955   Pottery Types of the Southwest, *Ceramic Series 3*, Museum of Northern Arizona, Flagstaff.

ADAMS, WILLIAM Y. AND NETTIE K.
  1959   An Inventory of Prehistoric Sites on the Lower San Juan River, Utah, *Bulletin 31*, Museum of Northern Arizona, Flagstaff.

AGOGINO, GEORGE A.
  1960   The San Jose Sites: A Cochise-like Manifestation in the Middle Rio Grande, *Southwestern Lore*, Vol. 26, No. 2.
  1960   The Santa Ana Pre-ceramic Sites: An Archaic Seed Gathering Culture in Sandoval County, New Mexico, *Southwestern Lore*, Vol. 25, No. 4.

AMSDEN, CHARLES AVERY
  1931   Man Hunting, *Masterkey*, Vol. 5, No. 2, July-August.
  1932   The Loom and Its Prototypes, *American Anthropologist*, Vol. 34, No. 2.
  1934   Navaho Weaving, Fine Arts Press, Santa Ana, California.
  1936   An Analysis of Hohokam Pottery Design, *Medallion Paper 23*, Gila Pueblo, Globe, Arizona.
  1938   The Ancient Basketmakers, *Masterkey*, Vol. 12, No. 6, November and following.
  1949   Prehistoric Southwesterners from Basketmaker to Pueblo, Southwest Museum, Los Angeles, California.

AMSDEN, MONROE
  1928   Archaeological Reconnaissance in Sonora, *Southwest Museum Paper 1*, Los Angeles, California.

ANTEVS, ERNST
  1936   Dating Records of Early Man in the Southwest, *American Naturalist*, Vol. 70, Lancaster, Pennsylvania.
  1959   Geological Dating of the Lehner Mammoth Site, *American Antiquity*, Vol. 25, No. 1.

ANTEVS, ERNST, AND EDGAR B. HOWARD
  1935   The Occurrence of Flints and Extinct Animals in Fluvial Deposits Near Clovis, New Mexico, and Age of the Clovis Lake Clays, *Proceedings of the Academy of Natural Sciences of Philadelphia*, Vol. 87.

BALDWIN, GORDON C.
  1935   Dates from Kinishba Pueblo, *Tree Ring Bulletin*, Vol. 1, No. 4.
  1938   An Analysis of Basket Maker III Sandals from Northeastern Arizona, *American Anthropologist*, Vol. 40, No. 3.
  1938   Basket Maker and Pueblo Sandals, *Southwestern Lore*, Vol. 4, No. 1.
  1938   Excavations at Kinishba Pueblo, Arizona, *American Antiquity*, Vol. 4, No. 1.
  1939   Dates from Kings Ruin, *Tree Ring Bulletin*, Vol. 5, No. 3.

BANCROFT, H. H.
  1889   History of Arizona and New Mexico, in The Works of Hubert Howe Bancroft, 1882 to 1890, Vol. 17, A. L. Bancroft & Co., San Francisco, California.

BANDELIER, A. F.
  1890   Investigations Among the Indians of the Southwestern United States,

Carried on Mainly in the Years from 1800 to 1885, *Papers of the Archaelogical Institute of America,* American Series III, Part I, Peabody Museum of American Archaeology and Ethnology, Harvard University, Cambridge, Massachusetts.

1890   Contributions to the History of the Southwestern Portion of the United States, *Papers of the Archaeological Institute of America,* American Series V, Peabody Museum of American Archaeology and Ethnology, Harvard University, Cambridge, Massachusetts.

BANNISTER, BRYANT

1959   Tree-Ring Dating of Archaeological Sites in the Chaco Canyon Region, New Mexico, Ph.D. dissertation, University of Arizona, Tucson, University Microfilms Inc., L.C. Card No. MIC 60-584.

1960   Southwestern Dated Ruins, VII, *Tree Ring Bulletin,* Vol. 23, Nos. 1-4.

1962   The Interpretation of Tree-Ring Dates, *American Antiquity,* Vol. 27, No. 4.

1962   Ed. Andrew Ellicott Douglass, *Tree Ring Bulletin,* Vol. 24, Nos. 3-4.

BARBER, E. A.

1876   The Ancient Pottery of Colorado, Utah, Arizona, and New Mexico, *American Naturalist,* Vol. 10, Cambridge, Massachusetts.

BARTLETT, KATHARINE

1930   Stone Artifacts; San Francisco Mountain Region, *Museum Notes,* Vol. 3, No. 6.

1931   Prehistoric Pueblo Foods, *Museum Notes,* Vol. 4, No. 4.

1933   Pueblo Milling Stones of the Flagstaff Region and Their Relation to Others in the Southwest, *Bulletin 3,* Museum of Northern Arizona, Flagstaff.

1933   Life in Pueblo II, *Museum Notes,* Vol. 6, No. 3.

1934   Material Culture of Pueblo II in the San Francisco Mountains, Arizona, *Bulletin 7,* Museum of Northern Arizona, Flagstaff.

1935   Prehistoric Mining in the Southwest, *Museum Notes,* Vol. 7, No. 10.

1936   The Utilization of Maize Among the Ancient Pueblos, *Bulletin 296,* University of New Mexico, Albuquerque.

1943   A Primitive Stone Industry of the Little Colorado Valley, Arizona, *American Antiquity,* Vol. 8, No. 3.

BEALS, RALPH L., G. W. BRAINERD, AND WATSON SMITH

1945   Archaeological Studies in Northeast Arizona, *Publications in American Archaeology and Ethnology,* Vol. 44, No. 1, University of California Press, Berkeley.

BICKFORD, F. T.

1890   Prehistoric Cave Dwellings, *Century Magazine,* October, New York City.

BLUHM, ELAINE A.

1957   The Sawmill Site, a Reserve Phase Village, Pine Lawn Valley, Western New Mexico, *Fieldiana: Anthropology,* Vol. 47, No. 1, Chicago Natural History Museum.

1960   Mogollon Settlement Patterns in Pine Lawn Valley, New Mexico, *American Antiquity,* Vol. 25, No. 4.

BOLTON, H. E.
    1916 Spanish Exploration in the Southwest, 1542 to 1706, Charles Scribner's
          Sons, New York City.
BOTELHO, GEORGE W.
    1955 Pinto Basin Points in Utah, *American Antiquity*, Vol. 21, No. 2.
BRADFIELD, WESLEY
    1929 Cameron Creek Village, a Site in the Mimbres Area in Grant County,
          New Mexico, School of American Research, Santa Fe, New Mexico.
BRAIDWOOD, ROBERT J., AND GORDON R. WILLEY
    1962 Eds. Courses Toward Urban Life, *Viking Fund Publications in An-*
          thropology, No. 32, New York City.
BRAND, DONALD
    1938 Aboriginal Trade Routes for Sea Shells in the Southwest, *Yearbook of*
          the Association of Pacific Coast Geographers, Vol. 4, Cheney, Wash-
          ington.
BRANDES, RAY
    1960 Archaeological Awareness of the Southwest as Illustrated in Literature
          to 1890, *Arizona and the West*, Vol. 2, No. 1, Tucson, Arizona.
BRETERNITZ, DAVID A.
    1959 Excavations at Nantack Village, Point of Pines, *University of Arizona*
          Anthropological Paper 1, Tucson.
    1959 Excavations at Two Cinder Park Phase Sites, *Plateau*, Vol. 31, No. 3,
          Museum of Northern Arizona, Flagstaff.
    1963 Archaeological Interpretation of Tree Ring Specimens for Dating South-
          western Ceramic Styles, Ph.D. dissertation, University of Arizona, Tuc-
          son.
BREW, J. O.
    1937 The First Two Seasons at Awatovi, *American Antiquity*, Vol. 3, No. 2.
    1946 Archaeology of Alkali Ridge, Southeastern Utah, *Papers of the Pea-*
          body Museum of American Archaeology and Ethnology, Vol. 21, Har-
          vard University, Cambridge, Massachusetts.
BRYAN, FRANK
    1938 A Review of the Geology of the Clovis Finds Reported by Howard
          and Cotter, *American Antiquity*, Vol. 4, No. 2.
BRYAN, KIRK
    1941 Geologic Antiquity of Man in America, *Science*, Vol. 93, No. 2422, New
          York City.
BRYAN, KIRK, AND L. L. RAY
    1940 Geologic Antiquity of the Lindenmeier Site in Colorado, *Smithsonian*
          Miscellaneous Collections, Vol. 99, No. 2, Washington, D.C.
BRYAN, KIRK, AND JOSEPH H. TOULOUSE, JR.
    1943 The San Jose Non-ceramic Culture and Its Relation to a Puebloan Cul-
          ture in New Mexico, *American Antiquity*, Vol. 8, No. 3.
CAMPBELL, E. W. AND W. H.
    1935 The Pinto Basin Site, *Southwest Museum Paper 9*, Los Angeles, Cali-
          fornia.
CAMPBELL, E. W. AND W. H., ERNST ANTEVS, CHARLES AVERY AMSDEN, J. A.

BARBIERI, AND F. D. BODE
  1937 The Archaeology of Pleistocene Lake Mohave, *Southwest Museum Paper 11*, Los Angeles, California.
CAYWOOD, LOUIS R., AND EDWARD H. SPICER
  1935 Tuzigoot, the Excavation and Repair of a Ruin on the Verde River Near Clarkdale, Arizona, Field Division of Education, National Park Service, Berkeley, California.
CHAPIN, FREDERICK H.
  1892 The Land of the Cliff Dwellers, W. D. Clark and Co., Boston.
COLE, FAY-COOPER, AND THORNE DEUEL
  1937 Rediscovering Illinois, University of Chicago Press.
COLTON, HAROLD S.
  1918 The Little Known Small House Ruins in the Coconino National Forest, *Memoirs of the American Anthropological Association*, Vol. 6, No. 4, Lancaster, Pennsylvania.
  1918 The Geography of Certain Ruins Near the San Francisco Mountains, Arizona, *Bulletin of the Geographical Society of Philadelphia*, Vol. 16, No. 2.
  1930 A Brief Survey of the Early Expeditions into Northern Arizona, *Museum Notes*, Vol. 2, No. 9.
  1932 Sunset Crater, the Effect of a Volcanic Eruption on an Ancient Pueblo People, *Geographical Review*, Vol. 22, No. 4, American Geographical Society, New York City.
  1932 A Survey of Prehistoric Sites in the Region of Flagstaff, Arizona, *Bulletin 104*, Bureau of American Ethnology, Washington, D.C.
  1935 Stages in Northern Arizona Prehistory, *Museum Notes*, Vol. 8, No. 1.
  1936 The Rise and Fall of the Prehistoric Population of Northern Arizona, *Science*, Vol. 84, No. 2181, New York City.
  1938 Names of the Four Culture Roots in the Southwest, *Science*, Vol. 87, No. 2268, New York City.
  1939 The Reducing Atmosphere and Oxidizing Atmosphere in Prehistoric Southwestern Ceramics, *American Antiquity*, Vol. 4, No. 3.
  1939 Primitive Pottery Firing Methods, *Museum Notes*, Vol. 11, No. 10.
  1939 An Archaeological Survey of Northeastern Arizona in 1938, *Bulletin 16*, Museum of Northern Arizona, Flagstaff.
  1939 Prehistoric Culture Units and Their Relationships in Northern Arizona, *Bulletin 17*, Museum of Northern Arizona, Flagstaff.
  1941 Winona and Ridge Ruin, Part II. Technology and Taxonomy of the Pottery, *Bulletin 19*, Museum of Northern Arizona, Flagstaff.
  1942 Archaeology and the Reconstruction of History, *American Antiquity*, Vol. 8, No. 1.
  1945 The Patayan Problem in the Colorado River Valley, *Southwestern Journal of Anthropology*, Vol. 1, No. 1.
  1945 A Revision of the Date of the Eruption of Sunset Crater, *Southwestern Journal of Anthropology*, Vol. 1, No. 3.
  1946 The Sinagua. A Summary of the Archaeology of the Region of Flagstaff, Arizona, *Bulletin 22*, Museum of Northern Arizona, Flagstaff.
  1953 Potsherds, *Bulletin 25*, Museum of Northern Arizona, Flagstaff.

1955   Check List of Southwestern Pottery Types, *Ceramic Series 2,* Museum of Northern Arizona, Flagstaff.

1955   Pottery Types of the Southwest, *Ceramic Series 3,* Museum of Northern Arizona, Flagstaff.

1956   Pottery Types of the Southwest, *Ceramic Series 3C,* Museum of Northern Arizona, Flagstaff.

1958   Pottery Types of the Southwest, *Ceramic Series 3D,* Museum of Northern Arizona, Flagstaff.

1960   Black Sand: Prehistory in Northern Arizona, University of New Mexico Press, Albuquerque.

COLTON, HAROLD S., AND LYNDON L. HARGRAVE

1933   Pueblo II in the San Francisco Mountains, Arizona, and Pueblo II Houses in the San Francisco Mountains, Arizona, *Bulletin 4,* Museum of Northern Arizona, Flagstaff.

1937   Handbook of Northern Arizona Pottery Wares, *Bulletin 11,* Museum of Northern Arizona, Flagstaff.

COLTON, M. R. F. AND HAROLD S.

1918   The Little-Known Small House Ruins in the Coconino Forest, *Memoirs of the American Anthropological Association,* Vol. 4, No. 4, Lancaster, Pennsylvania.

COSGROVE, C. B.

1947   Caves of the Upper Gila and Hueco Areas in New Mexico and Texas, *Papers of the Peabody Museum of American Archaeology and Ethnology,* Vol. 24, No. 2, Harvard University, Cambridge, Massachusetts.

COSGROVE, C. B. AND H. S.

1932   The Swarts Ruin, a Typical Mimbres Site in Southwestern New Mexico, *Papers of the Peabody Museum of American Archaeology and Ethnology,* Vol. 15, No. 1, Harvard University, Cambridge, Massachusetts.

CUMMINGS, BYRON

1910   The Ancient Inhabitants of the San Juan Valley, *Bulletin of the University of Utah,* Second Archaeological Number, Vol. 3, No. 3, Part 2, Salt Lake City.

1915   Kivas of the San Juan Drainage, *American Anthropologist,* Vol. 17, No. 2.

1935   The Archaeology of the Southwest, *The Kiva,* Arizona Archaeological and Historical Society, Arizona State Museum, Tucson.

1940   Kinishba, a Prehistoric Pueblo of the Great Pueblo Period, Hohokam Museums Association, University of Arizona, Tucson.

1953   First Inhabitants of Arizona and the Southwest, Cummings Publication Council, Tucson, Arizona.

DAIFUKU, HIROSHI

1952   A New Conceptual Scheme for Prehistoric Cultures in the Southwestern United States, *American Anthropologist,* Vol. 54, No. 2.

DANSON, EDWARD BRIDGE

1957   An Archaeological Survey of West Central New Mexico and East Central Arizona, *Papers of the Peabody Museum of American Archaeology and Ethnology,* Vol. 44, No. 1, Harvard University, Cambridge, Massachusetts.

DAVIS, JEROME
   1927   An Introduction to Sociology, D. C. Heath and Co., Boston, Massa-
          chusetts.
DICK, HERBERT W.
   1954   The Bat Cave—Pod Corn Complex: A Note on Its Distribution and
          Archaeological Significance, *El Palacio*, Vol. 61, No. 5.
DI PESO, CHARLES C.
   1951   The Babocomari Village Site on the Babocomari River, Southeastern
          Arizona, No. 5, the Amerind Foundation, Inc., Dragoon, Arizona.
   1958   The Reeve Ruin of Southeastern Arizona, No. 8, the Amerind Founda-
          tion, Inc., Dragoon, Arizona.
DITTERT, ALFRED E., JR.
   1958   Navajo Project Studies, I. Preliminary Archaeological Investigations in
          the Navajo Project Area of Northwestern New Mexico, *Papers in An-
          thropology 1*, Museum of New Mexico, Santa Fe.
DITTERT, ALFRED E., JR., FRANK W. EDDY, AND BETH L. DICKEY
   1963   Evidences of Early Ceramic Phases in the Navajo Reservoir District,
          El Palacio, Vol. 70, Nos. 1-2.
DITTERT, ALFRED E., JR., JAMES J. HESTER, AND FRANK W. EDDY
   1961   An Archaeological Survey of the Navajo Reservoir District, Northwest-
          ern New Mexico, *Monograph 23*, Museum of New Mexico, Santa Fe.
DIXON, RONALD
   1928   The Building of Culture, Charles Scribner's Sons, New York City.
DOUGLASS, A. E.
   1928   Climatic Cycles and Tree Growth, *Carnegie Institution Publication 289*,
          Washington, D.C.
   1929   The Secret of the Southwest Solved by Talkative Tree Rings, *National
          Geographic Magazine*, December, Washington, D.C.
   1935   Dating Pueblo Bonito and Other Ruins of the Southwest, *Pueblo Bonito
          Series 1*, Contributed Technical Papers, National Geographic Society,
          Washington, D.C.
   1936   The Central Pueblo Chronology, *Tree Ring Bulletin*, Vol. 2, No. 4.
   1936   Climatic Cycles and Tree Growth, Vol. III, A Study of Cycles, Carnegie
          Institution, Washington, D.C.
   1937   Tree Rings and Chronology, *University of Arizona Bulletin*, Vol. 8, No.
          4, Tucson.
   1938   Southwestern Dated Ruins: V, *Tree Ring Bulletin*, Vol. 5, No. 2.
EDDY, FRANK W., AND BETH L. DICKEY
   1961   Excavations at Los Pinos Sites in the Navajo Reservoir District, *Papers
          in Anthropology 4*, Museum of New Mexico, Santa Fe.
EULER, ROBERT C.
   1963   Archaeological Problems in Western and Northwestern Arizona, 1962,
          Plateau, Vol. 35, No. 3, Museum of Northern Arizona, Flagstaff.
EULER, ROBERT C., AND HENRY F. DOBYNS
   1962   Excavations West of Prescott, Arizona, *Plateau*, Vol. 34, No. 3, Museum
          of Northern Arizona, Flagstaff.
EZELL, PAUL H.
   1963   Is There a Hohokam-Pima Culture Continuum? *American Antiquity*,
          Vol. 29, No. 1.

FEWKES, JESSE WALTER
  1898   Archaeological Expedition to Arizona in 1895, *Seventeenth Annual Report*, Part II, Bureau of American Ethnology, Washington, D.C.
  1904   Two Summers' Work in Pueblo Ruins, *Twenty-second Annual Report*, Bureau of American Ethnology, Washington, D.C.
  1907   Excavations at Casa Grande, Arizona, *Smithsonian Miscellaneous Collections*, Vol. 50 (quarterly issue, Vol. 4, Part 3), Washington, D.C.
  1909   Antiquities of the Mesa Verde National Park: Spruce Tree House, *Bulletin 41*, Bureau of American Ethnology, Washington, D.C.
  1910   Cremation in Cliff-Dwellings, *Records of the Past*, Vol. 9, Part III, Washington, D.C.
  1911   Antiquities of Mesa Verde National Park: Cliff Palace, *Bulletin 51*, Bureau of American Ethnology, Washington, D.C.
  1912   Casa Grande, Arizona, *Twenty-eighth Annual Report*, Bureau of American Ethnology, Washington, D.C.
  1917   Archaeological Investigations in New Mexico, Colorado, and Utah, *Smithsonian Miscellaneous Collections*, Vol. 68, No. 1, Washington, D.C.
  1919   Designs on Prehistoric Hopi Pottery, *Thirty-third Annual Report*, Bureau of American Ethnology, Washington, D.C.
  1924   Designs on Prehistoric Pottery from the Mimbres Valley, New Mexico, *Smithsonian Miscellaneous Collections*, Vol. 76, No. 6, Washington, D.C.
  1924   Additional Designs on Prehistoric Mimbres Pottery, *Smithsonian Miscellaneous Collections*, Vol. 76, No. 6, Washington, D.C.
  1926   An Archaeological Collection from Youngs Canyon, Near Flagstaff, Arizona, *Smithsonian Miscellaneous Collections*, Vol. 77, No. 10, Washington, D.C.
FRANKE, PAUL R.
  1933   New Dates from Mesa Verde Ruins, *Mesa Verde Notes*, Vol. 4, No. 1.
  1935   Mesa Verde's Place in the Southwest Story, *Southwestern Lore*, Vol. 1, No. 2.
FULTON, W. S.
  1941   A Ceremonial Cave in the Winchester Mountains, Arizona, No. 2, the Amerind Foundation, Inc., Dragoon, Arizona.
FULTON, W. S., AND CARR TUTHILL
  1940   An Archaeological Site Near Gleeson, Arizona, No. 1, the Amerind Foundation, Inc., Dragoon, Arizona.
GETTY, H. T.
  1935   Dates from Spruce Tree House, *Tree Ring Bulletin*, Vol. 1, No. 4.
  1935   New Dates from Mesa Verde, *Tree Ring Bulletin*, Vol. 1, No. 3.
GIFFORD, E. W.
  1928   Pottery-Making in the Southwest, *Publications in American Archaeology and Ethnology*, Vol. 23, No. 8, University of California Press, Berkeley.
GLADWIN, H. S.
  1928   Excavations at Casa Grande, Arizona, *Southwest Museum Paper 2*, Los Angeles, California.
  1937   Excavations at Snaketown II, Comparisons and Theories, *Medallion Paper 26*, Gila Pueblo, Globe, Arizona.

1940 Methods and Instruments for Use in Measuring Tree-Rings, *Medallion Paper 27*, Gila Pueblo, Globe, Arizona.

1940 Tree-Ring Analysis, Methods of Correlation, *Medallion Paper 28*, Gila Pueblo, Globe, Arizona.

1942 Excavations at Snaketown III, Revisions, *Medallion Paper 30*, Gila Pueblo, Globe, Arizona.

1943 A Review and Analysis of the Flagstaff Culture, *Medallion Paper 31*, Gila Pueblo, Globe, Arizona.

1944 Tree-Ring Analysis. Problems of Dating I. The Medicine Valley Sites, *Medallion Paper 32*, Gila Pueblo, Globe, Arizona.

1945 The Chaco Branch, Excavations at White Mound and in the Red Mesa Valley, *Medallion Paper 33*, Gila Pueblo, Globe, Arizona.

— Tree-Ring Analysis. Tree-Rings and Droughts, *Medallion Paper 37*, Gila Pueblo, Globe, Arizona.

1948 Excavations at Snaketown IV, Reviews and Conclusions, *Medallion Paper 38*, Gila Pueblo, Globe, Arizona.

GLADWIN, H. S., EMIL W. HAURY, E. B. SAYLES, AND NORA GLADWIN

1937 Excavations at Snaketown, Material Culture, *Medallion Paper 25*, Gila Pueblo, Globe, Arizona.

GLADWIN, WINIFRED AND H. S.

1928 A Method for Designation of Ruins in the Southwest, *Medallion Paper 1*, Gila Pueblo, Globe, Arizona.

1928 The Use of Potsherds in an Archaeological Survey of the Southwest, *Medallion Paper 2*, Gila Pueblo, Globe, Arizona.

1929 The Red-on-Buff Culture of the Gila Basin, *Medallion Paper 3*, Gila Pueblo, Globe, Arizona.

1930 The Red-on-Buff Culture of the Papagueria, *Medallion Paper 4*, Gila Pueblo, Globe, Arizona.

1930 The Western Range of the Red-on-Buff Culture, *Medallion Paper 5*, Gila Pueblo, Globe, Arizona.

1930 An Archaeological Survey of the Verde Valley, *Medallion Paper 6*, Gila Pueblo, Globe, Arizona.

1930 A Method for the Designation of Southwestern Pottery Types, *Medallion Paper 7*, Gila Pueblo, Globe, Arizona.

1930 Some Southwestern Pottery Types, Series I, *Medallion Paper 8*, Gila Pueblo, Globe, Arizona.

1931 Some Southwestern Pottery Types, Series II, *Medallion Paper 10*, Gila Pueblo, Globe, Arizona.

1933 Some Southwestern Pottery Types, Series III, *Medallion Paper 13*, Gila Pueblo, Globe, Arizona.

1934 A Method for the Designation of Cultures and Their Variations, *Medallion Paper 15*, Gila Pueblo, Globe, Arizona.

1935 The Eastern Range of the Red-on-Buff Culture, *Medallion Paper 16*, Gila Pueblo, Globe, Arizona.

GLOCK, WALDO S.

1934 The Language of Tree Rings, *Scientific Monthly*, Vol. 38, Lancaster, Pennsylvania.

1937   Principles and Methods of Tree-Ring Analysis, *Carnegie Institution Publication 486,* Washington, D.C.

GREGORY, H. E.
   1915   The Navaho Country, *Bulletin 380,* United States Geological Survey, Washington, D.C.

GUERNSEY, SAMUEL J.
   1931   Explorations in Northeastern Arizona, *Papers of the Peabody Museum of American Archaeology and Ethnology,* Vol. 12, No. 1, Harvard University, Cambridge, Massachusetts.

GUERNSEY, SAMUEL J., AND ALFRED VINCENT KIDDER
   1921   Basket Maker Caves of Northeastern Arizona, *Papers of the Peabody Museum of American Archaeology and Ethnology,* Vol. 8, No. 2, Harvard University, Cambridge, Massachusetts.

GUNNERSON, JAMES H.
   1956   A Fluted Point Site in Utah, *American Antiquity,* Vol. 21, No. 4.

HACK, JOHN T.
   1942   The Changing Physical Environment of the Hopi Indians of Arizona, *Papers of the Peabody Museum of American Archaeology and Ethnology,* Vol. 35, No. 1, Harvard University, Cambridge, Massachusetts.

HALL, E. T., JR.
   1942   Archaeological Survey of Walhalla Glades, *Bulletin 20,* Museum of Northern Arizona, Flagstaff.

   1944   Early Stockaded Settlements in the Governador, New Mexico, *Columbia Studies in Archaeology and Ethnology,* Vol. 2, Part 1, New York City.

HALSETH, ODD S.
   1936   Prehistoric Irrigation in the Salt River Valley, *Bulletin 296,* University of New Mexico, Albuquerque.

HARGRAVE, LYNDON L.
   1929   Elden Pueblo, *Museum Notes,* Vol. 2, No. 5.

   1931   Prehistoric Earth Lodges of the San Francisco Mountains, *Museum Notes,* Vol. 3, No. 5.

   1932   Guide to Forty Pottery Types from the Hopi Country and the San Francisco Mountains, Arizona, *Bulletin 1,* Museum of Northern Arizona, Flagstaff.

   1933   The Museum of Northern Arizona Archaeological Expedition, 1933, Wupatki National Monument, *Museum Notes,* Vol. 6, No. 5.

   1935   Archaeological Investigations in the Tsegi Canyons of Northeastern Arizona in 1934, *Museum Notes,* Vol. 7, No. 7.

   1935   Report on Archaeological Reconnaissance in the Rainbow Plateau Area of Northern Arizona and Southern Utah, University of California Press, Berkeley.

   1936   The Field Collector of Beam Material, *Tree Ring Bulletin,* Vol. 2, No. 3.

   1938   Results of a Study of the Cohonina Branch of the Patayan Culture in 1938, *Museum Notes,* Vol. 11, No. 6.

HARGRAVE, LYNDON L., AND HAROLD S. COLTON
   1935   What Do Potsherds Tell Us? *Museum Notes,* Vol. 7, No. 12.

HARGRAVE, LYNDON L., AND WATSON SMITH
   1936   A Method for Determining the Texture of Pottery, *American Antiquity,* Vol. 2, No. 1.

HARLAN, T. P.
  1962 A Sequence of Ruins in the Flagstaff Area Dated by Tree-Rings, Master's thesis, University of Arizona, Tucson.
HARRINGTON, M. R.
  1933 Gypsum Cave, Nevada, *Southwest Museum Paper 8*, Los Angeles, California.
  1948 An Ancient Site at Borax Lake, California, *Southwest Museum Paper 16*, Los Angeles, California.
HARRINGTON, M. R., I. HAYDON, AND L. SCHELLBACK
  1930 Archaeological Explorations in Southern Nevada, *Southwest Museum Paper 4*, Los Angeles, California.
HAURY, EMIL W.
  1931 Minute Beads from Prehistoric Pueblos, *American Anthropologist*, Vol. 33, No. 1.
  1931 Kivas of the Tusayan Ruin, Grand Canyon, Arizona, *Medallion Paper 9*, Gila Pueblo, Globe, Arizona.
  1932 Roosevelt: 9-6, a Hohokam Site of the Colonial Period, *Medallion Paper 11*, Gila Pueblo, Globe, Arizona.
  1932 The Age of Lead Glaze Decorated Pottery in the Southwest, *American Anthropologist*, Vol. 34, No. 3.
  1934 The Canyon Creek Ruin and the Cliff Dwellings of the Sierra Ancha, *Medallion Paper 14*, Gila Pueblo, Globe, Arizona.
  1935 Dates from Gila Pueblo, *Tree Ring Bulletin*, Vol. 2, No. 1.
  1935 Tree Rings—the Archaeologist's Time-Piece, *American Antiquity*, Vol. 1, No. 2.
  1936 Some Southwestern Pottery Types, Series IV, *Medallion Paper 19*, Gila Pueblo, Globe, Arizona.
  1936 The Mogollon Culture of Southwestern New Mexico, *Medallion Paper 20*, Gila Pueblo, Globe, Arizona.
  1936 The Snaketown Canal, *Bulletin 296*, University of New Mexico, Albuquerque.
  1937 A Pre-Spanish Rubber Ball from Arizona, *American Antiquity*, Vol. 2, No. 4.
  1938 Southwestern Dated Ruins, II, *Tree Ring Bulletin*, Vol. 4, No. 3.
  1940 Excavations in the Forestdale Valley, East-Central Arizona, *University of Arizona Social Science Bulletin 12*, Tucson.
  1942 Some Implications of the Bluff Ruin Dates, *Tree Ring Bulletin*, Vol. 9, No. 2.
  1943 The Stratigraphy of Ventana Cave, *American Antiquity*, Vol. 8, No. 3.
  1943 A Possible Cochise-Mogollon-Hohokam Sequence, *Proceedings of the American Philosophical Society*, Vol. 86, No. 2, Philadelphia.
  1945 The Excavation of Los Muertos and Neighboring Ruins in the Salt River Valley, Southern Arizona, *Papers of the Peabody Museum of American Archaeology and Ethnology*, Vol. 24, No. 1, Harvard University, Cambridge, Massachusetts.
  1945 Painted Cave, Northeastern Arizona, No. 3, the Amerind Foundation, Inc., Dragoon, Arizona.
  1945 The Problem of Contacts Between the Southwestern United States and Mexico, *Southwestern Journal of Anthropology*, Vol. 1, No. 1.

1950   The Stratigraphy and Archaeology of Ventana Cave, Arizona, University of New Mexico Press, Albuquerque.

1953   Artifacts with Mammoth Remains, Naco, Arizona: Discovery of the Naco Mammoth and the Associated Projectile Points, *American Antiquity*, Vol. 19, No. 1.

1960   Association of Fossil Fauna and Artifacts of the Sulphur Springs Stage, Cochise Culture, *American Antiquity*, Vol. 25, No. 4.

1962   HH-39: Recollections of a Dramatic Moment in Southwestern Archaeology, *Tree-Ring Bulletin*, Vol. 24, Nos. 3-4.

1962   The Greater American Southwest, in Courses Toward Urban Life, ed. by Robert J. Braidwood and Gordon R. Willey, *Viking Fund Publications in Anthropology*, No. 32, New York City.

HAURY, EMIL W., AND CARL M. CONRAD
1938   The Comparison of Fiber Properties of Arizona Cliff-Dweller and Hopi Cotton, *American Antiquity*, Vol. 3, No. 3.

HAURY, EMIL W., AND I. F. FLORA
1937   Basket-Maker III Dates from the Vicinity of Durango, Colorado, *Tree Ring Bulletin*, Vol. 4, No. 1.

HAURY, EMIL W., AND LYNDON L. HARGRAVE
1931   Recently Dated Pueblo Ruins in Arizona, *Smithsonian Miscellaneous Collections*, Vol. 82, No. 11, Washington, D.C.

HAURY, EMIL W., AND E. B. SAYLES
1947   An Early Pit House Village of the Mogollon Culture, Forestdale Valley, Arizona, *University of Arizona Social Science Bulletin 16*, Tucson.

HAURY, EMIL W., E. B. SAYLES, AND WILLIAM W. WASLEY
1959   The Lehner Mammoth Site, Southeastern Arizona, *American Antiquity*, Vol. 25, No. 1.

HAWLEY, FLORENCE M.
1929   Prehistoric Pottery Pigments in the Southwest, *American Anthropologist*, Vol. 31, No. 4.

1934   The Significance of the Dated Prehistory of Chetro Ketl, Chaco Canyon, New Mexico, *University of New Mexico Bulletin*, Monograph Series, Vol. 1, No. 1, Albuquerque.

1936   Field Manual of Prehistoric Southwestern Pottery Types, *University of New Mexico Bulletin 291*, Albuquerque.

HESTER, JAMES J.
In Press Blackwater Locality No. 1, a Stratified Paleo-Indian Site in Eastern New Mexico, Texas Memorial Museum, Fort Burgwin Research Center.

HEWETT, EDGAR L.
1906   Antiquities of the Jemez Plateau, New Mexico, *Bulletin 32*, Bureau of American Ethnology, Washington, D.C.

1930   Ancient Life in the American Southwest, Bobbs-Merrill Co., Indianapolis, Indiana.

HIBBEN, FRANK C.
1937   Association of Man with Pleistocene Mammals in the Sandia Mountains, New Mexico, *American Antiquity*, Vol. 2, No. 4.

1938   The Gallina Phase, *American Antiquity*, Vol. 4, No. 2.

1948   The Gallina Architectural Forms, *American Antiquity*, Vol. 13, No. 1.

1949   The Pottery of the Gallina Complex, *American Antiquity*, Vol. 14, No. 3.

HIBBEN, FRANK C., AND BRYAN KIRK
  1941 Evidences of Early Occupation in Sandia Cave, New Mexico, and Other Sites in the Sandia-Manzano Region, with an Appendix: Correlation of the Deposits of Sandia Cave, New Mexico, with the Glacial Geology, *Smithsonian Miscellaneous Collections*, Vol. 99, No. 23, Washington, D.C.

HODGE, F. W.
  1920 Hawikuh Bonework, *Indian Notes and Monographs*, Vol. 3, No. 3, Museum of the American Indian, Heye Foundation, New York City.
  1923 Circular Kivas Near Hawikuh, New Mexico, *Contributions*, Vol. 7, No. 1, Museum of the American Indian, Heye Foundation, New York City.

HOOVER, J. W.
  1929 The Indian Country of Southern Arizona, *Geographical Review*, Vol. 19, No. 1, American Geographical Society, New York City.
  1929 Modern Canyon Dwellers of Arizona, *Journal of Geography*, Vol. 28, No. 7, Chicago.
  1930 Tusayan, the Hopi Indian Country of Arizona, *Geographical Review*, Vol. 20, No. 3, American Geographical Society, New York City.
  1935 House and Village Types of the Southwest as Conditioned by Aridity, *Scientific Monthly*, Vol. 40, New York City.
  1936 Physiographic Provinces of Arizona, *Pan-American Geologist*, Vol. 65, Geological Publishing Co., Des Moines, Iowa.

HOUGH, WALTER
  1903 Archaeological Field Work in Northeastern Arizona. The Museum Gates Expedition of 1901, Smithsonian Institution, Washington, D.C.
  1907 Antiquities in the Upper Gila and Salt River Valleys in Arizona and New Mexico, *Bulletin 35*, Bureau of American Ethnology, Washington, D.C.
  1914 Culture of the Ancient Pueblos of the Upper Gila and Salt River Region, New Mexico and Arizona, *Bulletin 89*, United States National Museum, Washington, D.C.
  1919 Explorations of a Pit House Village at Luna, New Mexico, *Proceedings of the United States National Museum*, Vol. 55, Washington, D.C.

HOWARD, EDGAR B.
  1935 Evidences of Early Man in North America, *Museum Journal*, Vol. 24, Nos. 2-3, University Museum, University of Pennsylvania, Philadelphia.
  1936 An Outline of the Problem of Man's Antiquity in North America, *American Anthropologist*, Vol. 38, No. 3.

JEANCON, J. A.
  1923 Excavations in the Chama Valley, New Mexico, *Bulletin 81*, Bureau of American Ethnology, Washington, D.C.
  1929 Archaeological Investigations in the Taos Valley, New Mexico, During 1920, *Smithsonian Miscellaneous Collections*, Vol. 81, No. 12, Washington, D.C.

JENNINGS, JESSE D.
  1955 The American Southwest: A Problem in Cultural Isolation, in Seminars in Archaeology: 1955, *American Antiquity*, Vol. 22, No. 2, Part 2.
  1957 Danger Cave, *Memoirs of the Society for American Archaeology*, No. 14, Salt Lake City, Utah.

1960   The Aboriginal Peoples, *Utah Historical Quarterly,* Vol. 28, No. 3, Salt Lake City.

JENNINGS, JESSE D., AND EDWARD NORBECK
1955   Great Basin Prehistory: A Review, *American Antiquity,* Vol. 21, No. 1.

JENNINGS, JESSE D., AND ERIK K. REED
1956   The American Southwest, a Problem in Cultural Isolation, *Memoirs of the Society for American Archaeology,* No. 11, Salt Lake City, Utah.

JOHNSON, FREDERICK
1951   Radiocarbon Dating, *American Antiquity,* Vol. 17, No. 1, Part 2.

JONES, VOLNEY H.
1936   A Summary on Data on Aboriginal Cotton in the Southwest, *Bulletin 296,* University of New Mexico, Albuquerque.

JUDD, NEIL M.
1926   Archaeological Observations North of the Rio Colorado, *Bulletin 82,* Bureau of American Ethnology, Washington, D.C.
1930   Dating Our Prehistoric Pueblo Ruins, from Explorations and Field Work of the Smithsonian Institution in 1929, Smithsonian Institution, Washington, D.C.
1930   The Excavation and Repair of Betatakin, *Smithsonian Institution Publication 2828,* Washington, D.C.
1940   Progress in the Southwest, in Essays in Historical Anthropology of North America, *Smithsonian Miscellaneous Collections,* Vol. 100, Washington, D.C.
1954   The Material Culture of Pueblo Bonito, *Smithsonian Miscellaneous Collections,* Vol. 123, Washington, D.C.

KIDDER, ALFRED VINCENT
1924   An Introduction to the Study of Southwestern Archaeology, Phillips Academy, Andover, Massachusetts.
1927   Southwestern Archaeological Conference, *Science,* Vol. 66, No. 1716, New York City.
1932   The Artifacts of Pecos, Phillips Academy, Andover, Massachusetts.
1936   The Archaeology of Peripheral Regions, *Southwestern Lore,* Vol. 2, No. 3.
1958   Pecos, New Mexico: Archaeological Notes, *Papers of the Peabody Foundation,* Vol. 5, Phillips Academy, Andover, Massachusetts.

KIDDER, ALFRED VINCENT, AND CHARLES AVERY AMSDEN
1931   The Pottery of Pecos, Vol. I, Phillips Academy, Andover, Massachusetts.

KIDDER, ALFRED VINCENT, AND SAMUEL J. GUERNSEY
1919   Archaeological Explorations in Northeastern Arizona, *Bulletin 65,* Bureau of American Ethnology, Washington, D.C.

KIDDER, ALFRED VINCENT, AND ANNA O. SHEPARD
1936   The Pottery of Pecos, Vol. II, Department of Archaeology, Phillips Academy, Andover, Massachusetts, Yale University Press, New Haven, Connecticut.

KING, DALE S.
1949   Nalakihu, Excavations at a Pueblo II Site on Wupatki National Monument, Arizona, *Bulletin 23,* Museum of Northern Arizona, Flagstaff.

KRIEGER, ALEX D.
  1962 The Earliest Cultures in Western United States, *American Antiquity,* Vol. 28, No. 2.
KROEBER, A. L.
  1916 Zuni Potsherds, *Anthropological Papers,* Vol. 18, Part I, American Museum of Natural History, New York City.
LANCASTER, J. A., AND D. W. WATSON
  1943 Excavation of Mesa Verde Pit Houses, *American Antiquity,* Vol. 9, No. 2.
LEHMER, DONALD J.
  1948 The Jornada Branch of the Mogollon, *University of Arizona Social Science Bulletin 17,* Tucson.
LINDSAY, ALEXANDER J., JR.
  1961 The Beaver Creek Archaeological Community on the San Juan River, Utah, *American Antiquity,* Vol. 27, No. 2.
LISTER, ROBERT F.
  1960 Plugging the Cultural Gap, *Desert, Magazine of the Outdoor Southwest,* Vol. 23, No. 12, Palm Desert, California.
  1961 Twenty-Five Years of Archaeology in the Greater Southwest, *American Antiquity,* Vol. 27, No. 1.
LOCKETT, H. CLAIBORNE
  1934 Northern Arizona's First Farmers, *Museum Notes,* Vol. 7, No. 4.
LOCKETT, H. CLAIBORNE, AND LYNDON L. HARGRAVE
  1953 Woodchuck Cave; a Basketmaker II Site in Tsegi Canyon, Arizona, *Bulletin 26,* Museum of Northern Arizona, Flagstaff.
MARTIN, PAUL S.
  1936 Lowry Ruin in Southwestern Colorado, *Anthropological Series,* Vol. 23, No. 1, Field Museum of Natural History, Chicago.
  1938 Archaeological Work in the Ackmen-Lowry Area, Southwestern Colorado, 1937, *Anthropological Series,* Vol. 23, No. 2, Field Museum of Natural History, Chicago.
  1940 The SU Site, Excavations at a Mogollon Village, Western New Mexico, *Anthropological Series,* Vol. 32, No. 1, Field Museum of Natural History, Chicago.
  1941 The SU Site, Excavations at a Mogollon Village, Western New Mexico. Second Season, *Anthropological Series,* Vol. 32, No. 2, Field Museum of Natural History, Chicago.
  1959 Digging into History. A Brief Account of Eighteen Years of Archaeological Work in New Mexico, *Chicago Natural History Museum Popular Series,* Anthropology, No. 38.
MARTIN, PAUL S., AND JOHN B. RINALDO
  1947 The SU Site, Excavations at a Mogollon Village, Western New Mexico, *Anthropological Series,* Vol. 32, No. 3, Field Museum of Natural History, Chicago.
  1950 Turkey Foot Ridge Site, a Mogollon Village, Pine Lawn Valley, Western New Mexico, *Fieldiana: Anthropology,* Vol. 38, No. 2, Chicago Natural History Museum.

1950   Sites of the Reserve Phase, Pine Lawn Valley, Western New Mexico, *Fieldiana: Anthropology*, Vol. 38, No. 3, Chicago Natural History Museum.

1951   The Southwestern Co-Tradition, *Southwestern Journal of Anthropology*, Vol. 7, No. 3.

1960   Excavations in the Upper Little Colorado Drainage, Eastern Arizona, *Fieldiana: Anthropology*, Vol. 51, No. 1, Chicago Natural History Museum.

1960   Table Rock Pueblo, Arizona, *Fieldiana: Anthropology*, Vol. 51, No. 2, Chicago Natural History Museum.

MARTIN, PAUL S., JOHN B. RINALDO, AND ERNST ANTEVS
1949   Cochise and Mogollon Sites, Pine Lawn Valley, Western New Mexico, *Fieldiana: Anthropology*, Vol. 38, No. 1, Chicago Natural History Museum.

MARTIN, PAUL S., JOHN B. RINALDO, AND ELOISE R. BARTER
1957   Late Mogollon Communities, Four Sites of the Tularosa Phase, Western New Mexico, *Fieldiana: Anthropology*, Vol. 49, No. 1, Chicago Natural History Museum.

MARTIN, PAUL S., JOHN B. RINALDO, AND ELAINE A. BLUHM
1954   Caves of the Reserve Area, *Fieldiana: Anthropology*, Vol. 42, Chicago Natural History Museum.

MARTIN, PAUL S., JOHN B. RINALDO, ELAINE A. BLUHM, AND HUGH C. CUTLER
1956   Higgins Flat Pueblo, Western New Mexico, *Fieldiana: Anthropology*, Vol. 45, Chicago Natural History Museum.

MARTIN, PAUL S., JOHN B. RINALDO, ELAINE A. BLUHM, HUGH C. CUTLER, AND ROGER GRANGE, JR.
1952   Mogollon Cultural Continuity and Change: The Stratigraphic Analysis of Tularosa and Cordova Caves, *Fieldiana: Anthropology*, Vol. 40, Chicago Natural History Museum.

MARTIN, PAUL S., JOHN B. RINALDO, AND WILLIAM A. LONGACRE
1961   Mineral Creek Site and Hooper Ranch Pueblo, Eastern Arizona, *Fieldiana: Anthropology*, Vol. 52, Chicago Natural History Museum.

MARTIN, PAUL S., JOHN B. RINALDO, WILLIAM A. LONGACRE, CONSTANCE CRONIN, LESLIE G. FREEMAN, JR., AND JAMES SCHOENWETTER
1962   Chapters in the Prehistory of Eastern Arizona, 1, *Fieldiana: Anthropology*, Vol. 53, Chicago Natural History Museum.

MARTIN, PAUL S., AND ELIZABETH S. WILLIS
1940   Anasazi Painted Pottery in Field Museum of Natural History, *Anthropology Memoir 5*, Field Museum of Natural History, Chicago.

MASON, RONALD J.
1962   The Paleo-Indian Tradition in Eastern North America, *Current Anthropology*, Vol. 3, No. 3, University of Chicago.

McGINNIES, W. G.
1963   Dendrochronology, *Journal of Forestry*, Vol. 61, No. 1, Washington, D.C.

McGREGOR, JOHN C.
1930   Tree Ring Dating, *Museum Notes*, Vol. 3, No. 4.

1935   Additional Houses from Beneath the Ash of Sunset Crater, *Museum Notes*, Vol. 8, No. 5.

1936 Dating the Eruption of Sunset Crater, Arizona, *American Antiquity*, Vol. 2, No. 1.
1936 Culture of Sites Which Were Occupied Shortly Before the Eruption of Sunset Crater, *Bulletin 9*, Museum of Northern Arizona, Flagstaff.
1937 Winona Village, *Bulletin 12*, Museum of Northern Arizona, Flagstaff.
1938 How Some Important Northern Arizona Pottery Types Were Dated, *Bulletin 13*, Museum of Northern Arizona, Flagstaff.
1938 Some Southwestern Dated Ruins: III, *Tree Ring Bulletin*, Vol. 4, No. 4.
1940 Burial of an Early American Magician, *Proceedings of the American Philosophical Society*, Vol. 86, No. 2, Philadelphia.
1941 Southwestern Archaeology, John Wiley and Sons, Inc., New York City.
1941 Winona and Ridge Ruin, Part I: Architecture and Material Culture, *Bulletin 18*, Museum of Northern Arizona, Flagstaff.
1951 The Cohonina Culture of Northwestern Arizona, University of Illinois Press, Urbana.

McKern, W. C.
1939 The Midwestern Taxonomic Method as an Aid to Archaeological Culture Study, *American Antiquity*, Vol. 4, No. 4.

Mera, H. P.
1931 Chupadero Black on White, *Technical Series Bulletin 1*, Laboratory of Anthropology, Santa Fe, New Mexico.
1932 Wares Ancestral to Tewa Polychrome, *Technical Series Bulletin 4*, Laboratory of Anthropology, Santa Fe, New Mexico.
1933 A Proposed Revision of the Rio Grande Glazed Paint Sequence, *Technical Series Bulletin 5*, Laboratory of Anthropology, Santa Fe, New Mexico.
1934 A Survey of the Biscuit Ware Area in Northern New Mexico, *Technical Series Bulletin 6*, Laboratory of Anthropology, Santa Fe, New Mexico.
1934 Observations on the Archaeology of the Petrified Forest National Monument, *Technical Series Bulletin 7*, Laboratory of Anthropology, Santa Fe, New Mexico.
1935 Ceramic Clues to the Prehistory of North Central New Mexico, *Technical Series Bulletin 8*, Laboratory of Anthropology, Santa Fe, New Mexico.
1938 Reconnaissance and Excavation in Southeastern New Mexico, *Memoirs of the American Anthropological Association*, No. 51, Lancaster, Pennsylvania.
1938 Some Aspects of the Largo Culture Phase, Northern New Mexico, *American Antiquity*, Vol. 3, No. 3.

Mera, H. P., and W. S. Stallings, Jr.
1931 Lincoln Black on White, *Technical Series Bulletin 2*, Laboratory of Anthropology, Santa Fe, New Mexico.

Miller, Carl F.
1934 Report on Dates on the Allantown, Arizona, Ruins, *Tree Ring Bulletin*, Vol. 1, No. 2.
1935 Additional Dates from Allantown, *Tree Ring Bulletin*, Vol. 1, No. 4.

Mindeleff, Cosmos
1896 Aboriginal Remains in the Verde Valley, *Thirteenth Annual Report*, Bureau of American Ethnology, Washington, D.C.

1896 Casa Grande Ruin, *Thirteenth Annual Report*, Bureau of American Ethnology, Washington, D.C.

1897 The Cliff-Ruins of Canyon de Chelly, Arizona, *Sixteenth Annual Report*, Bureau of American Ethnology, Washington, D.C.

MINDELEFF, VICTOR

1891 A Study of Pueblo Architecture in Tusayan and Cibola, *Eighth Annual Report*, Bureau of American Ethnology, Washington, D.C.

MONTGOMERY, ROSS GORDON, WATSON SMITH, AND J. O. BREW

1949 Franciscan Awatovi, *Papers of the Peabody Museum of American Archaeology and Ethnology*, Vol. 36, Harvard University, Cambridge, Massachusetts.

MORRIS, EARL H.

1919 The Aztec Ruin, *Anthropological Papers*, Vol. 26, Part I, American Museum of Natural History, New York City.

1919 Preliminary Account of the Antiquities of the Region Between the Mancos and La Plata Rivers in Southwestern Colorado, *Bulletin 33*, Bureau of American Ethnology, Washington, D.C.

1921 The House of the Great Kiva at the Aztec Ruin, *Anthropological Papers*, Vol. 26, Part II, American Museum of Natural History, New York City.

1927 The Beginnings of Pottery Making in the San Juan Area; Unfired Prototypes, and the Wares of the Earliest Ceramic Periods, *Anthropological Papers*, Vol. 28, Part II, American Museum of Natural History, New York City.

1928 An Aboriginal Salt Mine at Camp Verde, Arizona, *Anthropological Papers*, Vol. 30, Part III, American Museum of Natural History, New York City.

1936 Archaeological Background of Dates in Early Arizona Chronology, *Tree Ring Bulletin*, Vol. 2, No. 4.

1939 Archaeological Studies in the La Plata District, Southwestern Colorado and Northwestern New Mexico, *Carnegie Institution Publication 519*, Washington, D.C.

1949 Basketmaker II Dwellings Near Durango, Colorado, *Tree Ring Bulletin*, Vol. 15, No. 4.

MORRIS, EARL H., AND ROBERT F. BURGH

1941 Anasazi Basketry, Basketmaker II Through Pueblo III: A Study Based on Specimens from the San Juan River Country, *Carnegie Institution Publication 533*, Washington, D.C.

1954 Basketmaker II Sites Near Durango, Colorado, *Carnegie Institution Publication 604*, Washington, D.C.

MORRIS, ELIZABETH ANN

1959 A Pueblo I Site Near Bennett's Peak, Northwestern New Mexico, *El Palacio*, Vol. 66, No. 5.

MORSS, NOEL

1931 Notes on the Archaeology of the Kaibito and Rainbow Plateaus in Arizona, *Papers of the Peabody Museum of American Archaelogy and Ethnology*, Vol. 12, No. 3, Harvard University, Cambridge, Massachusetts.

1954 Clay Figurines of the American Southwest, *Papers of the Peabody Museum of American Archaeology and Ethnology*, Vol. 49, No. 1, Harvard University, Cambridge, Massachusetts.

NESBITT, PAUL H.
1938 Starkweather Ruin, *Bulletin 6*, Logan Museum Publications in Anthropology, Beloit, Wisconsin.

NORDENSKIOLD, G.
1893 The Cliff-Dwellers of the Mesa Verde, tr. by D. Lloyd Morgan, P. H. Norstedt & Söner, Stockholm.

NUSBAUM, JESSE L.
1922 A Basket Maker Cave in Kane County, Utah, with notes on artifacts by A. V. Kidder and S. J. Guernsey, *Miscellaneous Paper 29*, Museum of the American Indian, Heye Foundation, New York City.

O'BRIEN, DERIC
1950 Excavations in Mesa Verde National Park, *Medallion Paper 39*, Gila Pueblo, Globe, Arizona.

PEPPER, GEORGE H.
1902 Ancient Basket Makers of Southern Utah, *American Museum Journal*, Vol. 2, No. 4, Supplement, New York City.
1920 Pueblo Bonito, *Anthropological Papers*, Vol. 27, American Museum of Natural History, New York City.

PRUDDEN, T. MITCHELL
1918 A Further Study of Prehistoric Small House Ruins in the San Juan Watershed, *Memoirs of the American Anthropological Association*, Vol. 5, No. 1, Lancaster, Pennsylvania.

REED, ERIK K.
1946 Sources of Upper Rio Grande Pueblo Culture and Population, *El Palacio*, Vol. 56, No. 6.
1946 The Distinctive Features and Distribution of the San Juan Anasazi Culture, *Southwestern Journal of Anthropology*, Vol. 2, No. 3.
1950 East-Central Arizona Archaeology in Relation to the Western Pueblos, *Southwestern Journal of Anthropology*, Vol. 6, No. 2.
1951 Types of Stone Axes in the Southwest, *Southwestern Lore*, Vol. 17, No. 3.
1954 Transition to History in the Pueblo Southwest, *American Anthropologist*, Vol. 56, No. 4, Part 1.
1955 Trends in Southwestern Archaeology, in New Interpretations of Aboriginal American Culture History, Seventy-fifth Anniversary Volume of the Anthropological Society of Washington, Washington, D.C.

RENAUD, E. B.
1931 Prehistoric Flaked Points from Colorado and Neighboring Districts, *Proceedings of the Colorado Museum of Natural History*, Vol. 10, No. 2, Denver.
1932 Yuma and Folsom Artifacts (New Material), *Proceedings of the Colorado Museum of Natural History*, Vol. 11, No. 2, Denver.
1934 The First Thousand Yuman-Folsom Artifacts, Department of Anthropology, University of Denver, Denver, Colorado.

RICE, STUART
  1931   Ed. Methods in Social Science, University of Chicago Press.
RINALDO, JOHN B.
  1950   An Analysis of Culture Change in the Ackmen-Lowry Area, *Fieldiana: Anthropology*, Vol. 36, No. 5, Chicago Natural History Museum.
  1959   Foote Canyon Pueblo, Eastern Arizona, *Fieldiana: Anthropology*, Vol. 49, No. 2, Chicago Natural History Museum.
ROBERTS, FRANK H. H., JR.
  1929   Recent Archaeological Developments in the Vicinity of El Paso, Texas, *Smithsonian Miscellaneous Collections*, Vol. 81, No. 7, Washington, D.C.
  1929   Shabik'eschee Village, a Late Basket Maker Site in the Chaco Canyon, New Mexico, *Bulletin 92*, Bureau of American Ethnology, Washington, D.C.
  1930   Early Pueblo Ruins in the Piedra District, Southwestern Colorado, *Bulletin 96*, Bureau of American Ethnology, Washington, D.C.
  1931   The Ruins at Kiatuthlanna, Eastern Arizona, *Bulletin 100*, Bureau of American Ethnology, Washington, D.C.
  1932   The Village of the Great Kivas on the Zuni Reservation, New Mexico, *Bulletin 111*, Bureau of American Ethnology, Washington, D.C.
  1935   A Survey of Southwestern Archaeology, *American Anthropologist*, Vol. 37, No. 1.
  1936   Problems in American Archaeology, *Southwestern Lore*, Vol. 1, No. 4.
  1937   Archaeology in the Southwest, *American Antiquity*, Vol. 3, No. 1.
  1937   New World Man, *American Antiquity*, Vol. 2, No. 3.
  1937   The Material Culture of Folsom Man as Revealed at the Lindenmeier Site, *Southwestern Lore*, Vol. 2, No. 4.
  1939   Archaeological Remains in the Whitewater District, Eastern Arizona, *Bulletin 121*, Part I, Bureau of American Ethnology, Washington, D.C.
  1940   Developments in the Problem of the North American Paleo-Indian, *Smithsonian Miscellaneous Collections*, Vol. 100, Washington, D.C.
  1940   Archaeological Remains in the Whitewater District, Eastern Arizona, *Bulletin 126*, Part II, Bureau of American Ethnology, Washington, D.C.
ROGERS, MALCOLM J.
  1929   Report of an Archaeological Reconnaissance in the Mohave Sink Region, *Archaeology*, Vol. 1, No. 1, San Diego Museum, San Diego, California.
  1941   Aboriginal Cultural Relations Between Southern California and the Southwest, *San Diego Museum Bulletin*, Vol. V, No. 3, San Diego, California.
  1945   An Outline of Yuman Prehistory, *Southwestern Journal of Anthropology*, Vol. 1, No. 2.
  1958   San Dieguito Implements from the Terraces of the Rincon-Pantano and Rillito Drainage System, *The Kiva*, Vol. 24, No. 1, University of Arizona, Tucson.
ROOSA, WILLIAM B.
  1956   The Lucy Site in Central New Mexico, *American Antiquity*, Vol. 21, No. 3.

ROUSE, IRVING
  1954   On the Use of the Concept of Area Co-Tradition, *American Antiquity,*
         Vol. 19, No. 3.
SAUER, CARL, AND DONALD BRAND
  1930   Pueblo Sites in Southeastern Arizona, *Publications in Geography,* Vol.
         3, No. 7, University of California Press, Berkeley.
SAYLES, E. B.
  1936   An Archaeological Survey of Chihuahua, Mexico, *Medallion Paper 22,*
         Gila Pueblo, Globe, Arizona.
  1936   Some Southwestern Pottery Types, Series V, *Medallion Paper 21,* Gila
         Pueblo, Globe, Arizona.
  1945   The San Simon Branch, Excavations at Cave Creek and in the San
         Simon Valley. I. Material Culture, *Medallion Paper 34,* Gila Pueblo,
         Globe, Arizona.
SAYLES, E. B., AND ERNST ANTEVS
  1941   The Cochise Culture, *Medallion Paper 29,* Gila Pueblo, Globe, Arizona.
SCHROEDER, ALBERT H.
  1957   The Hakataya Cultural Tradition. Facts and Comments, *American
         Antiquity,* Vol. 23, No. 2, Part 1.
  1960   The Hohokam, Sinagua and the Hakataya, *Archives of Archaeology,*
         No. 5 (on 4 microcards), Society for American Archaeology and the
         University of Wisconsin Press, Madison.
  1961   The Pre-eruptive and Post-eruptive Sinagua Patterns, *Plateau,* Vol. 34,
         No. 2, Museum of Northern Arizona, Flagstaff.
  1961   An Archaeological Survey of the Painted Rocks Reservoir, Western
         Arizona, *The Kiva,* Vol. 27, No. 1, University of Arizona, Tucson.
  1961   The Archaeological Excavations at Willow Beach, Arizona, 1950, *Uni-
         versity of Utah Archaeological Paper 50,* Salt Lake City.
  1963   Navajo and Apache Relationships West of the Rio Grande, *El Palacio,*
         Vol. 70, No. 3.
SCHULMAN, EDMUND
  1956   Tree Rings and History in Western United States, *Economic Botany,*
         Vol. 8, No. 3, Lancaster, Pennsylvania.
  1956   Dendroclimatic Changes in Semiarid America, Laboratory of Tree-Ring
         Research, University of Arizona, Tucson.
SCHWARTZ, DOUGLAS W.
  1955   Havasupai Prehistory: Thirteen Centuries of Cultural Development,
         Ph.D. dissertation, Yale University, New Haven, Connecticut.
  1956   Demographic Changes in the Early Periods of Cohonina Prehistory, in
         Prehistoric Settlement Patterns, ed. by Gordon R. Willey, *Viking Fund
         Publications in Anthropology,* No. 23, New York City.
  1957   Climatic Change and Culture History in the Grand Canyon Region,
         American Anthropologist, Vol. 22, No. 4.
SELLARDS, E. H.
  1940   Early Man in America, Index to Localities and Selected Bibliography,
         Bulletin of the Geological Society of America, Vol. 51, New York City.
  1952   Early Man in America, a Study in Prehistory, University of Texas Press,
         Austin.

1960   Some Early Stone Artifact Developments in North America, *Southwestern Journal of Anthropology*, Vol. 16, No. 2.

SENTER, FLORENCE HAWLEY

1938   Southwestern Dated Ruins; IV, *Tree Ring Bulletin*, Vol. 5, No. 1.

SHEPARD, ANNA O.

1942   Rio Grande Glaze Paint Ware. Contributions to American Anthropology and History, No. 39, *Carnegie Institution Publication 528*, Washington, D.C.

SMILEY, TERAH L.

1951   A Summary of Tree-Ring Dates from Some Southwestern Archaeological Sites, *University of Arizona Bulletin*, Vol. 22, No. 4, Tucson.

1952   Four Late Prehistoric Kivas at Point of Pines, Arizona, *University of Arizona Social Science Bulletin 21*, Tucson.

1955   Geochronology, *University of Arizona Physical Science Bulletin 2*, Tucson. "Dendrochronology," with Bryant Bannister.

SMILEY, TERAH L., STANLEY A. STUBBS, AND BRYANT BANNISTER

1953   A Foundation for the Dating of Some Late Archaeological Sites in the Rio Grande Area, New Mexico: Based on Studies in Tree-Ring Methods and Pottery Analysis, *University of Arizona Bulletin*, Vol. 24, No. 3, Tucson.

SMITH, H. V.

1930   The Climate of Arizona, *University of Arizona Bulletin 130*, Tucson.

SMITH, WATSON

1952   Excavations in Big Hawk Valley, Wupatki National Monument, Arizona, *Bulletin 24*, Museum of Northern Arizona, Flagstaff.

1952   Kiva Mural Decorations at Awatovi and Kawaika-a; with a Survey of Other Wall Paintings in the Pueblo Southwest, *Papers of the Peabody Museum of American Archaeology and Ethnology*, Vol. 37, Harvard University, Cambridge, Massachusetts.

SPENCER, J. E.

1934   Pueblo Sites of Southwestern Utah, *American Anthropologist*, Vol. 36, No. 1.

SPICER, EDWARD H.

1934   Pueblo I Structures of the San Francisco Mountains, Arizona, *Museum Notes*, Vol. 7, No. 5.

1954   Spanish-Indian Acculturation in the Southwest, *American Anthropologist*, Vol. 56, No. 4.

SPICER, EDWARD H., AND LOUIS R. CAYWOOD

1934   Tuzigoot, a Prehistoric Pueblo of the Upper Verde, *Museum Notes*, Vol. 6, No. 9.

1936   Two Pueblo Ruins in West Central Arizona, *University of Arizona Social Science Bulletin 10*, Tucson.

SPIER, LESLIE

1918   Notes on Some Little Colorado Ruins, *Anthropological Papers*, Vol. 18, Part IV, American Museum of Natural History, New York City.

1919   Ruins in the White Mountains, Arizona, *Anthropological Papers*, Vol. 18, Part V, American Museum of Natural History, New York City.

SPUHLER, J. N.
  1954 Some Problems in the Physical Anthropology of the American Southwest, *American Anthropologist*, Vol. 56, No. 4, Part 1.

STALLINGS, W. S., JR.
  1931 El Paso Polychrome, *Technical Series Bulletin 3*, Laboratory of Anthropology, Santa Fe, New Mexico.
  1932 Notes on the Pueblo Culture in South Central New Mexico and in the Vicinity of El Paso, Texas, *American Anthropologist*, Vol. 34, No. 1.
  1933 A Tree-Ring Chronology for the Rio Grande Drainage in Northern New Mexico, *Proceedings of the National Academy of Sciences*, Vol. 19, No. 9, Washington, D.C.
  1937 Some Southwestern Dated Ruins; I, *Tree Ring Bulletin*, Vol. 4, No. 2.
  1939 Dating Prehistoric Ruins by Tree-Rings, *General Series Bulletin 8*, Laboratory of Anthropology, Santa Fe, New Mexico.

STEEN, CHARLIE, LLOYD M. PIERSON, VORSILA L. BOHRER, AND KATE PECK KENT
  1962 Archaeological Studies at Tonto National Monument, *Technical Series*, Vol. 2, Southwestern Monuments Association, Globe, Arizona.

STEWARD, JULIAN H.
  1933 Archaeological Problems of the Northern Periphery of the Southwest, *Bulletin 5*, Museum of Northern Arizona, Flagstaff.
  1936 Pueblo Material Culture of Western Utah, *University of New Mexico Bulletin*, Anthropological Series, Vol. 1, No. 3, Albuquerque.
  1937 Ancient Caves of the Great Salt Lake Region, *Bulletin 116*, Bureau of American Ethnology, Washington, D.C.

STUBBS, STANLEY A., AND W. S. STALLINGS, JR.
  1953 The Excavation of Pindi Pueblo, New Mexico, *Monographs of the School of American Research and the Laboratory of Anthropology*, No. 18, Santa Fe, New Mexico.

TAYLOR, DEE C.
  1954 The Garrison Site, *University of Utah Anthropological Paper 16*, Salt Lake City.

TAYLOR, WALTER W.
  1948 A Study of Archeology, *American Anthropologist*, Vol. 50, No. 3, Part 2.
  1954 Southwestern Archeology, Its History and Theory, *American Anthropologist*, Vol. 56, No. 4, Part 1.

TOULOUSE, JOSEPH H., JR., AND ROBERT L. STEPHENSON
  1960 Excavations at Pueblo Prado, *Papers in Anthropology 2*, Museum of New Mexico, Santa Fe.

TURNEY, OMAR A.
  1929 Prehistoric Irrigation in Arizona, Arizona State Historian, Capitol Building, Phoenix.

TUTHILL, CARR
  1947 The Tres Alamos Site on the San Pedro River, Southeastern Arizona, No. 4, the Amerind Foundation, Inc., Dragoon, Arizona.

VALLIANT, GEORGE C.
  1932 Some Resemblances in the Ceramics of Central and North America, *Medallion Paper 12*, Gila Pueblo, Globe, Arizona.

WASLEY, WILLIAM W.
   1960   Salvage Archaeology on Highway 66 in Eastern Arizona, *American Antiquity*, Vol. 26, No. 1.
   1960   A Hohokam Platform Mound at the Gatlin Site, Gila Bend, Arizona, *American Antiquity*, Vol. 26, No. 2.
WAUCHOPE, ROBERT
   1956   Ed. Seminars in Archaeology: 1955, *American Antiquity*, Vol. 22, No. 2, Part 2.
WENDORF, FRED
   1950   A Report on the Excavation of a Small Ruin East of Point of Pines, East Central Arizona, *University of Arizona Social Science Bulletin 19*, Tucson.
   1953   Archaeological Studies in the Petrified Forest National Monument, *Bulletin 27*, Museum of Northern Arizona, Flagstaff.
   1954   A Reconstruction of Northern Rio Grande Prehistory, *American Anthropologist*, Vol. 56, No. 2, Part 1.
   1960   The Archaeology of Northeastern New Mexico, *El Palacio*, Vol. 67, No. 2.
WHEAT, JOE BEN
   1954   Southwestern Cultural Interrelationships and the Question of Area Co-Tradition, *American Anthropologist*, Vol. 56, No. 4, Part 1.
   1954   Crooked Ridge Village (Arizona W:10 15), *University of Arizona Social Science Bulletin 24*, Tucson.
   1955   Mogollon Culture Prior to A.D. 1000, *American Antiquity*, Vol. 20, No. 4, Part 2.
WHEAT, JOE BEN, JAMES C. GIFFORD, AND WILLIAM W. WASLEY
   1958   Ceramic Variety, Type Cluster, and Ceramic System in Southwestern Pottery Analysis, *American Antiquity*, Vol. 24, No. 1.
WILLEY, GORDON R., AND PHILIP PHILLIPS
   1955   Method and Theory in American Archaeology II: Historical Developmental Interpretation, *American Anthropologist*, Vol. 57, No. 4.
WINSHIP, GEORGE P.
   1896   The Coronado Expedition, *Fourteenth Annual Report*, Part I, Bureau of American Ethnology, Washington, D.C.
WISSLER, CLARK
   1917   The American Indian, Oxford University Press, New York City.
   1917   Man and Culture, T. Y. Crowell Co., New York City.
WOODBURY, RICHARD B.
   1954   Prehistoric Stone Implements of Northeastern Arizona, *Papers of the Peabody Museum of American Archaeology and Ethnology*, Vol. 34, Harvard University, Cambridge, Massachusetts.
   1961   Prehistoric Agriculture at Point of Pines, Arizona, *Memoirs of the Society for American Archaeology*, No. 17, Salt Lake City, Utah.
WOODWARD, ARTHUR
   1931   The Grewe Site, *Occasional Paper 1*, Los Angeles Museum of History, Science, and Art, Los Angeles, California.

WORMINGTON, H. M.
  1955 A Reappraisal of the Fremont Culture, *Proceedings of the Denver Museum of Natural History*, No. 1, Denver, Colorado.
  1957 Ancient Man in North America, *Popular Series 4*, Denver Museum of Natural History, Denver, Colorado.

Index